QUATTRO PRO 5 MADE EASY

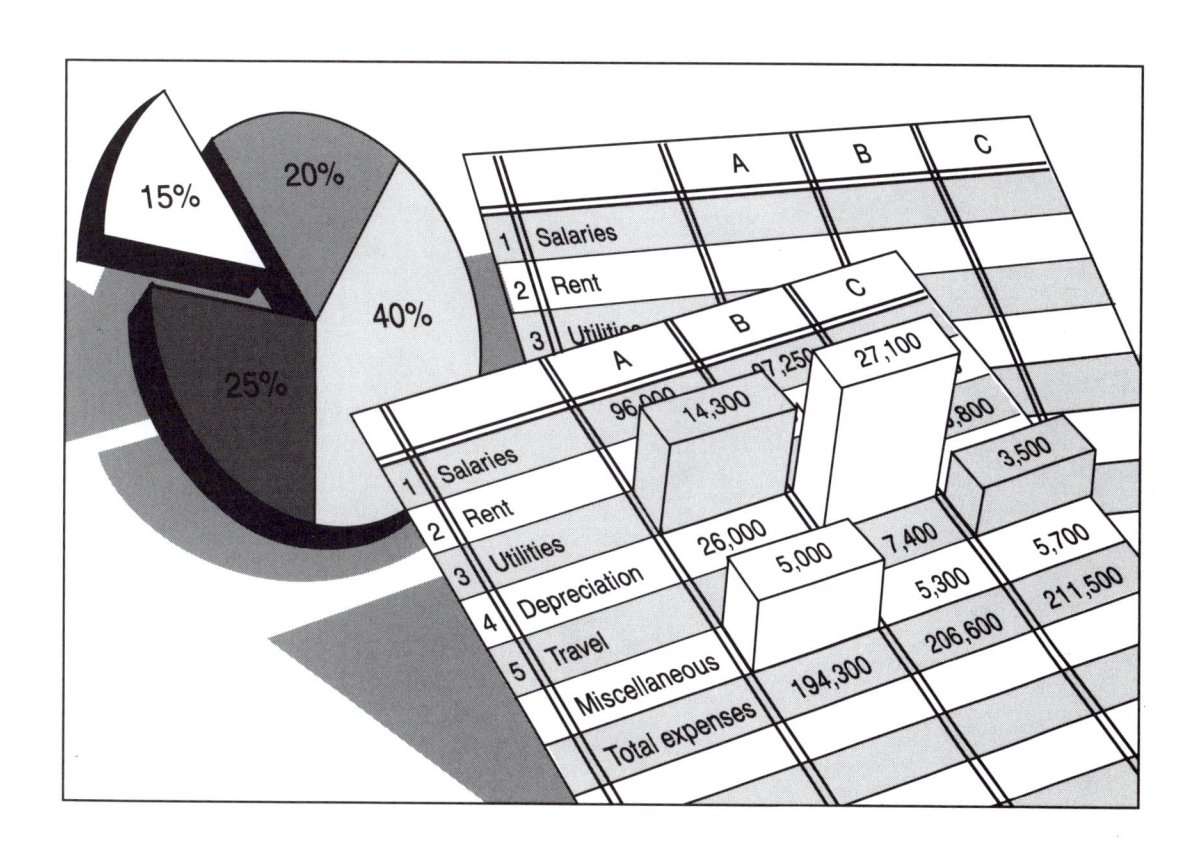

QUATTRO PRO 5 MADE EASY

Lisa Biow and Deborah Craig

Osborne **McGraw-Hill**

Berkeley New York St. Louis San Francisco
Auckland Bogotá Hamburg London Madrid
Mexico City Milan Montreal New Delhi Panama City
Paris São Paulo Singapore Sydney
Tokyo Toronto

Osborne **McGraw-Hill**
2600 Tenth Street
Berkeley, California 94710
U.S.A.

For information on translations or book distributors outside of the U.S.A., please write to Osborne **McGraw-Hill** at the above address.

Quattro Pro 5 Made Easy

Copyright © 1994 by McGraw-Hill. All rights reserved. Printed in the United States of America. Except as permitted under the Copyright Act of 1976, no part of this publication may be reproduced or distributed in any form or by any means, or stored in a database or retrieval system, without the prior written permission of the publisher, with the exception that the program listings may be entered, stored, and executed in a computer system, but they may not be reproduced for publication.

234567890 DOC 9987654

ISBN 0-07-881963-6

Acquisitions Editor
Scott Rogers

Associate Editor
Kristin D. Beeman

Technical Editor
Jim Ploss

Project Editor
Wendy Rinaldi

Copy Editor
Heidi Steele

Proofreaders
Hannah Raiden
Jeff Barash

Indexer
Deborah Craig

Computer Designer
Lance Ravella

Illustrator
Marla J. Shelasky

Cover Designer
Compass Marketing

Information has been obtained by Osborne **McGraw-Hill** from sources believed to be reliable. However, because of the possibility of human or mechanical error by our sources, Osborne **McGraw-Hill**, or others, Osborne **McGraw-Hill** does not guarantee the accuracy, adequacy, or completeness of any information and is not responsible for any errors or omissions or the results obtained from use of such information.

*To our siblings, Cindy and David Biow,
and Sarah, Walter, and Ruth Craig*

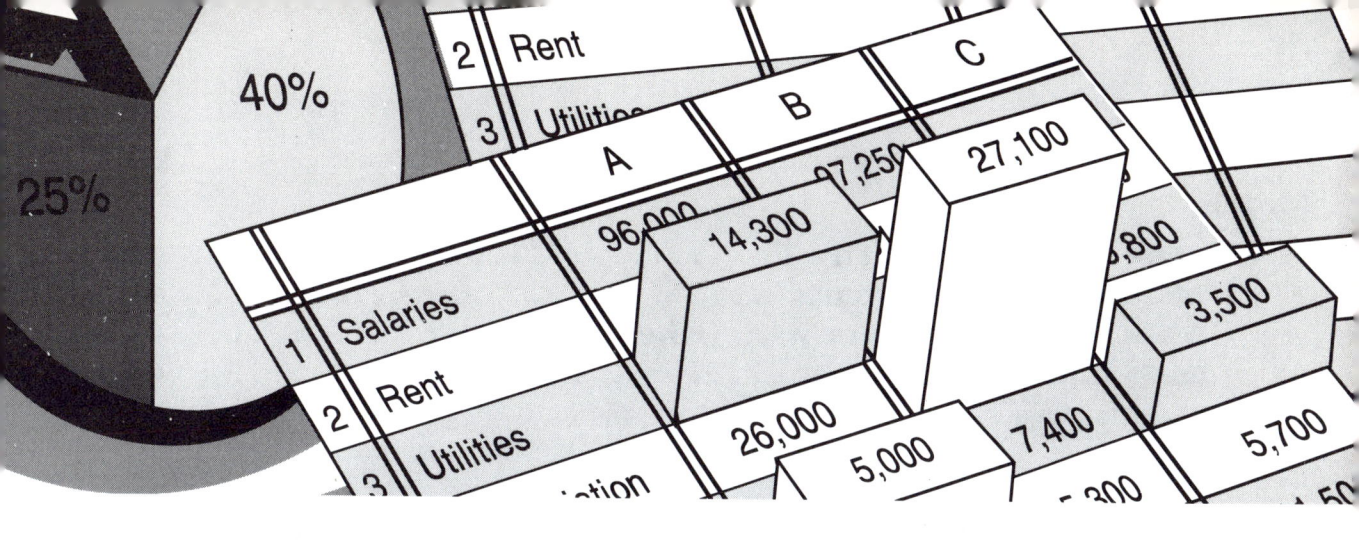

CONTENTS AT A GLANCE

1	Getting Started	1
2	Entering Text and Numbers	25
3	Formulas	43
4	Rearranging the Spreadsheet	59
5	Formatting Your Notebook	81
6	Printing Notebooks	107
7	Functions	133
8	More About Formulas	155
9	Advanced Editing and Formatting Commands	173
10	Dates and Times	189
11	Working with Windows	205
12	Working with Notebooks	223
13	Customizing the Environment	241
14	Creating Graphs	259
15	Customizing and Annotating Graphs	299
16	Designing and Using Databases	331
17	Selecting Records from Your Database	351
18	Managing Your Files	367
19	Combining, Extracting, and Linking Files	391
20	Introduction to Macros	415

A	Installing Quattro Pro	441
B	Keys and Shortcuts	449
C	Exchanging Data with Other Programs	457
	Index	489

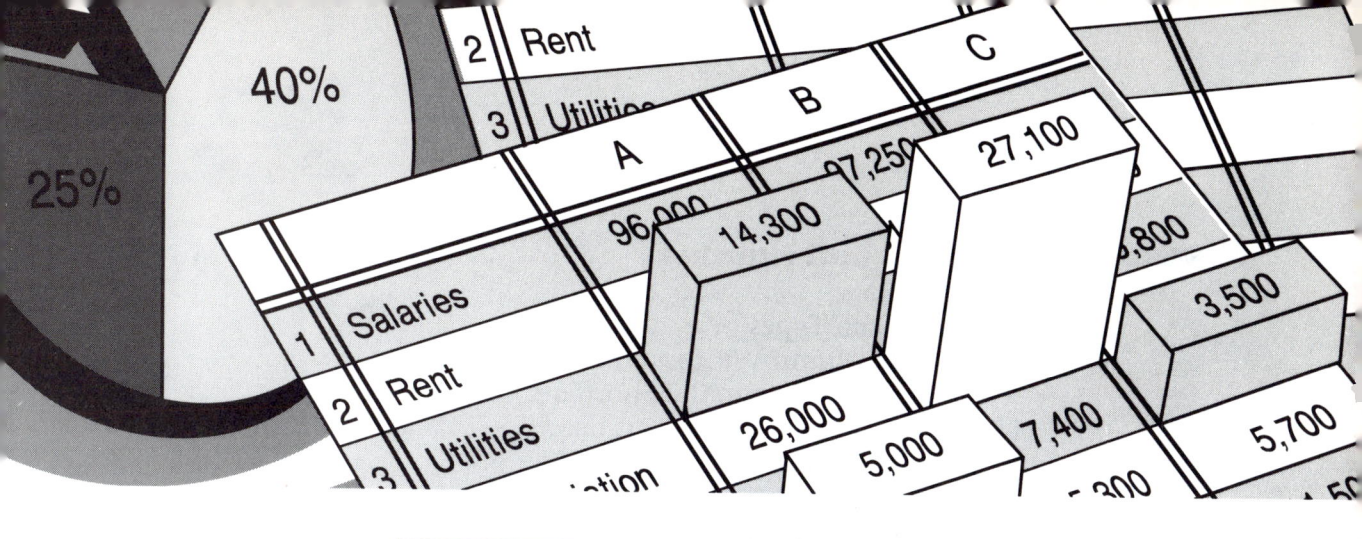

CONTENTS

1 Getting Started 1
    A Few Basic Concepts 2
        What Is a Spreadsheet? 2
        What Is a Database? 3
        Graphics 4
    Starting Up 5
    The Quattro Pro Display 6
        The Notebook Area 7
        The Input Line 8
        The Status Line 8
        The WYSIWYG Display Mode 9
    The Quattro Pro Keyboard 10
        Movement Keys 10
        Function Keys 12
    The Quattro Pro Menu System 13
        The "Hold Everything" Keys 15
    Getting Help 16
    Using a Mouse in Quattro Pro 17
        Basic Mouse Techniques 18
        The SpeedBars and Other Mouse Tools 18
    Leaving Quattro Pro 21

2 ▬ Entering Text and Numbers 25
Entering Data 26
Data Types 27
Changing Column Widths 29
Menu Command Shortcuts 30
Label Alignment 31
Entering Numbers 32
Entering Dates 33
Editing Data 34
Saving and Retrieving Notebooks 36
Saving Your Notebook for the First Time 37
Resaving Your Notebook 38
Retrieving Files 39

3 ▬ Formulas 43
Arithmetic Operators 44
Cell References 45
Automatic Recalculation 47
Pointing 48
Order of Calculation 49
Referencing Blocks of Cells 50
Designating Blocks 51
Common Mistakes in Formulas 53
Circular References 53
ERR Values 55
Building an Income Statement Model 55

4 ▬ Rearranging the Spreadsheet 59
The Undo Feature 60
Inserting and Deleting Rows and Columns 61
Inserting Rows 61
Deleting Rows 62
Inserting and Deleting Columns 63
Manipulating Blocks 64
Pointing Out Blocks in Commands 64
Copying Cells 68
Copying Formulas 70
Notes of Caution on Moving and Copying
Blocks 73
Using the [End] Key to Define Large Blocks 74

      Erasing a Block 74
      Inserting and Deleting Rows or Columns
          Within a Block 75
   Putting Blocks to Work on Your Spreadsheet 76

5 ▗▖ Formatting Your Notebook **81**
   Default Formats 82
   Adjusting Column Widths 82
      Changing the Width of Several Columns at
          Once 83
   Display Formats 85
      The Default Format Setting 85
      Quattro Pro's Ten Display Formats 85
      Changing the Notebook's Numeric Format 87
      Changing the Numeric Format of a Block 88
   Aligning Blocks of Data 92
      Aligning Labels 92
      Aligning Numeric Values 94
   More About Default Formats 94
   Line Drawing and Shading 95
      Drawing Lines on the Notebook 95
      Shading Cells 99
   The / Edit | Copy Special Command 100
   Using Custom Styles 101
      Defining Custom Styles 101
      Applying Custom Styles 102
      Predefined Styles and the Normal Style 103
      Editing and Erasing Styles 103
      Saving and Retrieving Custom Styles 104

6 ▗▖ Printing Notebooks **107**
   Selecting Printers 108
      Telling Quattro Pro About Your Printers 108
      Saving Your Printer Specifications 109
   Standard Quattro Pro Reports 110
      Draft-Quality Versus Final-Quality Printing 112
   Page Layout 113
      Adding Headers and Footers 114
      Margins, Page Breaks, and Dimensions 115
      Printing in Landscape and Banner Mode 116

Saving and Resetting Print Settings	116
Printing Larger Notebooks	117
Displaying Your Print Block	117
Defining Headings	118
Inserting Page Breaks	121
Printing to Fit and Scaling	121
Printing 3-D Blocks	122
Using Fonts	122
Applying Fonts to Sections of the Report	123
Using Different Fonts to Print LEARN1.WQ2	125
The Screen Previewer	127
Special Print Options	128
Printing Formulas	128
Adding Bullets to a Report	129
Printing in the Background	129
Monitoring the Print Queue	130

7 ■ Functions — 133

Types of Functions	134
Function Syntax	135
The Functions Key	136
Basic Statistical Functions	136
Functions for Dropping Decimal Places	139
The @IF Function	141
Complex Operators	143
@VLOOKUP and @HLOOKUP	144
String Functions	148
Financial Functions	149
Getting Help with Functions	152

8 ■ More About Formulas — 155

Absolute Versus Relative Cell Referencing	156
Mixed Cell References	160
Using Named Blocks	160
Naming a Block	162
The Choices Key	162
An Exercise in Naming Cells	163
Changing and Deleting Block Names	164
Naming Blocks Using Adjacent Labels	165
Creating a Table of Block Names	166

  Attaching Notes to Named Blocks 166
 Converting Formulas to Their Values 167
 Using the Audit Feature 169
  Viewing Dependencies 169
  Auditing Circular References 170
  Finding Labels, Blanks, ERR Values, and Links 170

9   Advanced Editing and Formatting Commands 173
 Searching and Replacing 174
  Performing the Search 175
  The Other Search & Replace Options 176
 Filling a Block with Values 178
 Reformatting Text 179
 Transposing Blocks 181
 Hiding and Exposing Columns 182
 Protecting Your Notebook 184
  Protecting Formulas 186

10   Dates and Times 189
 Working with Dates 190
  Date Arithmetic 192
  Date Functions 193
  Using Functions to Enter Dates 196
  Creating Month Headings 198
 Working with Times 199
  Time Arithmetic 202

11   Working with Windows 205
 Customizing Individual Windows 206
  Using Titles 206
  Splitting a Window in Two 209
  Synchronizing Panes 211
  Eliminating Column and Row Borders 212
  Map View 212
 Opening and Closing Windows 213
  Saving All Open Notebooks 214
  Moving Among Windows 215
 Rearranging and Resizing Windows 215
  Tiling and Stacking Windows 215
  Zooming Windows 216

Moving and Resizing Windows	217
Saving and Retrieving Workspaces	219
Copying and Moving Data Between Windows	219

12 — Working with Notebooks — 223

Notebook Basics	224
Navigating Between Pages	225
Naming Pages	226
Using Groups	227
Creating Groups	227
Working in Group Mode	228
Manipulating 3-D Blocks	232
Moving, Inserting, and Deleting Pages	237
Moving Pages	237
Inserting and Deleting Pages	238

13 — Customizing the Environment — 241

The Different Types of Defaults	242
Telling Quattro Pro About Your Hardware	242
Customizing Quattro Pro's Colors	243
The International Settings	245
Changing the Display Mode	247
Defining Startup Settings	250
Changing the SpeedBars	251
The "Other" Default Settings	252
Recalculation Settings	252
Updating the Global Defaults	253
Menu Command Shortcuts	254

14 — Creating Graphs — 259

Choosing a Graph Type	260
Line Graphs	260
Bar Graphs	261
Area Graphs	263
Pie Graphs	264
Column Graphs	265
XY Graphs	265
Bubble Graphs	267
High-Low (Open-Close) Graphs	267
Text Graphs	268

Three-Dimensional Graph Types	269
The Graphing Process	269
Adding Text to Your Graph	272
Hands-On Practice	273
Shortcuts for Creating Graphs	275
Zooming and Panning Graphs	279
Saving, Changing, and Restoring Graphs	280
Copying Graphs	282
Resetting Series and Graphs	282
Defining Pie Graphs and Column Graphs	283
Defining XY Graphs and Bubble Graphs	284
Creating Three-Dimensional Graphs	286
Graphing Data on Multiple Pages	288
Printing Graphs	289
Adjusting Print Speed and Quality	290
Changing the Graph Print Layout	291
"Printing" to Disk	291
Graph Slide Shows	292
Slide Show Transitions	292
Inserting Graphs in a Notebook	294
Printing an Inserted Graph	296

15 Customizing and Annotating Graphs ... 299

Customizing Series	300
Customizing Colors	300
Altering Fill Patterns	300
Changing Lines and Markers	301
Changing the Width of Bars	301
Labeling Points on a Graph	301
Overriding the Graph Type	302
Using a Second Y-Axis	303
Resetting Graph Settings	304
Updating Graph Settings	305
Customizing Pie and Column Graphs	305
Changing the Label Format	305
Eliminating Tick Marks	306
Changing Pie or Column Fill Patterns	306
Altering Colors	307
Exploding Pie Slices	307
Customizing the Axes	307
Scaling Axes Manually	307

Changing the Tick Marks	308
Eliminating the Scaling Display	308
Logarithmic Scaling	309
Customizing Graphs as a Whole	309
Customizing Grid Lines	310
Changing the Background Color	311
Framing the Graph	311
Displaying Graphs in Black and White	311
Eliminating the Three-Dimensional Effect	311
The Annotator Environment	311
The Toolbox	314
Adding Text and Lines to the Graph	315
Drawing Curves	317
Hands-On Practice	317
Modifying Graph Elements	319
Resizing Elements	319
Changing Design Properties	320
Aligning and Modifying Several Elements at Once	321
Using a Grid to Position Objects	322
Modifying Non-Annotator Elements	322
Fine-Tuning Text Elements	322
Editing Text Elements	323
Changing Text Design Properties	323
Creating Text Graphs	324
Linking Elements to Points on the Graph	324
Using the Clipboard	326
Cutting and Pasting Graph Elements	326
Creating and Using Clip Art Files	326
Moving Elements Between Foreground and Background	327

16 Designing and Using Databases   331

Database Terminology	332
Designing a Database	333
Field Content	333
Values or Labels?	333
Field Names	334
Cell Referencing in Databases	334
Data Entry Commands	336
Building a Sample Database	337

Adding and Deleting Records	340
Modifying Your Database	341
Improving the ORDERS Database	341
Sorting Your Database	344
Sort Order	344
Single-Key Sorts	345
Multiple-Key Sorts	346
Changing the Sort Rules	347

17 ▬ Selecting Records from Your Database 351

Database Query Commands	352
Preparing a Query	352
Criteria Tables	353
Exact Matches	353
Using Wild Cards	354
Locating Records One at a Time	354
The Query Key	354
Hands-On Practice	355
Defining Complex Searches in a Criteria Table	356
Using Formulas in a Criteria Table	358
Complex Conditions in Logical Formulas	360
Putting Your Selections to Work	361
Extracting Records	361
Extracting Unique Records	362
Deleting Selected Records	364
Resetting the Query Settings	365

18 ▬ Managing Your Files 367

Using Different Directories	368
Loading Quattro Pro from Other Directories	368
Changing the Default Directory	368
Using Subdirectories	369
Manipulating File Lists	370
Displaying More Informative File Lists	370
Searching Through File Lists	371
Displaying More Specific File Lists	371
Shortcuts for Retrieving Files	372
Using Passwords	372
Managing Disk Space	373

Compressing Files	374
Managing Memory	375
Determining How Much Memory Is Available	375
Running Out of Memory	375
Backing Up Files	376
Exiting to the Operating System	377
The File Manager Utility	377
The Control Pane	379
Switching Drives or Directories	379
Selecting Files to Display	379
Opening a File	380
Searching for a File	380
The File List Pane	380
Sorting File Lists	382
Manipulating Files	384
Selecting Files	384
Opening Files	384
Copying Files	385
Copying a Group of Files to Multiple Disks	385
Moving Files	386
Deleting Files	386
Duplicating Files	386
Renaming Files	386
Displaying and Using Directory Trees	387
Resizing the Directory Tree	388
Other File Manager Options	388
Rereading the File List	388
Making Directories	389
Printing the Contents of a File Manager Window	389

19 ■ Combining, Extracting, and Linking Files 391

Extracting Files	392
Copying or Moving Versus Extracting Data	392
Combining Files	393
The / Tools	Combine	Copy Command	394
The / Tools	Combine	Add Command	394
The / Tools	Combine	Subtract Command	395
Hands-On Practice	395
Linking Notebooks	398
Creating Notebook Links	399

Hands-On Practice	402
Opening Linked Notebooks	406
Linking Notebooks Hierarchically	407
Updating Notebook Links	408
Copying and Moving Link Formulas	410
Graphing Linked Notebooks	411
Linking Versus Combining Files	412

20 Introduction to Macros … 415

Creating Macros	416
Recording Macros	416
A Macro for Date-Stamping a Notebook	418
Pasting Macros into the Notebook	418
Naming Macros	419
Where to Store Your Macros	420
Interpreting Macros	421
Editing Macros	427
Sample Database Macros	428
Applications for Recorded Macros	432
The Macro Language	432
Maintaining and Using Macros	433
Documenting Your Macros	433
Renaming and Deleting Macros	433
Copying Macros to Another Notebook	434
Using Macro Libraries	435
Changing the Macro Recording Method	436
Playing Macros Automatically	437
Startup Macros	437
Autoloading Macros	437

A Installing Quattro Pro … 441

Copying the Quattro Pro Disks	442
Starting the Installation	443
Upgrading from Earlier Versions of Quattro Pro	444
Reading the README File	445

B Keys and Shortcuts … 449

Ready Mode SpeedBar	450
Edit SpeedBar	451
Editing Keys	451

Preassigned Shortcuts	453
Function Keys	454

C — Exchanging Data with Other Programs — 457

Exchanging Data with Lotus 1-2-3	458
Retrieving Version 3.0 Files	458
Retrieving Allways and Impress/WYSIWYG Files	460
Saving in 1-2-3 File Formats	461
Trading Data with Other Spreadsheet Programs	461
The "Desktop Settings are Removed" Message	462
Exchanging Data with Harvard Graphics	462
Trading Data with Paradox, dBASE, and Reflex	462
Reading Paradox, Reflex, and dBASE Files	463
Writing Paradox, Reflex, and dBASE Files	464
Modifying the File Structure	465
dBASE and Paradox Memo Fields	466
Potential Problems in Exchanging Data with Database Programs	467
Linking to External Databases	468
Accessing Paradox	470
Stand-Alone Configuration	471
Network Configuration	473
Finishing the Configuration	473
Using Paradox Access	473
Loading Paradox Tables While in Quattro Pro	475
Working with Paradox Temporary Files	476
Loading a Table or Spreadsheet Automatically	477
Exporting Data to Word Processing Software	478
Exporting Data to Other Types of Software	479
Importing Data into Quattro Pro	480
Importing Delimited Files	480
Parsing ASCII Text Files	481
Creating Format Lines	483
Editing Format Lines	485
Defining Input and Output Blocks	487
Initiating the Parse	487

Index — 489

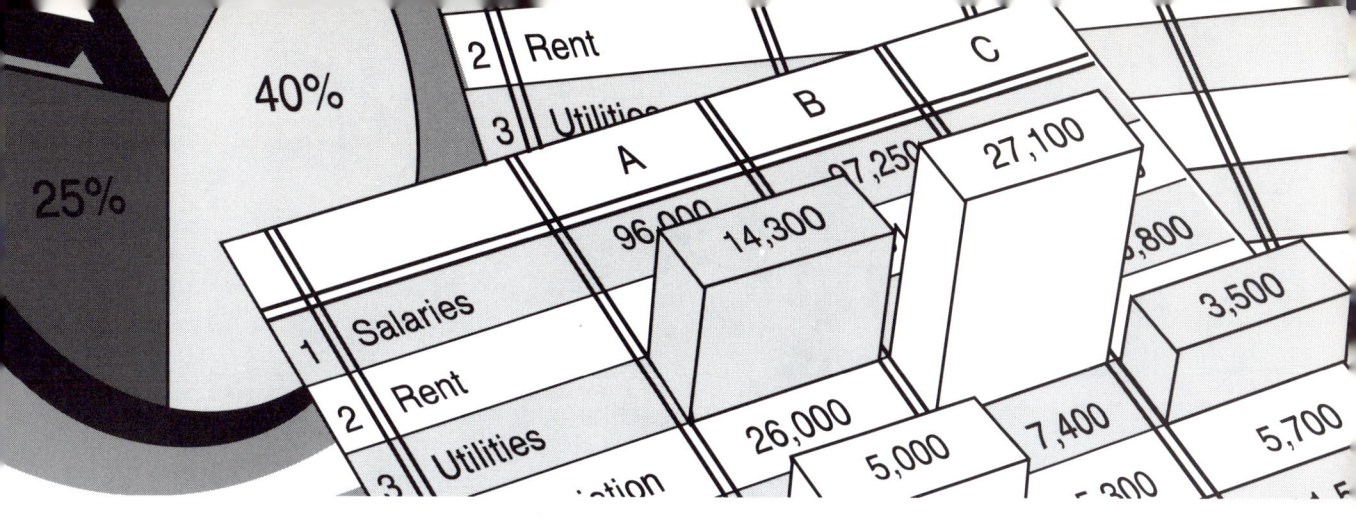

ACKNOWLEDGEMENTS

Several terrific people helped us through this latest rewrite:

- ◆ Heidi Steele did an outstanding job on the copy edit, as well as capturing all the screens, catching minor and major technical errors, scanning pages proofs, and bringing her dog Joss over to keep Moki entertained during the long haul.
- ◆ Jim Ploss contributed a superb technical edit, hand-delivering most chapters, providing expert phone advice, and going way beyond the call of duty by working over the Fourth of July weekend. Ted McGavin also pitched in, meeting over margaritas and checking up on the intricacies of notebooks.
- ◆ Madhu Prasher filled in briefly as Project Editor, most certainly getting this project off on the right foot.
- ◆ Wendy Rinaldi is our favorite Project Editor. She blends competence with humor, and skill with patience. (She also has a great Godzilla T-shirt.)
- ◆ Scott Rogers, Acquisitions Editor, kept us on track while managing to stay as good-natured as usual under pressure.
- ◆ Proofreaders Hannah Raiden and Jeff Barash caught the mistakes that somehow mysteriously slipped past the rest of us.
- ◆ Lance Ravella deserves credit for the high quality of the screens, which he spent many hours manipulating until they were just right.

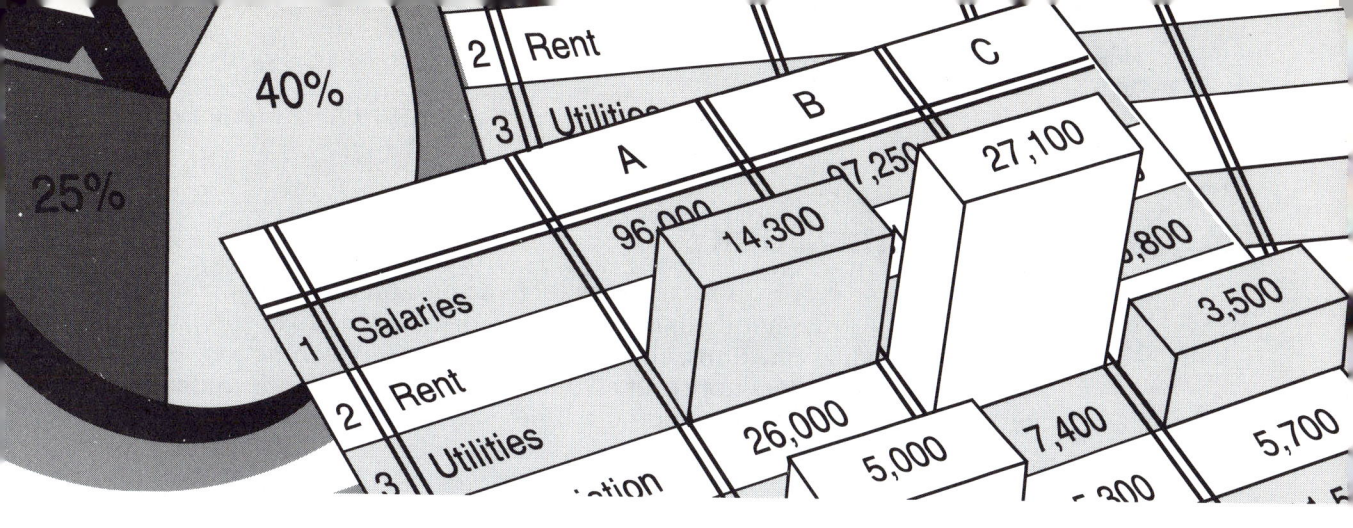

INTRODUCTION

When it was introduced in 1989, Quattro Pro was heralded as one of the most exciting software packages ever developed. Versions 2 through 4 added even more features to an already rich product. Quattro Pro 5 has gone further still. Its graphing talents continue to rival or exceed those of any other spreadsheet on the market. The SpeedBars have been expanded so that even more features are available with a single mouse click. And—perhaps what's most exciting—the new notebook feature permits you to organize your data on different "pages" within a single file. Notebooks are a tremendous organizational asset, since they permit you to place different sets of data on different pages within a single file. They can also drastically cut down on your typing and formatting chores, since you can enter data and apply formatting to multiple pages at once if you choose.

Quattro Pro 5 is a combination spreadsheet, database, and graphics program that is both easy to use and extremely powerful. Given the range of its capabilities, Quattro Pro 5 can be used by almost anyone who needs to work with numbers, rapidly organize and access information, or speculate with different sets of data. Quattro Pro 5 is also supremely adaptable, providing a range of options for customizing the program to your own taste, information needs, and style of working. And while newcomers to Quattro Pro 5 (and to spreadsheets in general) can learn to build functional worksheets in a matter of hours, experts will find that the program provides all the features, speed, and versatility they need.

About This Book

Quattro Pro 5's set of tools for entering, organizing, and extracting information includes hundreds of commands, over one hundred special operators known as functions, and well over a dozen special function keys. Although this book does not cover all of these tools in depth, it introduces you to most of them. More important, it provides you with a thorough grounding in the basic concepts of spreadsheet design; you can build on this foundation as you continue to explore Quattro Pro 5's more esoteric elements on your own.

This book presumes no experience with spreadsheets, graphics, or databases, although it does assume that you know how to turn your computer on, are familiar with the basic keyboard layout, and have a rudimentary knowledge of DOS (the disk operating system for IBM PCs and compatibles).

While you don't need to know anything about Quattro Pro 5 to read this book, you can expect to know quite a bit by the time you finish. Most chapters alternate between explanations of new ideas and techniques, and instructions for trying them out yourself. In general, the discussion of each command and function not only covers what that tool does, but also how and when to apply it. The emphasis is on general concepts—how a spreadsheet works or the implications of Quattro Pro 5's way of linking different items of data through formulas, for example—as well as on specific techniques.

How to Learn a New Program

If you are new to electronic spreadsheets, the good news is that they are not only extremely useful, they are also fun. Creating your own models, changing a few numbers and watching the effects ripple instantly through the data, and creating graphics can be dramatic and exciting. You can learn Quattro Pro 5's fundamentals quickly, and the rewards are almost immediate.

Perhaps the most important assets you can bring to the learning process are a sense of adventure and a willingness to experiment. As mentioned, this book will walk you through most of the commands and techniques that Quattro Pro 5 offers, providing hands-on practice exercises wherever possible. You should use these exercises as a starting point, applying what you learn to data and situations of your own choosing. Try, when possible, to use real-life examples, drawn from your business or area of study. The more you apply Quattro Pro 5 to the problems that concern you, the more you will appreciate Quattro Pro 5's potential and the more likely you will be to remember particular commands and techniques.

Introduction XXV

As you follow the exercises in this book, be aware that there is often more than one way to accomplish something in Quattro Pro 5. If the text dictates one method of doing something and you think of another, try it your own way. In some cases, you will discover that the particular commands or sequence of actions used in the text were chosen for some objective reason; in other cases, you will find that the choice was simply a matter of taste and that you are free to use whichever method feels most natural to you.

For those of you who are new to computers and are wary of rampant experimentation, no command or random set of characters that you type in Quattro Pro 5 can in any way harm your equipment. At worst, you can damage or erase part of your data, making it necessary to redo some work. Assuming you are working with practice data, such mishaps are hardly worth worrying about, and in any case you can minimize potential damage by frequently saving your work to disk and backing up your data files.

How This Book Is Organized

In Quattro Pro 5, spreadsheet files are called notebooks.

This book is organized into several groups of chapters that introduce and then explore each of Quattro Pro 5's major functional areas. Chapters 1 through 6 cover the basics of creating and using Quattro Pro 5 notebook files, including entering and editing data, saving and retrieving notebooks, manipulating blocks of data, rearranging and formatting notebooks, and printing reports. Chapters 7 through 13 build on that foundation, introducing more advanced concepts and techniques for manipulating your data, including the use of functions, as well as methods of customizing Quattro Pro 5 to suit your own work style.

Chapters 14 and 15 cover all the fundamentals of designing, displaying, printing, and customizing graphs. Chapters 16 and 17 cover everything you need to know about creating, using, and sorting Quattro Pro 5 databases. Chapters 18 through 20 cover more advanced topics, including commands for combining worksheet files, file management techniques, and macros (miniprograms that allow you to initiate an entire series of actions with a single keystroke). If you have not already installed Quattro Pro 5, Appendix A walks you through the process. Appendix B is a quick reference list of Quattro Pro's SpeedBar buttons, preassigned menu command shortcuts, editing keys, and function keys. And Appendix C explores the intricacies of exchanging data with other programs.

Depending on your needs and your schedule, you might work your way through this book in a matter of a few weeks, or you may decide to cover only a section at a time, postponing your study of graphs or databases until you have a need for those features, for example. If you do decide to take a break before finishing the book, you should at least skim Chapter 18, which covers File Management. Although you may not understand all of it if you have not read the previous chapters, you can at least pick up the basic concepts and learn some important techniques that can greatly enhance your work.

Conventions Used in This Book

The following terms and conventions are used throughout this book for consistency and ease of understanding:

- Special keyboard keys are printed like this: [Pg Up] or [Home].
- Characters that you are supposed to type are displayed in boldface within numbered sequences.
- The word "type" means just type the characters indicated, while "enter" means type the characters indicated and then press the [Enter] key.
- File names, block names, and cell references are always shown in uppercase, but entering them in lowercase will yield the same results.

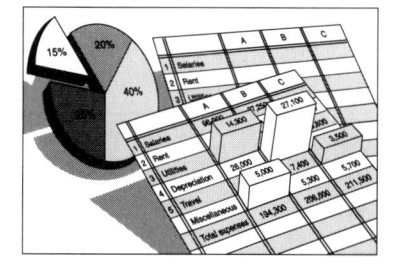

CHAPTER

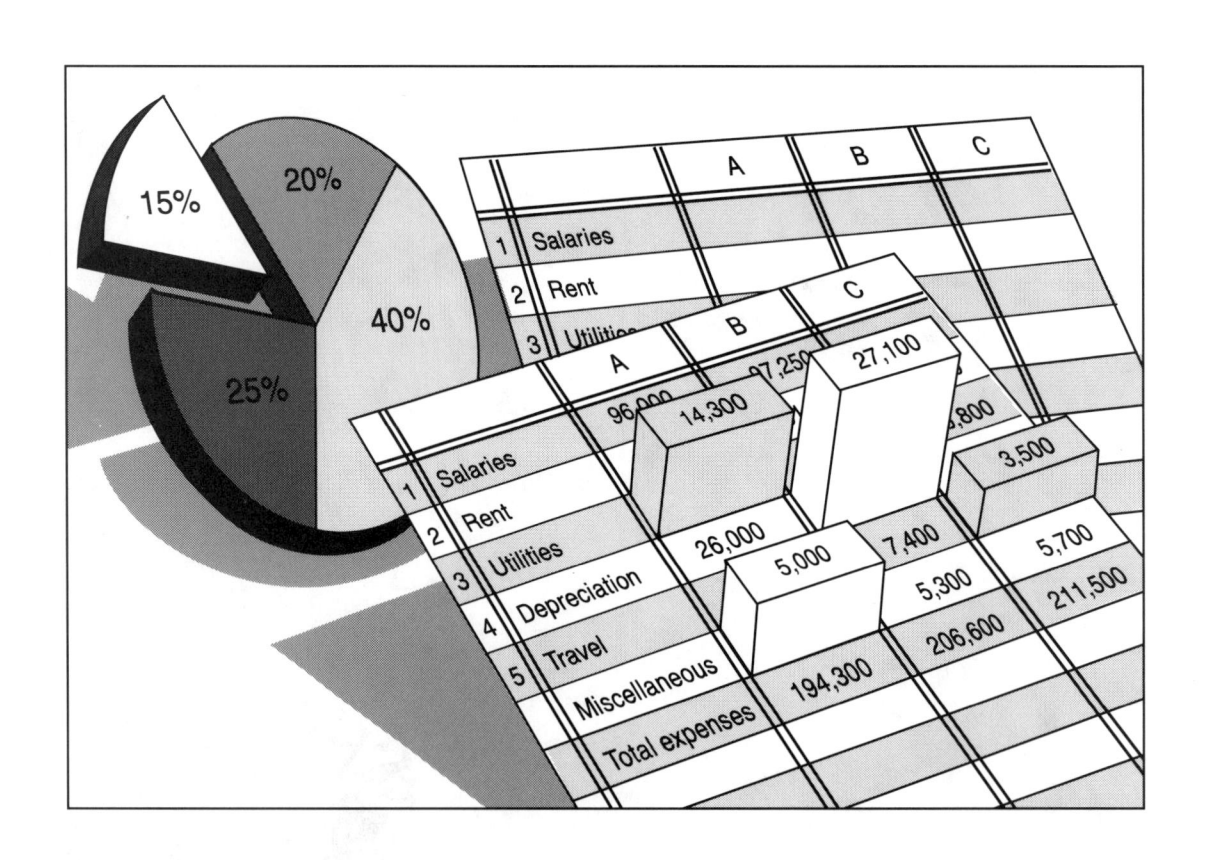

1
GETTING STARTED

Quattro Pro 5 combines three types of programs: spreadsheet, graphics, and database management. It is designed for organizing and manipulating data, particularly numeric data, and for translating that data into graphic form.

This book acquaints you with both the basic techniques of using Quattro Pro and the essential concepts of spreadsheet, graph, and database design. By reading the next six chapters, you will learn everything you need to know to build simple spreadsheets. From there you can delve into more advanced techniques, and then branch out into database management and into graphs.

A Few Basic Concepts

Before you begin working with Quattro Pro, you need to understand what spreadsheets, databases, and graphs are and what you can do with them.

What Is a Spreadsheet?

A *spreadsheet* is a grid of rows and columns in which you enter, edit, and view data. A spreadsheet program, such as Quattro Pro, is like an electronic ledger pad—it presents you with a largely empty screen on which you can enter and manipulate numbers and text. The notebook pages in the Quattro Pro spreadsheet are like the individual sheets of paper in a ledger pad.

NOTE: In Quattro Pro 5, spreadsheet files are now called *notebook files* and are divided into a large number of *notebook pages* that can contain discrete sets of information. You'll learn more about this enormously useful feature in a moment, as well as in Chapter 12. If you're accustomed to an older version of Quattro Pro or another spreadsheet, don't become confused: What was once called a spreadsheet is now often called a notebook.

Spreadsheets can be employed for everything from the simplest expense reports to the most complex loan calculations or statistical analyses. Some of the more typical applications are budgets, income statements, profit and loss projections, schedules of accounts payable and receivable, production schedules, loan analyses, and tax statements.

When you use a spreadsheet program, you generally begin by entering numbers and descriptive text; then you enter instructions that tell the program how to manipulate that data. For example, you might start a budget by entering a list of line items in one column, and then enter corresponding dollar amounts in the next column to the right. At the bottom of the numbers column, you would enter a set of instructions, known as a *formula*, directing the program to add all the numbers and display the result. A simple personal budget appears in Figure 1-1.

At this level the spreadsheet acts as little more than a glorified calculator. However, Quattro Pro offers several capabilities not available with calculators:

◆ It can perform *automatic recalculation*. Once you have told the spreadsheet program what calculations to perform, you can "plug in" any set of numbers and the results are updated automatically. For example, as soon

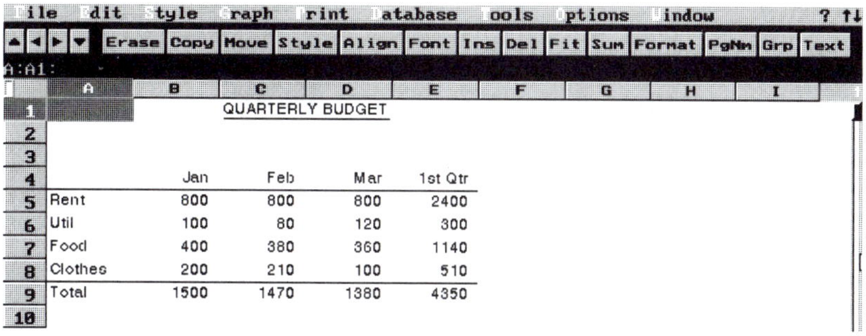

Getting Started

A simple personal budget
Figure 1-1.

	A	B	C	D	E
1			QUARTERLY BUDGET		
2					
3					
4		Jan	Feb	Mar	1st Qtr
5	Rent	800	800	800	2400
6	Util	100	80	120	300
7	Food	400	380	360	1140
8	Clothes	200	210	100	510
9	Total	1500	1470	1380	4350
10					

as you change any of the amounts allocated for food in the budget shown in Figure 1-1, the total changes to reflect that modification.

✦ It can perform sophisticated calculations. Besides addition and subtraction, Quattro Pro can easily handle over 100 other types of calculations, including financial, mathematical, and statistical calculations.

✦ It can consolidate data from multiple notebook pages, and can also link separate spreadsheet files. You might, for example, create individual notebook pages for each department, product line, or month in the year, and then design a separate notebook page that calculates the totals for all departments, products, or months. If you're working on a larger, more complex model, you can also create separate notebook files for each category and then link them when needed.

✦ You can create macros to automate particular sequences of keystrokes that you repeat frequently. Using a macro is similar to speed-dialing on a telephone: You press one button and the machine responds as if you had pressed a series of buttons, one after another.

What Is a Database?

A *database* is any structured collection of data about people, organizations, things, or events. Two characteristics distinguish databases from other groups of data: how they are organized and how they are used. A database always includes the same categories of information for every entity it contains. A phone book, for example, is a database of people and businesses that contains the names, addresses, and phone numbers for a set of individuals or organizations. A customer list might include the name, contact person, address, phone, date of last order, and credit limit for each organization on the list. In the personnel database shown in Figure 1-2, the categories of information include first name, last name, date hired, department code, position, and salary.

4

Quattro Pro 5 Made Easy

	A	B	C	D	E	F	G
1	PERSONNEL DATABASE						
2							
3	FIRST NAME	LAST NAME	HIRED	DEPT	POSITION	SALARY	
4	Maria	Cooper	10/01/87	FIN	Junior Accountant	24000	
5	Dennis	Mathews	11/15/87	FIN	Accountant	28000	
6	William	Weiss	03/04/88	MIS	Junior Programmer	18500	
7	Alicia	Tower	10/31/88	MIS	Senior Programmer	26500	
8	Timothy	Walker	03/05/89	MIS	Systems Analyst	36000	
9	Richard	Curry	07/21/89	PER	Accounting Clerk	16000	
10	Pat	Hernandez	10/27/89	FIN	Data Entry Clerk	15000	
11	Carol	Barnes	04/03/90	MIS	Executive Secretary	22000	
12	Thelma	Morgan	09/30/90	MIS	Junior Programmer	18500	
13	John	Mcdermott	11/03/90	PER	Senior Accountant	40000	
14	Lynne	Diamond	01/19/91	PER	Administrative Assistant	19000	
15	Alan	Frank	03/21/91	FIN	Data Entry Clerk	16000	
16	Martha	Walker	07/18/91	FIN	Accountant	32000	
17	Lauren	Albert	09/16/91	MIS	Senior Programmer	26000	
18	Anne	Mason	06/03/92	MIS	Data Entry Clerk	15500	
19	Hector	Santiago	07/21/92	MIS	Admistrative Assistant	22500	
20	Jennifer	Hoffman	08/18/92	PER	Senior Accountant	42000	
21	Tony	Santini	03/07/93	FIN	Junior Accountant	25000	
22	Marie	Thibaut	06/19/93	MIS	Systems Analyst	37500	

A personnel database
Figure 1-2.

In a Quattro Pro database, each column represents a single category of information, and the information for each person, organization, or thing in the database is located on a single row. You might not fill in every column of every row, but you leave space for every category of data.

Databases are also distinguished from other groups of data by the types of operations you perform on them, including sorting the data into a particular order, isolating data that meet particular criteria, and generating summary information or statistics. These operations form the crux of *database management*—the process of organizing, manipulating, and extracting information from databases.

In Quattro Pro, you can treat any area of a notebook as a database. When you work with a database, you use the same keys and many of the same commands that you would use when working with any other type of data on a notebook. The difference lies solely in the way you manipulate the data.

Graphics

Quattro Pro's third capability is displaying and printing graphs. Used properly, graphs are a succinct and engaging way to present information. Quattro Pro allows you to translate data from your spreadsheet or database into a graphic format quickly and easily. It offers 15 graph types—including

Getting Started

4 three-dimensional graph types—enabling you to summarize a tremendous amount of data in a format that is easy to grasp.

While Quattro Pro makes it easy to create simple graphs, it also provides an extensive array of tools for customizing and embellishing graphs, as you can see in Figure 1-3. You can mix graph types, change fill patterns and colors, alter fonts, and add labels to particular points in the graph. Quattro Pro's Annotator feature also lets you add descriptive elements—such as arrows and lines, boxes, and custom-drawn shapes or pictures.

Starting Up

When starting Quattro Pro, first make sure you are on the drive containing the Quattro Pro program (usually C or D). Then switch to the Quattro Pro directory, using the DOS change directory (CD) command. The form for this command is CD*directory name*. For example, if Quattro Pro is stored in the QPRO directory on drive C, you type **CD\QPRO** and press Enter. Next load the Quattro Pro program by typing **Q** and pressing Enter. Load Quattro Pro now so that you can follow the examples in this chapter.

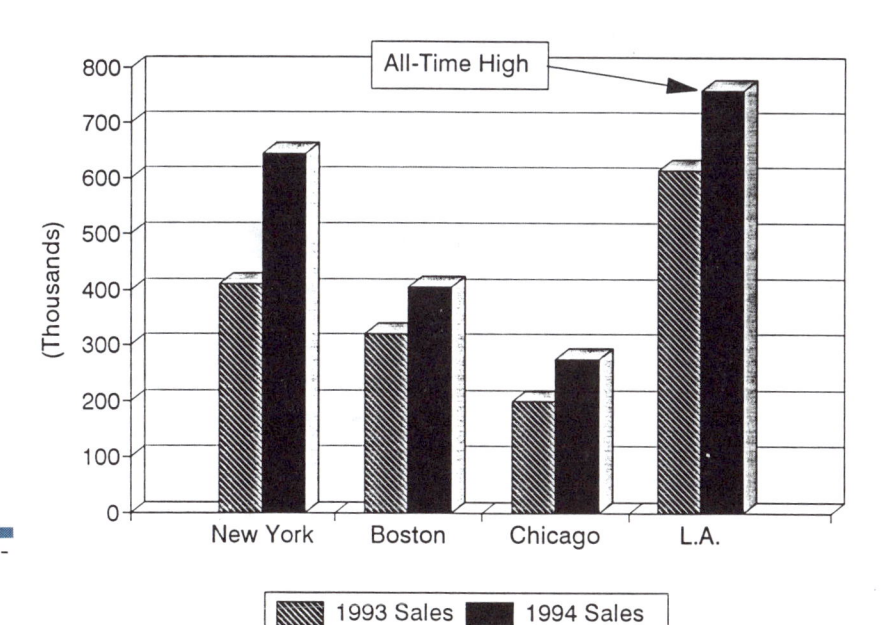

A presentation-quality graph
Figure 1-3.

Quattro Pro 5 Made Easy

The Quattro Pro Display

The Quattro Pro display consists of five sections, as shown in Figure 1-4.

- **The main menu bar** A list of nine options (File, Edit, and so on) on the first line of the screen.
- **The SpeedBar** If you have installed a mouse and loaded your mouse software, a SpeedBar appears at the top or right edge of the screen, depending on whether you're in WYSIWYG or a character-based display mode. You'll learn more about display modes later in this chapter.
- **The input line** The line below the SpeedBar in WYSIWYG display mode or below the menu bar in character-based display modes.
- **The notebook area** The majority of the Quattro Pro display, bounded by a column of numbers along the left, a row of letters across the top, a shaded "scroll bar" at the right, and lettered page tabs at the bottom. (These items are described in more detail under "The SpeedBar and Other Mouse Tools").
- **The status line** The last line of the Quattro Pro display, immediately below the notebook area.

The notebook area, input line, and status line are discussed here. The menu bar and SpeedBar are covered in the sections "The Quattro Pro Menu System" and "Using a Mouse in Quattro Pro," later in this chapter.

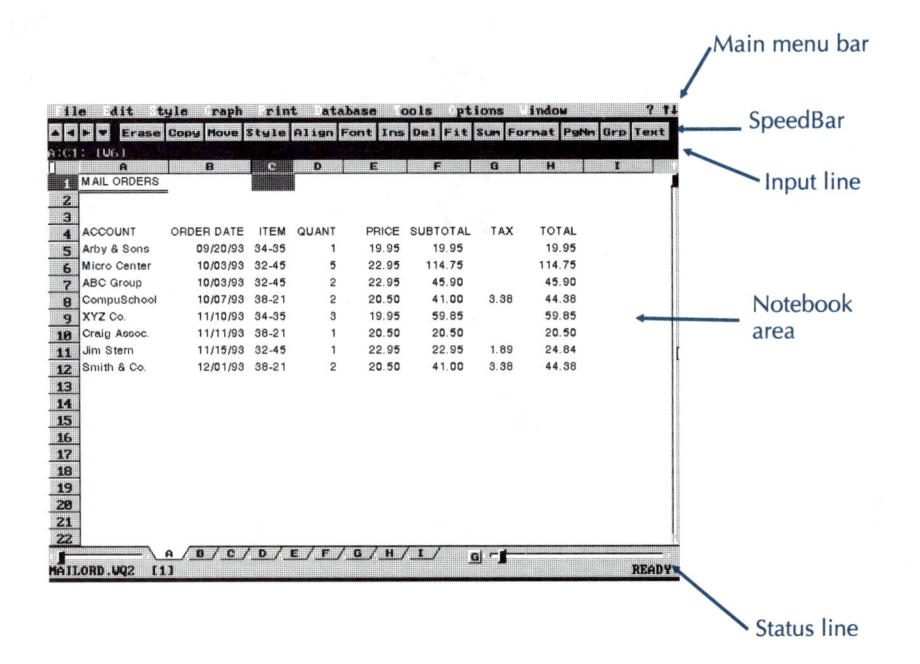

Sections of the Quattro Pro display
Figure 1-4.

Getting Started

Remember, if you do not have a mouse installed, you won't see the SpeedBar.

If you're using a relatively new color monitor (an EGA or VGA monitor), your screens will probably look like those shown so far in this book. If you're using a monochrome or CGA monitor, your screen will look more like the one shown in Figure 1-5. This is one of the available character-based—as opposed to graphics-based—display modes. For more on display modes, see "The WYSIWYG Display Mode" section later in this chapter.

The Notebook Area

The notebook area is the section in which you enter and view your data. This area is actually a window onto a much larger notebook surface that is 256 columns wide and 8192 rows long. (Columns are labeled A through Z, AA through AZ, BA through BZ, and so on up to IV.) As you will see, you can move this window to view different sections of the notebook. The important thing to note is that what you see on the screen is only a small part of a large landscape: There may be more data beyond the borders of your display and there is definitely more room for data.

The notebook area consists of individual *cells*—rectangles formed by the intersection of one row and one column. Every piece of data that you enter into a notebook is placed in a single cell. Each cell is referred to by its column letter and row number. Cell A1, for example, is located in the upper-left corner of the notebook. This letter and number combination is known as the cell's *coordinates,* or its address. In Quattro Pro 5, a cell's address also includes its notebook page number. For example, cell A:A1 is the upper-left cell in the first page of the current notebook.

The rectangular highlight that marks the currently selected cell is known as the *cell pointer.* When you first enter Quattro Pro, the cell pointer is

Notebook displayed in the 80x25 character-based display mode
Figure 1-5.

positioned in cell A1, or the *home cell*. Whenever Quattro Pro is ready to accept data, the cell pointer is positioned in a single cell, which is referred to as the *current cell*. If you start entering data, it will be placed in the current cell as soon as you press [Enter].

To determine the address of the current cell, you can look at the top and left borders of the notebook area, where the current cell's coordinates are displayed in reverse video or a contrasting color. For example, in Figure 1-6 the cell pointer is in cell E6, so the letter "E" is highlighted on the upper border of the notebook area and the number 6 is highlighted on the left border. The coordinates of the current cell are also displayed at the left side of the input line. (The A: just before E6 indicates the current notebook page.) If the cell contains data, the cell contents are displayed to the right of the cell address.

The Input Line

The information on the input line depends on the operation you are performing. When you enter data, the characters you type initially appear on the input line. They are transferred to the current cell when you press [Enter] or one of the cursor-movement keys. When you edit data, a copy of the contents of the current cell is displayed on the input line. You then modify the data on this line, and press [Enter] or one of the arrow keys to transfer your changes back to the cell. When you issue a command, Quattro Pro often displays messages or questions on the input line prompting you for more information. Your response appears on this same line. In all other cases, the input line simply displays the address and contents of the current cell.

The Status Line

The status line—the last line of the screen—is divided into left, middle, and right sections—and each displays information about the current working environment. In Quattro Pro 5, there are some new features just above the

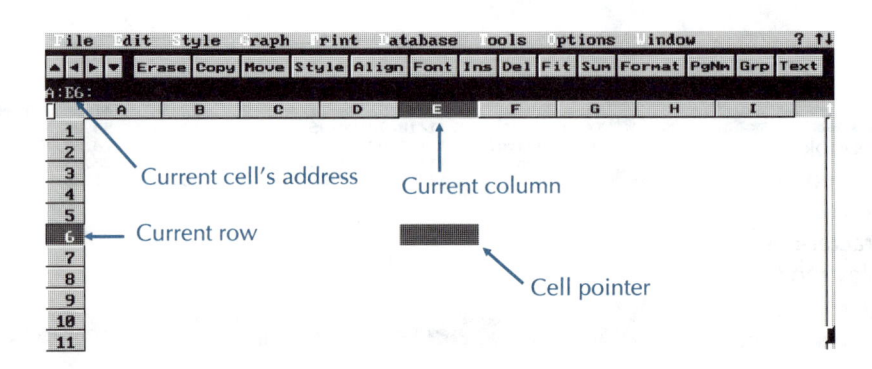

Determining the address of the current cell
Figure 1-6.

Getting Started

status line, most notably the lettered notebook tabs that let you move between and manipulate notebook pages. These are covered later in the chapter, under "The SpeedBars and Other Mouse Tools."

The information that appears on the left side of the status line depends on what you are doing. If you are simply moving around the notebook, the left side of the status line contains the name of the notebook and the number of the window that the notebook occupies. (The number helps you determine where you are when you are working with several notebooks at once.) If you are editing previously entered data, the data currently stored in the cell appears on this line until you press [Enter] to replace the old cell contents with the new. If you are using a menu, this line contains information about the currently highlighted menu option. If Quattro Pro is displaying a message or question on the input line, the status line displays the address and contents of the current cell.

The middle of the status line displays information on the status of various keys. If [Caps Lock] is turned on, for example, the letters "CAP" appear here.

At the right side of the status line, Quattro Pro always displays a *mode indicator*, specifying in which mode the program is currently operating. When you first enter Quattro Pro, the program is in Ready mode, meaning that it is ready to accept data. Quattro Pro's other modes include Help, when a help screen is displayed; Edit, when you are editing the contents of a cell; and Menu, when you activate the menu system.

The WYSIWYG Display Mode

WYSIWYG stands for "what you see is what you get."

When you install Quattro Pro, you are asked to choose a default display mode. If you chose the WYSIWYG mode, your screen will look much like most of the ones displayed in this book. You can only use WYSIWYG mode if you have an EGA or VGA graphics adaptor board. Assuming you have such a board, you can change from one display mode to another during the course of any work session and can also switch your default display mode so that Quattro Pro automatically instates the display mode of your choice every time you load the program.

The full range of display modes available in Quattro Pro is covered in Chapter 13. Your basic choice is between the various character-based modes and WYSIWYG. In character-based modes, your computer uses a built-in set of characters to construct images on your screen. In graphics display modes, such as WYSIWYG, your computer constructs all shapes—including letters, numbers, lines, squares, and so on—out of dots, allowing it to display virtually any two-dimensional image.

WYSIWYG mode offers a much closer approximation of what your notebook will look like when printed than do the character-based display modes. In

Quattro Pro 5 Made Easy

particular, you can see the exact point size and typeface of any fonts that you applied to your text. If you have a mouse installed, the icons on the SpeedBar appear more three-dimensional and sculpted in WYSIWYG mode. The colors are also generally different from those used in character-based modes, and Quattro Pro allows you to choose your own colors for most of the screen elements. WYSIWYG also permits you to see graphs inserted into the notebook.

You cannot print a readable image of your screen using the Prt Sc key in WYSIWYG mode.

You can also adjust WYSIWYG's "zoom" setting, which determines the degree to which the image is enlarged or reduced. The default zoom setting is 100%, which approximates what the notebook will look like when printed. If you increase this percentage, you will see a smaller section of the notebook in greater detail. If you decrease it, you will see a larger block of cells displayed with smaller characters.

Assuming you have a VGA or EGA board, the choice between character-based display modes and WYSIWYG is yours. If you often use a variety of fonts and inserted graphs, you may decide to work primarily in WYSIWYG mode. However, since character-based modes can be a bit easier to read and a bit faster—particularly on relatively slow computers—you may prefer working in the character-based mode most of the time and switching to WYSIWYG mode only as necessary.

If you are completely new to Quattro Pro, you will learn how to issue commands later in this chapter.

To change display modes, you issue the / **O**ptions | **D**isplay Mode command. If you are using a mouse, you can switch from a character-based display mode to WYSIWYG by clicking the WYS button on the SpeedBar (you may need to click on the BAR button first) and switch to character-based mode by clicking the Text button. If you want to change your default display mode—so that 80x25 mode is turned on automatically whenever you load Quattro Pro for example—select the desired display mode and then issue the / **O**ptions | **U**pdate command.

The Quattro Pro Keyboard

Quattro Pro assigns its own meanings to many of the nonalphanumeric keys on your keyboard. Because there are a wide variety of computer keyboards, it is impossible to specify exactly where these keys will be on your system. If you are not already familiar with your keyboard, take some time to locate each of the following keys, which are listed in Table 1-1.

Movement Keys

On the right side of all computer keyboards is a numeric keypad. You can use this keypad either for cursor movement or, if you press Num Lock, for entering numbers. When Number Lock is off, pressing any of the arrow keys moves the *cursor* or cell pointer in the direction indicated by the arrow.

Getting Started

Table 1-1. Keys on the Keyboard

Key	Function
Enter	Sometimes labeled Return or simply with a ↵ symbol
Esc	The Escape key, often located in the upper-left corner of the keyboard
Break	Generally shares a key with Scroll Lock or Pause, in the upper-right section of the keyboard
Ctrl	The Control key
Alt	The Alternate key
Backspace	A leftward-pointing arrow or a key labeled Backspace to the right of the number keys near the top of the keyboard
Caps Lock	The Capitals Lock key
Tab	Generally located to the left of the Q key
Function keys	Located either at the top or at the left edge of the keyboard, labeled F1 through F10 or F12
Numeric keypad	A set of number or cursor-movement keys, laid out like a calculator, located at the right side of the keyboard
Directional keypad	On newer keyboards, an extra set of cursor-movement keys like those on the numeric keypad; generally located to the left of the numeric keypad
Num Lock	The Number Lock key, usually located at the top of the numeric keypad at the right edge of the keyboard
Ins	The Insert key; shares a key with the number 0 on the numeric keypad and, on newer keyboards, has its own key above the directional keypad
Del	The Delete key; shares a key with the decimal point on the numeric keypad and, on newer keyboards, has its own key above the directional keypad

Some keyboards contain a second set of arrow keys—the directional keypad—so you can use that set for moving around on the screen and reserve the numeric keypad for numbers.

NOTE: [Num Lock] is like the SHIFT LOCK key on a typewriter. When it is off, the lower character printed on each key in the numeric keypad is active; when it is on, the upper characters (the numbers) are active.

Several keys allow you to make large leaps on the notebook. In addition to the arrows, the numeric keypad contains the four cursor-movement keys [Home], [End], [Pg Up], and [Pg Dn]. The [Home] key is a shortcut to the top-left corner of the notebook, immediately repositioning the cursor on cell A1 of the current notebook page. The [Pg Up] key moves the notebook display window up a screen, while maintaining the relative position of the cursor within the window. In contrast, the [Pg Dn] key moves the notebook display down one screen.

You will learn how to use the [End] key in Chapter 4, after you have entered more data.

[End] is always used in combination with another key. In combination with the arrow keys, it is used to move the cell pointer from one block of data on the notebook page to another. The [End]-[Home] key combination (pressing [End] and then pressing [Home]) moves the cell pointer to the last cell that contains data on the notebook page.

Quattro Pro also provides keys for jumping sideways on the notebook page. [Tab] moves the display a screenful of columns to the right. Holding down one of the [Shift] keys and pressing [Tab] moves the display a screenful of columns to the left. [Ctrl]-[→] (holding the [Ctrl] key while tapping the [→] key) is the equivalent of [Tab], and [Ctrl]-[←] is the equivalent of [Shift]-[Tab].

Function Keys

The function keys are labeled [F1] through [F10] or [F12], depending on your keyboard, and are located at either the top or the left side of the keyboard. Most of the function keys have different effects depending on whether you use them alone or in combination with other keys. For example, pressing [F2] places Quattro Pro in Edit mode, allowing you to change the contents of the current cell. However, holding down the [Shift] key while pressing [F2] places Quattro Pro in Debug mode, which is used for locating errors in macros.

If you accidentally press [F10] (the Graph key), the screen goes blank. Just press [Esc] to return to your notebook.

Most of the function keys are explained in this book as they become relevant in the learning process. The discussion here is limited to [F5], the GoTo key. When you press this key, Quattro Pro displays the prompt "Enter address to go to." To the right of this prompt, the coordinates of the current cell are displayed. These cell coordinates are the default—the setting that Quattro Pro assumes unless you specify otherwise. You will encounter similar default settings throughout your work with Quattro Pro. If you want to accept the default, press [Enter]; otherwise overwrite the default by typing in a setting of

Getting Started

your choice and pressing [Enter]. In this case, Quattro Pro moves the cell pointer directly to the specified cell, moving the notebook area if this cell is not already visible on the screen. Notice that the default cell coordinates include the notebook page. If you are staying on the same page, however, you don't need to reenter the page number.

The Quattro Pro Menu System

Much of your work in Quattro Pro will involve moving the cell pointer around on the notebook, and entering and editing data. However, Quattro Pro also offers over 200 commands for such tasks as changing the notebook environment; altering the appearance of data; printing, graphing, and saving your work; and retrieving notebook files from disk. You issue these commands by choosing options from one or more menus and, in some cases, entering additional information as requested by the program.

The top line of the Quattro Pro screen always contains a menu bar. When you first enter the program, you see the options File, Edit, Style, Graph, Print, Database, Tools, Options, and Window. This Main menu is your point of entry into the Quattro Pro menu system. Most options on this menu lead to other, more detailed menus.

Access the menu system with the slash (/) that shares a key with the question mark rather than the backslash (\\).

When you first enter Quattro Pro, the menu system is dormant. To activate the menus, you press either [F3] or, more commonly, the / (slash) key. If you have a mouse, you can activate the menu system just by clicking on one of the nine options in the Main menu.

As soon as you press /, Quattro Pro highlights the first option on the menu, File. At this point, you still see only the Main menu bar. If you select any of the options on this bar, Quattro Pro displays a pull-down menu, as shown in Figure 1-7. If you're using a mouse, clicking on one of the options in the Main menu automatically "pulls down" the associated menu.

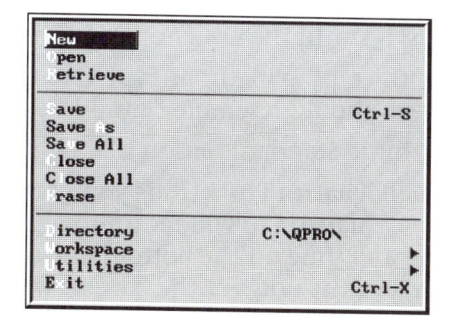

Opening the
File menu
Figure 1-7.

```
New
 pen
 etrieve

 ave                        Ctrl-S
Save  s
Sa e All
 lose
C ose All
 rase

 irectory        C:\QPRO\
 orkspace                      ▶
 tilities                      ▶
E it                        Ctrl-X
```

Quattro Pro 5 Made Easy

There are three methods of selecting menu options in Quattro Pro:

- **The pointing or point-and-shoot method** Use the arrow keys to highlight the desired option, and then press [Enter] to select it.
- **The typing method** Type the highlighted letter within an option name.
- **The clicking method** If you have a mouse, move the mouse pointer to the desired option and click the left mouse button.

You'll find more information on mouse usage under "Basic Mouse Techniques" later in this chapter.

Try activating the menu system now:

1. Type /. The File option on the menu bar becomes highlighted and the mode indicator in the lower-right corner of the screen changes from READY to MENU, indicating that Quattro Pro is now in Menu mode.
2. Press [→] to move through the options on the Main menu. Notice that the descriptions on the status line change as you move from one option to the next.
3. Use [→] or [←] to highlight the File option, and press [Enter] to open the File menu, which is shown in Figure 1-7. The triangles that appear to the right of some menu options indicate options that lead to other, more specific menus.
4. Press [↓] to move through the options. Again, note the menu option descriptions on the status line.
5. Press [→] to move through the options on the Main menu bar. This time, because you have already opened one menu, you will see the menus associated with each option on the menu bar. If you move past the last option on the menu bar (the Window option), you cycle back to the first option.

Now try issuing a command that directs Quattro Pro to display the current date and time (according to your computer's clock) on the status line.

1. Press [→] or [←] until the Options menu is open.
2. Press [↓] until the Other option is highlighted; then press [Enter].
3. Try the typing method: Type **C** to select Clock. At this point, your screen should resemble Figure 1-8.
4. With the Standard option highlighted, press [Enter].
5. When Quattro Pro returns you to the Options menu, type **Q** to select Quit. Quattro Pro will return to Ready mode. You should now see the date and time on the bottom line of the screen. This date and time display lasts only for the current work session.

Chapter 13 explains how to make settings such as this date and time setting permanent.

Getting Started

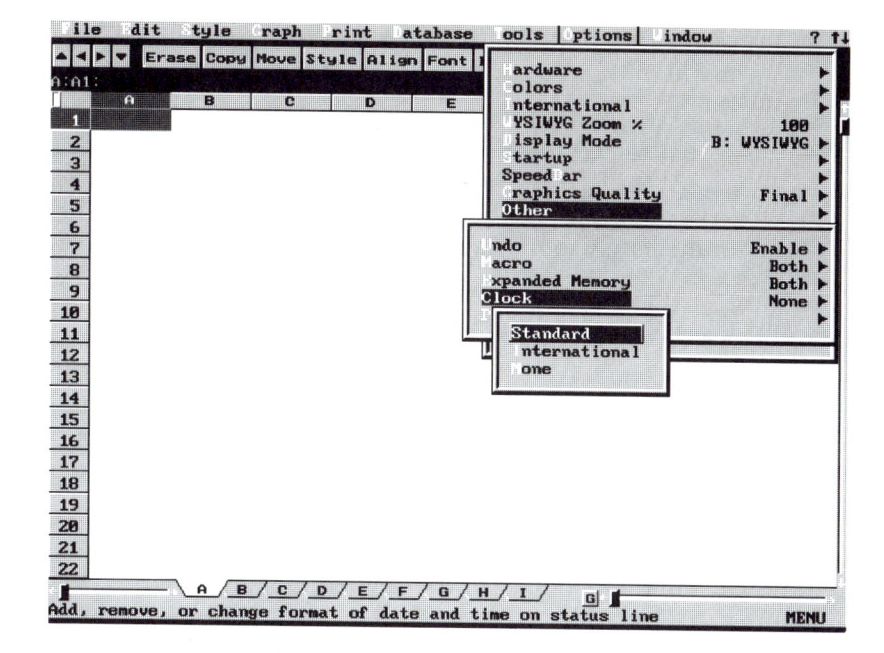

Issuing the /**O**ptions | **O**ther | **C**lock | **S**tandard command
Figure 1-8.

In many cases, Quattro Pro returns to Ready mode as soon as it carries out your command. Sometimes it returns to the menu from which you made your selection or to the previous menu, on the assumption that you may want to make another selection. From there you can issue another command, or choose the Quit option or press [Esc] to return to the previous menu level (or to Ready mode if you are already on one of the Main menu bar's menus).

Quattro Pro commands are referred to by the sequence of menu selections required to execute them. The command that you just issued, for example, is the / **O**ptions | **O**ther | **C**lock | **S**tandard command. Commands are written with vertical bars separating one menu option from the next. The letter you type to select each menu option is printed in boldface. Quattro Pro menus are referred to by the option or, in some cases, the series of menu options, that you select to display that menu. For example, the menu displayed when you select the Other option from the Options menu is called the Other menu or perhaps the Options | Other menu.

The "Hold Everything" Keys

As you work with Quattro Pro, you will undoubtedly change your mind sometimes in the midst of a command sequence. There are two means of backing out of a command. The [Esc] (Escape) key generally takes you back one step in the command sequence. For example, if you are on the Clock menu and decide not to continue with the / **O**ptions | **C**lock | **S**tandard command, pressing [Esc] takes you back one menu level—from the Clock menu to the Other menu.

You can undertake an even more dramatic escape from a command sequence with the [Ctrl]-[Break] key combination. To use [Ctrl]-[Break], hold down one of the [Ctrl] keys and tap the [Break] key, which generally occupies the same key as [Pause] or [Scroll Lock] in the upper-right corner of the keyboard. [Ctrl]-[Break] immediately returns you to Ready mode.

Getting Help

When you use Quattro Pro, help is always available at the touch of the [F1] (Help) key. If you press [F1] while a menu is displayed on the screen, Quattro Pro displays a screenful of information on the highlighted menu option. Otherwise it displays a Help Topics screen listing the main categories of information covered in the Help system.

Keywords are displayed in boldface or a contrasting color.

A help screen contains a list of keywords on the current subject. To display information on one of the keyword topics, use the arrow keys to highlight the word and then press [Enter], or click on the word with your mouse. Most help screens also contain a list of related topics at the bottom of the screen. This list always includes an option for returning to the Help Topics screen, and often an option for returning to the previous help topic you selected. As with the keywords, you can select one of these topics by highlighting the topic name and pressing [Enter], or by clicking on the word with your mouse.

If you press [F1] while in the Help system, Quattro Pro displays a screen with information on using the Help system itself. If you press the [Backspace] key, Quattro Pro redisplays the previous help screen. Pressing [Esc] or [Ctrl]-[Break] deactivates the Help system.

NOTE: Letters that you type to find a Help Index topic appear after the "Search for" prompt in the status line. Continue typing to add letters to the search string, or press [Backspace] to delete letters if you want to rephrase your search or begin a brand new search.

You can also press [F3] while in the Help system to display a Help Index—an alphabetical list of help topics. You can move through this list using the cursor-movement keys. In addition, you can type the first few letters of the desired topic to move to that location in the list. Once you've highlighted the topic you want, just click on it or press [Enter] to display a help screen on that topic.

Try out these Help keys now:

Getting Started

1. Press F1. You should immediately see the Help Topics screen shown in Figure 1-9. The cursor should be positioned on the keyword Help.
2. Press ↓ to move to the keyword Basics, and press Enter to select it. Quattro Pro displays a screen labeled "Introduction to Quattro Pro."
3. Press ↓ to highlight the keyword Starting and press Enter to select it. You should see a screen entitled "Starting a Quattro Pro Work Session." On this screen, the keywords are embedded in the text itself. When you first display the screen, the words "enter data" are highlighted.
4. Press the → key nine times to move through all the keywords. Press Enter to select the Help Topics key word at the bottom of the screen.
5. Press F3 to display the Help Index.
6. Type **H** to move down to the entry for Hardware Options. Then type **EL** to move directly to the Help entry. You should see the letters "HEL" after the Search for prompt in the status line.
7. Press Enter to display information about the Quattro Pro Help system.
8. Leave the Help system by pressing Esc.

Using a Mouse in Quattro Pro

As you probably know, a *mouse* is a hand-operated device for pointing to various objects or locations on your screen and making selections. Although you do not need a mouse to use Quattro Pro, it can be a very useful supplement to the keyboard.

In Quattro Pro, you can use a mouse to activate or deactivate the menu system and select menu options; move the cell pointer; point out a block of

The Help Topics screen
Figure 1-9.

```
Quattro Pro Help Topics
  Help      How to use help.           Functions      @Functions.
  Basics    A guide to Quattro Pro.    Macros         Macros.
  Keys      Description of special     Menu Commands  Descriptions of
            keys in Quattro Pro.                      menu commands.
  1-2-3     Quattro Pro for            File Manager   Using the File
            1-2-3 users.                              Manager.
  Mouse     How to use a mouse         Error Messages Descriptions of
            in Quattro Pro.                           error messages.
  Graphs    Creating graphs            Formulas       Creating formulas
            in Quattro Pro.                           in Quattro Pro.
  Printing  Printing notebooks         Glossary       Common terms
            in Quattro Pro.                           in Quattro Pro.
  Use arrow keys to move around this screen, Enter to choose topic.
```

cells on the notebook in preparation for moving, copying, deleting, or formatting data; accept or cancel cell entries or entries in a dialog box; scroll through lists of options; change the size of a column; resize or reposition windows; draw lines, boxes, and pictures to embellish graphs using the Annotator; switch between character-based display modes and WYSIWYG; and switch between pages in the current notebook.

If you have a mouse installed and your mouse software is loaded, a mouse pointer appears on your screen as soon as you load Quattro Pro. This pointer is initially displayed as a small highlighted rectangle in character-based display modes and as an arrow in WYSIWYG.

Basic Mouse Techniques

If you have never used a mouse, there are a few terms that you need to know. *Point* means move the mouse until the mouse pointer is positioned on the desired object or spot on the screen. *Click* means press and release the left button on the mouse. *Drag* means hold down the left button while you move the mouse pointer on the screen. These three actions form the repertoire of mouse techniques you use in Quattro Pro.

NOTE: By default, you use the left mouse button in Quattro Pro. If you prefer, you can specify the right button as the active button, as discussed in Chapter 13.

To move the cell pointer with a mouse, simply point to the desired cell and click. Other techniques for moving around on the notebook surface will be discussed shortly.

To activate the menu system, click on any option on the Main menu bar. Once you are in Menu mode, you can select menu options by clicking on them. To leave the menu system, click on any cell in the notebook area. Note that clicking on a cell when you are in Menu mode deactivates the menu system but does not move the cell pointer to that cell. This enables you to leave the menu system without changing your position on the notebook.

The SpeedBars and Other Mouse Tools

When you load Quattro Pro with a mouse installed and mouse software loaded, an extra set of symbols, known as a SpeedBar, appear at the top or the right edge of the screen. This SpeedBar can look quite different in character-based display modes (Figure 1-10) than in WYSIWYG mode

Getting Started

SpeedBar in
80x25
character-based
display mode
Figure 1-10.

(Figure 1-11). SpeedBars are designed to streamline your work with Quattro Pro. Most of the SpeedBar buttons let you instantly issue a frequently used command—such as the command for copying or erasing data. Other buttons allow you to duplicate the effects of different keys on your keyboard, particularly the function keys. (Chapter 13 explains how to customize SpeedBars by changing the names and functions of the buttons.)

> **NOTE:** In character-based display modes, there is not room for all the mouse buttons on the SpeedBar. Click the BAR button to see the additional buttons. Click BAR again to return to the previous SpeedBar display.

There are actually two different SpeedBars available in Quattro Pro. The Ready mode SpeedBar (shown in Figures 1-10 and 1-11) appears when you first load Quattro Pro and contains a wide range of buttons for moving the cell pointer, erasing, copying, and moving data, inserting and deleting columns and rows, and more. The Edit SpeedBar, shown in Figure 1-12, appears whenever you enter or edit the data in a cell. It contains buttons to help you change an entry or construct formulas.

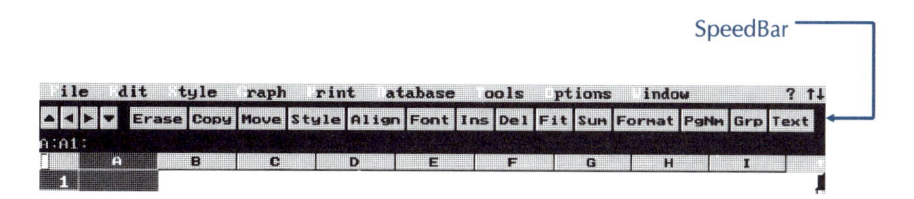

SpeedBar in
WYSIWYG
mode
Figure 1-11.

The Edit SpeedBar
Figure 1-12.

The Edit SpeedBar

The buttons on the two SpeedBars will be explained as they become relevant. In the meantime, you can experiment with some of the other mouse tools available on the Quattro Pro screen, as shown in Figure 1-13. The two adjacent arrows in the upper-right corner of the screen are known as the *zoom icon.* If you are using a character-based display mode and the current window occupies the entire screen, clicking on the zoom icon shrinks the window. Otherwise, clicking on this icon expands the window so that it fills the screen. In WYSIWYG, unless you already have multiple windows on the screen Quattro Pro simply beeps if you click on the zoom icon; if you already have multiple windows on screen, you can use the zoom icon to expand one of them but not to shrink it again. (Chapter 11 explains how to change the size of windows and work with multiple windows on the screen at once.)

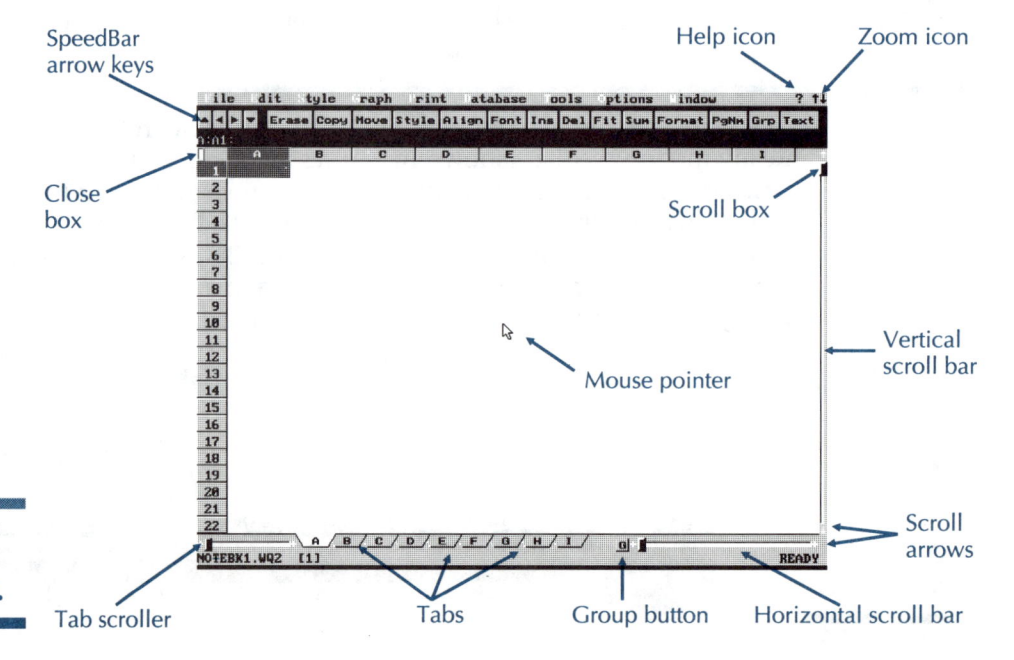

Other mouse icons
Figure 1-13.

Getting Started

*If you click the close box accidentally, issue the **File** | **New** / command to reopen the notebook window.*

To the left of the zoom icon is the Help icon (?), which is the mouse analogue for the F1 (Help) key. Click on this symbol to activate the Quattro Pro Help system.

The set of four arrows on the SpeedBar are for moving around the spreadsheet. When you're not in Edit mode, clicking on one of these arrows has the same effect as pressing the corresponding arrow key on your keyboard after pressing the End key (see Chapter 4 for details).

In the upper-left corner of the screen, just below the input line, is a close box, displayed as ⌐ in character-based display modes, and as a solid rectangle in WYSIWYG. Clicking on this icon closes both the current notebook file and the currently selected window.

At the right side and bottom right edge of the screen are *scroll bars*, shaded bars with small rectangles indicating the current position of the cell pointer. (In Quattro Pro 5, the bottom, or horizontal, scroll bar does not occupy the full width of the screen.) You can use these bars to move quickly through the notebook surface as well as to scroll through lists. At either end of the scroll bars are *scroll arrows*; clicking on the scroll arrows scrolls the window up or down a row at a time or left or right a column at a time. Each scroll bar also includes a *scroll box* that you can click on and drag with your mouse to move rapidly through the notebook. This feature is particularly handy when your notebook is too large to fit on the screen.

Quattro Pro 5 also includes several mouse tools for navigating through the pages of your notebooks and for taking advantage of the new notebook features. To the left of the horizontal scroll bar are a number of *page tabs*. You can click on these tabs to move to the various pages in your current notebook. By default, the page tabs are marked with letters, but you can also assign names to them, as you'll learn in Chapter 12. To the left of the notebook tabs is another scroll bar known as the *tab scroller*. This scroll bar operates much like the horizontal and vertical scroll bars, but allows you to display tabs for notebooks pages that are not currently visible. Once you've displayed the desired tab, simply click on it to move to the notebook page of your choice. Finally, immediately to the left of the horizontal scroll bar is the Group button (marked with a "G"). Click on this button to switch to *group mode,* in which you can perform actions on multiple pages at the same time. You'll learn much more about working with multiple notebook pages in Chapter 12.

Leaving Quattro Pro

The last operation covered in this chapter is the / **F**ile | **Ex**it command. If you issue this command before entering any data, Quattro Pro immediately returns you to the operating system. If you have entered or changed data and have not yet saved your work, Quattro Pro displays a dialog box with the message "Lose your changes and Exit?" at the top, followed by the three options No, Yes, and Save & Exit. If you choose No, Quattro Pro returns you to the notebook. If you select Yes, Quattro Pro discards any data you have entered or changed since the last time you saved your notebook and returns you to the operating system. If you select Save & Exit, Quattro Pro saves the notebook (asking you for a name if you just created the notebook and otherwise using the previously assigned name) and then returns you to the operating system.

When you first install Quattro Pro, certain control keys known as *shortcuts* are assigned to some of the most commonly used menu options. These key combinations allow you to execute a command by holding down [Ctrl] and tapping the assigned letter. For example, the shortcut for the / **F**ile | **E**xit command is [Ctrl]-[X]. Using this key combination has exactly the same effect as choosing Exit from the File menu. In fact, when you open the File menu, the shortcut key combination is displayed next to the Exit option as a reminder. Other preassigned shortcuts are introduced in this book as they become relevant.

Try leaving Quattro Pro now, using either the menus or the [Ctrl]-[X] shortcut to issue the / **F**ile | **E**xit command. Then, if you want to continue on to the next chapter, just enter **Q** to reload the program.

This chapter presented an overview of Quattro Pro's tools and capabilities. If this is your first exposure to spreadsheet or database software, the chapter may have covered more material than you can absorb at once. If so, don't worry and don't try to memorize the various keys and commands introduced so far. All you need at this point is a sense of the basic types of resources available with Quattro Pro. You will master the details easily once you begin putting these tools to work.

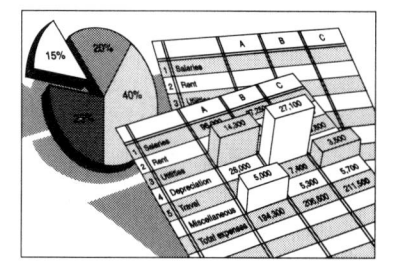

CHAPTER

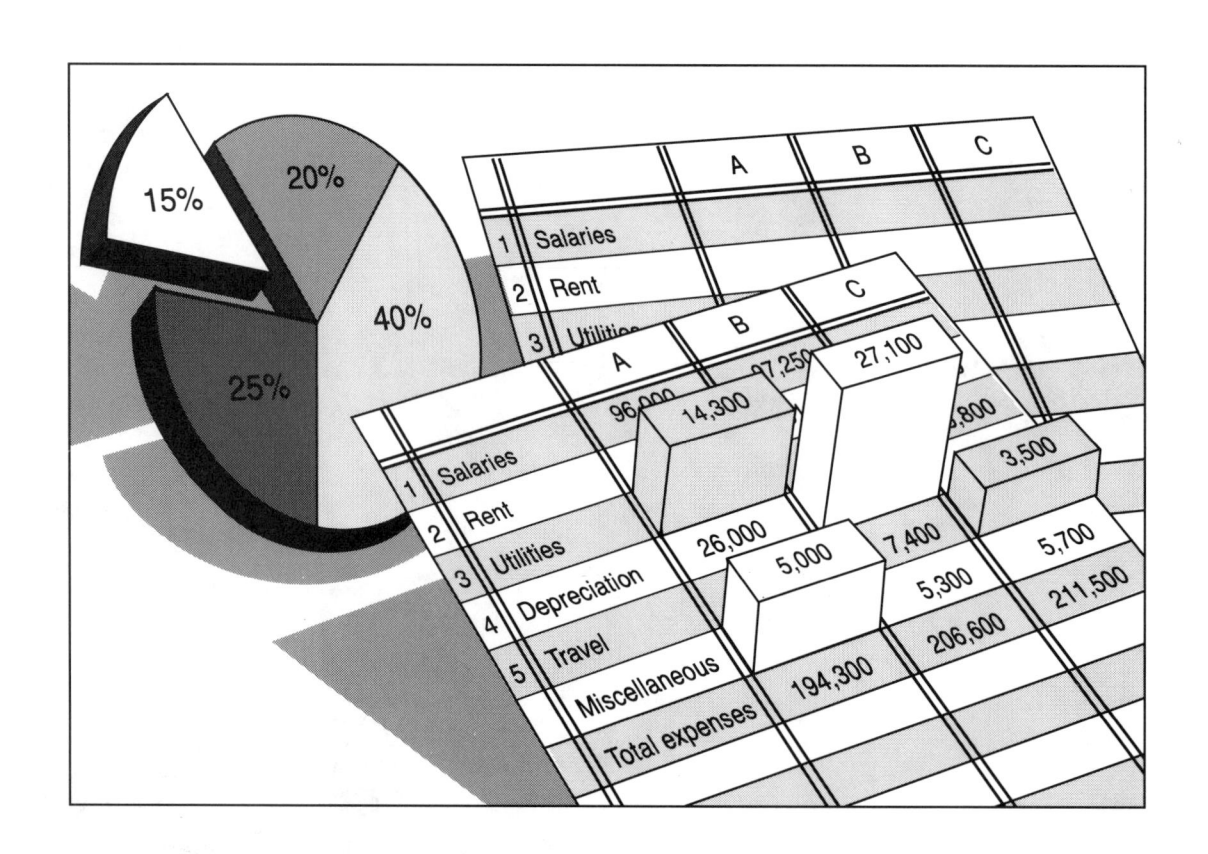

2
ENTERING TEXT AND NUMBERS

In this chapter you learn how to enter text, numbers, and dates. You also learn how to edit data, and how to save and retrieve your work. Much of your work in this and the following chapters will involve building and refining a sample notebook. This notebook is a model for projecting a company's income for 1994 and comparing it to actual income for 1993. Creating this typical financial model will acquaint you with the fundamentals you need to build any Quattro Pro notebook.

Figure 2-1 shows the notebook as it should look by the time you have completed this chapter. Illustrations of the notebook-in-progress appear throughout the next three chapters to ensure that you are on the right track.

Entering Data

Entering data into a cell entails three steps: First you must move the cell pointer to the cell in which you want the data to appear. Next you type the data. As you type, the characters appear on the input line at the top of the screen. If you make mistakes while you are typing, you can use the [Backspace] key to erase characters to the left of the cursor, and then reenter them as necessary. Finally, you press either the [Enter] key or one of the cursor-movement keys to copy the data from the input line into the cell itself. If you press [Enter], the cell pointer remains in the same cell. Using one of the cursor-movement keys to finish making the entry has the same effect as pressing [Enter] and then pressing the cursor-movement key.

NOTE: If you are using a mouse, the mouse control buttons [Enter] and [Esc] are displayed on the input line whenever you enter or edit data. Clicking on [Enter] is equivalent to pressing the [Enter] key. Clicking on [Esc] is equivalent to pressing [Esc].

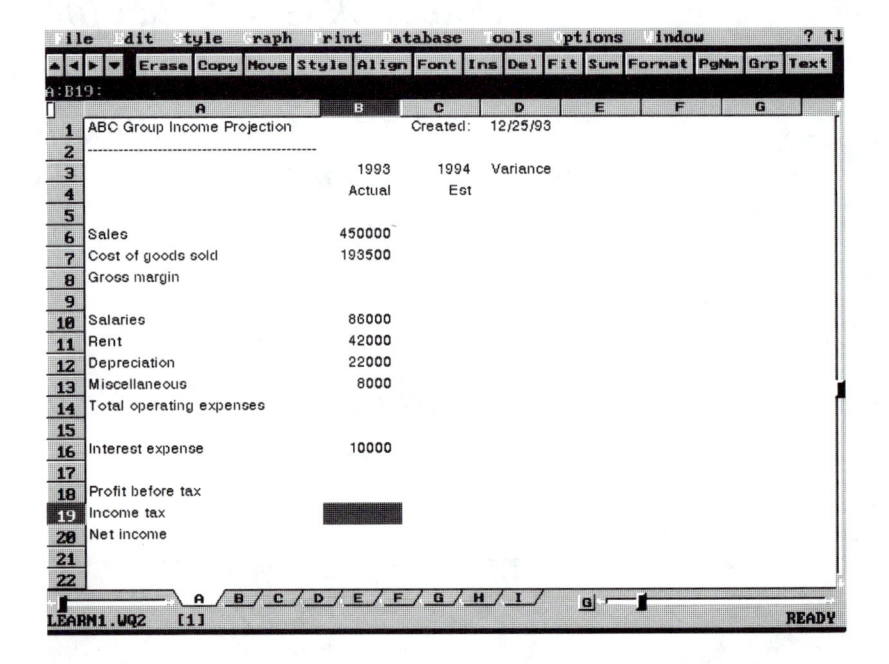

The Chapter 2 notebook
Figure 2-1.

Entering Text and Numbers

If you notice a mistake before you have finished entering data into a cell, you can use the [Backspace] key to back up, erasing characters as you go. You can also press [Esc] to discard everything on the input line. If you notice a mistake after you have entered the data, just pretend the cell is empty and enter the data again. As soon as you press [Enter] or one of the arrow keys, the new data replaces the old. If you want to erase the cell contents altogether, move the cell pointer to the cell you want to erase and press the [Del] key.

Data Types

You can enter two basic types of data into cells: values and labels. A *value* is anything that can be evaluated numerically, including numbers, dates, and mathematical formulas. A *label* is a string of characters generally used for descriptive text, such as report titles or column headings. Labels can consist of any combination of letters, numbers, and punctuation and can include up to 254 characters.

Quattro Pro decides what type of data you are entering as soon as you press your first key. If the first character you type is a letter, a punctuation mark, or a blank space, Quattro Pro decides that you are entering a label and changes the mode indicator to LABEL. If the first character you type is a digit or one of the symbols associated with values (such as a plus or minus sign), Quattro Pro assumes that you are entering a number, date, or formula, and changes the mode indicator to VALUE.

To start entering data into your notebook,

1. If the cell pointer is anywhere other than A1, press the [Home] key.
2. Type **Income Statement Projection** and press the [Enter] key or click the [Enter] button.

Because the entire label does not fit into a single cell, some of the characters appear to spill into cells B1 and C1.

When you press [Enter], the data is copied from the input line to the current cell and Quattro Pro returns to Ready mode. The characters that you typed still appear on the input line, only now they are preceded by the cell address, as shown below. When you are not entering or changing data, the input line displays the address and contents of the current cell. (The apostrophe at the beginning of the data will be discussed soon.) If you move the cell pointer to an empty cell, you see only the current cell address on the input line. If you then move back to A1, the cell contents reappear.

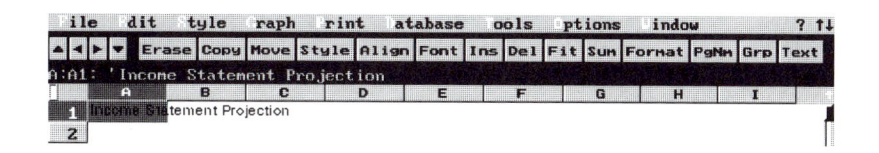

Follow these steps to enter the rest of the labels in column A of the notebook:

1. Press the ⬇ key five times to move to A6 and type **Sales**.
2. Press ⬇ both to enter the data into the cell and move the cell pointer down to A7. Then type **Cost of goods sold**.
3. Press ⬇ once and, in A8, type **Gross margin**.
4. Press ⬇ twice and, in A10, type **Salaries**.
5. Press ⬇ once and, in A11, type **Rent**.
6. Press ⬇ and, in A12, type **Depreciation**.
7. Press ⬇ and, with the cell pointer in A13, type **Miscellaneous**.
8. Press ⬇ and, in A14, type **Total operating expenses**.
9. Press ⬇ twice and, in A16, type **Interest expense**.
10. Press ⬇ twice and, in A18, type **Profit before tax**.
11. Press ⬇ and, in A19, type **Income tax**.
12. Press ⬇ one last time, type **Net income** in A20, and press [Enter].

Your notebook should resemble the one shown in Figure 2-2.

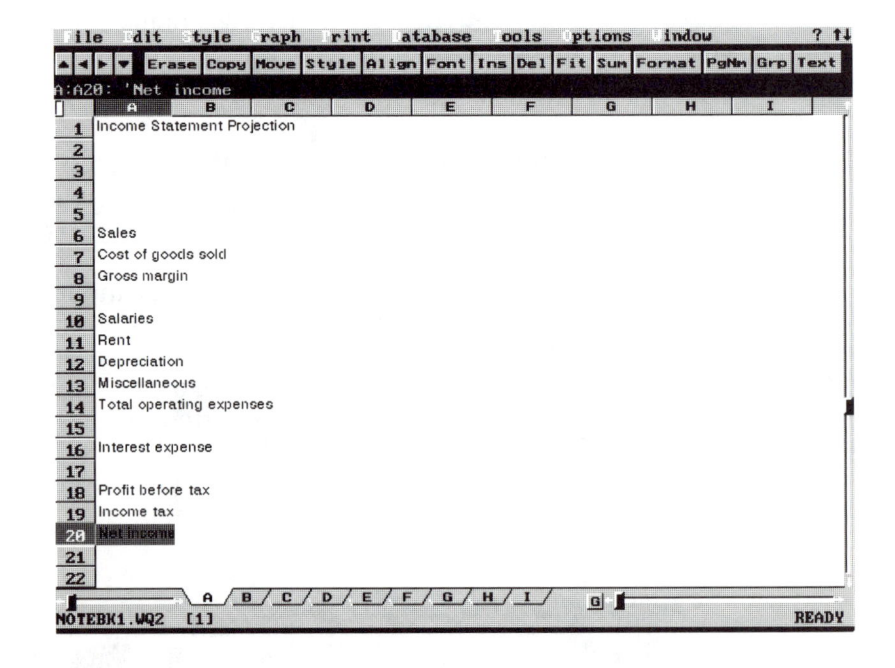

The notebook with labels
Figure 2-2.

Entering Text and Numbers

Changing Column Widths

Longer labels would spill into as many adjacent cells as needed, provided those cells were blank.

As you can see, the contents of several cells in column A spill into the next column to the right. This did not cause a problem at the time, but now enter data in column B and see what happens.

1. Press the F5 (GoTo) key and, when prompted for an address to go to, type **B7** and press Enter.
2. Type the number **193500** and press the ← key.

   The new data is written over part of the data that was entered into A7, as shown in Figure 2-3. However, the input line shows that none of the data in A7 has actually been lost; Quattro Pro displays only as much data as fits within the cell's borders.

3. Move back to B7 and press Del to delete the contents of the cell so that the "missing" piece of A7's data reappears on the notebook.

Values cannot spill into adjacent columns in this manner.

This exercise illustrates one of the most important aspects of working with electronic spreadsheets: understanding the distinction between the way data is displayed on the spreadsheet and the way it is stored in your computer's memory. As far as your computer's memory is concerned, there is plenty of room in A7 for the label "Cost of goods sold" (or for any other label of up to 254 characters). When you first entered this label, however, it appeared to occupy three different cells because Quattro Pro lets the data spill over into adjacent cells on the notebook, as long as they do not contain data of their own. In general, the information displayed on the input line is a more accurate version of what is stored in a particular cell than what appears in the cell itself.

A number that overlaps a label
Figure 2-3.

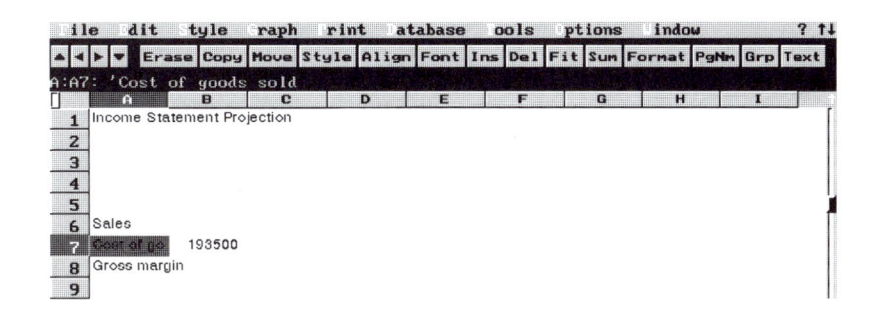

Now widen column A using the /**S**tyle | **C**olumn Width command so that all the labels fit within the column:

1. Press [Home] to move to A1.
2. Either type / to activate the Main menu and then type **S** to select and pull down the Style menu, or click on the Style menu option.
3. Type **C** or click on Column Width to select the Column Width option. Quattro Pro displays the prompt "Alter the width of the current column [1..254]: 9" on the input line. The current default column width setting is 9, and the width of a column can range from 1 to 254 characters. You can change the default width either by using [→] or [←] to expand or shrink the column, or by simply typing in the desired width.
4. To accommodate the labels you have just entered, press [→] several times to widen the current column. Keep pressing until the label "Income Statement Projection" fits within the cell pointer and the column width indicated on the input line is 27 characters (wide enough to fit the characters in either display mode). Then press [Enter] to lock in the new width.

Make sure to click on the Style option on the menu bar, not the Style button on the SpeedBar.

The cell pointer immediately widens to reflect the change. The column width code [W27] now appears on the input line, indicating the new column width of 27 characters.

If you are using a mouse, you can click on the associated column letter on the top border of the notebook area and drag it to the left or right to narrow or widen a column. Make sure that the mouse pointer is on or next to the column letter when you release the mouse button; otherwise Quattro Pro leaves the column width unchanged. You can also change column widths by clicking on the Fit button on the SpeedBar (see Chapter 5) and specifying which columns to widen. The column width will expand or shrink to accommodate the longest entry in the column.

Menu Command Shortcuts

You will come to use some Quattro Pro commands often in almost every work session. Chapter 13 explains how to create command menu shortcuts for quickly selecting your favorite commands. These shortcuts allow you to execute a command just by holding down [Ctrl] and pressing a letter key. When you first install Quattro Pro, several shortcuts are already assigned. Quattro Pro displays the assigned keys for a particular menu option to the right of the command name on the menu. For example, when you open the Style menu, the shortcut keys assigned to the Alignment, Numeric Format, and Column Width options appear.

Entering Text and Numbers

Label Alignment

As you enter labels, you may notice an apostrophe on the input line at the beginning of each label. In Quattro Pro every label begins with a *label prefix character;* if you do not enter one, Quattro Pro automatically inserts the default alignment character—generally an apostrophe, indicating flush-left alignment. There are three label prefix characters in Quattro Pro:

Character	Effect
'	Align flush left
"	Align flush right
^	Center within cell

When you begin a label with one of these three characters, Quattro Pro aligns the text accordingly; it does not display the prefix character in the cell itself. If you ever want to enter a label that actually begins with one of the label prefix characters, type an additional label prefix character before the label itself. Quattro Pro reads this first character as a label prefix, and then reads and displays the second character as part of the label text.

Besides determining the positioning of text within a cell, label prefix characters also indicate that the data being entered constitute a label. This can be useful when you are entering a label that begins with a number. For example, suppose that you want to enter a column heading that starts with the current year. If the heading consists entirely of numerals, Quattro Pro accepts the entry without complaint. However, if your heading also includes letters or punctuation, Quattro Pro beeps and displays an error message (shown here) because you are trying to include unacceptable characters in what it considers to be a value. You can clear the message from the screen by pressing [Esc] or [Enter].

```
Error (press F1 for help)
Invalid cell, block, or page
```

Because Quattro Pro determines the type of data you are entering from the first character you type, entering an alignment character before a number directs Quattro Pro to treat the data as a label rather than a value. To see how this works, follow these steps:

1. Use the [F5] (GoTo) key to move to B3, and type "**1993**. As soon as you type the quotation mark, the mode indicator changes to LABEL. If you had omitted this character, the mode indicator would have said VALUE.
2. Press [↓] to move to B4, and type "**Actual**.
3. Press [→] to move to C4, and type "**Est**.

4. Press ↑ to move to C3, and type "**1994**.
5. Press → and type "**Variance** in D3. Then press Enter.

Quattro Pro also uses two other label prefix characters. The vertical bar (|) is used as the prefix for printer command codes, and is covered in Chapter 6. The backslash (\ ) is used to repeat one or more characters across the width of a cell. When you enter \ as the first character in a cell, Quattro Pro replicates whatever character(s) you type after that across the entire cell. For example, if you entered **ABC** in a 9-character wide cell, Quattro Pro would display ABCABCABC in that cell. If you later changed the column width to 11 characters, you would see ABCABCABCAB displayed in the cell.

The \ prefix is particularly useful for drawing borders and underlines to improve the appearance of the notebook. For example, you can fill an entire cell with dashes, as shown in Figure 2-4, by moving to A2, typing \ followed by a hyphen (-), and pressing Enter. If you do, a line (a set of dashes) should now appear underneath your notebook title.

Entering Numbers

It's easy to enter numbers in Quattro Pro, but you should keep a few rules in mind. You can only use numerals, plus or minus signs, percent signs, or a single decimal point; you cannot use dollar signs, parentheses, or commas. Chapter 5 explains how to display numbers with any of these symbols by changing the display format of the cell.

Like a label, a number can be up to 254 characters long. Unlike labels, however, numbers do not spill into adjacent cells if they do not fit within the borders of the current cell. Instead, they are displayed either in scientific (exponential) notation or as a row of asterisks, depending on the cell's display format. Even if you see a row of asterisks, the number is stored in its entirety—up to 16 digits—in Quattro Pro's memory; you only need to widen the cell to correct the display on the notebook.

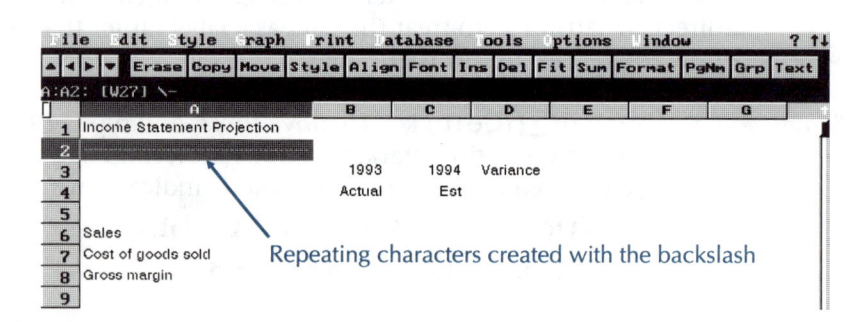

The notebook with column headings and dashes
Figure 2-4.

Entering Text and Numbers

To practice entering numbers in your notebook, follow these steps:

Remember not to type in commas when you enter numbers in Quattro Pro.

1. Move to B6, and type **450000**.
2. Press ↓ to move to B7, and type **193500**.
3. Press ↓ three times to move to B10 and type **86000**.
4. Press ↓ and, in B11, type **42000**.
5. Press ↓ and, in B12, type **22000**.
6. Press ↓ and, in B13, type **8000**.
7. Press ↓ three times, type **10000** in B16, and press [Enter] or click on the [Enter] button with your mouse.

Your notebook should now look like the one shown in Figure 2-5.

Entering Dates

A date may be entered as a label or a value. To create a date label with the month, day, and year separated by slashes, you would enter a date in the form **12/25/93**. This method is fine if you plan to use the date merely as descriptive text. If you enter dates as values, however, you can use them to perform date arithmetic, such as adding a specified number of days to a date or calculating the number of days between two dates. You enter date values in Quattro Pro using a special date prefix: [Ctrl]-[D]. Just hold down [Ctrl], type

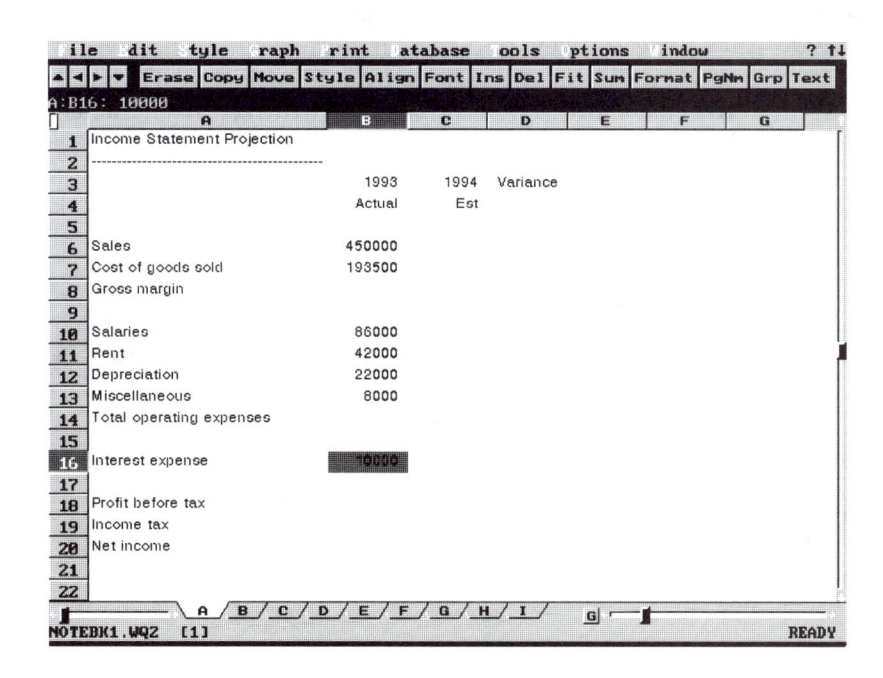

The notebook after entering numbers
Figure 2-5.

D, and then enter a date in one of several acceptable formats (see Chapter 10). For now, try using the familiar MM/DD/YY format:

1. Move to C1 and type the label "**Created:**.
2. Press → and, in D1, press Ctrl-D. Notice that Quattro Pro displays DATE in place of READY as the mode indicator.
3. Type today's date using the MM/DD/YY format, and then press Enter or click on [Enter] with your mouse.

The date in your notebook should now look like Figure 2-6. Note the information A:D1: 34328 on the input line. D1 refers to the coordinates of the current cell. The numeral (probably not 34328 on your notebook) is the numeric equivalent of the date that you entered, calculated in terms of the number of days since the turn of the century.

Editing Data

When you enter data into cells, Quattro Pro gives you a limited number of options for correcting mistakes. If you want to change the data you have entered, you can either erase characters using the Backspace key and then reenter them, or press Enter and then replace the entire contents of the cell by entering the data a second time.

You'll learn more about the End key and the arrow keys on the Edit SpeedBar in Chapter 4.

If you want to edit the contents of a cell—replacing or deleting existing characters or inserting new ones—you must switch to Edit mode by pressing F2, the Edit key, or by clicking on the input line with your mouse. The mode indicator will change from READY to EDIT. Use ← or → to reposition the cursor without erasing or overwriting any characters. Press Home to move the cursor to the first character in the cell, and press End to move the cursor to the right of the last character. You can also reposition the cursor by clicking in the desired location with the mouse, or by using the left and right

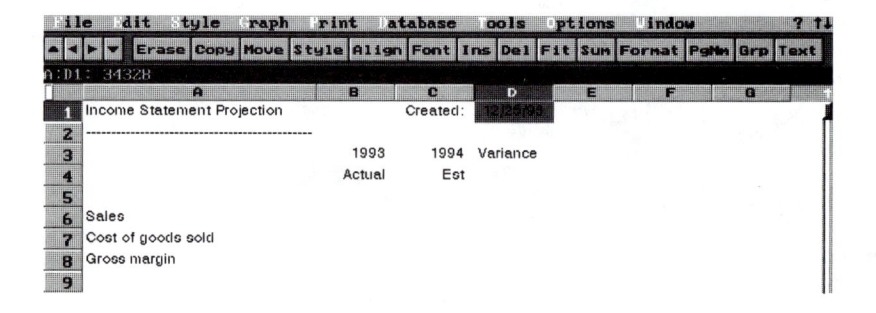

Entering a date value
Figure 2-6.

Entering Text and Numbers

arrows on the Edit SpeedBar to move through the text one character at a time. Clicking on the up and down arrows on the SpeedBar returns you to Ready mode and moves you in the direction of the arrow.

To erase characters, you can use either [Backspace] to move the cursor to the left, erasing as you go, or [Del] to delete the character located at the cursor. When you first enter Edit mode, Quattro Pro automatically switches to Insert mode, meaning that any characters you type are inserted into the data immediately to the left of the cursor. If you want to replace existing characters rather than insert new ones, you need to turn Insert mode off by pressing the [Ins] key. When you do, the letters "OVR" on the status line indicate that you are in Overwrite mode. To turn Overwrite mode off, simply press [Ins] a second time. The changes that you make while in Edit mode are not recorded in the current cell until you press [Enter]. Until then, if you press the [Esc] key, the changes are canceled and the cell contents are not changed.

Follow these steps to edit the title of your notebook:

1. Make sure you're in Ready mode and press the [Home] key to move to A1.
2. Press [F2] (Edit) and then press [Home] to move to the beginning of the text.
3. Tap [→] once to move the cursor to the right of the apostrophe (the flush-left alignment character).
4. With the editing cursor positioned on the letter "I" of "Income," type **ABC Group**.
5. Press the [Spacebar] to insert a space between "Group" and "Income."
6. Hold down the [→] key until the cursor reaches the "S" in "Statement." Move back with [←] if you overshoot your mark.
7. Press [Del] ten times to erase the word "Statement" and the extra space that follows. Then press [Enter] to incorporate your changes into the cell and exit from Edit mode. The title should now read "ABC Group Income Projection."

You can use any combination of keyboard keys and mouse commands when editing.

You have now seen the commonly used editing keys. A full list of editing keys appears in Table 2-1. As mentioned, you can also use a mouse to edit data. To enter Edit mode using a mouse, point to the cell you want to edit and click to move the cell pointer to that cell. Then point to the input line and click again to copy the cell's contents to that line. You can move the cursor by pointing to the desired spot and clicking. When you are done editing, click on [Enter] to enter your changes into the cell or click on [Esc] to discard your changes.

Key	Function
Esc	Erases the input line. If you press Esc again or press Enter without entering any data, Quattro Pro discards any changes you made and returns to Ready mode.
Enter	Copies the data as it appears on the input line into the current cell.
←	Moves the cursor one character to the left.
→	Moves the cursor one character to the right.
Home	Moves the cursor to the first character on the input line.
End	Moves the cursor to the last character on the input line.
Tab or Ctrl-→	Moves the cursor five characters to the right.
Shift-Tab or Ctrl-←	Moves the cursor five characters to the left.
Backspace	Deletes the character to the left of the cursor.
Ins	Toggles between Insert mode and Overwrite mode.
Del	Deletes the character at the cursor.
Ctrl-\	Deletes all characters from the cursor to the end of the input line.

Editing Keys
Table 2-1.

Saving and Retrieving Notebooks

When you create a new notebook, it exists only in the computer's memory until you save it to disk. A computer's memory is analogous to a blackboard—a temporary reading and writing surface that is wiped clean as soon as the "class" is over. If you want to retain the notebook's contents beyond the current work session, you need to record them somewhere else. Saving a notebook essentially means copying the data currently in your computer's memory to a more permanent storage place: a disk file. When you save a Quattro Pro notebook to disk, the resulting file contains not only the data you have entered but also formatting information, printing specifications, and graphs.

Once you have saved a notebook to disk, you can erase the screen, load another notebook into memory, or leave Quattro Pro without worrying about losing the contents of the notebook. The next time you want to work with that notebook, you can load Quattro Pro and *retrieve* the file—copying

Entering Text and Numbers

its contents from disk into memory, where you can again view and manipulate the data.

You should save your work periodically throughout your work session, rather than waiting until you are done with a particular notebook or ready to leave Quattro Pro. First, if you lose power or experience problems with your computer hardware, you could lose all your work. Second, it is fairly easy to wreck a notebook. An ill-chosen command or an accidental deletion can reduce even a finely honed model to chaos. If you wreak havoc on your notebook, you can discard the version currently in memory and retrieve the previous version from the disk file. A good rule of thumb is that you should save your work before you reach the point where you would be miserable if you had to reenter the data.

Saving Your Notebook for the First Time

Quattro Pro has three commands for saving notebooks: / **F**ile | **S**ave, / **F**ile | Sa**v**e All, and / **F**ile | Save **A**s. The / **F**ile | Sa**v**e All command is primarily used when you are working with multiple notebooks (see Chapter 11). If you are working with only one notebook, it works exactly like / **F**ile | **S**ave.

NOTE: You can't have more than one file with the same name in a particular directory. If you select a file name from the list of existing files you'll replace that file with the notebook currently in memory.

If you are saving a notebook for the first time, the / **F**ile | **S**ave and / **F**ile | Save **A**s commands function identically. In both cases Quattro Pro displays a dialog box with the message "Enter save file name" at the top, as well as the default data directory and a list of any notebook files already stored in that directory, as shown in Figure 2-7.

Save your notebook under the name LEARN1.WQ2 on the drive and directory that Quattro Pro displayed when prompting you for a file name (probably C:\QPRO). You will use this file name to retrieve your notebook from disk and load it into memory in future work sessions.

1. Type **/FS** to issue the / **F**ile | **S**ave command.
2. Type **LEARN1** and press ⟨Enter⟩, or click on Enter with your mouse. You don't need to type the WQ2 extension; Quattro Pro assigns it automatically.

The file name also appears in the lower-left corner of the screen. You can always tell whether the currently displayed notebook has been saved to disk

Saving a file
Figure 2-7.

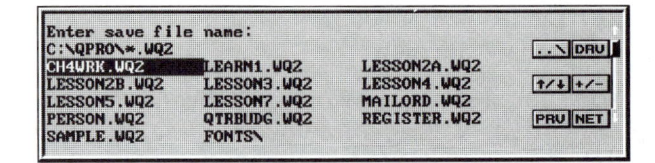

```
Enter save file name:
C:\QPRO\*.WQ2
CH4WRK.WQ2      LEARN1.WQ2      LESSON2A.WQ2    [..\][DRV]
LESSON2B.WQ2    LESSON3.WQ2     LESSON4.WQ2     [↑/↓][+/-]
LESSON5.WQ2     LESSON7.WQ2     MAILORD.WQ2
PERSON.WQ2      QTRBUDG.WQ2     REGISTER.WQ2    [PRV][NET]
SAMPLE.WQ2      FONTS\
```

by looking in this spot. If the notebook has not yet been saved, you will see a name such as NOTEBK1.WQ2, a temporary name that Quattro Pro assigns to a notebook. Once you save the file to disk, Quattro Pro displays the name that you assigned to the file. If you want to store your notebook somewhere other than the drive and directory that Quattro Pro suggests when you issue the / **F**ile | **S**ave command, you must press [Esc] twice—once to erase the file name and a second time to erase the default drive and directory. Then enter the drive letter, directory, and file name of your choice.

Resaving Your Notebook

The / **F**ile | **S**ave command has a preassigned shortcut of [Ctrl]-[S].

The differences between the / **F**ile | **S**ave and / **F**ile | Save **A**s commands emerge when you save a file that you have previously saved to disk. In this case, if you want to save your data under the same name you use the / **F**ile | **S**ave command. Quattro Pro displays a dialog box like the one shown below, warning you that there is already a file with that name in the current directory. At this point, select Cancel to cancel the save operation and return to Ready mode, select Replace to confirm that you want to overwrite the existing file with this name, or select Backup to copy the old version of the file to a new file with the extension BAK before overwriting.

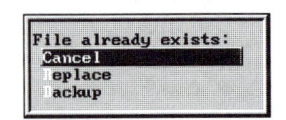

```
File already exists:
Cancel
Replace
Backup
```

Occasionally you will want to save the current version of your notebook under a new name, leaving the old version intact. For example, to use last year's budget notebook as the starting point for this year's model, you could retrieve the old notebook, update the figures, and then save it under a new name. To save a notebook under a new name, use the / **F**ile | Save **A**s command. Quattro Pro prompts you for a file name and displays the current name of the file. Just type in the new name and press [Enter]. To edit an existing file name, use the editing keys described earlier.

Entering Text and Numbers

Note that saving a file under a new name means creating a new disk file, not renaming the old one. If you simply want to change a notebook's name, it is more efficient to use Quattro Pro's File Manager utility (see Chapter 18) or the DOS RENAME command.

Retrieving Files

The command for retrieving files is / **F**ile | **R**etrieve. When you issue this command, Quattro Pro displays a list of all the files in the default data directory that have an extension beginning with "W," as shown in Figure 2-8. (This will include files created in all versions of Quattro Pro and Lotus 1-2-3. You can use such files in Quattro Pro, just as you would Quattro Pro's own WQ2 or WQ1 files.)

The mouse buttons in this file name list are covered in depth in Chapter 18.

Files are listed alphabetically from left to right across each row. If Quattro Pro cannot fit all files in the default directory in the file name box, simply press ⬇ or Pg Dn, or use the scroll bar on the right side of the screen to view additional file names. To the left of this scroll bar are six mouse buttons that you can use to manipulate the file list. For example, you can click on the +/– button to show more information about the files.

To select a file from the file list, highlight the desired file and press Enter, or click on the file name. You can also type the name of the file you wish to retrieve, which may be more efficient if you have a large number of files stored in the default directory.

If the notebook file's extension is WQ2, you do not need to type it when entering the file name. If the file name extension starts with a letter other than "W," however, the file does not appear in the file list and you must type in the entire file name, including extension, to retrieve it. If you want to retrieve a file that is stored somewhere other than in the default data directory, press Esc twice to erase the default disk drive and directory, and then enter the drive and directory before the file name using the form *drive:\directory\filename*. For example, to retrieve the LEARN1 notebook from

Retrieving a notebook from disk
Figure 2-8.

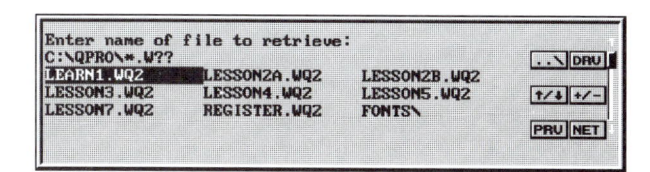

```
Enter name of file to retrieve:
C:\QPRO\*.W??                                            ..  DRV
LEARN1.WQ2      LESSON2A.WQ2    LESSON2B.WQ2
LESSON3.WQ2     LESSON4.WQ2     LESSON5.WQ2      ↑/↓  +/-
LESSON7.WQ2     REGISTER.WQ2    FONTS\
                                                 PRV  NET
```

the QDATA directory on drive C, you would issue the / **F**ile | **R**etrieve command, press Esc twice, and then enter **C:\QDATA\LEARN1**.

If you have been working with another notebook and have not saved your work, when you issue the / **F**ile | **R**etrieve command, Quattro Pro displays a dialog box asking whether you want to lose your changes. Select Yes to discard the latest version of your work or No to cancel the command.

You will use the techniques covered in this chapter in all the work you do with Quattro Pro. If this is the first time you have created a notebook or if you are at all uncertain about the techniques covered, you should practice what you have learned before moving on. In particular you should be comfortable moving around the notebook and entering, editing, and deleting data. You should also understand the different types of data and how Quattro Pro distinguishes among them.

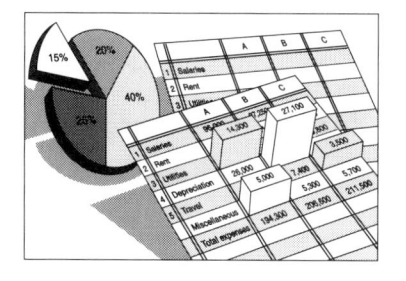

CHAPTER

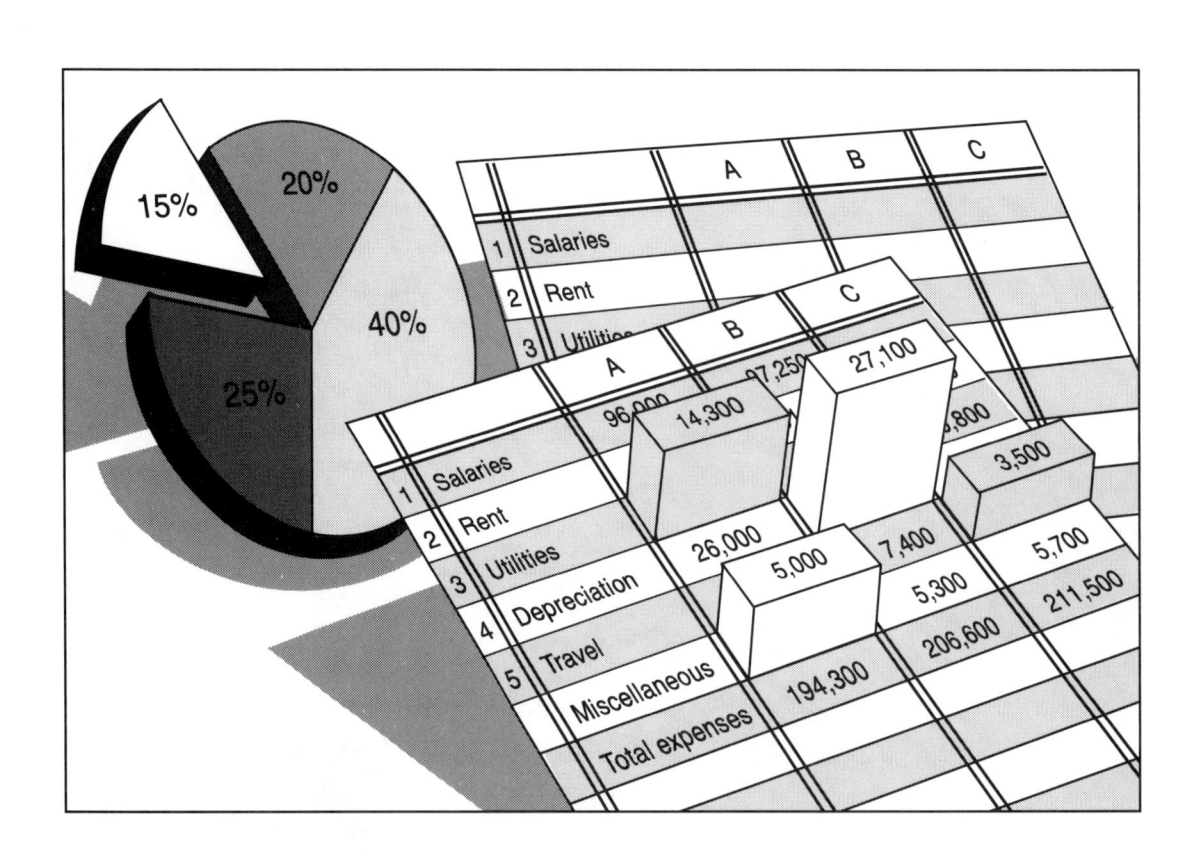

3

FORMULAS

Formulas are the heart of any notebook. They determine what the notebook does and how it links and processes a set of numbers. Once you have mastered the formula basics in this chapter, you will have all the essential tools for building modest notebooks of your own.

A formula *is a set of instructions for performing a calculation and displaying the result in a cell. The types of calculations you can perform in Quattro Pro range from the simple, such as adding a group of numbers, to the complex, like sophisticated* statistical and trigonometric operations. You can create three types of formulas in Quattro Pro notebooks: *arithmetic, text,* and *logical.* In this chapter you learn to construct arithmetic formulas—the most common type of formula and the easiest to understand. Text and logical formulas are introduced in Chapters 7 and 17.

First you'll experiment on a blank practice notebook, trying out various types of formulas, using different methods of entering formulas, and learning to avoid, spot, and correct common formula mistakes. Later you'll get a chance to apply some of what you've learned to the LEARN1 notebook that you started in Chapter 2.

Arithmetic Operators

The values in formulas can consist either of numbers or of references to cells that contain numbers.

Arithmetic formulas are made up of values and operators such as plus and minus signs. To enter a formula, you move the cell pointer to the appropriate cell and start typing. Then you press (Enter) or one of the cursor-movement keys to record the formula in the cell and return to Ready mode.

Formulas can be up to 240 characters long and can include numbers, cell references, arithmetic operators, and functions (specialized operators that are covered in Chapter 7). The simplest formulas contain only numbers and these arithmetic operators:

Symbol	Operation
^	Exponentiation
+	Addition
–	Subtraction
*	Multiplication
/	Division

Once you press (F2), you are in Edit mode and must press (Enter) rather than an arrow key to complete your entry.

Note that you can enter most of these operators by using the Edit SpeedBar. To do so, simply press (F2) to display the Edit SpeedBar if it's not already displayed and click on the button representing the appropriate operator. If you are not using the mouse, you may prefer to use the operator symbols on the numeric keypad on the right side of your keyboard instead of those on the top row of number keys: This way you can avoid pressing (Shift) to get the correct symbol.

The easiest way to learn how to construct and enter formulas is to perform experiments on a blank notebook page. If LEARN1 is currently on your screen, save it with the / **F**ile | **S**ave command, and then issue the / **F**ile |

Formulas

Erase command by typing **/FE** to remove the notebook from memory and clear the notebook area on the screen.

With the cell pointer at A1, type **1+1+1** and press (Enter). The result of the calculation now appears in A1, while the input line still displays the formula, as shown in Figure 3-1.

Cell References

Although you can use formulas to perform arithmetic on numbers typed directly into the formula itself, to truly tap Quattro Pro's power, you need to create formulas that perform calculations on data in other cells. Rather than adding 2 and 4, for example, you might add the value in A1 to the value in A2. To see how this works, perform the following steps:

1. With the cell pointer still in A1, type **100**.
2. Press ⬇ and type **50** in A2.
3. Press ⬇ again, type **+A1+A2** in A3, and press (Enter).

Your results should resemble those in Figure 3-2. When Quattro Pro evaluates a formula that contains a cell reference, it uses the current value of the referenced cell. That is, the formula in A3 adds the number currently stored in A1 to the number currently stored in A2.

Notice that the first character entered in A3 is a plus sign. Recall from Chapter 2 that Quattro Pro determines the data type by looking at the first character. If your formula starts with a cell reference, you must precede that reference with another character that indicates you are entering a value. Otherwise, Quattro Pro will assume that you are entering a label. Try deleting the first plus sign to see the problem. With the cell pointer in A3, press (F2) (Edit) or click on the input line. Move to the first character in the cell—the plus sign—press (Del) to delete it, and press (Enter). The input line now shows an apostrophe where there was previously a plus sign. Once you delete the plus sign, Quattro Pro interprets the formula as a label rather than

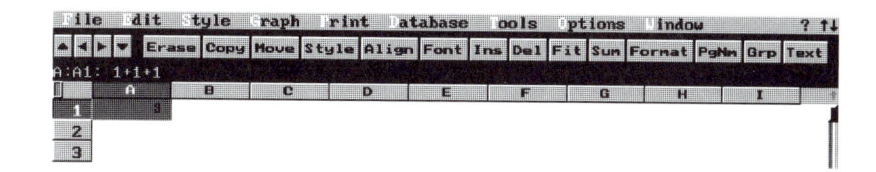

A simple formula
Figure 3-1.

Referencing other cells
Figure 3-2.

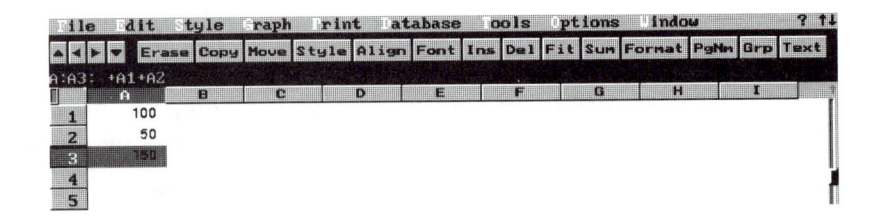

a value, inserts the default label alignment character, and displays the characters A1+A2 in the cell.

> **NOTE:** In this context the + and - signs don't indicate an addition or subtraction operation, but simply tell Quattro Pro to treat what follows as values rather than labels.

A formula can begin with any of the following characters:

0 1 2 3 4 5 6 7 8 9 . (+ − @ $ #

You will encounter the @ symbol later in this chapter and the last two symbols in later chapters; the other symbols should already be familiar. If you want to start a formula with a cell reference, you usually precede the cell reference with a plus sign or enclose the entire formula in parentheses.

To undo the "damage" you have just done,

1. Still in A3, press [F2] (Edit) or click on the input line.
2. Press [Home] or use your mouse to move to the first character on the input line, and press [Del] to delete the apostrophe.
3. Type (or click on the (button on the Edit SpeedBar.
4. Press [End] to move past the last character, type) or click on the) button on the SpeedBar, and press [Enter] or click on [Enter].

So far you have entered formulas that contain numbers and operators or cell references and operators. You can also combine numbers and cell references within one formula and reference cells that contain formulas of their own. Whenever Quattro Pro evaluates a formula that references another formula, it uses the referenced formula's current result in its calculations. To see this in action:

Formulas

1. Press ⬇ twice and, in A5, type **+A1*3**.
2. Press ⬇ again, type **+A5*2** in A6, and press Enter.

Your notebook should now resemble Figure 3-3. The value of A6 depends on the value of A5, which in turn depends on the value of A1. At the moment, 100 (the value of A1) times 3 is 300 (the value of A5) times 2 is 600 (the value of A6).

Automatic Recalculation

In a sense, entering formulas that contain cell references is a means of "teaching" Quattro Pro how to perform a particular set of calculations. In an income statement notebook, you must teach the program to calculate net income by subtracting the value in the total expenses cell from the value in the total revenue cell. It is worth doing this because you only have to teach Quattro Pro how to perform a particular calculation once. After you enter the formula, you can change the numbers at will. Quattro Pro remembers your instructions and automatically reexecutes them, generating a new result.

This feature is known as *automatic recalculation*. It means that any time you change the value in a cell that is referenced by formulas in other cells, the results of those formulas are automatically and, in most cases, immediately recalculated. It is this feature that lets you use Quattro Pro to experiment with numbers, testing the effect of changing one or more items of data. What will happen to your net income, for example, if the cost of goods sold increases by 3%? Automatic recalculation also means that you can "recycle" your notebooks by using the same set of labels and formulas with a different set of numbers.

While automatic recalculation is impressive even in the case of a single formula, the benefits are magnified when one cell is referenced directly or indirectly by several formulas across the notebook. As you have already seen, you can construct a formula that references cells containing formulas of their own. When you do, the second formula "piggy backs" on the first, so

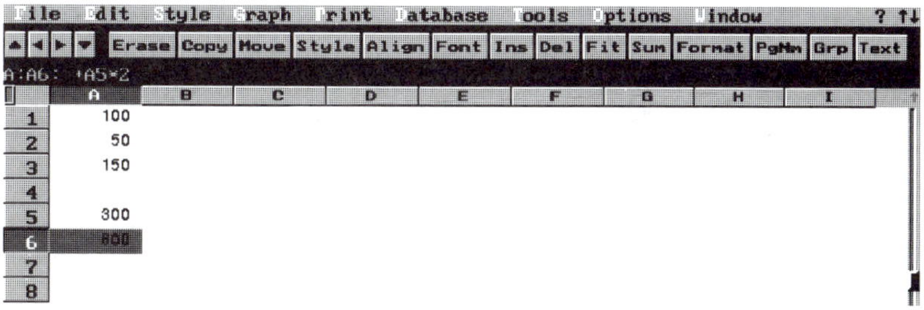

Referencing other formulas
Figure 3-3.

that changes in cells referenced by the first formula are passed on to the second formula. For instance, try moving to A1 and typing **200**. Keep your eyes on cells A3 through A6 while you press (Enter). The values displayed there should immediately change to reflect the new value in that cell.

The value of A6 changes even though its formula does not include any direct reference to the cell you changed. The formula in A6 refers *indirectly* to A1, by referring to A5, which in turn has a formula that refers to A1. Many real-life notebooks contain elaborate chains of references, with a formula in one cell referring to a formula in another, which refers to a formula in a third, and so on. A single change in data ripples through the entire notebook, as dozens of formulas are recalculated.

Chapter 5 explains how to display all the formulas on the notebook as formulas.

Now that you have several numbers and formulas on your notebook, you may have noticed that you cannot tell which numbers on the notebook are the results of formulas and which are *constants*—numbers that you entered as numbers and that therefore have a set, unchanging value. The only way to determine whether a value is the product of a formula is to move to that cell and look at the input line. The fact that numbers and numeric formulas look the same on the notebook makes it all too easy to overwrite a formula accidentally. You will learn how to protect formulas from being overwritten in Chapter 9.

Pointing

There are actually two ways to include cell references in a formula: typing cell coordinates, which you have already tried, and pointing to cells with the cell pointer. Although the typing method can be quite efficient if you know the exact address of the cells you want to reference, the pointing method is less likely to result in errors.

The cell-pointing method consists of three steps. First, if you are at the beginning of the formula, enter a plus sign or opening parenthesis. If you are in the middle of a formula, enter any character that is allowable immediately before a cell address, such as an opening parenthesis, one of the arithmetic operators, or a comma.

Second, if you are using a mouse, simply click on the cell that you want to reference. Otherwise, use the arrow keys to move to the cell. As soon as you move the cell pointer, Quattro Pro places you in Point mode, as indicated by the mode indicator on the status line. This means that as you move the cell pointer, the address of the current cell appears at the end of your formula on the input line.

Third, if you want to keep adding to the formula, type another operator. This locks the coordinates of the cell to which you were pointing into the

Formulas

formula and returns the cell pointer to the formula cell. You can then continue typing or point to another cell. When you are done entering the formula, press [Enter] or one of the arrow keys. This writes the coordinates of the current cell into your formula, returns the cell pointer to the cell in which you are entering the formula, and records the entire formula in that cell.

To use the pointing method to enter the formula +A1+A3/A2 in A7, follow these steps:

1. Press [↓] until you reach A7, and type +.
2. Press [Home] to move to A1. The instant you move the cell pointer, the mode indicator changes from VALUE to POINT—you are now in Point mode. Notice also that A:A1 now appears on the input line after the +.
3. Type another +. This locks in the address of the current cell and adds a second plus sign to the formula. Notice that the cell pointer has returned to A7, the formula cell.
4. Press [↑] four times to move to A3. The address of each cell you cross is displayed on the input line.
5. Type / to lock in the reference to A3 and add a / to your formula.
6. Press [Home] again, and then press [↓] to move to A2.
7. Press [Enter] to add the address A2 to your formula and to enter the entire formula into A7. The number 205 should now appear in A7 on your notebook.

Order of Calculation

Formulas that contain more than one operator are subject to strict rules governing the order of calculation. In some cases these rules cause Quattro Pro to evaluate a formula in a sequence other than the one you expected and to generate unintended results. The order of precedence among arithmetic operators is

1. Exponentiation
2. A minus or plus sign occurring at the beginning of a formula
3. Multiplication and division
4. Addition and subtraction

For example, you may have expected the formula you just entered to return 9 rather than 205. If Quattro Pro had read the formula from left to right, it would have added the value of A1 (200) plus the value of A3 (250) to get 450 and then divided that amount by the value of A2 (50) for a final result of 9.

Instead, because division takes precedence over addition, Quattro Pro first divided A3 by A2 (250/50) and then added the value of A1 to the result (200+5).

If you want operations within a formula to be carried out in a sequence other than the one dictated by the rules of precedence, you need to use parentheses to group sets of numbers and operators. Any expression within a set of parentheses is evaluated first. If a formula contains nested sets of parentheses—sets of parentheses inside other sets of parentheses—the innermost set is evaluated first.

To edit your formula so it produces the expected result,

1. With the cell pointer in A7, press [F2] or click on the input line.
2. Press [Home] or click to move to first character on the input line, press [Del] to erase the +, and type **(** or click **(** on the Edit SpeedBar.
3. Use [→] to move the editing cursor to the slash, type **)** or click **)** on the Edit SpeedBar, and press [Enter] or click on [Enter].

The formula should now read (A1+A3)/A2, and the result that appears in A7 should be 9. Technically, you don't need to erase the plus sign at the beginning of the formula, but once you add parentheses, the + only makes the formula harder to read.

Referencing Blocks of Cells

Adding numbers with the plus sign is fine when you want to add only two or three numbers at a time. It is less adequate when you want to add an entire column or row of values. If you had a budget with 102 line items, you would not be happy typing **+B2+B3+B4** and so on until you reached +B102. Fortunately, there is a way to have Quattro Pro add up all the values that fall between two points on the notebook.

In Quattro Pro 5, you can also create 3-D blocks that span several pages. You'll learn how to do this in Chapter 12.

So far all the formulas you have created have referred to one or more individual cells. Formulas can also refer to a group of cells—known as a block—at one time. A *block* is any rectangular group of cells. It can range from a single cell to an entire notebook page, provided it forms an uninterrupted rectangular group. It can contain several cells within one row, several cells within one column, or cells in multiple rows and columns. Blocks are used in two situations: in formulas and in commands, particularly some of the commands on the Edit and Style menus.

All formulas that refer to blocks of cells contain *functions*—operators used to perform specialized calculations beyond those performed by the arithmetic operators (see Chapter 7 for details). The function used for totaling the values in a block of cells is called @SUM. Its form, for this purpose, is

@SUM (*first cell address..last cell address*)

with the cell addresses defining the block of cells that will be summed. All Quattro Pro functions start with an @ sign. You type it by holding down [Shift] and typing **2**, located near the top of the keyboard.

Designating Blocks

When specifying a block in a formula, you can either type in cell addresses or you can point to them. In Quattro Pro, cell blocks are generally designated by the addresses of their upper-left and lower-right corners. For example, a block that includes the rectangle of cells spanning rows 1 through 4 and columns B through E would be referred to as B1..E4. (As described in Chapter 12, you need to use a special syntax to refer to blocks that span multiple pages.)

Typing Block Coordinates   In Quattro Pro, the coordinates of the upper-left corner are always shown first, followed by two periods, and then the coordinates of the lower-right corner. However, when you specify a block, you can use the addresses of either of its two diagonally opposed corners, in either order. For example, you could refer to block B1..E4 as E4..B1, E1..B4, or B4..E1. You can also type in only one period between cell addresses, and Quattro Pro fills in the second period for you.

To enter a formula that contains the @SUM function, follow these steps:

1. Move the cell pointer to C1, type **1**, and press [↓].
2. Next type **2** in C2, type **3** in C3, type **4** in C4, and type **@SUM(C1.C4)** in C5.
3. Press [Enter] to enter the formula. You should see a result of 10 in C5.

You might think of the formula you just entered as "sum C1 through C4" because it adds any values found within the specified block, including its starting and ending cells.

Pointing Out Block Coordinates   To use the pointing method to enter a formula containing the @SUM function, type **@SUM(** and move the cursor to the first corner of the block. When you move the cell pointer, Quattro Pro enters Point mode. Type a period to anchor the cell pointer, and then move the cell pointer to the diagonally opposite corner. (Usually, you use @SUM to add values in a single row or single column, so the diagonally opposite corner of the block is in the same row or column as the first corner.) As you move, the cell pointer expands. As soon as you have highlighted the entire group of cells you want to sum, you are ready to finish the formula. If you press [Enter] at this point, Quattro Pro displays an error message because it "knows" the formula is not yet complete. Instead, you must type in the closing parenthesis and press [Enter] again to enter the completed formula into the cell.

Creating @SUM Formulas with a Mouse   You can use a similar method to construct @SUM formulas with a mouse. Just type **@SUM(**, click on one corner of the block, drag to the other corner, and release the mouse button. Remember to select the closing parenthesis before clicking on [Enter].

There is, however, an even easier route for constructing @SUM formulas using the mouse: the Sum button on the SpeedBar. To use this button, simply drag to select the cells to be added, including in the block the cell immediately below a column of values or immediately to the right of a row of values that you want to add. Then click the Sum button and Quattro Pro constructs the formula for you. To see this feature in action:

1. Press [Del] to erase the @SUM formula in cell C5.
2. Move the mouse pointer to cell C1, hold down the left mouse button, drag to cell C5, and then release the button. Cells C1 to C5 should be highlighted.
3. Click the Sum button on the SpeedBar. Quattro Pro should enter the formula @SUM(C1..C4) in cell C5, and display a result of 10.

You can also use the Sum button to create several @SUM formulas at once. You can even use it to construct @SUM formulas along the entire bottom and right edge of a block. Try this now:

1. With C5 highlighted, press [Del] to erase the @SUM formula there.
2. Enter the numbers **4**, **3**, **2**, and **1** in cells D1, D2, D3, and D4.
3. Use your mouse to highlight the block from C1 through E5—that is, a block that includes an extra row of cells at the bottom and an extra column of cells at the right.
4. Click the Sum button on the SpeedBar. Then click in G1 just to remove the highlighting from C1..E5. Your spreadsheet should now resemble Figure 3-4. Move the cell pointer to cells C5, D5, E1, E2, E3, E4, and E5 and note that Quattro Pro has created @SUM formulas for all the columns and rows in the block.

Formulas

Summing a block with the Sum button **Figure 3-4.**

Common Mistakes in Formulas

Remember that to clear the error message from the screen, you press either Esc *or* Enter*.*

One of your first challenges in building notebooks is learning to find and fix your mistakes. Table 3-1 lists the most common error messages you will receive when entering formulas, along with suggested solutions to the problems they indicate. Whenever Quattro Pro displays an error message, it also attempts to place the cursor on or near the mistake on the input line. You should therefore start hunting for the problem at the cursor position.

The most frequent mistakes in formulas are typos, such as typing an equal sign when you mean a plus or inserting a space where it doesn't belong. The second most common mistake is forgetting to start the formula with a number or some symbol indicating that you are entering a value. (This includes omitting the @ in @SUM.) Some of these errors cause Quattro Pro to display an error message, but often it will simply return the wrong answer (sometimes displaying the formula itself rather than its result).

Circular References

A *circular cell reference* is a reference that refers to the formula cell itself. As an example, move to A8, type **+A6+A7+A8**, and press Enter. At first the result, 1209, looks fine. Quattro Pro gets this result by adding the value of A6 (1200) to the value of A7 (9) and the value of A8 (which was initially 0). But now try changing the value in A7 to 10; the result has changed to 2419. As soon as you changed one of the numbers referenced in the formula, Quattro Pro recalculated the result. This time Quattro Pro has added 1200 plus 10 plus the previous value in A8 (1209). If you change the value in A6 or A7 again, Quattro Pro again reevaluates the formula, producing an even larger result.

Formulas containing the @SUM function are a common breeding ground for circular references. Particularly if you use the typing method, it is easy to name the formula cell as one end of the block.

Common Error Messages When Entering Formulas
Table 3-1.

Error Message	Problem and Solution
Incomplete formula	Something is missing. Look for operators not followed by cell references or numbers.
Invalid cell or block address	You entered something that Quattro Pro is interpreting as a nonexistent cell or block name. Look for typos or, if you are using named blocks (see Chapter 8), make sure you have named the blocks properly.
Invalid character	You entered a character that does not make sense in its current position. Look for extra commas or other inappropriate punctuation.
Missing operator	You omitted an operator between two values or cell references. Enter the missing operator.
Missing right parenthesis	You opened more sets of parentheses than you closed. Look for an extra left parenthesis or missing right parenthesis.
Syntax error	You made an error that does not fall into one of the above categories. Check for typos or syntactical mistakes.

Quattro Pro does not prevent you from including circular references in formulas because certain complex financial and engineering calculations require them. However, Quattro Pro does warn you about such references. Whenever your notebook contains one or more circular references, you will see CIRC on the status line.

The most common circular references are found in formulas that refer directly to themselves—that is, they contain their own cell address—but these are not the only type. If a formula in A9 refers to a formula in A5 that refers to a formula in A1 that refers to A9, you have an indirect circular reference, with the same inherent problems as a direct one. These references can be much harder to find and correct because you must trace back through the entire chain of references to look at all the cells that it refers to, and then at all the cells those cells refer to, and so on. In large, complex notebooks, this process can be difficult and time-consuming.

Fortunately, Quattro Pro provides a tool to assist in this process. If your notebook contains a circular reference, Quattro Pro displays the address of the problematic formula on the Recalculation menu that is displayed when you issue the / **O**ptions | **R**ecalculation command. If you issue this

Formulas

command now, for example, you can see the address A:A8 on the Circular Cell line, as shown here:

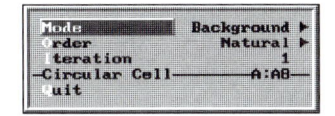

```
Mode            Background ▶
 rder            Natural ▶
 teration              1
Circular Cell——A:A8
 uit
```

You can also track down circular references by using the Circular option on the Tools | Audit menu (see Chapter 8). When you select this option, Quattro Pro uses diagrams to point out any circular relationships in your notebook.

ERR Values

When you make certain types of mistakes in formulas, Quattro Pro displays ERR in the formula cell and, in most cases, in any formula cells that refer to that cell. These characters signify what is known as an *ERR value*. This does not indicate a syntactical error; there is nothing structurally wrong with the formula. Instead, there is some problem with one of the cells your formula references. Correcting the problem entails changing data in one of the referenced cells rather than editing the formula itself.

The most common cause of ERR values is an attempt to perform division by zero, by referencing a cell that either contains a zero or is blank. For example, if you type **+C5/C6** in C7 and press (Enter), you'll receive an ERR value in C7. Entering a value in C6 will correct the problem.

Any formula that references an ERR value returns an ERR value itself. For example, 2 times ERR equals ERR. If you have a relatively complex notebook with formulas that reference other formulas that reference other formulas, one attempt to divide by zero can produce multiple ERR values across the notebook. To find the problem you should look at the last cell you changed, and then at all the formulas that reference that cell.

Building an Income Statement Model

You can now add formulas to the LEARN1.WQ2 notebook that you started in Chapter 2.

1. Issue the / **F**ile | **R**etrieve command and select Yes when asked whether you want to lose your changes. Now select LEARN1.WQ2 from the list or type **LEARN1.WQ2** and press (Enter). Quattro Pro displays the LEARN1 notebook on the screen.

2. Move to B8 and type **(B6-B7)**.
3. Press ⬇ six times and enter **@SUM(** in cell B14.
4. Press ⬆ and type a period to anchor the cell pointer in B13.
5. Press ⬆ three times and, in B10, type **)** and press Enter. The formula on the input line should now read @SUM(B10..B13) and the result should be 158000.
6. Press ⬇ four times and, in B18, enter the formula **(B8-B14-B16)**. The result should be 88500.
7. Press ⬇ again and, in B19, type **(.4*B18)**.
8. Press ⬇, type **(B18-B19)** in B20, and press Enter. You have just created the model for an income statement: Revenue minus expenses equals profit before tax, and profit before tax less the tax (calculated as a percentage of profit before tax) equals net income. At this point, you can vary one or more of the variables on the notebook (for example, Sales or Depreciation) and the effect of that change will ripple through the entire model.
9. Press ⬆ four times to move to B16, and type **10500**.
10. Press Enter while keeping your eye on cells B18 through B20. The notebook should now look like the one shown in Figure 3-5.

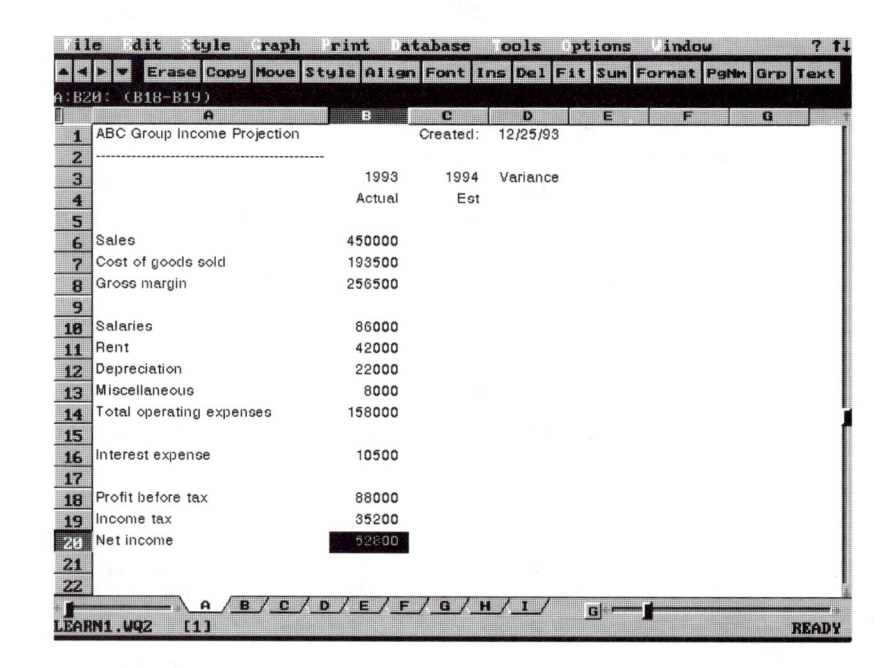

Adding formulas to LEARN1.WQ2
Figure 3-5.

Formulas

When you ask what any particular notebook "does," you are essentially asking how it links and processes a collection of numbers—or how its formulas work. And just as formulas are the heart of any notebook, learning to construct formulas is central to the art of building notebooks. Your ability to obtain useful results from a notebook depends on your ability to translate into formulas the relationships among the numbers pertinent to your business. The challenge is learning to translate what you already know—your business and your informational needs—into a form that Quattro Pro can use.

CHAPTER

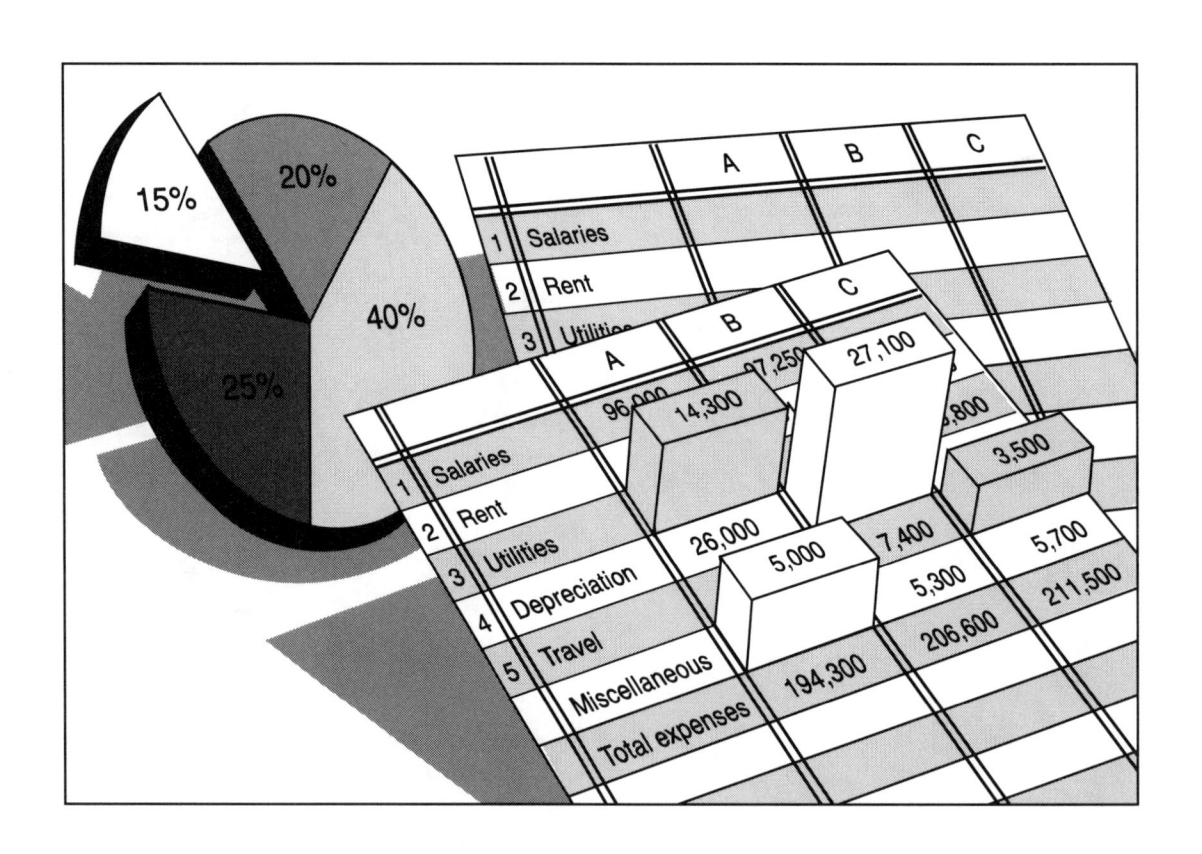

4
REARRANGING THE SPREADSHEET

This chapter introduces several commands for moving, copying, and deleting data. These commands are Quattro Pro's equivalents of scissors and paste—they are tools for "cutting and pasting" groups of data on the notebook.

Most of the commands covered in this chapter can be issued in one of three ways: by selecting menu options using either the keyboard or the mouse, by issuing menu command shortcuts, or by clicking on SpeedBar buttons if you are using a mouse.

Try not to be overwhelmed by the number of choices: All the methods accomplish the same end. Once you've experimented with the various techniques, simply use the one you find easiest.

Because this chapter furnishes you with several tools that can wreak havoc on your notebook, it also introduces Quattro Pro's Undo feature, which allows you to cancel the effect of all the cut and paste commands, as well as many other operations.

The Undo Feature

Even the most experienced spreadsheet builders make mistakes. The more complex the spreadsheet, the more disastrous errors can be. Fortunately, Quattro Pro has a special Undo feature that allows you to change your mind about many operations after the fact.

TIP: Undo is disabled by default when you first load Quattro Pro. However, once Undo is enabled, you can issue the / **O**ptions | **U**pdate command to save that setting to disk, so that the Undo feature is automatically enabled every time you load Quattro Pro.

Undoing an operation takes two steps. The first is to turn on Quattro Pro's Undo feature by issuing the / **O**ptions | **O**ther | **U**ndo | **E**nable command. Once you have enabled this feature, you can use the / **E**dit | **U**ndo command to undo a particular action. The operations you can undo with this command include entering data into a cell, editing data, and deleting a cell's contents; moving, copying, or erasing blocks of cells; inserting or deleting columns and rows; deleting graph names or block names; erasing the entire notebook; and retrieving files.

*The function key equivalent for / **E**dit | **U**ndo is [Alt]-[F5].*

The / **E**dit | **U**ndo command always works on the last "undoable" operation, no matter how much time has elapsed since you performed it. For example, suppose you insert a row, move the cell pointer to another cell, activate the menus, start to issue a command, and then press [Esc]. If you then issue the / **E**dit | **U**ndo command, Quattro Pro removes the inserted row, because that was the most recent operation that / **E**dit | **U**ndo can reverse. If you issue the / **E**dit | **U**ndo command when the Undo feature is not enabled, Quattro Pro displays the error message "Undo is disabled. Cannot undo it."

If you have LEARN1 on the screen, save it by issuing the / **F**ile | **S**ave command and choosing Replace, and then erase the screen with / **F**ile | **E**rase. If you have just reloaded Quattro Pro, you are ready to begin.

Start by enabling the Undo feature:

Rearranging the Spreadsheet

1. Issue the / **O**ptions | **O**ther | **U**ndo | **E**nable command.
2. Select the Update option from the Options menu to save that setting permanently, and then select **Q**uit to return to Ready mode. Now you can try the Undo feature.
3. In A1, type **111** and press Enter.
4. Issue the / **E**dit | **U**ndo command. (Remember, you can use the Alt-F5 shortcut if you like.)

> You can undo the effects of an undo operation by issuing the / **E**dit | **U**ndo command again.

The rest of this chapter covers commands for reorganizing and copying data on the notebook. If you make a mistake and obtain a different result from that shown in the figures, use Alt-F5 to undo your last command and try again.

Inserting and Deleting Rows and Columns

As you construct notebooks, you will frequently need to insert new rows and columns—to add a new line item to a budget, to create another level of subtotals, or to make room for a title at the top of the notebook. You also need a way to delete rows and columns—closing up empty space on the notebook or removing data that is no longer needed.

Inserting Rows

At its simplest, the / **E**dit | **I**nsert | **R**ows command can be used to insert a single row immediately above the current cell. When you issue this command, Quattro Pro displays the prompt "Enter row insert block" followed by a default block consisting of the current cell. If you want to insert one row immediately above the current cell, you can simply press Enter.

If you are using a mouse, you can click on the Ins button on the SpeedBar to insert rows. As soon as you click the button and click on Rows, Quattro Pro displays the prompt "Enter row insert block" and you can click on [Enter] to insert a single row.

How Inserted Rows Affect Formulas

As you learned, using the @SUM function rather than several plus signs to add a series of numbers can save you time and keystrokes. It has another advantage: When you sum a group of cells with the @SUM function, new cells you insert in the block will automatically be included in the sum.

NOTE: Since you are familiar with the basics of data entry, you no longer need as much detail in the instructions. *Enter,* from this point, will mean type the specified data and press [Enter] (or one of the cursor-movement keys) or click on [Enter] with your mouse to enter data into a cell or complete a command. *Type* will mean type the specified characters without pressing [Enter].

1. Enter **300** in A4, **400** in A5, **500** in A6, and **@SUM(A4.A6)** in A7.
2. If you are using a mouse, click on the Ins button on the SpeedBar. Otherwise, press the [Ctrl]-[I] shortcut.
3. Press [Enter] to select Rows from the Insert menu.
4. Now insert two rows at once. When Quattro Pro suggests A:A7..A7 as the "row insert block," move the cell pointer to A6 and press [Enter] or click on [Enter] to specify the block A:A7..A6. Note that Quattro Pro inserts new rows 6 and 7, pushing all the data in or below what was row 6 down two rows.
5. Move to A9 and notice that Quattro Pro has adjusted the formula to read @SUM(A4..A8).
6. Enter **100** in A6 and A7 and note that these new numbers are automatically included in the total. If instead you had used the formula +A4+A5+A6 and then inserted two new rows, you would have needed to edit the formula to include the new cells.

Quattro Pro has no way of discerning whether a cell located above or below a block's boundaries is related to the block. As a result, it only adjusts block references in formulas when you insert new rows within the borders of the original block. If you add rows above the uppermost row or below the lowermost row of a block reference, the scope of the block reference remains unchanged.

*Clicking the Del button on the SpeedBar and clicking on Rows is equivalent to issuing / **Edit** | **Delete** | **Rows**.*

Deleting Rows

When you issue the / **E**dit | **D**elete | **R**ows command, Quattro Pro prompts you for a block of cells and deletes the rows specified within the block. It also automatically adjusts any formulas that reference cells relocated by the command. Try the following:

1. Move to A2 and type **/EDR**.
2. Press [Enter] to accept the default of A:A2..A2 as the "block of rows to delete."

Rearranging the Spreadsheet

Whenever you delete a row, any data within that row is lost. If any of the cells within the row are referenced by formulas in other rows, those formulas return a value of ERR since they will, in effect, be referencing cells that no longer exist.

If you delete rows that include cells that fall inside the boundaries of a block referenced by a formula, Quattro Pro simply adjusts the block coordinates as necessary. However, if you delete a row that contains one of the coordinate cells of a block, any formula that references that block returns a value of ERR. To see this in action:

1. Move to A7, type **/EDR**, and press [Enter] to delete row 7. ERR appears in A7, and the formula in that cell reads @SUM(ERR).
2. Press [Alt]-[F5] to undo the last command.

This is a particularly useful application for the Undo feature because, as you have just seen, once you delete a row containing a block corner cell, the block coordinates are entirely replaced by ERR. This makes it difficult to reconstruct the original formula even after you recognize the problem.

Inserting and Deleting Columns

You can use the Ins and Del buttons on the SpeedBar in place of these commands.

The / **E**dit | **I**nsert | **C**olumns and / **E**dit | **D**elete | **C**olumns commands work exactly like / **E**dit | **I**nsert | **R**ows and / **E**dit | **D**elete | **R**ows, except that they operate on columns. Columns are always inserted to the left of the cell block that you specify.

Here's an exercise that involves inserting and deleting columns:

1. In any cell in column A, press [Ctrl]-[I]. Then select Columns.
2. When Quattro Pro prompts you for a "column insert block," press the [→] key to move to column B and press [Enter] to insert two columns to the left of column A. Look at the formula in C8, noting that the cell references have been adjusted to refer to column C.
3. Move back to column A and issue the / **E**dit | **D**elete | **C**olumns command.
4. Again, move to column B, expanding the block to two columns, and press [Enter] to delete what are now columns A and B. The two empty columns should disappear and your data should now be back in column A.

As with rows, when you delete columns you must be careful not to eliminate any cells referenced by formulas in other columns on the notebook (including any cells used as block coordinates).

NOTE: Inserting and deleting columns or rows affects the entire length or width of the current notebook page. This can present problems if you have discrete sets of information in different areas of a single notebook page. In such cases, you can use the block insert commands to insert partial rows or columns, opening up space in one section of the notebook page without affecting other areas. For details, consult the section "Inserting and Deleting Rows or Columns Within a Block" later in this chapter.

Manipulating Blocks

These three commands have equivalents on the SpeedBar: the Move, Copy, and Erase buttons.

So far you have changed the position of data on your notebook indirectly by inserting or deleting rows or columns. Quattro Pro's / **E**dit | **M**ove command also allows you to move a block of cells from one location to another. In addition, you can copy blocks with / **E**dit | **C**opy and erase them with / **E**dit | **E**rase Block.

When you issue any block command, Quattro Pro prompts you for the block's coordinates and displays the current cell as the default. In most cases, Quattro Pro displays two addresses on the input line. If, for example, the cell pointer is positioned at D4 when you issue the command, Quattro Pro displays a message something like "Source block of cells: A:D4..D4."

You now have several options for defining the block. If you want to accept the default block of the current cell, you can simply press [Enter]. Otherwise, you can use either the typing or pointing method to define an alternative block. To use the typing method, type the address of one corner of the block, one or two periods, and the address of the diagonally opposite corner. Then press [Enter] or one of the cursor-movement keys. The pointing method, described next, takes a bit more getting used to.

Pointing Out Blocks in Commands

Pointing with a mouse to select blocks is covered shortly.

When you issue a block command, Quattro Pro assumes that you will be pointing to cells and enters Point mode immediately. It also assumes that you will use the current cell as one of the defining corners of your block. If the current cell is, in fact, located at one corner of the block you want to specify, you need only perform two steps to define the block using the keyboard: First, use the arrow keys to move to the opposite corner of the block. As you do, the cell pointer remains anchored at the first cell and the entire block of cells is highlighted. Second, when you reach the opposite corner, press [Enter].

If the cell pointer is not already located in a corner of the desired block, you must take three steps: First, press [Esc] or [Backspace] to unanchor the cell pointer from the current cell. When you do this, Quattro Pro erases the second corner of the default block from the input line. Second, move to the cell you want to designate as the first corner of the block, and type a period to re-anchor the cell pointer in this location. Third, move to the diagonally opposite corner of the block and press [Enter].

If you get lost while using this method, look at the number of addresses on the input line. If only one set of cell coordinates appears on the input line, Quattro Pro thinks you are still defining the first corner of the block. If you press one of the cursor-movement keys, the cell pointer moves in the specified direction and the address on the input line changes to reflect that position. When you reach one corner of the desired block, you must type a period to anchor the cell pointer there. Quattro Pro then displays a second address on the input line.

If you see two coordinates on the input line, Quattro Pro thinks that you have already finished defining your first corner and are now pointing to the second. If you press one of the cursor-movement keys, the first address on the input line stays the same, the second address changes to reflect your current position, and the cell pointer expands to highlight all the cells in between those two addresses.

Start by moving the contents of block A6..A8 to C6..C8 using / **E**dit | **M**ove. When you issue this command, Quattro Pro asks you for two pieces of information: the source block (the block of cells you want to move) and the destination (the spot that you want to move them to).

1. In A8, issue the / **E**dit | **M**ove command. Quattro Pro displays the prompt "Source block of cells: A:A8..A8."
2. Move to A6. Notice that as you move the cell pointer, Quattro Pro displays the current cell's address as the second address on the input line, and illuminates the block of cells that would be specified if you chose the current cell as the second corner of the block. When you reach A6, A6 through A8 are highlighted.
3. Press [Enter] or click on [Enter] to designate A8..A6 as the source block for this command. Quattro Pro displays the prompt "Destination for cells: A:A8." Now Quattro Pro is asking you to specify the upper-left corner of the area where you want to move the block. Because blocks always retain their shape when moved, you must specify a new location only for the upper-left corner; the rest of the block will "tag along" intact. To specify a different location as the destination, you can either move to another cell or type the cell's address.
4. Move to C6 and press [Enter] or click on [Enter]. The block should now appear in cells C6 through C8. The total displayed in C8 is still correct, even though you have moved only part of the referenced block.

5. Move to C8. Look at the input line and notice that the formula in cell C8 reads @SUM(A3..C7).

Even though you have separated the cells specified in the formula, Quattro Pro has appropriately adjusted the cell references. Whenever you move cells that are referenced in a formula, Quattro Pro adjusts the references to fit the data's new location. Because Quattro Pro keeps track of blocks by keeping track of their upper-left and lower-right corners, moving one of those corner cells, in effect, changes the size of the block itself.

Remember, Quattro Pro only remembers a block's corners.

In the previous exercise, for example, moving the data in A7, the original block's corner, meant expanding the block referenced in the formula. Quattro Pro adjusted the coordinates of that block to fit the new location of the corner cell, C7. Because cell blocks must be rectangular, there is no way to keep C7 within the block without also including cells B3 through B7, C3 through C5, and the now empty cells A6 and A7. If those additional cells contained values, or if you entered values in them now, those values would automatically be included in your total. In contrast, if you move a cell that falls within the middle of a referenced block, Quattro Pro does not adjust the block references at all. For example, if you had moved only the value in A6 to C6, the formula in A8 would remain the same, and the value in C6 would be excluded from the total.

If you move cells that are individually referenced by a formula, Quattro Pro adjusts the formula accordingly. For example, if cell A3 contained the formula +A1+A2 and you moved the contents of A1 to C1, Quattro Pro would change the formula in A3 to +C1+A2. No new cells would be included in the total.

Now try moving the same block of cells back to its original position. This time you will either use the [Ctrl]-[M] shortcut for / **E**dit | **M**ove or click on the Move button on the SpeedBar and, for practice, you will start in the destination cell rather than in one corner of the source block.

1. Move to A6 and press [Ctrl]-[M] or click on the Move button. Quattro Pro displays the message "Source block of cells: A:A6..A6."
2. Press [Esc] or click on [Esc] to unanchor the cell pointer from A6. Only one address is now displayed on the input line; this means that you can now redefine the first corner of the source block.
3. Move to C6 and type a period to re-anchor the cell pointer. The cell coordinate C6 should appear twice on the input line.
4. Move to C8 and press [Enter] or click on [Enter] to specify a source block of C6..C8.

Rearranging the Spreadsheet

5. When Quattro Pro requests a destination for the block, press [Enter] or click on [Enter] to accept the default of A6.

If you preselect a block for a particular operation, it remains selected after the operation is complete.

Pointing Out Blocks in Advance   Quattro Pro also lets you point out the blocks of cells you want to manipulate before you issue a command. To move a block, for example, you can first highlight the source block; then issue the / **E**dit | **M**ove command, and define the destination block by moving the cell pointer to one corner of the block. To point out a block in advance, you start by pressing [Shift]-[F7]. Quattro Pro displays EXT on the status line, indicating that it now expects you to extend the cell pointer to highlight the block. Next you move to the opposite corner of the block and issue the / **E**dit | **M**ove command. Try this now.

1. Move to A3 and press [Shift]-[F7]. Notice that EXT appears on the status line.
2. Move to A8. The entire block A3..A8 should be highlighted.
3. Issue the / **E**dit | **M**ove command or click on the Move button. Quattro Pro automatically uses the predefined block of A3..A8 as the source block and asks you only for a destination.
4. Enter **B3** as the destination.

Most examples in the next two chapters instruct you to specify blocks when you are prompted to do so during a command. Feel free to select those blocks in advance if you prefer.

Pointing Out Blocks with a Mouse   You can also point out blocks with a mouse, before or during a command, by using one of two methods. One method involves clicking on one corner of the block, holding down the left mouse button while you drag to the opposite corner (Quattro Pro highlights the block as you move the pointer), and then releasing the button. The second method involves clicking on one corner of the block, moving the mouse pointer to the opposite corner of the block, and holding down the right button on the mouse while you click the left button.

If you are using a mouse, you might try these methods in some of the upcoming exercises, substituting either method whenever Quattro Pro prompts for a source block. In this case, you can ignore instructions about anchoring the cell pointer. Note that you can also use these techniques for pointing out blocks when defining formulas.

Copying Cells

*The shortcut for / **E**dit | **C**opy is ⌈Ctrl⌉-⌈C⌉; or, you can click the Copy button on the SpeedBar.*

Edit | **C**opy is one of the most useful commands in Quattro Pro's repertoire. It can be used to copy a block of cells from one location on the notebook to another. As with / **E**dit | **M**ove, Quattro Pro asks for a source block and a destination. As soon as you specify the destination, Quattro Pro replicates the source block in the desired location. Try this now.

1. In B3, issue the / **E**dit | **C**opy command.
2. When prompted for the source block, move to B6, and press ⌈Enter⌋ to define the block B3..B6.
3. When prompted for the destination, type **C3** and press ⌈Enter⌋. You have now copied the data in block B3..B6 to block C3..C6.

Although this exercise simply replicated a block of cells in a new location, you actually have four possible source block/destination block combinations with / **E**dit | **C**opy: You can copy a block, consisting of one or more cells, to another block of the same size and shape. You can copy a single-cell block to a multiple-cell block. And you can copy a multiple-cell source block across a row or down a column. You have already tried the first of these combinations. Now try the others.

Copying a Single Cell Across a Block As you have seen, when you copy one block of cells to another block of the same dimensions, you specify two cell addresses for the source block and only one address—the upper-left corner—for the destination. In all other cases, you specify two addresses for the source block and two for the destination. Try this now.

1. Enter **111** in cell A1.
2. While still in A1, press ⌈Ctrl⌋-⌈C⌋, the shortcut for / **E**dit | **C**opy, or click on the Copy button on the SpeedBar.
3. When prompted for the source block, press ⌈Enter⌋ or click [Enter] to accept the default A:A1..A1.
4. When prompted for a destination, type a period to anchor the cell pointer in A1.
5. Move to F1 and press ⌈Enter⌋ to define a destination block of A:A1..F1. Your notebook should now look like the one in Figure 4-1.

Note that you can include the source block (A1..A1) in the destination block (A1..F1) since this has no real effect on the content of A1. It just saves you the trouble of moving to B1 before anchoring the cell pointer.

Rearranging the Spreadsheet

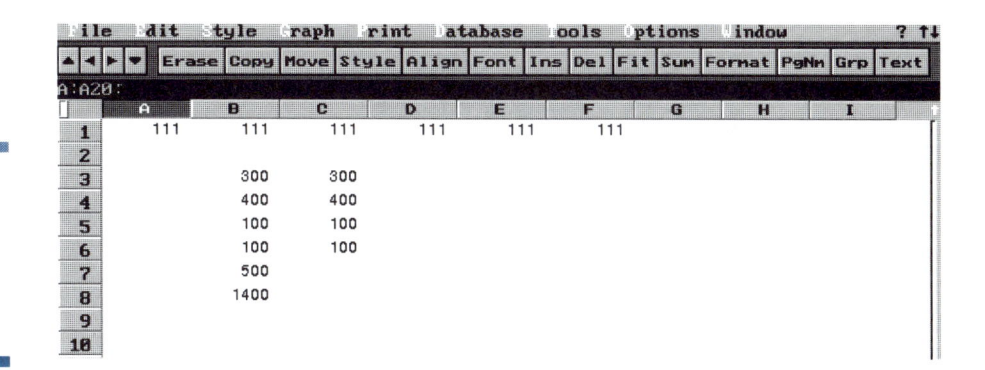

The effect of copying cell A1 across a multiple-cell block

Figure 4-1.

Copying Multiple-Cell Blocks Across Rows or Down Columns In certain circumstances, you can copy a multiple-cell source block across a row or down a column by specifying two cell addresses for the destination rather than one. To illustrate, try copying cells C3 and C4 across part of row 5.

1. In C3, press Ctrl-C or click on the Copy button.
2. When prompted for a source block, press the ↓ to move to C4 and press Enter.
3. When prompted for a destination, type or point to the block D5..F5.
4. Press Enter. Your notebook should now look like Figure 4-2.

NOTE: If you try to copy a block that spans multiple rows and columns across a larger block, Quattro Pro simply replicates the source block once rather than many times.

You can use / **E**dit | **C**opy to replicate a multiple-cell block across a larger destination block (as you just did) in only a few situations. The source block has to consist of cells in a single row or a single column. When the source block falls within one column, you can only copy it across a row, creating adjacent duplicate columns. When the source block falls within one row, you can only copy it down a column, creating adjacent, duplicate rows.

Notice that the cells used to designate the destination block in the last exercise were within the top row of the block. This is actually consistent

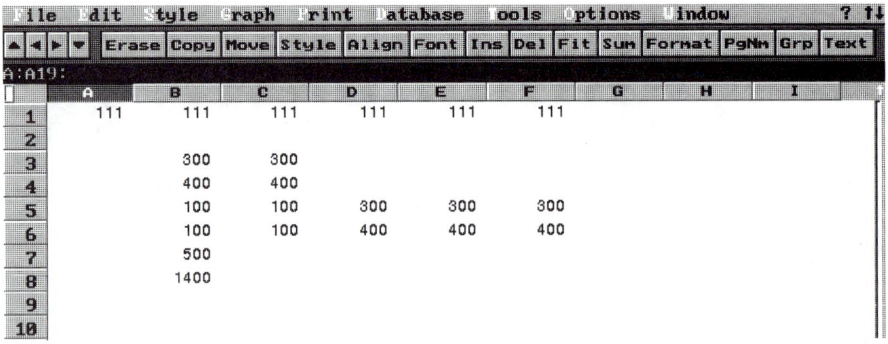

Copying a multiple-cell block across a row
Figure 4-2.

with the way you have specified destinations in previous commands. When you copy or move a block, you usually specify only an upper-left corner for the destination; the rest of the block simply follows along when copied or transported. Similarly, when you copy a block across a row or down a column, you must specify only the top row or the left column. This is like specifying the upper-left corner for each one of a series of replications.

Copying Formulas

So far the / **E**dit | **C**opy command has been fairly predictable. When you copy formulas, however, the outcome is less obvious. When you copy a formula, Quattro Pro abandons the actual addresses of the referenced cells and remembers only their locations *relative to the formula cell*. Cell B8, for example, currently contains the formula @SUM(B3..B7). If you copy the contents of this cell to C8, Quattro Pro evaluates that formula as "add together the contents of the five cells located immediately above the current cell." In C8, the formula @SUM(B3..B7) is therefore transformed into @SUM(C3..C7)—cell references are adjusted to fit the new location.

To see how this works, follow these steps:

1. Move to B8 and issue the / **E**dit | **C**opy command by pressing Ctrl-C or clicking on the Copy button.
2. When prompted for the source block, press Enter or click [Enter] to accept A:B8..B8.
3. When prompted for the destination, press the → key to move the cell pointer to G8, and type a period to anchor the cell pointer. Then point to I8 and press Enter. (If you are using a mouse, simply highlight G8..I8 and click on [Enter]). Your notebook should now look like the one in Figure 4-3.

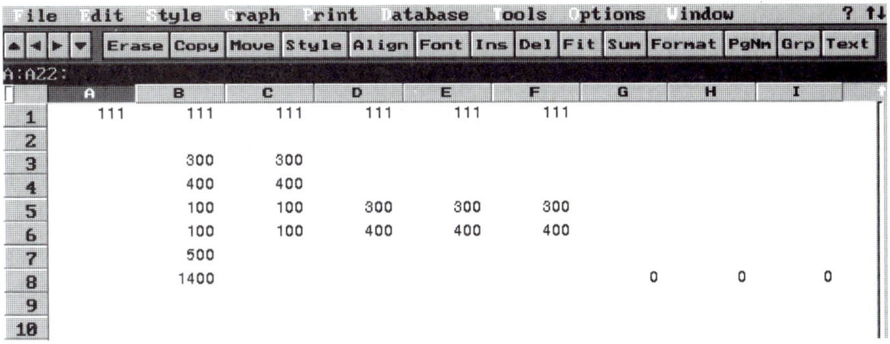

Rearranging the Spreadsheet

The notebook after copying the @SUM formula
Figure 4-3.

	A	B	C	D	E	F	G	H	I
1	111	111	111	111	111	111			
2									
3		300	300						
4		400	400						
5		100	100	300	300	300			
6		100	100	400	400	400			
7		500							
8		1400					0	0	0
9									
10									

4. Now look at the formulas in G8, H8, and I8. They add up values in the five cells immediately above themselves; Quattro Pro has adjusted the formula to fit each of the columns. If those cells had already contained numbers, these new formulas would have calculated their total. Quattro Pro shows zeros instead because the cells that the formulas reference are currently empty.

5. Fill in all the cells in the block G3..I7 and watch Quattro Pro automatically add up the columns, as shown in Figure 4-4.

When you copied the formula, you created three new formulas, each of which replicates the general function of the formula in B8 (adding a column of five numbers) rather than its literal contents.

This method of handling cell references lets you build typical spreadsheets quickly. In most business spreadsheets, the same basic set of calculations is performed in several adjacent rows and columns. For example, Figure 4-5 shows a notebook that calculates total monthly sales revenues in each of four sales regions. In this case a single formula—@SUM(B4..B7)—was entered

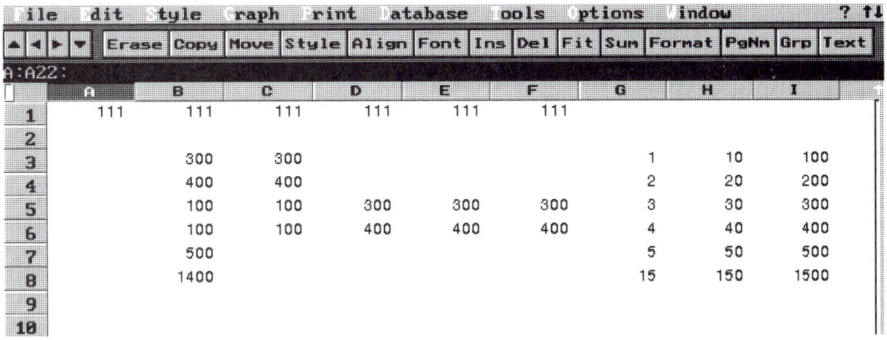

Filling in cells referenced by the new formulas
Figure 4-4.

	A	B	C	D	E	F	G	H	I
1	111	111	111	111	111	111			
2									
3		300	300				1	10	100
4		400	400				2	20	200
5		100	100	300	300	300	3	30	300
6		100	100	400	400	400	4	40	400
7		500					5	50	500
8		1400					15	150	1500
9									
10									

in B8 to calculate total sales in January. This formula was then copied to C8 through G8 to calculate totals for the next five months. Next the formula @SUM(B4..G4) was entered in H4 to calculate sales revenue in the Northeast region over a six-month period. This formula was then copied to H5 through H7 to calculate six-month totals for the other regions, and to cell H8 to add the six monthly totals for all regions. Altogether, only two formulas were typed in the notebook; the other nine were generated from those first two.

All the cell references you have entered in formulas are what are called *relative cell references*. Whenever Quattro Pro replicates a relative cell reference, it "thinks" in terms of the referenced cell's position relative to the formula cell, rather than in terms of a fixed location on the notebook. Sometimes you want Quattro Pro to leave some or all of your cell references as is, no matter where you copy them. In such cases you can make the cell references absolute rather than relative (see Chapter 8). *Absolute cell references* do not change when copied; they always refer to exactly the same location.

If you change the original formula, you need to reissue the / **E**dit | **C**opy command if you want the copies to change accordingly. This may seem strange: Once you get used to Quattro Pro's automatic recalculation of formulas, you may expect it to reexecute other operations as well. However, formulas, unlike commands, are actually stored in the notebook. Quattro Pro can recalculate formulas because they are retained in your computer's memory. In contrast, when you issue a command, Quattro Pro may request information, but it discards your answers as soon as the operation is complete. With / **E**dit | **C**opy, once you have finished copying a formula to several other cells, Quattro Pro "forgets" about the entire operation; there is no longer any link, in the notebook or in memory, between the original formula and its copies.

Quattro Pro features another copy command, / **E**dit | **C**opy Special, that allows you to copy either just the contents or just the formatting in a block

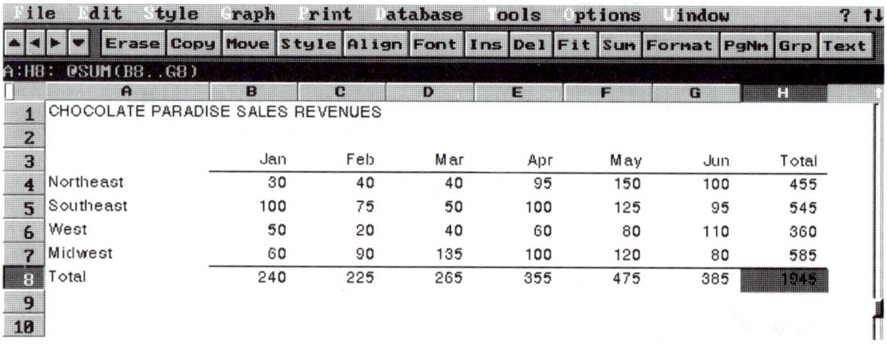

A spreadsheet built by copying formulas
Figure 4-5.

of cells (see Chapter 5). You can use this command to copy a formula without including any style information such as shading and alignment, or you can use it to copy only style information, leaving behind the actual contents of the copied cells.

Notes of Caution on Moving and Copying Blocks

When you move a block of cells, be careful not to overwrite any cells that are referenced by formulas. If you do, the cell reference is replaced with ERR and the formula yields a result of ERR on your notebook. You can experience similar problems if you overwrite cells in a block that is referenced by a formula. If you overwrite cells in the middle of a referenced block, the formula is simply recalculated with the new values. However, if you overwrite a corner, or coordinate, cell of a block, Quattro Pro responds as if you had overwritten any cell references within a formula, replacing the block reference with the value ERR and evaluating the formula as ERR on the notebook. Execute the following steps to see how this problem occurs:

1. Move to A1 and issue the / **E**dit | **M**ove command.
2. Accept the default source block of A1..A1 and, when prompted for a destination, move to B3 and press Enter.
3. Move to B8 and note that the formula in that cell now reads @SUM(ERR). Then press Alt-F5 (Undo) to undo the damage.

If any other formulas on the notebook referenced B8, they too would have been changed to ERR. As explained in Chapter 3, an ERR value in one cell can, like any other change in value, ripple through your entire notebook.

Overwriting cells with / **E**dit | **C**opy rather than / **E**dit | **M**ove does not produce the same problems. For this reason, you should be that much more careful about copying one block of cells over another one. Quattro Pro does not produce warnings or generate ERR values, so it is easy to damage your notebook by copying something to the wrong location.

You can also experience problems with / **E**dit | **C**opy if you copy a formula to a location that requires Quattro Pro to reference a cell off the edge of the notebook. For example, if you enter a formula in column D that refers to a cell in column C and then attempt to copy that formula to column A, Quattro Pro tries to adjust the formula so that it refers to the column that is to the left of column A. Since there is no column to the left of A, Quattro Pro "wraps around" to the other edge of the notebook, referencing a cell in column IV, the rightmost column on the notebook. Because no error message is displayed in this case, this unintended result can easily go undetected.

In addition, if you try to copy or move a block of cells to a destination too close to the borders of the notebook, Quattro Pro displays the error message "Out of worksheet boundary." For example, you would see this error message if you tried to copy or move block A1..A3 to the destination A8192 (the lower-left corner of the notebook).

Using the [End] Key to Define Large Blocks

The [End] direction key is particularly useful for pointing out blocks. In this context, [End] is always used in conjunction with one of the arrow keys or with [Home]. You press the [End] key first, release it, and then press the other key. (With most other key combinations, such as those including the control key, you instead hold down [Ctrl] *while* tapping the second key.) If you're using a mouse you can press the arrow buttons on the Ready mode SpeedBar rather than pressing [End] followed by one of the regular arrow keys.

If the current cell contains data, the [End]-arrow key combination moves the cell pointer in the direction of the arrow key to the next cell immediately before or after an empty cell. If the current cell is empty, it moves the cell pointer in the specified direction to the next cell that contains data. Essentially, the [End] key combinations move the cell pointer from one edge of a block of data to the next.

You might also find it helpful to keep two rules in mind. The [End]-arrow key combination always moves the cell pointer to an edge—either the edge of a block of cells (the boundary between a cell that contains data and one that is empty) or the edge of the notebook itself. It also moves the cell pointer to a filled cell (that is, a cell that contains data) if there is such a cell in the indicated direction.

One last [End] key combination, [End]-[Home], always moves the cell pointer to the lower-right corner of the section of the notebook that contains data. This corner cell is the intersection of the rightmost column that currently contains data, and the lowest row that currently contains data. This cell may or may not contain data itself. In your current notebook, for example, [End]-[Home] would move the cell pointer to I8. However, if there were data in J1, [End]-[Home] would move the cell pointer to J8, whether or not it contained data.

Erasing a Block

The shortcut for / **Edit** | **Erase Block** is [Ctrl]-[E].

The / **Edit** | **Erase Block** command erases all data in a specified block of cells, as if you had moved the cell pointer to every cell in the block and pressed [Del]. If you're using a mouse, you can instead use the Erase button on the SpeedBar. Keep in mind that Quattro Pro does not make you confirm your

Rearranging the Spreadsheet

intention before erasing a large block. If you do erase cells by accident, be sure to issue the / **E**dit | **U**ndo command immediately, before you perform another "undoable" operation.

To practice using / **E**dit | **E**rase Block, follow these steps:

1. Use the [F5] (GoTo) key to move to G3.
2. This time try defining the block in advance using the [End] key.
3. Press [Shift]-[F7] (Select) and then press [End]-[→] to extend the block to G3..I3.
4. Press [End]-[↓] to extend the block to G3..I8.
5. Issue the / **E**dit | **E**rase Block command by pressing [Ctrl]-[E] or clicking on the Erase button. Quattro Pro erases all the data in the predefined block.

CAUTION: Be careful not to erase cells referenced as the denominator in a division formula elsewhere on the notebook. For example, if a cell contained the formula (B3/B4) and you erased a block that included B4, the formula would evaluate to ERR because you cannot divide by zero (a blank cell is read as the equivalent of zero).

Inserting and Deleting Rows or Columns Within a Block

When you insert or delete rows or columns, the entire row or column is affected. For example, if you position yourself in row 2 and insert a new row, all the data from that row is moved down to row 3, whether it's in column A or column IV. Similarly, if you insert a new column while in column B, all the information that was formerly in column B moves over to column C, whether it's in row 1 or row 8192.

In some cases, however, you may want to insert space in only one section of a notebook, leaving other sections unchanged. You can do this by using the / **E**dit | **I**nsert | Row **B**lock command. When Quattro Pro prompts you for a "row insert block," it then inserts only the specified cells, rather than inserting a row across the entire notebook page. To delete a block of rows without affecting any data to the right or left of the selected block, follow the same procedure but use the / **E**dit | **D**elete | Row **B**lock command.

You can also insert and delete *columns* in a specified area using the / **E**dit | **I**nsert | Column B**l**ock and / **E**dit | **D**elete | Column B**l**ock commands. These commands move data within the specified block to the right (if you insert) and to the left (if you delete), without affecting information above or below the selected block.

Quattro Pro 5 Made Easy

Putting Blocks to Work on Your Spreadsheet

Now that you have learned the mechanics of cutting and pasting data, try putting this knowledge to work on your sample notebook. The following instructions tell you only the operations to perform. You can choose between menu selections and command shortcuts, and pointing and typing methods. You can also use the SpeedBar buttons if you're working with a mouse.

1. Issue the / **F**ile | **R**etrieve command and select Yes when asked whether you want to lose your changes. When prompted for the name of a file to retrieve, either move the cursor to LEARN1.WQ2 and press [Enter] or click on LEARN1.WQ2 with your mouse.

2. Suppose you have decided that the notebook would look less crowded with an extra row before the column headings, and that the word "Variance" would look better down one cell. Move to row 3 and issue the / **E**dit | **I**nsert | **R**ows command. Press [Enter] or click on [Enter] to accept the default row insert block.

3. Move to D4 and issue the / **E**dit | **M**ove command. Accept the default source block of A:D4..D4 and enter a destination of D5.

4. Now insert a row within the block specified in the Total operating expenses formula and add another expense category. Move to B13 and issue the / **E**dit | **I**nsert | **R**ows command.

5. Press [Enter] when Quattro Pro displays the prompt "Enter row insert block: A:B13..B13" to insert a row between Rent and Depreciation.

6. Enter **15500** in B13, and enter **Utilities** in A13.

7. Move to B16 and notice that the formula has been adjusted to include the new line item. The total displayed in cell B16 should be 173500.

8. Now you want to copy the data in column B to column C, on the assumption that most of the ABC Group's revenues and expenses will be the same in 1994 as they were in 1993. Use / **E**dit | **C**opy to copy cells B7 through B22 (the source block) to cell C7 (the destination). Your notebook should now look like Figure 4-6.

9. Assume that some of your revenue and expense items are likely to increase by 5% in 1994. You can make this adjustment by entering a formula for calculating the 5% increase in one cell in column C and then copying that formula to several other cells in the column. Move to C7 and enter the formula (**B7*1.05**).

10. Use / **E**dit | **C**opy ([Ctrl]-[C]) or the Copy button) to copy C7 to cells C8, C11..C13, and C15. You need to issue the command three times, defining C7..C7 as the source block each time and C8, C11..C13, and C15 as the various destinations. Leave Depreciation and Interest

Rearranging the Spreadsheet

expense at the same levels as the previous year. Your notebook should now look like Figure 4-7.

11. Now use / **E**dit | **C**opy to fill column D with a set of formulas that calculate the variance between 1993's actual figures and the estimates for 1994. Move to D7 and enter **(C7-B7)**.

12. Use / **E**dit | **C**opy to copy this formula to the destination block D7..D22. Note that zeros now appear in cells D10, D17, and D19, because the formulas generated in those cells by the / **E**dit | **C**opy command reference cells that are blank.

13. Delete the contents of cells D10, D17, and D19 using the [Del] key. (Be careful not to delete the zeros in D14 and D18; they are legitimate results.) Then compare your notebook to Figure 4-8. Make any corrections that are necessary to achieve a total of 3150 in D22.

14. Issue the / **F**ile | **S**ave command and choose Replace.

LEARN1 is beginning to resemble the kind of notebook you might use in your business. In subsequent chapters, you will enhance its appearance, print it, and improve its design, but even at this point it is a viable and realistic model.

This chapter has introduced some ideas—such as relative cell referencing—that are often difficult for beginners. If you are not yet comfortable with the concept, take more time to experiment with copying formulas. You might also want to practice pointing out blocks. Much of your

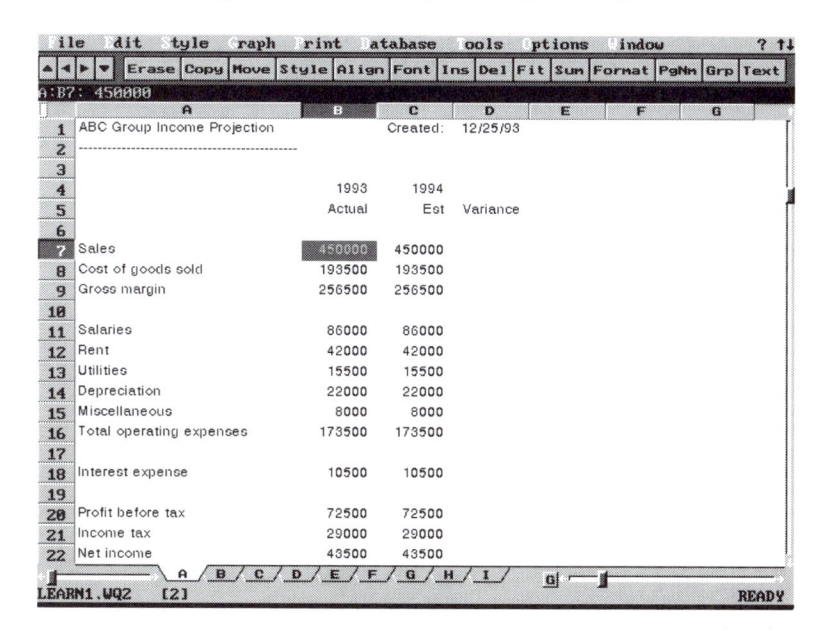

LEARN1 after copying B7..B22 to column C
Figure 4-6.

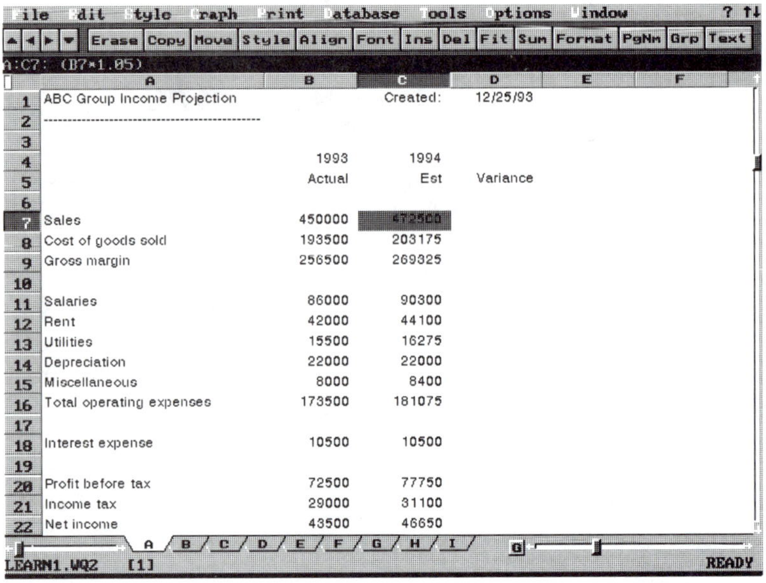

A:C7: (B7*1.05)

	A	B	C	D
1	ABC Group Income Projection		Created:	12/25/93
2	--			
3				
4		1993	1994	
5		Actual	Est	Variance
6				
7	Sales	450000	472500	
8	Cost of goods sold	193500	203175	
9	Gross margin	256500	269325	
10				
11	Salaries	86000	90300	
12	Rent	42000	44100	
13	Utilities	15500	16275	
14	Depreciation	22000	22000	
15	Miscellaneous	8000	8400	
16	Total operating expenses	173500	181075	
17				
18	Interest expense	10500	10500	
19				
20	Profit before tax	72500	77750	
21	Income tax	29000	31100	
22	Net income	43500	46650	

LEARN1.WQ2 [1] READY

Projecting revenue and expense increases in 1994
Figure 4-7.

work in subsequent chapters draws and builds on the ideas and procedures introduced in this one. The better you understand the basics of block operations now, the easier it will be to master the complexities later.

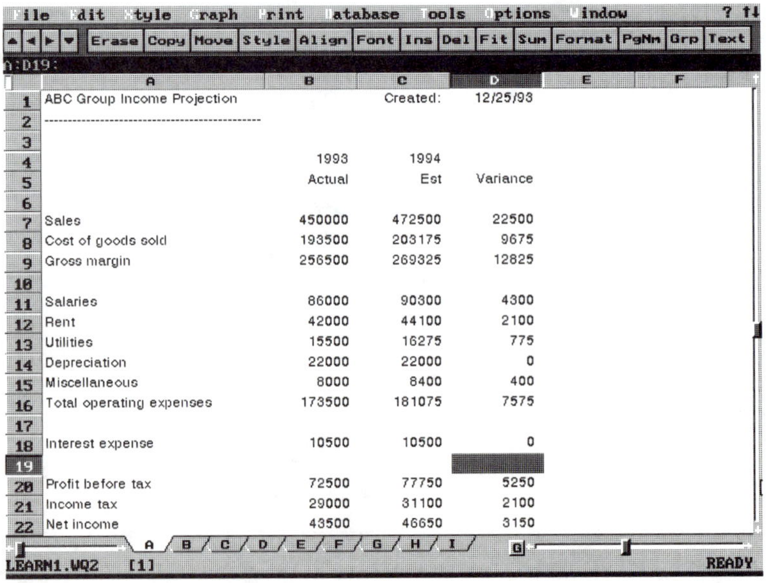

A:D19:

	A	B	C	D
1	ABC Group Income Projection		Created:	12/25/93
2	--			
3				
4		1993	1994	
5		Actual	Est	Variance
6				
7	Sales	450000	472500	22500
8	Cost of goods sold	193500	203175	9675
9	Gross margin	256500	269325	12825
10				
11	Salaries	86000	90300	4300
12	Rent	42000	44100	2100
13	Utilities	15500	16275	775
14	Depreciation	22000	22000	0
15	Miscellaneous	8000	8400	400
16	Total operating expenses	173500	181075	7575
17				
18	Interest expense	10500	10500	0
19				
20	Profit before tax	72500	77750	5250
21	Income tax	29000	31100	2100
22	Net income	43500	46650	3150

LEARN1.WQ2 [1] READY

LEARN1 after constructing the Variance column
Figure 4-8.

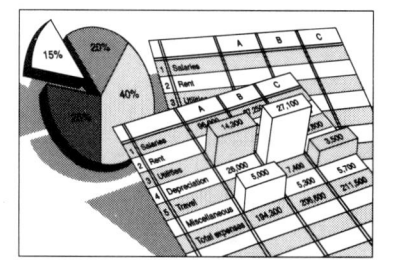

CHAPTER

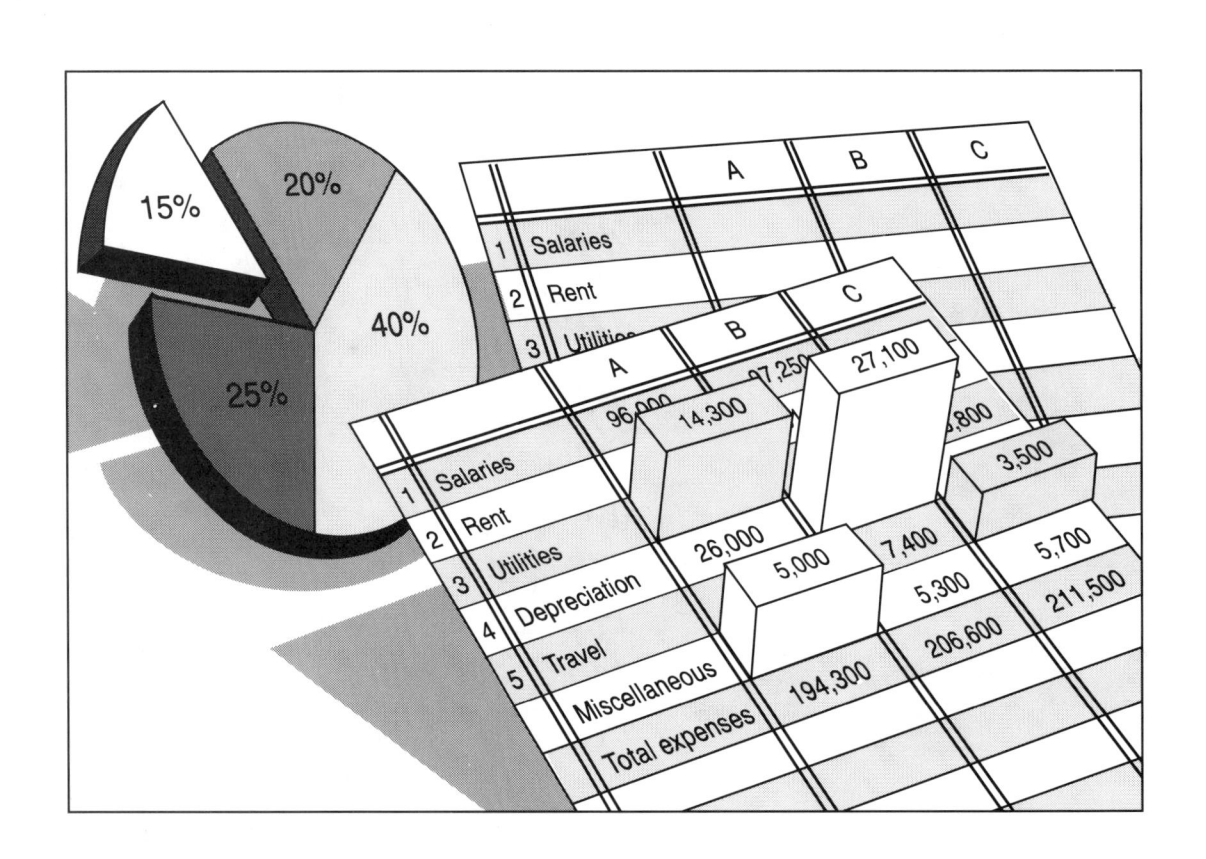

5
FORMATTING YOUR NOTEBOOK

The layout and appearance of your notebook are often as important as the data it contains. Proper formatting can transform a mass of numbers and text into a storehouse of readable, usable information. Even if you intend to be the sole user of a notebook, careful design can make your work easier to understand when you return to it next month or next year. If you expect others to read the notebook, its appearance is even more important.

This chapter covers most of Quattro Pro's formatting

commands—commands that let you change the appearance of your notebook without altering the data itself. You learn to change the width of columns and the alignment of labels. You also learn to change the display format of numbers—add dollar signs, commas, and percent signs, control the number of decimal places, and so on. Then you learn to draw lines and boxes and add shading to selected cells. In addition, you learn about the Copy Special command, which permits you to copy just the formatting attributes or only the contents of a selected block of cells. Finally, you learn how to save a group of formatting attributes as a custom style. This way you can assign many style attributes at once, instead of having to apply them one by one.

Default Formats

Column widths, label alignment, and the display format of numeric values can all be defined on two levels: You can either assign a new format to a particular set of cells or you can change the default setting for the notebook as a whole. For example, every notebook has a default column width, which is used for all columns that you do not otherwise format with a column width command. Similarly, every notebook has a default label alignment (usually flush left) that is used for every new label you enter. If you want particular labels aligned differently, you must type an alignment prefix character or issue a label alignment command. Each notebook also has a default format for displaying numeric values. This format determines the appearance of every numeric value to which you have not explicitly given a different format.

NOTE: The commands for altering the notebook defaults are located on the Options | Formats menu. The commands for formatting sections of the notebook are located on the Style menu.

Several Style menu commands have equivalents on the Ready mode SpeedBar.

It's usually most efficient, in terms of both keystrokes and the size of the notebook file, to use the notebook default settings to format the majority of the notebook. For example, if you want most columns to be 13 characters wide, but you want column A to be 30 characters wide, it is best to change the default column width to 13 and then change the width of column A (the exception to the general rule) to 30.

Adjusting Column Widths

The default column width is initially nine characters. You can change this setting with / **O**ptions | **F**ormats | **G**lobal Width. When you issue this

Formatting Your Notebook

command, Quattro Pro asks you to reset the default column width and displays the current setting. You can either enter a new column width or use → or ← to adjust the columns manually.

Try applying this command to the LEARN1.WQ2 notebook.

1. With LEARN1.WQ2 on your screen, issue the / **O**ptions | **F**ormats | **G**lobal Width command.
2. Press → twice and then press (Enter) and press (Esc) twice to return to Ready mode.

Note that columns B, C, D, and all columns to the right widen from 9 to 11 characters, while the width of column A remains unchanged. The cells in column A all contain a column width code—inserted when you issued the / **S**tyle | **C**olumn Width command in Chapter 2—that overrides the global column width setting. This code is an instruction to display the column as 27 characters wide, regardless of the global column width setting. This allows you to reset the global width without changing the width of any individually formatted columns. The only way to eliminate column width codes is by issuing the / **S**tyle | **R**eset Width or / **S**tyle | **B**lock Size | **R**eset Width command; these commands affect the current column and all the columns in a specified block, respectively.

Try resetting column A to the current global width of 11 characters by moving to any cell in column A and issuing the / **S**tyle | **R**eset Width command. The column width code [W27] no longer appears on the input line as you move through cells in column A. Notice also that some of the labels now appear truncated.

Changing the Width of Several Columns at Once

As you saw in Chapter 2, you can change the width of a single column by using the / **S**tyle | **C**olumn Width command ((Ctrl)-(W)), or by clicking and dragging the column letter on the top border of the notebook area. Quattro Pro also offers commands for adjusting the width of several columns simultaneously.

/ **S**tyle | **B**lock Size | **S**et Width adjusts the widths of all columns in a specified block. When you issue this command, Quattro Pro asks you for a block of columns. Specify a block that includes all the columns that you want to change. Quattro Pro asks you to indicate a column width of 1 to 254 characters. Type the desired width, or use the arrow keys to adjust the width manually. As soon as you press (Enter), Quattro Pro changes every column in the block to the specified width.

If you use the Fit button, Quattro Pro automatically places one space between columns.

Quattro Pro offers another command—/ **S**tyle | **B**lock Size | **A**uto Width (or the Fit SpeedBar button)—that lets you widen one or more columns to fit the width of the existing entries. When you issue this command, Quattro Pro asks for the number of extra spaces between columns, from 0 through 40 (with a default of 1). Quattro Pro adds the number you specify to the width of the column's longest entry to calculate the column's new width. Next, Quattro Pro asks you to specify the block of columns. This time the row coordinates of the specified block actually make a difference. If you specify a block containing just one row, Quattro Pro looks only at entries in that row and the rows below when calculating the column width. If you specify a multiple-cell block, Quattro Pro just considers the entries within that block in its calculation.

NOTE: When the longest entry in the block of cells you are formatting is a numeric value, Quattro Pro makes the column one character wider than it would if the value were a label. This prevents numbers in one column from running into numbers in adjacent columns.

Try the / **S**tyle | **B**lock Size | **A**uto Width command now to adjust the width of column A.

1. Move to A11, and issue the / **S**tyle | **B**lock Size | **A**uto Width command or click on the Fit button on the SpeedBar.
2. If Quattro Pro asks for the number of characters between columns, press [Enter] to accept the default of one character.
3. When asked for a block of columns, press [↓] twice to expand the block to A13. Press [Enter].

Quattro Pro reduces the column width. If you made the change from within character-based mode, the new width will be 10 characters—the exact width of the longest entry in the specified block plus the one extra character you specified. If you're working in WYSIWYG mode, the proportional fonts will take up somewhat less space and your column width will be less than 10. Now, specify a column block consisting of the first cell in the column.

1. Press [Home] to move to A1 and issue the / **S**tyle | **B**lock Size | **A**uto Width command or click on the Fit button.
2. Accept **1** as the number of characters between columns, if applicable.
3. Press [Enter] to accept the default column block of A:A1..A1.

Because you specified a single-cell block, Quattro Pro looks at all of the entries in or below that cell—which, in this case, means all of the entries in

Formatting Your Notebook

the entire column. Quattro Pro then widens the column to match the width of the longest entries in that block—the entries in A1 and A2. (The column width will be slightly larger if you're in character-based rather than WYSIWYG mode.)

Display Formats

Quattro Pro's display formats determine how values are displayed on the notebook. As you know, the only characters you can use when entering numbers are the digits, the plus sign, the minus sign, and the decimal point. Fortunately, Quattro Pro gives you far more flexibility in displaying numbers. Changing the display format of a cell has no effect on the data itself; it affects the data's form but not its content. As far as calculations are concerned, 0.5 is equivalent to 50%, and 25.00 is equivalent to 25.

The Default Format Setting

Every Quattro Pro notebook has a default format for displaying values. Most of the time, this default is the General format, which approximates the way Quattro Pro actually stores values. In the General format, only decimal places that affect the value of a number are displayed, any trailing zeros to the right of a decimal point are dropped, and percentages are displayed as decimals, even if you enter a percent sign. In addition, decimals are always preceded by a zero to the left of the decimal point (you'd see 0.14 rather than .14, for example). Finally, if the value is too long to fit within a cell, Quattro Pro displays as much of it as possible. If the portion to the left of the decimal point fits within the cell, Quattro Pro displays that portion, a decimal point, and as many decimal places as possible. Otherwise Quattro Pro displays the value in exponential notation. (In most of the other numeric formats, Quattro Pro merely displays asterisks if the number does not fit within its cell.) Whenever Quattro Pro truncates a value to display it in the specified format or to fit it within a cell, it rounds the number.

The General format is similar to the way Quattro Pro actually stores numbers; in most cases what you see in the cell is the same as what appears on the input line. This is not true of Quattro Pro's other display formats, where you enter the data in one form, but Quattro Pro may store it in a second form and display it in a third.

Quattro Pro's Ten Display Formats

Quattro Pro supplies ten display formats for values. Depending on your data, you may choose to display all notebook values in one format or to mix and match formats within the same notebook. Table 5-1 illustrates six of the ten formats. (The Code is explained in "Changing the Numeric Format of a Block," later in this chapter.)

Display Formats for Values
Table 5-1.

Format	Decimals	Value	Display	Code
General	NA	9876.543	9876.543	(G)
	NA	−9876.543	−9876.543	(G)
Fixed	0	9876.543	9877	(F0)
	2	9876.543	9876.54	(F2)
	4	−9876.543	−9876.5430	(F4)
, (comma)	2	9876.543	9,876.54	(,2)
	0	9876.543	9,877	(,0)
	2	−9876.543	(9,876.54)	(,2)
Currency	2	9876.543	$9,876.54	(C2)
	0	9876.543	$9,877	(C0)
	2	−9876.543	($9,876.54)	(C2)
Percent	1	.123	12.3%	(P1)
	2	.123	12.30%	(P2)
	0	1.23	123%	(P0)
Scientific	0	10	1E+01	(S0)
	.2	100	1E+02	(S2)
	.1	333	3.33E+02	(S1)

The Fixed format displays values with the number of decimal places you specify, regardless of whether you typed more or fewer decimal places when entering the value.

The Scientific format displays values in scientific (exponential) notation. In scientific notation, values are expressed as the product of two numbers, one of which is a number between 1 and 10 and the other of which is a power of 10. For example, when displayed in scientific notation, the number 1420 appears as 1.42E+3. The letter E in this format represents "10 to the power of," so the entire expression can be read as 1.42 times 10 to the power of 3, or 1.42 × 1000.

The Currency format displays values preceded by a currency symbol. The default symbol is $, but you can change it with the / **O**ptions | **I**nternational | **C**urrency command (see Chapter 13). The Currency format also inserts commas every three digits as you move left from the decimal point, and displays negative numbers in parentheses.

The , (comma) format inserts commas every three digits as you move left from the decimal point and displays negative numbers in parentheses.

Formatting Your Notebook

The General format generally displays numbers as entered, but displays only decimal places that affect the value of the number, drops decimal places as necessary to accommodate the column width or, if that is insufficient, displays the value in scientific notation.

The +/– format translates numbers into bar graphs, displaying plus signs for positive numbers, minus signs for negative numbers, and periods for zeros. For example, 5 would be displayed as + + + + +; –3 would be displayed as – – –.

The Percent format displays values as percentages, in effect multiplying the value by 100 and following it with a percent sign. The value 0.75, for example, is displayed as 75% in Percent format.

The five Date formats and four Time formats are considered numeric formats because Quattro Pro stores both dates and times as numbers. To select one of these formats, choose Date from the Style | Numeric Format menu. If you want to choose a time format, choose Time from the resulting submenu. (See Chapter 10 for details.)

The Text (Show Formulas) format displays all formulas as entered rather than displaying the results of their calculations. This format is extremely useful for tracking down potential problems or errors in your notebook's logic, or examining the notebook's structure.

You can "unhide" cells by assigning them any other display format or by using the Reset option.

The Hidden format conceals data so that a cell actually containing data appears to be empty. This is the only Quattro Pro display format that affects labels as well as values; both text entries and values disappear from the notebook. The Hidden format is particularly useful for hiding comments or confidential information before you print the notebook. It does not really hide anything from users who will be viewing the notebook on screen because, even in Hidden format, you can display a cell's contents on the input line by moving the cell pointer to that cell.

Changing the Notebook's Numeric Format

You can alter a cell's numeric format in two ways: You can define a format for a block of cells with / **S**tyle | **N**umeric Format, or you can change the default format for the entire notebook with / **O**ptions | **F**ormats | **N**umeric Format. (You can use the `Ctrl`-`F` shortcut or the Format SpeedBar button to issue the / **S**tyle | **N**umeric Format command.) When you issue either command, Quattro Pro displays a menu with the ten numeric formats and a User Defined option (which is beyond the scope of this book). The Style | Numeric Format menu also contains a Reset option for changing the display format back to the notebook default. If you select the Fixed, Scientific, Percent, Comma, or Currency format, Quattro Pro asks you to specify the number of decimal places. In the case of / **O**ptions | **F**ormats | **N**umeric

Format, Quattro Pro then executes the command immediately, changing the notebook's values to the specified format. However, if you use the / **S**tyle | **N**umeric Format command, Quattro Pro asks you for a block to modify, and then executes the command.

Try changing the default format for LEARN1.WQ2 to the comma format with 0 decimal places.

1. Issue the / **O**ptions | **F**ormats | **N**umeric Format command.
2. Type **,** or click on the comma to select the comma format.
3. When prompted for the number of decimal places, enter **0**.
4. Press Esc twice or type **Q** (for Quit) twice to return to Ready mode. Your notebook should now look like Figure 5-1.
5. Save the notebook in its current form by pressing Ctrl-S and choosing Replace.

Changing the Numeric Format of a Block

The / **S**tyle | **N**umeric Format command changes the appearance of values within a specified block of cells. When you issue this command, you actually are applying numeric formats to particular cells rather than to the values those cells contain. Quattro Pro "remembers" the format of a cell, regardless

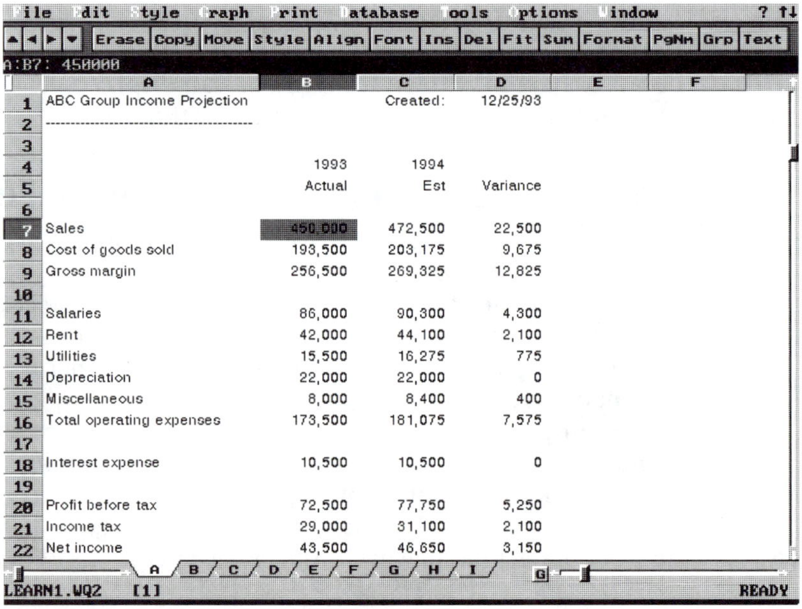

	A	B	C	D
1	ABC Group Income Projection		Created:	12/25/93
2	--			
3				
4		1993	1994	
5		Actual	Est	Variance
6				
7	Sales	450,000	472,500	22,500
8	Cost of goods sold	193,500	203,175	9,675
9	Gross margin	256,500	269,325	12,825
10				
11	Salaries	86,000	90,300	4,300
12	Rent	42,000	44,100	2,100
13	Utilities	15,500	16,275	775
14	Depreciation	22,000	22,000	0
15	Miscellaneous	8,000	8,400	400
16	Total operating expenses	173,500	181,075	7,575
17				
18	Interest expense	10,500	10,500	0
19				
20	Profit before tax	72,500	77,750	5,250
21	Income tax	29,000	31,100	2,100
22	Net income	43,500	46,650	3,150

The , (comma) format

Figure 5-1.

Formatting Your Notebook

of changes in cell contents, by inserting numeric format codes in cells that are formatted with the / **S**tyle | **N**umeric Format command. Even if you delete the contents of a formatted cell, with either the [Del] key or / **E**dit | **E**rase, the formatting code remains intact and affects the appearance of any data that you enter later. In addition, numeric formatting that you assign in this way will always override formatting assigned with the / **O**ptions | **F**ormats | **N**umeric Format command.

You can always change a cell's format code by reformatting it, but the only way to get rid of the code altogether is with / **S**tyle | **N**umeric Format | **R**eset. Once you remove a cell's numeric format code with this command, the cell's format reverts to the numeric format of the notebook as a whole. Table 5-1 shows most of the numeric format codes. The formats that do not appear on that table are

Format	Code
+/–	Represented by the code (+).
Text	Represented by the code (T).
Date	Both Date and Time formats are represented by the code (D) followed by the option number of the specific format, enclosed in parentheses. For example, (D2) represents Date format 2.
Hidden	Represented by the code (H).

When you issue the / **S**tyle | **N**umeric Format command ([Ctrl]-[F]), Quattro Pro displays the Numeric Format menu. Once you select a format, Quattro Pro usually asks for the number of decimal places you want to display. Lastly, Quattro Pro asks you to specify the block to be formatted.

Try applying the command to data on the LEARN1 notebook.

1. Move to C7 and type **/SN** or click on the Format button on the SpeedBar to display the Style | Numeric Format menu.
2. Type **C** or click on Currency to select the Currency option.
3. When prompted for a number of decimal places, enter **0** and press [Enter].
4. At the "Block to be modified" prompt, specify C7..C22 and then press [Enter] or click on [Enter].
5. Try a different format on column D by moving to D7, pressing [Ctrl]-[F] or clicking on the Format button, and selecting Fixed.
6. Specify zero decimal places and designate a block of D7..D22. Your notebook should now look like the one shown in Figure 5-2.

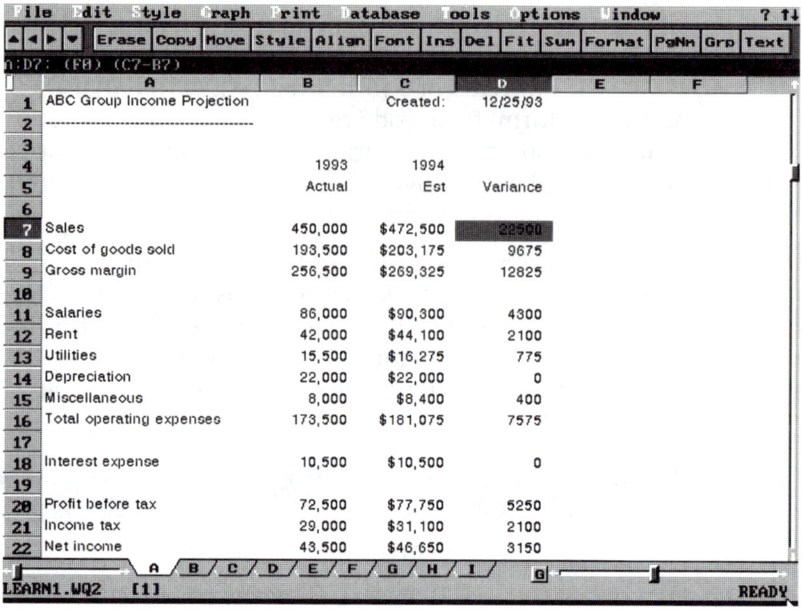

	A	B	C	D
1	ABC Group Income Projection		Created:	12/25/93
2	--			
3				
4		1993	1994	
5		Actual	Est	Variance
6				
7	Sales	450,000	$472,500	22500
8	Cost of goods sold	193,500	$203,175	9675
9	Gross margin	256,500	$269,325	12825
10				
11	Salaries	86,000	$90,300	4300
12	Rent	42,000	$44,100	2100
13	Utilities	15,500	$16,275	775
14	Depreciation	22,000	$22,000	0
15	Miscellaneous	8,000	$8,400	400
16	Total operating expenses	173,500	$181,075	7575
17				
18	Interest expense	10,500	$10,500	0
19				
20	Profit before tax	72,500	$77,750	5250
21	Income tax	29,000	$31,100	2100
22	Net income	43,500	$46,650	3150

Trying different numeric formats
Figure 5-2.

Note that you cannot use the / **E**dit | **U**ndo command (Alt-F5) to reverse changes made with the / **S**tyle | **N**umeric Format command. Instead, you have to issue another / **S**tyle | **N**umeric Format command to reinstate the desired format.

Whenever you relocate or copy cells with / **E**dit | **M**ove or / **E**dit | **C**opy, the format moves or is copied along with the cell. In addition, if you insert columns or rows in a block that has been formatted, the new cells will take on the formatting either from the column to the left or the row above.

Now that you have formatted most of the values on your notebook, see what happens if you change the numeric format for the notebook as a whole, using the / **O**ptions | **F**ormats | **N**umeric Format command.

1. Press Home to move back to A1.
2. Issue the / **O**ptions | **F**ormats | **N**umeric Format | **F**ixed command.
3. Press Enter to accept the default number of two decimal places.
4. Press Esc twice to return to Ready mode.

The only values that change are those in column B. The other values retain their appearance because they contain formatting codes that override the default format. As mentioned, the only way to eliminate those codes is with another / **S**tyle | **N**umeric Format command.

Formatting Your Notebook

Hiding Zeros

The Options | Formats menu contains another option—Hide Zeros—that allows you to conceal all the zero values on your notebook page. Some people prefer this default format for most notebooks, particularly when generating formal reports. When you save the notebook, the Options | Formats | Hide Zeros setting is saved with its notebook page.

> **NOTE:** The Hide Zeros option only affects true zero values; it does not hide values that are displayed as zeros because of rounding imposed by a numeric format.

The Text (Show Formulas) Format

Spreadsheet programs typically show the results of formulas rather than displaying the formulas themselves. Although this is exactly what you want most of the time, it can make it difficult to find errors or decipher an unfamiliar spreadsheet. To examine a formula or even to determine whether a particular cell contains a formula, you generally need to move the cell pointer to the cell in question and examine the input line.

The Text (Show Formulas) format is designed to remedy this problem by exposing all the formulas within a block of cells. Whenever you display cells in Text format, the literal contents of every cell appears on the notebook itself, just as it would appear on the input line if you pointed to that cell. (When you use this display format, you must often widen columns to see the formulas in their entirety.) Try the Text format now.

1. Issue the / **S**tyle | **N**umeric Format | **T**ext command (press Ctrl-F) or the Format button and then select Text).

2. When prompted for a block, type **B1..D22** and press Enter. Notice that not every formula may fit neatly within its cell.

3. If you need to widen the columns, issue the / **S**tyle | **B**lock Size | **A**uto Width command and press Enter to accept the default of one extra space between columns. Specify a column block of B1..D1. Because the formulas are displayed with flush-left alignment, the data in the columns do not line up well at these widths, but you can see all the formulas. Your notebook should now resemble Figure 5-3.

One problem with the Text format is that it is just like any other numeric format. This means that if you use the / **O**ptions | **N**umeric Format | **T**ext format command, the only cells affected are those that do not already have numeric formatting codes. However, if you use the / **S**tyle | **N**umeric Format | **T**ext format command, the Text format codes replace any numeric format

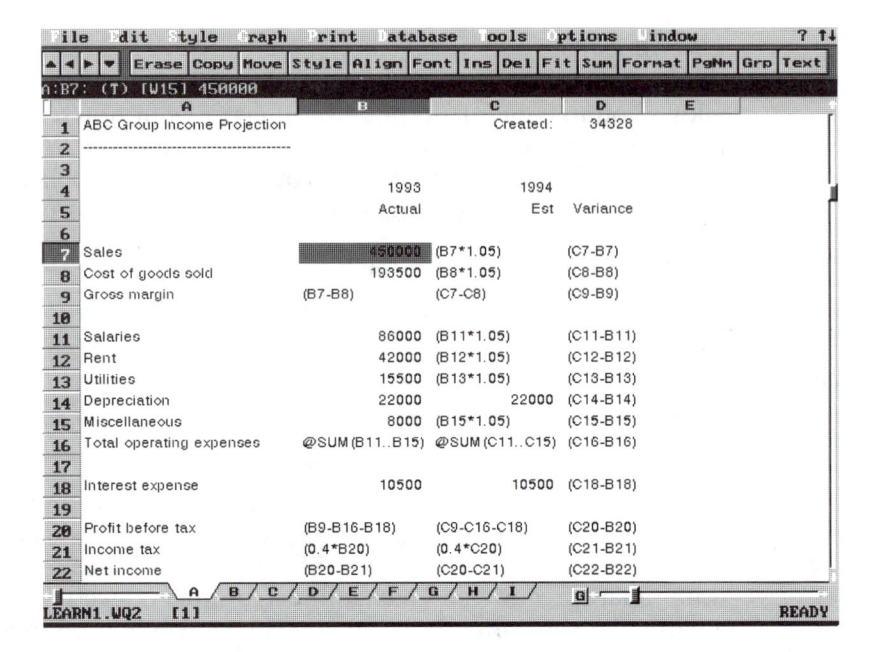

The Text (Show Formulas) format
Figure 5-3.

codes already in the specified block, making it difficult to restore the notebook to its previous appearance.

You can circumvent these problems by saving the notebook and then using the / **S**tyle | **N**umeric Format | **T**ext command. When you are done viewing your notebook in this form, discard the new format and retrieve the previous version of your notebook from disk. In this case, you can retrieve the version of the notebook saved immediately after issuing the / **O**ptions | **F**ormats | **N**umeric Format | **,** (comma) command.

1. Issue the / **F**ile | **R**etrieve command and select Yes when asked whether you want to lose your changes.
2. Select LEARN1.WQ2 from the file list.

Aligning Blocks of Data

Quattro Pro allows you to change the alignment of labels and numeric values, including dates. However, it aligns the two types of data somewhat differently.

Aligning Labels

As you learned in Chapter 2, when you enter labels they assume the label alignment of the notebook as a whole unless you type in a different

Formatting Your Notebook

alignment character. In most notebooks the default alignment for labels is flush left, so if you enter a label that does not begin with an alignment character, Quattro Pro automatically inserts an apostrophe (the left alignment character). If you want to assign a different alignment, you can start the label with a quotation mark (flush-right) or a caret (centered). You can change the default label alignment for a notebook with / **O**ptions | **F**ormats | **A**lign Labels. You can change the alignment of blocks of labels using the / **S**tyle | **A**lignment command or the Align button on the SpeedBar.

*The shortcut for the / **S**tyle | **A**lignment command is Ctrl-A.*

When you issue the / **O**ptions | **F**ormats | **A**lign Labels command, Quattro Pro displays a menu with the choices Left, Right, and Center. When you issue the / **S**tyle | **A**lignment command (or click on the Align SpeedBar button), you will see a menu with the same three choices, plus a fourth choice, General, which will be discussed momentarily.

In some ways, aligning labels is just like assigning numeric formats. You can either change the notebook default or you can format a block of cells. However, there are also important differences. First, label alignment characters are not really formatting codes. Rather, they are part of the labels themselves. If you delete a label, the label alignment character is deleted as well, unlike numeric formatting codes. In addition, you cannot apply a particular alignment to a blank cell; you can only align data within cells.

Second, you cannot enter a label *without* a label alignment character; either you enter one or Quattro Pro does it for you. For this reason, changing the default alignment only affects those labels that you enter in the future. It tells Quattro Pro which alignment character to include in any label that does not already start with such a character.

To see the / **S**tyle | **A**lignment command in action, follow these steps:

1. Issue the / **S**tyle | **A**lignment command (Ctrl-A or click the Align button).
2. Select the Center option from the Alignment submenu and, when prompted for a block to align, designate A1..A22 and press Enter. All the labels in column A should now be centered. Note that Quattro Pro has inserted the ^ alignment character at the beginning of each label in the block (with the exception of \-).
3. Move to A5, type **test**, and press Enter. Although this cell falls within the block that you designated for the / **S**tyle | **A**lignment command, the label's alignment is derived from the default alignment setting of flush left. Press Del to erase the data in A5.
4. Issue the / **S**tyle | **A**lignment command again, this time using the Ctrl-A shortcut, and return column A's labels to their previous state by left-aligning block A1..A22.

Aligning Numeric Values

While / **O**ptions | **F**ormats | **A**lign Labels affects labels only, / **S**tyle | **A**lignment affects numeric values as well. In practice, you will probably center or left-align blocks of numeric values only if they have exactly the same number of digits. Otherwise the numbers will be difficult to read.

Quattro Pro aligns labels and numeric values somewhat differently. When you modify a block of cells with / **S**tyle | **A**lignment, Quattro Pro changes the alignment character at the beginning of every cell within the block. As mentioned, these alignment characters are not formatting codes but are part of the labels themselves.

At the same time, / **S**tyle | **A**lignment stores a hidden alignment code in each cell of the specified block. These codes have no effect on any new labels you enter. The alignment of new labels is always determined by the default label alignment setting for the notebook (unless you enter a label alignment character). However, these hidden alignment codes will affect numeric values you enter later. Like numeric format codes, they are independent of the data currently stored in the cell. If you enter a numeric value into a cell that was left-aligned with / **S**tyle | **A**lignment, the new value is automatically left-aligned.

The only way you can eliminate these hidden alignment codes is by issuing / **S**tyle | **A**lignment | **G**eneral. This command is analogous to / **S**tyle | **N**umeric Format | **R**eset: It restores all the cells in the specified block to the default format of the notebook, effectively right-aligning all values within the block. The labels in the block are aligned according to any default label alignment setting for the notebook.

More About Default Formats

As you have seen, Quattro Pro has default settings for several notebook attributes: numeric format, label alignment, and column width. Formatting a block of cells amounts to overriding the default format for one of those attributes within a specified section of the notebook. Quattro Pro also allows you to change the default settings themselves, specifying formats for every cell on the notebook that does not contain a formatting code to the contrary. The default numeric format, for example, determines the appearance of values within every cell that does not contain a display code.

Whenever you change the label alignment, numeric format, or column width default settings and then save your file, the current default settings are stored with the notebook. When you retrieve the notebook later, those settings are retrieved. Although this feature is extremely useful, it can sometimes be confusing. Quattro Pro has no codes to indicate the default settings for a particular notebook, so you have only two ways to determine

Formatting Your Notebook

what those settings are. First, you can open the Options | Formats menu and look at the settings displayed at the right side of the menu. Second, you can enter data in unformatted cells and watch what happens.

If you want to use a numeric format, label alignment, or column width other than the current system default for most of your notebook, it is generally a good idea to use a default setting. Even when you want to use more than one format, you should set a default for the format you want to use most and format the exceptions with block formatting commands. Default settings have three main advantages over block formatting commands: They require fewer keystrokes; they save memory and disk space; and they are generally more efficient if you decide to change formats later.

Line Drawing and Shading

The / **S**tyle | **L**ine Drawing and / **S**tyle | **S**hading commands allow you to add solid lines or boxes and shading to your notebook. You can use these attributes to highlight elements of the notebook, making it more visually appealing and easier to read, or to group together elements on a notebook. Unlike the other formatting tools discussed in this chapter, lines and shading are always applied to a particular cell or blocks of cells; there are no notebook-wide or system-wide default settings. There are also no line or shading codes stored in the cells. Nonetheless, as you'll learn shortly, the lines or shading will remain until you remove them explicitly with another line or shading command.

When drawing lines, you may want to switch to WYSIWYG display mode even if you normally prefer a character-based display mode. In character-based displays, Quattro Pro inserts extra space between rows and columns to accommodate any lines that you add with the / **S**tyle | **L**ine Draw command. In WYSIWYG mode, lines appear on the borders between cells, as they do when printed.

Drawing Lines on the Notebook

The / **S**tyle | **L**ine Drawing command lets you underline or draw boxes around notebook titles, column headings, or other text, or to separate columns or rows for emphasis. You can even use this command to add a grid of horizontal and vertical lines to your notebook, which can often make your data easier to read, particularly when printed.

NOTE: If you have a color monitor, you can change line colors using Spreadsheet | Drawn Lines or Spreadsheet | WYSIWYG Colors | Drawn Lines on the Options | Colors menu.

After issuing the / **S**tyle | **L**ine Drawing command, you must specify the block you want to draw lines around. Quattro Pro then displays a Placement menu that you use to specify where you want the lines drawn, relative to the specified block.

In the Placement menu, the All option draws a box around the specified block, and draws vertical and horizontal lines between all cells in the block, producing a grid. The Outside option draws a box around the block. The Top option draws a horizontal line above the block, while the Bottom option draws a horizontal line below the block. The Left option draws a vertical line along the left edge of the block, and the Right option draws a vertical line along the right edge of the block. The Inside option draws vertical and horizontal lines between all cells in the block, producing a grid but with no outer border. The Horizontal option draws horizontal lines between each row in the block, and the Vertical option draws vertical lines between each column in the specified block. Finally, the Quit option returns you to Ready mode.

Once you specify the placement, Quattro Pro displays a Line Types menu with the options Single, Double, Thick, and None. Select the desired option, or select None to remove existing lines from the specified block.

When Quattro Pro is done executing the / **S**tyle | **L**ine Drawing command, it returns you to the Placement menu and automatically highlights the last Placement option you selected. This makes it easy for you to experiment with different line types around the same block of cells. If you want to draw lines around a different block, press (Esc). Quattro Pro displays the prompt "Enter block to draw lines" on the input line and displays the block you last specified. You then can type or point to a new block and press (Enter). If you are done drawing lines, simply select Quit from the Placement menu.

Try adding lines to LEARN1.WQ2:

1. Move to B5 and issue the / **S**tyle | **L**ine Drawing command.
2. When prompted for a "block to draw lines," specify a block of B5..D5 and then press (Enter).
3. Select Bottom from the Placement menu, and then select Single from the Line Types menu.
4. When the Placement menu reappears, press (Esc) to move back one step. You will see the prompt "Enter block to draw lines" on the input line. Enter the block coordinates **B22..D22**.
5. Select Top from the Placement menu and then select Single from the Line Types menu.
6. When Quattro Pro redisplays the Placement menu, select Quit. Then move to cell A2 and press (Del) to get rid of this extra line. Your notebook should resemble Figure 5-4 if you are in WYSIWYG mode.

Formatting Your Notebook

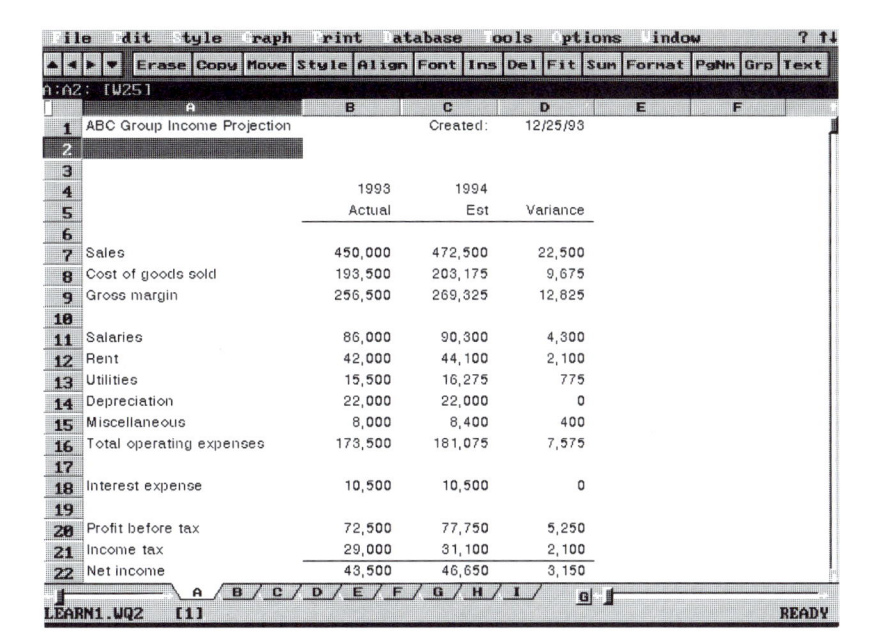

LEARN1.WQ2 in WYSIWYG mode
Figure 5-4.

Because lines are drawn *in between* cells, they are not that easy to get rid of. Suppose you decide to delete the line between rows 21 and 22. Because the line is not stored in any particular cell, you cannot use Del or even / **E**dit | **E**rase to erase it. Even the / **E**dit | **U**ndo command is powerless in this context. Fortunately, you can reissue the / **S**tyle | **L**ine Drawing command, specify the same block and placement you chose last time, and choose a line type of None.

1. Issue the / **S**tyle | **L**ine Drawing command and specify a block of B22..D22.
2. Select Top from the Placement menu and then select None from the Line Types menu. Then select Quit when Quattro Pro redisplays the Placement menu.
3. Issue the / **F**ile | **S**ave command (Ctrl-S shortcut), and select Replace from the submenu.

This is an attractive but judicious use of line drawing. Now try being a little more adventurous. Start by drawing a box around the notebook title and then add a grid of lines to the notebook.

1. Press Home to move to A1, and issue the / **S**tyle | **L**ine Drawing command.

2. Press Enter to accept the default block of A:A1..A1.
3. Select Outside from the Placement menu and then select Single from the Line Types menu. When Quattro Pro redisplays the Placement menu, select Quit. (In 80 × 25 display mode, the right edge of the box may obscure the final characters of the label in A1. If so, you can solve the problem by widening the column as needed.)
4. Move to A7 and press Shift-F7 (Select). Then move to D22 and press Enter. If you prefer, you can also preselect the block with your mouse.
5. Issue the / **S**tyle | **L**ine Drawing command again. Quattro Pro does not prompt you for a block this time because you predefined one.
6. Select All from the Placement menu, select Single from the Line Types menu, and select Quit from the Placement menu.

Now use / **E**dit | **D**elete | **R**ows to delete row 6, row 9, row 15, and row 16, one at a time. Figure 5-5 shows the resulting notebook in WYSIWYG mode. If you like this version, save it with the / **F**ile | Save **A**s command, and assign it any name other than LEARN1.

No matter which option you select from the Style | Line Drawing | Placement menu, Quattro Pro considers a line to be an attribute of the cell to which you assigned it. For example, if you place a line at the bottom of cell C4 and then move or copy that cell to A1, A1 will also have a line at the bottom. However, if you move C5, which would appear to have a line at the top in

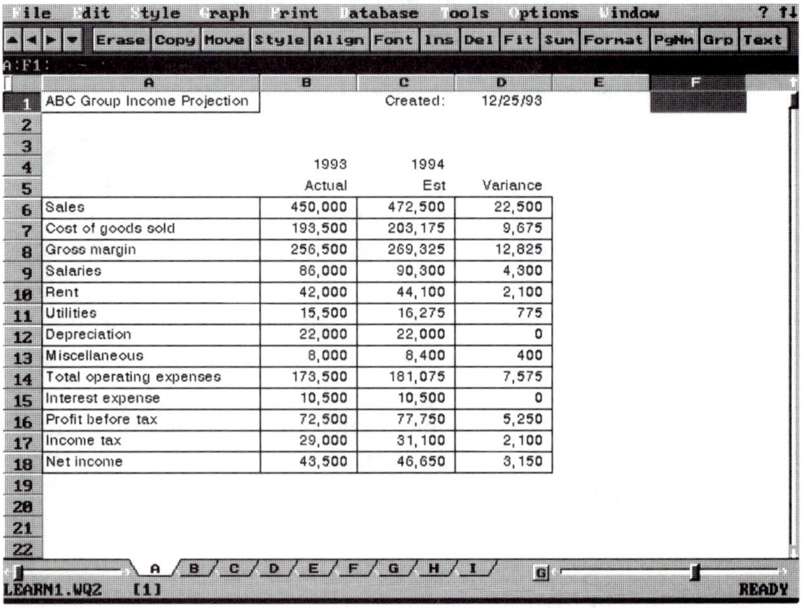

	A	B	C	D
1	ABC Group Income Projection		Created:	12/25/93
2				
3				
4		1993	1994	
5		Actual	Est	Variance
6	Sales	450,000	472,500	22,500
7	Cost of goods sold	193,500	203,175	9,675
8	Gross margin	256,500	269,325	12,825
9	Salaries	86,000	90,300	4,300
10	Rent	42,000	44,100	2,100
11	Utilities	15,500	16,275	775
12	Depreciation	22,000	22,000	0
13	Miscellaneous	8,000	8,400	400
14	Total operating expenses	173,500	181,075	7,575
15	Interest expense	10,500	10,500	0
16	Profit before tax	72,500	77,750	5,250
17	Income tax	29,000	31,100	2,100
18	Net income	43,500	46,650	3,150
19				
20				
21				
22				

LEARN.WQ2 in WYSIWYG mode with a grid of lines
Figure 5-5.

Formatting Your Notebook

this situation, no line will be moved—this is because the line is a property of cell C4, not cell C5.

Most of the time this behavior is fairly intuitive. However, you may occasionally get lines you didn't want, or not get lines when you wanted them. In these cases, it's probably easiest to add or remove lines with the Line Drawing feature rather than redoing the move or copy operation. If you want to ensure that lines—as well as any other formatting—are not copied, you can copy just the cell contents using the / **E**dit | C**o**py Special command that is described shortly.

CAUTION: One word of caution about using text and lines together: If a cell has a line at its right border, your text won't be able to spill over into the adjacent cells to the right. In addition, if your text does spill over into an adjacent cell, lines drawn at the top or bottom of the cell won't extend to the full length of the text entry; they'll stop at the end of the cell to which they were assigned. If you want to lengthen the lines, you can increase the column width.

Shading Cells

In character-based display modes, gray shading only appears in between the characters.

Shading can be an effective means of highlighting data on the notebook or setting off one group of cells from another. When used sparingly, shading also enhances the appearance of printed reports, particularly if you have a high-resolution printer and direct Quattro Pro to print in final-quality mode.

To shade a block of cells, issue the / **S**tyle | **S**hading command. Quattro Pro displays a Shading menu with the options None, Gray, and Black. After you select an option, Quattro Pro prompts you for a block to shade. Once you specify the block, Quattro Pro adds the shading and returns to Ready mode.

TIP: When you apply shading to a cell and enter text in that cell that spills into the adjacent cell, any portion of the text that appears in the adjoining cell will not be shaded. The easiest solution is to increase the column width so that all the text to be shaded fits entirely within its column.

In the following exercise, you will add shading to the totals at the bottom of LEARN1.WQ2.

1. Issue the / **F**ile | **R**etrieve command and select LEARN1.WQ2 from the file list. The previous version of the notebook (before you added the grid) reappears on the screen.

2. Move to B22, issue the / **S**tyle | **S**hading command, and select Gray from the Shading menu.
3. When prompted for a block to shade, press `→` twice and press `Enter` to specify B22..D22.
4. Save the notebook by pressing `Ctrl`-`S` and selecting Replace.

Even if you delete the contents of a shaded cell with the `Del` key or / **E**dit | **E**rase, the shading remains. If you want to erase the shading as well, you must reissue the / **S**tyle | **S**hading command, include the cells whose shading you want to remove in the shading block, and select None as the type of shading.

The / Edit | Copy Special Command

You can copy formatting from just one cell to as many cells as you like.

You can use the / **E**dit | **C**opy Special command to copy style attributes without copying cell contents, and vice versa. When you issue this command, you'll see the choices Contents and Format. The Format option is useful for duplicating formatting features that you've already applied to one area of your notebook. If you've already boldfaced, italicized, and shaded the totals in your notebook, you can apply those style features to other areas of the notebook without having to issue three separate Style commands. You can use / **E**dit | **C**opy Special to copy shading, lines, numeric formatting, alignment, boldfacing, italic, point size, typeface, and even color. The Contents option is handy for stripping the formatting from labels, values, or formulas as you copy them. For example, you could copy formulas without copying style information such as lines or numeric formatting.

Try copying just the style information from the Net income figures that you shaded in the previous exercise, and applying that shading to the notebook title. First, however, add bold to those numbers, so you can copy more than one style attribute at once.

1. Point out the block B22..D22 and issue the / **S**tyle | **F**ont | **B**old command to boldface the numbers in those three cells. Then select Quit to return to Ready mode.
2. Issue the / **E**dit | **C**opy Special | **F**ormat command.
3. Select B22 as the source block and press `Enter` or click on [Enter]. (Make sure you select only a single cell as the source block, otherwise you may format more cells than you anticipate.)
4. Enter A1 as the destination block, the block that you want to format. The shading and boldfacing that you copied will be applied to that cell.

Formatting Your Notebook

As you can see, if you copy formatting only, the contents in the destination block are preserved, and are simply reformatted with the new style attributes. At the same time, any existing formatting is overridden. You can also use the / **E**dit | **C**o**p**y Special command to copy style information to blank cells. If you then enter data into those cells, it is formatted with the style information that you copied.

When you copy just the contents of a cell, the data that you've moved takes on any formatting that exists in the destination cell. For this reason, make sure that there are not unwanted formatting attributes in the destination cell.

If you don't like the results of a / **E**dit | **C**o**p**y Special command, you can undo the damage with / **E**dit | **U**ndo when you've copied just the contents of a cell. You can also use the / **S**tyle command (but not the Undo feature) to get rid of any unwanted formatting you may have copied. However, this method is laborious if much formatting is involved because you have to get rid of each style attribute separately. Fortunately, you can eliminate unwanted formatting with the Normal style, which you'll learn about in a moment.

Using Custom Styles

Quattro Pro provides eight predefined styles. Each notebook file can hold up to 120 custom styles, including these eight.

You can use / **E**dit | **C**o**p**y Special if your current notebook contains style information that you want to copy to another part of the notebook. However, if you frequently use the same set of style attributes, it's much more efficient to create a *custom style*. For example, if you always make your notebook titles 14 point, bold, Dutch, you can create a custom style called TITLES that includes this information, and can format your notebook title—or any other text or data—simply by applying the custom style to it. You can save fonts, lines, shading, alignment, and numeric formatting in this manner. Once you've saved this formatting information as a custom style, you can use it repeatedly in the current notebook or in other notebooks. In addition, if you edit the style later—perhaps you decide to use a Swiss font instead—those changes are reflected automatically in any cells formatted by the style.

Defining Custom Styles

To create a custom style of your own, issue the / **S**tyle | **D**efine Style | **C**reate command, enter a name for the style, and then specify the various formats that you want the style to include. Follow these steps to create a custom style called TITLES that includes a 14 point bold and underlined Dutch-SC font:

1. From a blank cell within the LEARN1 notebook, issue the / **S**tyle | **D**efine Style | **C**reate command.
2. Type **TITLES** as the style name and then click on [Enter] or press Enter to display a menu of style attributes.
3. Select Font and then select Typeface to display a list of available fonts. Select Dutch-SC.
4. Select Point Size and choose 14 point, select Bold and Underlined, and then select Quit. Quattro Pro returns you to the main style attributes menu, where you can see your menu selections.
5. Select Quit twice to return to Ready mode. You've just created the custom style TITLES, which you'll use in a moment.

The list of fonts displayed may depend on your printer type. Consult Chapter 6 for details.

You can also create a custom style using formatting information that already exists in the notebook. To do this, just select the cell that includes the desired styles, issue the / **S**tyle | **D**efine Style | **C**reate command, and name the style. If you use this method, it's a good idea to double-check that the correct attributes have been selected by glancing at the style attributes menu. You can even use this method as the first step in creating a custom style, and then build on the existing formatting information once you get into the style attributes menu.

Applying Custom Styles

Custom styles may overwrite some of the existing formatting in the block to which they are applied.

Once you've created a custom style, you can apply it by selecting / **S**tyle | **U**se Style from the menu or clicking on the Style button on the SpeedBar, selecting the desired style from the list that appears, choosing the block to which to apply the style, and pressing Enter. After you apply a style, its name shows up on the input line when the cell pointer is located in the relevant cells. These style codes are similar to some of the other codes that you have encountered—such as the numeric formatting codes: They remain even if you delete the cell's contents, and are applied to other text or data that you may enter in that cell. You can, however, change a cell's style by overwriting it with custom style. You can also erase styles, as described a bit later in the chapter.

TIP: You may want to save your notebook before applying a custom style so you can retrieve the original if you want to discard the changes.

Formatting Your Notebook

Predefined Styles and the Normal Style

As mentioned, every new notebook comes with eight predefined styles. (You will see these styles listed every time you issue the / **S**tyle | **D**efine Style | **C**reate or / **S**tyle | **U**se Style command.) You can use these styles as is, modify them, or replace them with new styles of your own. The predefined styles are as follows:

Style Name	Description
Currency	Currency numeric format with two decimal places
Comma	Comma numeric format with two decimal places
Date	A numeric format that represents date serial numbers as the name of the month, followed by the date, and a four-digit year, as in August 6, 1994. (See Chapter 10.)
Fixed	Fixed numeric format with two decimal places
Heading1	Swiss-SC 18-point bold
Heading2	Swiss-SC 12-point bold
Percent	Percent numeric format with two decimal places
Total	Double line drawn on bottom, single line on top

When you apply the Normal style to a cell, no style name shows up on the input line when you highlight that cell.

The Normal style is not really a style at all. Instead, it is a means of removing custom styles—as well as any other formatting—from a block of cells. (You should take care not to delete formatting, such as date formatting, unintentionally.) If you apply the Normal style to a cell that was previously formatted with a custom style, its format reverts to the default formats for the notebook.

The Normal style is also an alternative means of setting default formats for the notebook. For example, if you change the numeric format for Normal to Currency with two decimal places, you will see this change reflected in the Options | Formats menu, and that format will be used for all values that have not been assigned a specific numeric format or custom style. You can also set the default font by changing the Normal style, as you'll learn in the next chapter.

Editing and Erasing Styles

You can use / **S**tyle | **D**efine Style | **C**reate to edit existing styles as well as create new ones. Just specify the name of the style you wish to edit, and then make the desired changes in the resulting style attributes menu. When you do this, any areas of the notebook formatted with this custom style will change to reflect your modifications.

To edit a specific cell that has a named style applied to it—rather than the style itself—simply highlight the desired cell or cells, get into the Style menu, and make the desired changes.

To clear a custom style from a block, use / **S**tyle | **D**efine Style | **E**rase. The style name no longer appears on the input line, but all formatting information is retained. You might do this if you didn't want these particular cells to change when you next changed the style that had been applied to them. To clear all formatting from a block, use / **S**tyle | **U**se Style | **N**ormal.

To delete a custom style from the entire notebook, issue the / **S**tyle | **D**efine Style | **R**emove command and select the name of the custom style you want to delete. If the style was used within the notebook, you are asked to confirm the deletion. Blocks to which the custom style has been applied will retain their formatting. If you wish to eliminate all formatting, you can apply the Normal style.

Saving and Retrieving Custom Styles

When you save your notebook, any custom styles it contains are saved along with your data. You can also save a custom style to a separate style file so that you can use it to format other notebooks. To use the custom style later in a different notebook, issue the / **S**tyle | **D**efine Style | **F**ile | **R**etrieve command. Try saving and retrieving the custom style TITLES now.

1. Issue the / **S**tyle | **D**efine Style | **F**ile command.
2. Choose Save, type **TITLES**, press [Enter], and select Quit.
3. Issue the / **F**ile | **S**ave command and select Replace to save the TITLES style with the notebook, replacing the previous version of LEARN1.
4. Issue the / **F**ile | **E**rase command to clear LEARN1 from memory. Then enter the title **Styles and Tribulations** in cell A1 of the blank notebook.
5. Issue the / **S**tyle | **D**efine Style | **F**ile | **R**etrieve command and select TITLES.STY from the file list box, retrieving that style into your new blank notebook. Then select Quit.
6. Make sure you're in cell A1; you're going to apply the TITLES style to this cell.
7. Issue the / **S**tyle | **U**se Style command, select TITLES, and press [Enter] to apply it to cell A1. Notice that the text changes to 14 point, bold, underlined Dutch-SC, and that the style name TITLES shows up within brackets on the input line. If you saved your notebook at this time, the TITLES style would be saved with it for future use.

As you master Quattro Pro's formatting tools, it is easy to get carried away with the possibilities. Few, if any, notebooks really merit hours of formatting, unless you are simply experimenting for fun. If restraint is the first rule of formatting, then, the second rule is proper timing. Whenever possible, formatting should be the last step in creating a notebook. If you worry about your notebook's appearance prematurely, your efforts may be wasted, particularly if you later rearrange data, add or delete rows, and make other modifications to the structure. Instead, start with the essentials—entering the numbers, labels, and formulas; making sure that the formulas work as intended; and then saving your work to disk. Next work on the aesthetics. Here, too, sequence is important. Begin by deleting rows and columns and adjusting column widths. Then format the numbers, adjust column widths if necessary, align the data, and add lines and shading if desired.

CHAPTER

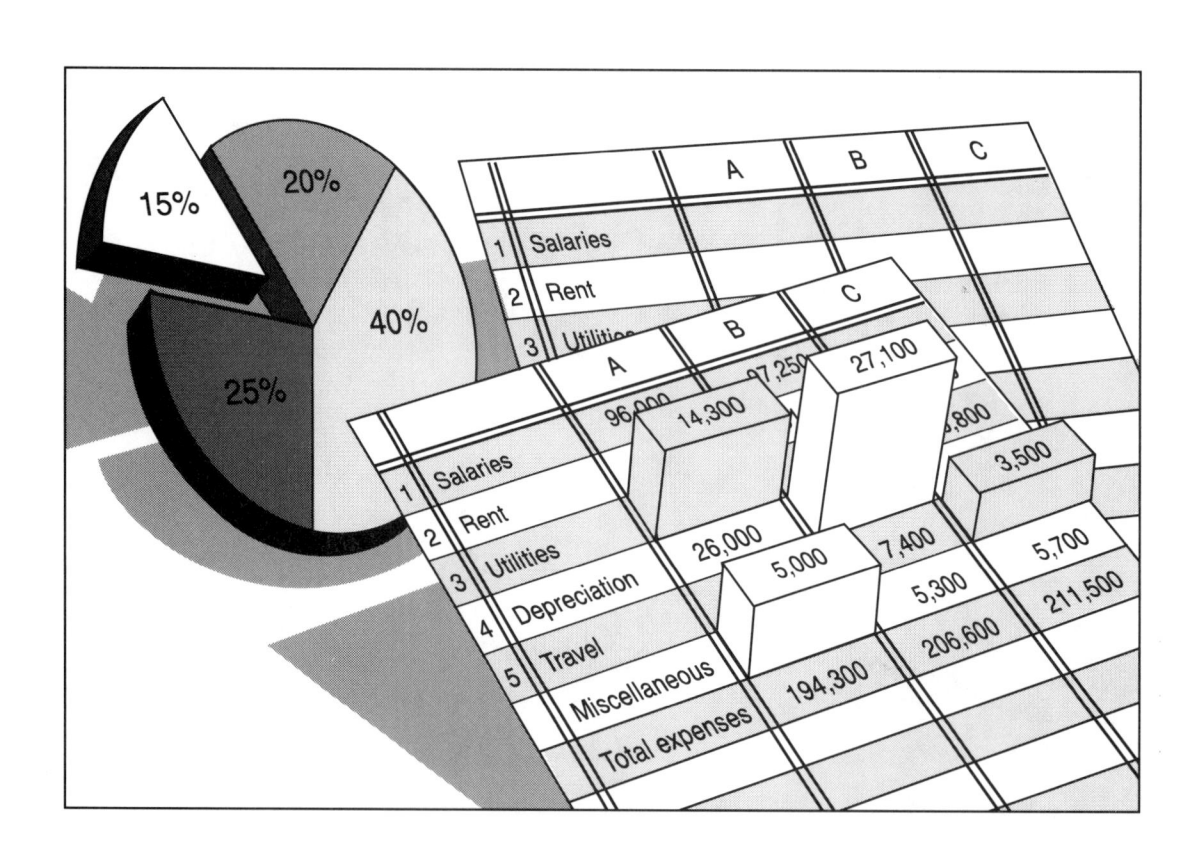

6

PRINTING NOTEBOOKS

Printing notebooks in Quattro Pro can be extremely simple or quite complicated, depending on how customized or elaborate you want your output to be. At the easy end of the spectrum, you can create a printed copy of all or part of your notebook by simply defining the block to be printed and directing Quattro Pro to print. At the more complex end, you can add headers and footers, specify unusual page lengths and widths, define borders to be displayed on each printed page, add page numbers, choose special fonts for all or part of the notebook, and insert page breaks at specific places in the notebook. In other words, you can produce attractive, visually interesting, and professional reports working only with Quattro Pro.

Selecting Printers

When you install Quattro Pro, you are prompted for information on your graphics printer—the printer you intend to use for printing both graphs and final-quality reports. If you do not plan to print graphs or use special fonts, you do not need to specify a graphics printer during installation and can now skip ahead to the "Standard Quattro Pro Reports" section.

You only need to supply Quattro Pro with additional printer information if you did not already tell Quattro Pro about your printer during installation or have changed your mind about what printer you want to use, you plan to use more than one printer to print graphs or final-quality reports, or your printer is connected to a port other than the first parallel port on your computer. If none of these is true, skip directly to "Standard Quattro Pro Reports."

Telling Quattro Pro About Your Printers

Only use the Baud rate, Parity, and Stop bits options if your output device is a serial port.

To supply Quattro Pro with information on printers, you change the 1st Printer or 2nd Printer settings on the Options | Hardware | Printers menu. The printer you specified during installation (if any) is considered to be the 1st Printer. Here is the submenu Quattro Pro displays when you select either the 1st Printer or 2nd Printer option.

```
Type of printer                                            ▶
Make                                            HP Printers
Model                    LaserJet II           (Additional RAM
Mode                          300 x 300 dpi (8.5 x 11)
Device                                          1 Parallel-1 ▶
Baud rate                                       Leave as is  ▶
Parity                                          Leave as is  ▶
Stop bits                                       Leave as is  ▶
Quit
```

To specify a new printer, select the Type of printer option to see a list of printer manufacturers. Once you select the appropriate manufacturer from the list, Quattro Pro displays a list of printer models produced by that manufacturer. Select a printer model, and Quattro Pro displays a Mode submenu. For most printers, you are given a choice between low-, medium-, and high-resolution printing. These settings determine how many dots per

Printing Notebooks

inch Quattro Pro will print. The smaller the number of dots, the faster the output and the poorer the print quality.

Next Quattro Pro returns you to the 1st Printer or 2nd Printer submenu. If your printer is connected to anything other than your computer's first parallel port, select the Device option and specify a different output device.

If you plan to use two different printers to print graphs or final-quality notebooks, use the 2nd Printer option to tell Quattro Pro about the second device. Once you have defined a second printer, be sure to select the desired printer, using the Default Printer option on the Printers menu, before attempting to print a notebook or graph.

The five other options on the Options | Hardware | Printers menu (or simply the Printers menu) are Plotter Speed, Fonts, Auto LF, Single Sheet, and Background.

- The Plotter Speed option applies only to printing graphs, and is beyond the scope of this book.
- The Fonts option leads to a submenu with two more options: Cartridge Fonts and Autoscale Fonts. If you plan to use font cartridges, you must use the Cartridge Fonts option to tell Quattro Pro about them. The Autoscale Fonts option applies only to printing graphs.
- The Auto LF (Automatic Line Feed) option on the Printers menu lets you specify whether your printer automatically inserts a carriage return and line feed at the end of each line. The default setting is No. If your reports appear double-spaced, you may need to change it to Yes. Before you try this, however, try printing a very small print block—a few columns wide and a few rows long. If it is not double-spaced, the problem is probably caused by a right margin setting that is too high for your printer.
- The Single Sheet option specifies whether you are hand feeding sheets of paper to your printer, one at a time. The default setting is No. If you change it to Yes, Quattro Pro pauses between pages of a multiple-page report to give you a chance to insert the next page.
- The Background option should be set to Yes if you want to be able to print in the background. For additional details, see "Printing in the Background" at the end of this chapter.

Saving Your Printer Specifications

Printer definition settings last only as long as the current work session, unless you explicitly save them with the Update option on the Options menu. Be aware that when you select Update, Quattro Pro saves all the settings that you have changed in this work session, not just the printer settings. For example, if you have changed screen colors or any of the startup options, those settings are saved as well. These other default settings are covered in Chapter 13.

If you have changed any of the Printers settings, press Esc or type **Q** for Quit until you are back on the Options menu. Then select the Update option to save your changes and select Quit or press Esc to return to Ready mode.

Standard Quattro Pro Reports

The standard Quattro Pro report settings assume that you will be printing at 10 characters per inch (cpi) on 8 1/2-by-11-inch paper and that you want to use 4-character margins (almost 1/2 inch) at the left and right sides of the page and 2-line margins (1/3 inch) at the top and bottom. To produce a printout with these specifications and without extra embellishments, follow the steps outlined here.

First specify the block to print by selecting Block from the Print menu. The menu disappears temporarily, and Quattro Pro prompts you for a block. Then select the print destination using the Destination option on the Print menu. Choose Draft Printer to print simple draft-quality reports, without any desktop publishing features. Select Graphics Printer to employ special fonts or show line drawing and shading at their best. You should also select Graphics Printer if you want to print in landscape mode (horizontally across the page) and your printer does not have a built-in landscape font. (For the details, see "Printing in Landscape and Banner Mode" later in this chapter.)

NOTE: If there are lines around the outside of your print block and you're printing in draft mode, be sure to include an extra row at the bottom and an extra column at the right in your print block. Otherwise the right and bottom edge of the box will be omitted from your printout.

Next adjust the printer by making sure it is at the top of a new page and then selecting the Adjust Printer option and choosing Align. The Align option sets the line and page counts to zero and informs Quattro Pro that you are at the top of a page. If you skip this step, Quattro Pro may insert page breaks at the wrong points. If you are using a laser or inkjet printer, make sure the Form Feed light on the printer control panel is off, indicating that the printer has finished the last print job. Otherwise press the On Line button to take the printer off line, press the Form Feed button to eject the page, and then press On Line again. If you are using a dot matrix printer, use the Form Feed option on Quattro Pro's Adjust Printer submenu rather than your printer's control panel to eject pages from the printer. If you align your printer properly when you first start printing, the Form Feed option always brings you to the top of the next page. You should also use the Skip Line option on the Adjust Printer menu rather than hand-rolling the paper to align it properly, so that Quattro Pro can keep track of where you are on the page.

At this point, make sure your printer is turned on and on line, and issue the / **P**rint | **S**preadsheet Print command to initiate printing. (If necessary, you can interrupt printing before the report is finished by pressing [Ctrl]-[Break].) If you are printing in draft-quality mode, use the Form Feed option on the Adjust Printer menu to advance the printer to the top of the next page. Finally, choose Quit or press [Esc] to return to Ready mode.

> **NOTE:** If your printer has a large buffer (memory that stores characters sent from your computer), pressing [Ctrl]-[Break] may not stop printing right away. Turning your printer off and back on again may stop printing more quickly.

You can define the print block, select the destination, and align the printer in any order you like, as long as you perform all these steps before you initiate printing. Quattro Pro remembers your print block and destination settings, so you don't need to redefine them every time you print. When you issue the / **F**ile | **S**ave, / **F**ile | Save **A**s, or / **F**ile | Sa**v**e All command, Quattro Pro saves the Block setting along with any print layout settings you have defined. The Destination setting lasts only as long as the current work session.

Try producing a draft-quality printout of LEARN1.WQ2, as follows:

1. With LEARN1 on your screen, type **/P** to display the Print menu.
2. Select the Block option to define the block to be printed.
3. Press [Home] and type a period to anchor the cell pointer in cell A1. Press [End]-[Home] to expand the print block to A:A1..D22, and then press [Enter].
4. If you are using a dot matrix printer with a tractor feed, set your printer to the top of a page and turn the printer on. Then choose / **P**rint | **A**djust Printer | **A**lign.
5. If the Destination option is set to anything other than Draft Printer, select Destination and then select Draft Printer.
6. Select Spreadsheet Print to start printing.
7. When the report stops printing, select the Adjust Printer option again and then select the Form Feed option to eject the printed page. Finally, select Quit to return to Ready mode.

You have just printed Quattro Pro's standard report. If this format seems to be adequate for your needs, you can simply use the previous command sequence whenever you want to print all or part of your notebook.

TIP: If you're having trouble printing in draft mode on a LaserJet, try changing the page length setting to 60 (see the upcoming section "Page Layout"). Also, make certain that this setting matches your printer's default settings. (Check your printer's documentation for details.)

Note that you can print multiple copies of a notebook by selecting the Copies option on the Print menu and entering the desired number of copies. (The acceptable range is 1 to 1000.) Since the Print | Copies setting is saved as a system default when you issue the / **O**ptions | **U**pdate command, you should probably change the setting back to 1 after printing if you plan to use the / **O**ptions | **U**pdate command to save other system defaults in the current work session.

Draft-Quality Versus Final-Quality Printing

When you print a notebook, you use the / **P**rint | **D**estination command to tell Quattro Pro where to send the output. The Print | Destination menu shown here enables you to direct output to a printer (the Draft Printer and Graphics Printer options); a file (the Text File and Binary File options), in case you want to print later or import the output into a word processing program; or the screen (the Screen Preview option), for previewing final-quality printing).

```
─Draft Mode Printing─────
 Draft Printer
 Text File
─Final Quality Printing──
 Binary File
 Graphics Printer
 Screen Preview
```

Directing print output to a file is discussed in Appendix C. Directing output to the screen is covered under "The Screen Previewer" later in this chapter. For now, let's focus on the differences between draft-quality and final-quality printed output.

In WYSIWYG, your notebook appears very similar to the way it will look when printed in final-quality mode.

When you print in draft-quality mode (select the Draft Printer option), Quattro Pro uses your printer's own built-in character sets. When you print in final-quality mode (choose Graphics Printer), Quattro Pro sends instructions to the printer telling it how to construct each character. Draft-quality printing is considerably faster than final-quality printing, but final-quality output generally looks more polished, as you can see in Figure 6-1. There are three main areas of difference between draft-quality and

Printing Notebooks

final-quality printing: the appearance of lines/boxes and shading, the use of fonts, and landscape printing.

In draft-quality mode, Quattro Pro uses standard keyboard characters rather than graphics characters to produce any lines or boxes in your notebook. Lines are printed as dashes rather than as solid lines, and the corners of boxes are printed with plus signs. Quattro Pro also drops shading when you use draft-quality mode. To obtain better-looking lines and to include shading, you must print in final-quality mode.

A point is a typographic measurement equalling 1/72 of an inch.

The other main difference between draft-quality and final-quality printing lies in the use of fonts. A *font* is a set of type with a particular style (such as bold or italic), typeface, and point size. When you print in draft-quality mode, Quattro Pro always uses your printer's default font for the entire notebook. When you print in final-quality mode, Quattro Pro automatically uses one of its own special fonts. It also allows you to switch to another font, and to choose different fonts for different sections of the notebook. (For more details, see "Using Fonts" later in the chapter.)

Page Layout

Although Quattro Pro's standard layout is adequate for quick and simple reports, eventually, you will want to deviate from that standard—change margins to center the report on the page; add headers and footers to longer reports; print horizontally rather than vertically; produce compressed print.

LEARN1.WQ2 printed in final-quality mode
Figure 6-1.

ABC Group Income Projection		Created:	12/25/93
	1993 Actual	1994 Est	Variance
Sales	450,000	472,500	22,500
Cost of goods sold	193,500	203,175	9,675
Gross margin	256,500	269,325	12,825
Salaries	86,000	90,300	4,300
Rent	42,000	44,100	2,100
Utilities	15,500	16,275	775
Depreciation	22,000	22,000	0
Miscellaneous	8,000	8,400	400
Total operating expenses	173,500	181,075	7,575
Interest expense	10,500	10,500	0
Profit before tax	72,500	77,750	5,250
Income tax	29,000	31,100	2,100
Net income	43,500	46,650	3,150

The options for all of these operations are found in the Print Layout Options dialog box that appears when you issue the / **P**rint | **L**ayout command (as shown here). You can navigate in this dialog box by clicking with your mouse or by using the [Tab] key.

```
Print Layout Options:
            Header text:
            Footer text:
    Printer Setup string:
           Break pages: (*) Yes  ( ) No
    Notebook page skip: 0 Lines
              % Scaling: 100                              Margins
                                        Page Length: 66
        Orientation      Dimensions          Left: 4
        (*) Portrait     (*) Lines/Characters Top: 2
        ( ) Landscape    ( ) Inches          Right: 76
        ( ) Banner       ( ) Centimeters    Bottom: 2

                [Update]       [Reset...]       [Quit]
```

NOTE: If you don't see the Print Layout Options dialog box when you choose / **P**rint | **L**ayout, your dialog boxes may be turned off. The remedy is to issue the / **O**ptions | **S**tartup | **U**se Dialogs | **Y**es command.

Adding Headers and Footers

Don't confuse the Header option with the Headings option on the Print menu (see "Printing Larger Notebooks").

Headers and footers are single lines of text that appear at the top and bottom, respectively, of every page of the report. A typical header or footer might include the notebook name or description, or perhaps a date and page number. A footer might also include the page number or perhaps the name of the notebook's creator.

TIP: Whenever you include page numbers in a header or footer, select the Align option on the Print | Adjust Printer menu every time you print, or page numbering will start from the last page number you printed rather than from page 1.

There are three special characters that you can use to define header and footer text on the Print Layout Options dialog box: @, #, and |. The @ symbol is used to print the current date within headers and footers. The # symbol is used to print the current page number. The | character designates the position of text within headers and footers: left, center, and right. Text that is not preceded by the | character is printed in the left section of the header or footer; text preceded by a single | is printed in the center; text preceded by two | characters is printed in the right section. For example, issuing the / **P**rint | **L**ayout command and entering the footer @ || **Page** # produces a footer containing the current date on the left and the current page number on the right.

Margins, Page Breaks, and Dimensions

Quattro Pro's initial defaults for margins and page length are as follows:

- **Top margin** Two lines (approximately 1/3 inch) plus three lines for a header, whether or not you define one
- **Bottom margin** Two lines (approximately 1/2 inch) plus three lines for a footer, whether or not you actually define one
- **Left margin** Four characters (just under 1/2 inch)
- **Right margin** 76 characters (leaves a little less than 1/2 inch between the right edge of the text and the edge of the page)
- **Page length** 66 lines (only 62 of which are available for text, including the 6 reserved for the header and footer)

You can change any or all of these defaults in the Print Layout Options dialog box. You might want to change margins or page length when your report is only slightly too long or wide to fit on one page with the default settings, when you are printing on paper that is larger or smaller than 8 1/2 by 11 inches or you are printing in landscape mode, or when you are using condensed or expanded print. The default margin settings assume you are printing at 10 cpi; if not, you need to adjust the right margin accordingly. In each of these cases, you may need to experiment before finding the ideal settings.

Adding additional page breaks is covered under "Inserting Page Breaks" later in this chapter.

By default, Quattro Pro issues a page eject command to your printer whenever it reaches the bottom of the page. If you prefer not to have any page breaks in your report, set the Break pages option to No. You might want to do this when "printing" to a disk file.

The Dimensions setting determines what unit of measurement Quattro Pro uses to define page margins. By default, this is set to Lines/Characters. If you are printing in final-quality mode and are using proportional fonts or mixing several fonts in one report, you may find it easier to specify margins in inches or centimeters.

Printing in Landscape and Banner Mode

By default, Quattro Pro prints notebooks in portrait mode—that is, vertically on the page. When printing wide notebooks, you may prefer to print the data horizontally. You can do this by selecting landscape mode. In landscape mode, the notebook is simply printed horizontally across the page, with the usual headers and footers and, assuming you set an appropriate page length, with page breaks at the bottom of each page. Alternatively, if you are using a dot matrix printer, you can print in banner mode, printing lengthwise across several continuous sheets of paper.

There are actually three ways to print in landscape mode, not all of which can be used on all printers. If you have a late-model laser or inkjet printer, you can obtain landscape printing in draft mode using setup strings defined in the Print Layout Options dialog box. If you are printing in final-quality mode, you can select the Landscape option in the Print Layout Options dialog box. If you are using a LaserJet or PostScript printer in final-quality mode, you can select a LaserJet or PostScript landscape font.

Regardless of which method you use, you need to adjust the margins for landscape printing. Change the page length to 7.5 inches (45 lines at 6 lines per inch) on Hewlett-Packard LaserJet and inkjet printers, 8.5 inches (51 lines at 6 lines per inch) on all others. If you are printing at 10 characters per inch, try a left margin of 1/2 inch (5 characters at 10 characters per inch) and a right margin of 10 inches (100 characters at 10 characters per inch).

To print in banner mode, select the Banner option in the Print Layout Options dialog box. When you use this mode, Quattro Pro ignores your right margin setting and prints continously across the paper from left to right, without any page breaks. If you have defined headers and footers, they will be printed as if the entire printout were one wide sheet of paper. That is, left-justified text in your headers and footers will appear at the left edge of the first page and right-justified text will appear at the right edge of the last page. If you have defined headings (as described under "Printing Larger Notebooks"), they will only appear on the top and leftmost pages.

Saving and Resetting Print Settings

Whenever you issue the / **F**ile l **S**ave, / **F**ile l **S**ave **A**s, or / **F**ile l **S**ave All command, Quattro Pro saves your print settings along with your data. If you neglect to save your notebook after changing print settings, Quattro Pro asks whether you want to lose your changes when you issue a / **F**ile l E**x**it, / **F**ile l **E**rase, or / **F**ile l **R**etrieve command, even if you have not changed any data on the notebook. The settings saved include the print block, the Left Heading and Right Heading settings (if any), and all the settings in the Print Layout Options dialog box (including the Header and Footer settings). When

Printing Notebooks

you retrieve the notebook, those settings are automatically reinstated, even if you have defined different print settings for another notebook in the current work session.

If you use certain settings for almost all your reports, you may want to save these settings as defaults for all future notebooks. You can do this using the Update button in the Print Layout Options dialog box. The settings saved will include all the Print Layout settings except the Header and Footer settings, plus the Destination setting on the Print menu.

You can use Reset to restore some or all of the print options to their default settings. When you press this button, Quattro Pro displays a submenu with the options All, Print Block, Headings, and Layout. The All option clears the print block setting, clears any headings, and restores the Destination and all the layout options to the last set of defaults saved with the Update option on the Print Layout Options dialog box. Print Block erases the Print Block setting. Headings clears the settings from the Top and Left Heading options. Layout returns margin settings in the Print Layout Options dialog box to their default settings.

Printing Larger Notebooks

If you define a print block that is too large to fit on a single page, Quattro Pro automatically splits the output across as many pages as necessary. Unfortunately this often makes the output unattractive and difficult to read. There are several ways of managing the printing of larger notebooks, either squeezing the data onto one page or making multiple-page printouts more readable.

Displaying Your Print Block

*To remove the print block lines, just issue the / **W**indow | **O**ptions | **P**rint **B**lock | **H**ide command.*

When you work with all but the smallest notebooks, it can be very helpful to display the borders of your print block on screen. If you are using WYSIWYG mode, you can do this by issuing the / **W**indow | **O**ptions | **P**rint Block | **D**isplay command. Assuming the Print | Destination setting is either Graphics Printer, Screen Preview, or Binary File, the boundaries of the current print block will appear on the screen as dotted lines. If the print block is too large to fit on a single page, you will see additional horizontal or vertical dotted lines—indicating page breaks—within the borders of the print block. This allows you to see whether your print block is large enough to accommodate your data. If it is not, you can then decide how to handle the situation. You may choose to expand the print block, use a smaller font, change the page orientation, or use the Print-To-Fit option on the Print menu to squeeze the print block onto a single page.

Defining Headings

Exclude all the cells in the Left Heading or Top Heading block from the print block; otherwise they will be printed twice.

When Quattro Pro splits a print block across multiple pages, the output is often difficult to decipher because only the first page includes all the column and row headings needed to identify the values. Figure 6-2, for example, shows a draft-quality printout of a six-month income statement. Notice that the line items on the second page of this report (at the bottom) are impossible to identify.

```
                    ABC GROUP INCOME PROJECTION
                        FIRST HALF OF 1994

Income Tax Rate:                               25%
Monthly Growth Factor                        1.004

                         Jan         Feb       March     1st Qtr
                        ------------------------------------------

Sales                   37,500      37,650     37,801    112,951
Cost of goods sold      16,125      16,190     16,254     48,569
Gross margin            53,625      53,840     54,055    161,520

Salaries                 7,166       7,195      7,223     21,584
Rent                     3,500       3,514      3,528     10,542
Utilities                1,291       1,296      1,301      3,888
Depreciation             1,833       1,840      1,848      5,521
Miscellaneous              666         669        671      2,006
Total operating expenses 14,456     14,514     14,572     43,542

Interest expense           875         879        882      2,636

Profit before tax       38,294      38,447     38,601    115,342
Income tax               9,574       9,612      9,650     28,836
Net income              28,720      28,835     28,951     86,506
```

```
                         April        May       June    2nd Qtr   YTD Total
                        -----------------------------------------------------

                        37,952      38,104     38,256    114,312    227,263
                        16,319      16,385     16,450     49,154     97,723
                        54,271      54,488     54,706    163,465    324,985

                         7,252       7,281      7,310     21,843     43,427
                         3,542       3,556      3,571     10,669     21,211
                         1,307       1,312      1,317      3,936      7,824
                         1,855       1,863      1,870      5,588     11,109
                           674         677        679      2,030      4,036
                        14,630      14,689     14,747     44,066     87,608

                           886         889        893      2,668      5,304

                        38,755      38,910     39,066    116,731    232,073
                         9,689       9,728      9,767     29,184     58,020
                        29,066      29,182     29,299     87,547    174,053
```

Figure 6-2. Printout of a wide spreadsheet

Printing Notebooks

You can clear headings by using the Reset button in the Print Layout Options dialog box.

The / **P**rint | **H**eadings command solves this problem. When you select Headings from the Print menu, Quattro Pro displays a submenu with the options Left Heading and Top Heading. Use the Left Heading option to define a block of cells (generally row headings) to be printed at the left side of every page of the printout. This option is useful when you are printing notebooks that are too wide to fit on one page.

Use the Top Heading option to define a block of cells (generally column headings) to be printed at the top of every page, immediately below the report header. Be sure to exclude cells in the heading from the print block itself. You can use both the Top Heading and Left Heading options on the same report; just be sure that the Top Heading and Left Heading blocks do not overlap.

TIP: If you experience problems printing headings in final-quality mode, try typing SET DOWNLOAD=0 at the DOS prompt, or experiment with different printer drivers.

To appreciate the Headings options, you need to make your notebook large enough to require additional pages of printed output. Do this now, and then define a header and left heading, and print the report. (In this case, you'll leave the Destination setting set to Draft Printer.)

1. Move to B4 in LEARN1.WQ2 and issue the / **E**dit | **C**opy command ([Ctrl]-[C] shortcut). Press [End]-[Home] to expand the source block to B4..D22. Press [Enter] and then enter a destination of **E4**. The notebook is now seven columns wide.

2. Change the label in E4 to "**1995** and the label in F4 to "**1996**.

3. Issue the / **P**rint | **L**ayout command, click on Header text or press Tab once to display the cursor after Header text, and type @|**ABC GROUP INCOME PROJECTION**|**Page #**. Press [Enter] and then select Quit to return to the Print menu.

4. Select Headings on the Print menu. Then select the Left Heading option and, when the prompt "Row headings to print on the left of each page" appears, enter **A7.. A22**. Then select Quit.

5. Move to B3. Select the Block option on the Print menu. Type a period, and then press [End]-[Home] to expand the block to B3..G22. Press [Enter].

6. Select the Adjust Printer option and select Align to let Quattro Pro know that the printer is at the top of page 1.

7. Select the Spreadsheet Print option to start printing.

8. When the report has stopped printing, select the **Adjust Printer** option and then select **Form Feed**. Your report should resemble the one shown in Figure 6-3.

> **NOTE:** If you're used to printing in a word processor, you're probably accustomed to seeing page breaks when the text becomes too long to fit on a single sheet of paper. In Quattro Pro, page breaks are also introduced when a notebook is too *wide* to fit on a single page, as in the previous exercise.

There are, of course, other methods of printing reports that are too large for one page. Many people simply cut and paste printout pages so they can see the notebook in one continuous piece. Some try, whenever possible, to design notebooks in small, discrete sections that can fit neatly on one

```
06-Jun-93                   ABC GROUP INCOME PROJECTION                    Page 1

                                    1993         1994                       1995
                                  Actual          Est    Variance         Actual
                                  ------------------------------------
Sales                            450,000      472,500      22,500        450,000
Cost of goods sold               193,500      203,175       9,675        193,500
Gross margin                     256,500      269,325      12,825        256,500

Salaries                          86,000       90,300       4,300         86,000
Rent                              42,000       44,100       2,100         42,000
Utilities                         15,500       16,275         775         15,500
Depreciation                      22,000       22,000           0         22,000
Miscellaneous                      8,000        8,400         400          8,000
Total operating expenses         173,500      181,075       7,575        173,500

Interest expense                  10,500       10,500           0         10,500

Profit before tax                 72,500       77,750       5,250         72,500
Income tax                        29,000       31,100       2,100         29,000
Net income                        43,500       46,650       3,150         43,500


06-Jun-93                   ABC GROUP INCOME PROJECTION                    Page 2

                                    1996
                                     Est    Variance
                                  ------------------
Sales                            472,500      22,500
Cost of goods sold               203,175       9,675
Gross margin                     269,325      12,825

Salaries                          90,300       4,300
Rent                              44,100       2,100
Utilities                         16,275         775
Depreciation                      22,000           0
Miscellaneous                      8,400         400
Total operating expenses         181,075       7,575

Interest expense                  10,500           0

Profit before tax                 77,750       5,250
Income tax                        31,100       2,100
Net income                        46,650       3,150
```

Printing a large spreadsheet with a header and a left heading
Figure 6-3.

printed page. You can also print in landscape mode—in effect rotating the notebook 90 degrees and printing it broadside. In some cases you can squeeze a moderately wide report onto one page with this method.

A few additional Quattro Pro features are useful for printing long reports. Compressed print and narrow margins can sometimes make the difference between a single- and multiple-page report. Quattro Pro also allows you to insert page breaks wherever you like within a report or to print without any page breaks at all.

Inserting Page Breaks

Unless you set page breaks, Quattro Pro automatically breaks the page whenever necessary, as determined by the page-length setting. You can also insert your own page breaks to separate multiple-page reports into coherent, readable sections.

> *You will see the entire page break code on the input line, but only :: is displayed on the notebook itself.*

The code for a hard page break (a break inserted whether or not the printer has reached the bottom of a page) is a vertical bar followed by two colons (|::). Often the easiest way to insert a page break is to move the cell pointer to the first column of your print block within the row where you want to break the page and then issue the / **S**tyle | **I**nsert Break command. Quattro Pro inserts a blank row immediately above the current cell and enters the page break code in the cell immediately above the current cell; to get rid of the page break later, just delete the row. You must move to the first column in the print block before issuing this command to obtain the proper results. You can also enter a page break code manually. If you do not have any blank or unnecessary rows on your notebook where you want the page break to occur, use / **E**dit | **I**nsert | **R**ows to insert a row for this purpose.

Note that Quattro Pro respects your page break codes even if you change the Page Breaks setting in the Print Layout Options dialog box to No. If you decide you do not want those page breaks, you must delete the page break codes from the notebook itself.

Printing to Fit and Scaling

> *If you issue the / **P**rint | **P**rint-To-Fit command, Quattro Pro ignores the current Print | Layout | % Scaling setting.*

Quattro Pro offers two methods of shrinking print blocks so they fit on a single printed page: the / **P**rint | **P**rint-To-Fit command and the % Scaling option in the Print Layout Options dialog box. Both of these commands only work when you print in final-quality mode. No matter which method you use to shrink the print size, Quattro Pro does not shrink margins.

The Print-To-Fit option automatically adjusts the point size so that your print block fits on one page or, in the case of very large notebooks, a few pages. The moment you select this option, Quattro Pro determines how far it needs to shrink the point size, and then starts printing. If your print block is large, Quattro Pro prints on more than one page rather than shrinking the print until it is no longer readable.

The % Scaling option in the Print Layout Options dialog box lets you manually adjust the size of the print—shrinking characters by a specified percentage. The default setting is 100%. You can reduce it to as low as 1%. The % Scaling setting is saved with the notebook when you issue any of the Save commands. (The Reset button on the Print Layout Options dialog box restores the setting to 100%, meaning no reduction at all.)

Printing 3-D Blocks

Often your larger notebooks will contain data on more than one page. You can print data from multiple pages just by specifying a 3-D block as the print block before issuing a / **P**rint | **S**preadsheet Print command. When you do this, however, the information from each page is run together in a single stream of data. If you prefer, you can control the amount of space between the data from the various pages in your 3-D block using the / **P**rint | **L**ayout | **N**otebook Page Skip command.

If you want the data from each notebook page to begin on a new printed page, issue the / **P**rint | **L**ayout | **N**otebook Page Skip command and select Form Feed. To specify a particular number of lines between the data from the various pages in your 3-D block, issue the / **P**rint | **L**ayout | **N**otebook Page Skip command and select Skip Lines. Then enter the desired number of lines. (You can choose anywhere from 0 to 100 lines; 0 is the default.)

Using Fonts

When you print in draft-quality mode, Quattro Pro always uses your printer's default font. When you print in final-quality mode, Quattro Pro lets you select from three types of fonts. Hershey fonts are a set of basic fonts that can be produced in all available sizes on almost any screen and most printers, without special preparation. Quattro Pro comes with eight Hershey fonts: Roman, Roman Light, Sans Serif, Sans Serif Light, Script, Monospace, Old English, and Eurostyle. Bitstream fonts are a set of clearer and more attractive fonts. To use these fonts Quattro Pro must build a font file for each combination of typeface, style, and point size you use. Quattro Pro comes with three Bitstream typefaces: Dutch, Swiss, and Courier. The scalable Bitstream fonts (marked with SC) are faster. The other Bitstream fonts are

Printing Notebooks

provided solely for compatibility with earlier versions of Quattro Pro. Quattro Pro also supports other Bitstream fonts that you can purchase separately. Finally, printer-specific fonts are special fonts used only by PostScript or LaserJet printers.

> To switch to WYSIWYG mode, use / **O**ptions | **D**isplay Mode and select B: WYSIWYG, or click on the SpeedBar's WYS button.

If you are using a character-based display mode, changing fonts has no visible effect on your notebook: The difference only shows up when you actually print the notebook in final-quality mode. In WYSIWYG display mode, however, text appears in the font that will be used if you print in final-quality mode. The ability to see fonts on screen is so useful that you will want to use WYSIWYG whenever you apply fonts to a notebook.

However, WYSIWYG's representation of fonts is not always perfect. WYSIWYG gives you a good general sense of how a notebook will look when printed, but it is not infallible, particularly with regard to the spacing between characters. As a result, text in WYSIWYG mode may appear slightly wider or narrower than it will look when printed. The moral is that WYSIWYG is terrific for providing first impressions of notebook fonts, but only the Screen Previewer discussed later in this chapter provides a thoroughly reliable image of what your notebook will look like when printed.

Applying Fonts to Sections of the Report

> You can use the Font button on the SpeedBar as a substitute for the / **S**tyle | **F**ont command.

To apply fonts in Quattro Pro, you use the / **S**tyle | **F**ont command. (You can also apply font changes with styles, which were covered in the previous chapter.) Once you've issued this command, enter a block to which to apply your changes, and make your selections from the submenu that appears. The Style | Font menu contains the following options:

- ✦ **Typeface** The typeface determines the shape of individual characters. When you select the Typeface option, Quattro Pro displays a submenu with 14 typefaces supplied with the program. If you are using a LaserJet, Canon laser, or PostScript printer, the submenu includes additional printer-specific fonts.

- ✦ **Point Size** The range of point sizes is from 6- to 72-point. (Remember, there are 72 points to an inch; a 72-point font is one inch high.) The larger the number, the bigger the characters.

- ✦ **Color** When you select the Color option, Quattro Pro displays a submenu of 16 colors (or a palette of 16 colors, if you are in WYSIWYG mode)—in case you are directing your output to a color printer. If you are not using a color printer, Quattro Pro ignores your choice unless you are in WYSIWYG, in which case the colors you select are reflected on the screen.

- **Bold** Select the Bold option to turn on boldfacing. Select it again to turn off boldfacing.
- **Italic** Select the Italic option to turn on italic. Select it again to turn off italic.
- **Underlined** Select the Underlined option to turn on underlining, and select it again to turn off underlining.
- **Reset** Use the Reset option if you want to turn off the Underlined, Italic, and Bold options all at once.
- **Quit** The Quit option returns you to Ready mode and puts your changes into effect.

When you apply a font, the font is stored in each cell of the designated block, and is applied to any data that you enter in that cell. To change the font you can assign a new font with another / **S**tyle | **F**ont command, or you can use a predefined or custom style. In fact, if there are specific font changes that you use repeatedly, you might consider saving them as a custom style, as described in Chapter 5.

Printer-Specific Fonts

If you are using a LaserJet or PostScript printer, additional fonts specific to your printer appear at the bottom of the Typeface submenu, underneath the Bitstream and Hershey fonts. If you are using font cartridges with a LaserJet or Canon laser printer, use / **O**ptions | **H**ardware | **P**rinters | **F**onts | **C**artridge Fonts to tell Quattro Pro about them. Those additional fonts then are included in the Typeface submenu.

Do not attempt to change the attributes of the cartridge fonts. Just select the one that most closely matches what you want. If you attempt to modify the typeface, point size, or style, Quattro Pro either displays an error message or just ignores your changes.

Saving Your Fonts

When you edit fonts and then save the notebook, your font changes are saved to disk along with other print settings and your notebook data. However, those changes apply only to the current notebook. If you create another notebook, Quattro Pro reinstates its usual font.

If there are specific font settings that you wish to use repeatedly, you should create a custom style. For example, if you regularly create headings that are Dutch, 16 point, bold, you can create a custom style that includes those

Printing Notebooks

settings, and then save the style so that you can use it in any notebook. Consult Chapter 5 for the details on creating custom styles.

Changing the Default Font

You may want to change the default font that is used each time you open a new notebook, rather than just changing the font for a single notebook. To do this, you must alter and then save the Normal style, as described here:

> You must execute this command from the directory that contains your Quattro Pro System files—usually C:\QPRO.

1. Issue the / **S**tyle | **D**efine Style | **C**reate command.
2. Select the Normal style from the list of styles that appears and press [Enter] to bring up the style attributes menu.
3. Select Font and make the desired changes to the font being used. For example, you could select a typeface of Dutch-SC and a point size of 14 point.
4. Choose Quit twice to return to the Style | Define Style menu, noting that the changes you made have already been put into place in the current spreadsheet.
5. From the Style | Define Style menu, choose File and then select Save. Then choose QUATTRO.STY and choose Replace to overwrite the existing file. Now all new notebooks you create will incorporate these font changes. If you want to change the default font again or revert to the original default, just follow the same procedure and make the needed changes.

Using Different Fonts to Print LEARN1.WQ2

The following exercise requires a graphics printer—that is, a printer capable of producing graphics images.

1. If you have not already specified a graphics printer as Printer 1, do so now. (See the instructions under "Selecting Printers" at the beginning of this chapter.)
2. Discard the large notebook you built in the previous exercise and retrieve LEARN1 by typing **/FR**, answering Yes when asked whether you want to lose your changes, and selecting LEARN1.WQ2 from the files list.
3. Make sure that the Options | Graphics Quality option is set to Final rather than Draft. Select Quit to return to Ready mode.
4. Issue the / **P**rint | **B**lock command. Press [Home] if the cell pointer is not already in A1. Type a period, press [End]-[Home] to extend the block to A:A1..D22, and press [Enter].

5. Issue the / **P**rint | **D**estination | **G**raphics Printer command, select Adjust Printer, select Align, and then select Quit.
6. Move to cell A1 and issue the / **S**tyle | **F**ont command or click on the Font button on the SpeedBar. Press [End]-[Home] and then press [Enter] to accept A:A1..D22 as the "block to set font."
7. Select Typeface from the Font menu and then choose Dutch-SC. Set the point size to 14 point; also turn Bold off. Select Quit to return to the notebook screen, noting the font changes on the screen.
8. With cell A1 selected, issue the / **S**tyle | **S**hading | **N**one command and press Enter to accept A1 as the default block.
9. Issue the / **S**tyle | **F**ont command again and this time turn on Bold in cell A1. Choose Quit to return to the the notebook screen and see your changes.
10. Issue the / **P**rint | **S**preadsheet Print command. When the printing stops, issue the / **P**rint | **A**djust Printer | **A**lign command. Then press [Esc] to return to Ready mode. Your printout should resemble Figure 6-4.
11. If you like the results, save your notebook by pressing [Ctrl]-[S] and selecting Replace. Your new selection of fonts and the current print destination are saved to disk.

	1993 Actual	1994 Est	Variance
ABC Group Income Projection	Created:	12/25/93	
Sales	450,000	472,500	22,500
Cost of goods sold	193,500	203,175	9,675
Gross margin	256,500	269,325	12,825
Salaries	86,000	90,300	4,300
Rent	42,000	44,100	2,100
Utilities	15,500	16,275	775
Depreciation	22,000	22,000	0
Miscellaneous	8,000	8,400	400
Total operating expenses	173,500	181,075	7,575
Interest expense	10,500	10,500	0
Profit before tax	72,500	77,750	5,250
Income tax	29,000	31,100	2,100
Net income	43,500	46,650	3,150

LEARN1.WQ2 printed in two Dutch fonts
Figure 6-4.

Printing Notebooks

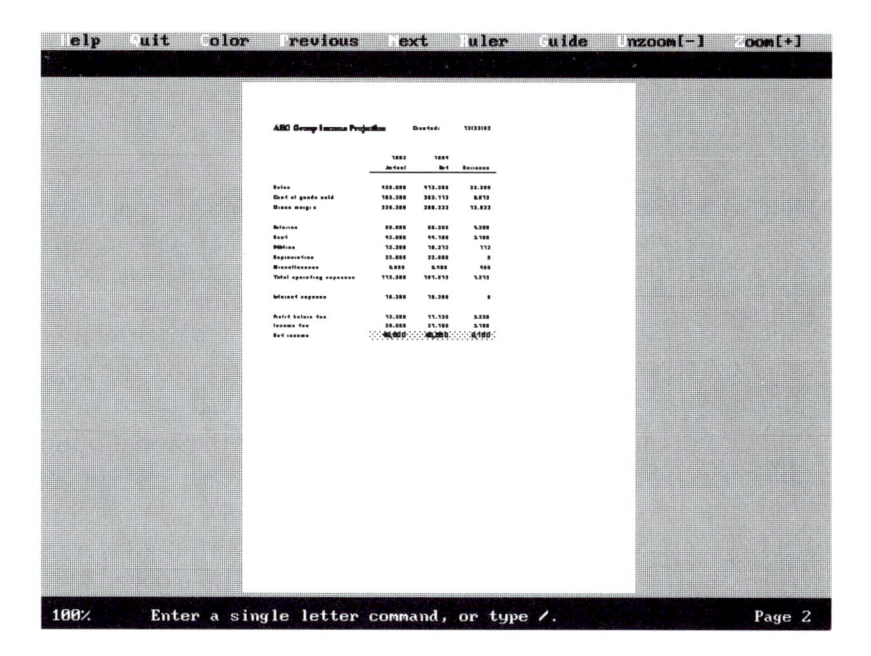

LEARN1.WQ2 in the Screen Previewer
Figure 6-5.

The Screen Previewer

The Screen Preview option in the Print I Destination menu allows you to view your report as it will look when printed in final-quality mode. This option only works if you have a graphics adaptor for your monitor. The Screen Previewer can save you a tremendous amount of time and paper, particularly if you are using a variety of fonts in your report. It can help you see how the data will be laid out and where the pages will break. If you are combining several fonts in one report, the Screen Previewer can give you a sense of how the fonts will look together and help you make adjustments if necessary.

To preview a report, define a print block using the / **P**rint I **B**lock command, change the Destination setting to Screen Preview and then "print" the report to your screen using the Spreadsheet Print option. Quattro Pro displays a screen like the one in Figure 6-5, showing the first page of your report. At the top of the screen is a menu bar with the following nine options:

✦ **Help** Displays a help screen with information on the Screen Previewer.
✦ **Quit** Returns you to the regular notebook display and the Print menu.
✦ **Color** Allows you to alter the colors used to display your report on the screen.
✦ **Previous** Displays the previous page of your report.

- **Next** Displays the next page of your report.
- **Ruler** Displays a grid over the previewed report to assist you in making exact modifications to the page layout. Select Ruler again to toggle the grid display off.
- **Guide** Displays a miniature page in the upper-right corner of the screen when the display is zoomed to 200% or 400%. This page guide includes a *zoom box* around the area currently shown on the rest of the Screen Previewer screen. To view a different section of your report, move the zoom box using the arrow keys or a mouse. If you are using a mouse, press [Enter] to redraw the screen. To remove the page guide from the screen, press [Del]. To restore it, press [Ins].

    Pressing the Guide option once turns the Guide display off; pressing it again turns it on (if the image is zoomed to at least 200%).

- **Unzoom[–]** Reverses the effects of the Zoom option, showing you more of the current page at once but with less detail.
- **Zoom[+]** Allows you to zoom in on a portion of the page currently on screen and view sections of your report in greater detail. There are three levels of Zoom: 100% displays the whole page, 200% displays half a page at twice the size, and 400% shows one-eighth of a page at four times the size. When you first enter the Screen Previewer, you are at a Zoom level of 100%. The current level of Zoom (if any) is displayed on the left end of the status line at the bottom of the screen.

Every time you print a report to the screen, Quattro Pro increases the page count (as reflected in the lower-right corner of the screen). You may want to reset the starting page number (by selecting Adjust Printer and then Align) before you select Spreadsheet Print, particularly if you are previewing multiple-page reports. If your report includes page numbers, be sure to use this method to reset the page count before you actually print the report.

Special Print Options

There are two last print options that you may want to use on occasion. / **P**rint | **F**ormat | **C**ell-Formulas allows you to print the contents of your notebook as stored rather than as displayed. Bullet characters allow you to create bulleted lists—to distinguish and highlight each item in a series.

Printing Formulas

Sometimes you may want to print a list of the literal contents of your notebook, including the formulas, display format codes, and column widths. / **P**rint | **F**ormat | **C**ell-Formulas generates such a list, printing exactly what you would see on the input line if you pointed to each cell in the print block in turn. This print option can be extremely useful when you are auditing a notebook to make sure that it is performing as intended. (When you print in Cells-Formula format, Quattro Pro ignores all other print options you have defined.)

Adding Bullets to a Report

Bullet characters work only in final-quality print mode.

Bullet characters are another design element you can use to dress up final-quality printed reports. Figure 6-6 shows the seven bullet characters you can use when printing Quattro Pro notebooks or graphs. To add bullets to a notebook, enter the characters \bullet #\ in the cell where you want the bullet to appear, where # is the number of the desired bullet character, as listed in Figure 6-6. For example, to use a checked box (bullet character 2), you would enter **\bullet 2**. You can enter this bullet command either in a cell by itself or before or after label text. If the bullet command is the first set of characters in a cell, you must preface it with a label alignment character. If you omit the alignment character, Quattro Pro interprets the \ character as an alignment character and attempts to repeat the entry as many times as will fit within the column width.

Printing in the Background

Quattro Pro includes a program known as the Borland Print Spooler (BPS) that lets you continue working while a notebook or graph prints in the background. This means you don't need to wait for your computer to finish sending data to your printer before you can go back to work. If you have taken the needed preparatory steps, whenever you print a notebook or graph, BPS temporarily saves your print job to disk and then returns you to Ready mode, leaving you free to resume working while BPS directs the print file to the printer in the background. With large or complex print jobs, the printing may take longer, but you needn't sit idle while it happens.

	Bullet Number	Description
☐	0	Box
■	1	Filled box
☑	2	Checked box
✓	3	Check
❑	4	Shadowed box
❑✓	5	Shadowed checked box
●	6	Filled circle

The seven Quattro Pro bullet styles
Figure 6-6.

Quattro Pro 5 Made Easy

> **NOTE:** Because BPS is a memory-resident program, it stays in memory even after you leave Quattro Pro. If you need to free up memory for use in another program, you can unload BPS by entering **BPS U** at the DOS prompt.

If you are familiar with DOS batch files, you may want to create a batch file that loads BPS and then loads Quattro Pro.

There are two steps you must take in order to use BPS. First, before you load Quattro Pro, you must switch to the Quattro Pro program directory and, at the DOS prompt, enter **BPS** to load the spooler into memory. Then go ahead and load Quattro Pro as usual. You must repeat this step every time you load Quattro Pro, unless you loaded BPS earlier in the day and have not yet turned off or rebooted your computer.

Second, issue the / **O**ptions | **H**ardware | **P**rinters | **B**ackground command and select Yes. Assuming that you want to use the spooler all or most of the time, you should select Update from the Options menu to save this setting as a default. (Once you select Update, you will not need to repeat this command in the future. You will only need to perform step 1.)

Once you have enabled BPS, your data is automatically directed to the spooler. From the time that you issue a print command until your notebook or graph is actually printed, your print job is said to reside in the *print queue*, a list of all pending print jobs.

When you unload BPS from memory or turn off your computer, all print jobs in the queue are suspended. However, they will continue to print the next time you load Quattro Pro after loading BPS. If you want to prevent them from printing, you can either delete any files with the extension .SPL from your Quattro Pro program directory, or remove them from the print queue using the / **P**rint | Print **M**anager | **J**ob command.

Monitoring the Print Queue

When you issue the / **P**rint | Print **M**anager command, Quattro Pro opens a window known as the Print Manager window. Assuming that BPS is loaded and you are either using a stand-alone computer or working on a network but sending print jobs to BPS rather than a network print spooler, this window displays information on all your currently pending print jobs. This information includes

- ◆ **Seq** The job sequence number, indicating the print job's place in line.
- ◆ **File Name** The name of the temporary file in which Quattro Pro has stored the data to be printed. This file will start with QPPRN, followed by the sequence number, followed by the extension .SPL.

- **Status** The current state of the print job. Active means the job is currently printing. Ready means the job is ready to print but not yet printing. Held means the job has been temporily suspended.
- **Port** The port to which the job is being sent (LPT1, LPT2, COM1, and so on).
- **File Size** The size of the print file, in bytes.
- **Copies** The number of copies to be printed, as determined by the Print | Copies setting.

At the top of the Print Manager window, you will see a menu bar with the options File, Queue, Job, and Window. The File and Window options let you open, close, zoom, tile, stack, move, resize, and select windows (see Chapter 11 for more on working with windows). If you are using a network, the Queue option lets you choose whether to view the BPS print queue or your network print queue. The Job option leads to a menu with the options Delete, Hold, and Release. You can use Delete to remove a print job from the queue. The Hold option temporarily suspends printing of a print job. (You will see its status change to Held in the print queue list.) The job will remain held until you select the Release option.

In this chapter, you learned to print Quattro Pro notebooks, producing output that ranges from the simplest draft-quality printouts to elaborate, highly customized reports. Try not to get overwhelmed by the myriad of options at this point. At its simplest, printing in Quattro Pro is extremely easy, and simple may be perfectly adequate for now. On the other hand, if you are thrilled at all the desktop publishing possibilities, you may want to experiment before moving on to other chapters—to get a sense of all the printing tools available.

CHAPTER

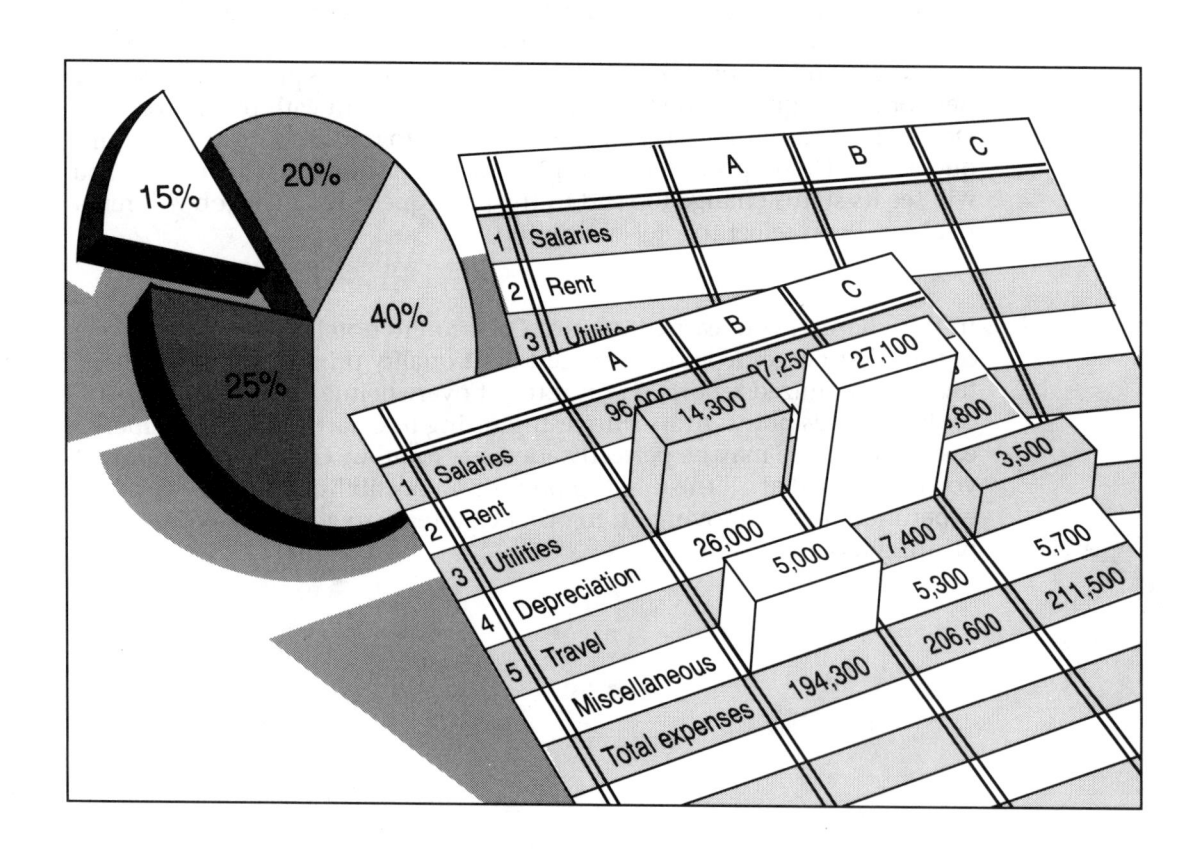

7
FUNCTIONS

Functions *are specialized operators that perform specific, often complex calculations. They allow you to manipulate values and text in ways that are difficult or impossible with traditional arithmetic operators. You have already tried the most commonly used function, @SUM. Quattro Pro furnishes over 100 of these tools to assist you in your work.*

This chapter introduces you to functions in general and then covers a few of the more commonly used functions in detail. Additional functions are introduced in later chapters as they become relevant. Because Quattro Pro has so many functions and not all of them will be relevant to your work, only the general-purpose functions are covered in this chapter. For the details about all of Quattro Pro's functions, consult your Quattro Pro documentation or take advantage of Quattro Pro's Help system.

Types of Functions

Quattro Pro functions can be classified into the following groups:

- *Mathematical functions* Used to perform mathematical calculations, such as finding the square root or natural logarithm of a number. This group includes functions for rounding and generating random numbers, and also includes several trigonometric functions.

- *Statistical functions* Used to calculate statistics about a block of cells on a notebook. @SUM falls in this category, along with functions that count the number of values in a block of cells and calculate the average, minimum, maximum, variance, and standard deviation.

- *Financial functions* Used primarily for investment calculations, such as determining mortgage payments or the value of long-term investments.

- *Logical functions* Allow you to build decision-making capabilities into your notebook by displaying different values or by performing different calculations depending on the value of a cell. These functions generally involve evaluating some kind of condition and taking different actions depending on whether the condition is true or false.

- *String functions* Allow you to manipulate text. String functions can be used to perform operations such as extracting part of a long string of text or converting all the characters in a label to uppercase.

- *Lookup functions* Let you look up a specified number or group of characters in a separate table or list of values.

- *Date and time functions* Used to enter and perform calculations on dates and times.

- *Database statistical functions* Used to perform statistical calculations on values in a database—for example, counting all the records in which a particular field has a particular value, or determining the average value in a field.

- *System functions* Return information about the Quattro Pro environment, including the currently selected menu item, the Quattro Pro version number, and the amount of available memory.

Functions

✦ *Miscellaneous functions* Let you enter the special values ERR and NA into a notebook, and determine the status of a cell or of the notebook as a whole.

*Once you load an add-in, it is automatically loaded in all future work sessions. You can unload it with / **Tools** | **Library** | **Unload**.*

Quattro Pro also lets you use additional functions that you purchase separately. To use such *add-in functions,* issue the / **Tools** | **Library** | **Load** command and choose from the list of add-in files or enter the name of the add-in file that you wish to load. (The add-ins list will automatically include every file in the default directory with the extension QLL.)

After you have loaded an add-in function, you can use it just as you would any other function, except that you need to specify the add-in name (without the QLL extension) as well as the function name. For information on the syntax and usage of add-in functions, refer to the add-in documentation.

Function Syntax

When you use a function in a formula, you type an @ character followed by the function name. In most cases the function name is followed by a set of parentheses containing the function's *arguments*—the raw data on which a function operates. For example, in the formula @SUM(A1..A5), the block A1..A5 is the argument; it is the portion of the expression on which Quattro Pro performs the calculation. This combination of function name, starting parenthesis, arguments list, and ending parenthesis in a formula is called a *function statement.* In some cases, function statements can also be part of longer formulas.

A few Quattro Pro functions do not require arguments, many functions require only one argument, and others require several arguments in a specific order. Whenever functions require more than one argument, the arguments must be separated by commas. Therefore, the general syntax for using Quattro Pro functions is

   @*function*(*argument1,argument2,...*)

In general, functions that require arguments also require that each argument evaluates to a particular data type: character strings, numbers, or blocks. When a character string argument is required, you can generally substitute any combination of characters enclosed in quotation marks, cell references, values, operators, and functions that evaluate to a string of text. When a function requires a numeric argument, you can usually use any combination of cell references, numbers, operators, and functions that evaluate to a single numeric value. When a function requires a block as an argument, you can enter block coordinates, a single cell address, a block name, or a combination of the above.

Using one function as the argument for another function is referred to as *nesting functions*. You can nest as many functions as you like, provided each function has its own matching set of parentheses and the entire expression does not exceed 240 characters. You should be wary of nesting too many functions in a single formula. The more functions you use, the more difficult it is to debug the formula if it generates either a Syntax Error or an unintended result.

The Functions Key

If you're using a mouse, you can click on the @ button on the Edit SpeedBar instead of pressing [Alt]-[F3].

Quattro Pro's Functions key, [Alt]-[F3], can make it easier to construct function statements, particularly if you forget the function's exact name. When you press this key combination, Quattro Pro displays a menu of functions. You can use the scroll bar or the cursor-movement keys to scroll through the options. Once you find the desired function, either click on it or highlight it and press [Enter] to insert the function name and an opening parenthesis into your formula.

You can also press the Functions key after you have started entering a formula. For example, if you want to multiply the sum of A1..A2 by 3, you start by typing **3***, and then use [Alt]-[F3] or the @ button to start adding the function statement.

Basic Statistical Functions

Quattro Pro offers several functions for aggregating and counting values. These functions can be applied to any list of numbers, cell references, and block references. The simple statistical functions require only one argument, but you can include as many as you like, separated with commas. Usually the argument is a single block of cells. Figure 7-1 shows a notebook illustrating the use of @SUM, @COUNT, @AVG, @MAX, and @MIN.

@SUM

The general syntax for the @SUM function is @SUM(*List*), where *List* is any series of cell references, block references, or expressions that evaluate to numbers. You have already used @SUM to calculate the total of a series of values within a column. You can also use @SUM to total the values in a single row, in a block consisting of several rows and columns, or in several blocks or cells. Here is a chart illustrating some of the possibilities:

Functions

Function Statement	Evaluates To
@SUM(A1,A3,B14)	The sum of the values in A1, A3, and B14
@SUM(A1..D2,B12)	The sum of the values in A1..D2, plus the value in B12
@SUM(*BlockName*)	The sum of the values in a named block (assigning names to blocks is covered in Chapter 8)
@SUM(A1,14)	The sum of the value in A1 plus the number 14

You cannot use the Sum button to add noncontiguous cells.

Chapter 3 explained that in certain contexts you can click on the Sum button on the SpeedBar instead of entering an @SUM formula. You can use this button to add the values in a row, column, or block. To do so, highlight the cells you want to total using either your mouse or Shift-F7 and the arrow keys. You also must include a blank row below and/or a column to the right of the selected values—this is where Quattro Pro will place the results of its calculation. Finally, click on the Sum button on the SpeedBar; Quattro Pro will display the results, inserting the appropriate @SUM formulas.

@COUNT

Quattro Pro's @COUNT function calculates the number of nonblank cells in a list of cells or blocks. Its syntax is @COUNT(*List*), where *List* consists of cell references, block coordinates, numbers, character strings, or other functions. For example, the function statement in E6 is @COUNT(B4..B10) in Figure 7-1. This function counts the number of nonblank cells in B4..B10. Because all the cells in this block contain data, the function returns a value of 7. The type of data a cell contains is irrelevant; the formula @COUNT(A4..A10) would have yielded the same results, for instance.

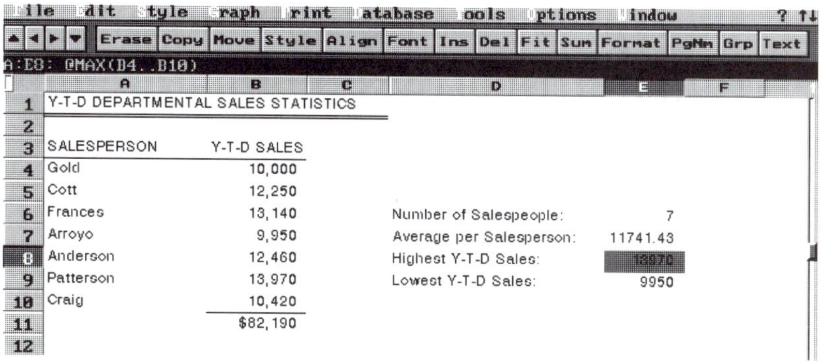

Notebook illustrating statistical functions
Figure 7-1.

@AVG

The @AVG function calculates the average value within a group, dividing the sum of the values by the number of values. Its syntax is @AVG(*List*), where *List* is any series of cell references, block references, or expressions that evaluate to numbers. In Figure 7-1 cell E7 contains the formula @AVG(B4..B10). Quattro Pro generates the result of 11741.43 by dividing the sum of all the values in the argument (82190) by the number of values in the argument (7).

@MAX and @MIN

Quattro Pro's @MAX function evaluates to the highest value within a group of values; the @MIN function evaluates to the lowest of the group. The syntaxes for these functions are @MAX(*List*) and @MIN(*List*), where *List* is a series of expressions that evaluate to numbers. In Figure 7-1, E8 contains the function statement @MAX(B4..B10) and evaluates to 13970, the highest number in the block B4..B10. The function in E9, @MIN(B4..B10), returns the value 9950, the lowest number in the block.

Blank Cells and Labels in Statistical Functions

One potential problem common to many statistical functions is that Quattro Pro treats any labels included in the arguments for a statistical function as zeros, whether they are named individually or included in a block. In the case of the @SUM function, this has no effect on the result. In other functions, however, including an unintended zero can skew the result. For example, if you include a label in the argument for an @AVG function, the result generally is lower than you intended because Quattro Pro treats that label as a zero for the purpose of the calculation.

You can encounter similar problems with the @MIN function. Whenever you include labels in the argument for an @MIN function, the function returns a value of zero (unless the argument happens to include negative numbers).

Similar issues arise if your argument list includes blank cells. Quattro Pro ignores any blank cells that occur within any blocks you specify as arguments for a statistical function. However, if you specify blank cells as arguments in themselves, Quattro Pro treats them as zeros for the purposes of the calculation. For example, if cell A3 happens to be blank, Quattro Pro ignores it when performing a statistical calculation on (A1..A5), but treats it as a zero if you use an argument such as (A1,A3,A5).

When using the @AVG function, you should avoid accidentally naming any labels (including the cells used in block references) in your argument or they will skew the result. (Fortunately, blank cells will not have the same effect.) If you use a block as your argument, you should also be careful not to leave

Functions

any cells within the block blank when you actually want them to be treated as zeros in the calculation. If you prefer not to see the zeros on your notebook, you can use the Hide Zeros format.

A Trick for Keeping New Rows Within an @SUM Block

With the @SUM function, you can actually take advantage of the fact that Quattro Pro treats labels as zeros. As previously discussed in Chapter 3, one of the benefits of using the @SUM function to add the values in a block (as opposed to using a formula with multiple plus signs) is that Quattro Pro automatically includes any new rows or columns you insert within the block's current borders.

However, if you're not careful while adding rows or columns to the edges of your block, Quattro Pro may not expand the block as needed. One way to solve this problem is to deliberately include labels in the referenced block when you enter the formula. In Figure 7-2, for example, a row of dashes was entered immediately above and below the line items in a budget. The formulas at the bottom of each column sum all the values in the block extending from the first row of dashes to the second row of dashes. The formula in B11, for example, is @SUM(B5..B10). Because Quattro Pro ignores labels in @SUM calculations, these dashes have no effect on the result. However, they do prevent a user from accidentally entering new rows outside the block's borders. As long as new rows are entered between the rows of dashes, they are automatically included in the @SUM results.

Functions for Dropping Decimal Places

Frequently you will enter a formula that returns more decimal places than you want to see on your notebook. You have three ways to solve this

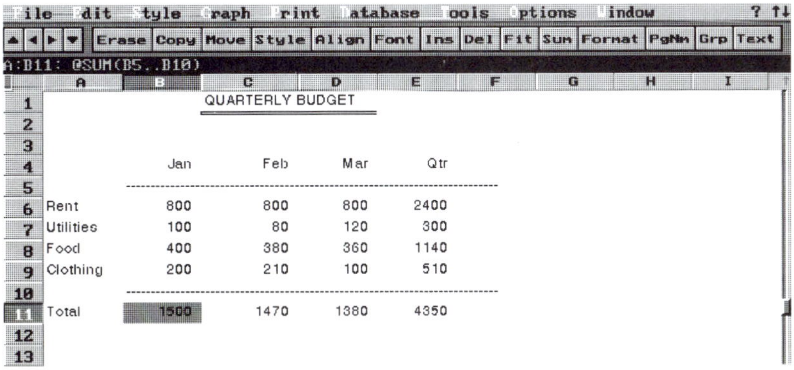

Including labels in an @SUM block
Figure 7-2.

problem: You can use a display format that limits the number of decimal places displayed; you can use the @ROUND function to round the result; in cases where you want no decimal places, you can use the @INT function, which returns the integer portion of a numeric value.

These three solutions generate different values (even if they sometimes look the same on the notebook) and can therefore have different impacts on your notebook's calculations.

@ROUND

Quattro Pro's @ROUND function rounds values to a specified number of decimal places. The syntax for this function is @ROUND (*Value,n*), where *Value* is any combination of numbers, cell references, and operators that evaluates to a number, and *n* is a number between –15 and 15 that specifies the number of significant digits you want to include in the result. Here are some examples of the @ROUND function and its results:

Function Statement	Result
@ROUND(1562.637,2)	1562.64
@ROUND(1562.637,0)	1563
@ROUND(1562.637,-1)	1560

If the second argument is negative, it indicates the number of digits to the left of the decimal that you want to round.

In the first two examples, the second argument in the @ROUND function statement specifies the number of decimals to include in the result. In the last example, the –1 argument directs Quattro Pro to not only round off all the decimal places, but also to round the digit one place to the left of the decimal point.

It is important to keep in mind the difference between displaying a series of numbers without decimal places and eliminating decimal places with @ROUND. These alternatives produce results that are identical in appearance but different in value. In general, displaying values with zero decimal places preserves a greater degree of mathematical accuracy than actually eliminating decimal places with @ROUND, because the numbers are still stored and used in calculations with all their digits. However, this method can also generate the appearance of rounding errors.

The choice between rounding numbers and simply displaying them without decimals depends, in most cases, on your data and the needs of your audience. If approximate values are good enough, rounded numbers may be less confusing. If accuracy is important, you should either display all the digits or omit them but note the apparent discrepancy in the numbers.

@INT

The @INT function is used to truncate numbers to integers. Its syntax is @INT(*Value*), where *Value* is any combination of numbers, cell references, and operators that evaluates to a number. The @INT function returns the number represented by *Value* stripped of its decimal places. For example, the function @INT(4623.7231) returns 4623.

There is an important difference between using the @INT function and rounding a number to zero decimal places with the @ROUND function, although they sometimes produce identical results. The @INT function simply drops any digits to the right of the decimal point, regardless of their value. The @ROUND function, in contrast, evaluates the digit to the right of the decimal point (when rounding to zero decimal places) and rounds to the next integer if that digit is 5 or greater. As shown in Figure 7-3, at times the two functions yield the same result, but at others they do not.

The @IF Function

The @IF function allows you to add decision-making capabilities to your notebook—to return different results depending on the value in one or more cells. The syntax of the @IF function is

> @IF(*Condition,Display if true,Display if false*)

When Quattro Pro encounters an @IF function, it begins by evaluating its first argument. If the first argument is true, Quattro Pro displays the result of the second argument; otherwise it displays the result of the third argument. The @IF function's first argument, *Condition,* therefore must be a *logical expression*—something that can be evaluated as either true or false. In a spreadsheet, logical expressions generally either make a comparison between two values, labels, or formulas, or test the contents of a particular cell.

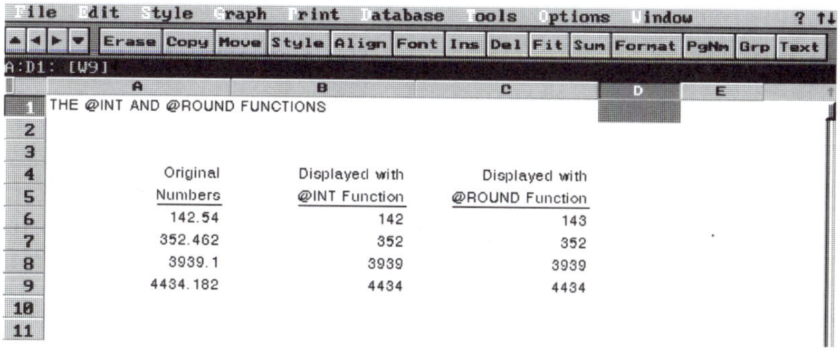

	Original Numbers	Displayed with @INT Function	Displayed with @ROUND Function
	142.54	142	143
	352.462	352	352
	3939.1	3939	3939
	4434.182	4434	4434

The effects of the @INT and @ROUND functions
Figure 7-3.

The most commonly used syntax for conditions is *X Operator Y*, where *X* and *Y* are expressions (consisting of numbers, character strings, cell references, arithmetic operators, and functions) that evaluate to numbers or text, and *Operator* performs some kind of comparison between those expressions. You can use six *comparison operators* to construct conditions:

Symbol	Meaning
=	Equal to
>	Greater than
<	Less than
>=	Greater than or equal to
<=	Less than or equal to
<>	Not equal to

Here are some examples of valid conditions:

```
A1 > 15
C2 <= D3
B14 <> "San Francisco"
```

Notice that "San Francisco" is enclosed in quotation marks. Whenever you want to treat a set of characters as text in a condition, you need to enclose them in quotes.

Now that you know the basic rules for the @IF function, let's explore a few applications. Figure 7-4 shows a notebook for calculating sales commissions. The commission rate on each sale depends on the gross sales amount: The rate for a gross sale greater than or equal to $12,000 is 14%; the rate for all other sales is 12%. For the first salesperson, B4 contains the sales amount and C4 contains the formula

```
@IF(B4>=12000,B4*0.14,B4*0.12)
```

The function is evaluated as follows: First, Quattro Pro determines whether the function's first argument is true or false for the value in B4. Second, if the value in B4 is greater than or equal to 12000, Quattro Pro displays the result of the function's second argument, multiplying the value in B4 by 0.14. If B4 is less than 12000 (the condition is false), Quattro Pro displays the result of the function's third argument, multiplying the value in B4 by 0.12.

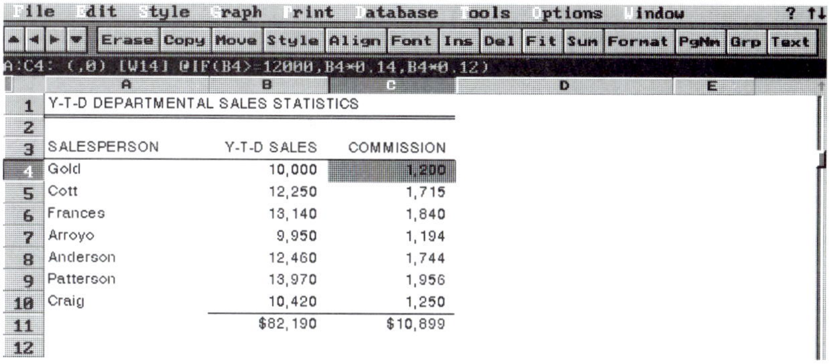

Functions

Using @IF to calculate sales commissions
Figure 7-4.

	A	B	C
1	Y-T-D DEPARTMENTAL SALES STATISTICS		
3	SALESPERSON	Y-T-D SALES	COMMISSION
4	Gold	10,000	1,200
5	Cott	12,250	1,715
6	Frances	13,140	1,840
7	Arroyo	9,950	1,194
8	Anderson	12,460	1,744
9	Patterson	13,970	1,956
10	Craig	10,420	1,250
11		$82,190	$10,899

Complex Operators

In some cases you need to create more elaborate conditions than you can manage with the basic comparison operators. Quattro Pro provides three complex logical operators for this purpose: #AND#, #OR#, and #NOT#. #AND# and #OR# are used to combine two or more conditions into a single complex condition. When two conditions are combined with the #AND# operator, the result is true only if both parts are true. For example, the condition A4>0#AND#A4<10 is true if A4 contains a value that is both greater than 0 and less than 10.

When two conditions are combined with the #OR# operator, the resulting condition is considered true if either condition is true. The expression A4=C3#OR#A4>100 is true if the value in A4 equals the value in C3 or if the value in A4 is greater than 100.

The last complex operator, #NOT#, provides an alternative means of creating negative conditional tests. #NOT# is used as a preface to a single simple or complex condition, rather than as a means of combining two conditions. When a condition is preceded by #NOT#, the resulting condition is considered true if the initial condition (before it was prefaced by #NOT#) is false. For example, the condition #NOT#A1=A2 is true if the value in A1 does *not* equal the value in A2. #NOT# is a convenient tool for negating a long or complicated condition. Rather than reentering the entire condition in modified form, you can enter **#NOT#(** at the beginning of the condition and add a closing parenthesis at the end. The result is a new condition that is exactly the opposite of the old one.

Figure 7-5 illustrates the use of the #OR# operator in a check register notebook. The formula

```
@IF(E6>0#OR#F6>0,G5+E6-F6," ")
```

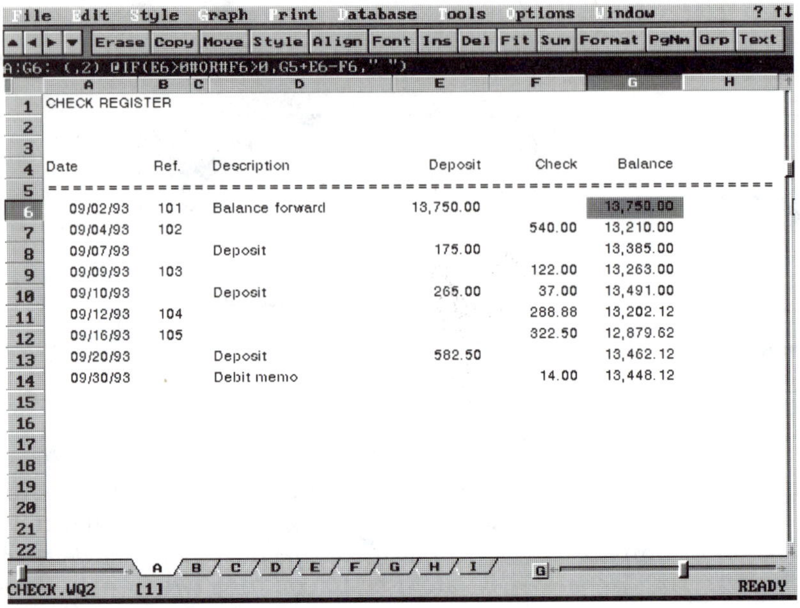

A check register using the @IF function
Figure 7-5.

[Screenshot of Quattro Pro check register spreadsheet]

	A	B	C	D	E	F	G
1	CHECK REGISTER						
4	Date	Ref.		Description	Deposit	Check	Balance
6	09/02/93	101		Balance forward	13,750.00		13,750.00
7	09/04/93	102				540.00	13,210.00
8	09/07/93			Deposit	175.00		13,385.00
9	09/09/93	103				122.00	13,263.00
10	09/10/93			Deposit	265.00	37.00	13,491.00
11	09/12/93	104				288.88	13,202.12
12	09/16/93	105				322.50	12,879.62
13	09/20/93			Deposit	582.50		13,462.12
14	09/30/93			Debit memo		14.00	13,448.12

was entered in G6 and then copied down column G. The resulting formulas determine whether an amount has been posted in either the Deposit or Check column. If a value appears in either column, the new balance (G5+E6-F6) is displayed; otherwise a blank is displayed in the balance column. This allows you to copy a formula to rows that are not yet used without displaying values in column G. Note that the formula in G6 is evaluated as 0 + 13750 - 0 because Quattro Pro treats the label in G5 as a zero for the purpose of the calculation.

@VLOOKUP and @HLOOKUP

@VLOOKUP and @HLOOKUP are two of the most useful functions in Quattro Pro's repertoire. Both allow you to look up specified values in tables located elsewhere on your notebook. For example, you can look up rates in a tax table, locate prices in an inventory price list, or pull commission rates from a commission rates table. Because @VLOOKUP and @HLOOKUP work similarly, we will cover the former in detail and then extrapolate to the latter. The syntax for @VLOOKUP is

@VLOOKUP(*Lookup Value,Table Block,Offset*)

where *Lookup Value* is a number, numeric expression, character string, or cell reference that you want Quattro Pro to look up; *Table Block* is the block containing the lookup table, and *Offset* is the column that Quattro Pro uses to locate the value to return. An *Offset* of 2, for example, directs Quattro Pro

Functions

to return the value located two cells to the right of that cell within the table block in which Quattro Pro found the lookup value.

When performing numeric lookups, Quattro Pro always begins at the top of the table and looks down the table's leftmost column until it finds a number greater than or equal to the lookup value. If the number it finds is equal to the lookup value, Quattro Pro returns the offset value in that row. Otherwise, Quattro Pro returns the offset value in the previous row.

In the notebook shown in Figure 7-6, B15 contains the following formula:

```
@VLOOKUP(B14,A5..B12,1)
```

Quattro Pro handles this function statement by looking down the first column of the lookup table (which occupies cells A5 through B12) until it finds a value greater than or equal to the value in B14. Since B14 contains the value 13,210, Quattro Pro stops when it reaches A10, which contains the value 15,000. If this were an exact match (if B14 contained the value 15,000), Quattro Pro would simply return the value one cell to the right. Because it is not an exact match, Quattro Pro goes back to the previous row to the nearest match that is lower than the lookup value (12,500) and returns the value located one cell to the right of that cell (325).

Given Quattro Pro's method of executing numeric lookups, all values in the first column of your lookup block must be in order from the lowest to the

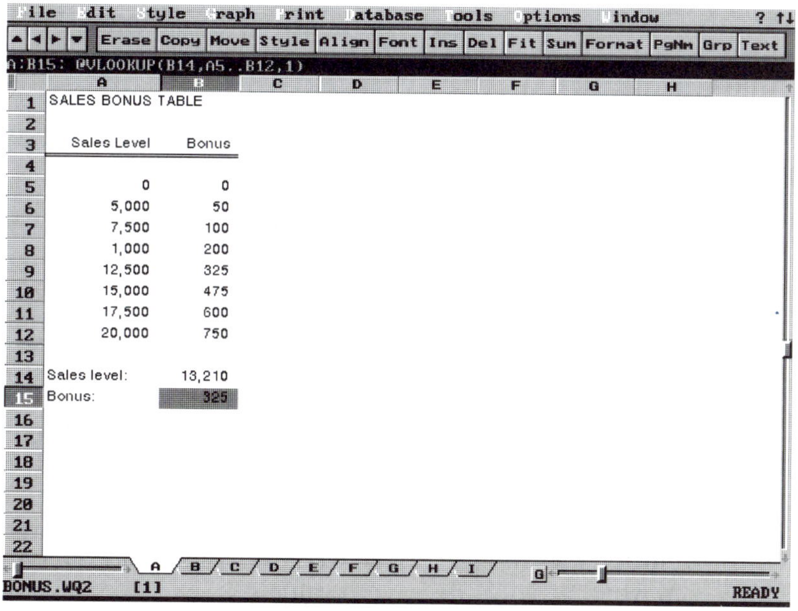

Looking up bonuses with @VLOOKUP
Figure 7-6.

highest. The first column should also include the lowest possible lookup value, because Quattro Pro returns the value ERR when you specify a lookup value lower than the first value in the table. If you specify a lookup value greater than the last number in the leftmost column, Quattro Pro returns the value corresponding to the last and highest number in the column.

NOTE: If you look up a blank cell in a lookup table, Quattro Pro always returns the value in the table's first row. For example, if cell C16 were blank in Figure 7-7, the formula in C17 would return 26.95.

Quattro Pro handles text lookups somewhat differently, beginning its search at the top of the leftmost column of the table, but stopping its search only when it finds an exact match. In the notebook shown in Figure 7-7, the @VLOOKUP function is used to find the costs and prices of inventory items by looking up their part numbers on an inventory table. (The part numbers have been entered as labels because they include dashes.) The formula in C17

`@VLOOKUP(C16,A6..D12,2)`

directs Quattro Pro to find the set of characters in C16 (240-52) in the first column of the lookup table and then return the value located two cells to the right (offset 2). The formula in C18

`@VLOOKUP(C16,A6..D12,3)`

directs Quattro Pro to find the same set of characters in the lookup table and then return the value located three cells to the right (offset 3). In both cases, because Quattro Pro is looking for an exact match for the specified part number (and will stop as soon as it finds one), the order of items within the table is inconsequential. What is important is that you do not have duplicate entries for any single lookup value and that the value can be found within the lookup table. If Quattro Pro cannot find the lookup value in the table, it returns an ERR value.

The @HLOOKUP function works exactly like @VLOOKUP except that the lookup table is arranged horizontally rather than vertically: Quattro Pro searches for the lookup value within the top row of the lookup table rather than the leftmost column. The offset value is interpreted as the number of rows below the top row in which to locate the return value. In Figure 7-8, the formula in B10 is @HLOOKUP(B9,A3..E4,1). This formula directs Quattro Pro to look up the current value of B9 in the table contained within the block A3..E4, and to return whatever value is located one cell below the cell in which it finds the lookup value.

Functions

Finding a character string in a lookup table
Figure 7-7.

In the preceding examples, @VLOOKUP and @LOOKUP were used to cross-reference single values or labels. In most real notebooks, however, lookup functions are used to look up each cell within an entire column or row of values. In these cases, you would generally enter a lookup function in one cell—using absolute cell references to designate the lookup table—and then replicate it across a row or column using / Edit | Copy. Absolute cell references are covered in Chapter 8.

As mentioned, you can also link notebooks so that values in one notebook can be based on values in another (see Chapter 19). The ability to link

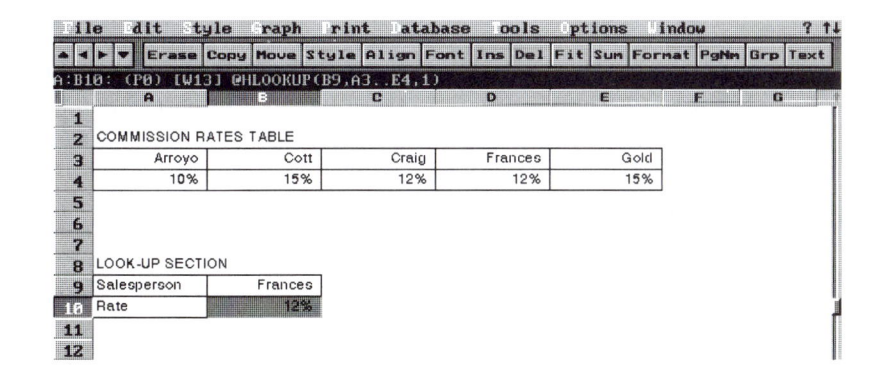

Looking up commission rates with @HLOOKUP
Figure 7-8.

notebooks allows you to store commonly used lookup tables (a tax table perhaps, or a product code list) in one notebook and use lookup functions to refer to that table from other notebooks.

String Functions

Quattro Pro offers several functions for manipulating text. Many of these functions are used primarily in complex macro operations, and most of them typically are used in database applications.

Quattro Pro handles three types of formulas: numeric, text, and logical. The simplest text formula is *concatenation,* which means combining two character strings. The operator used for concatenation is the ampersand (&). Concatenation is commonly used to combine a column of first and last names, or cities and states, for printing on a report. In such cases, you would generally create a new column with formulas concatenating the labels in two or more other columns.

You can specify arbitrary character strings as well as cell references in text formulas. Whenever you designate a character string within a formula, however, you need to enclose the string in quotation marks to let Quattro Pro know that you are referring to an arbitrary set of characters, rather than a cell, block, or function.

The ampersand is the only simple operator designed for use with character data. All other text formulas involve the use of string (text) functions. Some of the simplest are @UPPER, @PROPER, @LENGTH, and @REPEAT.

@UPPER

The @UPPER function changes text so that all letters are in uppercase. The syntax for the @UPPER function is @UPPER(*String*), where *String* is a character string, cell reference, or combination of the two. For example, if D14 contained the label "New York," the formula @UPPER(D14) would return "NEW YORK". The @UPPER function (and the @PROPER function) can be useful for standardizing data that has been entered in different formats.

@PROPER

The @PROPER function modifies text so that the first letter of each word is uppercase and the remaining letters are lowercase. For example, if A12 contained the label "SCURRILOUS," the function statement @PROPER(A12) would return "Scurrilous."

@LENGTH

The @LENGTH function returns the number of characters in a label or other character string. Its syntax is @LENGTH(*String*), where *String* is a cell address, a character string enclosed in quotes, or a text formula such as A1&A2.

@REPEAT

The @REPEAT function repeats whatever character you specify as many times as you wish across a given row. The syntax is @REPEAT(*String,# of Repetitions*). @REPEAT is often used for replicating a character string across a row or column to create decorative borders or underlining. @REPEAT creates a specific number of characters. In contrast, the backslash character that you used earlier to create a repeating character sequence simply generates enough characters to fill the width of the specified cell.

In character-based display modes, you can use @REPEAT in combination with @LENGTH to generate a character string that is exactly the same length as the text located in another cell; this can be extremely useful for underlining.

Financial Functions

Quattro Pro offers a total of 18 financial functions, which do everything from calculate depreciation to help compute loan amortization schedules. What follows are discussions of only four of the simpler and more commonly used financial functions. If you have a need for other similiar types of calculations, refer to Quattro Pro's documentation.

When using any of the financial functions, you can employ any valid combination of numeric constants, cell references, arithmetic operators, and other functions for the function arguments.

@PMT

The @PMT function lets you calculate the amount required to pay back a loan in equal payments. The syntax for this function is

@PMT (*Principal,Rate,Periods*)

where *Principal* is the amount borrowed, *Rate* is the periodic interest rate, and *Periods* is the number of periods in the loan. The tricky aspect of using @PMT and many other financial functions is that the period used for the *Rate* and *Periods* arguments must be the same. If the loan will be paid in monthly installments, for example, the interest rate must be expressed as a rate per month. Since interest rates are normally expressed in terms of interest per year, you will usually have to divide the annual interest rate by

12. For example, Figure 7-9 shows a notebook for calculating payments on a car loan. In the formula in cell C7

`@ROUND(@PMT(C3,C4/12,C5),2)`

the second argument is the interest in C4 divided by 12 to yield the monthly interest rate. If the amount in C5 were the number of years in the loan rather than the number of months, the formula would need to read

`@ROUND(@PMT(C3,C4/12,C5*12),2)`

Note that the result of the @PMT function is rounded to two decimal places, to eliminate fractions of a cent.

Once you have calculated the payment per period using @PMT, you can also calculate the total amount paid over the term of the loan by multiplying the payment per period by the number of periods. For example, cell C9 of Figure 7-9 contains the formula +C7*C5. Cell C11 calculates the amount of interest paid with the formula +C9–C3, which subtracts the original loan amount from the total paid.

@NPER

The @NPER function lets you calculate the time required to attain two very different ends: either to meet an investment goal or to pay off a loan. By using negative numbers for the *Payment* and *Present Value* arguments—representing money going out, a decrease in your own assets—you can calculate the number of periods required to achieve a particular investment goal. If you use positive numbers for the *Present Value* argument, you can calculate the number of periods required to pay off a loan.

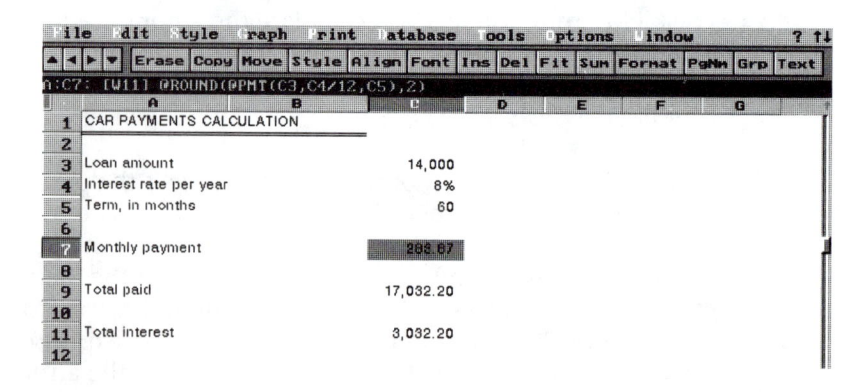

Using the @PMT function
Figure 7-9.

Functions

If you omit the Type argument, Quattro Pro assumes 0.

The syntax for the @NPER function is

@NPER(*Rate,Payment,Present Value,Future Value,Type*)

where *Rate* is the periodic interest rate and *Payment* is the amount of each payment. In the case of a loan repayment calculation, *Present Value* is the amount of the loan. In the case of an investment calculation, *Present Value* is the amount you have already invested, if any. The last two arguments are used only in investment calculations. *Future Value* is your financial goal and *Type* indicates whether the payments will be made at the beginning or end of each period, with 0 indicating the beginning and 1 indicating the end.

Let's start with an investment example: To calculate how many payments of $250 per month you would need to make to reach a goal of $20,000 when you are earning 9.5% interest per year and already have $3,000 invested, you would use the following formula:

```
@NPER(.095/12,-250,-3000,20000,0)
```

The answer is approximately 51 payments, which, at one payment per month, would take approximately 4 years and 3 months. If you find it easier to express the interest rate as a percent, you can enter

```
@NPER(9.5%/12,-250,-3000,20000)
```

To calculate how long it would take to pay off a $10,000 car loan in monthly $200 installments at an interest rate of 12%, you would enter the formula

```
@NPER(.12/12,-200,10000)
```

The answer is 70 months (or 69 months and about 20 days).

@CTERM

The @CTERM function determines how long it will take for a single investment to grow to a specified amount given a particular interest rate. The syntax for this function is

@CTERM(*Rate,Future Value,Present Value*)

where *Rate* is the periodic interest rate, *Future Value* is the investment goal, and *Present Value* is the amount you are investing. To calculate how long it will take for $10,000 to grow to $12,500 at a fixed interest rate of 10%, you would enter

```
@CTERM(.1,12500,10000)
```

Because the interest rate is expressed in years, the answer—the number 2—will also be expressed in years. For an answer expressed in months, use the monthly interest rate, in this case .1/12 or 10%/12.

@FVAL

If you omit the Type argument, Quattro Pro assumes 0.

The @FVAL function is only one of the many Quattro Pro functions that let you determine the value of an investment or compare the values of two investments. @FVAL calculates the future value of a series of equal periodic investments. Its syntax is

@FVAL(*Rate,Periods,Payment,Present Value,Type*)

where *Rate* is the periodic interest rate, *Periods* is the number of periods, and *Payment* is the amount of each payment. The *Present Value* and *Type* arguments are both optional. *Present Value* is the amount you have invested so far (if any), and a *Type* argument of 0 or 1 indicates whether the payments are made at the beginning or end of each period, respectively. Both the *Payment* and *Present Value* arguments should be expressed as negative numbers to indicate that they are cash outflows.

For example, to calculate the amount you will save if you invest $500 in a savings account at the beginning of each year, over a 5-year period, and earn 6.5% annual interest, you would enter

```
@FVAL(.065,5,-500)
```

The result is approximately $2,847. If you have already saved $1,000 and plan to make your $500 investments at the end of each year, you would enter

```
@FVAL(.065,5,-500,-1000,1)
```

with a result of approximately $4,402.

Getting Help with Functions

As you work with Quattro Pro, you will undoubtedly find applications for the functions introduced in this chapter, and you will probably start exploring other functions on your own. For a quick tour of Quattro Pro's functions or a quick reminder of a particular function's syntax, you may find it easiest to refer to Quattro Pro's Help system.

Functions

There are two ways to look up functions in the Help system. You can press `F1` from Ready mode, and select Functions from the Help Topics list to display the @Function Topics screen. If you are in the middle of entering a formula, you can press `Alt`-`F3` or click on the @ button on the Edit SpeedBar to display the Functions List, and then press `F1` to immediately display the Function Index. When you select a function from the @Function Index, Quattro Pro displays a help screen on the type of function you selected, with the syntax and a brief description of each function in the group.

This chapter has introduced you to only the most commonly used, general-purpose functions. There are about 100 functions not even mentioned here. Although several other functions are introduced in later chapters, most of the more specialized functions are not discussed at all. Once you begin to develop your own notebooks, take time to experiment with those groups of functions that are most relevent to your work.

CHAPTER

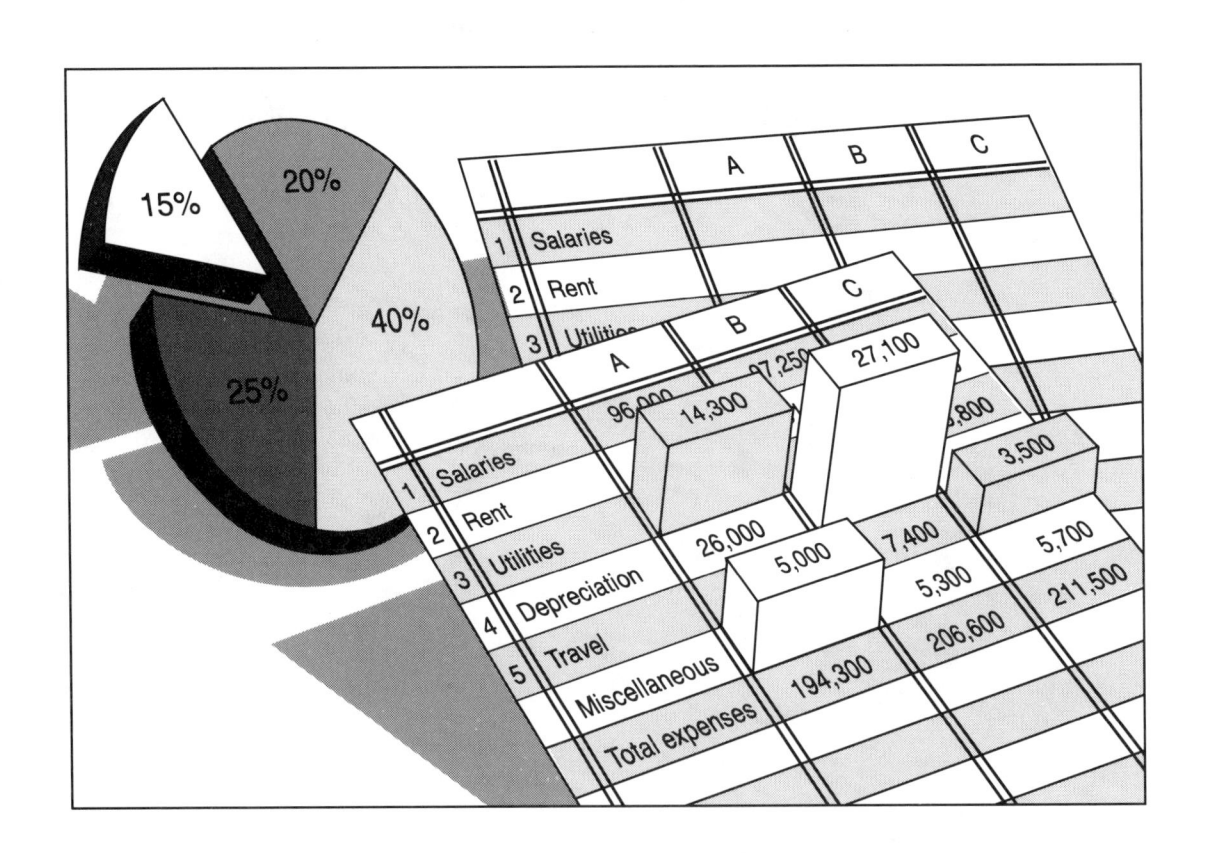

8

MORE ABOUT FORMULAS

This chapter covers four more advanced topics in formulas: using absolute references, using named blocks, converting formulas to their current values, and auditing your notebook. Defining absolute references and converting formulas to values allow you to exercise more control over your formulas—either by keeping them from changing when copied or by keeping them from responding to changes in other sections of the notebook. Named blocks make your formulas easier to enter and to read. The Audit feature helps you troubleshoot your notebook by pointing out circular references, cell dependencies, ERR values, and more.

Absolute Versus Relative Cell Referencing

When you copy formulas Quattro Pro generally "thinks" of the formula's cell references in terms of their position relative to the formula cell itself. For example, if you copy the formula (B1–B2) from B3 to E11, Quattro Pro translates the source formula into "subtract the value one cell above this one from the cell two cells above this one." When copied to E11, this formula becomes (E9–E10).

In some cases you may want some of the cell references in a formula to stay the same when copied to a new location. For example, in the LEARN1 notebook you multiplied several 1993 revenue and expense figures by 1.05 to arrive at the 1994 projections. Suppose, however, that you put the estimated rate of increase in a cell by itself and then referenced that cell in calculating the 1994 figures, as shown in Figure 8-1. This allows you to experiment with different rates simply by changing the value in a single cell (B5) rather than re-creating all the formulas in column C. However, if you entered the formula **+B11+(B11*B5)** in C11 and then copied that formula down the column, the new formulas would be wrong. For example, the formula in C12 would be +B12+(B12*B6) rather than +B12+(B12*B5). To

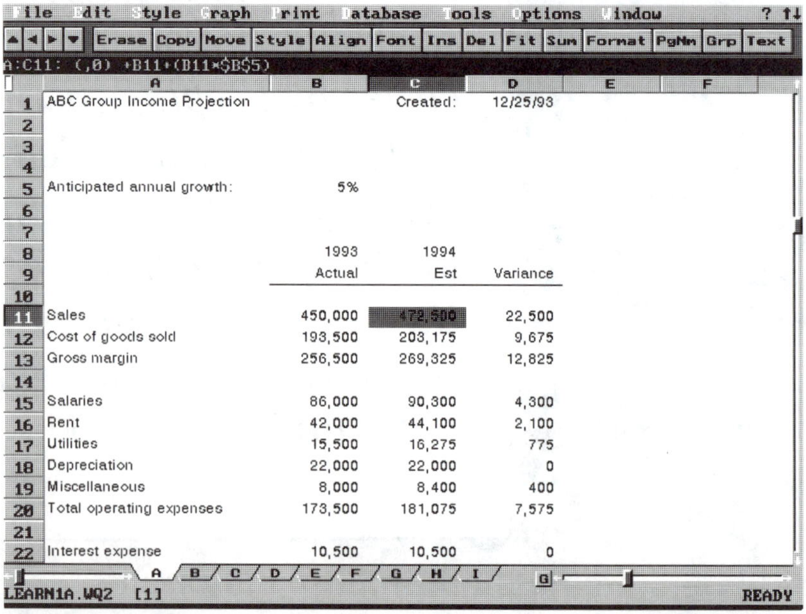

Using absolute references to reference a growth rate
Figure 8-1.

More About Formulas

keep the reference to cell B5 unchanged when copied, you must make that cell reference absolute by attaching it to one particular cell on the notebook.

Relative and absolute cell referencing can be compared to two sets of directions: "Go to the corner, turn left, walk past three houses, and enter the fourth" and "Go to the Smiths' house." The first set of directions is entirely relative to your current position; where it leads depends on where you are at the moment. The second set of directions is independent of your current position; it will always lead you to the same spot (the Smiths' house) regardless of your current location.

Note that an absolute reference is a reference, within a formula, that does not change when you *copy* the formula cell. However, if you do something to *move* the cell the formula refers to, the formula will be adjusted. In other words, if you have a formula in cell A10 that includes an absolute reference to cell C15, any copies you make of that formula will refer to C15. If you move cell C15 itself, however, all references to that cell will be adjusted accordingly, whether they're absolute or not. That is, making a reference absolute only affects what happens when you copy the formula cell. It doesn't change what happens when you move either the formula cell or the cell that the formula refers to.

You can also create mixed cell references, in which one coordinate is absolute and the other relative.

To make a cell reference absolute, you simply enter dollar signs ($) before its column, row, and page coordinates. You can type the dollar signs while entering or editing a formula, or you can use [F4], the Abs key. To use the Abs key while entering a formula, just type in a cell reference and then press [F4]. To use the Abs key when editing a formula, press [F4] while the cursor is on or immediately after the cell reference you want to change. As soon as you press [F4], Quattro Pro immediately inserts dollar signs before all three coordinates of the cell reference that is at or just to the left of the cursor, making the entire reference absolute. If you press [F4] repeatedly, Quattro Pro cycles through the following eight possibilities:

Option	Example
All three coordinates absolute	$A:$B$5
Page and row coordinate absolute	$A:B$5
Page and column coordinate absolute	$A:$B5
Page coordinate absolute	$A:B5
Column and row coordinates absolute	+A:$B$5
Row coordinate absolute	+A:B$5
Column coordinate absolute	+A:$B5
All coordinates relative	+A:B5

Quattro Pro 5 Made Easy

> As an alternative, you could use the formula (1+$B$5)*B11.

If you're using a mouse, you can employ the Abs button on the Edit SpeedBar instead of F4. Generally, you should use absolute references when you want several formulas in a single row or column to refer to the same cell. In the previous example, the reference to the increase rate in B5 should be absolute so it doesn't change when you copy the formula to other rows. Leave the reference to B11 relative, however, because you want this reference to change when copied. The appropriate formula for C11, therefore, is +B11+(B11*$B$5).

You also should use absolute cell references when you refer to lookup tables with the @VLOOKUP or @HLOOKUP functions. Generally, you want the reference to the lookup table block—which is a group of cells outside the main body of the notebook—to stay the same when copied. This requires designating both corners of the block as absolute. The other option is to place the lookup table on a separate notebook page. You'll learn more about working with notebook pages in Chapter 12.

Another rule of thumb is that you should use relative references when referring to a cell in the same row as the formula cell if you intend to copy the formula down a column, or in the same column as the formula cell if you intend to copy the formula across a row.

Take a moment to experiment with relative and absolute cell references.

1. Unless your notebook area is already blank, save your work and then issue the / **File** | **Erase** command.
2. Issue the / **Options** | **Formats** | **Numeric Format** | **Fixed** command. Press Enter to accept the default setting of two decimal places.
3. Select Global Width from the Options | Formats menu and enter **15**.
4. Type **Q** (for Quit) twice to return to Ready mode.
5. Enter **Sales Commissions Spreadsheet** in A1; enter **Commission rate** in A3; enter **.15** in B3; enter **Invoice amount** in A6; enter **200** in A7; enter **150** in A8; enter **250** in A9; enter **100** in A10; enter **275** in A11; and enter **Commission** in B6.

Now try entering a formula to calculate the commission on each sale. First see what happens if you enter a formula using all relative references in B7, and then copy that formula down the column.

1. Move to B7 and enter **+A7*B3**.
2. Issue the / **Edit** | **Copy** command (Ctrl-C or the Copy button). Press Enter to accept the default source block of A:B7..B7, and specify a destination block of A:B7..B11. Your notebook should now look like the one in Figure 8-2.

More About Formulas

```
File Edit Style Graph Print Database Tools Options Window        ? ↑↓
     Erase Copy Move Style Align Font Ins Del Fit Sum Format PgNm Grp Text
A:B7: (F2) +A7*B3
          A              B           C           D           E
  1  Sales Commissions Spreadsheet
  2
  3  Commission rate         0.15
  4
  5
  6  Invoice amount       Commission
  7         200.00            30.00
  8         150.00             0.00
  9         250.00             0.00
 10         100.00             0.00
 11         275.00          8250.00
 12
```

Problems in copying relative cell references
Figure 8-2.

The reference to B3 is relative, so it changes to B4 when the formula is copied to B8, B5 when copied to B9, and so on. The result is a series of useless formulas. The number 0 appears in B8, B9, and B10 because the formulas in those cells multiply the value to their left by a cell with a value of 0 (B4, B5, and B6). The number 8250 appears in B11 because the formula in that cell multiplies the cell to the left (275) by the value in B7 (30).

Now make the reference to B3 (the cell containing the commission rate) absolute in B7's formula. From B7, press F2 to get into Edit mode and then press F4 or the Abs button on the Edit SpeedBar. The formula should change to +A7*$A:$B$3. (Notice that A7 is not changed, since the cursor was not on that cell reference.) Press Enter and then issue the / Edit | Copy command a second time. Accept the default source block of A:B7..B7, and specify a destination of A:B7..B11. Your notebook should now look like the one shown in Figure 8-3. This time the first cell reference in the formula (A7)

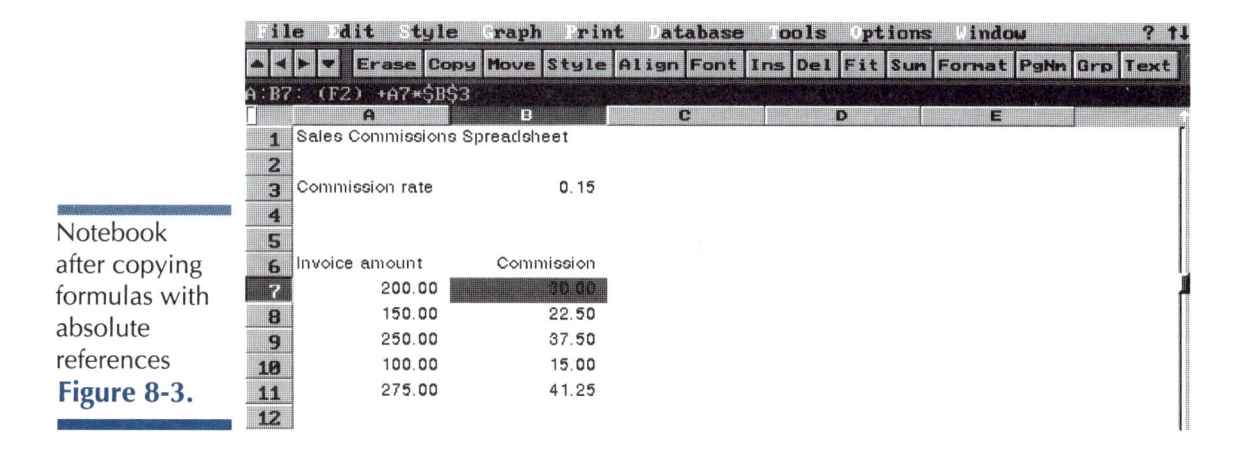

```
File Edit Style Graph Print Database Tools Options Window        ? ↑↓
     Erase Copy Move Style Align Font Ins Del Fit Sum Format PgNm Grp Text
A:B7: (F2) +A7*$B$3
          A              B           C           D           E
  1  Sales Commissions Spreadsheet
  2
  3  Commission rate         0.15
  4
  5
  6  Invoice amount       Commission
  7         200.00            30.00
  8         150.00            22.50
  9         250.00            37.50
 10         100.00            15.00
 11         275.00            41.25
 12
```

Notebook after copying formulas with absolute references
Figure 8-3.

changes to reference whatever cell is located immediately to the left as you copy it down the block, while the second cell reference (B3) remains stable.

Mixed Cell References

As mentioned, you also can make one cell coordinate absolute while leaving the other relative. When you copy formulas containing such mixed references, the absolute coordinate remains the same, while the relative one changes in relation to the location of the formula on the notebook. This can be useful in some cases where you want to copy a formula across more than one row or down more than one column.

For example, the notebook in Figure 8-4 was constructed by entering the formula +B6/B$12 in cell C6 and copying that formula to C6..C10 and E6..E10. The resulting formulas calculate the percentage of total sales represented by each of several products. The reference to row 12 is made absolute because the total number of units sold is always in that row. If the row coordinate were relative, it would change when copied down columns.

If you were copying the original formula down only column C, you could make the entire reference to cell B12 absolute, so that the formula would be +B6/$B$12. By leaving the column coordinate relative, however, you allow all the references to column B to change to column D as you copy the formula down column E. As the formula is copied to cell E6, for example, it becomes +D6/D$12.

Using Named Blocks

So far you have designated blocks by using the coordinates of their corner cells. Quattro Pro also allows you to assign names to blocks of cells and to

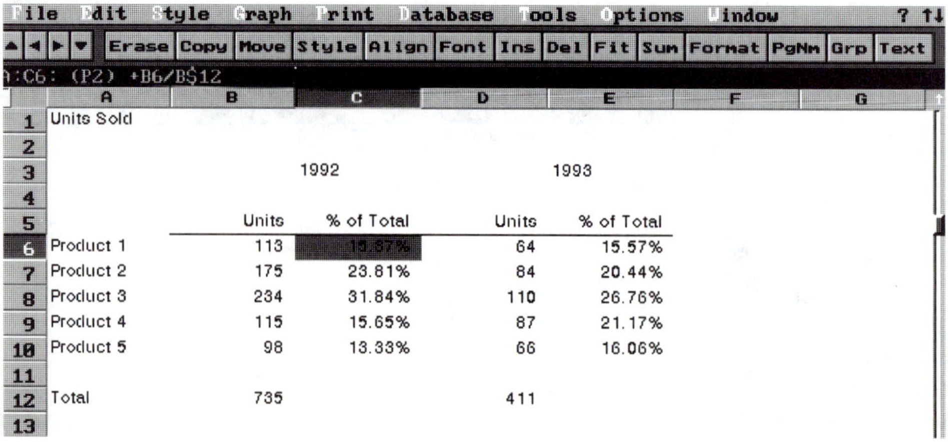

A spreadsheet with mixed cell references
Figure 8-4.

More About Formulas

As you'll learn in Chapter 12, you can also assign names to notebook pages.

refer to those blocks—in formulas, functions, and commands—by name rather than by coordinates.

Using block names can make formulas more understandable. For example, if you name a block of cells containing a tax rate lookup table TAX TABLE, you can enter lookup formulas by this name rather than by less informative coordinates. Block names are also easier to remember than block coordinates. In most cases a name like FEB EXPENSE comes to mind more quickly than coordinates such as G17..G29. In addition, using block names increases accuracy. If you make a mistake when you enter block coordinates, Quattro Pro has no way of catching your error. If you specify a nonexistent block name in a command or formula, however, Quattro Pro immediately displays an error message.

F3 works only if there is already at least one named block in the current notebook.

When entering or editing formulas, you can use F3, the Choices key, to reference named blocks in formulas or commands. F3 displays a menu of all the named blocks on the current notebook, as shown in the following illustration. To select a block name from this list, move the cursor to the name and press Enter, or point and click with your mouse. You can also use the Choices key to move quickly to different sections of the notebook—pressing F5 (GoTo) and then F3 (Choices) and selecting a block name from the list. Quattro Pro moves the cell pointer to the upper-left corner of the specified block. The Choices key is covered in more depth in a moment.

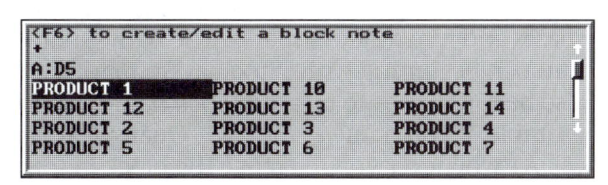

```
<F6> to create/edit a block note
+
A:D5
PRODUCT 1      PRODUCT 10     PRODUCT 11
PRODUCT 12     PRODUCT 13     PRODUCT 14
PRODUCT 2      PRODUCT 3      PRODUCT 4
PRODUCT 5      PRODUCT 6      PRODUCT 7
```

When you name a block, Quattro Pro adjusts all formulas that currently reference that block. For example, if your notebook already contains formulas that reference the block D4..G12 when you assign that block a name, Quattro Pro displays the block name on the input line (in place of the block coordinates) whenever you move the cell pointer to one of those formulas. If you delete the block name later, the formulas revert to referencing the block coordinates. If you edit a formula that references a named block, Quattro Pro displays the block's coordinates (rather than its name) on the input line until you press Enter. This allows you to change one or more of the block coordinates.

Quattro Pro also makes appropriate adjustments in the coordinates of a named block when you insert or delete rows within the block's borders or if you move the entire block. As with any block, you must be careful not to overwrite the corner cells of named blocks with / **E**dit | **M**ove. Even if you refer to a block by name, Quattro Pro still identifies it by its corner cells. If you overwrite those coordinates, Quattro Pro "loses its place" and returns ERR values in those cells and in any formulas that reference them. You also need to be careful not to accidentally expand the block: If you use / **E**dit | **M**ove to move one of the block's corner cells without moving the other, Quattro Pro expands the block to include all cells between the corner cells.

As with other cell references, you must precede block names at the beginning of formulas with a parenthesis or arithmetic operator to inform Quattro Pro that you are entering a value rather than a label. This is true even when you pull the block name from the Choices list.

When you refer to a block by name you can place a dollar sign before it (by either typing **$** or pressing [F4]) to make all the block coordinates absolute. Unfortunately, you cannot make a named block absolute by typing **$** and then popping up a Choices list using [F3]. Also, if you type a plus sign (or other arithmetic operator), select a name from the Choices list, and then press [F4] (Abs) or click on Abs on the Edit SpeedBar, Quattro Pro simply beeps.

Naming a Block

The simplest way to create a named block is to issue the / **E**dit | **N**ames | **C**reate command. Quattro Pro prompts for a "name to create/modify." Block names can be up to 15 characters long and can include any character, including spaces and punctuation marks. The name should always start with a letter or a number; beginning with punctuation marks can cause problems. You should also be careful not to create a block name that looks like a cell reference. For example, if you name a block A1, Quattro Pro assumes you are referring to the cell A1 whenever you reference the block in formulas or commands.

If you assign the same name to more than one block at the same time, Quattro Pro simply assigns that name to the new block and removes it from the old one. Although it is possible to assign more than one name to the same block, it is not recommended. If you highlight a formula that references that block, Quattro Pro displays only one of the names (the most recently assigned one) on the input line. It is, however, permissible to create a named block that includes another named block.

The Choices Key

You can also click the Name button on the Edit SpeedBar to display the list of named blocks.

The Choices key, [F3], has different functions in different contexts. If you press this key while in Ready mode, Quattro Pro simply activates the menu bar, as if you had typed a slash (/). If you are entering a formula or issuing a command and you have already named one or more blocks of cells on the current notebook, [F3] displays a list of all those named blocks. Before displaying a list of block names while entering a formula, you must get to a

More About Formulas

point where it would make sense to enter a cell or block reference—such as after typing the characters @SUM(or @AVG(, or after typing an arithmetic operator such as a plus or minus sign. Once the Choices list is on screen, pressing [F3] zooms the list so that it occupies a larger portion of the screen.

If the list of block names is too long to fit in the Choices box, you can use the cursor-movement keys or the scroll bar to scroll through the list. To see the coordinates of the blocks, type a plus sign (+). Type a minus sign (–) to remove the coordinates from the display.

If you have not yet named any blocks of cells on the notebook and you press [F3] while building a formula, Quattro Pro automatically enters Point mode, if the last character was an operator or opening parenthesis. If the last character you typed was neither an operator nor a parenthesis, Quattro Pro accepts the entry (as though you had pressed [Enter]) and activates the menu system (as if you had typed /).

An Exercise in Naming Cells

To name a single-cell block on your current notebook, follow these steps:

1. Move to B3 and issue the / **E**dit | **N**ames | **C**reate command. When prompted for "name to create/modify," enter **COMMISSION RATE**. Accept the default block coordinates of A:B3..B3. Then move through the formulas in column C and note that they now all reference $COMMISSION RATE rather than $B$3.

2. Move to B7 and issue the / **E**dit | **N**ames | **C**reate command again. This time enter **COMMISSIONS** as the name to create/modify. Press [End]-[↓] to expand the block to A:B7..B11, and then press [Enter].

3. Move to B12 and enter "---------- to draw a row of dashes under the commissions list.

4. Move to B13 and type **@SUM(**. Press [F3] to display a list of currently named blocks. Note that the mode indicator changes to NAMES, indicating that Quattro Pro is expecting you to select a block name from the list.

5. Type **+** to expand the menu to include the block coordinates on the Choices list, and then select COMMISSIONS from the list, inserting that block name into your formula.

6. Type **)** or click on) on the Edit SpeedBar and press [Enter] to finish entering the formula @SUM(COMMISSIONS) into your notebook.

7. Issue the / **S**tyle | **N**umeric Format | **P**ercent command. Enter **0** as the number of decimal places. When prompted for a block to modify, press

F3 and select COMMISSION RATE from the list of block names. Your notebook should now look like Figure 8-5.

8. Press Home to move to A1. Press F5 and, when prompted for an address to go to, press F3. Select COMMISSIONS from the list to move directly to the upper-left corner of that block.

As you can see, even on a small and simple notebook, block names can make your formulas more readable. They also make it easier to reference blocks when entering formulas or issuing commands. These advantages are magnified on larger, more complex notebooks, and also hold true for named pages, which are covered in Chapter 12. The judicious use of block names is an excellent tool for clarifying your formulas and increasing your efficiency.

Changing and Deleting Block Names

Once you have created a block name, you can change the block to which the name refers. To do so, you simply issue the / **E**dit | **N**ames | **C**reate command again, pick that block name from the list of named blocks, and designate a different set of coordinates for the name. There is no direct method of changing the name assigned to a particular block, however. If you decide to change a block name, simply create another block with a different name but the same coordinates. Then delete the old name for the block.

You can delete a block name by issuing the / **E**dit | **N**ames | **D**elete command and selecting the name you want to delete from the menu of block names. You can also delete all the block names on a worksheet by issuing the / **E**dit |

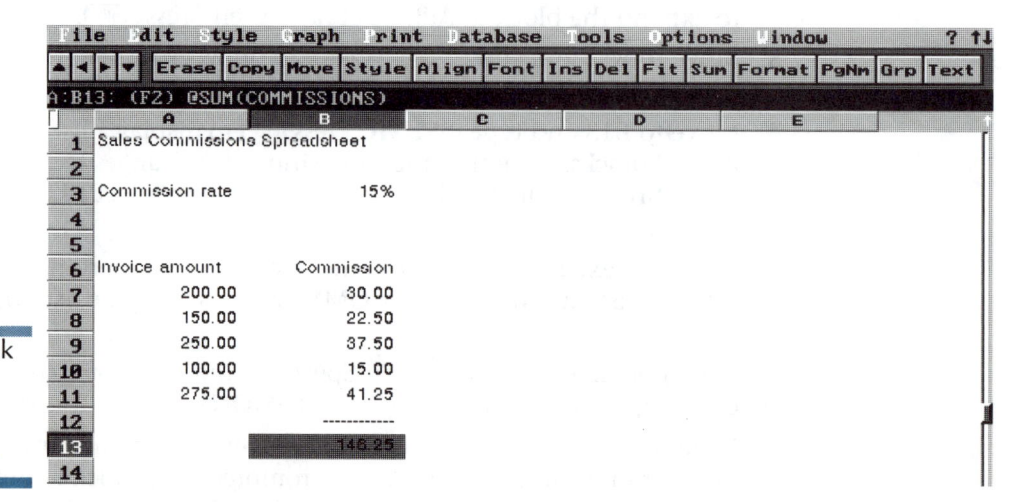

Using a block name in a formula
Figure 8-5.

More About Formulas

Names | **R**eset command. Be extremely careful with this command, however. If you delete one or all of your block names accidentally, use / **E**dit | **U**ndo immediately to restore them. If you have performed any other undoable operation since deleting one or more block names, there is no way to retrieve them.

Naming Blocks Using Adjacent Labels

The / **E**dit | **N**ames | **L**abels command uses the labels in a specified block to name a set of cells adjacent to that block. The specified block must fall within a single row or a single column. When you issue the / **E**dit | **N**ames | **L**abels command, Quattro Pro displays a submenu containing four options—Right, Down, Left, and Up—that determine which cells will be named by the command. If you choose Down, for example, Quattro Pro assigns the names to the cells located below the specified block of labels.

Once you have chosen an option from the Labels submenu, Quattro Pro prompts for a block of labels. If the block you specify contains labels that are longer than the 15-character limit for block names, Quattro Pro simply drops the extra characters. If the specified block contains values, they are ignored rather than used as names for the adjacent cells. Quattro Pro also ignores any blank cells in the block, which allows you to use this command with a block of labels that includes empty rows or columns.

In certain situations, / **E**dit | **N**ames | **L**abels can be an efficient way to assign names to an entire set of single-cell blocks. It is often used to label a set of cells with a group of adjacent column or row headings. It can also be used to name single-cell blocks using text already entered in an adjacent cell.

Try inserting a new column at the left edge of the notebook, entering invoice numbers, and then using those invoice numbers as block names for the invoice amounts in the adjacent column.

1. Press (Home) to move to A1, issue the / **E**dit | **I**nsert | **C**olumns command, and press (Enter) to accept the default of A:A1..A1 when prompted for a column insert block.
2. Issue the / **E**dit | **M**ove command, enter a source block of **B1..C3**, and accept the default destination of A:A1.
3. Enter **Inv. 111** in A7; enter **Inv. 112** in A8; enter **Inv. 113** in A9; enter **Inv. 114** in A10; and enter **Inv. 115** in A11.
4. Issue the / **E**dit | **N**ames | **L**abels command. Select Right from the submenu. Press (End)-(↑) to expand the label block to A11..A7 and press (Enter). You have named all the cells in the block B11..B7—the block to the right of A11..A7. You can prove this by examining the formulas in

C7 through C11 and noting that they now refer to cells in column B by name rather than by address, as shown on the input line in Figure 8-6.

Creating a Table of Block Names

The / Edit | Names | Make Table command creates a table of all the current named blocks on the notebook, including both the names and coordinates of the blocks. The table looks much like the expanded menu displayed with the Choices key. It is useful primarily when you are documenting the notebook by printing its formulas or when there are too many named blocks to fit within the Choices window. When you issue the / Edit | Names | Make Table command, Quattro Pro prompts you for a block in which to place the table. You need only specify the upper-left corner of this destination block.

The table created with / Edit | Names | Make Table is not updated if you add, delete, or change any named blocks. If you make such modifications, be careful to reissue the / Edit | Names | Make Table command.

Attaching Notes to Named Blocks

You can attach notes to named blocks to help you remember their purpose. When you display the list of block names, these notes appear whenever their associated blocks are highlighted. In addition, when you issue the / Edit | Names | Make Table command, the resulting table of block names includes block name notes.

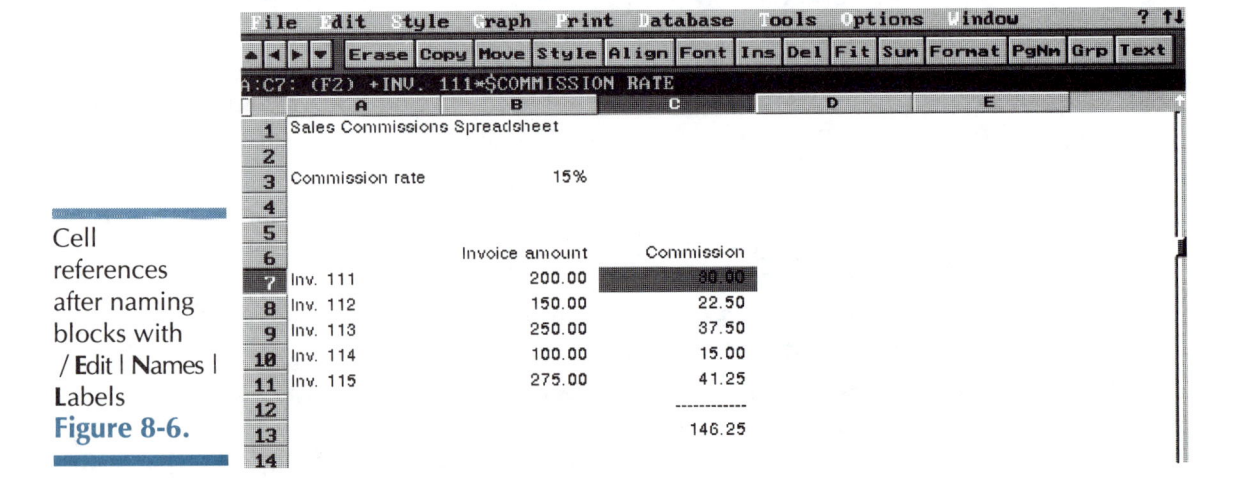

You can enter notes of up to 71 characters.

Cell references after naming blocks with / Edit | Names | Labels
Figure 8-6.

More About Formulas

Follow these steps to attach a note to the COMMISSION RATE block:

1. Issue the / **E**dit | **N**ames | **C**reate command, highlight the COMMISSION RATE named block, and press [F6].
2. At the prompt "Enter note to be attached to name," type **Rate as of 6/1/94** and press [Enter] or click on Enter. Your note should appear above COMMISSION RATE in the list of named blocks. (These notes appear when their named block is highlighted.)

To edit an existing note, simply highlight the desired named block, press [F6], and proceed to edit the note. You can navigate using [→], [←], [Home], and [End]. In addition, you can press [Ctrl]-[Backspace] to delete the entire text of the note and begin from scratch. When you're done, press [Enter] or click on Enter to incorporate your changes.

Converting Formulas to Their Values

Occasionally you will want a formula to stop acting like one; that is, you will want it to return the same result regardless of changes in other cells on the notebook. Quattro Pro provides the / **E**dit | **V**alues command for effectively freezing formulas. This command can be used to replace a block of formulas with their current results, transforming them into the numeric values or text currently displayed on the notebook. For example, / **E**dit | **V**alues would change the formula (1+2) to the value 3; it would replace the formula (A1–A2) with whatever value that formula returns at the time you issue the command.

You can use / **E**dit | **V**alues to prevent a cell from responding to changes in other cells. You may also want to use formulas to derive data initially, but then keep the results of those calculations stable. For example, you might create a budget for next year using formulas based on the current year's revenues and expenses. Once the budget has been approved, however, you want it to remain unchanged as you update figures for the current fiscal year.

Another reason for using / **E**dit | **V**alues is that values take up less space than formulas in memory and on disk. If you no longer need your formulas to respond to changes in data, you can save space, particularly in large notebooks, by converting all formulas to their values.

/ **E**dit | **V**alues works exactly like / **E**dit | **C**opy, except it transforms the source block as it copies by replacing formulas with their current results. When you issue the / **E**dit | **V**alues command, Quattro Pro asks for a source block and then a destination. Unless you plan to make duplicate copies of the source block, you need only specify the upper-left corner of the destination. Although you can use / **Edit** | **Values** to create a duplicate copy of the source block in another spot on the notebook, more often you will copy the source block over itself by using the block's upper-left corner as the destination.

Try the / **Edit** | **Values** command now:

1. Move to cell C7 and then issue the / **Edit** | **Values** command. Press [End]-[↓] to expand the source block to A:C7..C13 and press [Enter]. Specify a destination of D7.
2. Move through the cells in D7..D13 and notice that Quattro Pro displays numbers rather than formulas on the input line.
3. Move to D6, and enter the label **Commission at 15%**.
4. Change the value in B3 to 0.14. Then save the notebook as **COMMISS** so you can use it in the next chapter. Your notebook should now look like Figure 8-7. The change in commission rate had no effect on the values in column D, because those cells contain numeric constants rather than formulas.

Quattro Pro has a shortcut for changing individual cells to their values. Rather than using the / **Edit** | **Values** command and designating the same single cell as the source block and destination, you can simply press [F9], the Calc key, or click the Calc button on the Edit SpeedBar while you are either entering or editing the cell's data.

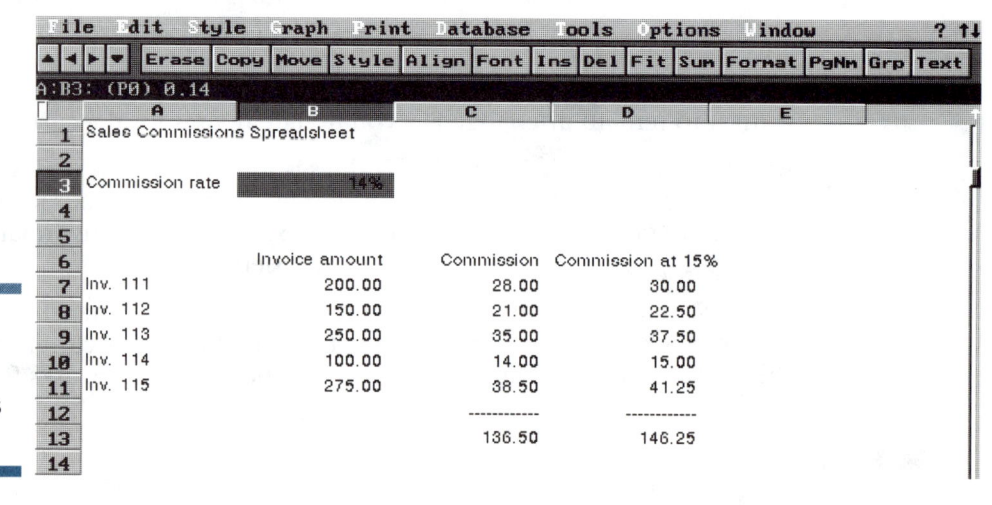

Changing the commission rate after / **Edit** | **Values**
Figure 8-7.

	A	B	C	D
1	Sales Commissions Spreadsheet			
2				
3	Commission rate	14%		
4				
5				
6		Invoice amount	Commission	Commission at 15%
7	Inv. 111	200.00	28.00	30.00
8	Inv. 112	150.00	21.00	22.50
9	Inv. 113	250.00	35.00	37.50
10	Inv. 114	100.00	14.00	15.00
11	Inv. 115	275.00	38.50	41.25
12			------------	------------
13			136.50	146.25
14				

More About Formulas

Using the Audit Feature

Quattro Pro's Audit feature is an excellent tool for both understanding and debugging your notebook. It can display graphic representations of circular cell references. It can diagram cell relationships so you can see in advance how changes to one cell will affect other, dependent, cells. It can also help you hunt down references to labels, blank cells, cells that return an ERR value, and cells that include formulas that refer to cells in other notebooks.

Viewing Dependencies

The / **Tools** | Au**d**it | **D**ependency command lets you know which cells in the notebook are dependent on other cells. For example, in the Sales Commissions notebook, cell C13 is *dependent* on cells C7 through C11, since it contains a formula that sums all of those cells. Prove this to yourself now by issuing the / **Tools** | Au**d**it | **D**ependency command from within the Sales Commissions notebook and selecting C7..C13 as the block to be audited. You should see a screen resembling Figure 8-8.

The data for the first cell in the selected block is shown first. This cell, which is highlighted, is also known as the *active* cell—the cell for which Quattro Pro displays any dependencies. The tree diagram in the figure tells you that C13 depends on C7 for data, and that C7 depends on both B3, the commission rate, and B7, the invoice amount.

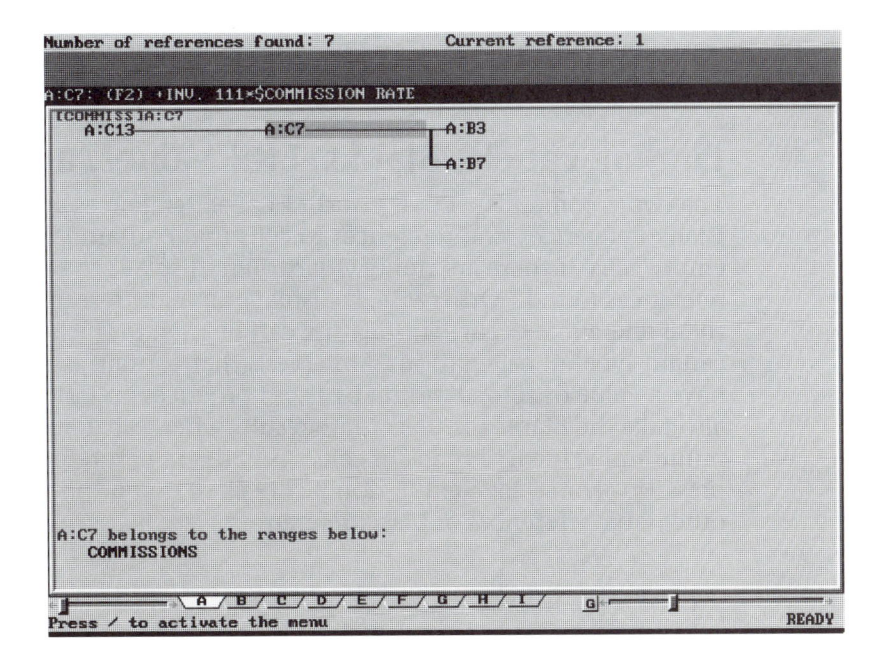

Audit screen showing cell dependencies
Figure 8-8.

You can move around the current diagram with the arrow keys or with your mouse. You can also change the active cell and see further dependencies in the notebook by pressing [Pg Dn] or by using the Next option on the audit screen menu that pops up when you press the forward slash (/). In this example, pressing [Pg Dn] will take you to C8, then to C9, and so on. You can press [Pg Up] or select the Previous option to view previous cells. You can also select the GoTo option from the audit screen menu or press [F5] to return to the notebook—you'll be located in the cell that was last active in the audit screen. In addition, you can use the Begin option (or the [Enter] key) to activate the highlighted cell, showing its dependent cells, if any. Finally, you can select the Quit option (or press [Esc]) to return to the notebook.

Auditing Circular References

Circular references in formulas refer, directly or indirectly, to the cell that contains the formula.

As you learned in Chapter 3, circular references in formulas can lead to very inaccurate results. The / **W**indow | **O**ptions | **M**ap View command (covered in Chapter 11) tells you whether cells contain circular references. However, the / **T**ools | Au**d**it | **C**ircular command provides many more details about circular references, mapping out the entire chain of formulas that constitute the referential circle. When you issue this command, Quattro Pro displays a tree diagram showing any circular references in your notebook. (If there are none, you receive the error message "No circular references found.")

After you've located a circular reference with the / **T**ools | Au**d**it | **C**ircular command, it's particularly critical to press [Pg Dn] or choose Next to search for additional circular references in your notebook, since Quattro Pro does not warn you if there are any. You can navigate through audit screens that are displayed using the same methods you used in the dependencies screen.

Finding Labels, Blanks, ERR Values, and Links

The two commands / **T**ools | Au**d**it | **L**abel References and / **T**ools | Au**d**it | **B**lank References find references to cells that contain labels and references to empty cells. If there are none, Quattro Pro displays the message "No such references found." Otherwise, it displays an audit screen that tells you where these references occur. This feature can be used to track down errors in certain types of calculations. Since cells that contain labels are considered to have a value of zero, dividing by them produces an ERR result. Labels can also take the blame for inaccurate results when calculating the average or minimum value in a block of cells. As with circular references, make sure to press [Pg Dn] or select Next to double-check that your notebook contains no other label references or blank references.

The / **T**ools | Au**d**it | **E**RR command finds cells that contain ERR values. Like the other Audit commands, it finds the first instance; make sure to press `Pg Dn` or select Next to find other cells that contain ERR.

The / **T**ools | Au**d**it | E**x**ternal Links command points out cells that include formulas that refer to cells in other notebooks. For more information on linking notebooks, consult Chapter 19.

You can also use the / **T**ools | Au**d**it | De**s**tination command if you want to send audit information to the printer (it's sent to the screen by default). However, be forewarned that Quattro Pro devotes one page to every cell in the audit block, which can result in a voluminous printout.

This chapter has introduced several techniques that enable you to manipulate formulas more easily. Absolute references allow you to copy formulas without necessarily adjusting all the references to fit their new locations. Named blocks make the formulas easier to read, offering a simple and rather elegant means of clarifying and documenting the notebook's logic. In addition, this chapter introduced / **E**dit | **V**alues—a tool for converting formulas to their results—and the Audit feature, an invaluable debugging tool.

CHAPTER

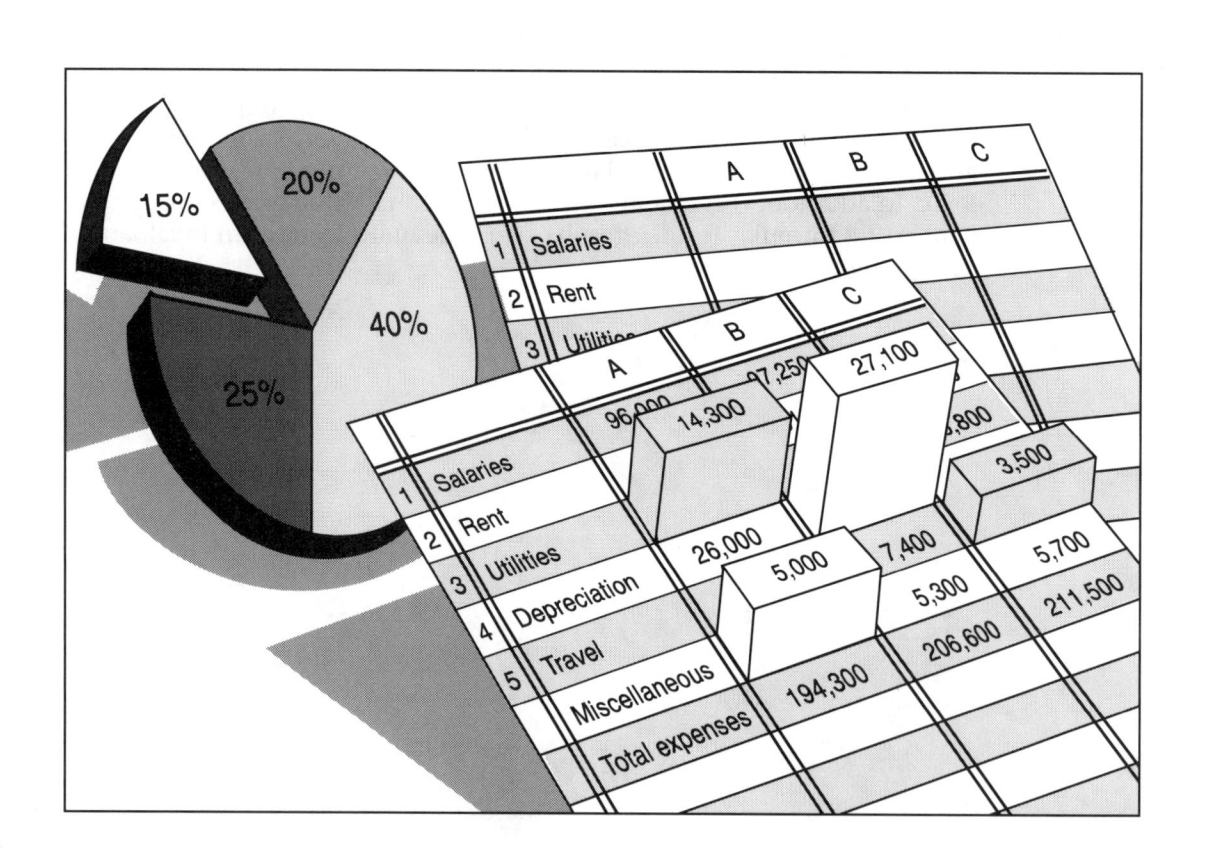

9

ADVANCED EDITING AND FORMATTING COMMANDS

*This chapter introduces a range of more advanced and specialized tools for changing the layout of data on the notebook. It covers all the commands on the Edit and Style menus that you have not already learned. These include a command for replacing one set of characters with another (/ **E**dit | **S**earch & Replace), for filling a block with sequential values (/ **E**dit | **F**ill), for word-wrapping text within a block (/ **T**ools |*

Reformat), for transposing (turning sideways) blocks of data (/ **E**dit | **T**ranspose), and for temporarily hiding one or more columns (/ **S**tyle | **H**ide Column). You will use most of these commands only occasionally, but when you do need them, they are extremely useful. This chapter also introduces Quattro Pro's protection feature, with which you can prevent inadvertent changes to your notebook. This feature is invaluable, particularly if you create notebooks to be used by others.

Searching and Replacing

Quattro Pro's / **E**dit | **S**earch & Replace command allows you to search for a specified set of characters and replace them with a different set. You must supply Quattro Pro with at least two pieces of information before initiating a search: a sequence of characters to look for (the search string), and a sequence of characters to replace them with (the replace string). The maximum length for both the search string and the replace string is 254 characters. Be careful not to include any unintended blank spaces when defining both the search and replace strings; Quattro Pro treats these blanks as characters just like any other.

CAUTION: If you conduct a search and replace operation without defining a replace string, Quattro Pro replaces each occurrence of the search string with nothing—in effect, deleting it from the notebook.

You can only delete a search block setting with Options Reset, which wipes out all Search & Replace settings.

The Block setting in the Edit | Search & Replace menu directs Quattro Pro to look for the search string within a particular section of the notebook. You can define a block within the current notebook page, or you can tell Quattro Pro to search a designated area within multiple pages by defining a 3-D search block. (3-D blocks are discussed in more detail in Chapter 12.) If you do not define a block, Quattro Pro searches the entire notebook. Even if you have a small notebook, defining a search block can prevent you from changing more data than you intend.

When it performs a search, Quattro Pro eventually finds every occurrence of the search string within the search block or, if no block was specified, the notebook. Three factors determine the order in which Quattro Pro will find these occurrences: the current position of the cell pointer, the option you choose to initiate the search (Next or Previous), and the Direction setting.

Quattro Pro always starts the search from the first page of the notebook. Within the first page, it begins searching from the current position of the cell pointer or, if the cell pointer is outside the search block or the area that contains data, from one corner of the search block or the area that contains data. If you want Quattro Pro to find occurrences of the search string in a particular order, move the cell pointer to the desired starting point before you initiate the search.

If you initiate the search with the Next option, Quattro Pro searches forward (moving down and right) from the current position of the cell pointer or from the upper-left corner of the search block (if the cell pointer is outside that block). If you use the Previous option to start the search, Quattro Pro searches backwards (moving up and to the left) from the current position of the cell pointer or from the lower-right corner of the search block (if the cell pointer is outside that block).

The Direction setting determines whether Quattro Pro searches by row or by column. If you select Row (the default), Quattro Pro searches from left to right in the first row of the specified block, then moves to the next row, and so on. If you select Column, Quattro Pro searches from top to bottom in the leftmost column, and then moves to the next column.

Performing the Search

If Quattro Pro does not find your search string within the specified block, it displays the error message "Not found." At this point you can press [Esc] or [Enter] to return to Ready mode. Otherwise Quattro Pro stops when it finds the first occurrence of the search string and moves the cell pointer to the cell in which the occurrence was found so you can see the cell contents on the input line. Quattro Pro then displays a menu with the five options Yes, No, All, Edit, and Quit.

The Yes option replaces an occurrence of the search string with the replace string, finds the next occurrence, and redisplays this menu. The No option does not replace an occurrence of the search string, but finds the next occurrence (if any) and redisplays this menu. The All option replaces occurrences of the search string found within the search block or, if no block has been specified, within the notebook—without redisplaying this menu. The Edit option does not replace an occurrence of the search string but allows editing of the cell in which the occurrence was found. When you select this option, Quattro Pro displays the contents of the cell on the input line and immediately places you in Edit mode. As soon as you press [Enter] or a cursor-movement key other than [←] or [→], Quattro Pro accepts your changes and looks for the next occurrence of the search string. Finally, the Quit option cancels the operation without performing any more replacements, and returns to Ready mode.

Try using / **E**dit | **S**earch & Replace to change "Inv." to "Invoice" in column A of the COMMISS.WQ2 notebook.

1. Press [Home] to move to A1 and issue the / **E**dit | **S**earch & Replace command.

2. Select Block and specify A7..A11.
3. Select Search String and enter **Inv.** (including the period at the end).
4. Select Replace String and enter the word **Invoice**.
5. Select Next to initiate the search. Quattro Pro stops at "Inv." in A7.
6. Select Yes to replace this first occurrence of the search string with the replace string and continue the search.
7. When Quattro Pro stops at the next occurrence of the search string, select All, directing Quattro Pro to replace all the remaining occurrences of the search string without waiting for your confirmation. Your notebook should now look like Figure 9-1.

You can also use the Search & Replace command to find and replace numeric digits—either within labels or within numeric values. In fact, whenever it conducts a search, Quattro Pro treats all cell entries like text, ignoring the meaning of the characters and looking only for an apparent match. This means that if you specify a search string of "100," Quattro Pro finds and replaces the "100" both in the value 100,000 and in the label "Invoice 1001." If this is not what you intend, you should be careful to replace occurrences of the search string one at a time rather than selecting the All option and having Quattro Pro replace the occurrences without your verification.

The Other Search & Replace Options

There are several other options on the Search & Replace menu that you can use to refine a search and replace operation. For instance, the Look In setting

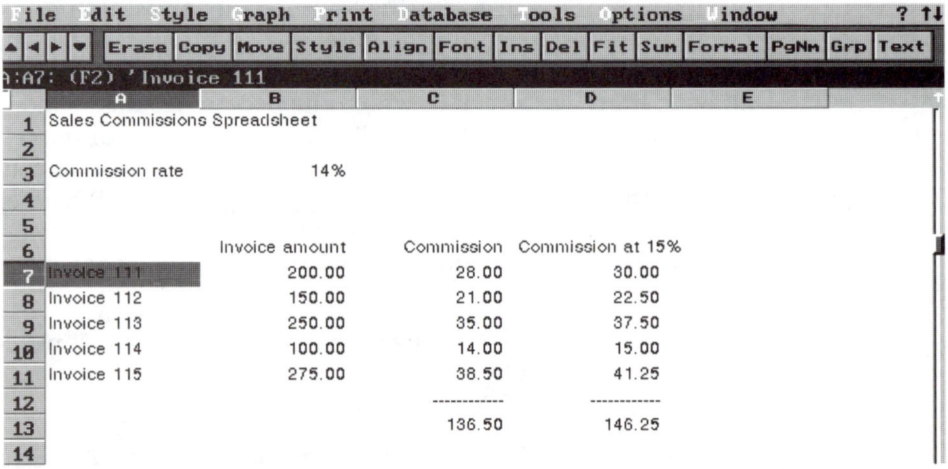

COMMISS.WQ2 after the search and replace operation
Figure 9-1.

Advanced Editing and Formatting Commands

determines what data Quattro Pro looks at in its search. The default setting, Formula, directs Quattro Pro to look for the search string within the formulas themselves. This setting finds values as they are stored—that is, as they appear on the input line. In contrast, if you select Value, Quattro Pro looks at the current values of formulas—that is, it examines the characters that appear on the notebook rather than at the formulas on which they are based. This setting finds values as they are displayed on the screen rather than as they appear on the input line. Both settings tell Quattro Pro to look at labels and numbers as well as formulas when conducting the search.

You cannot select Condition unless the search string is already a condition.

The third choice for the Look In setting—the Condition option—directs Quattro Pro to treat the search string as a condition. When entering the search string, either start with the address of the current cell or with a question mark to designate all cells (in which case Quattro Pro substitutes the address of the current cell as soon as you press [Enter]). For example, if you want Quattro Pro to consider only cells that have a value of 200 or more, select Search String and enter a formula such as **C1>=200** (assuming the cell pointer is in C1) or **?>=200**. Then change the Look In setting to Condition. If the search string you enter is not a valid condition, Quattro Pro beeps, displays an error message, and changes the Look In setting to Formula.

Setting the Look In option to Condition allows you to perform a simple search rather than a search and replace. When it searches for a condition, Quattro Pro simply moves the cell pointer to the first cell it finds that matches your criterion and then stops. (In this case Quattro Pro looks at the results of formulas rather than their actual contents.) If you want to change the contents of the cell, you must do so manually. To look for other cells that match your criterion, you must issue another / **E**dit | **S**earch & Replace command. The Condition setting is particularly handy for finding the next or previous cell that meets a specific condition in a large notebook.

The Match setting on the Search & Replace menu determines whether the search string must match the entire entry in a cell or just part of it. The default setting is Part, which means that Quattro Pro considers any cell that includes the search string to be a match. If you change the setting to Whole, Quattro Pro only considers a cell a match if its entire contents match the search string.

The Case Sensitive option on the Search & Replace menu is set to Any Case by default. In this case, Quattro Pro considers any string containing the same characters, regardless of case, to be a match. If you want it to look for exact matches, change the Case Sensitive setting to Exact Case.

The Options Reset option on the Search & Replace menu restores the default settings for all the Search & Replace options, including removing any settings you have defined for the Block, Search String, and Replace String options.

Filling a Block with Values

The / **E**dit | **F**ill command fills a block of cells with a sequence of values. It can be used to assign invoice numbers, account numbers, loan repayment dates—any series that is separated by even intervals. As discussed in Chapter 16, this command is also useful for numbering records in a database so that you can return records to their original order after sorting.

When you issue the / **E**dit | **F**ill command, Quattro Pro prompts you for the "Destination for cells"—that is, the block to be filled. In most cases this block consists of cells within a single row or a single column. If you designate a block with multiple rows and columns, Quattro Pro fills each column from top to bottom before moving on to the next column to the right (see the middle block in Figure 9-2).

You can preselect the block to be filled by using your mouse or Shift - F7 *and the arrow keys.*

Once you define the block, Quattro Pro requests three values: The *Start value* is the value to be placed in the first cell of the block. All values in the series increase or decrease from this starting point. The *Step value* is the interval between each value in the series. (Note that Step values can also be decimals—0.5 or 1.5, for example—rather than whole numbers.) The *Stop value* is the last value in the series, unless Quattro Pro reaches the last cell in the specified block before it reaches this value. Quattro Pro stops when it reaches this value or fills in each cell in the specified block, whichever comes first. (You can generate a decreasing series by entering a negative Step value and a Stop value that is lower than the Start value.)

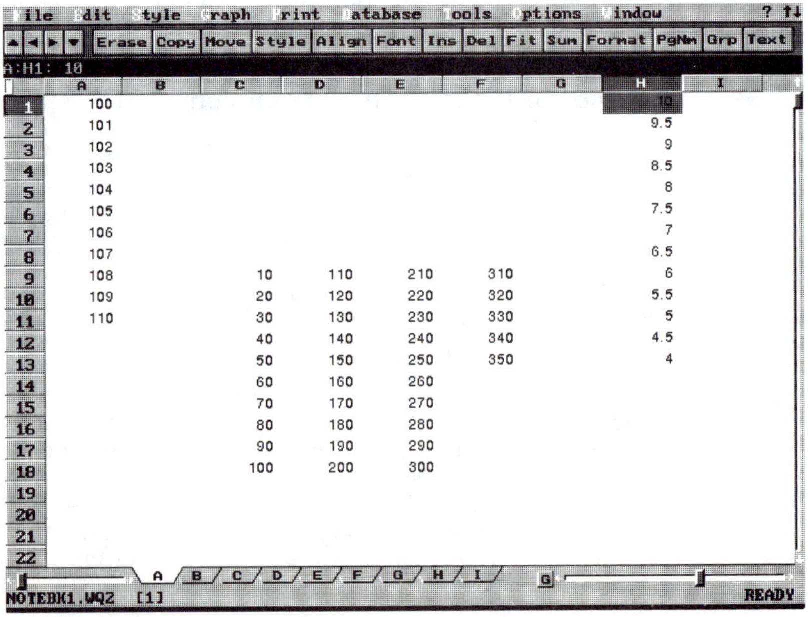

Blocks of values created with / **E**dit | **F**ill
Figure 9-2.

Advanced Editing and Formatting Commands

*All / **Edit** | **Fill** settings (destination block and Start, Step, and Stop value) are retrieved the next time you issue the command.*

Figure 9-2 shows three blocks of data created with / **Edit** | **Fill**. The block on the left was created by specifying the block A1..A11, a Start value of 100 and a Step value of 1, and accepting the default of 8191 for the Stop value. The middle block was created by specifying the block C9..F18, a Start value of 10, a Step value of 10, and a Stop value of 350. The right corner of the block is blank because Quattro Pro reached the Stop value of 350 before it filled in the entire block. The block on the right was created by specifying the block H1..H13, a Start value of 10, a Step value of –0.5, and a Stop value of 0. A descending series is created because the Step value is negative and the Stop value is lower than the Start value.

In all three examples, simple numbers were used as the Start, Step, and Stop values. You can also use formulas, including cell references and functions, for one or all of these values. If you do this, the formulas are evaluated and their end results are used as the basis for the command.

Reformatting Text

You cannot reformat cells and then enter text into them; you must first enter the text, and then reformat the cells.

Many notebooks, particularly those you plan to share with others, can benefit from comments, footnotes, and explanations. The / **Tools** | **Reformat** command facilitates inclusion of such descriptive text by breaking up long blocks of text into smaller blocks distributed neatly across several cells. The command performs a type of rudimentary word processing on one or more adjacent labels within the same column, word-wrapping text at a specified margin. Figure 9-3 shows a block of text that was entered as a single label in A3 and then reformatted over the block A3..E6 with / **Tools** | **Reformat**.

Before issuing the / **Tools** | **Reformat** command, you must place the cell pointer in the cell containing the text to be modified. (You can reformat several adjacent cells within the same column; in that case, first place the cell pointer in the topmost cell to be reformatted.) When you issue the

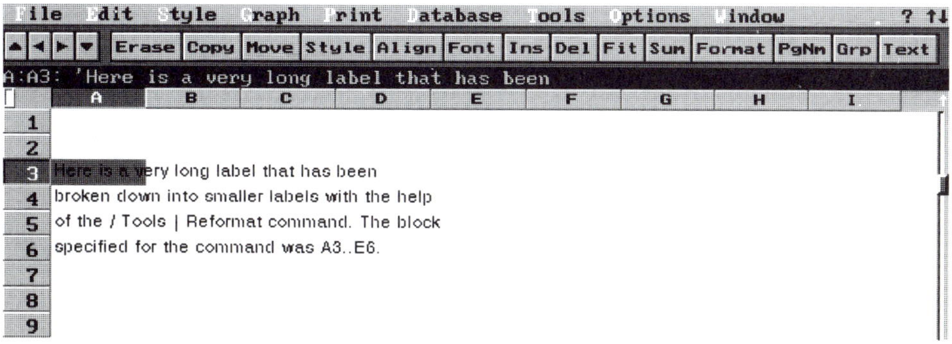

An example of reformatted text
Figure 9-3.

The topmost cell containing data to be reformatted must be the upper-left cell in the "block to be modified."

command, Quattro Pro prompts for a "block to be modified." You may find this prompt slightly confusing because Quattro Pro is actually asking you where you want the text to go, not where it is at the moment. The block that you specify determines the margins that Quattro Pro uses to break the text into rows. For example, if you specify the block A1..D4, Quattro Pro displays as much data as fits within the margins of cells A1 through D1 on the first line (without breaking a word), as much of the remaining data as possible on the second line (cells A2 through D2), and so on. The text in Figure 9-3 was entered in A3 and then reformatted over the block A3..E6. It is important to note, however, that even though / **T**ools | **R**eformat displays the data over the entire width of the designated block, the data itself is broken down into consecutive cells within the column that originally contained the data (A3, A4, A5, and A6 in the figure). The text appears in more than one column on the notebook because it spills into adjacent cells to the right, just as do any labels that do not fit within their cells. If the adjacent cells to the right contain data, that data obscures part of the reformatted text.

You must make sure to specify a block large enough to accommodate the text; otherwise Quattro Pro displays an error message and reformats only part of the label. Use [Alt]-[F5] to undo the damage and try again, using a larger reformat block. If possible, you should guess high when estimating how much space the reformatted text will occupy, including a row or two more than you think you actually need.

Try using the / **T**ools | **R**eformat command.

You cannot use [↑] or [↓] to move through the text, since Quattro Pro treats it as a single character string.

1. Retrieve COMMISS.WQ2 if it is not already on your screen.
2. Move to A24 and enter the following text. (As you type, the text wraps to another row on the input line when you fill a row. Don't worry if it wraps to the next row in the middle of a word.)

   ```
   This notebook allows you to compare commissions at a rate
   you specify to commissions at a rate of 15%. To use it,
   highlight cell B9, type in a new rate, and press ENTER.
   ```

   If you make a mistake, use [Backspace] to erase characters and then retype them. If you notice the mistake later, press [F2] (Edit) and edit as usual. The only way to back up through the text, unless you have a mouse, is with [←].

3. After you have pressed [Enter], issue the / **T**ools | **R**eformat command. To be safe, specify a block of A24..D26. (Remember, if you don't specify a large enough block, Quattro Pro displays an error message and only reformats as much of the text as it can.) Then press [Enter].

4. Look at the input line as you move from A24 to A25 to A26, and notice that the text has been distributed across these three cells. If you move to

Advanced Editing and Formatting Commands

column B, you will see that none of the text is actually contained within that column, even though it appears that way.

5. Move to A3, issue the / **E**dit | **I**nsert | **R**ows command, press ↓ five times to expand the block to A3..A8, and press Enter to insert six new rows above the Commission rate.
6. Issue the / **E**dit | **M**ove command. Specify a source block of A30..A32 and a destination of A4. Your notebook should look like Figure 9-4.

Transposing Blocks

The / **E**dit | **T**ranspose command is a specialized form of / **E**dit | **C**opy that allows you to rotate a block 90 degrees as you copy it. As you do this, the rows in the original block become columns in the new block; columns in the original become rows in the new.

CAUTION: Use / **E**dit | **T**ranspose to transpose blocks of labels or numeric constants, but *not* to transpose formulas. If you transpose a block that contains formulas with relative cell references, those references are not adjusted properly.

Reformatted text on COMMISS.WQ2
Figure 9-4.

Try turning the block A13..B17 from COMMISS.WQ2 on its side using / **Edit** | **Transpose**.

1. Move to A13 and issue the / **Edit** | **Transpose** command.
2. When prompted for a source block, press End-↓ and then → to expand the block to A:A13..B17. Then press Enter. When prompted for a destination, enter A22. Your notebook should now resemble Figure 9-5.
3. Press Alt-F5 to undo the effects of / **Edit** | **Transpose**.

In this example, the source block and destination block do not overlap. Although it is possible to overlap the two blocks, you should avoid doing so unless you are transposing a single column or row. Otherwise, only the top row or leftmost column is transposed. If you are transposing a rectangular block, you are generally better off transposing the block to a different location, deleting the original block, and then moving the new one to its desired location.

Hiding and Exposing Columns

Quattro Pro's / **Style** | **Hide Column** | **Hide** command can be used to temporarily conceal one or more columns on the notebook. You can use this command to view only summary data, such as subtotals and totals, rather

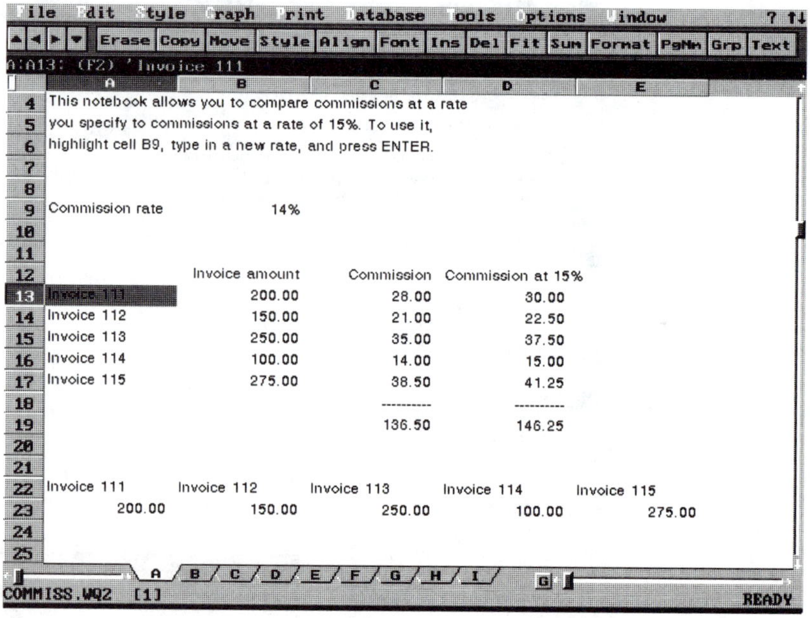

Transposing two columns on COMMISS.WQ2
Figure 9-5.

Advanced Editing and Formatting Commands

than all the detail. It allows you to customize the notebook—to display different levels of detail at different times or for different viewers. There is no analogous command for hiding rows.

When Quattro Pro executes the / **S**tyle | **H**ide Column | **H**ide command, all columns to the right of the hidden column are moved to the left so that no gaps remain between columns. You can always tell that a column has been hidden, however, because its letter is skipped.

When you issue the / **S**tyle | **H**ide Column | **H**ide command, Quattro Pro displays the prompt "Hide columns from view," and offers the current cell's coordinates as the default setting for the command. If you accept this default, Quattro Pro hides the current column. If you want to hide a different column, you can either type the coordinates of any cell in that column or move to that column and press (Enter) or click on [Enter]. To hide more than one column, designate a block spanning multiple columns.

To hide column D from view, follow these steps:

1. Move to any cell in column D, and issue the / **S**tyle | **H**ide Column | **H**ide command.
2. Press (Enter) or click on [Enter] to accept the default cell. Your notebook should now look like Figure 9-6. Notice that none of the text at the top of the notebook is hidden because it is actually stored in column A (even though some of it initially appeared to spill over into column D).

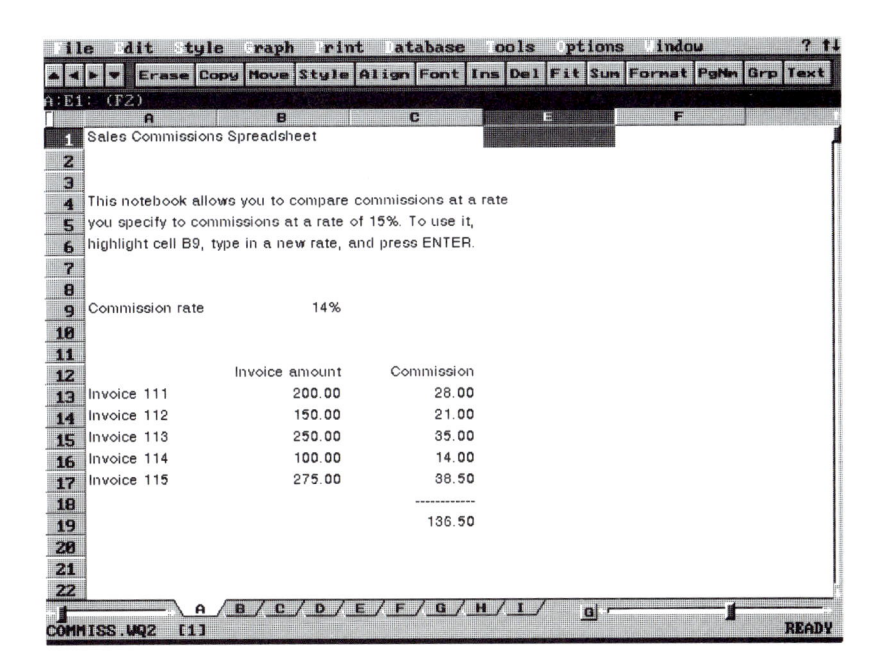

COMMISS.WQ2 after hiding column D
Figure 9-6.

The / **S**tyle | **H**ide Column | **E**xpose command undoes the effects of the / **S**tyle | **H**ide Column | **H**ide command. As soon as you issue this command, the previously hidden columns reappear on the screen, with asterisks to the right of their column letters at the top of the notebook area. At this point Quattro Pro displays the prompt "Expose hidden columns:" and offers the current column as a default. You can either move to the column you want to expose and press [Enter], or designate a block if you want to expose more than one adjacent column.

To expose the column you have just hidden, just issue the / **S**tyle | **H**ide Column | **E**xpose Column command, move to any cell in column D, and press [Enter] or click on [Enter].

The most common application for / **S**tyle | **H**ide Columns is in printing. You might print with hidden columns to squeeze a wide notebook on a single page by eliminating unessential columns. You might also hide columns when printing to limit the information displayed on particular reports—either to conceal confidential information or to create summary reports for people who want to see only the big picture.

Quattro Pro temporarily redisplays hidden columns during operations such as / **E**dit | **M**ove and / **E**dit | **C**opy so that you can place or access data within those columns. As soon as the operation is complete, the hidden columns in the original block disappear from view again. However, the hidden columns were in fact moved or copied, and are revealed in their new location. For example, suppose you hide columns B and C, select a block from column A through D, and copy that block to another location. There will be four columns' worth of information in the new location, even though columns B and C are still concealed.

Protecting Your Notebook

One of the side effects of Quattro Pro's flexibility is that it can take only a second to wreak havoc with a notebook. One wrong move and half the values on your screen can change to ERR. In many cases you can undo the damage with the Undo key, but only if you notice it before you perform another "undoable" operation. For this reason Quattro Pro offers you the option of protecting all or part of your notebook from modification. Once a particular cell has been protected, it cannot be edited, overwritten, or deleted. You also cannot delete a row or column that contains protected cells, and you can choose to protect just the formulas in your notebook.

You frequently will construct a notebook in one or two work sessions and thereafter modify it only slightly. Once you know the notebook works and are pleased with its appearance, you generally will change only a few items of data while leaving the basic structure of the notebook intact. You may

Advanced Editing and Formatting Commands

want to protect every cell on the notebook except those few that you want to be able to change easily. You will find this particularly useful when other people are using the notebook. By protecting every cell that normally will not be changed, you can guard the notebook's infrastructure against accidental modification.

Two factors determine whether a cell is modifiable: whether Quattro Pro's protection feature has been enabled on the current notebook page, and whether the cell itself has been designated as unprotected. When you first enable Quattro Pro's protection feature with / **O**ptions | **P**rotection | **E**nable, every cell on the current notebook page is immediately protected. At this point, if you move the cell pointer around that page, you will notice the code PR (for protected) on the input line when you highlight any cell. If you try to change the contents of a cell, Quattro Pro beeps and displays an error message.

If you save a notebook after enabling protection, Quattro Pro saves the protection setting with the notebook page—so the protection feature is automatically enabled on that page the next time you retrieve the file. To turn off protection you can simply issue the / **O**ptions | **P**rotection | **D**isable command. When you do, the protection codes are no longer displayed on the input line and you are again allowed to change any cell on the page in question.

Once you have enabled protection, you generally will want to unprotect selected cells or blocks while leaving the rest of the notebook protected. The command for unprotecting cells is / **S**tyle | **P**rotection | **U**nprotect. Quattro Pro displays unprotected cells in a different color or, on monochrome screens, in bolder text to distinguish them from the other cells on the notebook. It also displays a U on the input line when you point to any cell that has been marked unprotected with this command. When you mark a cell as unprotected, this setting stays with the cell even if you later disable protection with / **O**ptions | **P**rotection | **D**isable. Once you reenable the protection feature, the cell remains unprotected. This allows you to temporarily disable the protection feature to make adjustments in the structure of your notebook, and then enable it again without having to unprotect the same set of cells. If you save your file after unprotecting cells, their unprotected status is saved along with the notebook.

If you change your mind and decide to reprotect a set of cells that you previously unprotected, you can do so using / **S**tyle | **P**rotection | **P**rotect. When you reprotect a cell, the unprotected marker (the U at the beginning of the input line) is replaced by a protected marker (PR) again. Keep in mind that / **S**tyle | **P**rotection | **P**rotect cannot protect a cell if the protection feature is not currently enabled. It is used solely for removing the unprotected code from a set of cells that were previously unprotected with

/ **S**tyle | **P**rotection | **U**nprotect. Those cells revert to the protection status of the notebook as a whole. In this sense, it is similar to a reset command—it removes a code from a block of cells so they revert to the default setting for the notebook.

Try this exercise to see Quattro Pro's various protection commands in action.

1. Issue the / **O**ptions | **P**rotection | **E**nable command and select Quit to return to Ready mode. Note that every cell has a PR code after the cell address on the input line.
2. Try to change or delete any cell on the notebook and note the error message. Press [Enter] to clear the message from the screen.
3. Move to B9 and issue the / **S**tyle | **P**rotection | **U**nprotect command. Accept the default block of A:B9..B9. The code U now appears immediately after the display code on the input line and the cell is displayed in a different color or is highlighted. This way, users of the notebook can experiment with different commission rates but cannot otherwise alter the notebook.
4. Type a new value for B9 and press [Enter]. You can now change the content of this cell because it has been explicitly unprotected. Note that the change affects all the values in column C even though they remain protected.
5. Save the notebook again by issuing the / **F**ile | **S**ave command and selecting Replace.

Protected formulas still respond to changes in other cells, they just cannot be changed directly.

Protecting Formulas

You can protect just the formulas in your notebook using the / **O**ptions | **P**rotection | **F**ormulas | **P**rotect command. This command enables you to single out the areas in your notebook that are most likely to need protection. In addition, formula protection is particularly secure, since you need a password to disable it.

To protect the formulas in your notebook, follow these steps:

1. First issue the / **O**ptions | **P**rotection | **D**isable command to turn off protection for the entire notebook.
2. Issue the / **O**ptions | **P**rotection | **F**ormulas | **P**rotect command.
3. Enter a password and press [Enter]. Then verify your password by typing it again. (If you press [Enter] without typing a password, your formula will not be protected.) Note that case is significant when it comes to passwords. (Quattro Pro will not accept the password zany if you originally supplied the password ZANY.)

Advanced Editing and Formatting Commands

4. Select Quit to return to Ready mode; then go to a cell that contains a formula and attempt to change it. You'll receive the error message "Formula protection is enabled," even though there is no visible protection code on the input line. When formulas are protected, you can neither edit them nor overwrite them with commands such as move and copy.

CAUTION: Make sure to keep track of your password; the best policy is to write it down and store it in a safe place. Without it you cannot edit the formulas in your notebook.

If you want to remove formula protection from your notebook, issue the / **O**ptions | **P**rotection | **F**ormulas | **U**nprotect command and enter your password. If you do not disable formula protection, your password is saved when you save the notebook.

Protecting valuable notebooks from carelessness is a simple and yet extremely worthwhile procedure. An unprotected notebook can unravel in seconds, particularly in the hands of an inexperienced user. Even when you are the only one using a particular notebook, protection can prevent you from accidentally overwriting formulas or critical items of data. In most cases it is far easier to guard against such mishaps than to correct them later.

This chapter introduced several specialized commands for modifying, formatting, and rearranging data. Which of these commands you'll find most useful will depend on the type of work you do in Quattro Pro. If you frequently enter numbered lists, for example, you'll find / **E**dit | **F**ill indispensable. If you create notebooks for other people, you should apply protection commands to every model you create. Even if some of the commands introduced here seem esoteric now, file them away for future reference. Sooner or later, they'll be the perfect tools for the task at hand.

CHAPTER

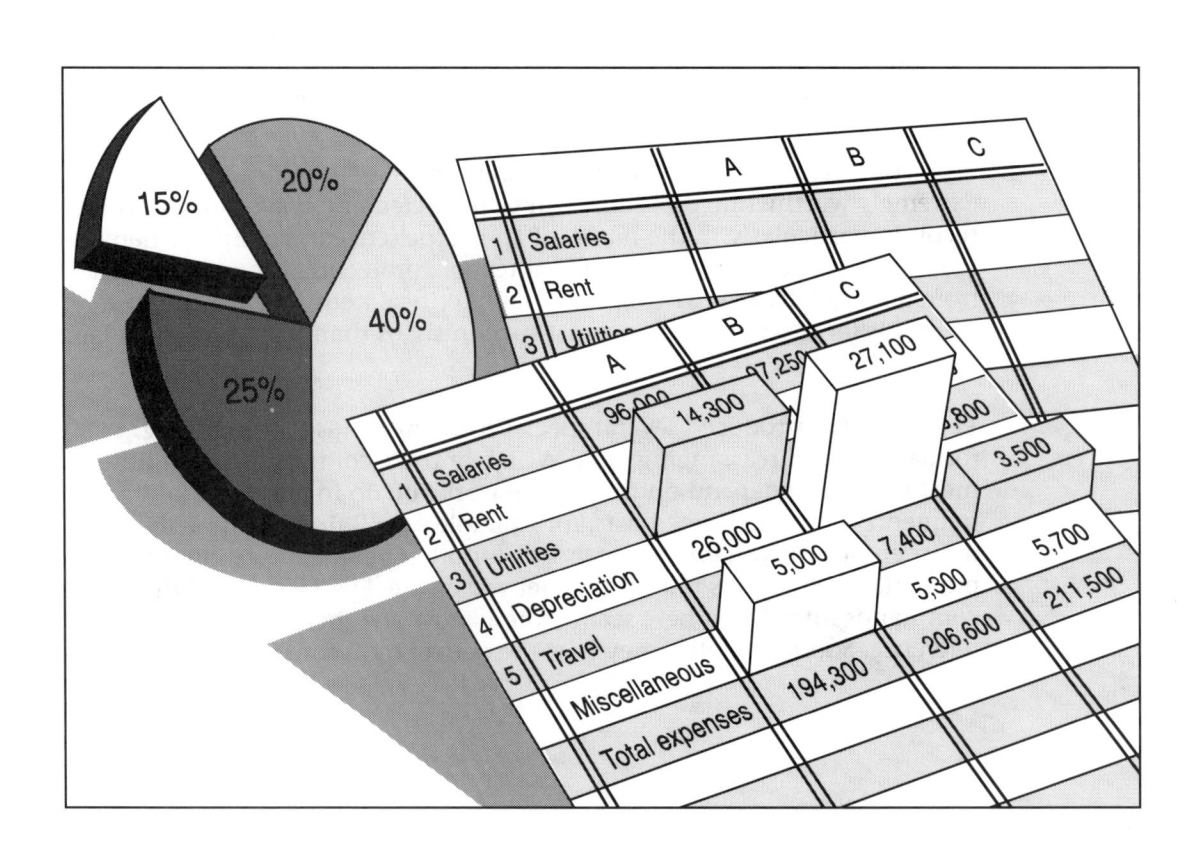

10

DATES AND TIMES

In Chapter 2 you learned to enter dates using the Ctrl-D prefix. This chapter covers how to enter times, use date and time functions, perform date and time calculations, and change date and time display formats.

Quattro Pro stores dates and times as numbers. This allows it to perform date and time arithmetic, manipulating those values in the same way it would any other numeric values. You can use date and time arithmetic on notebooks to determine the amount of time elapsed between two dates—for example, to calculate how long it has been since a customer placed an order. You can also calculate a series of dates spaced at regular intervals, such as a loan repayment schedule. And you can determine the amount of time elapsed between two points in time—for example, to evaluate timecards in payroll calculations. In addition, you can calculate a future date or time—for instance, to determine renewal dates in a subscription database. Finally, you can sort records in a database into date or time order—for example, to list customers in order by first or last order date.

Working with Dates

You'll learn more about the date formatting codes in a moment.

As discussed in Chapter 2, you cannot simply type a date into the notebook. If you enter **1/1/94**, Quattro Pro thinks you are trying to divide 1 by 1 by 94. You must use the Ctrl-D prefix to let Quattro Pro know that you intend to enter a date. When you press Ctrl-D, you can enter a date in one of the following five formats:

Format	Code	Example
DD-MMM-YY	D1	01-Mar-94
DD-MMM	D2	01-Mar
MMM-YY	D3	Mar-94
MM/DD/YY	D4	03/01/94
MM/DD	D5	03/01

If you use a different format—03-01-94 for example—Quattro Pro beeps to let you know there is a problem and then ignores the Ctrl-D prefix. Quattro Pro treats the entry of 03-01-94 as 3 minus 1 minus 94.

CAUTION: Be careful when entering dates using a format that omits the day or year. If you enter dates using the DD-MMM or MM/DD format, Quattro Pro assumes you are entering dates for the current year. If you enter a date using the MMM-YY format, Quattro Pro assumes you mean the first day of the month.

When you enter a date using Ctrl-D, the date appears in the format in which you entered it. If you look at the input line, however, you see that it is stored as a number. This *date serial number* indicates the number of days that have elapsed since December 31, 1899.

To practice entering a date on your notebook, perform the following steps:

Dates and Times

1. Save any data you currently have on screen, and then issue the / **F**ile | **E**rase command so you can start with a clean slate.
2. In A1, press Ctrl-D, and then enter **6/1/94**. The input line should now read 34486.

> **NOTE:** Quattro Pro provides a special tool—the / **D**atabase | **D**ata Entry | **D**ates Only command—that facilitates entry of a group of dates (see Chapter 16). This command lets you specify a block of cells as "dates-only" cells. When you enter data into one of these cells using any one of the five Quattro Pro Date formats, Quattro Pro automatically acts as if you had pressed Ctrl-D first.

As you have seen, the Ctrl-D prefix directs Quattro Pro to translate the characters you type into a date serial number while displaying that number in any one of the acceptable Date formats. Quattro Pro also allows you to apply a Date format to a number already on the notebook. This is extremely useful when you perform date calculations. If you add a number to a date, for example, the result is a date serial value displayed as a simple number. If you want the number to look like a date, you must use / **S**tyle | **N**umeric Format | **D**ate. Quattro Pro displays a submenu with the same five Date formats you can use when entering dates with Ctrl-D. You might also use / **S**tyle | **N**umeric Format | **D**ate to change a date from one format to another.

> **NOTE:** Both the Long International (option 4) and Short International (option 5) settings on the Style | Numeric Format | Date menu can be changed with the / **O**ptions | **I**nternational | **D**ate command discussed in Chapter 13. The forms for options 4 and 5 in the previous table are Quattro Pro's initial default settings.

*You can also click on the Format button on the SpeedBar to issue the / **S**tyle | **N**umeric Format command.*

Formatting a number as a date is slightly different from entering a date with Ctrl-D. When you use / **S**tyle | **N**umeric Format, Quattro Pro inserts a date format code in the cell. This format code, like any other numeric format code, remains in the cell even if you delete the data and affects any numeric values (including new dates) you subsequently enter in that cell. You can change the display code by reissuing / **S**tyle | **N**umeric Format and choosing a nondate format. The only way to eliminate these codes altogether is with / **S**tyle | **N**umeric Format | **R**eset.

Experiment now with all of Quattro Pro's date formats.

1. Issue the / **O**ptions | **F**ormats | **G**lobal Width command and specify a new column width of 12. Return to Ready mode by typing **Q** twice.

2. In A1, try all five date formats by issuing the / **S**tyle | **N**umeric Format | **D**ate command five times and selecting a different Date format each time. Accept the default block, and be sure to end with the first option on the date format menu (the DD-MMM-YY format).

3. Press [Del] to delete the date. Note that the format code (D1) still appears on the input line.

4. Enter the number **12345**. Quattro Pro formats the number as a date, displaying 18-Oct-33 in the cell.

5. Press [Ctrl]-[D] and enter **1/1/94**. Quattro Pro translates these characters into the date serial number 34335, formats that number as a date, and then displays 01-Jan-94.

You can also apply a date format to a cell by issuing the / **S**tyle | **U**se Style command and selecting the predefined style named DATE. This style displays dates with the name of the month spelled out, followed by the day of the month, followed by a four-digit year. The date 1/1/94, for example, is shown as January 1, 1994.

Date Arithmetic

The basic unit for all Quattro Pro date calculations is a single day. If you subtract one date from another date, Quattro Pro returns the number of days between those two dates. If you add a number to a date, Quattro Pro returns the date that occurs the specified number of days later.

Try performing some simple date arithmetic now.

1. Move to A3 and enter today's date using the MM/DD/YY format.

2. Move to A4 and enter **+A3+70** to calculate the date 10 weeks from today. To display the result of this calculation as a date, you need to assign it a Date format.

3. Issue the / **S**tyle | **N**umeric Format | **D**ate | **4** command, and accept the default block of A:A4..A4.

4. Move to A5 and enter **+A4−A3** to calculate the number of days elapsed between two dates. The answer should be 70.

This type of simple date arithmetic has numerous applications. Figure 10-1 shows a notebook designed to calculate discounts allowed for rapid payment of invoices. The policy of this business is that a 2% discount is applied to all invoices paid within 10 days of their invoice date. The formula

```
@IF(D4<>0#AND#D4-C4<=10,B4*0.02,0)
```

Dates and Times

was entered in E4 and copied down column E to perform the necessary calculations. This formula determines whether the payment date (D4) is both greater than 0 (not blank) and no more than 10 days after the invoice date (C4). If both conditions are true, the formula multiplies the invoice amount (B4) by 0.02; otherwise it returns zero.

Date Functions

You have now performed a few simple date calculations. You can perform more sophisticated operations on dates by using one or more of Quattro Pro's date-related functions.

Extracting Part of a Date   The @DAY, @MONTH, and @YEAR functions isolate an element of a date, extracting the numeric value of the day, month, or year. In each of these functions, the argument must be a number between -36463 (corresponding to March 1, 1800) and 73050 (corresponding to December 31, 2099). Quattro Pro ignores decimal fractions.

The @DAY(*DateTimeNumber*) function returns the day of the month of the date specified by the argument. (*DateTimeNumber* is used throughout this chapter to represent any date serial number, regardless of whether it is actually displayed as a date on the notebook). The function statement @DAY(34567), for example, yields the value 21, because 34567 is the serial value for August 21, 1994. The @MONTH(*DateTimeNumber*) function returns a number between 1 and 12 that corresponds to the month of the date specified in the argument; @MONTH(34567) returns 8, for August. The @YEAR(*DateTimeNumber*) function returns a number between –100 (the year 1800) and 199 (the year 2099) corresponding to the year of the date specified in the argument.

To see how these functions work, enter **@DAY(A3)** in B1, enter **@MONTH(A3)** in B2, and enter **@YEAR(A3)** in B3. Quattro Pro returns the current day, month, and year. You can use these three functions in several

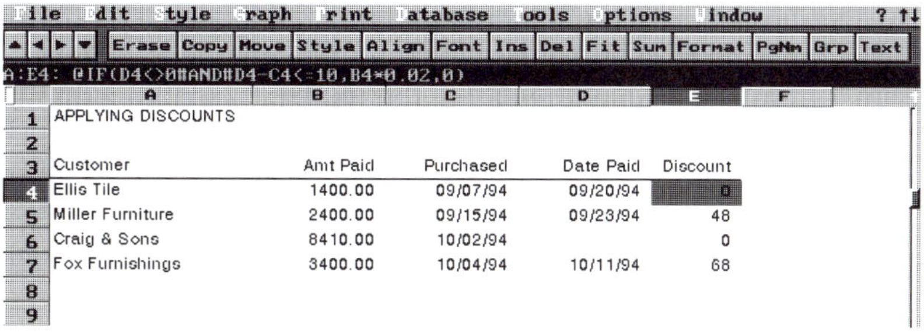

Using date arithmetic to calculate discounts
Figure 10-1.

situations. Suppose your fiscal year extends from July 1 of one year to June 30 of the next. After entering a series of order dates in column C, you could enter the formula

```
@IF(MONTH(C3)>6,1993,1994)
```

in D1 and copy it down column D to return the fiscal year that corresponds to each order date in column C.

The values returned by the @DAY, @MONTH, and @YEAR functions sometimes supply information in a form slightly different from what you intended—returning two digits when you want four or the number of a month when you want its name. Following are a few tricks to get the information in the form you need. You can generate a four-digit year rather than a two-digit year from the @YEAR function using the following formula:

@YEAR(*DateTimeNumber*)+1900

As described in the next sections, you can use @DAY and @MONTH in combination with other functions to display the names of days and months.

Determining the Day of the Week   The @MOD function is an arithmetic function that returns the remainder, or modulus, of a division operation. The syntax for the formula is @MOD(*Dividend,Divisor*), where *Dividend* is the numeric value you are dividing, and *Divisor* is the number you are dividing the *Dividend* by. Both arguments can be any expression that evaluates to a number, including cell references and function statements as well as numeric constants. For example, the formula @MOD(5,2) returns 1 because 5 divided by 2 equals 2 with a remainder of 1.

To determine the day of the week for a current date, enter a function statement with the form @MOD(*DateTimeNumber,7*). This function statement returns the remainder (modulus) that results from dividing the date value *DateTimeNumber* by the number of days in a week. A result of 1 corresponds to Sunday, 2 to Monday, and so on. A result of 0 corresponds to Saturday because Saturday is the seventh day of the week and 7 divided by 7 leaves a remainder of 0. (This works out neatly only because Quattro Pro's base date of December 31, 1899, happens to have been a Sunday.) If you want to display the day of the week rather than a number, you must use the function described next.

Displaying the Names of Months and Days of the Week   Figure 10-2 illustrates the use of lookup tables for displaying the name of the month and

Dates and Times

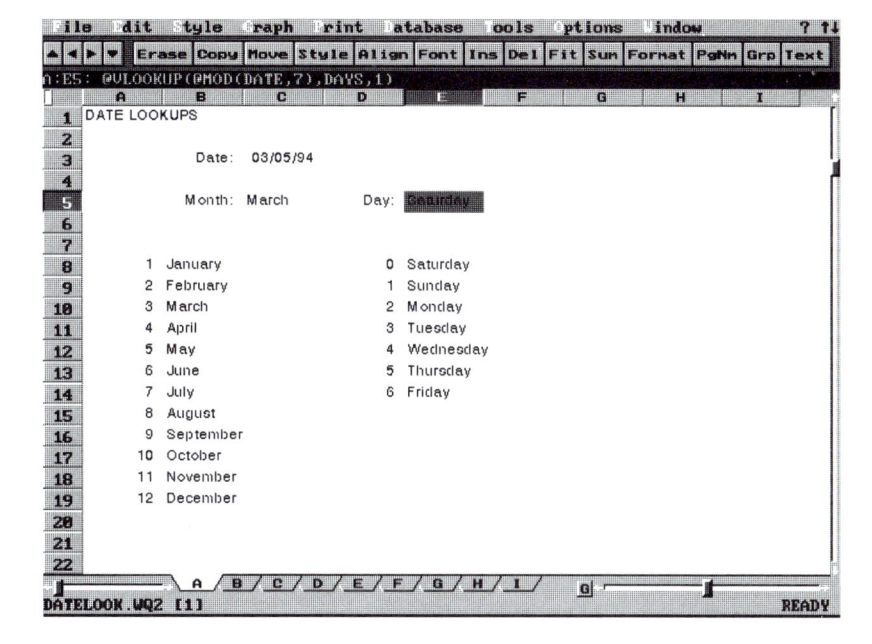

Looking up the names of months and days of the week
Figure 10-2.

[Screenshot of spreadsheet showing DATE LOOKUPS with Date: 03/05/94, Month: March, Day: Saturday, a months table (1 January through 12 December) and a days table (0 Saturday through 6 Friday)]

the name of the day corresponding to a particular date. The formulas use the following block names: DATE is the name assigned to C3, which contains the date to be looked up. MONTHS is the name assigned to the block A8..B19, which contains the months lookup table. DAYS is the name assigned to the block D8..E14, which contains the days lookup table.

The formula in C5, which returns the name of the month, is

`@VLOOKUP(@MONTH(DATE),MONTHS,1)`

It works by looking up the month portion of the cell named DATE (C3) in the lookup table MONTHS. When it finds that number, it returns the label in the cell one column to the right (an offset of one).

The formula in E5, which returns the day of the week, is

`@VLOOKUP(@MOD(DATE,7),DAYS,1)`

This formula looks up a number representing the day of the week (the modulus produced by dividing the date by 7) in the lookup table DAYS and returns the value one column to the right.

Using Functions to Enter Dates

Although you will enter most dates using the Ctrl-D prefix, Quattro Pro also provides three functions for entering dates: @TODAY, @DATE, and @DATEVALUE.

The @TODAY Function

The @TODAY function returns the numeric value of the current date. It does not require any arguments, but rather draws the date directly from the computer's system clock.

If your computer's clock is not set to today's date, this function will not work as expected.

Figure 10-3 shows a notebook calculating a schedule of accounts receivable. The formula in cell D5 (which was copied down column D) is

```
@IF(@TODAY-B5<=30,C5,0)
```

If the number of days elapsed between today and the date in column B is less than or equal to 30, the function returns the value in C5; otherwise it returns 0. The formula in E5 is slightly more complex because it must determine whether the number of days between today and the due date is both greater than 30 and less than or equal to 60. The exact formula is

```
@IF(@TODAY-B5>30#AND#@TODAY-B5<=60,C5,0)
```

Similarly the formula in F5 is

```
@IF(@TODAY-B5>60#AND#@TODAY-B5<=90,C5,0)
```

The formula in G5 is

```
@IF(@TODAY-B5>90,C5,0)
```

A schedule of accounts receivable
Figure 10-3.

	A	B	C	D	E	F	G
1	Accounts Receivable Aging Report			Date:	02/05/94		
4	Customer	Due Date	Amount	Current	Over 30	Over 60	Over 90
5	Mary Franklin	11/01/93	150.00	0.00	0.00	0.00	150.00
6	Bill Gross	11/15/93	210.00	0.00	0.00	210.00	0.00
7	Bob Ramirez	11/30/93	75.00	0.00	0.00	75.00	0.00
8	Ann Goldstein	01/01/94	125.00	0.00	125.00	0.00	0.00
9	Frank Stern	02/11/94	180.00	180.00	0.00	0.00	0.00
10	Ted Fisher	02/14/94	220.00	220.00	0.00	0.00	0.00
11	Pam Wynn	02/20/94	90.00	90.00	0.00	0.00	0.00
12			1,050.00	490.00	125.00	285.00	150.00

Dates and Times

The @DATE Function The syntax for @DATE is @DATE(*Year,Month,Day*), where *Year* is a numeric value between −100 and 199 (representing the years 1800 through 2099), *Month* is a numeric value between 1 and 12, and *Day* is a numeric value between 1 and 31. This function returns a serial number corresponding to the date specified with the three arguments. The @DATE function generates an ERR message if you use an invalid number for one of your arguments, specifying 15 for *Month*, for example. @DATE is often used to maintain compatibility with Lotus 1-2-3, which doesn't have any other tool for entering dates. You can also use this function to express a particular date value within a formula. Figure 10-4 shows a personnel database in which the formulas in column D calculate a salary increase based on the date each employee was hired. Employees hired prior to 1/1/93 receive a 5% increase, while employees hired after that date receive a 4% increase. To accomplish this, the formula

```
@IF(B6<@DATE(93,1,1),C6*0.05,C6*0.04)
```

was entered in D6 and copied down the column.

The @DATE function is particularly useful when you are constructing a date on the basis of a year (and possibly a month and day) entered elsewhere on the notebook. For example, if you want to display the first day of a year that was entered in another cell, you can use a formula such as @DATE(C1,1,1).

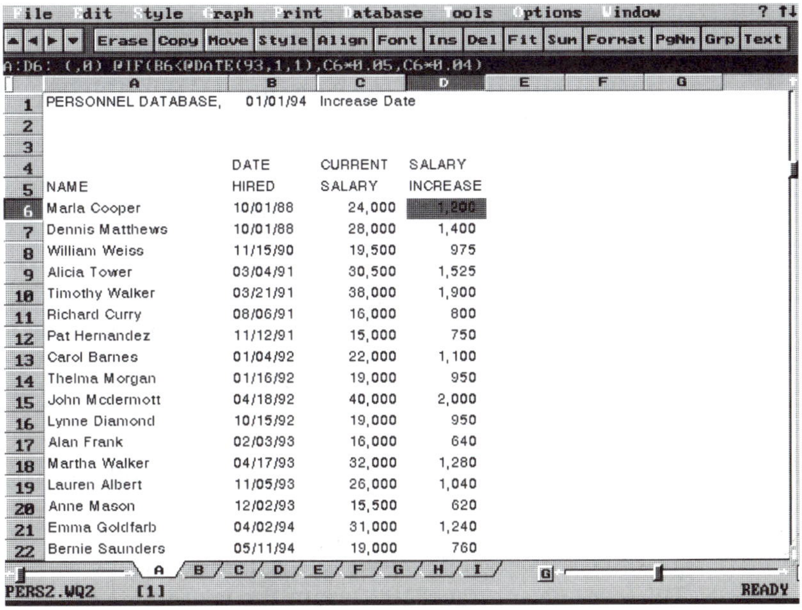

Using @DATE to calculate a salary increase
Figure 10-4.

The @DATEVALUE Function The @DATEVALUE function converts a character string that looks like a date into a date serial number that Quattro Pro can use in calculations. Its syntax is @DATEVALUE(*DateString*), where *DateString* is a string value—either a character string enclosed in quotation marks or a cell reference to a label on the notebook—that was entered in any one of Quattro Pro's five Date display formats. If *DateString* is in an invalid format, the function evaluates to ERR. Quattro Pro also returns a value of ERR if you specify an invalid date or neglect to enclose a character string in quotes.

The most common application for @DATEVALUE is transforming date data that was either imported as text from other software or was entered as a label by someone unfamiliar with Quattro Pro date manipulation. You can also use it as you do the @DATE function—to express a particular date within a formula.

Creating Month Headings

One common application for @DATEVALUE or @DATE is in creating monthly column or row headings for a notebook. To do this, you use the / **E**dit | **F**ill command and use @DATEVALUE or @DATE to specify the Start and Stop values.

1. Start with a clean notebook by issuing the / **F**ile | **E**rase command.
2. Issue the / **E**dit | **F**ill command, and specify a destination of A1..L1.
3. Enter a Start value of **@DATEVALUE("1/15/94")**, a Step value of **30**, and a Stop value of **@DATEVALUE("12/31/94")**. A series of date serial numbers will show up on your notebook.
4. Issue the / **S**tyle | **N**umeric Format | **D**ate | **3** command, and specify A1..L1 as the block to be modified. Your notebook should now have a row of month headings.

You could achieve the exact same result if you used a Start value of @DATE(94,1,15) and a Stop value of @DATE(94,12,31); the choice of functions is up to you.

Note that January 15 rather than January 1 was used as the Start value. This circumvents potential problems caused by the varying lengths of the months. The actual dates in this series are not all on the fifteenth day, but they do fall within consecutive months, resulting in the desired series of column headings.

You might want the column headings to change relative to other values on the notebook. This makes it easy for you to recycle your notebook year after year simply by changing a single value. For example, in Figure 10-5, the formula @DATE($C$1-1900,1,1) is used to display the column heading in B4. The formula subtracts 1900 from the year in C1 to produce the two-digit

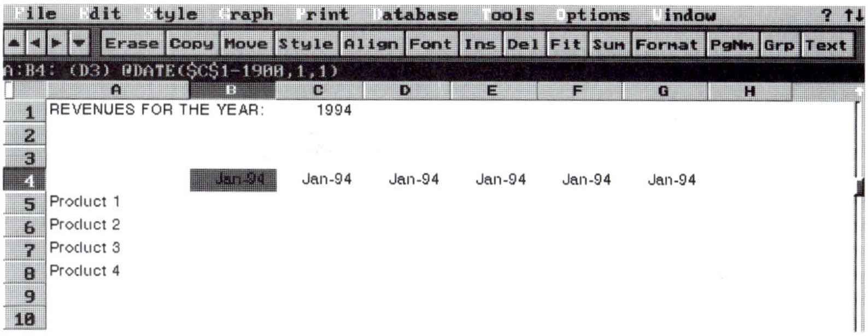

Dates and Times

Calculating dates for column headings
Figure 10-5.

year required by the @DATE function. The formulas in the other cells in row 4 are the same except for the second argument (the month), which increases by 1 in each column. The formula in D4 is @DATE($C$1–1900,2,1), for example. The entire row of column headings was formatted with Date format number 3.

To update this notebook for future years, you need only change the number in C1. Quattro Pro automatically recalculates the formulas in row 4, displaying appropriate column headings for the specified year.

Working with Times

Quattro Pro measures, stores, and represents time as a fraction of a day. For example, the time 12:00 noon is represented as 0.5 since it is halfway through any given 24-hour period (Quattro Pro starts counting at midnight). Similarly 6:00 AM is represented as 0.25 and 6:00 PM is represented as 0.75. As with dates, Quattro Pro stores times as numbers so it can easily perform calculations with the data. By treating times as numbers, Quattro Pro can use those values in arithmetic formulas and functions.

Quattro Pro has no equivalent to the Ctrl-D key combination for entering times. Generally, times are entered using the @TIME function and then formatted with one of Quattro Pro's four time display formats. Entering times in a notebook involves two steps: entering data with the @TIME function, and then formatting the value with a Time display format. The order in which you perform these steps does not matter. You can even omit the second step if you don't mind your times appearing as decimals on the notebook.

The @TIME function's syntax is @TIME(*Hours,Minutes,Seconds*), where *Hours*, *Minutes*, and *Seconds* specify the time you want to enter in the notebook. *Hours* must be an integer between 0 and 23, and *Minutes* and *Seconds* must be integers between 0 and 59. Arguments higher or lower than these integers return a value of ERR.

The command for formatting a block with a Time display format is / **S**tyle | **N**umeric Format | **D**ate | **T**ime. Once you issue this command, Quattro Pro displays a menu with the four Time display formats:

Format	Code	Form	Example
1	D6	HH:MM:SS AM/PM	1:17:35 PM
2	D7	HH:MM AM/PM	1:17 PM
3 (Long International)	D8	HH:MM:SS (24-Hour)	13:17:35
4 (Short International)	D9	HH:MM (24-Hour)	13:17

Notice that the display format codes for the Time formats all begin with D. Quattro Pro treats the entire Time format submenu as a continuation of the Date format menu: the code for Time format 1 is D6, for Time format 2 is D7, and so on.

To enter times into your notebook, follow these steps:

When entering times that occur after noon, you must convert them to a 24-hour format. For example, 1:00 PM is entered as 13 hours.

1. Move to cell B3 and enter the time 7:12 PM by typing **@TIME(19,12,0)** and pressing [Enter]. The time 7:12 PM is translated into 19 hours and 12 minutes for the @TIME function's arguments. This time is stored as the numeric value 0.8.

2. Issue the / **O**ptions | **F**ormats | **G**lobal Width command and enter **12**. Press **Q** or [Esc] twice to return to Ready mode.

3. Still in B3, try all the various Time display formats by issuing / **S**tyle | **N**umeric Format | **D**ate | **T**ime four times, choosing a different Time format each time.

The @NOW Function

The @NOW function allows you to insert the value of the current date and time into your notebook. Like @TODAY, @NOW does not require any user input. Instead, it draws all the data it needs from your computer's clock and returns a combined date/time value. The integer portion of the result represents the current date, and the decimal portion represents the current time. As with @TODAY, your computer's clock must be set correctly for this function to work.

There is no combined Date/Time display format.

Once you have calculated the value of @NOW, you must choose whether to display it as a date or as a time. If, for example, you display the value 34370.5 (the value of @NOW at noon on February 5, 1994) with Date format 4, you will see 2/5/94. If you display the same number with Time format 3, you will see 12:00:00. If you want to display both the date and the time value of @NOW, you should enter the function twice on the notebook and use two different formats.

Quattro Pro updates the value of the @NOW function every time the notebook is recalculated. If you are in automatic recalculation mode, Quattro Pro updates every time you enter or edit data on the notebook. If you are in manual recalculation mode, Quattro Pro updates every time you press F9 to recalculate the notebook. (The various recalculation modes are discussed in more depth in Chapter 13.)

Sometimes you may want to freeze the value of @NOW, so it is calculated upon entry but never updated. Suppose you want to use the @NOW function to "stamp" your notebook with the date and time you created it. You can enter the @NOW function as soon as you finish building the notebook. Then you either use the / **E**dit | **V**alues command or edit the cell and press F9 (Calc) to replace the function itself with its current numeric value.

Just as there is no format for displaying a combined date/time value, there is no function for entering one. If you want to enter a specific time on a specific date, you must use a combination of date and time functions. For example, you can use the formula

```
@DATE(94,2,5)+@TIME(12,0,0)
```

to enter the date/time serial value for noon on February 5, 1994. Then you can add or subtract other dates, other times, or combined date/times.

The @TIMEVALUE Function

The @TIMEVALUE function is the time equivalent of @DATEVALUE: It allows you to transform labels that look like times into the numeric form that Quattro Pro requires for performing time calculations. Its syntax is @TIMEVALUE(*TimeString*), where *TimeString* is either a character string enclosed in quotation marks or a label containing data in any of Quattro Pro's four Time formats. Omitting quotes (in the case of character strings) or using an invalid format generates a value of ERR. Like @DATEVALUE, this function is useful primarily for transforming data imported from other software into a form that Quattro Pro can use. You can also use it to express a specific time within a formula.

Try the @TIMEVALUE function now.

1. Enter the label **'12:28:53** in C3.
2. Move to D3 and enter **@TIMEVALUE(C3)**.

The result should be 0.52005787. If you changed the display format for cell D3 to Time format 1, it would be displayed as 12:28:53 PM.

Calculating payroll
Figure 10-6.

	A	B	C	D	E	F
1	Time Cards					
4		Time In	Time Out	Time In	Time Out	Hours
5	Jane Smith	08:48:00 AM	11:57:00 AM	01:04:00 PM	04:58:00 PM	7.05
6	Oscar Gomez	08:52:00 AM	12:14:00 PM	01:08:00 PM	05:12:00 PM	7.43
7	Herb Gold	09:08:00 AM	12:01:00 PM	01:16:00 PM	05:34:00 PM	7.18
8	Tom Williams	09:01:00 AM	12:45:00 PM	01:50:00 PM	05:03:00 PM	6.95
9	Fran Simpson	09:03:00 AM	01:12:00 PM	02:02:00 PM	05:52:00 PM	7.98

Time Arithmetic

There are several uses for time calculations in notebooks. For example, Figure 10-6 shows a model for calculating payroll. The formula in F5,

```
((C5-B5)+(E5-D5))*24
```

was copied down column F to calculate the amount of time worked by each employee on a given day. The formula calculates the time that has passed between the first time out (C5) and the first time in (B5), plus the amount of elapsed time between the second time out (E5) and the second time in (D5). The result of this calculation is a decimal that represents some fraction of the 24-hour period. This result is then multiplied by 24 to convert the decimal into a quantity of hours.

The decimal portion of the formula's result represents a fraction of an hour, not a number of minutes. The value 7.05 (F5) represents 7.05 hours (7 hours and 3 minutes) rather than 7 hours and 5 minutes. You can then multiply this result by the employee's hourly wage to determine her or his wages due for the day. If you want the amount of time worked to be represented in hours and minutes, you can use the formula ((C5–B5)+(E5–D5)) and format the result with the Time format. The result is 07:03.

This chapter has introduced you to Quattro Pro's Date and Time display formats and functions. It has also presented ideas and illustrations on how you might employ date and time calculations on your own notebooks.

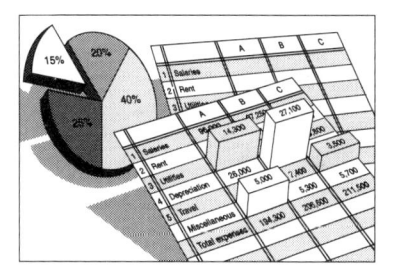

CHAPTER

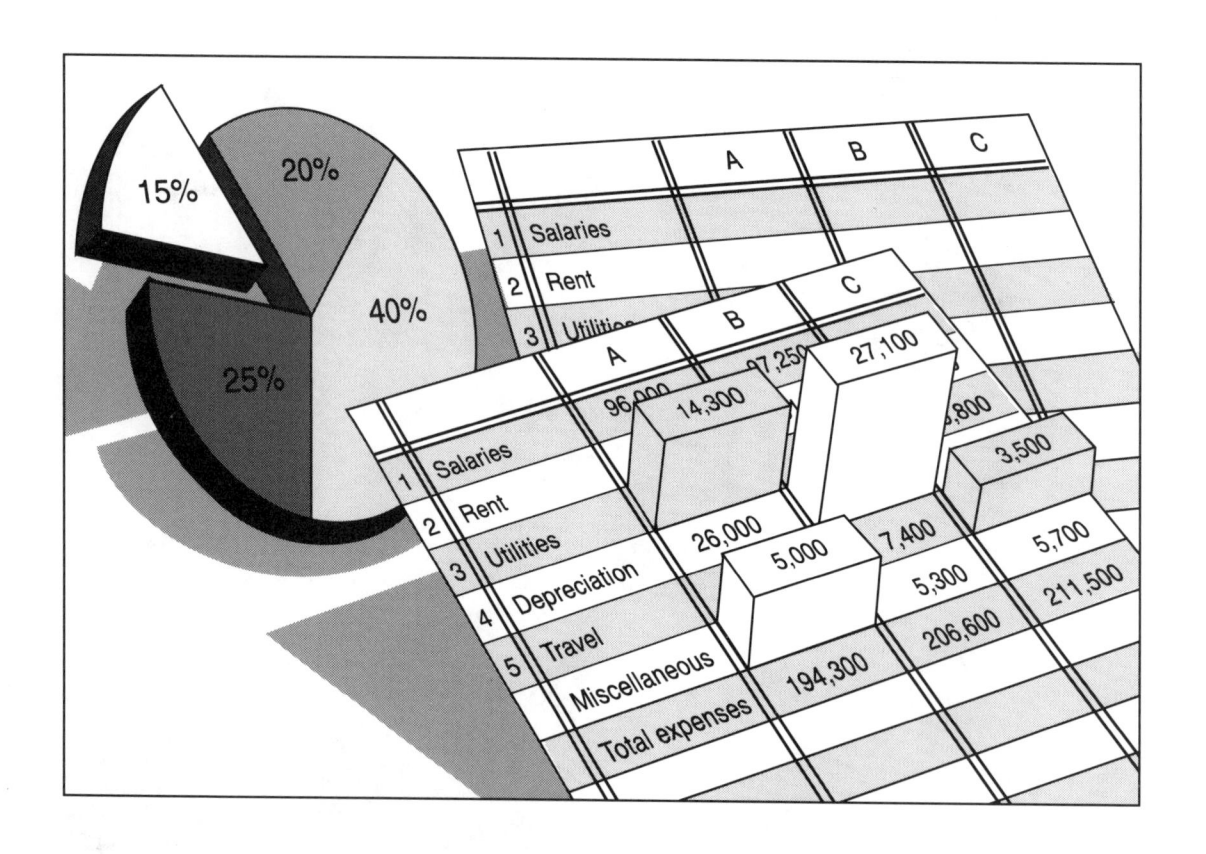

11

WORKING WITH WINDOWS

There are two types of windows in Quattro Pro: notebook windows and File Manager windows. You have been working with notebook windows since you first loaded Quattro Pro, although you learn more about them in this chapter. File Manager windows are covered in Chapter 18.

A notebook window *is a grid of rows and columns usually bordered by column letters at the top and row numbers at the left side, within which you can create or retrieve a single notebook. So far you* have worked with one notebook window at a time. Sometimes you have worked with several different notebooks within that window, building one file, saving it, retrieving another, and so on, but you have always worked within a single window.

Quattro Pro gives you several options for customizing the appearance and operation of individual notebook windows—for example, allowing you to split the window in two or to freeze selected rows or columns at the edges of the window. It also allows you to open up to 32 different windows at once, to display them in a variety of configurations, and to move or copy data between windows. This chapter introduces you to all these window options.

Customizing Individual Windows

All of the Window | Options settings are saved whenever you save your notebook.

All commands for customizing individual windows can be found on the Window | Options menu. The first five options on this menu—Horizontal, Vertical, Sync, Unsync, and Clear—pertain to dividing a window into sections so you can view two parts of a notebook at once. The Locked Titles option locks one or more rows and/or columns of labels as a set of titles at the top and/or left edges of the window. Once these titles are locked, they stay on screen even as you scroll through other data. The Row & Col Borders option allows you to erase the row and column borders at the left and top edges of the notebook area. The Map View option displays an overview of the notebook, with different codes indicating the position of labels, numbers, formulas, circular formulas, and linking formulas (formulas that refer to data in another notebook). The Grid Lines option displays a grid of lines between cells in WYSIWYG mode (or hides the grid lines if they are already displayed). Finally, the Print Block option displays a dashed line around the print blocks you specify using the / **P**rint | **B**lock command (as described in Chapter 6). Most of these commands are useful primarily when you are working with medium to large notebooks.

Using Titles

Most notebooks contain sets of labels—usually near the top or left edge of the notebook—that identify the contents of individual rows and columns. Because most notebooks cannot fit on a single screen, however, these column and row headings scroll off screen when you move beyond the current borders of the notebook area, making it difficult to identify individual items of data.

The / **W**indow | **O**ptions | **L**ocked Titles command solves this problem by letting you lock specific rows or columns at the left or top edge of the notebook area. Once a set of rows or columns have been locked, they remain in their current positions, regardless of how far you move the cell pointer.

Working with Windows

The Window | Options | Locked Titles menu includes the options Horizontal, Vertical, Both, and Clear. Horizontal locks all rows above the current position of the cell pointer. Vertical locks all columns to the left of the cell pointer. Both locks all rows above and columns to the left of the cell pointer. Make sure to move the cell pointer to the desired location before locking columns and/or rows.

You can remove the duplicate cells from the screen by moving the cell pointer past the current borders of the screen display.

Once you lock part of a notebook, those cells are shaded in a different color and you can no longer access them with any of the cursor-movement keys. You can only move the cell pointer to one of those cells by using the [F5] (GoTo) key. When you go to a locked cell, Quattro Pro displays duplicate copies of that cell. Any changes you make to these duplicate cells should appear in the original, still-locked cells when you press [Enter] or the next time the screen is redrawn. If you save a notebook that has locked titles, the titles are saved along with the data and are restored the next time you retrieve the file. The command for eliminating locked titles is / **W**indow | **O**ptions | **L**ocked Titles | **C**lear.

Before you can experiment with / **W**indow | **O**ptions | **L**ocked Titles or the various commands for splitting windows, you must construct a fairly large notebook, as described in the next exercise. This process gives you a chance to practice several of the commands and techniques covered in Chapter 9. It also introduces the @STRING function. This function is used to convert a numeric value to a character string, usually so it can be joined with another character string. Its syntax is

@STRING(*Value,Decimal places*)

where *Value* is a numeric value (usually a reference to a cell containing a number or numeric formula) and *Decimal places* is a numeric expression specifying the number of decimal places you want included in the resulting character string. If you specify a number of decimal places less than the number of meaningful decimals in the value itself, Quattro Pro rounds the value as necessary.

Start by entering data in two adjacent columns and then combining them in a single column. If necessary, save your data and issue the / **F**ile | **E**rase command to start with a blank notebook.

1. In A4, enter the label **Item No.** and issue the / **E**dit | **C**opy command. Press [Enter] to accept the default source block of A:A4..A4. Enter a destination block of **A4..A60**.

2. Issue the / **E**dit | **F**ill command. Enter a destination block of **B4..B60**, a Start value of **1**, a Step value of **1**, and a Stop value of **100**.

Recall that & is the operator used for concatenating character strings.

3. Move to C4 and enter the formula **+A4&" "&@STRING(B4,0)**, noting that this produces the label "Item No. 1".
4. Issue the / **E**dit | **C**opy command. Accept the default source block of A:C4..C4 and specify a destination block of C4..C60.
5. Issue the / **E**dit | **V**alues command. Specify a source block of C4..C60 and a destination of C4. You're going to convert the formulas in column C to values so that you can delete columns A and B without generating ERR values. (The input line now displays 'Item No. 1 rather than the formula you entered in step 3.)
6. Delete columns A and B by issuing the / **E**dit | **D**elete | **C**olumns command and specifying a block of A4..B4.
7. Use the / **S**tyle | **C**olumn Width command (Ctrl - W) to widen column A to 14 characters, and enter the label **Sample Notebook** in A1.
8. Issue the / **E**dit | **F**ill command. Enter a destination block of **B3..M3**, a Start value of **@DATE(94,1,15)**, a Step value of **30**, and a Stop value of **@DATE(94,12,31)**. You'll see date serial numbers across row 3.
9. Issue the / **S**tyle | **N**umeric Format command, select Date, and then select Date format 3. Again, specify the block B3..M3, and watch as the date serial numbers are transformed into formatted dates.
10. Issue the / **E**dit | **F**ill command one last time. Enter the block **B4..M60**, a Start value of **100**, a Step value of **2**, and a Stop value of **2000**.
11. Enter **TOTALS** in A62 and the formula **@SUM(B4..B60)** in B62.
12. Issue the / **E**dit | **C**opy command. Accept the source block of A:B62..B62 and specify a destination of B62..M62. Press Home .
13. Issue the / **F**ile | **S**ave command and assign the name **BIG** to the notebook which should now look like the one shown in Figure 11-1.

Now that you have enough data, lock the upper-left corner of the notebook with the / **W**indow | **O**ptions | **L**ocked Titles command.

1. Move to B4, issue the / **W**indow | **O**ptions | **L**ocked Titles command, and choose Both. All cells in column A and rows 1 through 3 are shaded to indicate that they are locked. Try moving the cell pointer up and to the left, and noting that column A and rows 1 to 3 are now inaccessible.
2. Press the → key until you reach the right edge of the notebook, and then keep moving, keeping your eye on the left side of the notebook. Note that column A remains locked as columns B, C, D, and so on scroll off the screen.
3. Press Home , and note that this key now takes the cell pointer to B4 rather than A1.

4. Press the ↓ key until rows begin to scroll off the top of the screen. Note that rows 1, 2, and 3 remain locked at the top of the notebook display.
5. Press F5 (GoTo) and enter **A1** as the address to go to. Your screen should now resemble Figure 11-2.
6. Change the contents of A1 to **SAMPLE NOTEBOOK**, and then press Pg Dn, Tab, and Home to clear the duplicate titles from the screen. Note that you were able edit A1, even though it was locked.
7. Issue the / **W**indow | **O**ptions | **L**ocked Titles | **C**lear command, and then press Home again. This time the cell pointer is moved to A1 because that corner of the notebook is now unlocked.

Splitting a Window in Two

The Vertical and Horizontal commands in the Window | Options menu split a single notebook window in two, enabling you to view two different sections of the notebook simultaneously. The two resulting window sections, known as *panes*, can be arranged either side by side (vertical panes) or one on top of the other (horizontal panes).

Splitting a window is particularly useful when you want to make changes in one set of cells and watch the effects of the changes on a distant section of the notebook. A split window can also allow you to make changes in two different parts of the notebook without having to move back and forth over large distances.

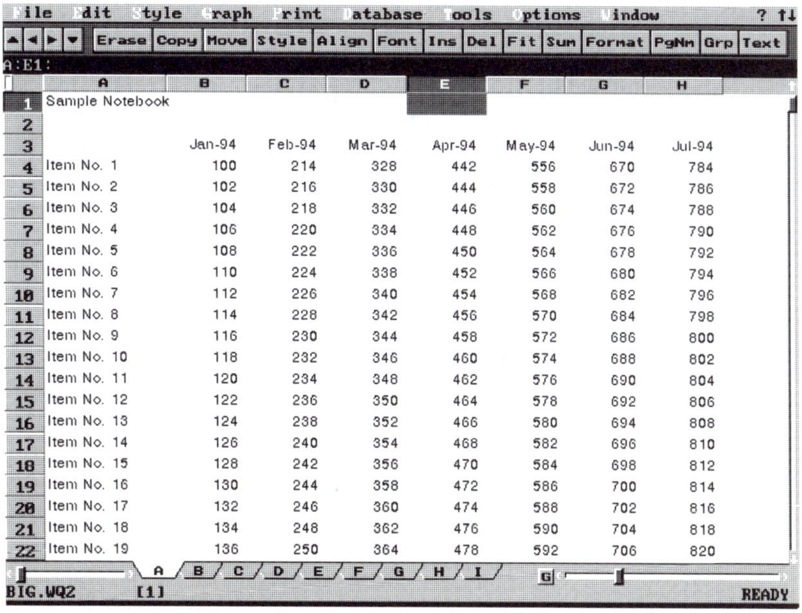

	A	B	C	D	E	F	G	H
1	Sample Notebook							
2								
3		Jan-94	Feb-94	Mar-94	Apr-94	May-94	Jun-94	Jul-94
4	Item No. 1	100	214	328	442	556	670	784
5	Item No. 2	102	216	330	444	558	672	786
6	Item No. 3	104	218	332	446	560	674	788
7	Item No. 4	106	220	334	448	562	676	790
8	Item No. 5	108	222	336	450	564	678	792
9	Item No. 6	110	224	338	452	566	680	794
10	Item No. 7	112	226	340	454	568	682	796
11	Item No. 8	114	228	342	456	570	684	798
12	Item No. 9	116	230	344	458	572	686	800
13	Item No. 10	118	232	346	460	574	688	802
14	Item No. 11	120	234	348	462	576	690	804
15	Item No. 12	122	236	350	464	578	692	806
16	Item No. 13	124	238	352	466	580	694	808
17	Item No. 14	126	240	354	468	582	696	810
18	Item No. 15	128	242	356	470	584	698	812
19	Item No. 16	130	244	358	472	586	700	814
20	Item No. 17	132	246	360	474	588	702	816
21	Item No. 18	134	248	362	476	590	704	818
22	Item No. 19	136	250	364	478	592	706	820

The BIG.WQ2 notebook
Figure 11-1.

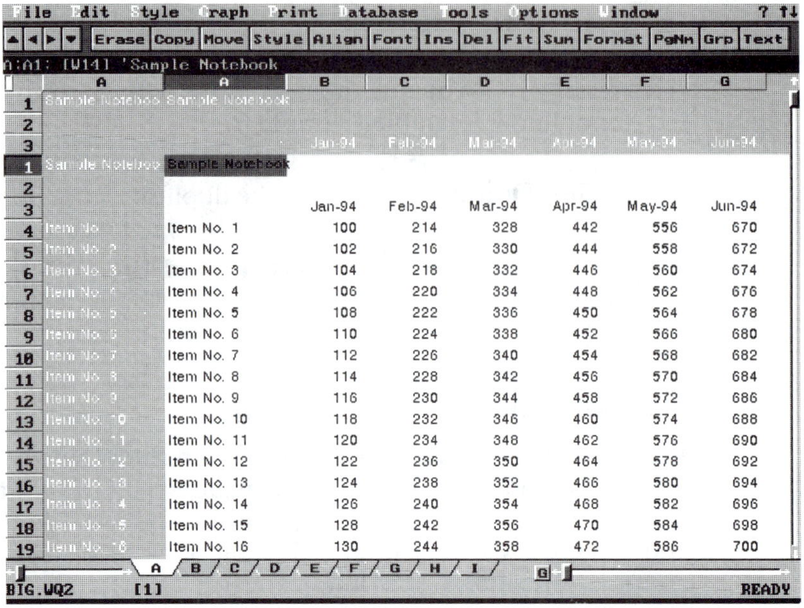

Quattro Pro 5 Made Easy

Going to a locked cell in BIG.WQ2
Figure 11-2.

Before you split a window, you must move to the spot where you want the division to occur. Then issue the / **W**indow | **O**ptions | **H**orizontal command to split the screen horizontally, immediately above the cell pointer, or issue the / **W**indow | **O**ptions | **V**ertical command to split the screen vertically, immediately to the left of the cell pointer.

To move between panes with a mouse, just click the pane you want to select.

As soon as you issue one of these two commands, Quattro Pro erases the Window | Options menu and divides the screen into panes. If you split the window horizontally, you will see a second column border just below the cell pointer. If you split it vertically, you will see a second row border, just to the right of the cell pointer. You can move panes by pressing F6, the Pane key. If you save your notebook while you have two panes open, the panes are saved and reappear the next time you retrieve the notebook.

Many commands that alter the screen display—including / **W**indow | **O**ptions | **L**ocked Titles, all commands related to columns, and all the / **O**ptions | **F**ormats commands—affect only the pane that currently houses the cell pointer. When you close the second pane with / **W**indow | **O**ptions | **C**lear, the only changes in column widths, window titles, and global formats that remain in effect are those that you made while the cell pointer was in the top or left pane. Column widths, global formats, or window titles established while the cell pointer was in the bottom or right pane are lost as soon as you close that pane.

Working with Windows

All other changes that you make to the notebook—including changes in data and changes made with any options on the Style menu other than those related to column widths—affect both panes and remain in effect when you close the second pane.

Synchronizing Panes

When you open a second pane, the two panes are automatically synchronized, so they scroll together as you move the cell pointer. Horizontal panes are only synchronized when you move right or left (both panes include the same columns) whereas vertical panes are only synchronized when you move up and down in the notebook (both panes include the same rows). This allows you to scan two ends of the same set of columns or rows. With synchronized panes you can, for example, watch how changes at the top of your notebook affect the bottom line. In some cases, however, you want the panes to be unsynchronized. The command for unsynchronizing panes is / **W**indow | **O**ptions | **U**nsync.

To create and use a horizontal pane on your sample notebook, follow these steps:

1. Press Home, and then move to A11 of the BIG.WQ2 notebook and issue the / **W**indow | **O**ptions | **H**orizontal command. Quattro Pro immediately divides the screen at row 11, so that rows 1 through 10 appear in the top pane and rows 11 through 20 appear in the bottom pane, as shown in Figure 11-3.

2. Press [Tab] to move one screen to the right. Notice that columns I through Q now appear in both panes. Press [Home], and note that columns A through H now appear in both panes. Because the panes are synchronized, the bottom pane scrolls along with the top one.

3. Issue the / **W**indow | **O**ptions | **U**nsync command. Press [Tab] again and note that different sets of columns now appear in the two panes. Because the panes have been unsynchronized, the bottom notebook is no longer affected by scrolling in the top pane. Press [Home] to return to A1. Type **/WOS** to resynchronize the panes.

4. Press [F6] (Pane) or click anywhere in the bottom pane to move to that pane.

5. In column A, issue the / **S**tyle | **C**olumn Width command ([Ctrl]-[W]), and change the column width to 12. Notice that the width of column A in the top pane is unchanged.

6. Press [Pg Dn] until the last rows are visible in the bottom pane.

7. Press [F6] or use your mouse to move back to the top pane. Keeping your eye on B62 in the bottom pane, change the value in B4 of the top

In character-based mode you'll see columns H through O, since less columns fit on the screen.

pane to 500. Press [Alt]-[F5] to undo the change and watch the total in B62 revert to 8892.

8. Issue the / **W**indow | **O**ptions | **C**lear command.

Eliminating Column and Row Borders

By default, all notebook windows include column letters at the top edge of the window and row numbers at the left edge. Occasionally you will want to erase these borders from the screen. The command for hiding the row and column borders in a notebook window is / **W**indow | **O**ptions | **R**ow & Col Borders | **H**ide. To redisplay the borders, use / **W**indow | **O**ptions | **R**ow & Col Borders | **D**isplay.

Map View

Quattro Pro's Map View affords a kind of aerial view of your work. You can survey a large section of a notebook and detect the type of data in each cell without seeing any of the details.

The command for changing to Map View is / **W**indow | **O**ptions | **M**ap View | **Y**es. The command for changing back to the regular notebook display is / **W**indow | **O**ptions | **M**ap View | **N**o.

BIG.WQ2 split horizontally **Figure 11-3.**

Working with Windows

> Note that in Map View you can still see the actual cell contents on the input line.

When you activate Map View, Quattro Pro narrows all columns to a single character and displays a code in each cell indicating the type of data the cell contains. The data type codes it uses are as follows:

Code	Type of Entry
l	Label
n	Number (or date)
+	Formula
–	Link formula
c	Circular formula
g	Inserted graph

You can also use Map View in conjunction with / **E**dit | **S**earch & Replace to locate particular types of data by searching for Map View data type codes. For example, if you want to find circular references, you can switch to Map View and specify a search string of "C." Make sure the **E**dit | **S**earch & Replace | **L**ook-In setting is Value rather than Formula or Condition. When you issue the / **E**dit | **S**earch & Replace command while in Map View, Quattro Pro does not let you edit or replace occurrences of the search string. It simply stops on the first cell that matches the search string. Remember, if you want more details on any circular references within your notebook, you can use the Audit feature (see Chapter 8).

Opening and Closing Windows

> You cannot open the same notebook in two different windows.

Quattro Pro allows you to open 32 windows at once. You might want to open more than one window to refer to one notebook when creating or modifying another, to copy or move data from one notebook to another, or to do several things at once, by switching from one notebook to another without having to constantly load and unload files from memory.

When you first load Quattro Pro, the program automatically opens a notebook window. To open additional windows, use either / **F**ile | **N**ew or / **F**ile | **O**pen. / **F**ile | **N**ew creates a new blank notebook in another window, without closing the current window. When you issue this command, Quattro Pro displays a second notebook window that completely overlays the first one. You can tell that you are in the second window only by looking at the window number displayed in brackets on the status line, just to the right of the notebook name.

The / **F**ile | **O**pen command retrieves an existing notebook from disk into another window. When you issue this command, Quattro Pro prompts you for a file name and displays the same list of files it displays when you issue the / **F**ile | **R**etrieve command. As soon as you select a file, Quattro Pro opens a new window and displays the selected notebook within it. The screen looks almost exactly as it does when you retrieve a file into the first window, except that the window number on the status line is increased by one.

Quattro Pro opens one window as soon as you load the program and fills it with a blank notebook temporarily named NOTEBK1.WQ2. Unless you want to build a new notebook in window 1, you should start by retrieving a notebook into that window. Then use / **F**ile | **O**pen to open additional notebooks in other windows.

You have used / **F**ile | **R**etrieve and / **F**ile | **E**rase many times in window 1. They work exactly the same way in other windows. Once you have opened a window, you can use / **F**ile | **R**etrieve to retrieve an existing notebook into it, replacing any notebook that was already there. You use / **F**ile | **E**rase to remove the notebook in the currently selected window from memory and from the screen, replacing it with a blank screen.

You can also close a window by clicking the close box in the window's upper-left corner.

Keep in mind that / **F**ile | **E**rase does not close the current window. To close a window, you issue the / **F**ile | **C**lose command. If you attempt to close a window without saving your latest changes to the notebook in that window, Quattro Pro displays a warning and gives you a chance to save your work. The command for closing all open windows is / **F**ile | **C**lose All. Whenever you close the last open window—either with / **F**ile | **C**lose or with / **F**ile | **C**lose All—Quattro Pro displays a mostly blank screen with a menu bar containing only the File option. You can open this File menu—which contains only five options—and select Open or New to open a notebook window. As soon as you do so, Quattro Pro displays the full menu bar, and you can proceed as usual.

Saving All Open Notebooks

There are actually three ways to save multiple notebooks at once. When you issue the / **F**ile | **C**lose All command, Quattro Pro closes the open windows one at a time, giving you a chance to save your work whenever it encounters a new or newly modified notebook. Similarly, when you issue the / **F**ile | **E**xit command, Quattro Pro checks whether you want to save any notebooks that have changed since the last time they were saved to disk. The / **F**ile | **S**ave All command lets you save all of your open notebooks. Issuing this last command is the equivalent of selecting each open notebook window in turn and issuing the / **F**ile | **S**ave command. As soon as Quattro Pro finishes saving all the open notebooks, it returns you to the notebook that was active when you issued the command.

Working with Windows

Even if you plan to leave Quattro Pro immediately after saving your work, / **F**ile | S**a**ve All is probably the safest way to save multiple files because if you mistakenly decide not to save a particular notebook, you can always issue another save command. (If you make the same error during the / **F**ile | C**l**ose All or / **F**ile | E**x**it command, your work is gone for good.) If you are creating or modifying several notebooks at once, you should also issue the / **F**ile | S**a**ve All command periodically to save your work in progress.

Moving Among Windows

Although you can have up to 32 windows open at any point, you can only work in one of those windows at a time. The window that contains the cell pointer is the *active window*. By default, any command that you issue applies to the active window.

When you first open a window, it is activated automatically. There are a number of ways of activating a window that is already open. If you are using a mouse and have arranged the windows so that at least part of several windows are visible, you can click on any portion of the desired window. If you're using the keyboard, you can press [Shift]-[F6], the Next Window key. Alternatively, you can hold down [Alt] and press the number of the window that you want to select; to select window 3, for example, you would press [Alt]-[3]. In addition, you can issue the / **W**indow | **P**ick command or either of its shortcuts [Alt]-[0] (use zero, not uppercase O) or [Shift]-[F5]. In this case, Quattro Pro displays a list of currently open notebooks and the windows in which they are displayed. Either click on the desired window, highlight it and press [Enter] to select it, or type the first letter of the notebook name.

Rearranging and Resizing Windows

When you first open multiple windows, Quattro Pro arranges them one on top of the other—rather like a neat stack of papers. Although you can shuffle through these windows using [Shift]-[F6] (Next Window), only the window currently on the top of the stack is visible. Quattro Pro allows you to change this arrangement and even provides commands for rearranging groups of windows in one of two common configurations: tiled and stacked. You can also shrink, expand, and reposition individual windows at will. The only commands you can use to rearrange windows in WYSIWYG are / **W**indow | **T**ile and / **W**indow | **Z**oom.)

Tiling and Stacking Windows

Both the / **W**indow | **S**tack command and the / **W**indow | **T**ile command rearrange all the currently open windows. When you issue the / **W**indow | **S**tack command while using a character-based display mode, Quattro Pro

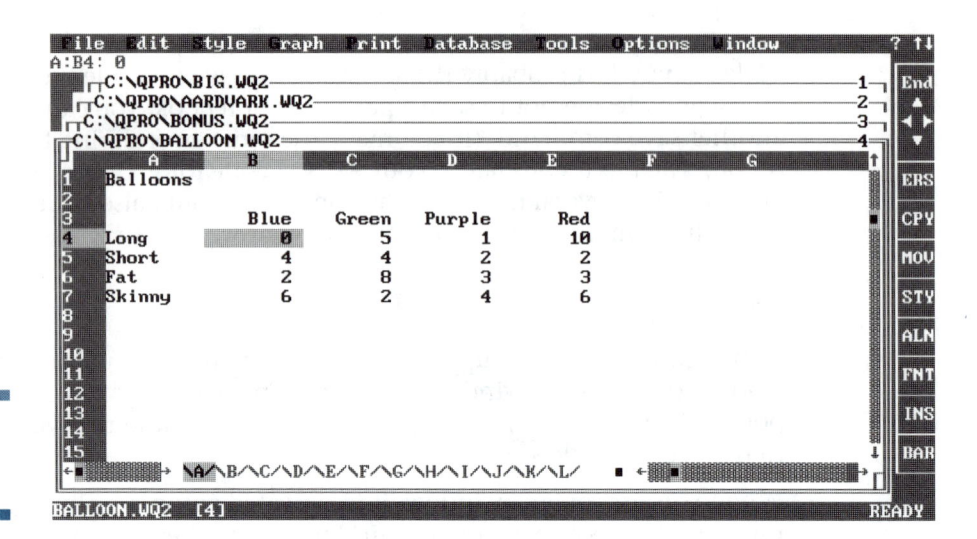

Stacked windows
Figure 11-4.

The menu command shortcut for / Window | Tile is Ctrl-T.

arranges the open windows in layers—the current window occupies most of the screen but the top edge of the other windows are visible above it. The resulting screen resembles a three-dimensional stack of papers, as you can see in Figure 11-4. You can use any of the usual methods to activate one of the windows: Shift-F6, Alt-0 or Shift-F5, Alt-# (Alt plus a window number), / Window | Pick, or clicking with the mouse. If you issue the / Window | Stack command in WYSIWYG mode, Quattro Pro simply beeps.

The / Window | Tile command splits the entire notebook area into sections—one for each open notebook. Figure 11-5 shows a screen with four tiled windows. The maximum number of windows you can display with / Window | Tile is 32—the same as the maximum number of notebooks you can open. If you have an EGA or VGA screen, you will find 43-line and 50-line display modes particularly useful when you are viewing several windows at once, because they allow you to see twice as much data. (You can switch to either of these display modes from the Options | Display Mode menu.) When you tile windows, all the open windows are visible on screen at once, but only one of those windows is active at any point. The active window is the one that includes scroll bars (in character-based mode it will also have double borders). In WYSIWYG, the active window's file name is displayed in a contrasting color.

Zooming Windows

To *zoom* means to expand a window temporarily until it occupies the entire area between the input line and the status bar. Zooming is particularly useful

Working with Windows

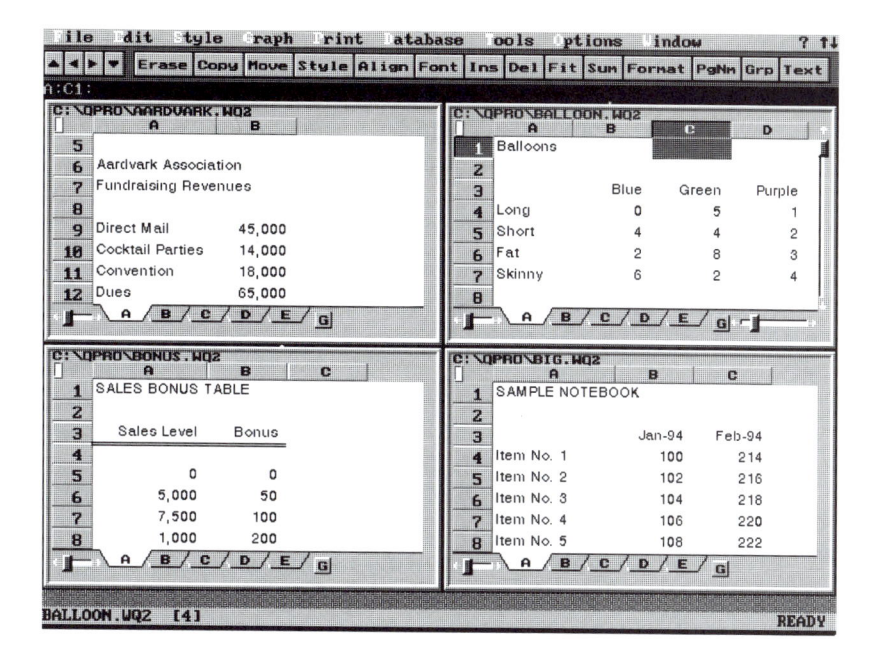

Tiled windows
Figure 11-5.

when you have several small windows on the screen and want to focus on one of them.

To zoom the active window, issue the / **W**indow | **Z**oom command or press `Alt`-`F6` (the Zoom Window key). If you are using a mouse, click the zoom icon, which is the two arrows just above the SpeedBar in the upper-right corner of the screen. Whenever you zoom a window, Quattro Pro remembers the size and position of all windows currently on the screen. As soon as you reissue the / **W**indow | **Z**oom command (or press `Alt`-`F6` again), Quattro Pro restores the previous window configuration. In WYSIWYG mode, once you have tiled windows, you can zoom one of them but you cannot use the Zoom Window key or the Zoom command afterward to return to the tiled configuration. You must issue the / **W**indow | **T**ile command again. In addition, if you switch between WYSIWYG and character-based modes with multiple windows open, Quattro Pro zooms the active window.

Moving and Resizing Windows

You cannot move or resize windows in WYSIWYG mode.

Although the window configurations produced by / **W**indow | **T**ile or / **W**indow | **S**tack are adequate in most situations, sometimes you may prefer a customized arrangement. You might want one window to occupy two thirds of the screen and another to occupy one third. Or you may want to arrange two windows one above the other rather than side by side. In these cases, you must move and resize the windows individually. Generally, it's easiest to tile the windows first and then adjust the resulting configuration.

To rearrange or resize windows in character-based display modes, use the / **W**indow | **M**ove/Size command ([Ctrl]-[R] shortcut). Quattro Pro displays a small box with the word "MOVE" in the upper-left corner of the active notebook. At the bottom of the screen you see the message "Press arrows to move, shift+arrows to resize."

> Quattro Pro indicates which mode you are in by displaying MOVE or SIZE in the upper-left corner of the window.

Once you issue the / **W**indow | **M**ove/Size command, you can either use the [Scroll Lock] key or type a period to toggle between Move and Size mode. If you are in Move mode, you can use the arrow keys to move the active window around on the screen. Press [Enter] when you're done to lock in the window's new position. Once you switch to Size mode, the arrow keys change the shape of the active window. To shrink the window, you can press either [↑] to move the bottom border up or [←] to move the right border to the left. To expand the window, press [↓] to move the bottom border down or [→] to move the right border further to the right. Once you start resizing a window, all the data in that window disappears temporarily. The data reappears as soon as you press [Enter].

To move a window using the mouse, drag any of its borders until the window reaches the desired location. To resize a window, drag the resize box in the bottom right corner of the window. (The resize box looks like ⌐.) The window frame changes size as you drag. When you move or resize a window with your mouse, there's no need to first issue the / **W**indow | **M**ove/Size command.

Quattro Pro also provides several single-key commands for rearranging the workspace once you are in Move/Size mode. T (top) moves the active window to the top half of the screen. B (bottom) moves the active window to the bottom half of the screen. L (left) moves the active window to the left half of the screen. R (right) moves the active window to the right half of the screen, and Z (zoom) expands the active window until it fills the screen. As soon as you press one of these keys, Quattro Pro performs the operation and immediately returns to Ready mode. To make further adjustments in your window configuration, you must reissue the / **W**indow | **M**ove/Size command.

When you save a notebook with the / **F**ile | **S**ave or / **F**ile | **S**ave **A**s command, Quattro Pro saves the current shape and location of the window in which the notebook is displayed. The next time you retrieve the notebook, it assumes that same shape and position. If you want to save a particular configuration of windows, including the notebooks they contain and their sizes and positions, you can use the / **F**ile | **W**orkspace command described next.

Working with Windows

Saving and Retrieving Workspaces

Once you have opened, sized, and positioned a set of windows, you may want to save the arrangement so that you can reuse it in the future. Using the / **F**ile | **W**orkspace | **S**ave command, you can create a special workspace file that contains all the details of the current window configuration, including the size and position of each window, and the name of the file displayed in each window.

When you issue the / **F**ile | **W**orkspace | **S**ave command, Quattro Pro prompts you for a workspace file name. Do not specify an extension; Quattro Pro automatically assigns the WSP extension. Once you have saved a workspace, you can restore it at any time using the / **F**ile | **W**orkspace | **R**estore command.

NOTE: If you have tiled windows in WYSIWYG mode, Quattro Pro expands them all to full-screen whenever you issue the / **F**ile | **W**orkspace | **S**ave command. When you restore the workspace later, just press Ctrl-T to tile the windows, reconstructing your previous window arrangement.

Workspace files do not contain any notebook data—they contain only the names of notebooks displayed in the windows that were open when you issued the / **F**ile | **W**orkspace | **S**ave command. This has two implications. First, you still need to save your notebooks as previously described under "Saving All Open Notebooks." Second, you need not worry about retrieving outmoded versions of your notebooks when you issue the / **F**ile | **W**orkspace | **R**etrieve command, even if you changed the notebooks after saving the workspace as a whole. Whenever you restore a workspace, Quattro Pro closes any open windows, reopens the workspace windows, and then fills those windows with the latest versions of your notebooks.

Copying and Moving Data Between Windows

Before you can move or copy data from one notebook to another, you must open both notebooks.

Quattro Pro allows you to copy and move data between any two open windows. The steps involved are the same as when you move or copy data within a single window: Issue the / **E**dit | **C**opy or / **E**dit | **M**ove command, specify a source block, and then specify a destination. The only difference is that either the source or the destination is in another unselected window.

When specifying cells in the second, nonactive window, you have a familiar choice between typing cell coordinates or pointing out cells on the notebook itself. To use the typing method, type the name of the notebook, enclosed in square brackets, followed by the cell or block coordinates. For example, to copy the block B10..B15 from XYZ.WQ2 into the active window, you would enter a source block of [XYZ]B10..B15. To copy cell A1 of the active window to cell B3 of the XYZ.WQ2 notebook, you would enter a destination of [XYZ]B3. When specifying the file name, you must include the extension only if it is something other than WQ2.

To use the pointing method, press [Shift]-[F6] (Next Window) or click in the desired window as soon as you are prompted for the source block or the destination. Then point to the cell or block and press [Enter]. Quattro Pro immediately returns the cell pointer to the notebook from which you issued the command.

When you move cells from one window to another, be careful not to create links between two notebooks accidentally. For now, whenever you move blocks of cells, be sure to keep formulas and the cells they reference together. Avoid moving a formula without also moving all the cells that it references; and refrain from moving cells without also moving any formulas in which they are referenced. Otherwise you will have formulas in one notebook that refer to (and are therefore affected by) cells in another notebook. Such formulas are easy to identify because they contain the name of a notebook in brackets. For example, the formula +A1*[XYZ]A:B15 multiplies the value of cell A1 in the current notebook by the value of A:B15 in a notebook called XYZ.WQ2. You can also ferret out linking formulas using Map View or the External Links option in the Audit menu.

There is nothing technically wrong with linking notebooks. It is a useful means of distributing and consolidating data across several notebook files. However, you should know all the implications of linking notebooks before you attempt this. The subject is covered in Chapter 19.

You don't have to worry about accidentally linking notebooks when you copy (rather than move) data from one window to another. Even if you copy a formula that contains absolute references, Quattro Pro assumes that you want to refer to the specified cell on the current notebook rather than on the notebook from which you copied the formula. Nonetheless, you should always check formulas after copying them to a new window. It is extremely easy to make mistakes such as copying a formula to column A that refers to the cell to its left (in which case Quattro Pro adjusts the formula to refer to the last column on the notebook).

Try opening an empty window and copying cells from the COMMISS.WQ2 notebook into the new, blank notebook.

1. Issue the / **File** | **E**rase command to clear BIG.WQ2 from your screen, and then retrieve the COMMISS.WQ2 notebook using the / **File** | **R**etrieve command.

Working with Windows

2. Issue the / **F**ile | **N**ew command to open a new blank notebook, move to A9, and issue the / **E**dit | **C**opy command.

3. When prompted for a source block, press [Alt]-[0] to display a list of open windows. Select the window that contains COMMISS.WQ2. Quattro Pro temporarily brings that notebook to the foreground so that you can see the data you are working with. The directory path and file name of the COMMISS.WQ2 notebook now appear on the input line as part of the default source block setting.

4. Press [Esc] to unanchor the cell pointer, move to A9 of the COMMISS notebook, and type a period. Press [End]-[Home] to expand the block to D19 and press [Enter]. Quattro Pro will redisplay the new, empty window.

5. Press [Enter] to accept the default destination of A:A9. The columns are too narrow to display all the data, and the numbers are displayed in General format.

6. Issue the / **O**ptions | **F**ormats | **G**lobal Width command, and enter a new column width of **15**.

7. Select Numeric Format from the Options | Formats menu and specify the Fixed format with two decimal places. Type **QQ** to return to Ready mode.

8. Save the notebook under any name you like, and then issue the / **F**ile | **Cl**ose All command to close the two open windows.

Quattro Pro does not copy any of the global formats when you copy data from one window to another.

You must copy the data to the same cells they occupied on COMMISS.WQ2, because the formulas in column D contain an absolute reference to cell B9. If you want to eliminate some of the blank rows at the top of the notebook, you can use / **E**dit | **D**elete | **R**ows after copying the data.

This chapter introduced you to a wealth of new tools for manipulating the Quattro Pro environment. You will find the commands such as those for locking titles and splitting a window into panes indispensable as soon as you start building notebooks that contain too much data to display in a single window.

CHAPTER

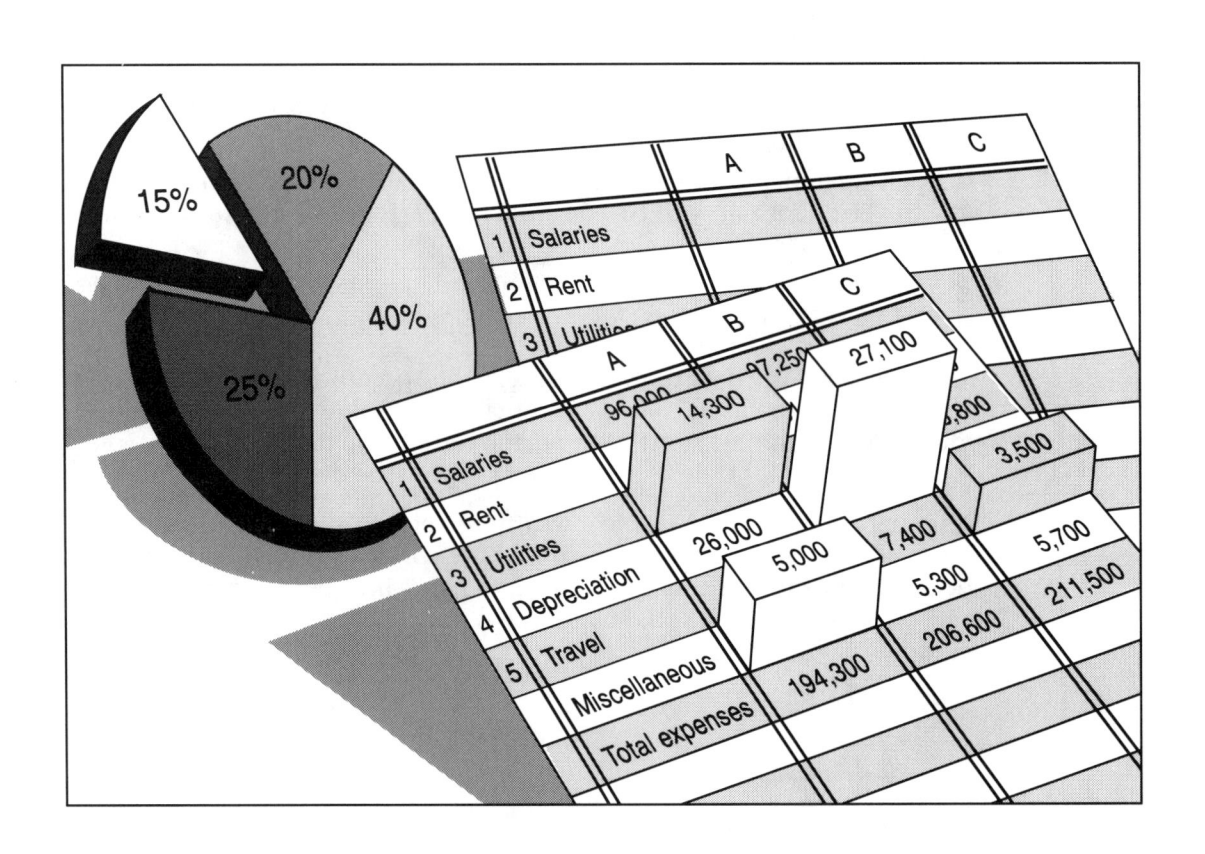

12

WORKING WITH NOTEBOOKS

After using Quattro Pro 5's new notebook feature for a while, you will probably find it indispensable. As you know by now, the term "notebook" is used to refer to any Quattro Pro file. However, what's new and exciting about notebooks is that they divide a single Quattro Pro file into 256 pages (A through IV), each of which consists of 256 columns and 8192 rows. In previous versions of Quattro Pro, each spreadsheet file essentially consisted of only one page. If you wanted to include various blocks of information in a single file, you had to place them in different locations on the same spreadsheet. The other alternative was to use multiple spreadsheet files, and then to link them via formulas if and when you needed to consolidate data. (Linking notebooks is covered in Chapter 19.)

Notebooks make it easier to organize your spreadsheets. If you want to include different types or sets of information within the same file, you can simply place them on different notebook pages. In the past, for example, you may have had inventory, payroll, and budget information in three separate files; now you can consolidate them into three pages of a single file. Placing discrete sets of data on separate pages also reduces the likelihood that you'll accidentally insert or delete rows or columns within data that is currently beyond your view, or erase blocks of information you forgot were there. In addition, you can assign unique names to notebook pages, which makes your spreadsheet's layout that much more apparent.

Notebook pages will also simplify your work whenever you need to enter duplicate or similar sets of information. If you're creating a balance sheet for all 12 months of the year, you can use a technique called "drilling" to enter all relevant text or data—including headings and line items—on all 12 pages at once, sparing you literally dozens of keystrokes. In addition, you can apply formatting across multiple pages. You'll learn to do both of these things later in the chapter, under "Using Groups."

This chapter begins with some notebook basics: You'll learn how to navigate between notebook pages and also how to name notebook pages, replacing the preset tabs that read A, B, C and so on. Then you'll learn how to create groups—essentially designating a contiguous set of pages on which you can operate simultaneously. Once you've created a group, you'll find out how to switch to Group mode so you can apply changes across multiple pages. You'll also learn all about working with 3-D blocks—that is, blocks that extend across multiple contiguous pages. Lastly, you'll learn some additional ways of manipulating notebooks, including moving, inserting, and deleting pages.

Notebook Basics

The only thing you really need to know before you can start using notebooks is how to get from one page to another. Naming pages is another basic operation that can both simplify your work with Quattro Pro and make your notebook files easier for others to read. Some other notebook basics—including moving, inserting, and deleting pages—will be covered later, after you've learned a bit more about manipulating 3-D blocks.

Working with Notebooks

Navigating Between Pages

The PgNm button is for naming pages, not for moving to specific page numbers, as you might at first think.

There are several ways of moving between notebook pages, some of which were introduced briefly in Chapter 1. One of the most straightforward ways to skip from page to page is simply to click on the page tabs at the bottom of the screen, which you can see in Figure 12-1. Try this out now by clicking on the tab for page D, noting that the cell address indicator on the input line now reads D:A1 and that the tab for page D at the bottom of the screen is highlighted. (If you see some other address, read the following paragraph for an explanation.) If you do not have a mouse, you can navigate between pages by using the (Ctrl)-(Pg Up) and (Ctrl)-(Pg Dn) key combinations; (Ctrl)-(Pg Up) moves backward one page, and (Ctrl)-(Pg Dn) moves forward one page.

The cell that you land in when you move to a particular page depends on two things: whether you have ever "visited" that page before, and, if you have, where your cell pointer was when you left the page. For example, when you moved to page D, you probably wound up in cell A1. However, if you had been to page D before, clicking on the tab for page D would have taken you to the cell you were in right before you left the page. (If you're in Group mode, you'll always wind up in the same cell when you move between pages in the group.)

If the tab for the desired page is not visible, you can use the tab scroller, shown just above the file name in Figure 12-1, to bring it into view. The tab scroller operates very much like the horizontal scroll bar; however, instead of moving you to the left or right on the current page, it displays more page tabs to the right or left of the current page. (Note that using the tab scroller does not move you to a new location; it simply makes it possible for you to move to a new location by bringing different page tabs into view.)

You can also use the GoTo key, (F5), to travel to a specific cell within a specific page. For example, you can press (F5) and enter **D:D8** to go to cell D8 on notebook page D. If you want to stay on the current (active) page, you don't need to specify a page letter or name while issuing the GoTo command.

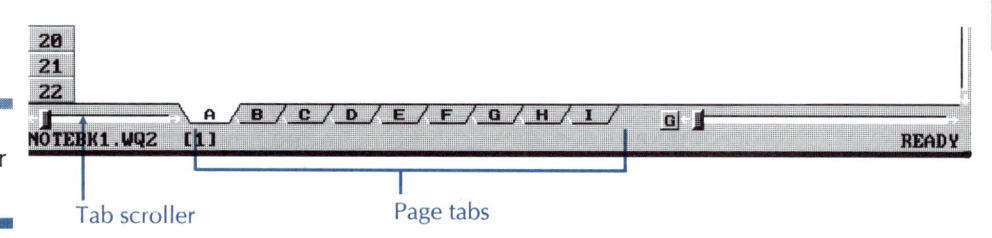

Page tabs and the tab scroller
Figure 12-1.

Naming Pages

You cannot assign a page a one- or two-letter name other than its default name.

When you open a new notebook file, all of its 256 pages are named with letters—the letters you see on the page tabs at the bottom of the screen. However, you can assign page names of up to 15 characters to any notebook page. (You can use letters, numbers, and the special characters ~, ', !, %, _, |, \, ', and ?, but you cannot use spaces in page names.) Naming pages has two advantages: It allows you to see at a glance what a page is for (January is more informative than A). In addition, as with block names, you can use page names in formulas; this both increases accuracy and makes formulas easier to decipher.

Note that you can still refer to renamed pages by their original one- or two-letter names. (The first 26 page tabs have one-letter names, and all page tabs after that have two-letter names such as AA.) For example, even if you rename page A to January, you can refer to it as January or as page A in cell references and 3-D block references—either in formulas or when specifying cell blocks in commands. This permits you to use a longer, more descriptive page name, but to save keystrokes by entering the single-letter page name.

The procedure for creating page names is extremely simple. Follow these steps to name the first four pages in an empty notebook:

The PgNm button on the SpeedBar is equivalent to the / Edit | Page | Name command.

1. With your cell pointer anywhere on page A of a blank notebook, issue the / **E**dit | **P**age | **N**ame command.

2. Press [Esc] or [Backspace] to delete the letter "A" after the "New page name" prompt, enter **Jan**, and then press [Enter] or click on the Enter button. Notice that the label "Jan" appears on the page tab at the bottom of the screen and also replaces A as the page reference on the input line. Before leaving the page, enter the title **January Chocolate Sales** in cell A:A1.

3. Press [Ctrl]-[Pg Dn] or click on page tab B to move to the next page, issue the / **E**dit | **P**age | **N**ame command, and change the page name to **Feb**. Enter the title **February Chocolate Sales** in cell B:A1. Then follow the same procedure to assign the names **Mar** and **1stQtr** to pages C and D, respectively. While you're at it, enter the title **March Chocolate Sales** in cell C:A1, and the title **First Quarter Chocolate Sales** in cell D:A1. At this point, your screen should resemble the one shown in Figure 12-2.

Renaming a page is as easy as naming it in the first place. Just follow the procedure outlined above, and type in the new name after the "New page name" prompt. If you want to reassign the page's default name, you can either type it in or delete everything after the prompt and press [Enter].

Working with Notebooks

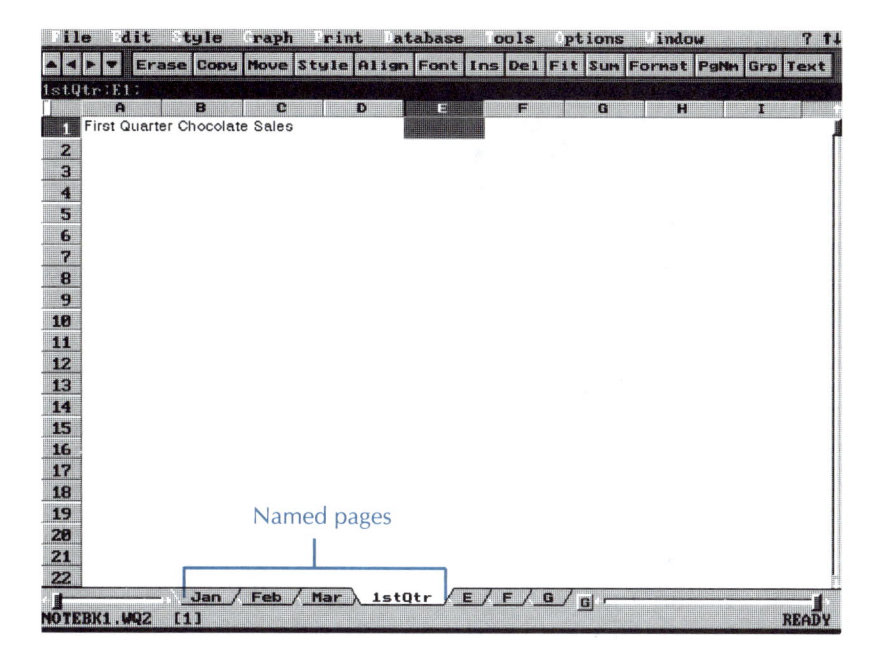

Four named pages
Figure 12-2.

Using Groups

In Quattro Pro 5, you can make changes to more than one page at a time by working in Group mode. This can present tremendous advantages. When you're in Group mode, any style and formatting changes that you make affect all pages in the designated group. For example, you can boldface a heading in a particular cell in all selected pages, and you can even insert or delete rows and columns on all pages in a group. In addition, you can use drilling to enter data in all pages of a group at once if you choose. Before you can use Group mode, however, you need to create one or more groups.

Creating Groups

The process of creating a group is exceedingly straightforward: You just issue the / **E**dit | **G**roup | **C**reate command, enter a group name, and tell Quattro Pro which pages to include in the group. The only restrictions on creating group names are that they cannot exceed 15 characters, cannot include spaces, and can include no special characters other than ~, ', !, %, _, |, \, ', and ?. In addition, group names within the same notebook must be unique. And finally, although you can have many groups within a single notebook, groups may not overlap. In other words, if you have one group that includes the pages A though F, you cannot create another group that includes the pages C through H.

The next exercise demonstrates how to create a group that consists of the four pages—Jan through 1stQtr—that you named a moment ago.

> You can use the Grp button on the SpeedBar in place of the / **E**dit | **G**roup | **C**reate command.

1. Issue the / **E**dit | **G**roup | **C**reate command. You will see a list of existing groups, if there are any, and the prompt "Group name to create/modify."
2. Type the group name **firstquarter** and press [Enter] or click on the Enter button.
3. When prompted for the "First page of group," type **a** and press [Enter]. When prompted for the "Last page of group," type **d** and press [Enter]. (You could also type **Jan** and **1stQtr** as the first and last pages.)

At this point, you'll return to Ready mode, and there will be no perceptible change to your notebook. However, if you click on the Grp button again, you'll see the group name FIRSTQUARTER, along with the names of any other groups that you may have created on your own.

Note that you can also modify existing groups by using the same procedure but choosing a group name from the list. For example, if you decided to modify the FIRSTQUARTER group so that it only included Jan through Mar, you could select FIRSTQUARTER from the list of group names, keep the same first page, but enter a last page of **c** or **Mar**. In addition, you can delete the names of groups you no longer use by issuing the / **E**dit | **G**roup | **D**elete command, selecting the name of the group you want to delete, and then pressing [Enter]. Keep in mind that deleting a group does not in any way affect the text, codes, or data you've already entered into those pages. It just tells Quattro Pro that it can no longer treat them as a group.

Working in Group Mode

> To turn off Group mode, click on the Group button again, or issue the / **E**dit | **G**roup | **M**ode | **D**isable command.

Naming groups is a preparatory step that you must take before you can work with multiple pages at the same time. Even if a page is part of a group, it is treated as a single entity unless you switch to Group mode. Switching to Group mode is a simple matter of either clicking on the Group button at the bottom of the screen—the button marked with a G (or a square, in text mode) to the right of the page tabs—or issuing the / **E**dit | **G**roup | **M**ode | **E**nable command ([Ctrl]-[F5] shortcut). (You can be anywhere in the notebook when you turn on Group mode; but you must be on one of the pages in the group in question before you can make changes that affect the entire group.) Being able to switch in and out of Group mode enables you to make changes to individual pages or to several pages at once, as you choose.

Working with Notebooks

> **HINT:** Don't confuse the Group button at the bottom of the screen with the Grp button on the SpeedBar. The Grp button is a shortcut for creating a group, whereas the Group (G) button enables you to switch to Group mode, in which you can apply changes to multiple notebook pages at once.

When you're in WYSIWYG mode and you switch to Group mode, a blue bracket will appear underneath the page tabs of all pages within the group, and the Group button will appear to have been pressed in. (If you have created multiple groups, they'll all have these brackets.) If you're in text mode, a G will appear on the Group button, and the page names at the bottom of the screen will be separated by two dots (like the two dots in block references) and will all appear on a single tab. For example, if you switch to Group mode, the tabs for the FIRSTQUARTER group will read Jan..Feb..Mar..1stQtr. Figure 12-3 shows the four pages you've named and grouped under the name FIRSTQUARTER, in WYSIWYG mode and with Group mode turned on. Note that if you're in Group mode when you save your notebook, you'll be returned to Group mode the next time you open the notebook.

Applying Formatting in Group Mode

If you want to apply changes to only a single page, you can just switch out of Group mode.

If Group mode is on, formatting changes you make within the group apply to all pages automatically. When you're in Group mode, changes to any one page in the group affect all pages, so it doesn't matter which page you're on. It does, however, matter which cell you're in. Try switching to Group mode now and applying a few simple changes to your notebook, noting that they affect all pages in the group.

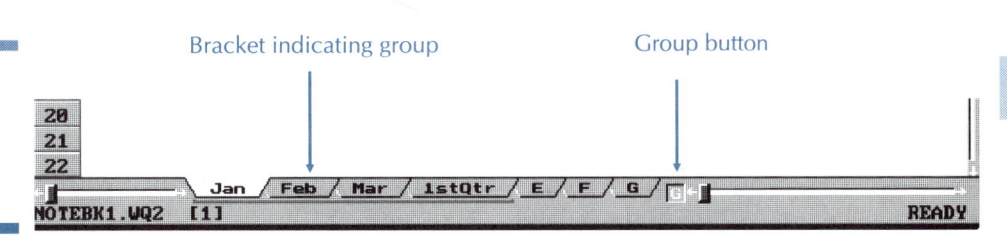

Several pages in a group with Group mode on Figure 12-3.

1. Switch to Group mode either by clicking on the Group button at the bottom of the screen or by issuing the / **E**dit | **G**roup | **M**ode | **E**nable command.
2. Move to cell Jan:A1, and then select / **S**tyle | **F**ont and press (Enter) to accept the default block. Note that the address on the input line reads FIRSTQUARTER:A1..A1; this is your indication that you're in Group mode and that changes will apply to all pages in the FIRSTQUARTER group.
3. In the Font menu that appears, choose Point Size and select 14 point; then choose Bold to turn on boldfacing. Choose Quit to return to Ready mode; right away you can see your changes on the current page. Nothing new so far.
4. Now click on the Feb tab or press (Ctrl)-(Pg Dn) to move to the next page in the group. Notice that the font changes have automatically taken hold here too. In fact, your changes have been applied to all four pages in the group, even though you made only a single change.
5. From the Feb page, issue the / **O**ptions | **F**ormats | **G**lobal Width command and enter a column width of 16. Choose Quit twice to return to Ready mode. Again, move from page to page in the group, noting that the change has taken place throughout. If you like, go to a page outside the group; you'll see that its column width has not changed.

When you're in Group mode, most other formatting changes are also automatically reflected across the designated cell or block in all pages in the group. For example, the majority of the commands on the Edit menu automatically apply to all pages in the group. You can insert and delete rows and columns, copy and move information, hide columns, and set column widths and row heights in all pages at once. You can also use the Undo ((Alt)-(F5)) option on the Edit menu to reverse the effects of changes you may have unintentionally made to all pages in a group. Undo might come in particularly handy if you use / **E**dit | **E**rase Block (or the Erase button on the SpeedBar) and then realize that you unintentionally deleted data in all notebook pages in the group.

In addition, most options in the Style menu automatically affect all pages in the block. You change the alignment and numeric format of specific cells, change column widths and row heights, add shading and lines, institute all types of font changes (of which you just experimented with a few), hide columns, and even apply styles across the entire group.

Entering Data in More Than One Page at Once

The one thing that does not happen completely automatically in Group mode is text and data entry. When you enter text or data in the normal

Working with Notebooks

fashion, it is only entered on the active page of a group, even when you're in Group mode. It is very easy, however, to use a technique called "drilling" to enter the identical text, data, or formulas in the same cells of all pages in the group. To drill an entry, make sure you're in Group mode, type the desired label or value in any page in the group, and press [Ctrl]-[Enter].

TIP: If you accidentally press [Enter] when you meant to press [Ctrl]-[Enter], it's easy to remedy the error without actually retyping your entry. Just move to the cell in question, press [F2] or click on the input line to get into Edit mode, and press [Ctrl]-[Enter]. Your entry will be drilled through to all pages in the group.

When you're in Group mode, you can also delete data from several pages at once. To do so, just highlight the desired cell or block of cells on any one page within the group. Then press [Ctrl]-[Backspace] to delete all entries in that particular cell or group of cells on all pages in the group. The other alternative is to use the / **E**dit | **E**rase Block command or the Erase button on the SpeedBar. In either case, you should proceed with caution. You may want to check all pages to be affected before you go ahead with the deletion. And, if you make an unintentional deletion, use the Undo command ([Alt]-[F5]) immediately. If you want to delete data in a single notebook page to be safe, just highlight the relevant area of the notebook and press the [Del] key. This technique works regardless of whether you're in Group mode.

Try out this exercise now to enter some data into your FIRSTQUARTER group:

1. Make sure you're in Group mode, go to cell A4 of the page Jan, type **Product**, and press [Ctrl]-[Enter]. (Remember, you can actually be in cell A4 of any page in the group when you do this.)

2. Go to cell A5, type **Truffles**, and press [Ctrl]-[Enter]. Then type **Chocolate Cigars** in cell A6 and press [Ctrl]-[Enter], type **Fudge Sauce** in cell A7 and press [Ctrl]-[Enter], and type **Chocolate Kisses** in cell A8 and press [Ctrl]-[Enter]. If you like, you can move to another page in the group at this point, noting that your entries have been applied there too.

3. Enter the label **Number Sold** in cell B4 and press [Ctrl]-[Enter]; next enter the label **Total Sales** in cell C4 and press [Ctrl]-[Enter]. Then boldface the three labels in cells A4..C4, and right-align cells B4 and C4 (this is so the numbers you enter in a moment will line up better with the labels you have just entered).

4. Use [Shift]-[F7] or drag with your mouse to select cells B9..C9 and issue the / **S**tyle | **L**ine Drawing | **T**op | **S**ingle command to create a line at the top of those two cells. This will separate the totals from the values above. Choose Quit to exit from the Placement menu.

5. Next you'll enter data in cells B5..C8 of the page for Jan. In this case, you *do not* want to drill the entries, since there will obviously be different sales amounts for the different months. Enter **99** in B5, **199** in B6, **299** in B7, and **399** in B8.

6. Type the formula **+B5*3** in C5 and press [Ctrl]-[Enter], type **+B6*2** in C6 and press [Ctrl]-[Enter], type **+B7*5** in C7 and press [Ctrl]-[Enter], and type **+B8*1** in C8 and press [Ctrl]-[Enter]. In this case, you unfortunately cannot enter a single formula and copy it down column C, since the chocolate items each have different price tags. However, you *can* drill the entries, since the same prices will apply in all months, and the formulas will pick up the Numbers Sold values to their left, even when they're copied to other pages.

7. Enter **@SUM(B5..B8)** in cell B9 and press [Ctrl]-[Enter]. In this case also, you should drill the entries in order to apply the formulas to all pages in the group. In cell C9, enter **@SUM(C5..C8)** and press [Ctrl]-[Enter]. (If you prefer, you can also copy B9's formula to C9.)

8. Move to the Feb page, noting that it has values of 0 in cells B9, C9, and C5 through C8. The formulas are there, but there are as yet no values in cells B5..B8—the cells upon which all the formulas depend. Enter some values in those cells now; the totals will be displayed in cells B9, C9, and C5 through C8. Go to Mar and again enter some values in cells B5 through B8.

9. Finally, for appearances, move to cell C9 and apply the Currency numeric format by issuing the / **S**tyle | **N**umeric Format | **C**urrency command, entering **0** as the number of decimal places, and pressing [Enter] to accept the default block of FIRSTQUARTER:C9..C9. Return to the Jan page, noting that this formatting change has automatically been applied to all notebook pages.

10. At this point, save your notebook by issuing the / **F**ile | **S**ave command and entering the file name **CHOCOLAT**. Your notebook should resemble the one shown in Figure 12-4.

Manipulating 3-D Blocks

You've already performed several operations that affect blocks of cells on multiple pages: Anytime you apply formatting such as boldfacing to one or more cells in Group mode, for example, those particular cells are formatted on all pages in the group. In a sense, then, you've already been working with 3-D blocks, which are simply blocks of cells that are extended across multiple consecutive pages.

Working with Notebooks

You'll learn how to move entire pages shortly.

Even when you're not working in Group mode, you can perform many operations on 3-D blocks. (In fact, it's usually less confusing and more convenient *not* to be in Group mode when you are explicitly defining 3-D blocks.) Among other things, you can copy, move, and erase 3-D blocks. As an example, you might want to copy a 3-D block spanning 12 pages to create a duplicate 12-month budget that you could then modify for the new year. You can also insert and delete columns and rows in 3-D blocks, and can even use the Fill command to fill across multiple pages. In fact, any operation that prompts you for a source block can be performed on a 3-D block. In addition, you can use 3-D block references in formulas. For example, you could decide to sum the cells in B5..B8 in pages A through C of a particular notebook. In some cases, you may want to switch out of Group mode so you can select a 3-D block that is just a portion of the group or that includes more than one group; you could do this to apply formatting to the first three pages of a 12-page group, as just one example.

See Chapter 4 for the details on selecting blocks.

There are two ways of entering a 3-D block reference. You can point out the block with either the keyboard or your mouse, and you can type in the 3-D reference. To point to a 3-D reference with the keyboard, go to the first or last page in the block and select a regular (2-D) block by pressing Shift-F7 and using the arrow keys. At this point, hold down the Shift key while pressing either Ctrl-Pg Up or Ctrl-Pg Dn until you get to the last or first page in the block. To point to a 3-D block with your mouse, move to the first or last page in the block and select a 2-D block by dragging with your mouse. Then

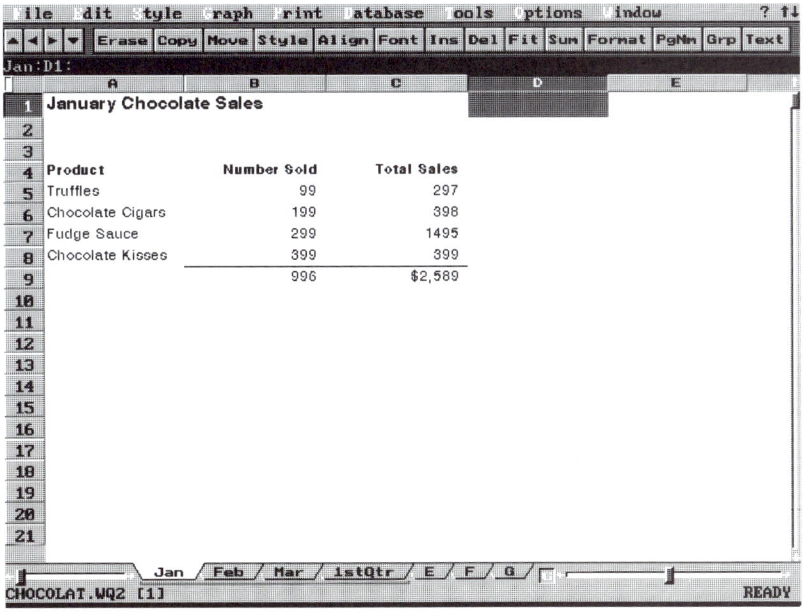

Drilling entries in your chocolate spreadsheet
Figure 12-4.

hold down the [Shift] key and click on the page tab of the last or first page of the block. (You may have to use the tab scroller to bring the desired page tab into view.) When you've pointed out a 3-D block, a black line appears underneath the tabs of the pages within the block if you're in WYSIWYG mode. (In character-based mode, underscores appear between the tabs. For example, if you select a block that spans pages X through Z, the page tabs will read X__Y__Z.)

When you type in a 3-D block reference, there are two syntax options. An example of the default syntax is X..Z:A1..B2, which refers to cells A1..B2 on pages X through Z. When you use this form, the second part of the syntax is exactly the same as when you enter normal, 2-D block references. The first part of the syntax merely includes the first and last pages in the block, separated by two dots. The alternate syntax is X:A1..Z:B2. This format is slightly less intuitive; it may help to think of it as representing the two corners of a 3-D block. X:A1, the first component, is the upper-left cell on the first page in the block. Z:B2, the second component, is the lower-right cell on the last page in the block. Anytime you enter a 3-D reference, Quattro Pro converts it into the first format; if you'd like the other style to be the default, however, you can issue the / **O**ptions | **S**tartup | **3**-D Syntax command and choose the second option.

When typing in 3-D references, you are free to use page names and even group names if you like. For example, you could enter Jan..Feb instead of A..B, or you could type in the group name instead of the first and last page in the group. In addition, Quattro Pro substitutes page and group names in your 3-D references wherever relevant. For instance, if the pages X through Z were grouped under the name CHOCOLATPROFITS, that page name would be substituted for X..Z in any block reference that included those three pages. The reference X..Z:A1..B1 would become CHOCOLATPROFITS:A1..B2, and so on. (This occurs no matter which way you designated the block to begin with.) In addition, when Group mode is on, the group name is used whenever you point out a block, regardless of whether you explicitly type in or point out multiple pages. This reminds you that any action will be performed on all pages in the group.

To experiment with 3-D references, try entering some formulas to calculate the totals from the first three months of the year in cells B5..B8 of the 1stQtr page in your CHOCOLAT.WQ2 notebook. (You won't have to enter formulas in C5..C8, or in B9 or C9, since you drilled formulas into those cells earlier.) Before you enter the formulas in column B, however, you have to modify the FIRSTQUARTER group so it only includes the pages Jan..Mar.

Working with Notebooks

1. Choose the / **E**dit | **G**roup | **C**reate command or click on the Grp button, choose the FIRSTQUARTER group name, retain the same first page (Jan), but change the last page to **Mar**.
2. Go to page 1stQtr of your CHOCOLAT.WQ2 notebook, and move to cell B5.
3. Enter the formula **@SUM(Jan..Mar:B5)**; this will add up all values in B5 in all pages in the group. The formula automatically changes to @SUM(FIRSTQUARTER:B5..B5); this is because the FIRSTQUARTER group now consists of pages A though C, and Quattro Pro automatically replaces page coordinates with page or group names where applicable.
4. Issue the / **E**dit | **C**opy command, press [Enter] to accept the source block of 1stQtr:B5..B5, and then enter a destination block of **B5..B8**. The cells B5 through B8 will now reflect the total numbers sold from those cells in the previous three pages, and the formulas that you drilled into cells C5..C8 will be updated to reflect the total dollar amounts for individual products for the quarter. In addition, the @SUM formulas you drilled into cells B9 and C9 will be updated to reflect the new data on the page. At this point, your screen should resemble Figure 12-5. (Your values will probably differ from those shown in the figure, depending on the numbers you entered on the Feb and Mar pages earlier in the chapter.)

Remember, you could enter the page coordinates A..C instead of Jan..Mar.

To double-check your results, you can try entering a different formula—@SUM(Jan..Mar:B5..B8)—that should produce the same results as those currently shown in cell B9. This time, to experiment, you'll try the pointing method of generating a 3-D reference.

1. Click on the Group button at the bottom of the screen to switch out of Group mode. Then move to cell B12 and type **@SUM(**. (Don't type the period.)
2. Click on the page tab for Jan, and then drag or use [Shift]-[F7] and your arrow keys to highlight the block B5..B8. At this point the input line should read @SUM(Jan:B5..B8.
3. Hold down the [Shift] key and click on the page tab for Mar. Note that the input line now reads @SUM(FIRSTQUARTER:B5..B8—Quattro Pro was intelligent enough to detect that you've pointed out the pages that comprise the FIRSTQUARTER group.
4. Finally, type a closing parenthesis or click on the) button on the Edit SpeedBar and press [Enter]. You should get the same results in B12 that you got in B9.

Entering formulas using 3-D block references
Figure 12-5.

When constructing formulas that refer to multiple pages, you are not confined to referring to *blocks*; you can refer to various cells on pages that need not be contiguous. For example, you could enter a formula such as

@SUM(A:A6..B10,I:Z100,Q:B3..B4)

to sum cell blocks or single cells scattered across the notebook. Or you could use the formula +A:A1-C:C1-E:E1 to subtract individual cells from various pages. This gives you tremendous flexibility to work with any of the thousands of cells within your notebook. You cannot, however, use this type of reference when issuing commands.

NOTE: Page references, like cell references, are relative by default. In other words, if you move the formula +A:A1+B1 from page A to page B, it will become +B:A1+B1. (When page or group names are used in 3-D references, the names don't change even if the formula is moved; nevertheless, the letter names for the pages are in fact being adjusted behind the scenes.) Most of the time this is what you want, but you may at times want to keep page references absolute. In such cases, you can either type a dollar sign in front of the page portion of the cell address, or use the Abs key (F4). Relative and absolute cell references are covered in more detail in Chapter 8.

Working with Notebooks

Moving, Inserting, and Deleting Pages

When your work involves multiple pages on a notebook, you will often have the occasion to delete pages that you no longer need, insert pages when you need extra workspace, and move pages if they are not currently in the optimum location. All of these operations are extremely easy. Moving pages is particularly simple if you're using a mouse. When you're moving, inserting, and deleting pages that are part of a group, you should turn Group mode off unless you wish to move, insert, or delete multiple pages.

Remember that page references, like cell references, are relative by default. In other words, if you delete page A, all references to cells that had been on page C change to references to page B. The same applies if you move or insert pages; all references are updated automatically to reflect the page's new location. (If you're using named pages, their names don't change when pages around them are moved, added, or deleted; however, the letter name that you can use to refer to them does. For instance, if you deleted Feb in your CHOCOLAT.WQ2 notebook, you could refer to the Mar page as either Mar or B.)

Moving Pages

You cannot, as you might think, move multiple pages by dragging the tab of a page that's part of a group.

You can move pages with either the keyboard or the mouse. Moving pages with the mouse is easy and intuitive. To move a single page, click on its page tab to select it if it's not already the active page. Then drag the page tab either to the left or the right until it's in the desired position—the tab will become highlighted when you begin to drag—and release the mouse button to deposit the page in its new location. If you're using a mouse and you drag any page included in a selected 3-D block, all of that block's pages move together.

You can also move pages with the keyboard by using the / **E**dit | **P**age | **M**ove command and then specifying the source and destination pages. (Pages being moved are deposited just to the left of the designated destination page.) This process is less visual than moving pages with the mouse, but may be easier than dragging if you're moving a page some distance, rather than just a few pages away. For example, if you wanted to move page A to page Z, dragging would be impractical. Note that when you move pages, the source and destination you specify must include a cell reference (to any cell) as well as a page reference.

When using / **E**dit | **P**age | **M**ove, you can just as easily move multiple contiguous pages by specifying multiple pages as your source block. For example, if you wanted to move pages A through D to another location, you would issue the / **E**dit | **P**age | **M**ove command and specify the source block A..D:A1 either by typing or pointing. In addition, you can move an entire group of pages by moving to any page in the group, switching Group mode on, issuing the / **Edit** | **P**age | **M**ove command, and accepting the default source block—which will be the group name. (Remember, you cannot move an entire group of pages by dragging page tabs.) No matter which method you use, when you move a multiple-page block, the block's rightmost page is inserted just before the specified destination page. For example, if you moved pages A through D and indicated a destination page of Z, the four moved pages would become pages V, W, X, and Y, respectively.

TIP: In most cases, moving a page beyond the boundaries of the group removes it from the group. And if you move a page into the boundaries of a group, that page becomes part of the group. The exception to this occurs when you move pages that are at either corner of a group. If you move the rightmost page in the group to the right, or the leftmost page to the left, the group will actually expand—much as moving either corner of a named block will expand the block. (Named blocks were covered in Chapter 8.)

Inserting and Deleting Pages

You can initiate either of these commands with the Ins or Del buttons on the SpeedBar.

You can insert one or more contiguous pages with the **E**dit | **I**nsert | **P**ages command. To do so, first move to the page in front of which you want to insert the pages. Then issue the / **E**dit | **I**nsert | **P**ages command. To insert a single page in front of the current page, press [Enter] to accept the default page block. If you want to insert multiple pages, expand the block before pressing [Enter]. Note that if you insert pages within a group, they're added to the group, whether or not Group mode is on. In addition, if you insert pages from within a group while Group mode is on, the group name is offered as the "page insert block" by default. If you press [Enter] to accept this default, multiple pages (as many pages as there are in your group) are inserted to the left of the group.

Deleting pages is not much different from deleting rows or columns, which you learned how to do in Chapter 4.

To delete pages you use the / **E**dit | **D**elete | **P**ages command. To delete a page, click on its page tab if it is not already the active page. (The cell pointer can be in any cell on the page.) Then issue the / **E**dit | **D**elete | **P**ages command. Press [Enter] at the "Delete one or more pages" prompt to delete the active page. You can expand the page block before pressing [Enter] if you want to delete several contiguous pages. If you're within a group and Group mode is on when you issue this command, the group name becomes the default list of pages to be deleted. Pressing [Enter] at this point deletes all pages in the group, and also deletes the group name itself.

Working with Notebooks

This chapter has provided you with a quick glimpse of what's possible with Quattro Pro 5's new notebook feature. You learned how to move between notebook pages, how to name notebook pages, and how to create groups and work in Group mode. In addition, you learned the details about when and how to use 3-D references. Finally, you discovered how to organize and reorganize your notebook in three dimensions, by moving, inserting, and deleting pages. Although this chapter has by no means been exhaustive, you should now have a solid grounding in the basics—enough so that you can begin to explore and experiment with this extraordinarily useful feature on your own.

CHAPTER

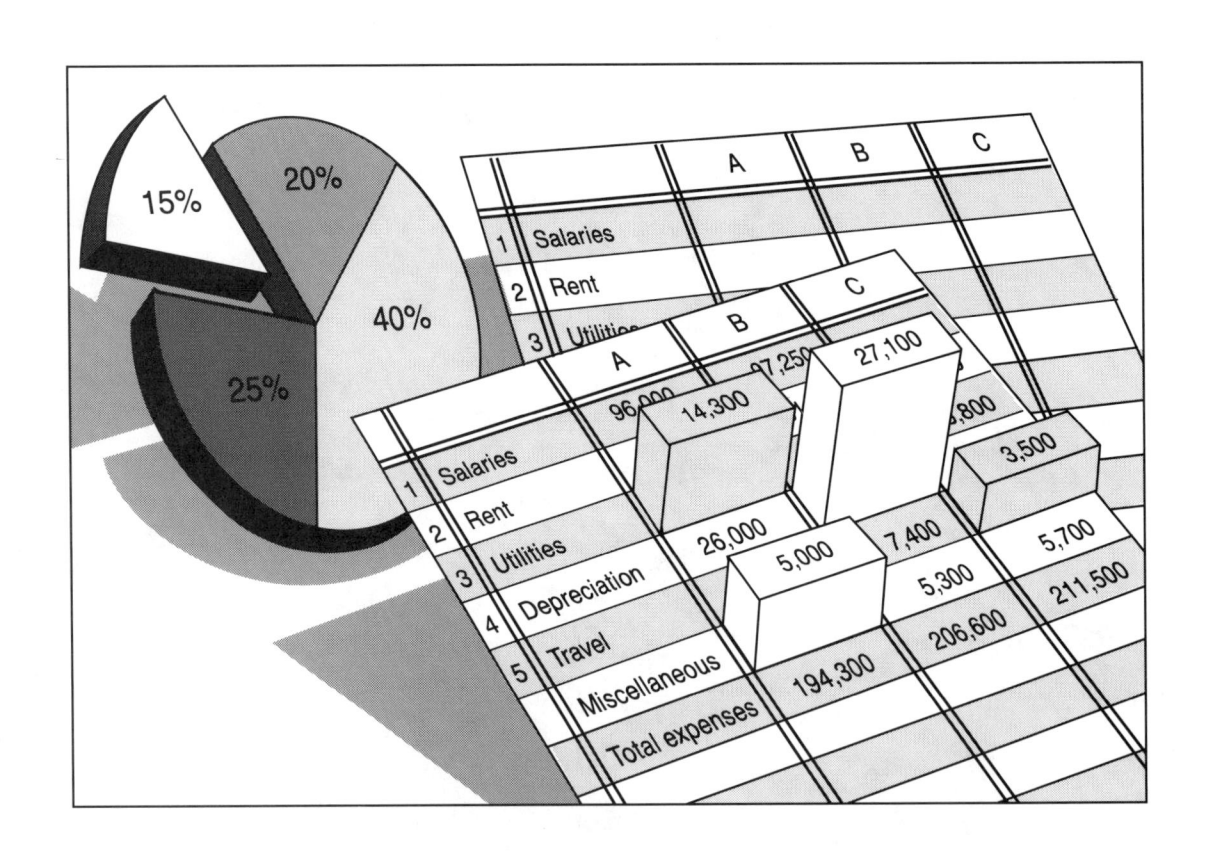

13

CUSTOMIZING THE ENVIRONMENT

So far you have used the working environment—including screen layout and colors, display mode, and SpeedBars—more or less as is. Quattro Pro actually allows you tremendous leeway in customizing this environment to your own tastes. This chapter explains how to change Quattro Pro's default settings for individual notebooks and, in some cases, individual notebook pages. In addition, you learn how to change global defaults. These defaults affect your entire work session, and—if you save them with the / **O**ptions | **U**pdate command—they can affect future work sessions as well. The chapter also covers another technique for customizing the environment: menu command shortcuts.

The Different Types of Defaults

Quattro Pro has default settings for everything from the extension it assigns to notebook files to the colors used on help screens. You can modify these default settings using various commands in the Options menu. Quattro Pro actually has three types of default settings. Some defaults—such as Global Width and Protection—only affect the notebook page on which you make the change; these are called *page defaults*. Other defaults—such as numeric format—affect the entire notebook, but do not affect new notebooks that you open, even during the current work session; these are called *notebook defaults*. Both page and notebook defaults are stored in the notebook file along with your data and placed in effect each time you retrieve that notebook from disk. These defaults have no effect on future notebooks: As soon as you create a new notebook, Quattro Pro reinstates the global defaults.

Still other defaults—including settings established with the Hardware, International, and SpeedBar options on the Options menu—affect the rest of the current work session; these are called *global defaults*. Global defaults remain in effect throughout the current work session, unless you explicitly change them. They are not saved when you issue any of the save commands, and are not automatically in effect for your next work session. You can, however, make them into permanent defaults by issuing the / **O**ptions | **U**pdate command.

If you change a page default while Group mode is on, the change is applied to all pages in the group.

Quattro Pro's global defaults include all settings in the Hardware, International, Display Mode, Startup, SpeedBar, Graphics Quality, Other, and Network submenus of the Options menu. Most of the color settings are also saved as global defaults, as is the WYSIWYG Zoom % setting. Notebook defaults include the Recalculation setting in the Options menu and the Numeric Format settings in the Options | Format menu. The page defaults include Protection, as well as Align Labels, Hide Zeros, and Global Width in the Options | Format menu.

Telling Quattro Pro About Your Hardware

The Options | Hardware menu, shown here, contains only three selectable options: Screen, Printers, and Mouse Button. The Screen and Mouse Button options are discussed shortly. The / **O**ptions | **H**ardware | **P**rinters commands are covered in Chapter 6. The other items on the menu are for display only; they cannot be changed. They include several items describing the amount of memory available in your computer. The Coprocessor setting at the

Customizing the Environment

bottom of the menu indicates whether a math coprocessor is installed in your computer.

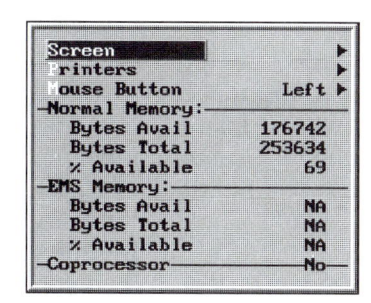

```
Screen                        ▶
Printers                      ▶
Mouse Button          Left    ▶
─Normal Memory:─────────────────
    Bytes Avail       176742
    Bytes Total       253634
    % Available           69
─EMS Memory:────────────────────
    Bytes Avail           NA
    Bytes Total           NA
    % Available           NA
─Coprocessor──────────────No────
```

Specifying Your Screen Type

The Options | Hardware | Screen options allow you to fine-tune the settings for your screen display. In most cases Quattro Pro automatically detects the type of video display card you are using and loads a special driver file that tells Quattro Pro how to display data on your screen. If you are using an unusual video display card, you may need to modify some of the settings yourself.

You cannot change the Screen Type option or the Resolution option from within WYSIWYG mode.

When you choose the Screen option, Quattro Pro displays a menu of screen types; select the appropriate type. The Resolution option lets you change the resolution used for displaying graphs. The default setting is the highest resolution available for your screen type. You may need to choose a lower resolution if you are using an external projection system to display graphs.

The Aspect Ratio option lets you change the way that Quattro Pro displays circles, so that the circle appears perfectly round when you draw pie charts. Use this option if your pie charts appear elongated. When you select this option, Quattro Pro displays a circle in the middle of the screen. Use the ↑ and ↓ keys to adjust the height of the circle until it appears round. Finally, the CGA Snow Suppression option lets you alleviate problems with flickering that sometimes occur on CGA screens.

Switching Mouse Buttons

Some left-handed people find it easier to click the right mouse button than the left. Quattro Pro lets you switch the active mouse button by using the / **O**ptions | **H**ardware | **M**ouse Button | **R**ight command. If you want to reactivate the left mouse button at some point, use / **O**ptions | **H**ardware | **M**ouse Button | **L**eft.

Customizing Quattro Pro's Colors

The / **O**ptions | **C**olors commands allow you to alter the colors used for menus, various sections of the notebook, and the help screens. They also include an option for defining *conditional colors,* which are used to highlight values that fulfill particular conditions, such as falling outside a particular numeric range.

You can use the / **O**ptions | **C**olors commands with a color or monochrome monitor. With monochrome, your choices are limited to Normal, Bold, Inverse, Underlined, and Empty. With color monitors, your choices expand to dozens of color combinations. After you select an item to define, Quattro Pro displays a box full of colors. Each row of this box represents a different background shade. The diamonds in the box represent various foreground shades. Select colors by moving the rotating cursor to the desired set of colors and pressing Enter. (When you use the / **O**ptions | **C**olors | **S**preadsheet | **W**YSIWYG Colors command, you instead see a gallery of colors, or a list of colors if you happen to be in character-based mode.)

Using Colors to Emphasize Data on a Notebook

Quattro Pro offers several commands that allow you to distinguish or highlight particular entries on a notebook. You can use the / **O**ptions | **C**olors | **S**preadsheet | **L**abels command to define colors for labels, and you can use the / **O**ptions | **C**olors | **S**preadsheet | **C**ells command to define colors for values. (Both of these commands only have an effect in character-based mode.) Similarly, you can use the / **O**ptions | **C**olors | **S**preadsheet | **U**nprotected command to change the color of cells that are unprotected on a notebook on which the protection feature has been enabled.

You can define a Smallest Normal Value without defining a Greatest Normal Value and vice versa.

The Options | Colors | Conditional menu contains options that allow you to designate colors for cells that fulfill particular conditions. For example, you can define a color for cells that return a value of ERR, so those cells are more noticeable. You can also define a range of values that you consider "normal" (using the Smallest Normal Value and Greatest Normal Value options) and then specify different sets of colors for normal, below-normal, and above-normal values.

NOTE: Conditional color settings do not take effect until you select the On/Off option on the Options | Colors | Conditional menu and change the setting from Disable to Enable. This allows you to define conditional colors but then turn them off temporarily without losing your settings.

All the color-related settings—for example, ERR and Below Normal Color—in the Options | Colors | Conditional menu are global defaults. However, the On/Off option, Smallest Normal Value option, and Largest Normal Value option are page defaults and are saved with your notebook.

Customizing the Environment

WYSIWYG Colors

Most of the / **O**ptions | **C**olors | **S**preadsheet commands have no visible effect in WYSIWYG mode. If you are using WYSIWYG display mode, you can issue the / **O**ptions | **C**olors | **S**preadsheet | **W**YSIWYG Colors command to further customize your display. When you issue this command, Quattro Pro displays a menu of screen elements. As soon as you select an element, it presents a gallery of available colors.

Reinstating Default Colors

Quattro Pro provides the / **O**ptions | **C**olors | **P**alettes command for returning all colors to their system default settings. When you issue this command, Quattro Pro displays a menu with the options Color, Monochrome, Black & White, Gray Scale, Version 3 Color, and Quit. To return the colors to normal, select the option appropriate to your screen. The Gray Scale option is useful for VGA screens that use gray tones rather than color. The Version 3 Color option sets your screen to the colors used in Quattro Pro 3.

The International Settings

The Options | International menu allows you to define special symbols or formats for displaying currency, negative numbers, punctuation, dates, and times. It also lets you choose how you want data sorted and accents displayed.

Currency   The International Currency option determines the appearance of values that are displayed in Currency format. The initial default setting is a dollar sign displayed before each formatted value. To display currency types other than dollars, you can select the Currency option on the Options | International menu, press (Esc) or (Backspace) to erase the current default symbol, and enter a new symbol.

You can use any symbol(s) you like, including special ASCII characters. You can enter special characters that do not appear on your keyboard, such as £, by holding down the (Alt) key while typing the ASCII code for the character. (As an example, the ASCII code for the British pound symbol shown above is 156.) You can also use a string like "Deutsche Marks" as a currency symbol. Once you have entered the new currency symbol, Quattro Pro asks whether this symbol is to be used as a prefix or suffix.

NOTE: You can use only one currency symbol per page. You cannot, for example, use $ in one area and £ in another.

> **TIP:** When entering ASCII codes, you must use the numbers on the numeric keypad rather than those at the top of the keyboard.

Displaying Negative Values   The Negative option determines whether negative numbers that are formatted with the Currency or comma format are displayed inside parentheses or preceded by a minus sign. The default setting is Parenthesis.

Punctuation   The Punctuation setting determines the punctuation characters that are used to designate a decimal point in numbers; to separate arguments in function statements and commands in macros; and to separate hundreds from thousands, thousands from millions, and so on in numbers displayed with the , (comma) and Currency formats. When you select the Punctuation option on the International menu, the character separating a1 from a2 in each of the menu options indicates the punctuation mark that you can use to separate arguments in functions and macros. The A option, Quattro Pro's initial default, uses periods to mark decimal places and commas to separate thousands. It also uses commas to separate arguments in functions and macros. You can choose one of the other seven options to alter this default setting.

Dates and Times   As mentioned in Chapter 10, you can modify the Long and Short International display formats for displaying dates and times using the Date and Time options in the Options | International menu. Note that all International Time formats use the 24-hour clock (two o'clock in the afternoon, for example, would be expressed as 14:00 in Short International format A option).

The following are alternative international date formats:

Format	Long Int'l	Example	Short Int'l	Example
A	MM/DD/YY	10/22/94	MM/DD	10/22
B	DD/MM/YY	22/10/94	DD/MM	22/10
C	DD.MM.YY	22.10.94	DD.MM	22.10
D	YY-MM-DD	94-10-22	MM-DD	10-22

Customizing the Environment

The following are alternative international time formats:

Format	Long Int'l	Example	Short Int'l	Example
A	HH:MM:SS	09:43:27	HH:MM	09:43
B	HH.MM.SS	09.43.27	HH.MM	09.43
C	HH,MM,SS	09,43,27	HH,MM	09,43
D	HHhMMmSSs	09h43m27s	HHhMMm	09h43m

Use Sort Table The Use Sort Table option lets you choose which set of rules Quattro Pro uses when sorting data. (Sorting is covered in Chapter 16.) The default sort order, ASCII, sorts uppercase before lowercase. Among other things, you can select INTL to use international sorting rules, in which sorts are not case sensitive.

LICS/LMBCS Conversion The LICS/LMBCS Conversion setting determines whether Quattro Pro converts characters from the Lotus International Character Set or the Lotus Multibyte Character Set to regular upper-ASCII characters. Issue the / **O**ptions | **I**nternational | **L**ICS/LMBCS Conversion | **Y**es command to convert any WK1 or WK3 file into ASCII characters when it is retrieved.

Overstrike Print The Overstrike Print option lets you print accented characters. The default setting is No. If you select Yes, your printer knows to print the letter, backspace, and then print the diacritical mark over the letter to form an accent. Note that if you chose the Standard European rather than the Standard U.S. character set when you installed the program, Quattro Pro can print many diacritical characters, even if Overstrike Print is set to No, provided you use final-quality printing.

Changing the Display Mode

If you have a monochrome or CGA monitor, you have only one choice for display mode—80x25 (80 characters wide, 25 lines long). If you have a high-resolution display (EGA or above), the Options | Display Mode menu will include a number of additional choices that you can use. The WYSIWYG (What You See Is What You Get) display mode is graphics-based; all the other display modes, like the 80x25 default setting, are character-based.

In graphics-based display modes such as WYSIWYG, each screen image is constructed from a pattern of dots. In character-based modes, characters are displayed using your hardware's built-in character sets. The various character-based modes that appear on the Options | Display Mode menu allow you to display these characters in different sizes. If you have any type of EGA or VGA monitor, you can use option C, EGA 80x43 mode, to display 43 lines on the screen. If you have a VGA monitor, you can also choose option D, VGA 80x50 mode, to display 50 lines on the screen. The remaining options are specific to different video adaptors and are primarily used for achieving 132-column mode.

If you select a display mode that your hardware cannot display properly, the screen display may be scrambled. In this case, press `Ctrl`-`Break` and then issue the / **O**ptions I **D**isplay Mode I **A**: 80x25 command.

Using WYSIWYG Mode

WYSIWYG mode requires an EGA or VGA monitor capable of 480x350 resolution. As mentioned in Chapter 1, several aspects of the screen appear different in WYSIWYG mode. In general, slightly more rows and columns fit on screen in WYSIWYG than in 80x25 mode. Also, the options on the menu bar and the buttons on the SpeedBar appear slightly sculpted and three-dimensional. Another difference is that some menus appear as *galleries* rather than conventional menus: Quattro Pro displays a series of images to represent options in place of the usual option names. In addition, lines added to the notebook with the / **S**tyle I **L**ine Draw command appear on the borderlines between cells rather than causing extra space to be inserted between rows or columns. You'll also notice that in WYSIWYG the screen closely resembles the way your notebook will look when it is printed in final-quality mode. Finally, if you insert graphs (as described in Chapter 14), they appear as part of your notebook on screen, just as they do when printed.

WYSIWYG also offers two other features not found in the character-based display modes—the ability to resize characters in the notebook and to adjust the heights of rows—that are described shortly.

The easiest way to alternate between WYSIWYG and 80x25 display modes is with a mouse: To select WYSIWYG, just click on the WYS button on the SpeedBar; for 80x25 mode, click on Text. (If you don't see the WYS button, try clicking on BAR first.) If you don't have a mouse, you must issue the / **O**ptions I **D**isplay Mode command whenever you want to switch from one mode to the other.

NOTE: WYSIWYG consumes more memory than the character-based display modes. If you are running short of memory, try switching to a character-based display.

Customizing the Environment

Zooming the WYSIWYG Display   By issuing the / **O**ptions | **W**YSIWYG Zoom % command and changing the setting to something less than 100%, you can view a greater number of rows and columns at one time. Figure 13-1 shows the BIG.WQ2 notebook created in Chapter 11, in a 12-point font zoomed to 70%; the amount of data you see on your screen may depend on the display mode or your monitor.(At 100%, only the first seven months' worth of data would be visible.) If you instead increase the zoom percentage beyond 100%, you can examine smaller sections of the notebook in greater detail.

Adjusting Row Heights   In WYSIWYG mode, Quattro Pro automatically adjusts row heights to a slightly larger point size than the largest font in the row, just as it does when printing in final-quality mode. (Quattro Pro does not, as you might expect, shrink rows if you use a small font in WYSIWYG mode.) If you prefer, you can adjust these row heights manually with the / **S**tyle | **B**lock Size | **H**eight command, which displays a menu with choices for Set Row Height and Reset Row Height. If you select Set Row Height, Quattro Pro asks you to specify a block of rows and then displays the current point size on the input line. You can adjust the size either by entering a new number or by pressing ↑ or ↓ to adjust the height manually.

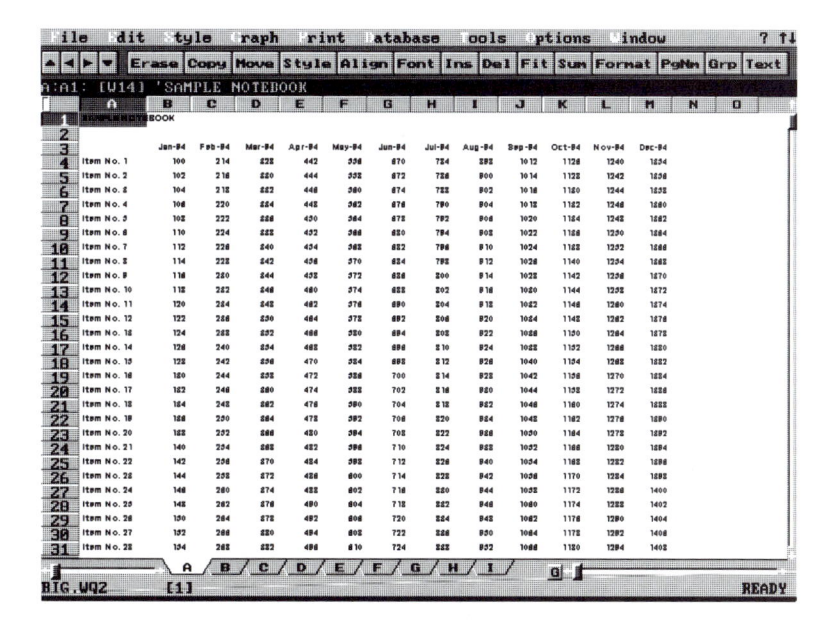

WYSIWYG display at 70%
Figure 13-1.

TIP: In WYSIWYG, you can also click and drag on a row's number to adjust it's height, much as you click and drag on a column letter to adjust that column's width.

Row height adjustments affect the notebook's printed appearance as well as the way it looks in WYSIWYG. If you specify a row height that is too small to accommodate some of the characters on the row, Quattro Pro will truncate the upper part of those characters, both when printing and in the WYSIWYG display.

Row height settings are automatically saved with the notebook page when you issue any of the file save commands. To return control over row heights to Quattro Pro, issue the / **S**tyle | **B**lock Size | **H**eight | **R**eset Row Height command and specify the block of rows to reset.

Defining Startup Settings

The / **O**ptions | **S**tartup commands direct Quattro Pro perform certain operations every time you load the program. The Directory option defines the default data directory—that is, the directory in which Quattro Pro looks for and stores notebook files unless another directory is specified. You can define a default data directory for the current work session using the / **F**ile | **D**irectory command, but that setting (unlike the Options | Startup | Directory setting) is not saved when you issue the / **O**ptions | **U**pdate command.

The Autoload File option designates a notebook file that will be loaded automatically whenever you load Quattro Pro. (If you specify a nonexistent file, Quattro Pro won't load any file automatically.) The Startup Macro option specifies a certain macro to be executed automatically every time you retrieve a notebook. The File Extension option designates default extensions for notebook files. If you are using the regular Quattro Pro menus, the initial default is WQ2, which you may want to change if you are planning to exchange notebooks with other programs frequently.

The Beep option causes your computer to sound a beep when you commit an error. The Menu System option displays a menu of options for using the Quattro menu tree, or any alternate menu systems you may have created with the Edit Menus option. The Edit Menus option lets you modify the Quattro Pro menu system: adding or deleting options and even moving commands from one menu to another (this option is not covered in this book). The Use Dialogs option determines whether Quattro Pro displays dialog boxes or menus when you issue commands such as / **P**rint | **L**ayout and / **G**raph | **C**ustomize Series; the default setting is Yes. Finally, the 3-D

Customizing the Environment

Syntax setting determines which syntax Quattro Pro uses by default for 3-D block references, which are covered in Chapter 12.

Changing the SpeedBars

You cannot redefine the arrow keys and the BAR button.

If you are using a mouse, the / **O**ptions | Speed**B**ar command allows you to customize the two SpeedBars—the palettes of buttons displayed at the top or right edge of your screen. When you choose / **O**ptions | Speed**B**ar, Quattro Pro displays a menu with the options READY mode SpeedBar, EDIT mode SpeedBar, and Quit. When you select either READY mode SpeedBar or EDIT mode SpeedBar, Quattro Pro displays a submenu with options for each of the definable buttons on that SpeedBar, and one or more extra options for defining new SpeedBar buttons. As soon as you select one of these buttons, you see a submenu with the options Short name, Long name, Macro, and Quit.

The BAR button is always visible in character-based mode.

Use the Short name and Long name options to define the description you want displayed on the SpeedBar button itself. Short name is the button's label (up to three characters) in character-based mode. Long name is the button's label (up to ten characters) in WYSIWYG mode. If you make your long names too long, the SpeedBar may no longer fit on a single screen, even in WYSIWYG mode. If so, a button labeled BAR appears on the end of the SpeedBar; click on this button to display the remaining buttons on the SpeedBar.

In both SpeedBars, you can define additional SpeedBar buttons using the undefined letters in the Options | SpeedBar | EDIT mode SpeedBar or Options | SpeedBar | READY mode SpeedBar menu. If you do so, your SpeedBar will not fit on the screen and Quattro Pro will display the BAR button at the edge of the SpeedBar.

To define a button's function, select the Macro option and enter a macro command. If you want clicking on a button to be equivalent to pressing a particular key on the keyboard, you must enter the appropriate macro keyboard command. For example, if you wanted the fifth button (button E) on the Ready mode SpeedBar to function like the [Tab] key, you could select the Short name option and enter **TAB**, select the Long name option and enter **Tab**, and then select the Macro option and enter the macro keyboard command **{TAB}**. Here is the Options | SpeedBar | READY mode SpeedBar | E Button submenu, with the settings necessary to make this button function like the [Home] key.

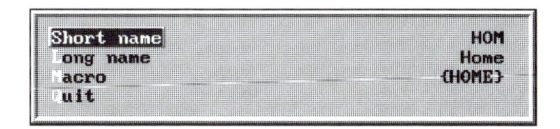

```
Short name                              HOM
 ong  name                              Home
 acro                                   {HOME}
 uit
```

Macro commands are beyond the scope of this book, but you can research the subject on your own using the Quattro Pro documentation. You can also use [Shift]-[F3] (Macros) or click on the Macro button on the Edit SpeedBar for a menu of macro command categories and then select the ones you are interested in. Press [F1] (Help) with one of these menus on the screen to display more detailed information.

The "Other" Default Settings

The Options | Other menu contains five options that don't fit into any of the other categories. The Undo option lets you enable or disable Quattro Pro's Undo feature. If Undo is enabled, you can use the / **E**dit | **U**ndo command or its shortcut [Alt]-[F5] to undo the effects of many commands.

*To have Undo enabled each time you start Quattro Pro, issue / **E**dit | **U**ndo and then select Update from the Options menu.*

The Macro option lets you specify which sections of the screen you don't want redrawn during macro execution (the less redrawing the faster the macro will execute). Your choices are Panel (menus), Window (including the status line and input line), Both, or None.

The Expanded Memory option determines what Quattro Pro stores in expanded memory (if your computer has such memory installed). Your choices are Both, Spreadsheet Data, Format, and None. While using expanded memory (EMS) allows you to work with very large notebooks, it can also slow down Quattro Pro's performance a bit for small notebooks. If you generally work with small notebooks, tell Quattro Pro to store only formatting codes (the Format option) or nothing at all (the None option) in EMS. If you are working with a large notebook and are running out of memory, direct Quattro Pro to store both notebook data and formatting codes in EMS (the Both option).

The Clock option allows you to display the date and time on the status line. When you issue the / **O**ptions | **O**ther | **C**lock command, Quattro Pro displays a menu with the three choices Standard, International, and None.

The Paradox option allows you to specify several network options if you plan to access Quattro Pro from within Paradox—a database management program distributed by Borland International. An in-depth discussion of networks is beyond the scope of this book.

Recalculation Settings

Unlike many other spreadsheet programs, Quattro Pro recalculates only formulas affected by new changes on the notebook, so recalculation time is minimized. The Options | Recalculation setting determines at what point Quattro Pro recalculates the values of formulas. When you select this option, Quattro Pro displays a menu with options for Mode, Order, and Iteration.

Customizing the Environment

The Options | Recalculation menu also contains one display-only item: Circular Cell. If your notebook currently contains one or more formulas with circular references, Quattro Pro displays the address of one of those cells to the right of the words "Circular Cell."

Recalculation Mode   If you select Mode, Quattro Pro displays a menu with the choices Automatic, Manual, and Background. The initial setting is Background, which means that Quattro Pro recalculates formulas between keystrokes, rather than forcing you to wait until recalculation is complete. The Automatic setting directs Quattro Pro to recalculate simultaneously all formulas affected by the most recent change in data, forcing you to wait until the recalculation is complete. The Manual setting directs Quattro Pro to postpone notebook recalculation until you press F9, the Recalculation key. Quattro Pro still recalculates individual formulas as you enter or edit them, but holds off recalculating existing formulas that refer to any newly changed cells. Whenever some of the notebook's formulas need recalculation, a CALC status indicator is displayed at the bottom of the screen.

Recalculation Order   When you issue the / **O**ptions | **R**ecalculation | **O**rder command, Quattro Pro displays a menu with the options Natural, Row-wise, and Column-wise. The Natural setting directs Quattro Pro to evaluate every cell in a notebook that is referenced in a formula before calculating the formula itself. As a result, each formula is evaluated using current values, ensuring the accuracy of the notebook. Row-wise and Column-wise orders—recalculation orders used in earlier spreadsheet programs—are included in Quattro Pro to allow you to replicate the sometimes-less-than-accurate results obtained by using these methods in other programs. They are also occasionally used in situations involving circular formulas that you want recalculated several times in a particular order.

The Number of Iterations   Some mathematical equations cannot be solved by entering a simple formula; they must be entered as one or more circular formulas that must be repeatedly recalculated with different values until the result is acceptably accurate. The Iteration option on the Options | Recalculation menu allows you to perform multiple evaluations of such circular formulas. When you issue the command, Quattro Pro prompts for a number of iterations. You can specify up to 255 iterations; the number you enter determines how many times Quattro Pro recalculates circular formulas every time it recalculates the notebook.

Updating the Global Defaults

The / **O**ptions | **U**pdate command transforms all the global default settings in effect for your current work session into defaults that are automatically placed in effect every time you enter Quattro Pro. By changing the global defaults and then selecting the Update option, you can customize Quattro Pro to your own tastes. For example, if you find that you like a particular set of colors, you can define them as the colors that you start with in every work session. (You can still override these defaults for a particular work session with an / **O**ptions | **C**olors command.)

When you issue the / **O**ptions | **U**pdate command, every global default setting currently in effect is saved for future work sessions. If you have issued several / **O**ptions commands in the current work session, you should verify them before you issue the / **O**ptions | **U**pdate command. The / **O**ptions | **V**alues command, which displays a list of many of the more commonly changed default settings, can aid in this process. Keep in mind that this list, shown here, includes many but not all of the settings saved with / **O**ptions | **U**pdate.

```
Macro Recording                           Logical
Default Printer                       1st Printer
Startup Directory
Autoload File                         quattro.wq2
Startup Macro                                  \0
File Extension                                WQ2
Graphics Quality                            Final
Undo                                       Enable
SQZ! Remove Blanks                             No
Screen Type                     Autodetect Driver
Clock                                        None
Sort Numbers Before Labels                     No
Label Order                                 ASCII
Paradox Access Load File               ANSWER.DB
Paradox Access Autoload                       Yes
International Currency                 $ (Prefix)
```

Unlike the equivalent commands in Quattro (Quattro Pro's predecessor) and Lotus 1-2-3, / **O**ptions | **U**pdate only saves defaults that apply to the program environment as a whole. It does not save print and graph settings, which you save using the Update buttons in the Print Layout Options and Graph Customize Series dialog boxes, respectively.

Menu Command Shortcuts

The shortcuts that you create or reassign must consist of the Ctrl *key followed by a letter.*

As you know, there are preassigned shortcuts for several of the most commonly used Quattro Pro commands. Table 13-1 lists all the preassigned shortcuts. As you work with Quattro Pro regularly, you may find that you repeatedly use commands for which there are no preassigned shortcuts. In such cases, you may want to define your own shortcuts, abbreviating the keystrokes needed to issue particular commands. You can also change some of the preassigned shortcuts, in case you want to assign one of those key combinations to a different menu command.

Customizing the Environment

Preassigned Menu Command Shortcuts
Table 13-1.

Shortcut	Command
Ctrl-A	/ **S**tyle	**A**lignment
Ctrl-C	/ **E**dit	**C**opy
Ctrl-D*	Date prefix
Ctrl-E	/ **E**dit	**E**rase Block
Ctrl-F	/ **S**tyle	**N**umeric Format
Ctrl-G	/ **G**raph	**F**ast Graph
Ctrl-I	/ **E**dit	**I**nsert
Ctrl-M	/ **E**dit	**M**ove
Ctrl-N	/ **E**dit	**S**earch & Replace	**N**ext
Ctrl-P	/ **E**dit	**S**earch & Replace	**P**revious
Ctrl-R	/ **W**indow	**M**ove/Size
Ctrl-S	/ **F**ile	**S**ave
Ctrl-T	/ **W**indow	**T**ile
Ctrl-W	/ **S**tyle	**C**olumn Width
Ctrl-X	/ **F**ile	E**x**it

*Not reassignable

To create a shortcut, follow these steps:

1. Highlight the menu option containing the command you want to abbreviate. (If you want to change a preassigned shortcut, just highlight the relevant option and follow the steps described here.)
2. Hold down Ctrl and press Enter to initiate creation of the shortcut. Quattro Pro displays the message "Hold down the Ctrl key and press any Letter, or <DEL>" on the status line at the bottom of the screen.
3. When prompted for a Ctrl key, hold down Ctrl and press any letter on the keyboard except D (Ctrl-D is reserved for entering dates). This combination of Ctrl and a second key becomes the key combination that you use to execute the command; it will appear in the menu to the right of the command name it's associated with. You should therefore choose a key that will be easy to associate with the command.

If you enter a letter that is already in use as a shortcut key, you'll get an error message.

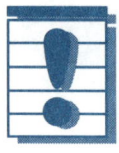

TIP: If you want to use a shortcut key combination that is already in use for some other purpose, you need to take two steps: First rename that shortcut by following the steps just listed. (You can also delete the shortcut, as described in a moment.) Then assign the shortcut in question to the desired command.

Quattro Pro allows you to assign shortcuts to any piece of a command. For example, you can assign shortcuts to the / **S**tyle command, the / **S**tyle | **B**lock Size command, or the / **S**tyle | **B**lock Size | **A**uto Width command. In each case, using the shortcut has exactly the same effect as highlighting the associated menu option and pressing (Enter).

Shortcuts are saved the moment you create them. The next time you reload Quattro Pro, the shortcuts in effect when you left the program remain in force. To delete a shortcut—including any of Quattro Pro's preassigned shortcuts—highlight the menu option to which the shortcut is assigned, press (Ctrl)-(Enter), and then press (Del) twice.

This chapter has introduced a wealth of commands for altering the Quattro Pro environment. Though you may use some of these commands only rarely, it is worth becoming familiar with all the available options. As you work with Quattro Pro, you undoubtedly will develop your own preferences in formatting, colors, shortcuts, and so on. As you do you can use the tools introduced in this chapter to fit Quattro Pro to your own informational needs, work style, and aesthetic.

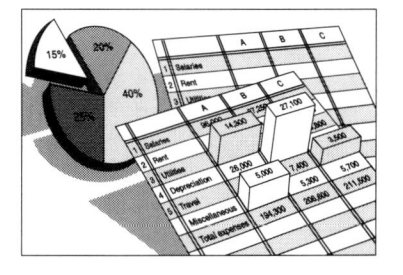

CHAPTER

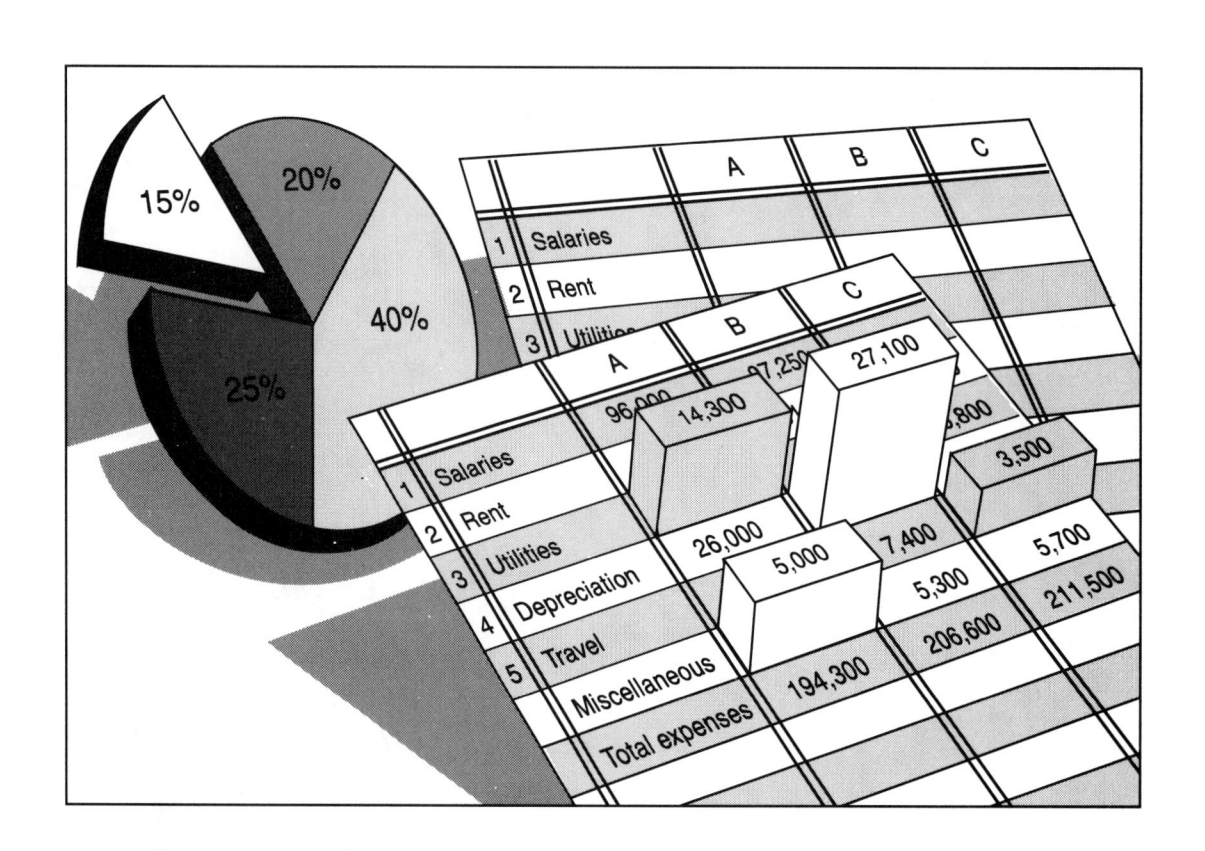

14

CREATING GRAPHS

Graphs are a means of presenting information in a concise and highly visual form. They can be used to summarize a set of numbers, highlight trends, or focus attention on critical aspects of your data. To create graphs in Quattro Pro, you begin by choosing a graph type, defining the blocks of notebook data (referred to as series) that you want to plot, and selecting the View option from the Graph menu or pressing F10 (Graph). You then modify, embellish, and customize the graph until you achieve the effect you want.

This chapter introduces you to the types of graphs you can create with Quattro Pro and covers the basics of defining and printing graphs. Chapter 15 covers techniques for improving, customizing, and annotating graphs.

Choosing a Graph Type

Quattro Pro offers 15 types of graphs: line graphs, area graphs, pie graphs, column graphs, XY graphs, high-low graphs, bubble graphs, text graphs, three types of bar graphs (regular, rotated, and stacked), and four types of graphs that use three-dimensional perspective (bar, step, ribbon, and area).

Line Graphs

In line graphs, lines, symbols, or a combination of lines and symbols map anywhere from one to six series of values at a time. If you plot more than one series of values, each series is represented by its own line. Line graphs are best suited to representing trends over time because they make it easy to see increases and decreases in a single series of values. The line graph in Figure 14-1 shows the rise and fall of a company's well production level over a six-month period.

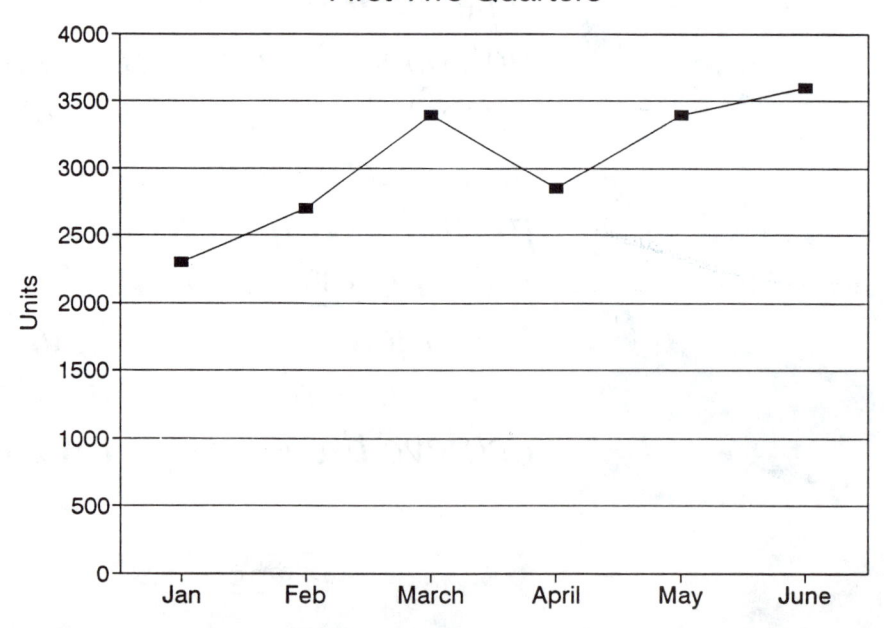

A line graph
Figure 14-1.

Creating Graphs

Bar Graphs

Remember, there is also a 3-D bar graph.

Bar graphs are most appropriate for comparing values at one (or more) specific points in time—for example, the expenses incurred in a company's different divisions. Quattro Pro offers three types of bar graphs: regular bar graphs, rotated bar graphs, and stacked bar graphs. Although there are some variations in usage—stacked bars are particularly well suited to representing multiple series of values, and rotated bars are good for representing progress toward a goal—the differences between the bar graph types are primarily aesthetic.

Regular bar graphs are appropriate for comparing the values in one or more series. For example, Figure 14-2 shows a graph of the travel expenses in four divisions. Each value in the series (in this case, each division) is represented by a single vertical bar. When you create a bar graph that plots more than one series of values, Quattro Pro displays the bars for the different series side by side and assigns each series a unique color or *fill pattern,* which is the pattern used to distinguish bars or other segments of a graph when the graph is displayed or printed in black and white.

Figure 14-2. A bar graph

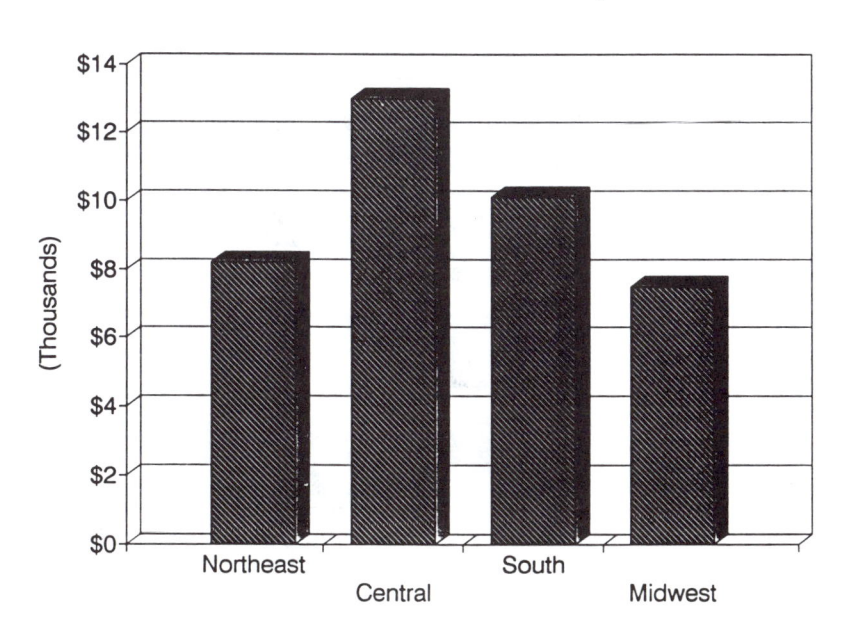

Rotated bar graphs are similar to regular bar graphs, except the bars extend from the left of the screen or paper rather than the bottom. They are often used for profit-and-loss charts, particularly when comparing actual to budgeted profits. The graph in Figure 14-3 compares year-to-date (Y-T-D) actual sales levels to the targeted sales for four different products. Note that the left-to-right direction of the bars is particularly appropriate for charting progress toward a goal.

Stacked bar graphs use segmented vertical bars to represent multiple series of values, with each segment of the bars representing one value from each series. For example, if you create a stacked bar graph that represents three series, each containing five values, the resulting graph contains five bars of three segments each. The first bar contains segments representing the first value in each of the three series; the second bar contains segments representing the second value in each of the three series, and so on. The height of the bar represents the sum of the values.

The graph in Figure 14-4 shows the sales of four products over a four-year period. Each bar represents the sales for one year. Each segment of each bar represents sales of a particular product within that year. This type of graph

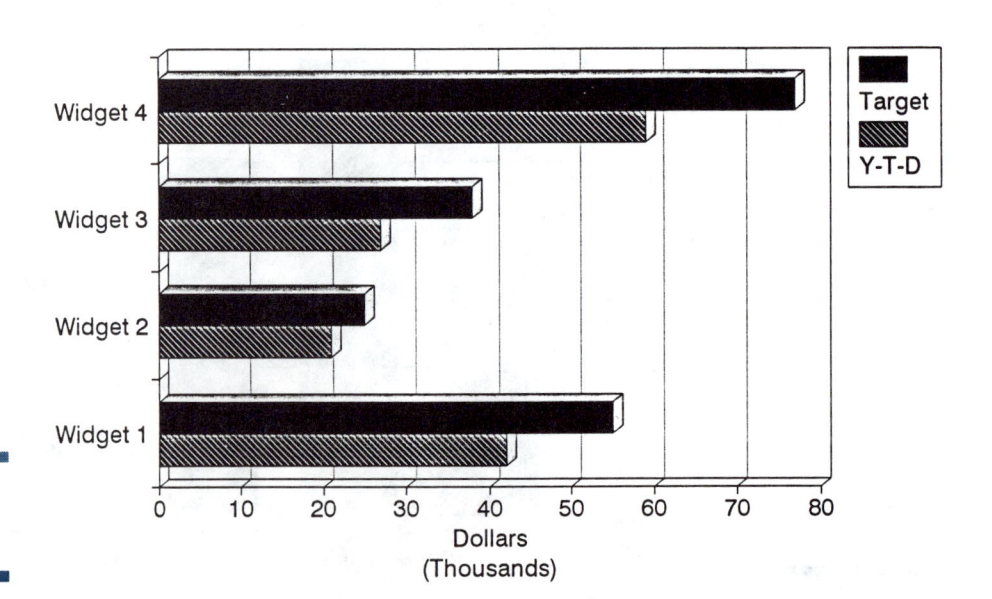

A rotated bar graph
Figure 14-3.

Creating Graphs

Widget Sales Comparison
1994 - 1997

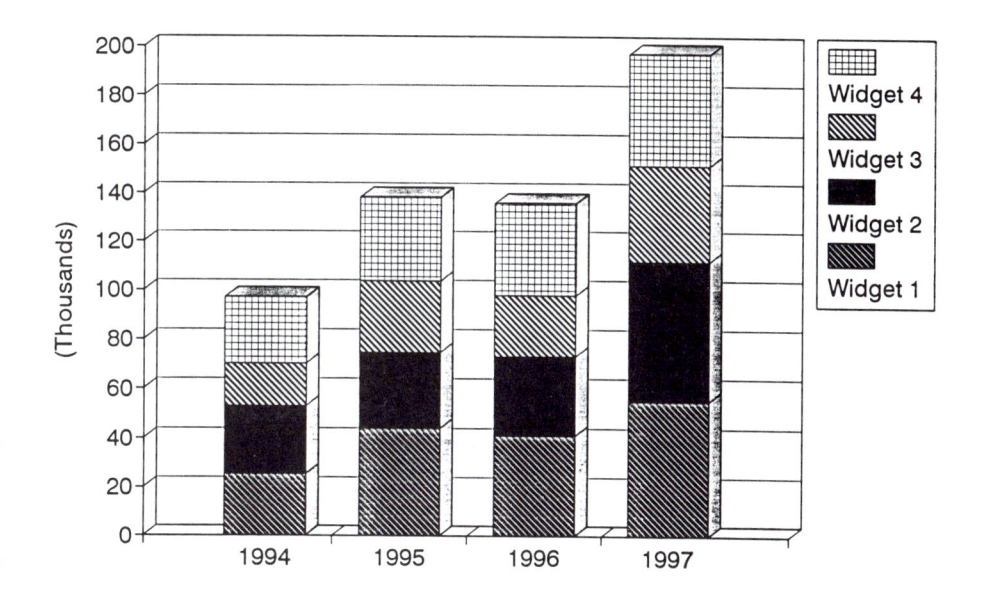

A stacked bar graph
Figure 14-4.

gives the reader a sense of each product's relative contribution to the year's total sales while presenting a visual comparison between the total sales levels for each of the four years. It is not particularly good for comparing values within a particular series—determining which was the best year for Widget 3 sales, for example.

Area Graphs

Area graphs share characteristics with line graphs and stacked bar graphs, using both lines and fill patterns to represent multiple series of values. Each series of values in the graph is represented by an area filled with a distinctive fill pattern. These areas are layered one on top of another, so the top edge of each area represents the cumulative total of the value series below. Like stacked bar graphs, area graphs are an effective means of showing how various components affect the whole over time. Like line graphs (of the cumulative totals rather than the individual series), they give you a feel for how the totals change over time.

Figure 14-5 shows an area graph that illustrates exactly the same data as that graphed in Figure 14-4—the sales of four products over a four-year period. Note that the graph is most useful for looking at the relative size of the sales level for each product and the rise and fall of the total product sales. It makes a poor and potentially misleading illustration of the increases in sales level of the individual products.

Pie Graphs

Pie graphs use a circle, or pie, to represent a single series of values. Each slice of the pie symbolizes an individual value within the series and is sized according to the percentage it represents of the series total. Pie graphs are useful for showing the sizes of different components in relation to the whole. For example, you might use a pie chart to show the portion of total sales represented by each of five product lines or the percentage of total travel expenses incurred by each of four departments. Figure 14-6 shows a graph that illustrates the relative contribution of each of five different financial sources to total fundraising revenues.

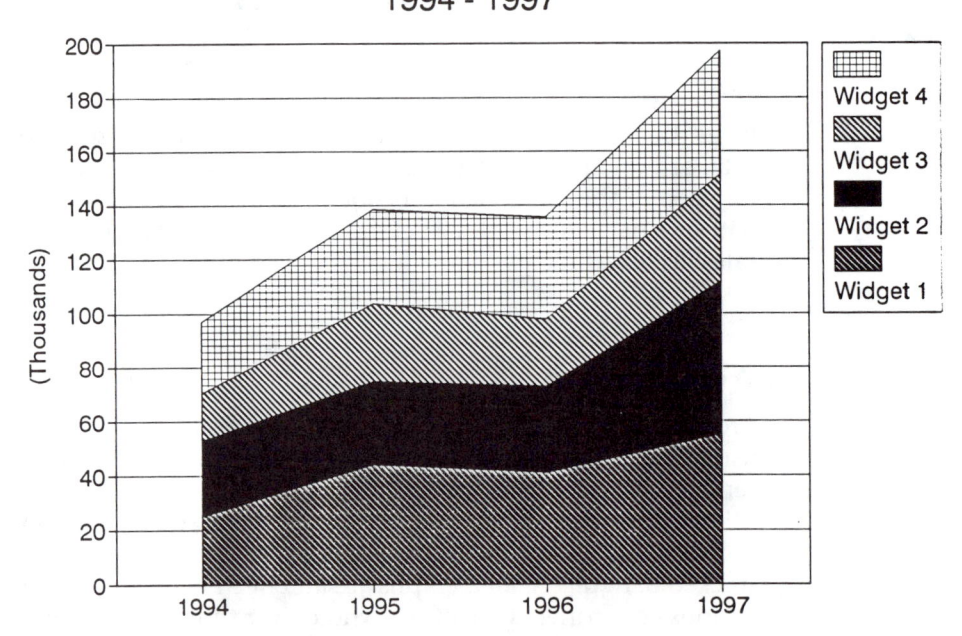

An area graph
Figure 14-5.

Creating Graphs

Fundraising Revenues

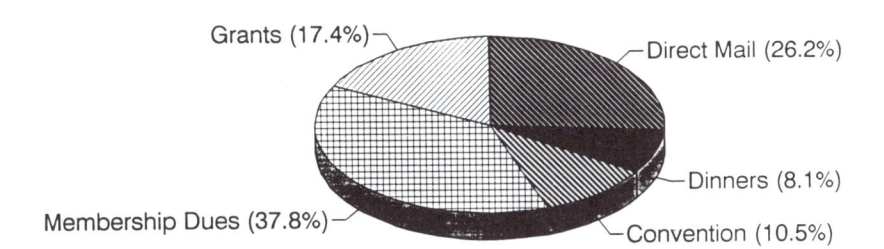

A pie graph
Figure 14-6.

Grants (17.4%)
Direct Mail (26.2%)
Dinners (8.1%)
Convention (10.5%)
Membership Dues (37.8%)

Column Graphs

Column graphs are essentially rectangular pie charts. Like pie graphs, they plot a single series of values, representing each value in the series as a percentage of the whole. However, a column graph represents the series values as a vertical column composed of multiple segments rather than as a pie with multiple slices. This layout often affords more room for labeling the individual values in the series. Figure 14-7 shows a column graph that plots the same values as those plotted in the pie graph in Figure 14-6.

XY Graphs

XY graphs show the relationship between two sets of values. They are most useful for illustrating the effect of one set of values (the *independent variable*) on a second set of values (the *dependent variable*). You can use an XY graph to map the effect of advertising investments or product pricing on sales volume or the effect of class size on student test scores. The graph shown in Figure 14-8 traces the correlation between years of post-high-school education and salary among ABC Group employees.

Fundraising Revenues

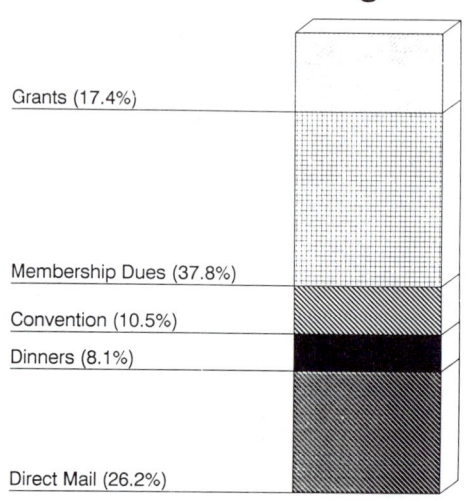

Grants (17.4%)

Membership Dues (37.8%)
Convention (10.5%)
Dinners (8.1%)

Direct Mail (26.2%)

A column graph
Figure 14-7.

Relationship of Education to Salary
ABC Group Employees

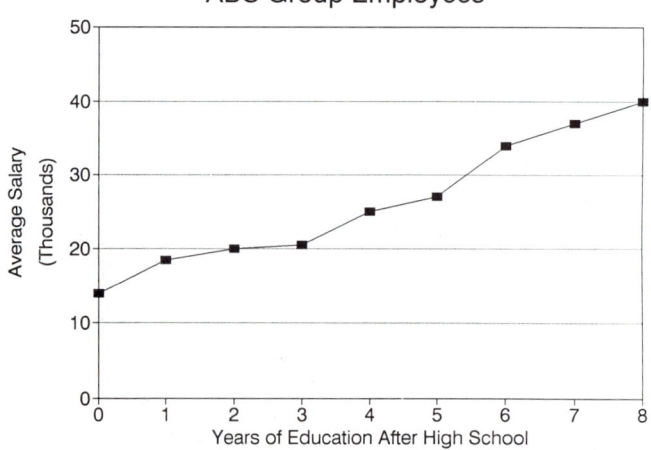

Average Salary (Thousands)

Years of Education After High School

An XY graph
Figure 14-8.

Bubble Graphs

Bubble graphs are similar to XY graphs, but they include an additional series that is represented by bubbles of relative size floating within the graph. (The center of the bubble marks the bubble's position on the graph.) You can use bubble graphs to show an additional piece of information in an XY graph. For example, suppose you want to illustrate the relationship between advertising expenditures and sales, and you also want to show the relative size of the various companies you're graphing. In a bubble graph, the company sizes can be illustrated as the different bubble sizes. Figure 14-9 shows a sample bubble graph.

High-Low (Open-Close) Graphs

High-low graphs are generally used to plot the daily rise and fall of stock prices, as shown in Figure 14-10. When creating a high-low graph, you define at least two series of values: the highest and lowest price each stock reached during the day. The top of the vertical line in the graph represents the highest price, the bottom represents the lowest.

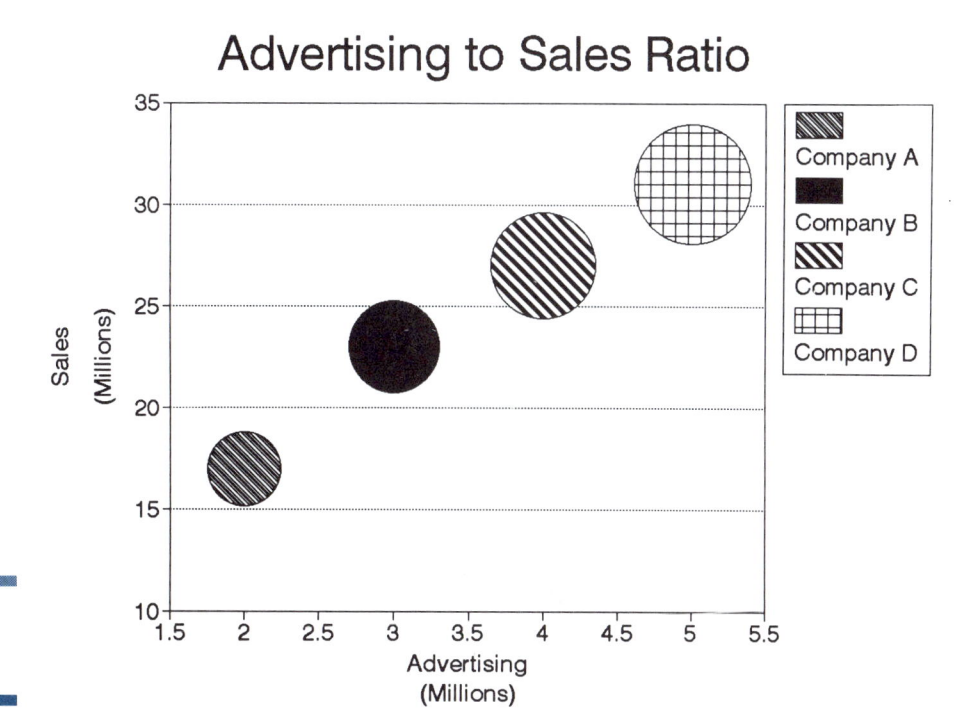

A bubble graph
Figure 14-9.

XYZ Stock

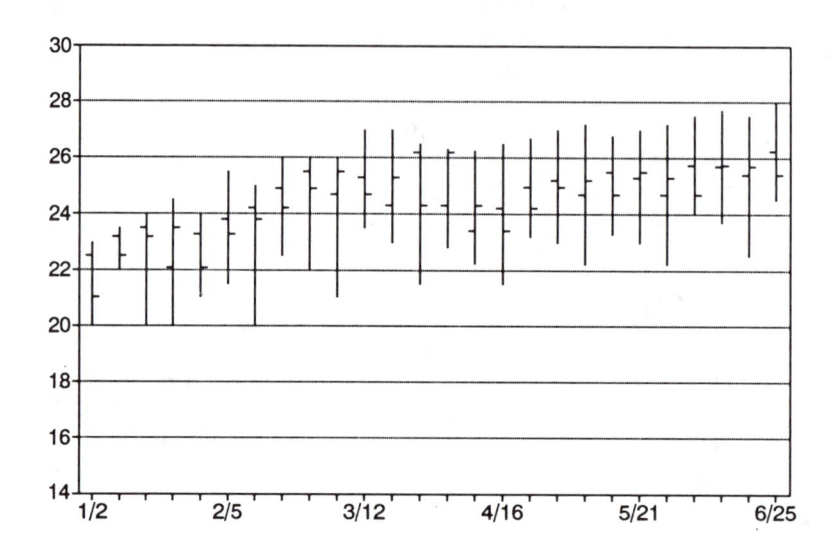

A high-low graph
Figure 14-10.

You can also define two additional series that represent the stocks' opening and closing prices. These are represented as tick marks extending from the vertical bars. Lines protruding to the left indicate the opening price (the third series value) and lines protruding to the right indicate the closing price (the fourth series value). You can define a fifth and sixth series of values to represent any additional information you like, such as the daily average price. These last two series are represented as lines with markers.

You can use high-low graphs to plot any other set of information involving a series of high and low values. You might use high-low graphs to plot retail and wholesale prices, units ordered and units shipped, or high and low temperatures in an experiment.

Text Graphs

The Annotator is introduced in the next chapter.

Strictly speaking, text graphs are not graphs at all because they do not involve plotting any data. They are pictures—often containing a large amount of text—that are created using Quattro Pro's Annotator feature. Typical applications include flow charts and organization charts, such as the one shown in Figure 14-11.

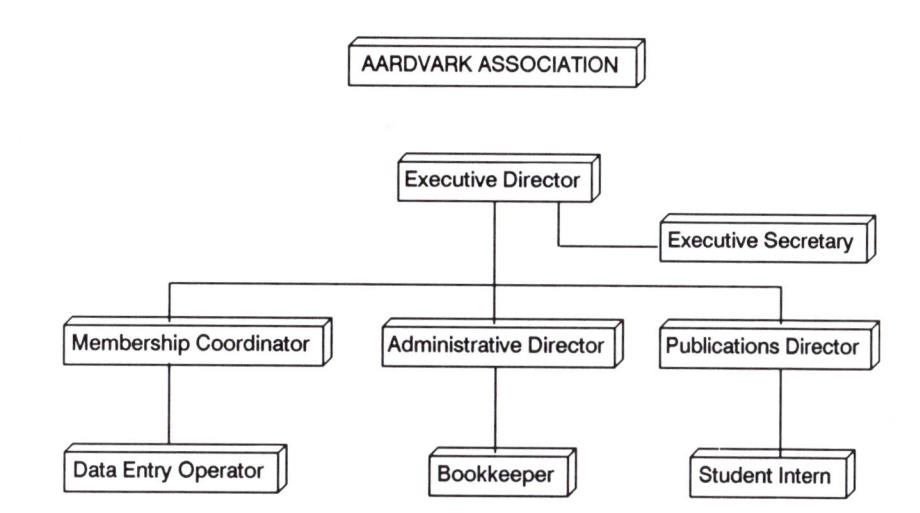

A text graph
Figure 14-11.

Three-Dimensional Graph Types

There are four "three-dimensional" graph types in Quattro Pro: bar, step, ribbon, and area—as shown in Figure 14-12. As you can see, the 3-D bar graph is similar to a regular bar graph, except that the bars are placed on a 3-D grid, with the bars for each series located in a separate row. The 3-D step graph is similar to the 3-D bar graph, but the bars are touching. The 3-D ribbon graph resembles a 3-D version of a line graph, with each line flattened out into a ribbon. Lastly, the 3-D area graph is like a ribbon graph in which the area between each ribbon and the bottom of the graph has been filled in.

Provided that each series you want to graph includes a distinct range of values, these 3-D graph types can offer a dramatic and effective means of representing multiple series of values. However, if your data series include values in the same range, a three-dimensional presentation may be harder to understand than a standard two-dimensional graph.

The Graphing Process

The first step in designing a graph is deciding what information you want to convey. Graphs are generally used to highlight patterns: the ebb and flow of sales over a period of time, the effect of a particular cost increase on profits, and so on. They should illuminate a few vital and well-chosen pieces of

Quattro Pro 5 Made Easy

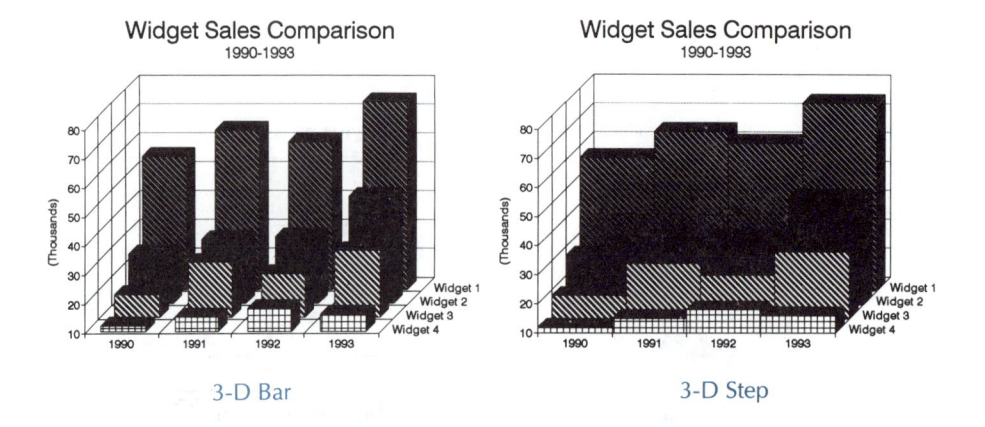

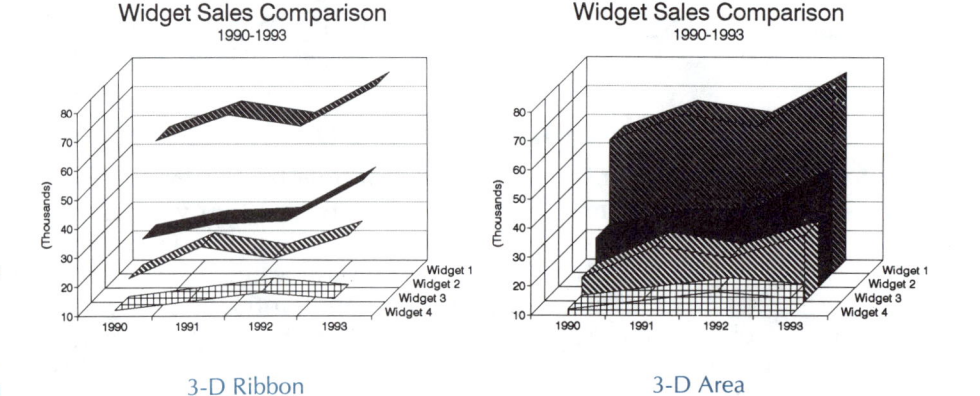

3-D Bar

3-D Step

3-D Ribbon

3-D Area

The 3-D graph types
Figure 14-12.

information from the mass of numbers on a notebook. If you find your graph becoming too cluttered, either find a way to consolidate your information or use more than one graph.

Following are the basic steps involved in creating a graph in Quattro Pro. The order of these steps is not written in stone (steps 2 and 3 can be reversed, for example, and you can define the graph type at any point prior to viewing), and not every graph requires every step in the process. Nonetheless, this is the basic sequence you should follow and the steps you should at least consider along the way.

Creating Graphs

1. **Pick the graph type**. Use the Graph Type option on the Graph menu to choose the type most appropriate for conveying the information being graphed.

2. **Select the Series option on the Graph menu**. Define the series of values to be plotted. For individual series, you need to designate sets of adjacent cells on the notebook. If you're plotting multiple series, however, they can be in various locations on the notebook, including on different pages. You can use the / **G**raph | **S**eries | **G**roup command to plot more than one series of values in one fell swoop if the values for each series are stored in adjacent columns or adjacent rows. Note that if you define a series that includes labels or blank cells, Quattro Pro ignores them when plotting the graph.

TIP: In certain situations you can use the Fast Graph option on the Graph menu to define multiple series, the X-axis series, and a legend all at once. (The / **G**raph | **S**eries | **G**roup command, in contrast, just defines several series of values at once.) For details, see the section "Shortcuts for Creating Graphs" later in this chapter.

3. **Define labels for the X-axis**. Use the X-Axis Series option on the Graph | Series menu. The block of cells that you define as the X-axis series is generally used as a set of labels identifying the different values that are represented on the graph. The X-axis series can actually contain either values or labels, although Quattro Pro always treats them simply as text unless you are plotting an XY graph.

Once you have defined a graph, you can view it while in either Ready or Menu mode by pressing F10, the Graph key.

4. **View the graph**. The Graph menu contains a View option that lets you display the currently defined graph on screen. After viewing the graph, you can return to the notebook display by pressing any key except the slash (/), which is used to activate Quattro Pro's Annotator.

5. **Add explanatory text**. Almost all graphs can benefit from explanatory text, including titles at the top and, in some cases, titles for the X-axis and Y-axis. Whenever you plot more than one series of values, you should also add a legend to the graph. The Graph | Text menu contains options for each of these items of text.

6. **Customize the graph.** Quattro Pro has many options for refining the graph display, including commands for changing colors, fill patterns, and marker symbols; for mixing and matching graph types; and for adding grids and borders to the graph as a whole. These options are covered in Chapter 15.

7. **Annotate the graph**. Quattro Pro's Annotator, covered in Chapter 15, allows you to add boxes filled with text, arrows, and a variety of geometric shapes to your graph.

8. **Print the graph**. The purpose of creating graphs is usually to present information to an audience, so you will almost always want to generate a printed copy of your product. The details of printing are discussed later in this chapter.

9. **Save the graph**. If you intend to create only one graph on a particular notebook, saving the graph is simply a matter of saving the notebook as a whole with one of the save commands. To save more than one graph on a notebook, you must assign graph names, as described in the section "Saving, Changing, and Restoring Graphs."

Adding Text to Your Graph

You can add several types of text to a graph. You can display titles at the top of the graph, a description of the values on the X-axis and Y-axis, and a legend identifying the different series of values. You can also label individual points on the graph using the Interior Label Block setting in the Graph Customize dialog box, and can add text anywhere on the graph using Quattro Pro's Annotator feature; both of these features are described in Chapter 15.

Titles   You can add three types of titles to Quattro Pro graphs: a main title to be displayed at the top of the graph, a title for the Y-axis, and a title for the X-axis. The main title consists of either one or two titles, which you enter through the 1st Line and 2nd Line options on the Graph | Text | Titles menu.

Cell references used to display graph text are not updated if you relocate the referenced cell using Move, Insert, or Delete.

Each graph title can be up to 39 characters long, and you can enter the text by typing it or by referencing a cell on the notebook that contains the desired text. If you use a cell reference, you must precede it with a backslash to let Quattro Pro know that it's a reference rather than straight text. When you use such cell references, the graph text is updated automatically if you change the referenced cell on the notebook. Figure 14-13 shows a graph with two titles at the top, titles for both axes, and a legend.

You can change the size, typeface, color, or style of a title using the Font option on the Graph | Text menu. This option works much like the / **S**tyle | **F**ont command introduced in Chapter 6, except that it includes an added style option: Drop Shadow. If you change the Drop Shadow setting to On, your titles will appear to have a shadow slightly behind and below the text. To return the style to normal, select the Reset option on the Style submenu.

Legends   Whenever you plot more than one series of values, you should add a legend to the graph to identify the colors, markers, or fill patterns that are used to represent each series. The Graph | Text | Legends menu contains

Creating Graphs

Widget Sales Comparison ← First title
1994 - 1997 ← Second title

(Graph showing Widget 1, Widget 2, Widget 3, Widget 4 sales for years 1994-1997, with Y-axis labeled "Dollars (Thousands)" from 0 to 80, X-axis labeled "Years")

Graph with titles and legend
Figure 14-13.

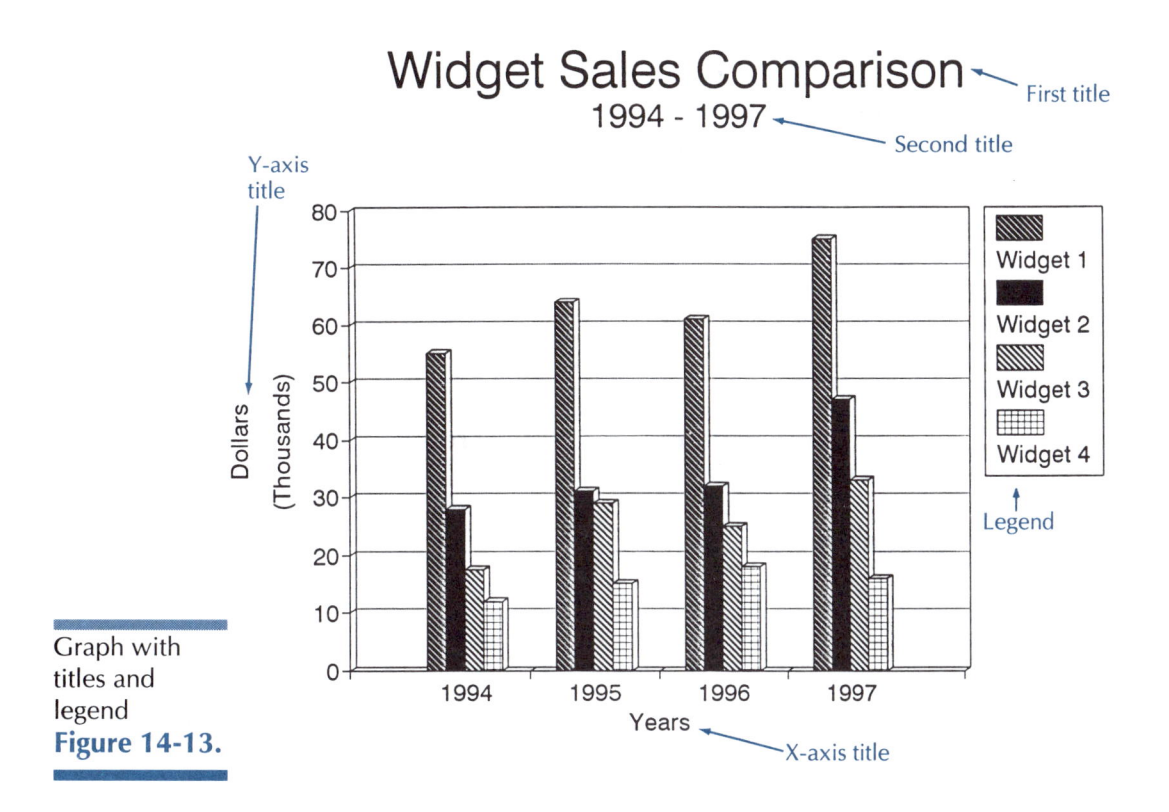

options for the first through the sixth series. To add labels to a graph legend, you select the option for the series you want to label and then type in the text (up to ten characters) that you want displayed. You can also refer to labels on your notebook by entering a backslash followed by a cell address. You can change the typeface, size, color, or style of the characters used in a legend with the / **G**raph | **T**ext | **F**ont | **L**egends command.

You cannot reposition legends on a 3-D graph.

The Position option on the Graph | Text | Legends menu lets you specify where you want the legend to appear on the screen. The default setting is Bottom. You can choose Right to display the legend at the right edge of the screen, or None to hide the legend temporarily.

Hands-On Practice

Begin by entering sample data that can be used as the basis for several different types of graphs.

1. If you have anything other than a blank notebook currently on your screen, issue the / **F**ile | **E**rase command. (Save your notebook first, if appropriate.)
2. Enter **Five-Year Sales Projection** in cell A1, **Product 1** in A4, **Product 2** in A5, **Product 3** in A6, and **Product 4** in A7.
3. Then move to column B and enter "**1994** in B3, **10000** in B4, **8500** in B5, **13000** in B6, and **18000** in B7.
4. In column C, enter "**1995** in C3, **12500** in C4, **9000** in C5, **12000** in C6, and **20000** in C7.
5. Next enter "**1996** in D3, **14500** in D4, **13000** in D5, **12500** in D6, and **23000** in D7.
6. Move to row E and enter "**1997** in E3, **16000** in E4, **15500** in E5, **12500** in E6, and **22000** in E7.
7. Finally, enter "**1998** in F3, **17500** in F4, **15500** in F5, **14000** in F6, and **25000** in F7.
8. Move to G9 and enter the formula **@SUM(B4..F7)**. The result of this formula should be 304000.
9. Save your work and assign the name GRAPH to the current notebook.

You now have a set of data appropriate for experimenting with most of Quattro Pro's graph types. Start by creating a simple line graph.

1. Issue the / **G**raph | **G**raph Type command and then choose the Line graph type. (If you are using WYSIWYG display mode, the graph types are displayed as a gallery, as shown in Figure 14-14, rather than as a menu.)
2. Select the Series option and then select 1st Series. Specify B4..F4 (the sales figures for Product 1) as the block to be used for the 1st Series values.

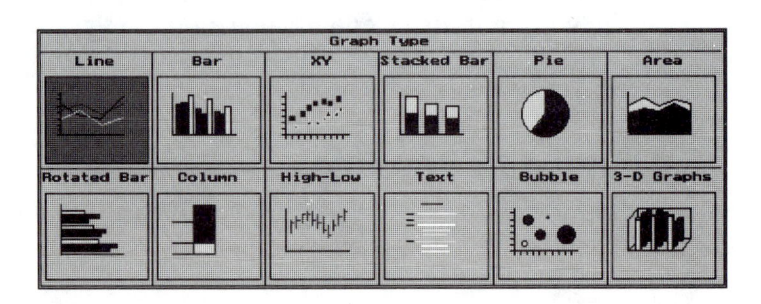

The gallery of graph types
Figure 14-14.

Creating Graphs

Chapter 15 explains how to manually scale axes, changing the starting point, ending point, and increment.

3. Select the X-Axis Series option and specify the block B3..F3 (the years 1994 through 1998) as labels to be displayed along the X-axis. Select Quit to return to the Graph menu.

4. Select the View option to see the results: a line graph mapping the progression of Product 1's sales level over the five-year period. Note that Quattro Pro automatically scales the Y-axis to accommodate the lowest and highest values in the series and inserts a title at the left edge of the graph to indicate that the numbers are expressed in thousands.

5. Now add a title to the graph. Press [Esc] to return to the notebook display, select the Text option on the Graph menu, select the 1st Line option, and enter **\A1** to designate the contents of cell A1 as the title to be displayed on the first line of the graph. Select the 2nd Line option and enter **\A4** to designate the contents of cell A4 as the title to be displayed on the second line of the graph.

6. Press [F10] (Graph) to view the results. It may take Quattro Pro a moment to build the necessary text fonts.

7. Press [Esc] twice to return to the Graph menu. Now try changing the graph type to see how the same data looks in a different form. Select Graph Type and change the graph type to Bar. Select View to take a look at the results.

Shortcuts for Creating Graphs

Several other sets of values in the current notebook can be graphed; however, rather than specifying them individually, you can save time by designating several graph series with a single command.

Fast Graphs   If all the data you want to graph is laid out in a single block on the notebook, you can use the / **G**raph I **F**ast Graph command to create a graph that represents up to six series of values, including both X-axis labels and a legend identifying the values in each series. (In contrast, the / **G**raph I **S**eries I **G**roup command only allows you to create multiples series of values, but not X-axis labels or a legend.) If the block of data contains more rows than columns, Quattro Pro treats each column of values as a single series. If the first column in the block contains labels, Quattro Pro uses them as X-axis labels; otherwise it defines them as the first series values. Quattro Pro treats each of the remaining columns as an additional series (up to a maximum of six). If the first row of the fast graph block contains labels, Quattro Pro uses them to create a graph legend. Otherwise Quattro Pro treats the first row entries as part of the values to be plotted.

If the number of columns equals or exceeds the number of rows in the block, Quattro Pro plots the values in each row (up to a maximum of six) as a series. If the block's first row contains labels, Quattro Pro uses them as X-axis labels. If the first column of the block contains labels, Quattro Pro uses them to create a graph legend.

*The shortcut for the / **G**raph | **F**ast Graph command is* Ctrl - G .

Creating a fast graph involves two steps. First, you issue the / **G**raph | **G**raph Type command and select the type of graph you want to create. Second, you issue the / **G**raph | **F**ast Graph command. Quattro Pro prompts for a block of data to graph. As soon as you specify the block, Quattro Pro displays the graph. Press any key other than / to return to the notebook. You can then use the options on the Graph menu to make additions or adjustments.

There are two potential pitfalls when using this command:

- ✦ If the entries you want to use as X-axis labels or legend text are numeric values, you must either change them to labels, or omit them from the fast graph block and define the X-axis labels and legend text later. Otherwise Quattro Pro treats them as values to be plotted on the graph. For example, if your X-axis labels are a series of years, you must *make certain* that you entered them with a label prefix character.

- ✦ The / **G**raph | **F**ast Graph command works properly only when the number of series you want to plot is smaller than the number of values in each series. If the number of series you want to plot is greater than the number of values in each series, use the / **G**raph | **S**eries | **G**roups command.

Defining a Group of Series   When you are plotting several series of values, the values in each series often are arranged in adjacent rows or adjacent columns on the notebook. In this case, you can use the / **G**raph | **S**eries | **G**roup command to define several series at once. This command does less than the / **G**raph | **F**ast Graph command; it does not automatically assign X-axis series or legends. However, it affords you more control over the graphing process by letting you tell Quattro Pro how to divide the specified block of values into series.

When you select Group, Quattro Pro displays a submenu with the choices Columns and Rows. Select Columns if the values in each series are stored within one column; select Rows if the values in each series are stored within one row. Next Quattro Pro asks for a block of values. If you have selected Columns, Quattro Pro assigns each column of values in the block to a series. The leftmost column of values becomes series 1, the next column to the right becomes series 2, and so on. If you have selected Rows, Quattro Pro assigns each row of values in the block to a series, starting from the uppermost row in the block.

Try using the two graph shortcuts just discussed to create graphs with multiple series. Start by creating a fast graph for all the data in the notebook.

Creating Graphs

Because the block contains more columns than rows, Quattro Pro plots each of the rows (products) as a series.

1. Issue the / **G**raph | **F**ast Graph command (Ctrl-G shortcut) and, when prompted for a block, enter **A3..F7**. Quattro Pro immediately displays a graph consisting of five groups of bars (representing the five years), each consisting of four bars (representing each of the four products). Quattro Pro uses the four labels at the left edge of the fast graph block (the product names) as legend text and uses the labels in cells B3..F3 (the years 1994 through 1998) as X-axis labels. Note that Quattro Pro also uses the titles from the last graph you displayed because the Fast Graph option does not affect any Text settings.
2. Press any key except / to return to the Graph menu and select Text. Pick the 2nd Line option, press Esc to erase the previous entry, and press Enter.
3. Press F10 (Graph) to view the results. Your graph should resemble Figure 14-15.

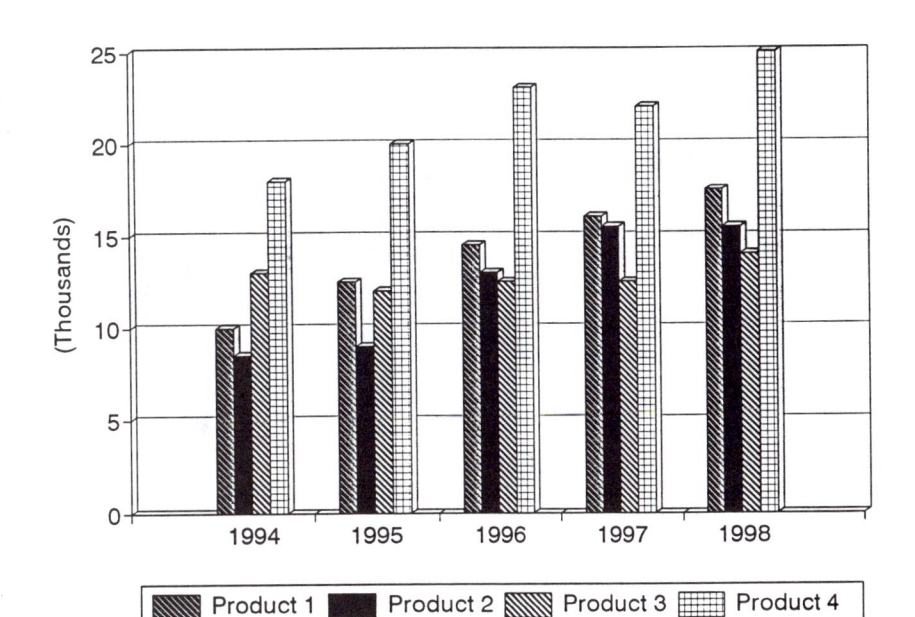

A fast graph generated for all five years of data
Figure 14-15.

Now try creating a fast graph using the values for years 1994 through 1996 only.

1. Press any key other than / to return to the Graph | Text menu and select the 1st Line option. Press (Esc) to erase the previous entry and enter **Three-Year Sales Projection.** Select Quit to return to the Graph menu.
2. Select the Fast Graph option and specify a block of **A3..D7**. The resulting graph should look like Figure 14-16. The specified block contains more rows than columns, so Quattro Pro plots each column (year) as a series rather than treating the products as series, as in the last graph.

The most efficient way to create a graph of this same set of values, treating each product (row) rather than each year (column) as a series, is by using the / **G**raph | **S**eries | **G**roup | **R**ows command. Try this now.

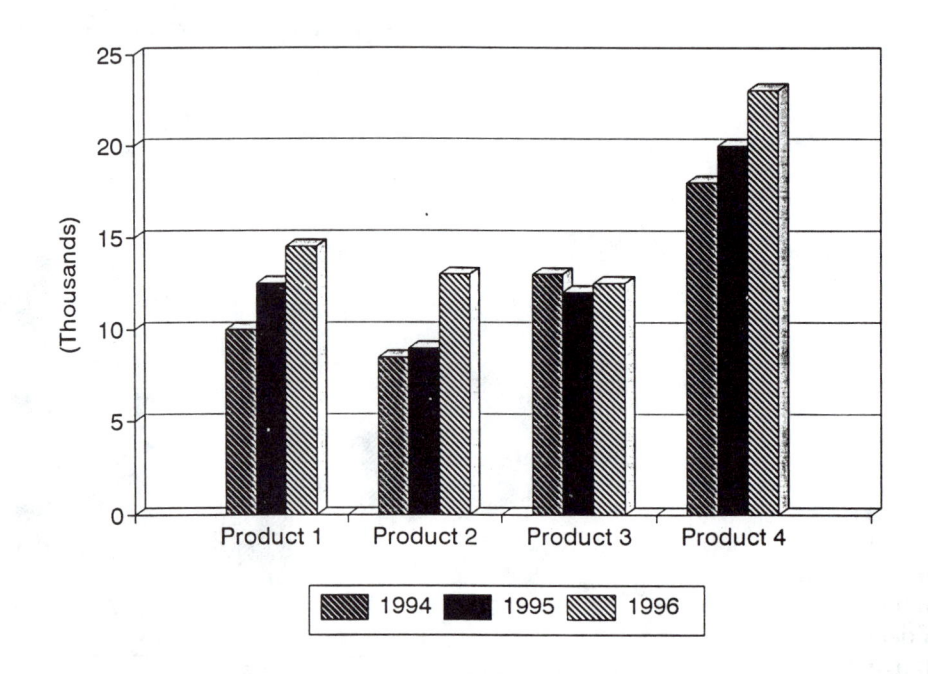

A fast graph generated for three years of data
Figure 14-16.

Creating Graphs

1. Press any key to return to the Graph menu, and then select Series. Notice that Quattro Pro filled in blocks for the first three series and the X-axis series in response to the last / **G**raph | **F**ast Graph command. Select Group from the Series menu, and then choose Rows. Enter a block of **B4..D7**. The settings for the first through fourth series should change immediately.

2. Select the X-Axis Series option and enter **B3..D3**. Select Quit to return to the Graph menu.

3. Select the Text option and then select Legends; you need to replace the existing entries generated by the Fast Graph command. Choose 1st Series and enter **\A4**; choose 2nd Series and enter **\A5**; choose 3rd Series and enter **\A6**; and choose 4th Series and enter **\A7**.

4. Press F10 (Graph) to view the results. When you are done, press Esc three times to return to the Graph menu.

At this point, try looking at this graph in several different forms by repeatedly changing the graph type.

Zooming and Panning Graphs

Quattro Pro's graph zooming feature lets you view portions of your graphs in greater detail. Once you have zoomed a graph, you can "pan" through it, moving back and forth to view details that have scrolled off-screen due to the zoom operation. (In certain cases, if you graph only a few series, you may not be able to zoom your graph.)

If you don't press the right and left mouse buttons at exactly the same time, you may remove the graph from view.

To zoom or pan a graph, display the graph by pressing F10 or selecting View from the Graph menu. Then click on the right and left mouse buttons simultaneously. You should see the zoom palette in the upper-left corner and a position bar at the top of the screen, as shown in Figure 14-17. The zoom palette contains three buttons for zooming and two for panning. Use the + + button to "zoom in" on a portion of your graph so you can see it in greater detail. When you do, Quattro Pro drops one or more points on the X-axis from the display. If you zoom a pie chart, slices of the pie disappear, leaving you with a pie that is proportionally divided among the remaining values.

Use the – – button to "un-zoom" the graph, displaying representations of more of the series values. Use the = = button to display the entire current graph, reversing the effects of any zoom operations. If you leave a graph zoomed, it will remain zoomed the next time you display it on the screen or retrieve it from disk; it will even print in this zoomed form. Since this can be confusing, you may want to click the = = symbol before leaving a graph.

Quattro Pro 5 Made Easy

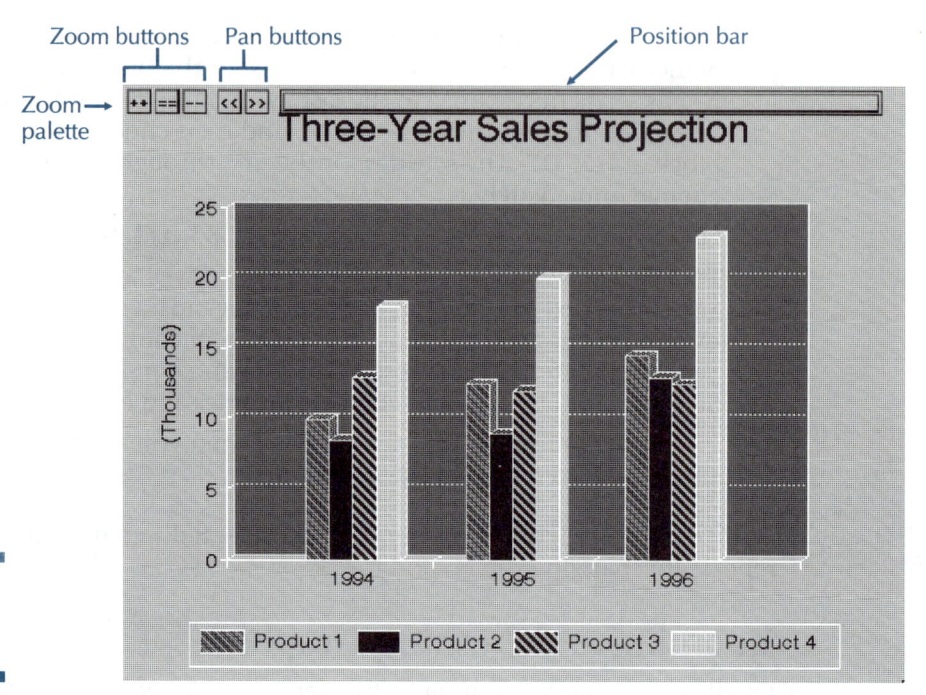

A zoomed graph
Figure 14-17.

(Figure shows a zoomed bar graph "Three-Year Sales Projection" with labeled Zoom buttons, Pan buttons, Position bar, and Zoom palette.)

The two pan buttons, << and >>, let you see portions of the graph that disappeared from view when you "zoomed in" on a graph. Click on >> to pan to the right (or down in a column or rotated bar graph) and click on << to pan to the left (up in a column or rotated bar graph). In the case of pie charts, panning moves you around the pie. You can pan repeatedly until you reach the edge of the graph. The position bar at the top of the screen displays your relative position in the graph as a whole and indicates what percentage of the graph you are currently viewing. To clear the zoom palette from the screen, make sure you are not pointing to a button on the zoom palette and click either mouse button.

Saving, Changing, and Restoring Graphs

When you create a graph and then save the notebook, the graph settings are saved along with the data. If you change any of the graph settings and resave the notebook, the new graph settings replace the old ones.

You also can save more than one set of graph settings for a particular notebook by assigning names to different groups of graph settings with the / **G**raph | **N**ame | **C**reate command. This command saves the current graph settings under the name you designate, so that you can recall them later. The / **G**raph | **N**ame | **C**reate command directs Quattro Pro to store the

Creating Graphs

settings for the current graph as part of the notebook's data in memory. You still must save the notebook as a whole to disk with one of the save commands to preserve those settings for future work sessions. Otherwise the graph settings are lost as soon as you leave the notebook.

When you save a graph by naming it, only the graph settings are saved, not the underlying data. If you modify the data and then recall a saved graph, the old settings are used to graph the new data, resulting in a different graph. However, if you change any of the graph settings—alter a title, for example—you must save the graph again. You can either issue the / **G**raph | **N**ame | **C**reate command again and specify the same graph name, or you can issue the / **G**raph | **N**ame | **A**utosave Edits | **Y**es command and Quattro Pro will automatically save your changes before executing any subsequent / **G**raph | **N**ame, / **P**rint | **G**raph Print | **N**ame, or / **G**raph | **V**iew commands. With Autosave Edits set to Yes, Quattro Pro also saves changes to a named graph when you press F10 to view the graph or when you issue any of the file saving commands.

Autosave Edits is particularly useful when you are modifying several existing graphs on a notebook. In this case, Autosave Edits prevents you from accidentally losing changes to one named graph when you display another. When you are creating new graphs, however, Autosave Edits can do more harm than good by making it easy to overwrite an existing graph with a new one. For example, suppose you turn Autosave Edits on and then display and perhaps modify an existing graph. Then you decide to create a new graph: You change the graph type, redefine the series, and press F10 to view the results. Unless you remembered to issue the / **G**raph | **N**ame | **C**reate command before you pressed F10, the new graph settings are saved under the old graph's name, overwriting the previous settings. Your only options are recreating the old graph and saving it under a new name, or retrieving the last version of the notebook from disk, thereby losing any changes you made since you last saved the file. To prevent such calamities, you should either make it a policy always to name new graphs before displaying them or turn Autosave Edits off whenever you create new graphs.

CAUTION: Quattro Pro does not display a warning when you reuse an existing graph name. You should therefore check your list of existing graph names before assigning a name to a new graph.

The command for recalling a stored graph to the screen is / **G**raph | **N**ame | **D**isplay. When you issue this command, Quattro Pro displays the named graph and replaces any graph settings that are currently in effect with the named graph's settings. (If you want to save the current settings, be sure to issue the / **G**raph | **N**ame | **C**reate command before you display a different graph.) You can eliminate named graphs with / **G**raph | **N**ame | **E**rase, which erases whatever named graph you specify, or with / **G**raph | **N**ame | **R**eset, which erases all named graphs for the current notebook. Because named graphs occupy space in memory, it is a good idea to delete any that you no longer need.

Copying Graphs

If the target notebook contains a graph with the same name as the graph being copied, the old graph is overwritten with the new one, with no warning.

The / **G**raph | **N**ame | **G**raph Copy command lets you copy a graph from one notebook to another. This can be particularly useful if you want to consolidate a whole group of graphs in one notebook, perhaps for a slide show. To copy a graph:

1. Open the notebook into which you want to copy the graph, using the / **F**ile | **O**pen or the / **F**ile | **N**ew command. This notebook is the *target notebook*.
2. Return to the notebook that currently contains the graph you want to copy (the *source notebook*) using any of the window selection commands (pressing [Shift]-[F6] is probably fastest).
3. Name the graph with the / **G**raph | **N**ame | **C**reate command.
4. Issue the / **G**raph | **N**ame | **G**raph Copy command. (If you are already on the Graph | Name menu, just type **G**.) Pick the graph that you want to copy from the list of named graphs.
5. When prompted, move back to the target notebook and press [Enter]. Quattro Pro returns you to the source notebook. If you wish to see the copied graph in the target notebook, type **Q** to leave the Graph menu, switch to the target notebook, issue the / **G**raph | **N**ame | **D**isplay command, and choose the graph you just copied.

If you are copying a text graph, the copy is completely independent of the source notebook. However, if the graph you are copying is based on one or more data series, the copied graph is automatically linked to the source notebook. (Notebook linking is covered in Chapter 19.) The graph will change to reflect changes in the graph series data on the source notebook, and changes in the target notebook will not affect the graph at all.

Resetting Series and Graphs

You can erase any setting except the series values and X-axis values by selecting the related menu option, pressing [Esc] to erase the current setting, and pressing [Enter]. If you try the same procedure with one of the series or X-axis values, however, Quattro Pro simply reinstates the previous setting.

Creating Graphs

The Reset button in the Graph Customize dialog box allows you to erase some or all of the series and X-axis values. When you press this button, Quattro Pro displays a menu with options for all six series and the X-axis. As soon as you select any of these options, Quattro Pro erases the current setting for the related item. This menu also contains an option called Graph, which erases all series, the X-axis settings, and all other graph settings so that you can create a new graph from scratch.

Defining Pie Graphs and Column Graphs

Pie graphs and column graphs show the relative values of the different components of a whole. For these graph types, you need only define values for the first series and, if you like, for the X-axis series. If you define any other series, Quattro Pro simply ignores them.

When you create a pie or column chart, Quattro Pro totals all the values in the first series and calculates the percentage that each value in the series represents of that total. The resulting graph represents the series as a whole, and individual values are portrayed as slices sized according to the percentage they represent of the total. Quattro Pro automatically displays these percentages next to each slice or segment of the pie or column, immediately after the X-axis label (if there is one).

Try saving the settings for the current graph and then resetting all the graph settings. Then create a pie chart from your data.

1. Select the Name option on the Graph menu and then choose Create. Enter the name **BARS**.
2. Select the Customize Series option on the Graph menu, select the Reset button, and then select Graph from the menu that appears.
3. Select Quit to return to the Graph menu. Note that the Graph Type setting automatically changes back to Stacked Bar, the default. Select the Series option and note that all the series are now undefined.
4. Select 1st Series and enter **B4..B7**, select X-axis Series and enter **A4..A7**, and then select Quit to return to the Graph menu.
5. Select Text, choose the 1st Line option, and enter **1994 Sales**.
6. Select Quit to return to the Graph menu, select the Graph Type option, and choose Pie. Then select the View option to see the results. Your screen should resemble Figure 14-18.
7. Press a key other than / to return to the Graph menu, select Name, and then choose Create. Enter the name **PIE**.
8. Select Graph Type and change the type to Column. Press F10 to view the results.

9. Press [Esc] to return to the Graph menu. Select Name, choose Create, and enter the name **COLUMN**.
10. Select Name. Then choose Display and enter **BARS** to view the previously named graph. Press any key to return to the Graph menu. Note that the Graph Type setting is now Bar because the BARS graph is the current graph.
11. Select Quit to return to Ready mode. Then issue the / **F**ile | **S**ave command and replace the previous version of the graph.

Defining XY Graphs and Bubble Graphs

XY graphs and bubble graphs differ substantially from most of the other graph types supported by Quattro Pro. In other graphs (except pie and column graphs) you define one or more series of values to be plotted against the X-axis. The X-axis is simply a baseline, and the only thing you can define about this axis is a series of labels used to identify the plotted values.

In an XY graph or bubble graph, you plot the points of intersection between two series. XY and bubble graphs treat one value series (the X-axis values) as the independent variable against which the other values (the series values) are plotted. In essence, an XY or bubble graph answers the question "When

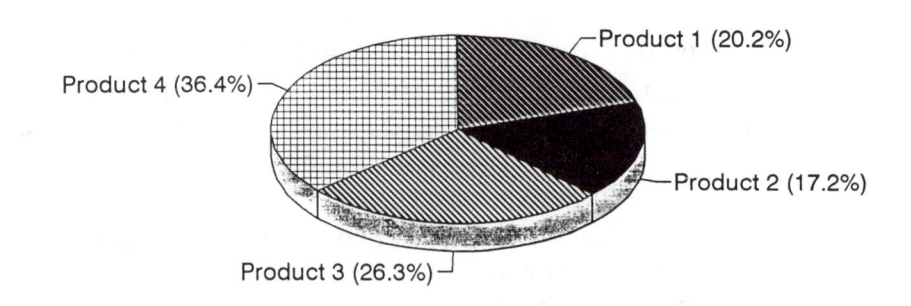

A pie graph of 1994 sales
Figure 14-18.

Creating Graphs

the X series is at this level, where is Y?" for every value of X that you specify. For example, the graph shown in Figure 14-8 answers the question "What is the average salary for people with X years of post-high-school education?" for nine different values of X. It is possible to plot several series on an XY or bubble graph, but in each case, the values that are plotted are the intersections between X-axis values and the values in one of the series.

There is no direct relationship between bubble size and Y-axis scale; the bubbles are scaled relative to each other.

There are two differences between an XY graph and a bubble graph. First, in a bubble graph, the intersections of the X and Y values are represented by bubbles rather than by markers. (The center of each bubble is located at the exact XY intersection.) Second, bubble graphs represent a third series of values, in addition to the X-axis series and 1st (Y-axis) series. This third series determines the size of the individual bubbles. For example, in the bubble graph shown in Figure 14-9, the X-axis series block includes the figures for advertising, the 1st series block includes the figures for sales, and the 2nd series block contains the figures for company size. The values in the 2nd series block determine the size of the bubbles, and the intersection of the values in the X-axis series and 1st series determine where the center of each bubble is located. The legend in Figure 14-9 was created by entering legend text for the first bubble as Graph | Text | Legends | 1st Series, legend text for the second bubble as Graph | Text | Legends | 2nd Series, and so on.

Try creating an XY graph now. First you must reset all current graph settings so that you can start your graph definition from scratch. Then you need to enter some additional data on your notebook.

1. Reset all graph settings by issuing the / **G**raph | **C**ustomize Series command, clicking on the Reset button, and selecting Graph. Then Select Quit twice to return to Ready mode.

2. Move the cell pointer to column A, issue the / **S**tyle | **C**olumn Width command ([Ctrl]-[W]), and widen the column to 11 characters.

3. Enter **Unit Price** in A14, enter **32** in B14, enter **33** in C14, enter **34** in D14, enter **35** in E14, enter **35.5** in F14, and enter **37** in G14. Then enter **Unit Sales** in A15, enter **400** in B15, enter **420** in C15, enter **460** in D15, enter **490** in E15, enter **530** in F15, and enter **550** in G15.

4. Issue the / **G**raph | **S**eries | **1**st Series command, and enter **B15..G15** as the block.

5. Select the X-Axis Series option and enter a block of **B14..G14**.

6. Select Quit to return to the Graph menu. Select Text, select 1st Line, and enter **Effect of Unit Price on Units Sold**.

7. Select the X-Title option on the Text menu and enter **\A14**; then select the Y-Title option and enter **\A15**.

8. Select Quit to return to the Graph menu, choose the Graph Type option, and pick XY.
9. Select the View option. Your graph should now look like the one shown in Figure 14-19.
10. Press a key other than / to return to the Graph menu, select Name, and choose Create. Enter the name **XY**, and then select Quit to return to Ready mode.

Creating Three-Dimensional Graphs

It's easier to see all values in ribbon graphs, since you can still see all the ribbons even if they crisscross at points.

In all of the three-dimensional graph types, the data for each series of values is graphed in front of data for previous series. As a result, in three-dimensional bar, step, and area graphs, you can only see all the values on the graph if there is little or no overlap between the values in different series, and if the series with the highest numbers is designated as series 1, the series with the second highest numbers is designated as series 2, and so on—so that the bars, area, or steps representing the highest numbers are in the back row of the graph.

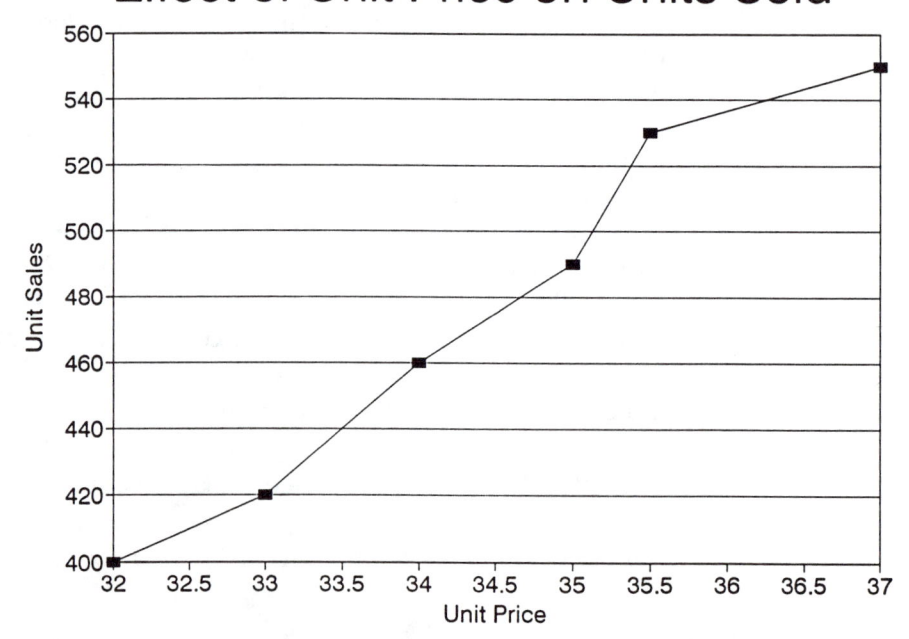

Creating an XY graph
Figure 14-19.

Creating Graphs

The legends for three-dimensional graphs always appear along the right edge of the bottom plane of the graph rather than in a legend box, regardless of the Graph | Text | Legends | Position setting.

If you would like to practice constructing three-dimensional graphs,

1. Create the notebook shown in Figure 14-20.
2. Issue the / **G**raph | **S**eries | **G**roup | **R**ows command and specify a block of B5..G8.
3. Select X-Axis Series from the Graph | Series menu and specify an X-axis range of B4..G4.
4. If you want to add a legend, choose Quit to return to the Graph menu, select Text, and then choose Legends. Choose 1st Series and enter **\A5**; choose 2nd Series and enter **\A6**; choose 3rd Series and enter **\A7**; and choose 4th Series and enter **\A8**.
5. Choose Quit twice to return to the Graph menu, select Graph Type, choose 3-D Graphs, and then choose Area. Now select View; your graph should resemble the one shown in Figure 14-21. Press any key to return to the Graph menu and try out the other 3-D graph types.

NOTE: Do not confuse the 3-D graph types with the effect achieved using the Add Depth option in the Graph Overall dialog box. As discussed in Chapter 15, the Add Depth setting determines whether individual bars, steps, ribbons, and areas are displayed with three-dimensional effects—in both three-dimensional graphs and in regular bar and area graphs. In contrast, choosing a three-dimensional graph type makes the graph as a whole appear three dimensional—with the values for each series lying in a different vertical plane.

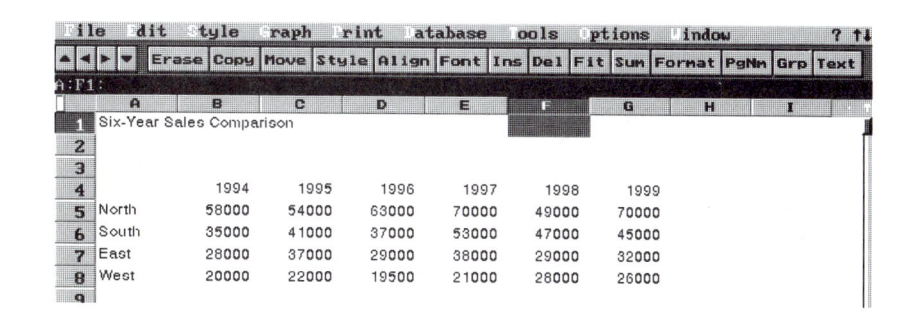

Notebook for generating 3-D graphs
Figure 14-20.

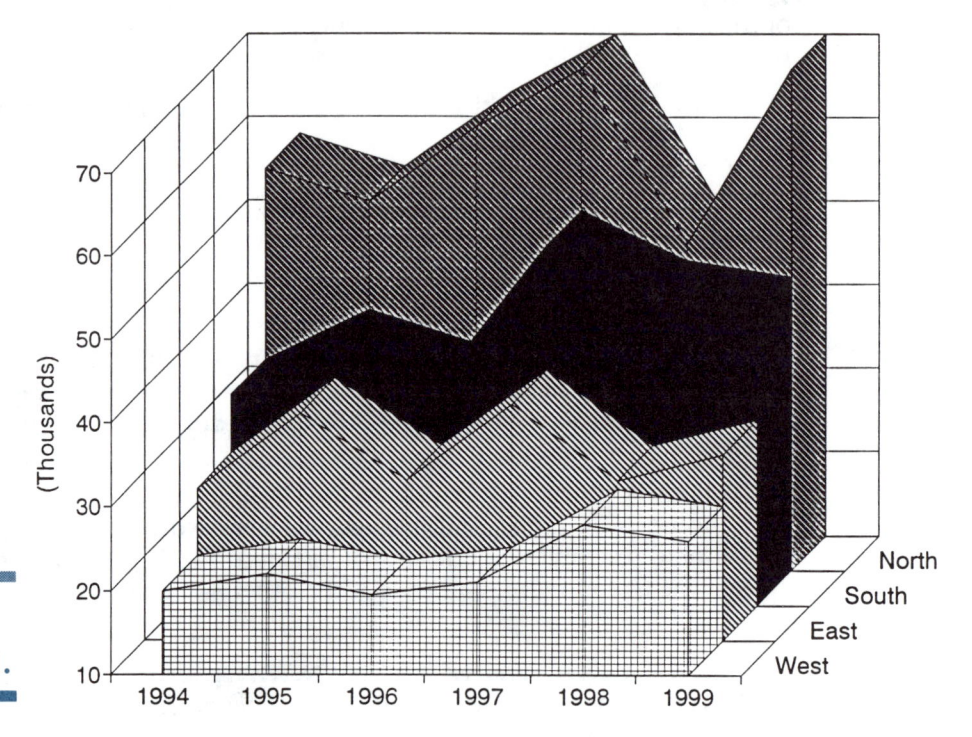

A 3-D area graph
Figure 14-21.

Graphing Data on Multiple Pages

As you learned in Chapter 12, Quattro Pro 5 allows you to enter data on multiple notebook pages if that suits your needs. Fortunately, this does not present a problem when you want to operate on the data on several pages: You can create groups and work in Group mode, or you can use 3-D block references in commands and formulas. Similarly, when you're graphing, it's a simple matter to graph the data from multiple notebook pages. Each series can be from a different page, or contiguous through multiple pages. (When graphing data from multiple pages, make sure you don't accidentally leave Group mode on; if you do, you may get unexpected results.)

If you created the CHOCOLAT.WQ2 notebook in Chapter 12, try following this exercise to create a stacked bar graph that graphs three series from three separate pages—Jan, Feb, and Mar. For the sake of simplicity, you'll only graph the first two items: truffles and chocolate cigars.

1. If necessary, clear your screen by issuing the / **F**ile | **E**rase command. Then retrieve the CHOCOLAT.WQ2 notebook. (If you didn't create this

Creating Graphs

notebook in Chapter 12, you can use any notebook that has similar data on multiple pages.) Turn off Group mode if you left it on the last time you saved the notebook.

2. Make sure you're on the page Jan, issue the / **G**raph I **G**raph Type command, and choose Stacked Bar if it's not already selected.

3. Choose Series from the Graph menu, select 1st Series, and then type or point to the cells Jan:C5..C6.

4. Choose 2nd Series from the Graph I Series menu, move to the Feb page, and select the cells Feb:C5..C6. Next choose 3rd Series and select Mar:C5..C6.

5. Choose X-Axis Series from the Graph I Series menu and highlight the cells A5..A6. (You can be on any page for this step, since these labels are identical on all pages in the notebook.)

6. Choose Quit to return to the Graph menu. Then choose Text, and choose Legends. Enter **Jan** under 1st Series, enter **Feb** under 2nd Series, and enter **Mar** under 3rd Series. Choose Quit to return to the Text menu.

7. If you like, enter 1st Line and 2nd Line descriptive titles for your graph. Then choose Quit to return to the Graph menu.

8. Finally, choose View from the Graph menu to survey your graph, which should be similar to the one shown in Figure 14-22. (Your graph will undoubtedly graph different values, depending on what numbers you entered into pages Feb and Mar.)

Printing Graphs

Printing graphs in Quattro Pro is very similar to printing notebooks. The basic steps are as follows:

1. Make sure that the graph you want to print is the current graph. If it is not, use the / **G**raph I **N**ame I **D**isplay command to make it the current graph.

2. Issue the / **P**rint I **G**raph Print command, and select the Layout option to change any layout options you wish.

3. Make sure the Destination setting on the Print I Graph Print menu is set to Graph Printer.

4. Check that the printer is turned on and the paper properly aligned.

5. Select the Go option on the Print I Graph Print menu.

If you want to preview the output before printing it, set the Print I Graph Print I Destination setting to Screen Preview. If you want to direct output to

Truffles Battle Cigars
First Quarter Showdown

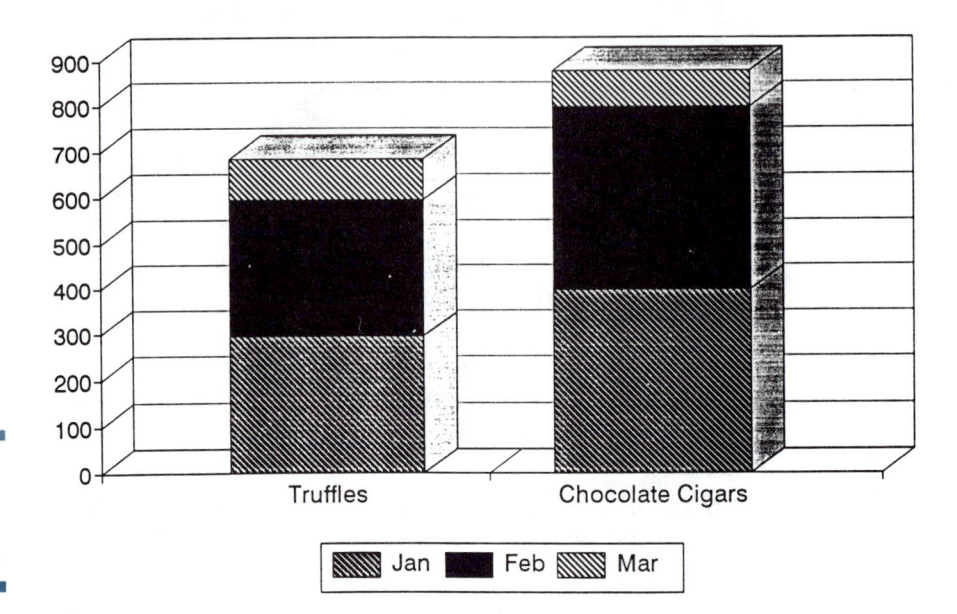

Graph created with data from multiple pages
Figure 14-22.

a disk file so that you can print it later, set the Destination to Binary File and enter a file name as prompted. (If you do not enter an extension, Quattro Pro automatically assigns the PRN extension.) Then select the Graph Print option, as if you were sending output to your printer. When you are ready to print the file, enter the following command from the DOS prompt (assuming your printer is connected to the LPT1 printer port):

    COPY *filename*.PRN LPT1: /B

If your printer is connected to a different port, substitute the appropriate port name, such as COM1, in place of LPT1.

Adjusting Print Speed and Quality

When you first tell Quattro Pro about a printer using the / **O**ptions | **H**ardware | **P**rinters | **1**st Printer | **T**ype of Printer or / **O**ptions | **H**ardware | **P**rinters | **2**nd Printer | **T**ype of Printer command, Quattro Pro often gives you a choice of print modes. These modes reflect a range of print densities. The higher the print mode, the larger the number of dots per inch and the slower the printer speed.

Changing the Graph Print Layout

The commands in the Print | Graph Print | Layout menu let you change the placement, size, and dimensions of a printed graph. The Left Edge option specifies the distance between the left edge of the page and the left edge of the graph itself. The default setting is 0 inch. The Top Edge option specifies the distance between the top edge of the page and the top edge of the graph. The default setting is also 0 inch. The Height option specifies the length of the graph from top to bottom. If you specify a height of less than 1 inch or more than 10 inches, Quattro Pro prints the graph full size. Because the default setting is 0, leaving the default setting unchanged amounts to directing Quattro Pro to print the graph full size. The Width option specifies the width of the graph across the page. The default setting is 0 inch. If you specify a width of less than 1 inch (either by entering a number less than 1 or leaving the default setting of 0) or more than 8 inches, Quattro Pro prints the graph full size.

The Dimensions option determines whether layout dimensions are expressed in inches or centimeters. The Orientation option specifies whether the graph will be printed in portrait or landscape mode; the default setting is Portrait. The 4:3 Aspect option determines whether Quattro Pro preserves a 4 to 3 width to height ratio when printing graphs or displaying inserted graphs on the screen. If you leave the 4:3 Aspect setting at Yes, Quattro Pro prints the largest graph it can within the height and width you specify while maintaining a 4 to 3 width to height ratio. If you change the 4:3 Aspect setting to No, Quattro Pro stretches the graph to fit whatever height and width you specify.

The Reset option reinstates the last set of print settings that you saved to disk with the Update option. Finally, the Update option saves the current graph print settings as permanent defaults, so they are reinstated every time you load Quattro Pro.

TIP: Although both the Print Layout Options dialog box and Print | Graph Print | Layout menus contain Dimensions and Orientation settings, these settings are saved separately. Setting the Orientation option for graphs to Landscape, for example, has no effect on the Orientation setting for notebooks.

"Printing" to Disk

As mentioned, you can "print" a graph to disk by changing the Destination setting to Binary File. This allows you to create files that you can later print from DOS. You can also use the / **P**rint | **G**raph Print | **W**rite Graph File command to create files for export to other software packages. When you issue this command, Quattro Pro displays a menu with the options EPS File, PIC File, Slide EPS, PCX File, and Quit. Select EPS File to create a PostScript file for use in word processing or desktop publishing programs that support PostScript page description language. Select PIC File to create graph files that can be printed through Lotus 1-2-3. Choose Slide EPS to create a file suitable for generating a 35mm slide. Select PCX File to create graph files that can be read by PC Paintbrush, Windows Paintbrush, and other programs that support the PCX file format.

Graph Slide Shows

You can enter the columns of slide show data on the same page as your data or on a different page.

The / **G**raph | **N**ame | **S**lide command allows you to display graph slide shows—a series of named graphs displayed on the screen one after another. To create a slide show, you must first enter two adjacent columns of data in a separate section of the notebook, away from your other data. In the first column enter the names of all the graphs that you want to display. In the second column enter the number of seconds that you want the graph to be displayed, or enter the number 0 if you want Quattro Pro to leave the graph on screen until you press a key. This second column is optional; if you leave it blank, Quattro Pro assumes a value of 0 and therefore displays each graph, waits for you to press a key, displays the next graph, and so on. Even if you enter a number greater than 0 in the second column, Quattro Pro displays the next graph as soon as you press a key. The interval only determines how long the graph stays on screen if you do not press a key. During a slide show, you can back up one slide by pressing (Backspace) or the right mouse button.

Once you have entered your one or two columns of data, issue the / **G**raph | **N**ame | **S**lide command and, when prompted, specify the block of graph names and their display intervals, if any. Quattro Pro displays each of the graphs in the block and then returns to the Graph menu.

Slide Show Transitions

By default, when you move from one slide to the next in a slide show, Quattro Pro simply erases one graph from the screen and replaces it with the next. If you prefer, you can customize your slide show transitions with both visual and sound effects. Quattro Pro offers a total of 24 different visual effects, including various types of fades, horizontal and vertical wipes, and dissolves. It also lets you use digitized sound files to produce sound effects during slide show transitions. Table 14-1 lists the 24 visual transition effects you can use.

Creating Graphs

Effect Number	Speed Range	Effect Produced
1	0	Instantaneous cut
2	0	Switch to black, then display new image
3	0	Wipe from left to right
4	0-16	Wipe from right to left
5	0-16	Wipe bottom
6	0-16	Wipe top
7	0-16	Barn door close, right/left to center
8	0-16	Barn door open, center to right/left
9	0-16	Barn door top/bottom to center
10	0-16	Barn door center to top/bottom
11	0-16	Iris close
12	0-16	Iris open
13	0-16	Scroll up
14	0-16	Scroll down
15	0-16	Vertical stripes right
16	0-16	Stripes right and then left
17	0-16	Spiral in
18	0-16	Dissolve, 2x1 rectangles
19	0-16	Dissolve, 2x2 squares
20	0-16	Dissolve, 4x4 squares
21	0-16	Dissolve, 8x8 squares
22	0-16	Dissolve, 16x16 squares
23	0-16	Dissolve, 32x32 squares
24	0-16	Dissolve, 64x64 squares

Slide Show Visual Effects
Table 14-1.

Recall that the first column contains the name of the slides and the second the number of seconds they'll be displayed.

To add transitions to a slide show, you add one to three additional columns to the slide show block. The types of visual effects are based on the values in the third column of a slide show block. (A zero or blank cell in the third column indicates no transition effect.) Their speed (how long it takes for the effect to transition from one slide to the next) is based on the values in the fourth column. Sound effects are based on the names of sound files in the fifth column.

You can also use visual transition effects to overlay one slide with another rather than simply replacing it. You do this by entering the transition effect number as a negative value. For example, if you enter –14, the new slide will scroll on top of the previous one.

If your computer contains a sound card that is compatible with Sound Blaster—including Sound Blaster, Sound Blaster Pro, and Adlib—Quattro Pro detects the card and uses it when generating sound effects.

Inserting Graphs in a Notebook

The / **G**raph | **I**nsert command allows you to insert a graph directly into your notebook, so it appears as part of the notebook rather than on a screen or printout by itself.

There are three reasons to insert a graph into a notebook: to see the graph change as you change data, to print the graph as part of the notebook when generating reports, and to print multiple graphs on a page. You can view inserted graphs on the screen only if you are using WYSIWYG display mode (see Figure 14-23). When Quattro Pro is in character-based display modes, an inserted graph appears as an empty highlighted block on the screen. This helps prevent you from accidentally entering data in this area.

In WYSIWYG mode, Quattro Pro redraws inserted graphs whenever the notebook is recalculated. Unless you have set the Recalculation mode to Manual, this means you must wait for Quattro Pro to redraw any inserted graphs that currently appear on your screen every time you enter or change data in any cell of the notebook. If you are making numerous changes to the notebook, you may either want to switch to a character-based display mode or set the Recalculation mode to Manual. When the Recalculation mode is Manual, Quattro Pro redraws the graph only when you press F9 (Calc) or scroll the screen display.

You can insert up to eight graphs in a single notebook. Quattro Pro always displays the name of the graph on the input line whenever you move the cell pointer into the block containing an inserted graph. If your notebook contains several inserted graphs, this is the easiest way to determine which one you are looking at.

Creating Graphs

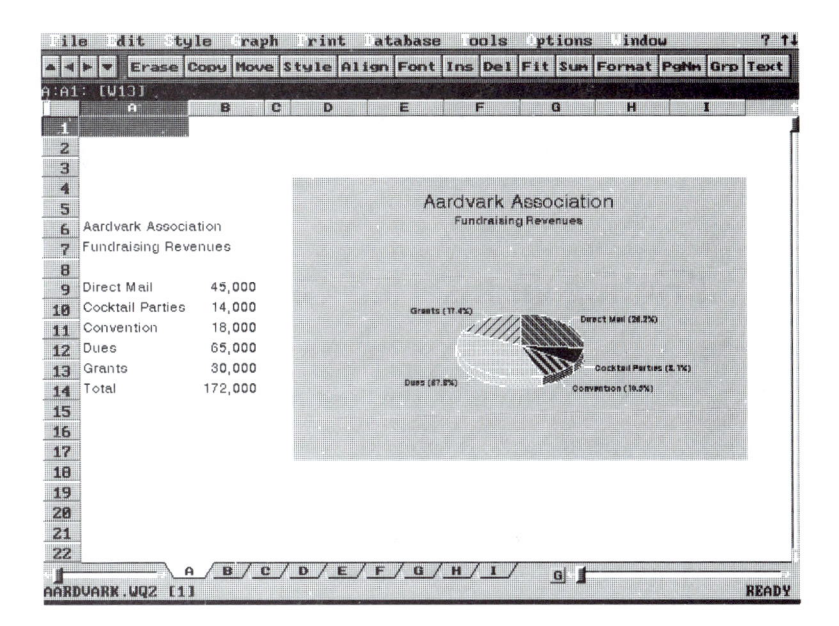

Notebook with inserted graph
Figure 14-23.

If you need a hint, the Graph menu shows the graph type of the current graph to the right of the Graph Type option.

Although you can have multiple graphs—and multiple inserted graphs—in a single notebook, only one of them can be the current graph. If you want a full-screen view of the current graph, just press F10 as usual. However, to display a full-screen view of an inserted graph that is not the current graph, you need to move the cell pointer into the graph block and press F10.

To insert a graph into your notebook, you perform the following steps:

1. If you have an EGA or VGA monitor, make sure that the Options | Display Mode setting is WYSIWYG.
2. Issue the / **G**raph | **I**nsert command. Quattro Pro prompts you for a graph to insert and displays a list of named graphs.
3. Choose a graph to insert. To specify the current graph, you can either choose the Current Graph option or the graph name.
4. When Quattro Pro prompts you for a block, specify the block using either the pointing or typing method. If the block you specify contains data, it is not erased by the inserted graph. The data is obscured by the inserted graph, however, and you can view or print it only by removing the graph from the notebook.

An inserted graph may be up to 12 columns by 32 rows. If this isn't large enough for your purposes, you can widen columns to increase width or attach larger fonts in the row to increase row height.

When you first insert a graph, Quattro Pro draws the graph using a 4 to 3 height to width ratio. If the block you specified has different proportions and you would prefer to have the graph stretched to fill the block, issue the / **P**rint | **G**raph Print | **L**ayout | **4**:3 Aspect | **N**o command. Quattro Pro does not actually redisplay the graph until it recalculates the notebook, so you may want to press F9 (Calc) after changing this setting so you can see its effects.

Printing an Inserted Graph

To print an inserted graph, just include the area that contains the graph in the print block, make sure Destination is set to Graph Printer, and select Spreadsheet Print from the Print menu.

If your print block is too wide to fit on one page, the graph generally breaks at the same column as the rest of the data in the notebook. As a result, part of the graph appears on one page and part on the next. You can fix the problem by moving the graph to a set of columns that fits on one page or, if the graph itself is too wide to fit on a page, by printing in landscape mode.

Removing an Inserted Graph

To remove an inserted graph from a notebook, issue the / **G**raph | **H**ide command. Quattro Pro displays a list of graphs—like the one it displays when you insert a graph. Select the graph you want to remove and press Enter. Quattro Pro erases the graph from the screen.

The name of this command is a bit misleading. The / **G**raph | **H**ide command does not temporarily conceal an inserted graph; it actually erases it. If you want to see the graph again later, you need to insert it again.

You have now learned all the basics of defining and printing graphs. Chapter 15 builds on this foundation while covering various options for refining, customizing, and annotating your graphs. If you anticipate using graphs frequently, you might want to experiment on your own with the other graph types, focusing on how series are represented in different graph types and which graphs work best for different types of applications.

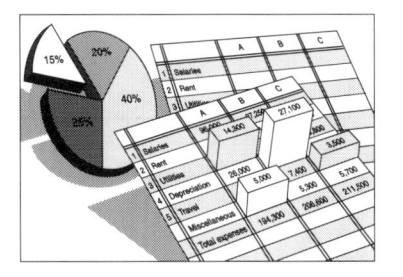

CHAPTER

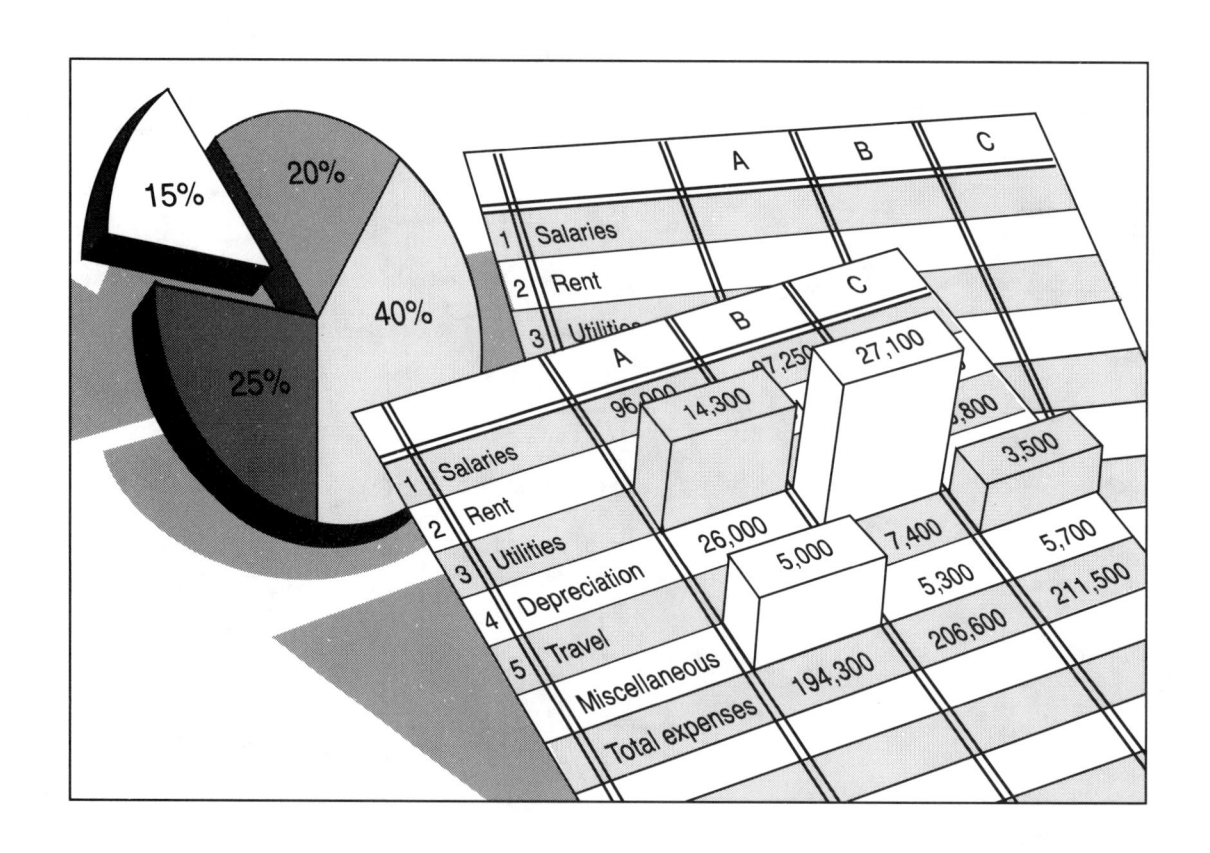

15

CUSTOMIZING AND ANNOTATING GRAPHS

Quattro Pro offers numerous commands for customizing and embellishing graphs, and also includes the Annotator— a sophisticated drawing tool that you can use to add text, lines, arrows, and shapes to your graph, as well as to rearrange existing graph elements. This chapter presents an overview of the possibilities for customizing and annotating your graphs. With this foundation you should have enough knowledge to experiment further on your own.

Customizing Series

When you create a graph, Quattro Pro automatically assigns a different color and, in area and bar graphs, a unique fill pattern to each series that you define. In line graphs it assigns each series a distinct marker type. You can change these and other series attributes using the / Graph | Customize Series command.

Customizing Colors

The options in the Graph Customize dialog box vary quite a bit depending on which graph type is selected.

If you have a color screen, Quattro Pro displays each series in a graph in a different color. You can change these colors using the Series and Color options in the Graph Customize dialog box, which is shown in Figure 15-1. To change the color for a series, select the appropriate series number and then select the desired color from the colors list.

The series colors are not the only graph colors you can control. To change the color of text, use / Graph | Text | Font and pick the item whose color you wish to change. To change the colors of the graph's background or the grid lines displayed on the surface of the graph, issue the / Graph | Overall command (discussed later in this chapter) and make your selections from the Graph Overall dialog box that appears.

Altering Fill Patterns

To customize the fill patterns to be used in bar, bubble, and area graphs, issue the / Graph | Customize Series command and make your selections from the Graph Customize dialog box. Just select a series and then choose from the 16 available fill patterns.

Quattro Pro uses the same fill patterns and colors for individual slices in pie and column graphs that it uses for individual series in other types of graphs.

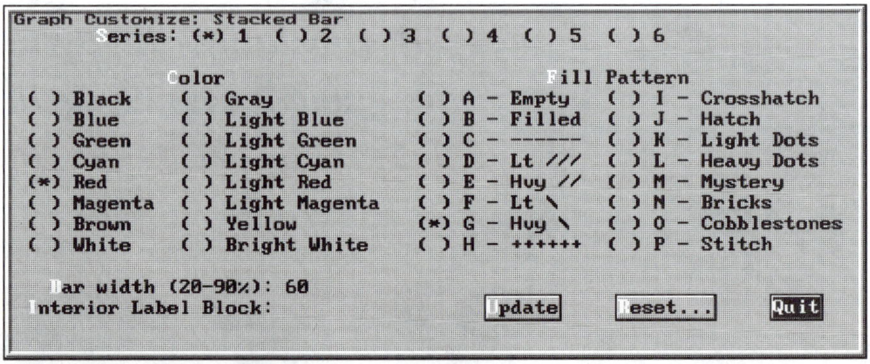

```
Graph Customize: Stacked Bar
      Series: (*) 1  ( ) 2  ( ) 3  ( ) 4  ( ) 5  ( ) 6

              Color                        Fill Pattern
   ( ) Black      ( ) Gray           ( ) A - Empty      ( ) I - Crosshatch
   ( ) Blue       ( ) Light Blue     ( ) B - Filled     ( ) J - Hatch
   ( ) Green      ( ) Light Green    ( ) C - ------     ( ) K - Light Dots
   ( ) Cyan       ( ) Light Cyan     ( ) D - Lt ///     ( ) L - Heavy Dots
   (*) Red        ( ) Light Red      ( ) E - Hvy //     ( ) M - Mystery
   ( ) Magenta    ( ) Light Magenta  ( ) F - Lt \       ( ) N - Bricks
   ( ) Brown      ( ) Yellow         (*) G - Hvy \      ( ) O - Cobblestones
   ( ) White      ( ) Bright White   ( ) H - ++++++     ( ) P - Stitch

      Bar width (20-90%): 60
   Interior Label Block:                    [Update]  [Reset...]  [Quit]
```

A Graph Customize dialog box
Figure 15-1.

Customizing and Annotating Graphs

For example, when you change the fill pattern assigned to the third series, the setting for the third slice changes as well.

Changing Lines and Markers

By default, Quattro Pro represents each data point in a line graph with a marker symbol and connects the markers for each series with a line. You may prefer to represent one or more series in a graph with marker symbols only or with lines only. (Lines are excellent for representing trends over time; markers are preferable for emphasizing individual values.) Quattro Pro also allows you to change the line style (solid, dotted, and so on) and marker symbol used for each series.

To change these characteristics of line graphs, you should issue the / **G**raph | **C**ustomize Series command with a graph type of Line selected. You'll see a Graph Customize dialog box with eight selections for Line Style, ten selections for marker types, and four selections for Format.

Under Format, choose Lines if you want Quattro Pro to use lines only, choose Symbols for symbols (markers) only, and select Both (the default setting) if you want markers connected by lines. Select Neither if you want Quattro Pro to display neither lines nor markers. You can use this option to temporarily remove a series from a graph. To specify the type of line or marker symbols used to plot each series, choose a series to change and select from the Line Style or Marker options on the Graph Customize dialog box.

Changing the Width of Bars

Make sure you've selected a bar graph type before changing the Bar width setting.

By default, when Quattro Pro draws a bar graph, it apportions 60% of the space on the X-axis among all the bars on the graph and reserves the remaining 40% for blank space between the bars. To change the bar widths on a graph, you adjust the percentage of X-axis space that Quattro Pro allocates to bars using the Bar width option on the Graph Customize dialog box. Enter a number from 20 through 90; the larger the number, the wider the bars. You can also narrow bars slightly by getting rid of the perspective lines at their right edge. See "Eliminating the Three-Dimensional Effect" later in this chapter.

Labeling Points on a Graph

You cannot use interior labels in pie, column, or area graphs.

In Chapter 14 you used X-axis labels to identify the values plotted on a graph. You may want to further identify these values by adding labels to the surface of the graph itself. These *interior labels* usually designate the numeric value of each point plotted on the graph. You might use them to indicate the value represented by each bar in a bar graph or the value of the points plotted in a line graph.

To define a set of interior labels, you select the desired series and select Interior Label Block in the Graph Customize dialog box. Quattro Pro prompts you for "Notebook data to label this series." After you specify a block of cells, Quattro Pro displays a submenu with the options Center, Left, Above, Right, Below, and None, which you use to indicate where you want the labels located in relation to the corresponding values. With bar graphs, you have no choice about the placement of labels; Quattro Pro automatically displays them above the bars in regular or stacked bar graphs and to the right of the bars in rotated bar graphs. You can use the None option on the Interior Labels menu to hide the labels temporarily so you can redisplay them later without having to redefine them.

You can use a block other than the series values block for interior labels. For instance, if you are labeling points that are fairly close together and the values themselves are long, you might need to create a second series of values on the notebook (you could divide each value by 100 or 1000) and use those as labels. As an example, suppose you had a bar graph that plotted values of 10,000,000, 20,000,000, and 30,000,000. To make the graph easier to read, you might want to display the abbreviated labels 10, 20, and 30 above each bar, instead of the actual values in millions. To do so, you would simply enter the values 10, 20, and 30 in adjacent cells in the notebook, and then choose those cells when prompted for "Notebook data to label this series."

Quattro Pro displays interior labels in the same format as the notebook values on which they are based. For example, if a set of interior labels is based on a block of numbers displayed on the notebook in Currency format, the labels also appear on the graph in Currency format.

Once you have defined a set of interior labels, they are not easy to eliminate. You can reset the entire series and thus erase the interior labels along with the series, or you can specify a block of blank cells as labels (but make sure the cells don't get filled later).

Overriding the Graph Type

The / **G**raph | **C**ustomize Series command lets you change the graph type used for one or more series to create graphs that use both lines and bars. You can override the graph type for a series only if the overall graph type is Bar or Line. In this case, you'll see the selection Override Type with the three options, Default (meaning the graph type for the graph as a whole), Bar, and Line. Figure 15-2 shows a bar graph in which the graph type for the fourth series was changed from Default to Line.

Customizing and Annotating Graphs

Five-Year Sales Projection

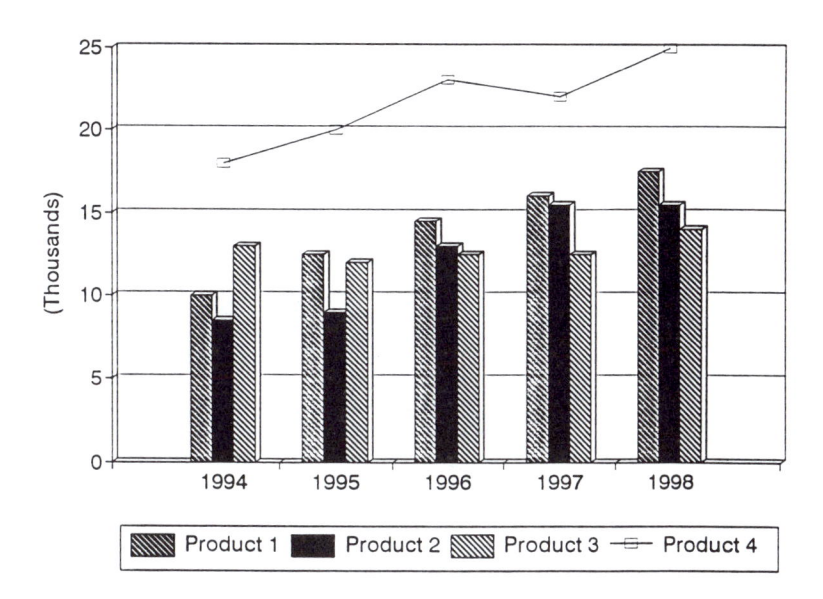

Mixing graph types
Figure 15-2.

Using a Second Y-Axis

You can define a second Y-axis only for line, bar, XY, rotated bar, high-low, 3-D bar, 3-D ribbon, and 3-D step graphs.

As you have seen, the Y-axis serves as a measuring stick to gauge the value of different data points on a graph. If you are graphing two or more series that differ widely in magnitude, you may want to define a second Y-axis so you can measure and compare two sets of values against two different scales. For example, Figure 15-3 shows a graph that plots two series of values—the number of bank loans made over a six-month period and the amount of those loans—against two different Y-axes. If you plotted both series against a single axis, the Y-axis scale would extend from 0 to 30000000 and the bars for the first series' values would be mere smudges near the bottom of the graph.

To define a second Y-axis, you use the Y-Axis selection in the Graph Customize dialog box (not the Y-Axis option on the Graph menu). Initially, all the series are set to Primary Y-Axis. To plot a series on a second Y-axis, select that series and change the setting to Secondary Y-Axis. Quattro Pro creates a separate Y-axis at the right edge of the graph and scales this axis on the basis of the range of values in all the series you have assigned it. Once you have defined a second Y-axis, you can use the / **G**raph | **Y**-Axis command and click on the 2nd Y-Axis button in the resultant dialog box to customize it.

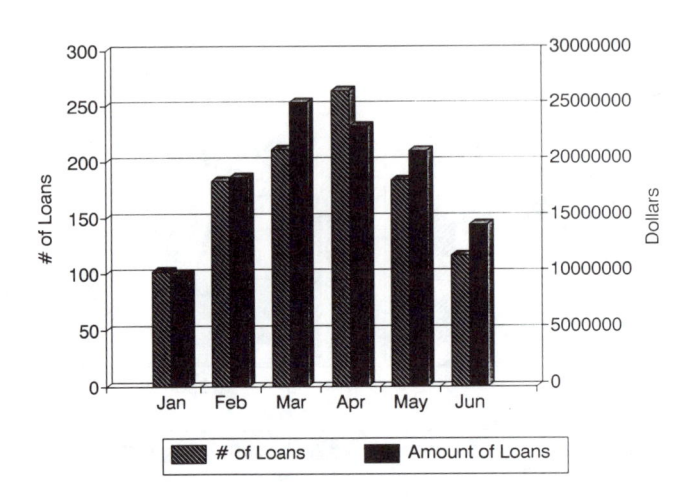

A graph with two Y-axes
Figure 15-3.

Resetting Graph Settings

The graph settings you establish stay in effect even if you change graph types. This allows you to experiment with different graph types without redefining the graph's series, text, and so on. However, if you create more than one graph on a particular notebook, the graph settings also carry over from one graph to the next, which is not always desirable.

The carryover of settings can be particularly problematic if you define one graph with several series and then define another with fewer series. You cannot simply select the appropriate option on the Graph | Series menu and press Esc to erase the setting. The only way to eliminate a series is with the Reset button in the Graph Customize dialog box. When you press this button, Quattro Pro displays a menu with options for each of the six possible series, along with the options for the X-Axis Series and for Graph (to reset all the graph settings).

When you reset a series, Quattro Pro erases the series values setting and the interior labels setting (if any), and sets the color, fill pattern, line style and marker symbol, and override type back to their defaults. If you select Graph from this submenu, Quattro Pro resets all the series, changes the graph type to Stacked Bar, and restores the bar width, the axes settings, and the overall settings back to the global defaults.

Customizing and Annotating Graphs

Updating Graph Settings

As mentioned, resetting a series means returning it to its global defaults. You can change those defaults with the Update button in the Graph Customize dialog box. Like other Quattro Pro update commands, the Update button in the Graph Customize dialog box stores a group of settings to disk so they can be recalled and placed into effect in future work sessions. When you issue this command, Quattro Pro saves the current graph type, Graph | Overall settings, Graph | X-Axis settings, Graph | Y-Axis settings, and every setting established through the Graph Customize dialog box except the interior label block. Once you have changed the graph defaults, Quattro Pro reinstates those settings every time you reload the program or select the Reset button from the Graph Customize dialog box and select the Graph option. You can, however, establish new defaults very easily just by choosing new settings and selecting the Update button again.

Customizing Pie and Column Graphs

There are a number of ways to fine-tune the appearance of pie and column charts through the Graph Customize dialog box. The attributes you can change include the colors and fill patterns of the pie slices or column segments, the format of the labels used to identify the slices or segments, and, in the case of pie charts, whether or not slices are exploded (pulled away) from the rest of the pie.

Changing the Label Format

When you first create a pie or column graph, Quattro Pro displays percentages next to each slice to indicate the percentage that slice represents of the whole pie or column. If you specify X-axis values for the graph, Quattro Pro displays these percentages next to the X-axis text.

X-axis labels are still displayed even if you choose the None option.

The Label Format option on the Graph Customize dialog box allows you to specify the information to be displayed next to each slice of the pie or section of the column. If you specify X-axis values for the graph, Quattro Pro displays the Label Format information immediately after the X-axis text. The Value option displays the series values exactly as they appear on the notebook. The % option (the default) displays the percentage that each slice represents of the whole pie or column. The $ option displays the series values in Currency format with zero decimal places; this option was used in the graph shown in Figure 15-4. The None option removes all labels from the chart.

If you want to display both the percentages and the notebook values, you can use the same block of data for the X-axis series as you use for series 1 and

Pie graph with exploded slice and labels displayed in Currency format
Figure 15-4.

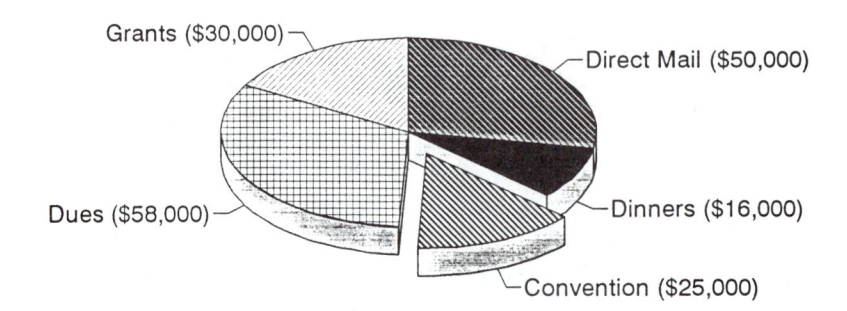

leave the Label Format option set to %. However, this means that you cannot use the X-axis series to display text that indicates what each slice of the pie or column represents.

Eliminating Tick Marks

By default, Quattro Pro displays lines between each slice in a pie or column graph and its identifying label. If you are plotting only a few values, these lines may be unnecessary. You can remove them by issuing the / **G**raph | **C**ustomize Series command and changing the Tick Marks setting to No.

Changing Pie or Column Fill Patterns

The graph slices are numbered beginning at the 12:00 position and proceeding clockwise.

You can choose fill patterns used for the slices of a pie or column graph in the same way you designate fill patterns for each series in a bar or area graph. When you issue the / **G**raph | **C**ustomize Series command, Quattro Pro displays a Graph Customize dialog box with options for the first nine pie slices. Once you select a slice to customize, you can select one of the 16 available fill patterns.

If you have more than nine slices in your pie or column, Quattro Pro recycles fill patterns beginning with the tenth slice: Slice 10 is displayed in the pattern that you specified for slice 1, slice 11 has the same pattern as slice 2, and so on.

Customizing and Annotating Graphs

Altering Colors

The Color options on the Graph Customize: Pie dialog box let you designate colors for the first nine slices of your pie or column graph. Simply select a slice and choose one of the 16 available colors. If you have more than nine slices in your pie or column, Quattro Pro reuses colors beginning with the tenth slice, so that the tenth slice is the same color as the first, and so on.

Exploding Pie Slices

If more than one series is selected when you generate a pie graph, all slices will automatically be exploded.

The Graph Customize: Pie dialog box also contains an option for exploding slices of a pie graph—separating them from the rest of the pie. You use this option to highlight one or more of the values represented in the graph. In the pie graph previously shown in Figure 15-4, slice 3 has been exploded. Once you select one of the slice options, select Explode to separate a slice from the rest of the pie. Select Don't Explode to return a slice to its original position.

Customizing the Axes

The dialog boxes displayed when you issue the / **G**raph I **X**-Axis and / **G**raph I **Y**-Axis commands each contain a range of options for changing the appearance of the axes of XY graphs, area graphs, line graphs, bubble graphs, high-low graphs, and bar graphs of all types. Because the choices on the two dialog boxes are almost identical, they are discussed together.

Scaling Axes Manually

You can adjust the Y-axis scale on any graph except pie and column graphs.

When you define a graph, Quattro Pro automatically scales the Y-axis and, in the case of XY graphs, the X-axis, meaning that it determines the starting and ending points for each axis and the intervals between those points. The X-Axis options and Y-Axis options dialog boxes allow you to adjust these scales manually. They also contain options for changing the display format and layout of the axis values.

On line graphs, XY graphs, high-low and bar graphs, the low point on the Y-axis is a round number equal to or slightly less than the lowest value plotted on the graph. The high point is a round number equal to or slightly greater than the highest value on the graph. You might occasionally prefer to scale the axes manually for several reasons. Sometimes extending the Y-axis to leave more room at the top of the graph can make the values easier to pinpoint or the axis labels easier to read. You may also modify the scaling to dramatize or downplay the differences among plotted values on a line or XY graph. In general, the narrower the range of values on the Y-axis, the more dramatic the differences among values appear. Conversely, the broader the range you use for scaling the axis, the smaller the apparent differences among plotted values.

Here are the steps involved in scaling an axis:

1. Issue the / **G**raph | **X**-Axis or / **G**raph | **Y**-Axis command.
2. Change the Scale setting from Automatic to Manual.
3. Next to the Low option, enter the number that you want to appear as the first number on the axis.
4. Next to the High option, enter the number that you want to display as the highest number on the axis.
5. Next to the Increment option, enter the interval you want between tick marks on the axis. If you leave the Increment setting at 0, Quattro Pro determines the tick marks interval itself.
6. If desired, customize the tick marks as described next.

Changing the Tick Marks

You can change the appearance of the axis tick marks using the No. of Minor Ticks option and the Format of Ticks button on the X-Axis options and Y-Axis options dialog boxes. Use the Format of Ticks button to change the display format for the numbers displayed along the axis. The default display format for graph tick marks is General.

Use the No. of Minor Ticks option to display ticks between the major (labeled) ticks on the axis. The No. of Minor Ticks setting does not increase the total number of ticks displayed along the axis. Rather, it determines how many of the existing ticks are changed from major (labeled) to minor (unlabeled) ticks. By setting No. of Minor Ticks to 1, you can replace every other label with a tick mark and make the remaining labels easier to read.

You also can alleviate overcrowding among X-axis labels using the Alternate Ticks option (available only on the X-Axis options dialog box). If you change the Alternate Ticks setting from No to Yes, Quattro Pro displays the X-axis labels at two alternating levels. This setting is particularly handy if you have long labels and/or many labels on the X-axis.

Eliminating the Scaling Display

When Quattro Pro plots a graph (other than a pie or column graph) that has one or more values over 10,000 along the Y-axis, it will divide those numbers by 10 or a multiple of ten, and then add a scale measurement indicator such as (Thousands) or (Millions) under the Y-axis title to the left of the axis. The same is true for the X-axis in XY graphs.

Customizing and Annotating Graphs

If you change the Display Scaling option from Yes to No, Quattro Pro omits these scale measurement labels and displays the full value of the tick marks on the axis. This can be useful if you enter data into your notebook in abbreviated form. When working with large numbers, you may occasionally choose to save keystrokes by dividing all values by 1000 as you enter them (entering **200** to mean 200,000, for example). If you graph these numbers and Quattro Pro divides them by 100 when defining the axis labels, the resulting scaling measurement, (Hundreds), would be more confusing than helpful. You're better off eliminating this scaling label and noting the measurement scale yourself on the axis or main title.

Logarithmic Scaling

When you scale an axis logarithmically, each tick mark represents ten times the value of the previous tick mark. This type of scaling can be useful for representing a series of values with a wide range of magnitude. Figure 15-5 shows two versions of the same graph: the one on the left has a normally scaled Y-axis and the one on the right has a logarithmically scaled Y-axis. If you find the profusion of horizontal grid lines confusing, you can eliminate the grid lines using the Graph Overall dialog box that appears when you issue the / **G**raph | **O**verall command (discussed shortly).

To specify logarithmic scaling, issue the / **G**raph | **Y**-Axis or / **G**raph | **X**-Axis command and change the Mode setting from Normal to Log. To return to regular scaling, change the setting back to Normal.

Customizing Graphs as a Whole

So far you have learned a variety of commands for customizing individual series on a graph and for adjusting the axes. Quattro Pro also offers several

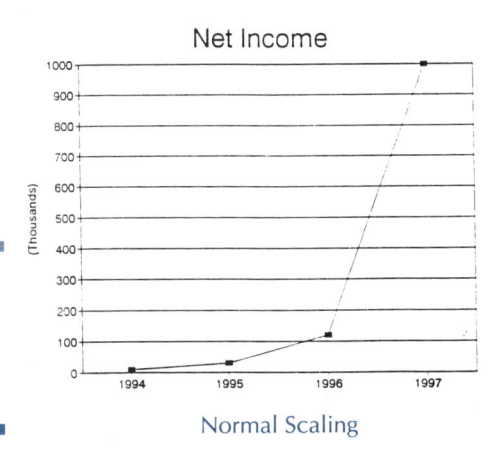

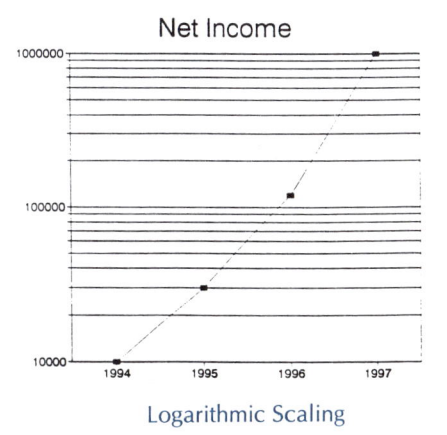

A graph with and without logarithmic scaling
Figure 15-5.

commands for changing the appearance of the graph as a whole. These commands are located in the Graph Overall dialog box (Figure 15-6), which is displayed when you issue the / **Graph** | **O**verall command. They include commands for changing the grid lines in the interior of the graph and drawing boxes around various graph elements or around the graph as a whole.

Customizing Grid Lines

When you first create a graph other than a pie, column, or text graph, Quattro Pro displays dotted lines running parallel to the bottom of the graph, perpendicular to the Y-axis. These grid lines can help you pinpoint individual values on a graph by gauging how high they extend on the Y-axis. You can change both the pattern and the color used for these grid lines using the various Grid options in the Graph Overall dialog box.

The Grid options define where the grid lines are displayed. Select the Vertical option to display grid lines that run parallel to the Y-axis. Select Horizontal (the default) to display grid lines running perpendicular to the Y-axis. Select Both if you want to display lines in both directions. Select Clear to eliminate grid lines altogether.

The Grid Line Style options control what the grid lines look like. You choose from the same eight line types you can use in a line graph: Solid, Dotted (the default), Center-line, Dashed, plus heavier versions of those same four styles. The Colors options let you change the color of the grid lines as well as the color displayed behind the grid lines, within the area bordered by the X- and Y-axes.

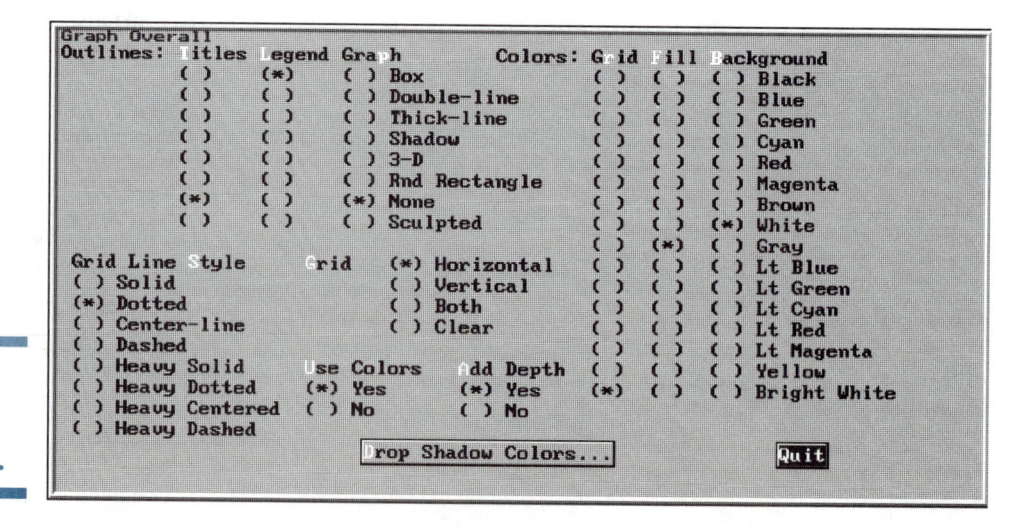

```
Graph Overall
Outlines:   Titles  Legend  Graph            Colors:  Grid  Fill  Background
   ( )       ( )    (*)    ( ) Box                    ( )   ( )   ( ) Black
   ( )       ( )    ( )    ( ) Double-line            ( )   ( )   ( ) Blue
   ( )       ( )    ( )    ( ) Thick-line             ( )   ( )   ( ) Green
   ( )       ( )    ( )    ( ) Shadow                 ( )   ( )   ( ) Cyan
   ( )       ( )    ( )    ( ) 3-D                    ( )   ( )   ( ) Red
   ( )       ( )    ( )    ( ) Rnd Rectangle          ( )   ( )   ( ) Magenta
   (*)       ( )    ( )    (*) None                   ( )   ( )   ( ) Brown
   ( )       ( )    ( )    ( ) Sculpted               ( )   ( )   (*) White
                                                      ( )   (*)   ( ) Gray
Grid Line Style         Grid     (*) Horizontal       ( )   ( )   ( ) Lt Blue
( ) Solid                        ( ) Vertical         ( )   ( )   ( ) Lt Green
(*) Dotted                       ( ) Both             ( )   ( )   ( ) Lt Cyan
( ) Center-line                  ( ) Clear            ( )   ( )   ( ) Lt Red
( ) Dashed                                            ( )   ( )   ( ) Lt Magenta
( ) Heavy Solid         Use Colors   Add Depth        ( )   ( )   ( ) Yellow
( ) Heavy Dotted        (*) Yes      (*) Yes          (*)   ( )   ( ) Bright White
( ) Heavy Centered      ( ) No       ( ) No
( ) Heavy Dashed
                              Drop Shadow Colors...            Quit
```

The Graph Overall dialog box
Figure 15-6.

Customizing and Annotating Graphs

Changing the Background Color

You can also use the Graph Overall dialog box to change the background color of a graph—that is, the color that is displayed outside the graph area. (To change the background color used inside the graph, instead change the fill color.)

Framing the Graph

The Outlines settings on the Graph Overall dialog box let you draw or erase boxes around the graph as a whole, the graph titles, and the legend. By default, Quattro Pro draws boxes only around legends. There are eight outline types—Box (a single-line box), Double-line, Thick-line, Shadow, 3-D, Rnd Rectangle (a rounded rectangle), Sculpted, and None. The default setting for Legend is Box and for Titles and Graph is None. Figure 15-7 shows a graph in which the Outlines setting for Legend is Shadow, for Graph is Rnd Rectangle, and for Title is Double-line.

Displaying Graphs in Black and White

The Use Colors setting has no effect with CGA, which always displays graphs in black and white.

The Use Colors setting on the Graph Overall dialog box lets you display graphs in black and white even if you are using a color monitor. You may find this useful if you are planning to print in black and white and want a more realistic preview of your printed graph.

Eliminating the Three-Dimensional Effect

By default, Quattro Pro draws most graphs three-dimensionally—that is, it uses perspective lines to simulate three dimensions. You can use the Add Depth option in the Graph Overall dialog box to add or remove the three-dimensional effect from a graph. In the case of bar graphs, this setting affects the display of perspective lines at the top and right edges of the bars and along the X- and Y-axes. Figure 15-8 shows the same bar graph, with and without the three-dimensional effect.

If your graph plots so many values that it would be unreadable in three dimensions, Quattro Pro displays it in two dimensions, regardless of the Add Depth setting.

The Annotator Environment

The process of annotating a graph involves defining and positioning various design elements—boxed text, lines, and shapes—on the surface of a graph. You perform these operations on a separate screen, known as the Annotator screen, which has its own menus and function key assignments. You can display the Annotator screen either by issuing the / **G**raph | **A**nnotate command or by typing / while displaying a full-screen graph.

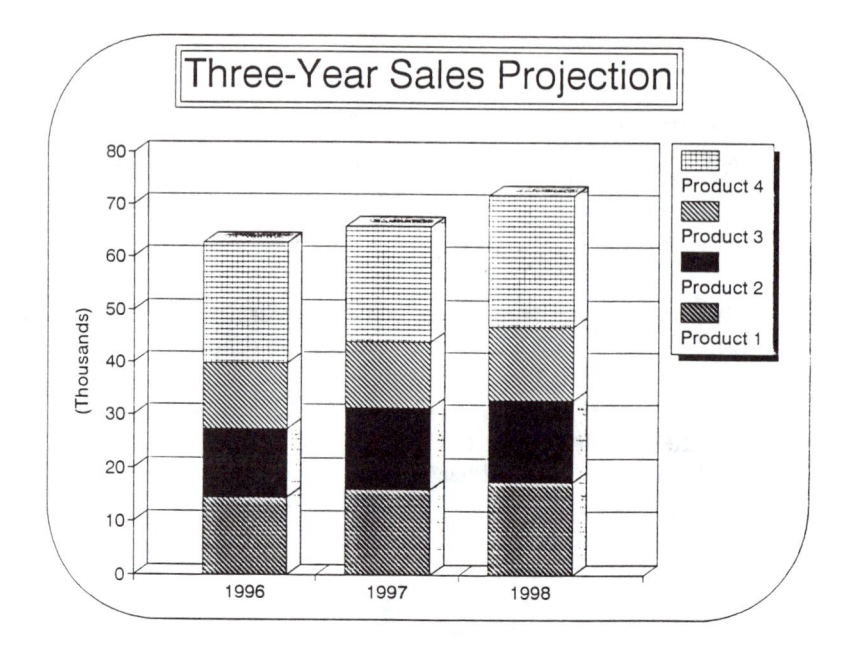

A graph with title, legend, and graph outlines
Figure 15-7.

NOTE: If you are annotating an existing graph (rather than building a new text graph) you should save your work with / **G**raph | **N**ame | **C**reate before accessing the Annotator. That way, if you don't like the modifications you make, you can leave the Annotator and use / **G**raph | **N**ame | **D**isplay to reinstate the old version.

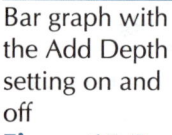

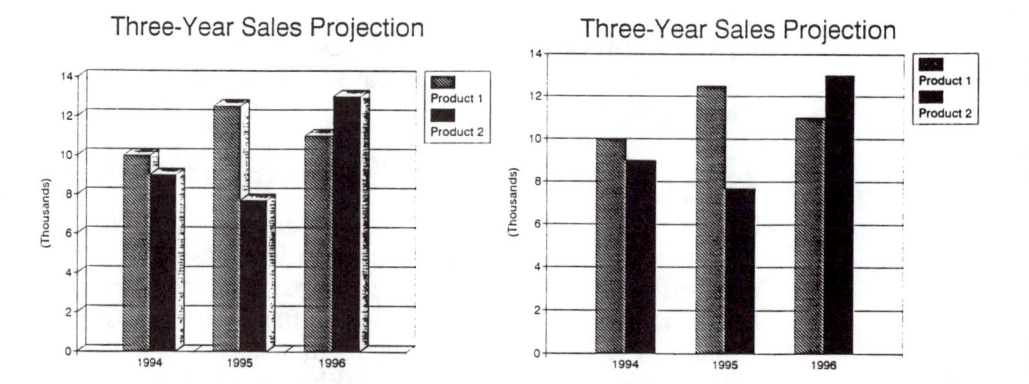

Bar graph with the Add Depth setting on and off
Figure 15-8.

Customizing and Annotating Graphs

The Annotator screen, shown in Figure 15-9, consists of five distinct areas.

- The **Toolbox** is the menu of icons (symbols) at the top of the Annotator screen. You use the options on this menu to create design elements, create and use clip art files, and leave the Annotator. To activate the Toolbox, type /. To return to the Draw Area without choosing a command, press (Esc).

- The **Draw Area** occupies most of the Annotator screen. It contains the graph, titles, and legend. You use this area to create, move, resize, copy, and delete annotation design elements.

- The **Property Sheet** is a menu of the properties that you can adjust for the current design element. For example, when you select a line element in the Draw Area or by highlighting one of the line icons in the Toolbox, the Property Sheet lists Color and Style. You can use the Property Sheet to modify the design element before or after you add the element to the graph. To activate the Property Sheet, press (F3). To return to the Draw Area without choosing a property, press (Esc).

- The **Gallery** displays a menu of options pertaining to the highlighted option on the Property Sheet. For example, if you highlight a Color option on the Property Sheet, the gallery displays all available colors. If you highlight the Box Type property on the Property Sheet, the Gallery displays the available box types.

- The **Status Box** at the bottom of the screen is where Quattro Pro displays instructions, keyboard shortcuts, and command descriptions. This area is essential for finding your way around the Annotator. If you are lost, check the Status Box for directions.

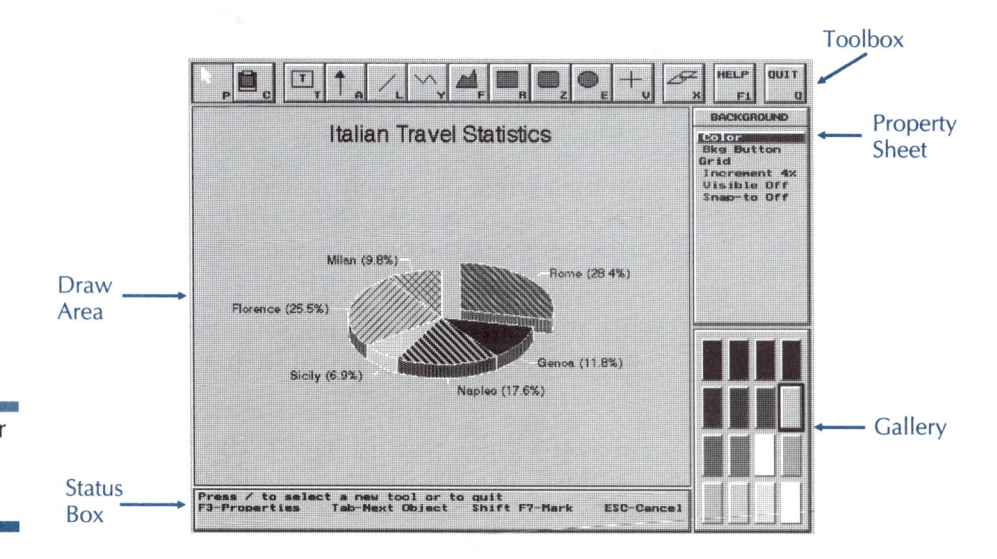

The Annotator screen
Figure 15-9.

The function keys have different effects in the Annotator than they do on the notebook screen. The one exception is F1, which activates the Help system from either environment. Table 15-1 lists the effect of function keys in the Annotator.

The Toolbox

The Toolbox is the Annotator's control center. It allows you to create new elements, and to copy or move elements from one graph to another. It also provides the only means of leaving the Annotator screen.

There are three ways to select options from the Toolbox: You can activate the menu by pressing /, and then highlight an icon and press Enter; you can activate the menu and type the letter displayed in the lower-right corner of the icon box; or, if you are using a mouse, you can click the icon. Figure 15-10 shows the Toolbox as it appears if you are using an EGA or VGA graphics adaptor.

The keystroke you can use to select each option is shown in parentheses after the option name.

The Pick or Edit icon (/P) looks like an empty arrow. You can use this icon to select various objects on the screen. You can also use it to deselect other tools on the Toolbox without selecting another design element, thereby returning to the Annotator's equivalent of Ready mode. The Clipboard icon (/C) allows you to cut and paste elements in and out of a section of memory called the Clipboard or in and out of a disk file. You can also use the Clipboard to move elements in the Draw Area in front of or behind other elements.

Effect of Function Keys in the Annotator
Table 15-1.

Key	Effect
F1	Activates the Help system
F3	Activates the Property Sheet
F7	With a group of elements selected, activates Proportional Resize mode so that you can adjust both the size of the selected elements and the space between them, thus resizing the group of elements as a single image.
Shift-F7	Retains the current element selection so you can use Tab or Shift-Tab to select additional elements without deselecting the currently selected element.
F10	Redraws the Annotator screen. This is useful when you are annotating a very complex graph (in which case Quattro Pro may only partially redraw the graph to avoid delays).

Customizing and Annotating Graphs

Figure 15-10. The Toolbox

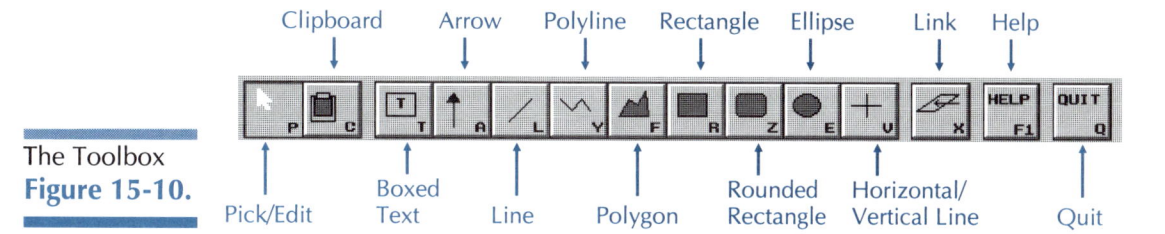

Labels (top): Clipboard, Arrow, Polyline, Rectangle, Ellipse, Link, Help
Labels (bottom): Pick/Edit, Boxed Text, Line, Polygon, Rounded Rectangle, Horizontal/Vertical Line, Quit

The design element icons (the third through eleventh icons in the Toolbox) let you add new design elements to your graph. You place and, in most cases, extend these various elements using your mouse or the arrow keys. Text (/T) adds a set of characters to the surface of the graph. The text is generally enclosed in a box, and can occupy multiple lines. Arrow (/A) draws a line with an arrowhead at one end. Line (/L) draws a straight line of any length. Polyline or Jointed Line (/Y) creates a straight line that is anchored in more than two places. The resulting element looks like a series of straight lines joined end to end. Polygon (/F) creates a multisided object of any size or shape. Unless you have a mouse, each edge of the element is a straight line. If you have a mouse, you can use the polygon icon to draw freehand any shape you like using the Curve Draw mode. Rectangle (/R) draws a rectangle of any dimensions. Round Rectangle (/Z) creates a rectangle with rounded corners. Ellipse (/E) draws a circle or ellipse of any size. Horizontal/Vertical Line (/V) draws horizontal or vertical lines parallel or perpendicular to the edges of the graph or screen.

In addition, the Link option (/X) lets you connect a design element to a particular point in the graph. If the point changes because you change the underlying value on the notebook, the design element moves along with it. The Help option (/H) lets you activate the Annotator Help system. And finally, the Quit option (/Q) lets you leave the Annotator and return to the regular notebook or the graph screen.

Adding Text and Lines to the Graph

To add a design element to a graph, activate the Toolbox by pressing / and then select the appropriate icon, or just click the icon with your mouse. Quattro Pro displays a symbol called the pointer in the middle of the graph. If you are using a mouse, the pointer looks like an arrow; otherwise it looks like a large plus sign. If you are using a mouse, place the pointer's tip where you want to start drawing the element. Otherwise place the middle of the plus sign in the desired spot.

What you do next depends on the type of element you are adding. To create a box of text using the Text tool, move the pointer to the spot where you want the upper-left corner of the box located. Type a period or click the mouse to anchor the box in that spot, and start typing text. The box expands to accommodate the characters you type. You can move to another line by pressing (Ctrl)-(Enter). You can use the cursor-movement keys to reposition the cursor and (Backspace) and (Del) to erase mistakes. When you are done entering text, press (Enter). (The section "Fine-Tuning Text Elements" explains how to create text elements without boxes.)

In most cases, it's far easier to draw lines and shapes with a mouse, if you have one.

To draw lines or arrows with the mouse, press the mouse button down in the spot where you want to start the line or arrow. Then drag the pointer until you reach where you want the line or arrow to stop, and release the button. (If you're drawing arrows, keep in mind that the arrowhead appears where you end the line.) If you're using a keyboard, move the cell pointer to the spot where you want to start the line or arrow and type a period. Then use the arrow keys to draw a line extending from that point. Press (Enter) when you are done.

To draw rectangles or ellipses, move the cell pointer to one corner. Press and hold down the mouse button while you drag the pointer to the opposite corner. Then release the button. If you are using the keyboard, move the cell pointer to one corner of the area where you want the rectangle or ellipse to appear and type a period. Then move the cell pointer to the diagonally opposite corner and press (Enter). If you're drawing an ellipse, Quattro Pro draws the largest ellipse that fits in the rectangle and erases the rectangle itself from the screen as soon as you press (Enter) or release the mouse button.

To draw polylines and polygons, move the pointer to the starting point, press the mouse button and hold it while you draw the first side, and then release the button. You can draw the rest of the lines in the element by moving the pointer where you want the next side of the element to end and clicking the mouse. As soon as you click the mouse, Quattro Pro draws a line from the last point in the polygon or polyline to the current position of the pointer. To complete the object, double-click the mouse or select any option from the Toolbox. If you are using a keyboard, move the pointer to your starting point and type a period. Then move the pointer until you reach a corner or turning point, and press (Enter). Next, move the pointer until you reach the next corner, press (Enter), and so on. You do not need to draw the last side of a polygon. As soon as you press (Enter) twice to complete the element, Quattro Pro draws a line from the arrow's current position to the element's starting point.

If you are using the keyboard, you can press (Esc) at any point between the time you start and the time you finish drawing a design element to erase the element from the screen. Then you can either start again or select another option from the Toolbox. Once you press (Enter), you can erase the element by placing the pointer on the element (if it is not already there) and then pressing (Del).

Customizing and Annotating Graphs

When you are finished creating a design element, Quattro Pro leaves the pointer on the screen in case you want to add another element of the same type. If you do want to add another element, follow the same steps. If you want to do something else, select another option from the Toolbox.

Quattro Pro treats design elements rather like titles, legends, or any of the graph settings—it carries them over to graphs you subsequently create on the same notebook. For example, if you create a blue polygon in one graph, it will automatically show up in the next graph you create. If you want to prevent this, issue the / **G**raph | **C**ustomize Series command, click the Reset button, and choose Graph before you create a new graph.

> Be sure to save your graph using the / **G**raph | **N**ame | **C**reate command if you want to return to it in the future.

Drawing Curves

If you have a mouse, you can draw curved lines and shapes using Quattro Pro's Curve Draw mode. Start by selecting the proper design element icon from the Toolbox: Use Polygon (/F) if you want to draw a closed shape or Polyline (/Y) to draw a line. Next, press [Scroll Lock] to turn on Curve Draw mode. Then position the pointer, press the mouse button, and drag the mouse. Release the mouse button when you're done. You can also enter Curve Draw mode by holding down [Shift] while you drag. This method is useful when you want to alternate between curves and straight lines.

In Curve Draw mode, Quattro Pro does not automatically draw in the last side of a polygon when you double-click or press [Enter] to complete the object. To close a polygon you can either click the polygon element in the Toolbox or turn off Curve Draw mode (by pressing [Scroll Lock] again or releasing [Shift]) and then double-click or press [Enter].

Hands-On Practice

The following exercise involves adding a box of text to the BARS graph created in Chapter 14 and drawing an arrow from that box to the highest bar on the graph. The result is shown in Figure 15-11.

1. Unless the GRAPH.WQ2 notebook is currently on your screen, save your work if necessary and then retrieve GRAPH.WQ2 using the / **F**ile | **R**etrieve command.
2. Issue the / **G**raph | **N**ame | **D**isplay command, and select BARS to make that the current graph. Then type / to activate the Annotator.
3. Type / to activate the Toolbox. The Pick option at the left end of the Toolbox should be highlighted. Click on the Text icon to select it. (If you're using the keyboard, press → twice to move to the Text icon, and press [Enter].)

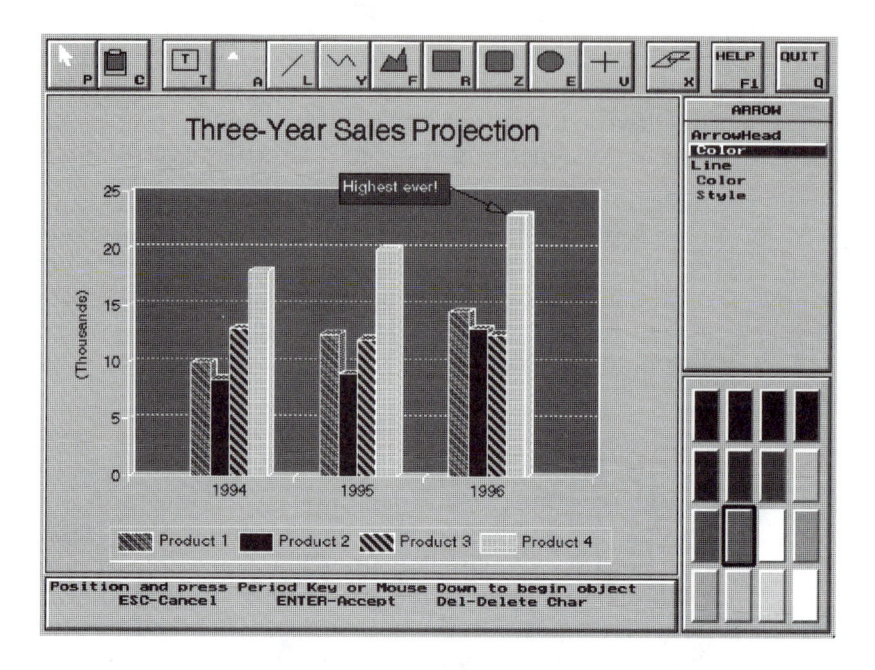

The BARS graph with a box of text and an arrow
Figure 15-11.

4. Move the pointer 1/4 inch above the top of the graph and directly below the left edge of the "S" in "Sales." Then click. (If you're using the keyboard, press ↑ and ← until the middle of the pointer is immediately below the left edge of the "S" in the word "Sales" in the graph title. Then type a period to anchor the text element.)

5. Type **Highest ever!** and press Enter. If you are not happy with the box of text, make sure the mouse pointer is over it and press Del to delete it. (You can also edit existing text in the Annotator, as you'll learn under "Editing Text Elements" later in the chapter.) The pointer remains in the Draw Area; you can move it to the desired location, press Enter or click with your mouse, and start typing to create another box.

6. Select the arrow icon from the Toolbox. Then move the pointer to the right side of the box of text you just entered, hold down the mouse button, drag the pointer to the bar for 1996 sales of Product 4, and release the mouse button to complete the arrow. (If you are using a keyboard, type a period to anchor the arrow, press ↓ and → to move the pointer to the top left corner of the highest bar on the graph, and press Enter.)

7. Select Quit from the Toolbox by typing **/Q** or by clicking the Quit option for a full-screen image of the results. (If you displayed the Annotator from the Graph menu rather than the graph screen, Quattro Pro returns you to that menu and you need to select View or press F10 to display your results on the full screen.)

Customizing and Annotating Graphs

Modifying Graph Elements

The first step in modifying a design element is to select it. To select an element with the keyboard, press Tab to move through all the elements in the Draw Area. Quattro Pro displays small boxes, called *handles,* around one element at a time to indicate that the element is currently selected. To select a design element using the mouse, simply click on the Pick tool and then on the element. When handles appear around the element you want to change, you are ready to delete, move, or modify it. If you have several overlapping elements on the screen, you may find it easier to select them using the keyboard instead of clicking with the mouse. Watch the first line of the Property Sheet (which indicates the selected element's type) to determine when the right element is selected.

To delete a selected element, just press Del. To reposition a selected element, use the arrow keys or drag it with the mouse. If you are using a mouse, be sure to place the pointer inside the element rather than on one of the handles. Dragging the handles changes the size of the element rather than its position.

Resizing Elements

The procedure for resizing an element depends on whether you are using the keyboard or mouse. If you are using the keyboard, start by selecting the element you want to resize. Type a period to enter Resize mode. Quattro Pro highlights the lower-right corner of the element, indicating that this is the corner it will use for resizing. If you prefer to resize the element by moving a different corner, keep pressing the period key until the box appears in that corner. Then use the arrow keys to move that corner to a new location. Quattro Pro displays an outline of the element to show you what the element would look like with the corner in each position. Once you press Enter to complete the resize process, Quattro Pro shrinks or expands the element to fill the outline.

If clicking doesn't produce selection handles, check that the Pick tool is selected.

If you are using a mouse, select the element you want to resize. Then point to the handle that you want to use to resize the element and drag it to the desired location. Use side handles to move one side of the shape; use corner handles to move two sides at the same time.

Quattro Pro lets you resize the graph itself as well as any of the design elements you have created through the Annotator. To resize graph text such as titles and legends within the Annotator, however, you must modify the text font using the font options in the Property Sheet.

Changing Design Properties

By default, any text elements you create are shown in 18-point Swiss-SC font, lines are solid, and two-dimensional shapes are completely filled in. You can change these design properties and others, such as colors and box types, using the Property Sheet on the right side of the Annotator screen.

You can change an element's design properties either before or after you add the element to your graph.

To define design properties before you create the element, you select the design element from the Toolbox and then activate the Property Sheet by either pressing [F3] or clicking one of the Property Sheet options with the mouse. Next you change any properties you like (as described shortly) and press [Esc] to return to the Draw Area. Then you proceed to place the element on the graph. To change the design properties of an existing element, you select the element, activate the Property Sheet, make the desired changes, and press [Esc] to deactivate the Property Sheet. Then you can either select other elements or choose another option from the Toolbox.

When you first activate the Annotator, you see the word "Background" at the top of the Property Sheet, which means if you activate the Property Sheet, you can change the display of the notebook's background. As soon as you select an element or choose a design element icon from the Toolbox, the Property Sheet changes accordingly. For example, if you select a text element or select the Text icon from the Toolbox, the Property Sheet title is "Boxed Text," and the options include all the display attributes you can define for text elements.

Once you activate the Property Sheet, Quattro Pro draws a second border around the Property Sheet section of the screen and displays a short description of the currently selected option in the Status Box. To view descriptions of the other options on the Property Sheet, just press [↓] to highlight each option in turn and look at the Status Box descriptions. As you highlight different options on the Property Sheet, the options in the Gallery also change, showing you the range of choices for the currently highlighted property.

You can select an attribute from the Property Sheet by highlighting it and pressing [Enter] or clicking it with the mouse. In response, Quattro Pro usually activates the gallery, displaying a second border around that portion of the screen, and draws a box around the currently selected option. Use the arrow keys to highlight the option you want and press [Enter], or click the option with the mouse.

When you are done changing properties, you must deactivate the Property Sheet by pressing [Esc]. The second border disappears from the Property Sheet section. Then you can select an option from the Toolbox or, if you are in the midst of creating an element, continue drawing the element on the graph.

Customizing and Annotating Graphs

Keep in mind that any settings you define for the various design properties affect all design elements of that type that you create afterward. For example, if you select a particular text element and change the box type to None, all text elements that you subsequently create will be displayed without a box, unless you explicitly assign them a different box type. (Preexisting elements will remain unchanged, however.)

Aligning and Modifying Several Elements at Once

You can perform all the same operations on a group of selected elements that you can perform on just one element. The first step in modifying a group of elements is to select all of them. The procedure for selecting multiple elements depends on whether you are using the keyboard or a mouse.

If you select multiple elements, the Property Sheet title changes to Group, indicating that your changes will affect a group of design elements.

First, make sure that the Pick icon is selected. Then, if you are using the keyboard, use [Tab] and [Shift]-[Tab] to move through the elements. When you reach one you want to select, press [Shift]-[F7]. This retains the current selection and keeps the handles on the element while allowing you to select additional elements. Next, press [Tab] until you reach the next element you want to select. Press [Shift]-[F7] again to retain that selection, use [Tab] to move to the next element you want to select, and so on.

If you are using a mouse, you can select all the elements in a particular section of the Draw Area by dragging from one corner of the area to the opposite corner. This draws a box around the entire area. As soon as you release the mouse button, Quattro Pro displays handles on all the elements in that area. To select several elements in different parts of the Draw Area, hold down the [Shift] key while you click each element.

To deselect a single element, tab past the element without pressing [Shift]-[F7]. To deselect all currently selected elements, press [Esc] or choose one of the design element icons from the Toolbox. If you're using a mouse, you can click anywhere that is not part of a selectable screen element.

If you are resizing a group of elements, Quattro Pro by default only resizes the elements themselves. It does not adjust the amount of space between the elements. This can create problems if you resize a set of elements that form a single image. To resize the space between elements while you resize the elements, you must activate Proportional Resize mode. If you are using the keyboard, you can do this by pressing [F7] after all the desired items are selected. If you are using the mouse, you can simultaneously select a group of elements and enter Proportional Resize mode by holding down the [Alt] key while you drag to select an area that encloses all the elements that you want to resize. Then release the [Alt] key and drag one of the handles to resize the group.

The first option on the Group property sheet is Align. This option lets you automatically align all the currently selected objects. When you choose this option, Quattro Pro displays a menu with the choices Left Sides, Right Sides, Vert Centers, Tops, Bottoms, and Horiz Centers. As soon as you select an option, the selected objects will jump into the designated alignment. If you select Left Sides, for example, Quattro Pro will line up the left edge of all the selected objects.

Using a Grid to Position Objects

The grid will not appear when you print the graph or display it outside of the Annotator.

The Background Property Sheet contains three options under the subheading Grid: Increment, Visible, and Snap-to. You can use these options to aid in object placement and alignment. To display a grid of dots in the Draw Area, select the Visible option on the Background Property Sheet. (This option is a toggle: Select it once to turn on the grid; select it again to turn off the grid.)

By default, Quattro Pro displays 19 rows and 25 columns of dots. You can increase or decrease the number of dots by changing the Increment setting on the Background Property Sheet. The default setting is 4%, meaning the dots are displayed at increments equivalent to 4% of the draw area. Increase the setting to decrease the number of dots; decrease the setting to display more dots.

While displaying the grid helps you align objects manually, the Snap-to setting lets you align new objects automatically. If you change the Snap-to setting to on, the grid acts like a magnet that automatically attracts any new elements placed near it. To align several elements, you simply place them close to the same grid line. The Snap-to setting is independent of the Visible setting. Even if you choose not to display a grid on the screen, an invisible grid—with dots at the currently specified increment setting—still attracts elements as you place them in the draw area.

Modifying Non-Annotator Elements

As mentioned, Quattro Pro allows you to select the graph's titles, legends, and the graph as a whole, as well as any of the elements you create through the Annotator itself. Once you have selected one of these elements, you can move it, change its design properties, or delete it. Any changes you make are recorded on the various Graph menus. For example, if you delete the title, Quattro Pro erases the 1st and/or 2nd Line setting on the Graph | Text menu.

Fine-Tuning Text Elements

There are too many design elements—each with too many design properties—to discuss in depth here. This chapter concentrates on text elements, since these are the most commonly used.

Customizing and Annotating Graphs

Editing Text Elements

You can only edit text elements that you've created within the Annotator; you cannot edit titles, legends, and so on.

To edit the contents of a text element, first select the element and then press `F2` (Edit). Quattro Pro displays a cursor just after the last character in the text element. Use the arrow keys, `Home`, `End`, `Backspace`, and `Del`, just as you do when editing data on the input line. If you want to move the cursor to the next line, press `Ctrl`-`Enter`. When you are done editing the text, press `Enter` to save your changes or `Esc` to discard them.

Changing Text Design Properties

You can modify four properties related to the text itself: color, justification, font, and graph button. Justification determines how multiple lines of text are aligned: by their left edges, right edges, or midpoints. It has no effect on boxes with only one line of text. You can also modify four properties of the box surrounding the text: the box type, interior color, fill pattern, and border color.

By default, the text color is white, the text is left-justified, the text font is 18-point Swiss-SC, the box type is single line, the interior color is light blue, the fill pattern is empty, and the border color is blue. To alter any of these settings, select the element you want to change, activate the Property Sheet, and select the appropriate option. Quattro Pro will either display a menu or activate a gallery of colors or box types immediately below the Property Sheet. Make your choice by highlighting the desired selection and pressing `Enter` or by clicking with your mouse.

One modification you might make to text elements is changing the box type to None. When you do this, Quattro Pro eliminates the entire box, fill pattern and all. This allows you to display text directly on the surface of the graph. It is also helpful when you are creating a text graph (as described in the next section) or when you want to place a shape, such as an ellipse, behind the text. The procedure for displaying text on shapes is described under "Using the Clipboard" later in this chapter.

You can also add drop shadows to boxed text, by choosing the Font option on the Boxed Text property sheet, choosing Style, and then choosing Drop Shadow. (Drop Shadow is a toggle: Selecting it once displays a drop shadow behind the selected text; selecting it again erases the drop shadow.) If you want to accentuate or otherwise change the placement of the drop shadow, select the Custom Shadow option from the Font | Style menu. Quattro Pro displays another menu with options for Right/Left Drop Shadow and Down/Up Drop Shadow. The default settings are 5% for Right/Left and 10% for Down/Up. You can change these settings to any value from -100 to 100. Entering a negative number for the Right/Left setting causes the drop shadows to appear to the left of your text rather than to the right. A negative number for the Up/Down setting causes the shadows to appear just above rather than just below the text. (To see your results, you must choose Quit twice to return to the Annotator screen.)

Creating Text Graphs

Text graphs are graphs that consist entirely of elements created through the Annotator. They are frequently used in graph slide shows. To create a text graph, you can either activate the Annotator when no series are selected or change the graph type to Text before activating the Annotator. When Quattro Pro displays the Annotator screen, the Draw Area is completely blank. You can fill it with any design elements you like.

Figure 15-12 shows an organization chart created as a text chart through the Annotator. It was created by setting the graph type to Text and then adding a text element for each position in the organization. The lines between elements were drawn using the horizontal/vertical lines option.

Linking Elements to Points on the Graph

In most cases, you will want a design element to maintain its position relative to a particular data point on the graph, even when your data changes. In the case of your BARS graph, for example, you want the arrow to point to the bar for 1996 sales of Product 4, even if you change the

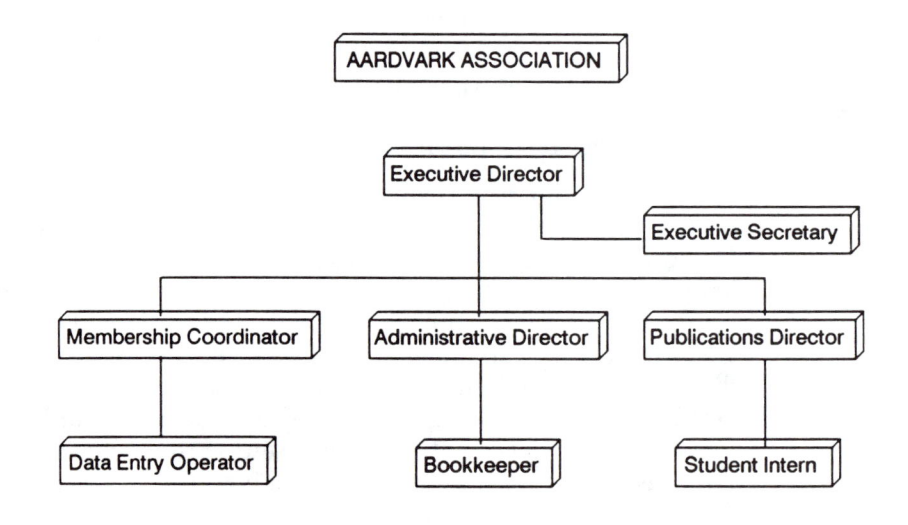

An organization text chart
Figure 15-12.

Customizing and Annotating Graphs

underlying value on the notebook. You can accomplish this by linking the design element (the arrow) to the data point (the 1996 sales figure for Product 4).

To unlink an element, select the element, choose the Link option from the Toolbox, and choose Unlink.

Linking a design element to a data point on your graph involves the following steps: First you select the design element you want to link. Then you select the Link icon (/X) from the Toolbox. Quattro Pro displays a menu of the six graph series in the Property Sheet section of the screen. Finally, you tell Quattro Pro which notebook value you want to link the element to. This is a two-step process. You start by selecting a series. Quattro Pro displays a box with the prompt "Enter link index," and you enter a number indicating where the value occurs within the specified series. For example, if you want to link a design element to the second value in the third series, you would select 3rd Series from the menu and then enter **2** as the link index.

Practice using this linking feature on the BARS graph. Try raising the amount for Product 4 in 1996 to see what happens when you change data without linking design elements. Then link the two design elements that you created (the text element and the arrow) to the data point, and change the data again.

1. Move to D7 and enter **30000**. Press F10 to view the graph, and note that the arrow no longer points to the top of the bar.
2. Press Esc to return to the notebook display, and enter **23000** so that the arrow now points to the desired spot on the bar.
3. Press F10 and then type / to activate the Annotator.

If you link just the arrow, the arrow moves with the data point but becomes disconnected from the box in the process.

4. Select both the arrow and the text elements by pressing Tab until handles appear around one of those elements. Then press Shift-F7 to select that element, and press Tab until handles appear around the other element. If you are using a mouse, you can simply drag the pointer to draw a rectangle around both elements.
5. Select the Link option from the Toolbox, and then select 4th Series from the Property Box. When prompted for a link index, enter **3**.
6. Press Esc to deactivate the Property Sheet, leave the Annotator by typing **/Q** or clicking the Quit option, and press Esc to return to the notebook display.
7. Enter **30000** in D7, and press F10 to view the results. This time the design elements rise with the associated bar.
8. Press Esc to return to the notebook display, issue the / **G**raph | **N**ame | **C**reate command, and enter **BARS2** to save the current graph.
9. Issue the / **F**ile | **S**ave command to save the notebook, replacing the previous version.

Using the Clipboard

The Clipboard option (the second option in the Toolbox) enables you to cut and paste design elements from one graph to another or to duplicate a design element within a graph. It also lets you create and use clip art (design elements saved as disk files). You can use Quattro Pro's clip art as well as third-party clip art files produced in the CLP file format. You can also use the Clipboard to move elements between the foreground and background when two or more elements overlap. This can be particularly useful for displaying text against a shape such as an ellipse.

Cutting and Pasting Graph Elements

You can use the Clipboard as a place to temporarily store design elements. You then can copy or move them from one graph to another. Cutting and pasting is particularly useful when you create a company logo or some other shape that you want to reuse. You can even paste whatever is in the Clipboard repeatedly during the current work session, until you copy or cut something else to the Clipboard. This is handy for creating repeating images.

To cut and paste a graph element, follow these steps:

1. Select the element or elements that you want to cut and paste and select Clipboard from the Toolbox.
2. Select the Copy option if you want to copy the selected elements from the current graph to the Clipboard. Choose Cut if you want to remove the selected elements from the current graph and transfer them to the Clipboard.
3. If you want to copy the elements to a different graph, choose the Quit icon from the Toolbox. Then display the other graph.
4. Once the graph in which you want to insert the Clipboard contents is displayed, activate the Annotator.
5. Select Clipboard and choose Paste. Quattro Pro inserts the element exactly where it was positioned in the original graph. The inserted element remains selected, so you can easily move or resize it.

Cutting and pasting works fine if you want to immediately copy or transfer from one graph to another. If you plan to reuse the element in a future work session, however, you must save it to a clip art file, as described in the next section.

Creating and Using Clip Art Files

A *clip art file* is a graphic image saved in a disk file. Quattro Pro is packaged with a set of clip art files with images ranging from airplanes to world maps.

Customizing and Annotating Graphs

It also lets you use any clip art files that are stored in the CGM (Computer Graphics Metafile) format.

To list clip art files from a different directory, press Esc twice and enter the full directory path, including the disk drive.

You can import clip art images into your own graphs using the Clipboard's Paste From option. As soon as you select the Paste From option, Quattro Pro displays a list of all the clip art files in the default data directory—clip art files that you have created as well as those packaged with the Quattro Pro program. As soon as you select a file from the list, Quattro Pro displays the clip art image in the center of the Draw Area, on top of any design elements that are already there.

Most of the Quattro Pro clip art files consist of design elements (some of them contain dozens) that form a single image. When you first insert clip art into your graph, all the design elements in the image are already selected. This makes it easy for you to resize or reposition the image. However, it also makes the image hard to see because of all the handles. If you have a mouse, you can easily reselect all the elements (unless they happen to be on top of other design elements) by dragging the pointer to draw a rectangle around the image. If you do not have a mouse, it may be extremely difficult to reselect all the elements later, particularly in images that consist of many small elements. In this case you must resize or reposition the image when you first copy it into your graph, before you do anything that deselects the elements.

CAUTION: Be sure to activate Proportional Resize mode by pressing F7 before resizing an image from one of the Quattro Pro clip art files. Otherwise the image may be distorted.

You may want to create your own clip art files to save one or more design elements for future use. To create a clip art file, simply select the element or elements that you want to save to the file, select Clipboard, and choose the Copy To option. Quattro Pro displays a list of clip art files in the current directory. Enter a file name or select one from the list if you want to overwrite an existing clip art file. Do not include a file extension because Quattro Pro automatically assigns the CLP extension.

When you want to retrieve the design elements from the clip art file into a graph, activate the Clipboard, select Paste From, and either enter the name of the clip art file or select it from the files list.

Moving Elements Between Foreground and Background

If two or more design elements on a graph overlap, you can use the Clipboard to determine which element will be placed on top. The To Bottom

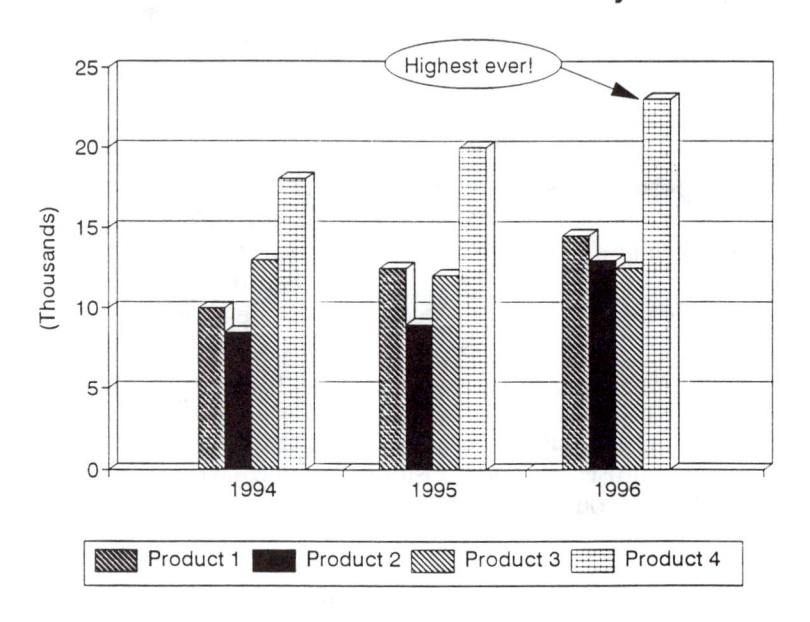

BARS graph with an ellipse behind the text element
Figure 15-13.

option moves the currently selected element to the bottom of the stack, and the To Top option places it on top. These options are particularly useful when you want to display text against a shape such as an ellipse. For example, Figure 15-13 shows a revised version of the graph you have been working on throughout this chapter. It was created by changing the box type for the text element to None, drawing an ellipse over the element, changing the fill pattern of the ellipse to None, and moving the ellipse to the background, behind the text element.

This chapter has covered a wide range of commands that allow you to embellish, fine-tune, and annotate your graphs. Used judiciously, these commands allow you to create attractive, professional graphs. You should be careful, particularly in the beginning, not to go overboard with custom colors, labels, mixed graph types, added text and shapes, and the like. Clutter and excessive embellishment tend to detract from your message rather than enhance it. Instead, aim for clarity and simplicity while still transmitting all the necessary information.

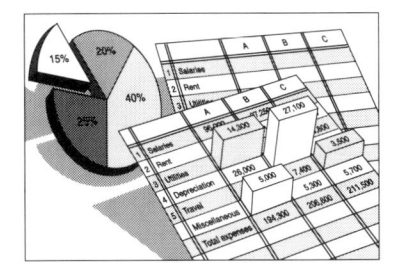

CHAPTER

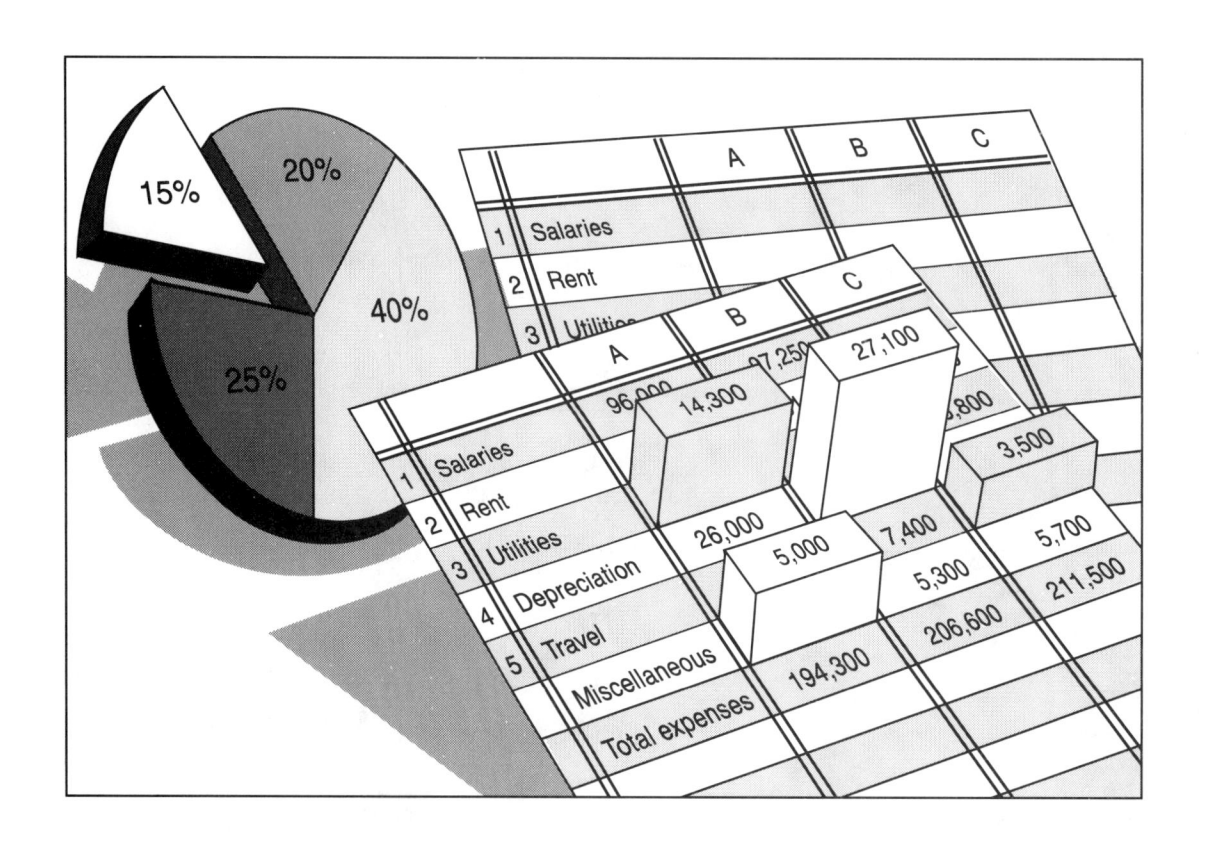

16 DESIGNING AND USING DATABASES

A database is a collection of data that share a common structure. In almost all cases, databases consist of information about a group of related people, things, or events, such as a set of customers, inventory items, or financial transactions. Phone books, customer ledger cards, and card catalogs are all examples of databases. In each case information is maintained about a particular type of entity (people who have telephones, customers, library books), and the same items of information (name, address, and phone number in the case of a phone book) are maintained for each person or thing in the group.

This chapter covers the creation of databases in Quattro Pro—from designing a database to entering and updating the data. It also explains how to sort your database—how to rearrange the data into particular orders. In the next chapter, you learn how to find or extract records that meet specified conditions.

Database Terminology

Figure 16-1 shows a database consisting of customer records. Note that each row contains the same items of information. The customer's first name is in column A, the last name is in column B, the street address is in column C, the city is in column D, the state is in E, and the ZIP code is in F. In database terminology, each logical unit in the database (in this case one customer) is called a *record*. Each item of information in the row is known as a *field*. In Quattro Pro databases, each record occupies a single row and all the fields line up in columns.

At the top of each column is a label indicating the column's contents. Such column headings are known as *field names*. As discussed in Chapter 17, these field names are frequently used to express instructions for locating or extracting selected records from a database.

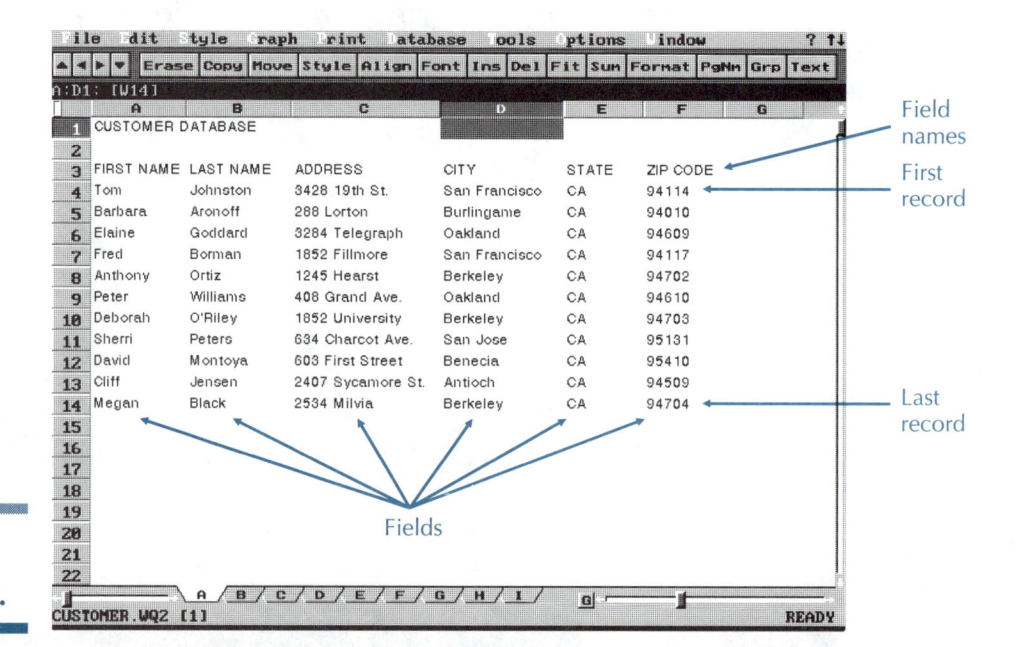

Database terminology
Figure 16-1.

Designing a Database

Although it is possible to add, delete, or rearrange fields after entering data, you can save a lot of time if you think out your application as carefully as possible beforehand. In general, it is a good idea to begin this design process by considering the type of output—lists, reports, statistics, graphs, and other kinds of information—that you need to generate. When you have a clear sense of what you want *out* of your database, you have a better idea of what to put *in*. When you know generally what the database will contain, you can begin planning the specifics—deciding what fields you want to include, their data types, and their order.

Field Content

The first issue to consider is how to separate your information into individual fields. Generally, you should create a separate field for every item of information you will use for sorting or selecting records. For example, if you plan to arrange all the records in your database alphabetically by last name, you must either place the last name before the first name in the name field or create separate fields for last name and first name.

Values or Labels?

Once you have decided what fields to include, you must determine the type of data you will enter in them. You should always use a consistent data type for each field, so you can easily manipulate the data later. The primary choice is between values and labels. In general, you should enter data as a value if you want to use it in any mathematical calculations or if you want to sort the database into numerical order on the basis of that field.

Another important factor in deciding whether to fill a field with labels or values is the way you want the field to be sorted. When you sort labels that consist entirely of digits, Quattro Pro orders the labels one digit at a time. For example, the label 12 is placed before the label 2. If you enter the same digits as values, however, and then sort those values, the database is arranged in numerical order and 2 comes before 12.

Quattro Pro disregards leading zeros in values, but not in labels.

There is another important difference in how Quattro Pro handles labels and values. If you enter a *leading zero* (a zero to the left of any other digits and the decimal point) in a value, that zero is dropped as soon as Quattro Pro stores the value. If you enter **01234**, for example, Quattro Pro records it simply as 1234 (which is disastrous if you are entering ZIP codes). In a label, a leading zero is treated as a distinct character when sorted.

Keep in mind that Quattro Pro treats your entry as a value if it starts with a number or arithmetic operator. This means that when you enter the phone number **555-1234**, Quattro Pro subtracts 1234 from 555 and returns the value –679. You encounter similar problems with social security numbers or any other entries that consist of only numbers and dashes. Until now you have prevented such problems by entering a label prefix character at the beginning of the entry to inform Quattro Pro that you want the data treated as text. You will learn a more efficient means of doing this under "Data Entry Commands" later in this chapter.

Field Names

Database field names serve a dual purpose: as column headings and as a means of identifying fields in selection criteria (see Chapter 17). You should observe a few rules when creating field names:

- Make each field name unique.
- Avoid using names that are already used for named blocks.
- Do not use decorative characters, such as dashes or asterisks, between the field names and the first record in the database. They are treated as rows in the database and can cause undesirable results when you try to sort, select, or analyze your data.
- Do not use more than 15 characters in a field name. As you will learn in Chapter 17, the process of selecting records from your database generally involves using the field names as block names, and the maximum length for block names is 15.
- Remember to enter all field names within a single row. If you want to use the field name ACCOUNT NUMBER, for example, enter both words in a single cell (abbreviate them if necessary) rather than entering **ACCOUNT** in one cell and **NUMBER** in the cell below.

Cell Referencing in Databases

Although most databases consist primarily of constants (values and labels entered directly into the notebook), they can also contain formulas. By entering formulas in your notebook, you create *calculated fields*—fields that are computed from other values rather than entered directly.

There are two rules for cell referencing in calculated fields. Unless you follow them carefully, the cell references will not be adjusted properly when you sort the database into a different order, and your formulas will yield incorrect results.

- **Rule 1** Whenever you enter a formula referencing another cell in the same row, make the row reference relative so that it is adjusted as it is

Designing and Using Databases

copied down the column and refers to the proper cell even if the record's row position changes as a result of sorting. In the database shown in Figure 16-2, for example, cell E11 contains the formula

@IF(C11=3,D11+365,D11+182)

which calculates the subscription expiration date based on the rate code (1, 2, or 3) in that record. (Code 3 indicates an annual subscription; the other two codes indicate a semiannual subscription.) If the rate code is 3, 365 days are added to the subscription date; otherwise 182 days are added to the subscription date. Note that all cell references in this formula are relative. As a result, if the database is sorted into alphabetical order by last name, for example, the cell references are adjusted to refer to the cells in columns C and D of the row to which the record is relocated.

+ **Rule 2** Whenever you reference cells outside the database, make the reference absolute so that it will not change as it is copied down columns of the database or when the database is sorted. The subscription database also contains the formula

@VLOOKUP(C11,$A$5..$B$7,1)

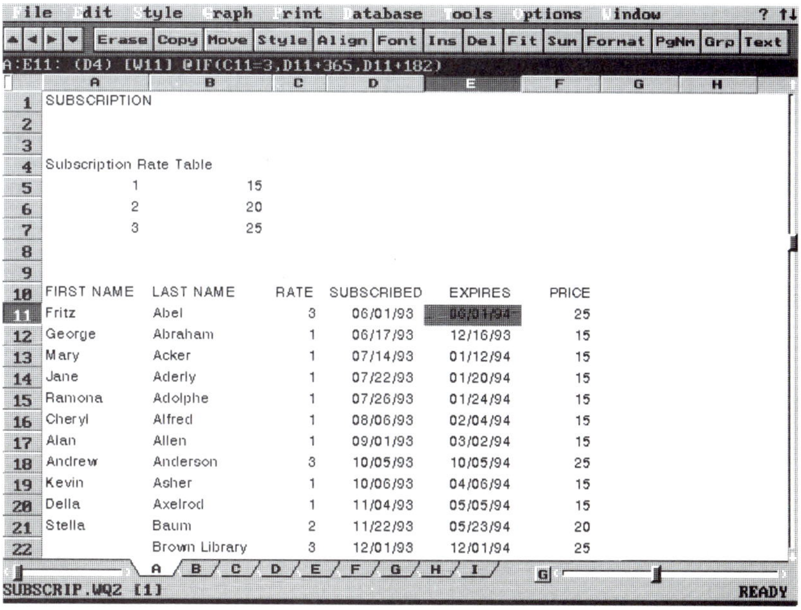

Relative cell referencing in a database
Figure 16-2.

in cell F11. This formula determines the price of each subscription by looking up the rate (C11) in a lookup table ($A$5..$B$7) located outside the database. Because the reference to the lookup table is absolute, it remains unchanged as it is copied down column F and when the records in the database are sorted into a different order.

Data Entry Commands

The / Database | Data Entry commands affect only new entries; they have no impact on previously entered data.

Quattro Pro offers two commands—/ **D**atabase | **D**ata Entry | **L**abels Only and / **D**atabase | **D**ata Entry | **D**ates Only—that allow you to restrict the type of data entered in a block of cells. The / **D**atabase | **D**ata Entry commands are most often used in database applications, where all the entries in an entire column are of the same data type. You can, however, use them in any notebook you like, whenever you want all the entries in a particular block to be either labels or dates.

You can use / **D**atabase | **D**ata Entry | **L**abels Only to allow only label entries within a specified block. If you then enter a number into one of the cells in that block, Quattro Pro automatically adds the default label prefix character to your entry, thus turning it into a label. This can be extremely useful when you are entering data such as phone numbers, social security numbers, and ZIP codes.

You can use / **D**atabase | **D**ata Entry | **D**ates Only to allow only date entries within a specified block. If you enter characters in any one of Quattro Pro's five Date formats or its four Time formats, Quattro Pro automatically translates your entry into a date serial number, as if you had pressed Ctrl-D at the beginning of the entry. If you enter a date that is not in one of the allowable formats, Quattro Pro beeps, displays the error message "Invalid date or time," and automatically enters Edit mode.

When you issue either the / **D**atabase | **D**ata Entry | **L**abels Only or / **D**atabase | **D**ata Entry | **D**ates Only command, Quattro Pro stores hidden codes in each cell of the specified block. You can always tell whether the current cell has been designated as a label cell or date cell by looking for the word "Label" or "Date" at the beginning of the input line. Note that in the case of dates, you will not see a date serial number on the input line; you'll see only the word "Date" followed by the cell address and the date just as it appears in the cell.

If you no longer want to restrict the type of data entered into a cell, you can issue the / **D**atabase | **D**ata Entry | **G**eneral command to remove the dates-only or labels-only designation. Any previously entered data will be unaffected: the dates will stay dates and the labels will remain labels.

Designing and Using Databases

Building a Sample Database

You can practice the various database commands and techniques by constructing a small sample database. This practice application is an order-tracking database for a mail order company that sells discount floppy disks. You will be building, refining, and manipulating this database for the remainder of this chapter as well as in Chapter 17. The database includes fields for account name, order date, item number, quantity ordered, price, subtotal, tax, total, payment date, payment amount, and amount due. Both the subtotal and total fields are calculated fields. Assume that most but not all the orders are paid for as they are placed and that customers generally order only one type of item at a time. Sales tax is applied only to orders within New York State. Assume that you are going to look up the tax rate for customers in New York as you enter the data.

1. Start with a blank notebook and adjust the column widths as follows: Change column A to 14 characters; change column B to 12 characters; change column C to 6 characters; change columns D and G to 7 characters; and change column I to 10 characters.

2. In cell A1, enter **MAIL ORDERS**.

3. Draw a double line under this title by issuing the / **S**tyle I **L**ine Drawing command, pressing [Enter] to accept the default block of A:A1..A1, selecting a Placement of Bottom, and choosing a Line Type of Double. Select Quit to return to Ready mode.

4. Enter the following field names: Enter **ACCOUNT** in A4; enter **ORDER DATE** in B4; enter **ITEM** in C4; enter **QUANT** in D4; enter **PRICE** in E4; enter **SUBTOTAL** in F4; enter **TAX** in G4; enter **TOTAL** in H4; enter **PMT DATE** in I4; enter **PMT AMT** in J4; and finally, enter **AMT DUE** in K4.

5. Right align the last seven field names by issuing the / **S**tyle I **A**lignment I **R**ight command and specifying the block E4..K4.

6. Issue the / **D**atabase I **D**ata Entry I **L**abels Only command and specify a block of C5..C12 (the ITEM field for eight records).

7. Issue the / **D**atabase I **D**ata Entry I **D**ates Only command and specify a block of B5..B12 (the ORDER DATE field for eight records). Issue the same command again and specify a block of I5..I12 (the PMT DATE field for eight records).

8. Enter the first record in your database: Enter **Arby & Sons** in A5; enter **8/20/94** in B5; enter **34-35** in C5; enter **1** in D5; and enter **19.95** in E5.

9. Enter the next seven records, as shown here. Leave the SUBTOTAL, TOTAL, and AMT DUE fields blank for now; many of the records have other blank fields as well.

In Cell	Enter	In Cell	Enter
A6	**Micro Center**	E9	**19.95**
B6	**9/3/94**	I9	**10/10/94**
C6	**32-45**	J9	**59.85**
D6	**5**	A10	**Craig Assoc.**
E6	**22.95**	B10	**10/11/94**
I6	**9/3/94**	C10	**38-21**
J6	**114.75**	D10	**1**
A7	**ABC Group**	E10	**20.50**
B7	**9/3/94**	A11	**Jim Stern**
C7	**32-45**	B11	**10/15/94**
D7	**2**	C11	**32-45**
E7	**22.95**	D11	**1**
I7	**9/3/94**	E11	**22.95**
J7	**45.90**	G11	**1.89**
A8	**CompuSchool**	I11	**10/15/94**
B8	**9/7/94**	J11	**22.95**
C8	**38-21**	A12	**Smith & Co.**
D8	**2**	B12	**11/1/94**
E8	**20.50**	C12	**38-21**
G8	**3.38**	D12	**2**
A9	**XYZ Co.**	E12	**20.50**
B9	**10/10/94**	G12	**3.38**
C9	**34-35**	I12	**11/1/94**
D9	**3**	J12	**44.38**

10. Move to F5 and enter **+D5*E5** to calculate the subtotal. Then copy the formula down column F by issuing the / **E**dit | **C**opy command, accepting the default source block A:F5..F5, and specifying the destination F5..F12.

11. Move to H5 and enter the total formula **+F5+G5**. Copy it down the block H5..H12.

Designing and Using Databases

12. Move to K5 and enter **+H5-J5** to calculate the amount due. Copy it down the block K5..K12. (Don't worry about the value in cell K9 for now.)
13. Change the default numeric format for the notebook by issuing the / **O**ptions | **F**ormats | **N**umeric Format command and specifying the , (comma) format with two decimal places. Type **Q** twice to return to Ready mode.
14. Format the values in the QUANT field by issuing the / **S**tyle | **N**umeric Format command, selecting the Fixed format, and specifying zero decimal places. Enter **D5..D12** as the block to be modified.
15. Save your work by issuing the / **F**ile | **S**ave command and entering the file name **ORDERS**. Your database should now look like the one shown in Figures 16-3 and 16-4.

Cell K9 contains the value (0.00). Before you changed the notebook's numeric format, the value appeared as –7.1E–15, which means .0000000000000071. This result is due to a slight rounding error generated by the formula in cell F9 (the subtotal column). When Quattro Pro multiplies the unit price by the quantity, it produces a result slightly lower than 59.85. When you subtract the payment of exactly 59.85 from this value, the result is a number slightly less than zero. Because the default display format is , (comma) with two decimal places, this value is rounded to two decimal places, yielding an apparently negative zero. You can eliminate this problem by including the @ROUND function in the formula in column F, as follows:

1. Move to F5 and change that cell's contents to **@ROUND(D5*E5,2)**.
2. Use the / **E**dit | **C**opy command to copy the formula to F5..F12.

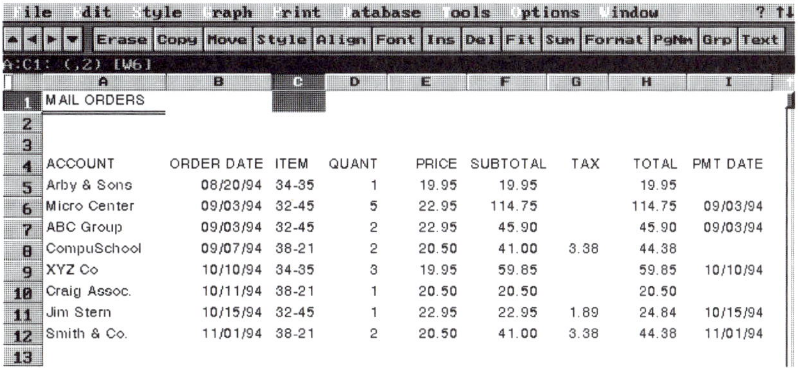

The first nine fields of the ORDERS database
Figure 16-3.

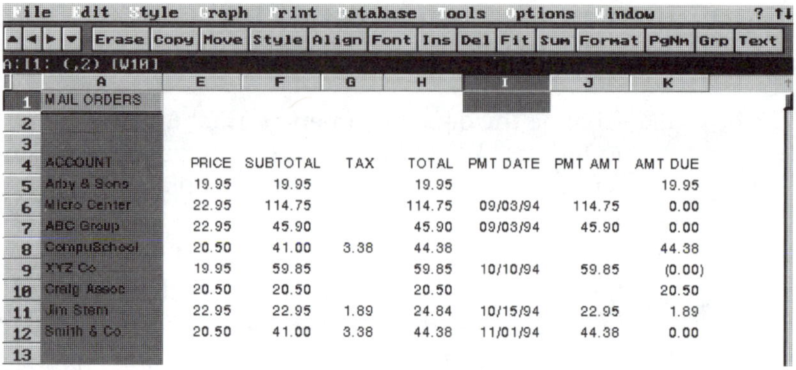

	A	E	F	G	H	I	J	K
1	MAIL ORDERS							
2								
3								
4	ACCOUNT	PRICE	SUBTOTAL	TAX	TOTAL	PMT DATE	PMT AMT	AMT DUE
5	Arby & Sons	19.95	19.95		19.95			19.95
6	Micro Center	22.95	114.75		114.75	09/03/94	114.75	0.00
7	ABC Group	22.95	45.90		45.90	09/03/94	45.90	0.00
8	CompuSchool	20.50	41.00	3.38	44.38			44.38
9	XYZ Co	19.95	59.85		59.85	10/10/94	59.85	(0.00)
10	Craig Assoc	20.50	20.50		20.50			20.50
11	Jim Stern	22.95	22.95	1.89	24.84	10/15/94	22.95	1.89
12	Smith & Co	20.50	41.00	3.38	44.38	11/01/94	44.38	0.00
13								

First field and last seven fields of the ORDERS database

Figure 16-4.

Adding and Deleting Records

In databases that contain calculated fields or different display formats for different fields, you can save time when you enter a new record by copying an entire adjacent record into the row you intend to use for the new record and then overwriting the data as necessary.

Try adding a new record to your database now.

1. Enter **Ace Personnel** in cell A13; enter **11/2/94** in B13; enter **34-35** in C13; enter **1** in D13; and enter **19.95** in E13. The results are probably not what you expected. Both the order date and the item number are treated as formulas because this new row was not included in the block for the / **D**atabase | **D**ata Entry commands issued earlier. Similarly, the format for the quantity is wrong, because cell D13 was not included in the block for the earlier / **S**tyle | **N**umeric Format command. You could solve the problem by reentering the date with the Ctrl-D prefix, reentering the item number with a label prefix character, and formatting the quantity field with / **S**tyle | **N**umeric Format. Then you must either enter formulas in cells F13, H13, and K13, or copy them from row 12. Instead, try an alternate method.
2. Copy the block A12..K12 to cell A13.
3. Now try again to enter the data you attempted to enter in step 1: Enter **Ace Personnel** in cell A13; enter **11/2/94** in B13; enter **34-35** in C13; enter **1** in D13; and enter **19.95** in E13.
4. Use Del to erase the entries in G13, I13, and J13 (the TAX, PMT DATE, and PMT AMT fields left over from row 12.)

The simplest way to add new records is to fill in the next empty row at the bottom of your database. If you add records frequently, however, you may

Designing and Using Databases

want to try a different approach. Several operations you perform on your database, such as sorting and selecting records, require specifying the block of cells that contains all the records in your database. If you add new records by entering data in the next available blank row at the bottom of the database, you must constantly adjust the coordinates for these blocks. You can solve this problem by inserting new records within the parameters of the established database coordinates (somewhere below the first record in the database and above the last one). Then the block coordinates automatically expand to accommodate the new row.

To delete a record from a database, you simply delete the row in which that data is stored. If you delete either the first or last row in the database block, you must adjust the coordinates of the sort block and of the database block specified in database selection criteria.

Modifying Your Database

After you enter your initial set of data, you may need to go back and improve the appearance of your database—to change the numeric formats for some of the fields or change field widths. To perform these operations you use the same commands you use on other notebooks—such as / **O**ptions | **F**ormats commands for changing notebook defaults and / **S**tyle | **N**umeric Format and / **S**tyle | **C**olumn Width commands for changing blocks of data.

Because it is easy to make a serious mistake when you move fields, you should always save your notebook first.

You may also decide, after entering some data, that you want to rearrange the order of fields in your database. You can do this by using the same set of cut-and-paste commands you use on other types of notebooks. First make room for the field in the desired location with the / **E**dit | **I**nsert | **C**olumns command. Then use / **E**dit | **M**ove to move the field to the new location, but be careful to include all the records in the database and the field name. You can then close up the space formerly occupied by this field with / **E**dit | **D**elete | **C**olumns.

Improving the ORDERS Database

So far you have created a simple and fairly standard database. Although it includes a few calculated fields, it does not yet fully exploit Quattro Pro's potential as a database manager. By making two substantial changes to your database, you can let Quattro Pro take over tasks currently performed manually, so it assumes more of the work involved in the order-tracking system.

The first modification involves adding a STATE field to the database, entering the current sales tax rate elsewhere on the notebook (outside the database), and changing the content of the TAX field to a formula. Once you make these changes, Quattro Pro automatically performs sales tax calculations as you enter data into the notebook.

1. Move to B4 and issue the / **E**dit | **I**nsert | **C**olumns command. Press [Enter] to accept the default block A:B4..B4.
2. Narrow the new column to six characters, and, in the new cell B4, enter the field name **STATE**.
3. Fill in the STATE field for the nine records currently in your database as follows: Enter **CA** in B5; enter **MA** in B6; enter **OH** in B7; enter **NY** in B8; enter **TX** in B9; enter **NJ** in B10; enter **NY** in B11; enter **NY** in B12; enter **MT** in B13.
4. Move to A3 and issue the / **E**dit | **I**nsert | **R**ows command. When prompted for a block, move the cell pointer down to row 10 (so that A3 through A10 are highlighted) and press [Enter].
5. Enter **Sales Tax Rate** in A3, and enter **.0825** in C3.
6. With the cell pointer still in C3, issue the / **S**tyle | **N**umeric Format command, select the Percent format, and specify two decimal places. Press [Enter] to accept the default block.
7. Issue the / **E**dit | **N**ames | **C**reate command, specify a block name of TAX RATE, and accept the default block A:C3..C3.
8. Move to H13 and enter the formula

    @IF(B13="NY",@ROUND(G13*$TAX RATE,2)," ")

    This formula calculates sales tax using the tax rate in cell C3 for those records in which the state field contains the characters NY.
9. Copy this formula to H13..H21. None of the numbers in the database should change since the formula results should be the same as the tax amount you previously entered manually.
10. Save the database.

You must make the TAX RATE block name absolute, so that the formula always refers to the interest rate in cell C3.

The second modification of the database entails adding a lookup table for the unit prices and changing the PRICE field to a calculated field employing the @VLOOKUP function. As a result, Quattro Pro assumes the work of looking up the price of each item ordered.

1. Construct a price lookup table by entering the following data: Enter **PRICE TABLE** in A5; enter **Item No.** in A6; enter **Price** in B6; enter **'32-45** in A7; enter **22.95** in B7; enter **'34-35** in A8; enter **19.95** in B8; enter **'38-21** in A9; and enter **20.50** in B9.

Designing and Using Databases

2. Create a block name for the lookup table by issuing the / **E**dit | **N**ames | **C**reate command. Enter **PRICE TABLE** and specify a block of A7..B9.
3. Move to F13 and enter the formula

   @VLOOKUP(D13,$PRICE TABLE,1)

   If Quattro Pro returns a value of ERR, the item number in D13 was not found in the price table. Check the item number entries in that cell and the first column of the price table.
4. Copy the formula to F13..F21. Your database should now look like Figure 16-5.

To see the effect of the changes you have just made, try adding a new record to the database.

1. Copy A21..L21 to A22.
2. Make the following changes in row 22: Enter **AAA Plumbing** in A22; enter **NY** in B22; enter **11/7/94** in C22; enter **38-21** in cell D22; and enter 3 in E22. Note that values for the PRICE, SUBTOTAL, TAX, and TOTAL fields have been entered automatically.
3. Save the database again.

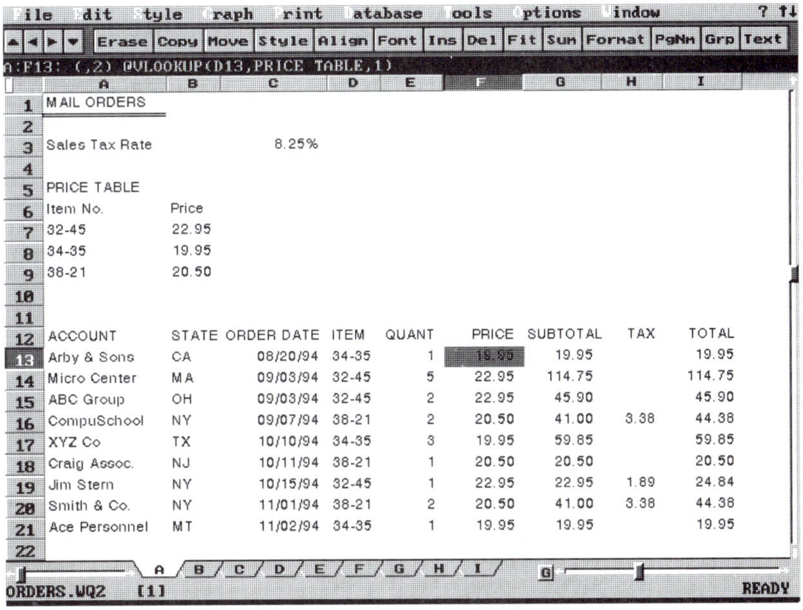

The improved ORDERS database
Figure 16-5.

Sorting Your Database

Sorting a database means arranging the records in a particular sequence based on the contents of one or more fields. The fields that you specify for this purpose are known as *sort keys* or *key fields*. The main reason for sorting a database is to make it easier to locate records. Sorting also allows you to group related records together so that you can compare, print, or gather statistics on subsets of your database.

The process of sorting a database consists of the following steps:

Be careful not to include the field names in the sort block.

1. Issue the / **D**atabase | **S**ort command to display the Sort menu.
2. Define the block of cells to be sorted by using the Block option on the Sort menu. In almost all cases, the sort block consists of all the records in your database. Be sure to include all the fields in the database; otherwise Quattro Pro rearranges the order of some fields in the database while leaving others in their current positions.
3. Define the sort key by selecting the 1st Key option on the Sort menu.
4. When prompted, indicate whether you want the records arranged in ascending or descending order.
5. If you want to sort on more than one key field, repeat steps 3 and 4 to define the additional sort keys. (Multiple-key sorts are explained later.)
6. Select Go to initiate the sort.

It is always a good idea to save your database before sorting, in case you make an error in defining the sort block or keys. Also, you can use [Alt]-[F5] to undo a sort, if you haven't already performed another undoable operation.

Sort Order

Quattro Pro sorts records in a specific but not necessarily intuitive order. As discussed later in this chapter, you can change this order with the / **D**atabase | **S**ort | **S**ort Rules command, but in most cases you will prefer to use the default order setting. The default sort order for an ascending sort is

- Blank cells
- Labels beginning with numbers, in numerical order
- Labels beginning with letters, in alphabetical order
- Labels beginning with punctuation marks or special nonkeyboard characters, such as ¢, in numerical order by ASCII code
- Values, in numerical order

Designing and Using Databases

The default sort order for a descending sort is

- Values, in reverse numerical order
- Labels beginning with punctuation marks or special nonkeyboard characters, in numerical order by their ASCII codes
- Labels beginning with letters, in reverse alphabetical order
- Labels beginning with numbers, in reverse numerical order
- Blank cells

Formulas are always sorted by their results rather than by the characters they contain. For example, the formula (3*25) comes before (2*50) in an ascending sort, because 75 is less than 100. Dates are always sorted by their serial numbers. For example, 12/31/93 comes before 01/01/94 in an ascending sort because the serial number for the former is 34334 and for the latter is 34335. Unless you change the Database | Sort | Sort Rules setting, Quattro Pro ignores capitalization when sorting.

Single-Key Sorts

The easiest type of sort is a single-key sort. You designate one field as the basis for the sort, and Quattro Pro arranges all the records in the database according to the content of that field. Try performing a single-key sort now by following these steps:

1. Move to A13 in the ORDERS.WQ2 database.
2. Issue the / **D**atabase | **S**ort | **B**lock command. Type a period to anchor the cell pointer, press End-Home to extend the block to A13..L22, and press Enter.
3. Select the 1st Key option, move to any cell in column A, and press Enter to designate the ACCOUNT field as the first sort key.
4. When prompted for the sort order, enter **A** to indicate Ascending, and then select Go to initiate the sort. Your database should now look like Figure 16-6.

The record for Jim Stern is now ordered by the first name because the name was entered first name first in the ACCOUNT field. To order by last name, you must enter the last name first, as follows:

1. Move to A19 and enter **Stern, Jim** to replace Jim Stern.

2. Issue the / **D**atabase | **S**ort | **G**o command. Since Quattro Pro remembers the previous sort block and sort key, you can issue the Go command without defining any settings.

If you have a database that contains a high proportion of individual names, you might want to create separate fields for first and last names and use the last name as the first key. If you have more than one record with the same last name, you can then use the first name field as the second key for the sort to achieve full alphabetical order.

Multiple-Key Sorts

It is possible to sort on up to five keys at once. Whenever you sort on more than one key, records are first arranged in order by the contents of the first key field. Then, within each first key field grouping, records are arranged by the contents of the second key field, and within each second key field grouping, they are arranged by the contents of the third key field, and so on.

To perform a multiple-key sort, you simply define additional sort keys by selecting the appropriate key options on the Sort menu and designating the columns containing the fields on which you want the sort to be based.

1. Issue the / **D**atabase | **S**ort | **1**st Key command. Move to any cell in column D, and press Enter to designate the ITEM field as the first sort key. When prompted for the sort order, enter **A** to specify Ascending.
2. Select the 2nd Key option, move to any cell in column E, and press Enter to designate the QUANT field as the second sort key. When prompted for the sort order, enter **D** to specify Descending.
3. Select Go to initiate the search. Your notebook should now look like Figure 16-7.

ORDERS.WQ2 database sorted on the ACCOUNT field
Figure 16-6.

	ACCOUNT	STATE	ORDER DATE	ITEM	QUANT	PRICE	SUBTOTAL	TAX	TOTAL
13	AAA Plumbing	NY	11/07/94	38-21	3	20.50	61.50	5.07	66.57
14	ABC Group	OH	09/03/94	32-45	2	22.95	45.90		45.90
15	Ace Personnel	MT	11/02/94	34-35	1	19.95	19.95		19.95
16	Arby & Sons	CA	08/20/94	34-35	1	19.95	19.95		19.95
17	CompuSchool	NY	09/07/94	38-21	2	20.50	41.00	3.38	44.38
18	Craig Assoc.	NJ	10/11/94	38-21	1	20.50	20.50		20.50
19	Jim Stern	NY	10/15/94	32-45	1	22.95	22.95	1.89	24.84
20	Micro Center	MA	09/03/94	32-45	5	22.95	114.75		114.75
21	Smith & Co.	NY	11/01/94	38-21	2	20.50	41.00	3.38	44.38
22	XYZ Co	TX	10/10/94	34-35	3	19.95	59.85		59.85

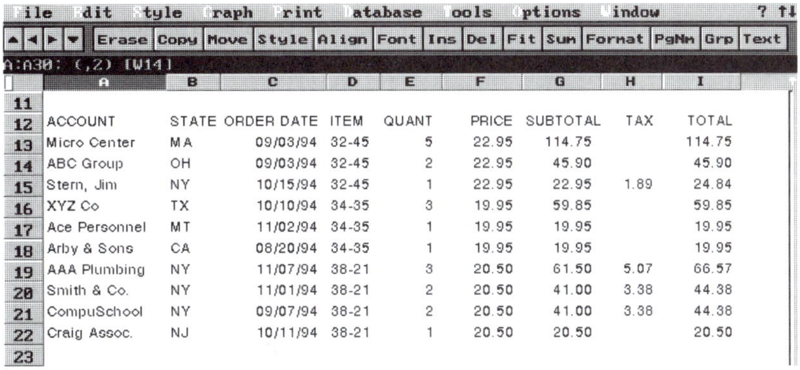

Designing and Using Databases

```
A:A30: (,2) [W14]
       A              B     C        D      E     F      G        H     I
11
12   ACCOUNT        STATE ORDER DATE ITEM  QUANT PRICE  SUBTOTAL  TAX   TOTAL
13   Micro Center    MA   09/03/94  32-45   5   22.95  114.75         114.75
14   ABC Group       OH   09/03/94  32-45   2   22.95   45.90          45.90
15   Stern, Jim      NY   10/15/94  32-45   1   22.95   22.95  1.89    24.84
16   XYZ Co          TX   10/10/94  34-35   3   19.95   59.85          59.85
17   Ace Personnel   MT   11/02/94  34-35   1   19.95   19.95          19.95
18   Arby & Sons     CA   08/20/94  34-35   1   19.95   19.95          19.95
19   AAA Plumbing    NY   11/07/94  38-21   3   20.50   61.50  5.07    66.57
20   Smith & Co.     NY   11/01/94  38-21   2   20.50   41.00  3.38    44.38
21   CompuSchool     NY   09/07/94  38-21   2   20.50   41.00  3.38    44.38
22   Craig Assoc.    NJ   10/11/94  38-21   1   20.50   20.50          20.50
23
```

ORDERS.WQ2 database sorted on multiple keys
Figure 16-7.

Sort Rules settings are not affected by the Reset command.

If you want to erase keys (to change from a five-key to a two-key sort, for example) you must use the Reset option on the Sort menu. This command erases the sort block setting as well as all the key settings so that you can begin defining your sort from scratch.

Changing the Sort Rules

The / **D**atabase | **S**ort | **S**ort Rules command allows you to alter the sequence in which Quattro Pro sorts records. When you select this option, Quattro Pro displays a menu that contains the options Numbers Before Labels, Sort Rows/Columns, Label Order, and Quit. If you select Numbers Before Labels, Quattro Pro displays a submenu with the options No (the default) and Yes. If you change this setting to Yes, Quattro Pro places values before labels (the order among the labels themselves is unaffected).

The Sort Rows/Columns option lets you determine whether to sort your database by rows (the default) or by columns. You can use this option if records are organized in columns rather than rows in your database. You can also use it to reorder the columns in any database.

The Label Order option allows you to change the way in which labels—as distinct from values—are sorted. When you select this option, Quattro Pro displays a submenu with two options: Dictionary and ASCII. The ASCII setting (the default) directs Quattro Pro to arrange labels by the ASCII codes of their first characters. This means that control characters (characters generated by holding down Ctrl while pressing another key) come first, followed by some punctuation marks, the digits 0 through 9, other punctuation marks, uppercase letters, a few other punctuation marks, lowercase letters, more punctuation marks, and lastly graphics characters, foreign letters, and other nonkeyboard characters. If you change this setting to Dictionary, Quattro Pro arranges labels alphabetically regardless of case, placing those labels that start with punctuation and special nonkeyboard characters at the end.

In this chapter you have learned basic database concepts and terminology and techniques for designing, constructing, and maintaining a database in Quattro Pro. You also learned how to sort the records in your database according to the data contained in one or more fields. A fairly sophisticated database was used as the sample application in order to acquaint you with the range of calculations possible within Quattro Pro. You will use this same database in the next chapter to select specified records from your database on the basis of their content.

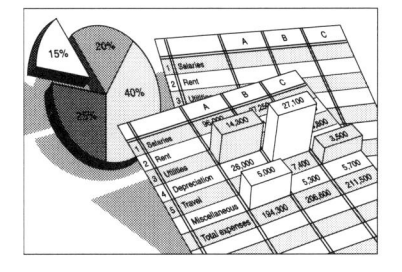

CHAPTER

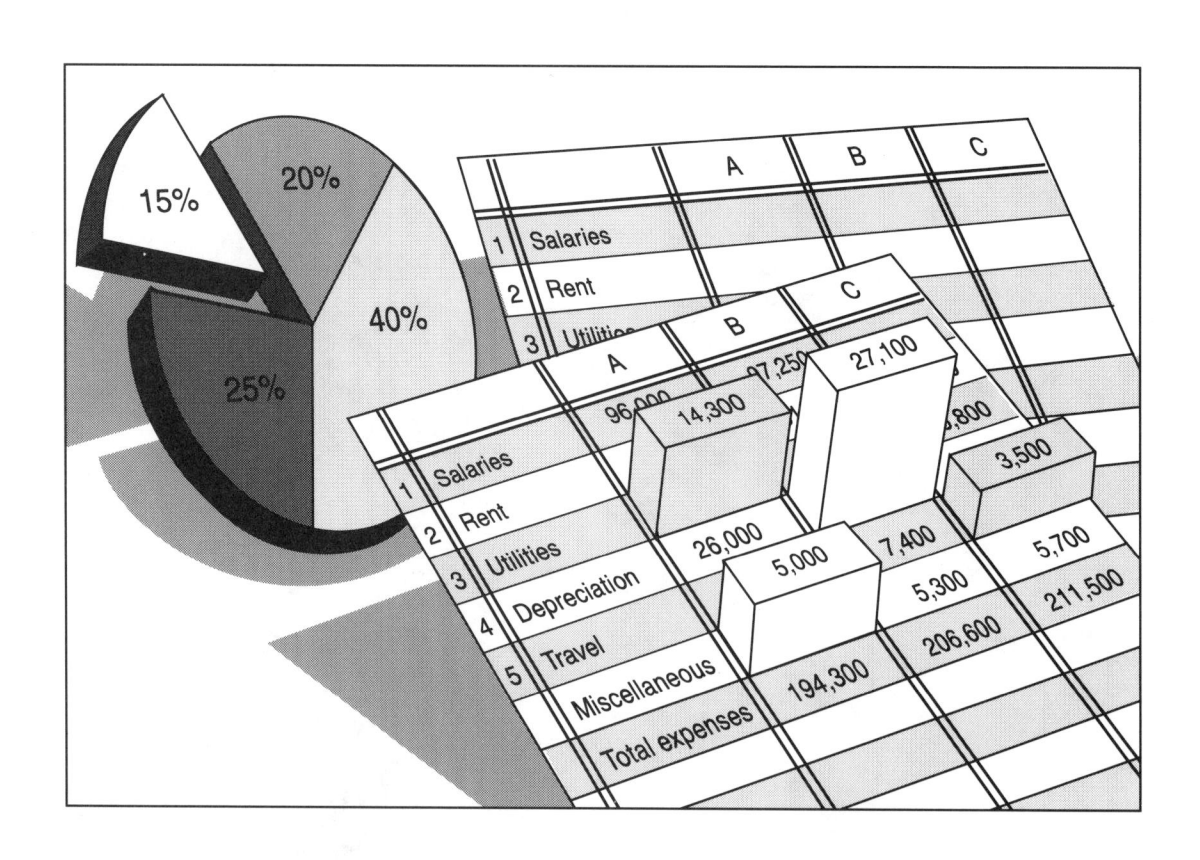

17

SELECTING RECORDS FROM YOUR DATABASE

One of the most useful operations you can perform on your databases is searching for and selecting records on the basis of their content. For example, in the mail order database you created in Chapter 16, you might want to extract all records that have a particular item code, order date, or order total. This chapter discusses the rules and techniques for constructing and using database selection criteria to locate, extract, delete, or perform calculations on subsets of your database.

Database Query Commands

Quattro Pro's / **D**atabase | **Q**uery commands allow you to find and manipulate the records that match a particular set of selection criteria. The criteria you can define range from simple (for example, all records that contain NY in the STATE field) to complex (all records in which the state is NY, the order date is prior to 10/1/94, the item code is either 32-45 or 34-25, and the quantity is greater than one).

Once you have defined your selection criteria, you can direct Quattro Pro to perform any of four operations on the selected records. You can locate the records one at a time, stopping at each record so that you can view and edit the data. You can extract all the records that match your selection criteria, creating copies of the selected records in a separate section of the notebook. You can extract unique records or unique portions of records, eliminating duplicates. Lastly, you can delete all the records that match your selection criteria.

Preparing a Query

Before searching for records, you need to take several preparatory steps:

You cannot assign names until you define the query block. Other than that, the order of these preparatory steps does not matter.

1. **Define the query block.** Before you perform a database query, you must use the / **D**atabase | **Q**uery | **B**lock command to tell Quattro Pro which block of cells to search through. The query block almost always consists of the entire database, including the field names.

2. **Assign names to fields in the first record if you want to reference fields by block name.** Most selection criteria are defined by referring to the fields in the first record on the database. For example, if you want to select ORDERS.WQ2 records in which the SUBTOTAL field contains a value greater than 41, you would specify that the value in cell G13 (the SUBTOTAL field of the first record in the database) must be greater than 41 to be selected. Quattro Pro then applies the same condition to every record in the database.

    The Assign Names option on the Database | Query menu facilitates the process of defining selection criteria by automatically assigning block names to each cell in the first row of the database block, using the field name immediately above each cell.

3. **Set up a criteria table on the notebook.** A *criteria table* is a block of cells on the notebook in which you enter criteria for a database query.

4. **Tell Quattro Pro where the criteria table is.** Before you initiate the query, you must tell Quattro Pro where to find the query criteria by issuing the / **D**atabase | **Q**uery | **C**riteria Table command.

Selecting Records from Your Database

5. **If necessary, define an output block.** If you want to extract the records that match your selection criteria and copy them to another section of the notebook, you must define an output block in which these records will be copied.

Once you have taken these steps, you are ready to tell Quattro Pro what to do with the selected records by choosing the Locate, Extract, Unique, or Delete option on the Database | Query menu.

Criteria Tables

Do not include any blank rows in the criteria block; if you do, Quattro Pro selects every record in the database.

A criteria table is a block of cells that contains the criteria for a database query. This block can be located anywhere on the notebook. The block consists of at least two rows; the exact number depends on the complexity of your selection criteria. The first row contains one or more field names from the database. The rows below contain the selection criteria.

Exact Matches

Any selection criterion that you can express in the form *Field = Value* can be entered in a criteria table by simply entering *Value* under the appropriate field name. For example, if you want to see all the records in which the STATE field equals CA, you can simply type CA below the field name STATE, as shown in Figure 17-1. The output block in this figure shows the one record found to match the table's criterion.

You can use this type of *exact match criteria* to search for values or labels. In either case, Quattro Pro pays attention only to the basic data, not the embellishments. If you are searching for values, for example, Quattro Pro ignores any differences in display format between the criteria you enter and the values for which you are searching. Similarly, if you are searching for labels, Quattro Pro ignores capitalization and label prefixes.

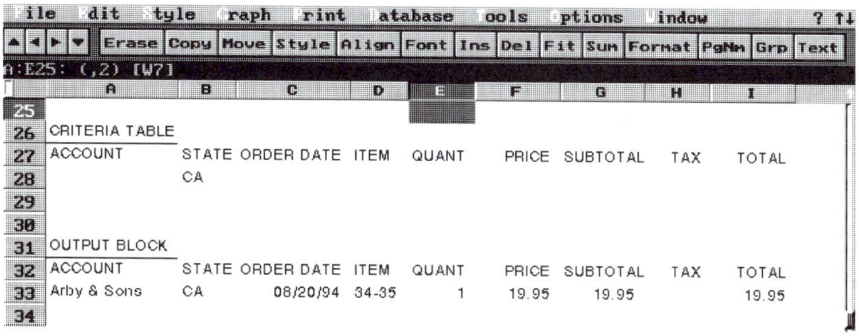

A query using an exact match criterion
Figure 17-1.

You can also search for the results of formulas using exact match criteria. For example, you can locate records in which the value displayed in the TOTAL field (which contains a formula adding SUBTOTAL to TAX) is 24.84 by entering **24.84** in the criteria table under the field name TOTAL. (This would find the record for Jim Stern.)

Using Wild Cards

Quattro Pro provides three wild-card characters you can use to define conditions in a criteria table. These characters increase the power of exact match criteria, allowing you to express conditions that may be difficult or impossible to express otherwise.

You can use the ? character to indicate any single character. For example, if you enter the selection criterion **N?** under the field name STATE in your criteria table, Quattro Pro selects all records in which the data in the STATE field consist of two characters (no more, no less) starting with N. You can use the * to indicate a series of characters of any length. For example, if you enter the selection criterion **A*** under the field name ACCOUNT in your criteria table, Quattro Pro selects all records in which the ACCOUNT field starts with the letter "A". You can use the ~ (tilde) to locate all records *except* those matching the specified selection criteria. For example, if you enter the selection criterion **~NY** under the field name STATE, Quattro Pro selects all records except those in which the STATE field is NY.

Locating Records One at a Time

When you issue the / **D**atabase | **Q**uery | **L**ocate command, Quattro Pro highlights the first record in the database that matches your selection criteria. Every time you press [↓], Quattro Pro highlights the next record that matches your criteria. You can press [Esc] or [Enter] to return to the Database | Query menu or the notebook (depending on where you initiated the query) at any point.

During a locate query operation, you can edit any of the records that match your criteria. When Quattro Pro highlights a record that you want to change, use [←] and [→] to move the cursor to the field you want to modify. If you want to replace the field, just type the new entry and press [Enter]. To change the contents of the field, press [F2] (Edit), use any of the usual editing keys to alter the data, and press [Enter].

The Query Key

You can press [F7] (Query) to repeat the last database query operation that you performed (Locate, Extract, Unique, or Delete) using the current settings

Selecting Records from Your Database

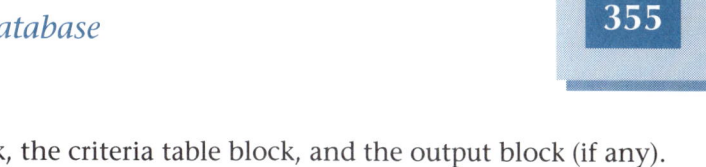

for the query block, the criteria table block, and the output block (if any). This key can save you numerous keystrokes, particularly when you want to change the contents of the criteria table and then reexecute a query.

Hands-On Practice

Try creating and using a criteria table by following these steps:

1. Retrieve ORDERS.WQ2 from disk.
2. Move to A26 and enter the label **CRITERIA TABLE**. Then use the / **S**tyle I **L**ine Drawing command to draw a single line underneath the label CRITERIA TABLE. Select Quit to return to Ready mode.
3. Issue the / **E**dit I **C**opy command. Specify the source block A12..L13 and the destination A27.
4. Issue the / **E**dit I **E**rase Block command and specify a block of A28..L28, erasing all the data in that row but leaving the formatting intact.
5. In B28 enter the criterion **NY**. Your notebook should now look like Figure 17-2.

In the next few steps you assign names to both the criteria table and the database as a whole.

6. Name the criteria block by issuing the / **E**dit I **N**ames I **C**reate command. Enter the block name **CRITERIA** and the coordinates **A27..L28**.
7. Name the database (including the field names) by issuing the / **E**dit I **N**ames I **C**reate command. Enter the block name **DATABASE** and the coordinates **A12..L22**.
8. Issue the / **D**atabase I **Q**uery I **B**lock command. Press (F3) (Choices), and choose DATABASE from the list of block names.
9. Select the Criteria Table option, press (F3) (Choices), and select CRITERIA from the list.
10. Select the Locate option on the Database I Query menu, and use ↓ to move through all the records for customers in New York State.
11. Press (Enter) or (Esc) to return to the Database I Query menu, and select the Quit option to return to Ready mode.
12. In B28, press (F2) (Edit), press ← twice so the cursor is on the "N" in NY, type ~, and press (Enter).
13. Press (F7) (Query) to locate the records for all customers in states other than New York. (Press ↓ to move through the selected records.)
14. When you reach the last record that matches your criteria, press (Enter) or (Esc).

Defining Complex Searches in a Criteria Table

You can use the exact match method to express conditions that involve multiple criteria by filling in more than one cell in the criteria table. Quattro Pro responds differently depending on whether you enter the criteria in the same or different rows. When you enter more than one criterion in the same row, Quattro Pro selects only those records that fulfill all of the criteria in the row. Figure 17-3 shows a criteria table for selecting records in which the state is NY, the item number is 38-21, and the quantity is 2. Below the table is an output block containing the two records that met these criteria. (You'll learn how to create output blocks shortly.)

When you enter criteria in different rows, Quattro Pro finds records that fulfill the criteria in any one of the rows in the criteria table. This is referred to as an #OR# criterion or #OR# condition. Figure 17-4 shows a criteria table for locating records in which the STATE field contains OH, MA, or MT.

You can also combine #AND# and #OR# conditions within the same criteria table. Again, Quattro Pro selects all the records that meet the criteria in any one row of the table. The criteria table in Figure 17-5 could be used to select those records in which the STATE field contains NY and the ITEM field contains the code 38-21, plus those records in which the state is MA and the item code is 32-45.

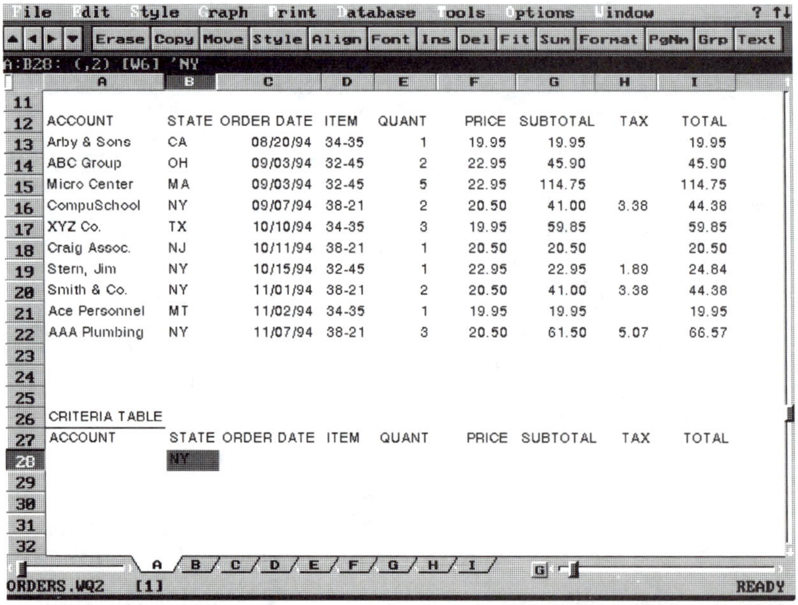

Creating a criteria table
Figure 17-2.

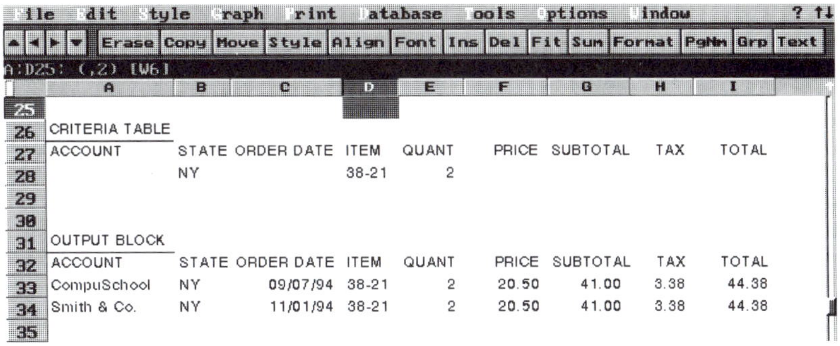

Selecting Records from Your Database

A criteria table that expresses an #AND# condition
Figure 17-3.

```
         A            B     C          D      E      F      G         H     I
 25
 26  CRITERIA TABLE
 27  ACCOUNT       STATE ORDER DATE ITEM  QUANT  PRICE SUBTOTAL  TAX   TOTAL
 28                 NY               38-21   2
 29
 30
 31  OUTPUT BLOCK
 32  ACCOUNT       STATE ORDER DATE ITEM  QUANT  PRICE SUBTOTAL  TAX   TOTAL
 33  CompuSchool    NY    09/07/94  38-21   2    20.50  41.00   3.38  44.38
 34  Smith & Co.    NY    11/01/94  38-21   2    20.50  41.00   3.38  44.38
 35
```

Whenever you enter criteria in more than one row of a criteria table, be sure to expand the criteria table's coordinates to include the extra rows. The criteria table in Figure 17-4, for example, is A27..L30. There are several ways to do this: You can manually change the Criteria Table setting on the Database | Query menu; you can use the / **E**dit | **I**nsert | **R**ows command to add one or more rows in the middle of the criteria table, immediately below the field names; or, if you've named the Criteria Table, you can use / **E**dit | **N**ames | **C**reate and redefine the block.

Be careful to readjust the criteria table's coordinates if you later perform a query that involves fewer rows of criteria. (Otherwise, Quattro Pro considers some rows of the table to be blank and selects all the records in your table.) To contract the table, you can either manually adjust the Database | Query | Criteria Table setting or delete the unnecessary rows from the middle of your criteria table with the / **E**dit | **D**elete | **R**ows command.

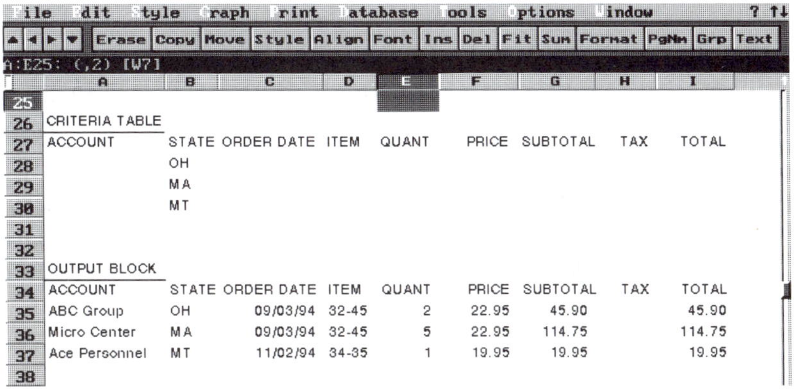

A criteria table with an #OR# condition
Figure 17-4.

```
         A            B     C          D      E      F      G         H     I
 25
 26  CRITERIA TABLE
 27  ACCOUNT       STATE ORDER DATE ITEM  QUANT  PRICE SUBTOTAL  TAX   TOTAL
 28                 OH
 29                 MA
 30                 MT
 31
 32
 33  OUTPUT BLOCK
 34  ACCOUNT       STATE ORDER DATE ITEM  QUANT  PRICE SUBTOTAL  TAX   TOTAL
 35  ABC Group      OH    09/03/94  32-45   2    22.95  45.90         45.90
 36  Micro Center   MA    09/03/94  32-45   5    22.95 114.75        114.75
 37  Ace Personnel  MT    11/02/94  34-35   1    19.95  19.95         19.95
 38
```

Quattro Pro 5 Made Easy

	A	B	C	D	E	F	G	H	I
25									
26	CRITERIA TABLE								
27	ACCOUNT		STATE	ORDER DATE	ITEM	QUANT	PRICE SUBTOTAL	TAX	TOTAL
28			NY		38-21				
29			MA		32-45				
30									
31									
32	OUTPUT BLOCK								
33	ACCOUNT		STATE	ORDER DATE	ITEM	QUANT	PRICE SUBTOTAL	TAX	TOTAL
34	Micro Center		MA	09/03/94	32-45	5	22.95 114.75		114.75
35	CompuSchool		NY	09/07/94	38-21	2	20.50 41.00	3.38	44.38
36	Smith & Co.		NY	11/01/94	38-21	2	20.50 41.00	3.38	44.38
37	AAA Plumbing		NY	11/07/94	38-21	3	20.50 61.50	5.07	66.57
38									

Combining #AND# and #OR# conditions
Figure 17-5.

Using Formulas in a Criteria Table

Logical formulas must begin with a plus sign, parenthesis, or number so Quattro Pro knows you are entering a formula rather than a label.

There are many selection criteria that cannot be expressed through exact match criteria, even with the help of wild-card characters. For example, you cannot select records in which the amount in the TOTAL field is greater than 50 by simply entering a value in a criteria table. You also cannot select records in which one field equals another. The only way to express such criteria is by entering a condition in the criteria table, usually consisting of a cell reference or block name that refers to a field in the first record of the database, followed by a comparison operator (such as < or >=), followed by the number, character string, or expression to which you want the field compared. For example, assuming you have assigned block names to each field in the first record of your database, you could use the condition +AMT DUE>40 to select records in which the value in the amount due field is greater than 40.

When you enter a condition in a notebook, Quattro Pro reads it as a *logical formula*—a formula that evaluates to the value True or False. Accordingly, Quattro Pro immediately performs the specified calculation and displays the result rather than the formula on the notebook. The value False is represented by the number 0, and the value True is represented by the number 1.

You can test this by entering the logical formula 3>4 in any cell of your notebook. Note that Quattro Pro returns the value 0 for False. If you change the formula to 4>3, Quattro Pro returns the value 1. Similarly, if you enter the condition +E13>2 anywhere on your notebook, Quattro Pro checks whether the value in the QUANT field in the first record in the database is

Selecting Records from Your Database

greater than 2. (Once you assign block names to the first record's fields, you can express this condition as +QUANT>2.) Because the condition is false, Quattro Pro returns a value of 0.

Figure 17-6 shows a criteria table in which the condition +SUBTOTAL<50 was entered in cell G28. The value 1 appears in that cell because the condition is true for the first record in the database. The output block below the criteria table contains the seven records that meet that criterion. Although the condition has been entered below the field name SUBTOTAL for clarity's sake, it could be entered anywhere in row 28.

Try entering a logical formula in row 28.

1. Issue the / **D**atabase | **Q**uery | **A**ssign Names command to automatically assign the field names at the top of the query block to the fields in the first record. This allows you to refer to fields by name when entering logical formulas. Select Quit to return to Ready mode.

2. Leave the criteria ~NY in cell B28, and enter **+TOTAL>=50** in cell B28, thereby defining an #AND# condition involving both criteria. Quattro Pro displays a 0 in the cell because the condition happens to be false for the first record in the database. The two decimal places are displayed because the global numeric format for the notebook is , (comma) with two decimal places.

3. Press F7 (Query) and then ⬇ to locate the two records for customers outside of New York State who placed orders worth $50 or more.

4. Press Enter to return to Ready mode.

You can enter a logical formula in any column in a criteria table.

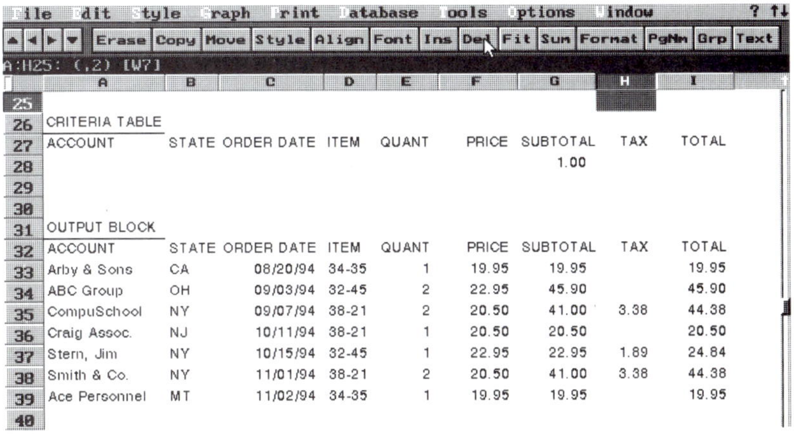

Extracting data with a logical formula
Figure 17-6.

Do not enter blank spaces before or after comparison operators; they can generate syntax errors.

There are a few rules to keep in mind when constructing logical formulas. First, you can use any of the comparison operators, including >, >=, <>, <, <=, and =. Keep in mind that you can use any of the comparison operators to compare character data as well as numeric values. For example, if you want to select all records in which the ACCOUNT field starts with the letter "M" or any letter that comes alphabetically after "M," you can use the formula criterion +ACCOUNT>="M".

You must enclose character strings within quotation marks in logical formulas. To select all records in which the STATE field contains CA, for example, you would enter the formula criterion **+STATE="CA"**. If you enter **+STATE=CA** instead, Quattro Pro assumes that CA, like STATE, refers to a block on the notebook, and returns a syntax error when it does not find a block with this name.

Although most logical formulas take the form of a field name followed by a comparison operator followed by a value, they can take other forms as well. You can compare two fields within the same record using the form *Field1 Operator Field2*. For example, the formula +ORDER DATE=PMT DATE selects all records for orders that were paid on the same day as they were placed. You can also use functions, references to cells outside the database, or any other expressions that evaluate to a value of True or False. You could use the formula +TOTAL*1.15>100 to find all records in which the total order amount would exceed $100 if you raised your prices by 15%. And, you could use a condition such as

```
ORDER DATE>@DATE(94,9,30)
```

to select records for orders placed after September 30, 1994.

The rule of thumb is that you can use any expression that does not violate rules of syntax and that always returns a value of True or False.

Complex Conditions in Logical Formulas

You can define more complex logical formulas using the #AND#, #OR#, and #NOT# operators. For example, to select orders for more than a single item that are less than 30 days old, you could enter this formula:

```
+QUANT>1#AND#@TODAY-ORDER DATE<30
```

Quattro Pro adheres to an order of calculation among the complex operators similar to the one it uses with mathematical operators: #NOT# operators have top priority and are always interpreted first; #AND# and #OR# operators share the same level of priority and are always evaluated from left to right. Unlike the order used with mathematical operators, however, the order used with

Selecting Records from Your Database

complex operators always results in a simple left to right sequence of interpretation. If you want a condition interpreted in another order, you must use parentheses to group those elements of the condition that you want to be interpreted first or arrange the components of the condition in a different order. Note that by default #NOT# operators apply just to the item immediately to the right; you must use parentheses if you want #NOT# to apply in a wider context.

Putting Your Selections to Work

In addition to locating records, you can use the / **D**atabase | **Q**uery commands to extract records to another section of the notebook, create lists of unique values, and delete selected records.

Extracting Records

Quattro Pro's / **D**atabase | **Q**uery | **Ex**tract command lets you create more meaningful and manageable subsets of your data by copying selected records (or selected fields within the records) to a new location on the notebook. Using this command, you can view all the records that match your criteria as a group. You can also perform all the same operations on this subgroup as you would on any other database, such as sorting, performing calculations, and generating lists, graphs, or reports.

Don't include blank columns in the output block; just enter the names of those fields that you actually want to extract.

Before you can extract records, you need to define an *output block*—a section of the notebook to which the selected records will be copied. You can place these records below the database and below the criteria table (if you have one), or on a separate page if you like. The output block is structured much like the database: The first row consists of field names and the subsequent rows hold the extracted records. Because you will probably want to extract all fields for each record in the same order as they appear in the database, you will usually fill in the first row of your output block by copying the field names from the top of your database. However, you can extract only some of the fields by including only selected field names in this row. You can also change the order of fields by entering the field names in a different sequence in the top row of the output block.

Once you have entered or copied the field names to the section of the notebook that you want to use as your output block, you need to select the Output Block option on the Database | Query menu and supply Quattro Pro with the block's coordinates. If there is no data below the output block, you need only specify the first row (the field names) and the extracted data will occupy as much space as necessary. If there is data below the output block, you should specify an output block that is large enough to accommodate the extracted records without encroaching upon the other data. If the block is not large enough to accommodate all the records selected in a particular query, Quattro Pro displays an error message. As soon as you press [Esc], Quattro Pro extracts as many records as fit in the block.

> **CAUTION:** When you reuse an output block for a new query, Quattro Pro erases the entire block before extracting the new set of data. If you have defined a single-row output block, Quattro Pro *erases any data below that row*, no matter how far down the notebook that data is located.

Whenever you extract data from a database, Quattro Pro converts any formulas in the extracted data to their results when copying them to the output block, functioning like a variation of the / **E**dit | **V**alues command. Once the formulas have been converted to numbers or, more rarely, to labels, they no longer respond to changes in data elsewhere on the notebook.

Extracting Unique Records

The / **D**atabase | **Q**uery | **U**nique command works exactly like / **D**atabase | **Q**uery | **E**xtract, except it automatically eliminates duplicates from the selected records before copying them to the output block. You can use / **D**atabase | **Q**uery | **U**nique to strip duplicate records from the database by specifying selection criteria that will be true for every record in the database (such as including a blank row in the criteria table) or leaving the criteria table empty. You can then erase the original database and use the new one.

You can also use this command to create lists of all the unique entries in a particular field. Leave the criteria table empty, and include only a single field name in your output block. For example, if you leave the criteria table blank, include only the ITEM field in your output block, and select the Unique option, Quattro Pro returns a list of the three item codes that occur throughout the ITEM column of ORDERS.WQ2. Similarly, you can create lists of all the unique combinations of entries in two or more fields by leaving the criteria table empty and including the combination of fields that you want to analyze in the output block. For example, if you include the names of both the ITEM field and the QUANT field in your output block, Quattro Pro generates a list of all the unique combinations of a particular item code with a particular quantity amount.

You can also enter criteria in the criteria table to produce a list of all the unique entries or combinations of entries that occur within the specified subset of records. For example, if you include only the ITEM field name in your output block, enter the criteria **ORDER DATE>@DATE(94,10,1)** in the criteria table or as a formula criterion, and then issue the / **D**atabase |

Selecting Records from Your Database

Query | **U**nique command, Quattro Pro returns a list of the unique item codes that occur in all records with an order date after October 1, 1994.

Try extracting selected records by following these steps:

1. In row 28, insert a single row by issuing the / **E**dit | **I**nsert | **R**ow command and pressing ⏎. This expands the coordinates of the criteria table so that new criteria you enter in row 28 are automatically included in the query.
2. Enter **+ORDER DATE<@DATE(94,10,1)** in A28.
3. Move to B29 and press ⌦ to erase ~NY from that cell. Leave the logical formula in A29; this formula and the one you just entered in step 2 are located on two different rows of the criteria table, so Quattro Pro treats them like an #OR# condition, selecting all records that fulfill either criterion.
4. Move to A32 and enter **OUTPUT BLOCK**. Then use the / **S**tyle | **L**ine Drawing command to place a single line at the bottom of cell A32.
5. Issue the / **E**dit | **C**opy command. Specify A27..L27 as the source block and A33 as the destination.
6. Issue the / **D**atabase | **Q**uery | **O**utput Block command. Enter the coordinates **A33..L33**. Note that the output block must include the column headings you just copied.
7. Select the Extract option on the Database | Query menu to copy the selected records to the output block.
8. Select the Quit option on the Database | Query menu to return to Ready mode. Your notebook should now look like the one shown in Figure 17-7, which lists all customers who either have a total of $50 or more, or whose order dates are prior to 10/1/94.
9. Enter **NY** in B28 and B29 to limit the records extracted to customers in New York. If you enter **NY** in cell B28 only, Quattro Pro extracts records in which the order date is less than 10/1/94 and the state is NY, plus records in which the total is greater than or equal to 50, regardless of the state. If you enter **NY** in cell B29 only, Quattro Pro extracts all orders placed before 10/1/94, regardless of the state.
10. Press F7 to initiate the query. Quattro Pro extracts only two records this time—the ones for CompuSchool (which matches the criteria in the first row of the criteria table) and AAA Plumbing (which matches the criteria in the second row). Notice that Quattro Pro automatically erased the output data before extracting the records for this query so that no data is left over from the previous query.

Because there's no data below the output block, you can specify a one-row block and let Quattro Pro use as much space as needed.

11. Erase all criteria in the criteria table by issuing the / **E**dit | **E**rase Block command and specifying a block of A28..B29.
12. Start creating a second output block by entering **STATE** in A44 and **ITEM** in B44.
13. Issue the / **D**atabase | **Q**uery | **O**utput Block command and specify **A44..B44**.
14. Select the Unique option on the Database | Query menu, and then select the Quit option to return to Ready mode. Your notebook should now look like Figure 17-8.

The new output block contains eight unique combinations of state abbreviations and item codes. Because no selection criteria were specified for this query, these represent every combination of state and item codes that occurs in the database.

Deleting Selected Records

When you select this Delete option, Quattro Pro asks for confirmation so you do not delete records accidentally.

The Delete option on the Database | Query menu allows you to delete all the records that match your selection criteria. For example, you could use this command to purge obsolete records by specifying selection criteria for all orders paid in full over six months ago.

When you issue the / **D**atabase | **Q**uery | **D**elete command, remaining records in the database move up to fill in blank rows, but any data located below the database remains where it is. Data to the right of the database is left intact and in the same location, and display format codes in the erased rows of the database are left as is. If you have created a named block for the database, its coordinates are not changed by the / **D**atabase | **Q**uery | **D**elete

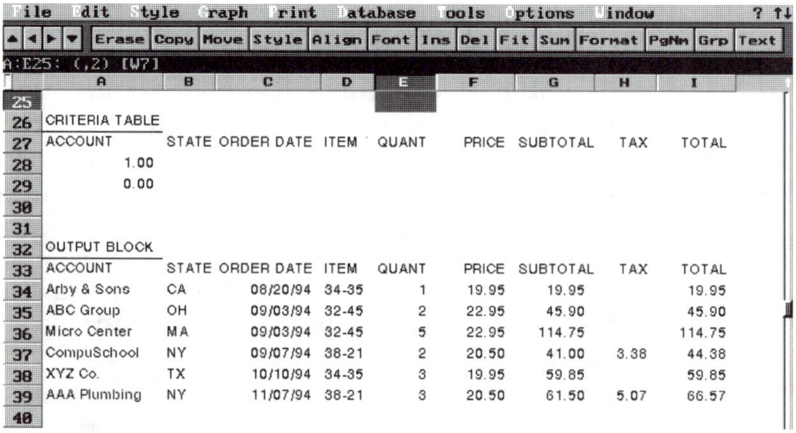

	A	B	C	D	E	F	G	H	I
25									
26	CRITERIA TABLE								
27	ACCOUNT	STATE	ORDER DATE	ITEM	QUANT	PRICE	SUBTOTAL	TAX	TOTAL
28	1.00								
29	0.00								
30									
31									
32	OUTPUT BLOCK								
33	ACCOUNT	STATE	ORDER DATE	ITEM	QUANT	PRICE	SUBTOTAL	TAX	TOTAL
34	Arby & Sons	CA	08/20/94	34-35	1	19.95	19.95		19.95
35	ABC Group	OH	09/03/94	32-45	2	22.95	45.90		45.90
36	Micro Center	MA	09/03/94	32-45	5	22.95	114.75		114.75
37	CompuSchool	NY	09/07/94	38-21	2	20.50	41.00	3.38	44.38
38	XYZ Co.	TX	10/10/94	34-35	3	19.95	59.85		59.85
39	AAA Plumbing	NY	11/07/94	38-21	3	20.50	61.50	5.07	66.57
40									

Extracting data with an #OR# condition

Figure 17-7.

Selecting Records from Your Database

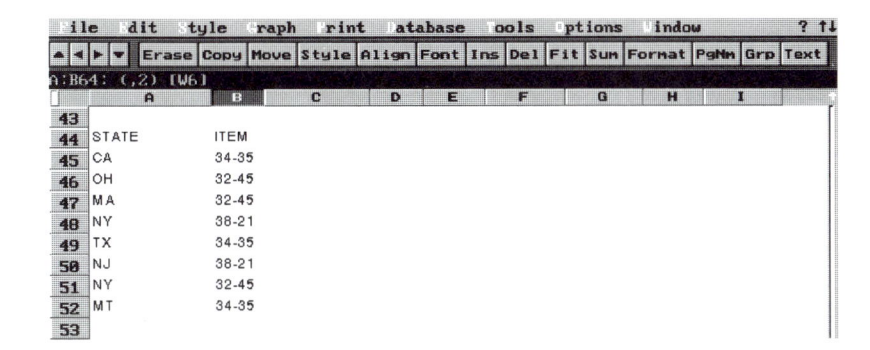

Extracting a unique list of state and item conditions
Figure 17-8.

command, so you will need to adjust them yourself after executing the command. The query block itself is automatically adjusted.

Resetting the Query Settings

If you want to change the parameters of your query, you can erase the Block, Criteria Table, and Output Block settings on the Database | Query menu with / **D**atabase | **Q**uery | **R**eset. This command is primarily used when you are querying more than one database on a single notebook.

This chapter has introduced you to Quattro Pro's / **D**atabase | **Q**uery commands. It also introduced you to the craft of defining selection criteria, which allows you to pinpoint information within a large and otherwise unwieldy mass of data. Using selection criteria correctly allows you to view and extract manageable and useful subsets of your database, focusing on only those records and fields that you want to work with at any given moment.

CHAPTER

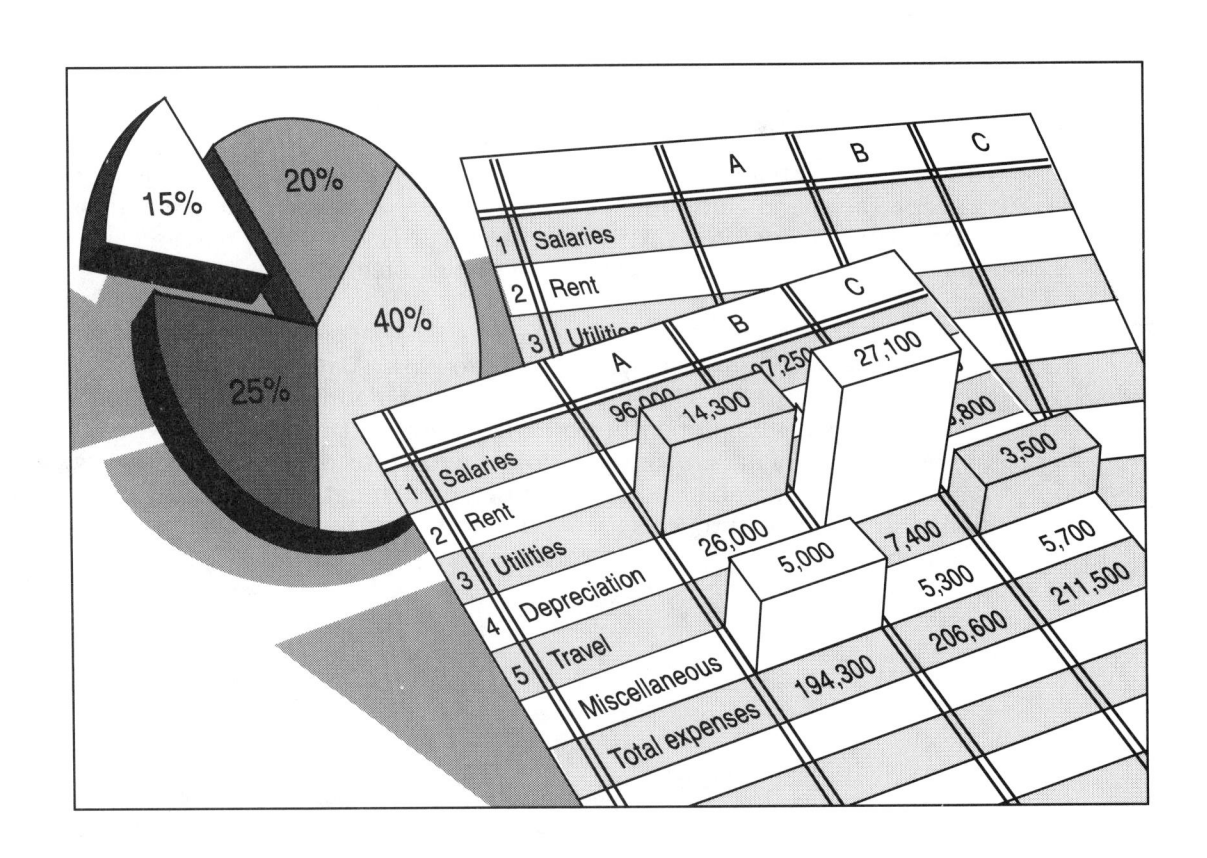

18 MANAGING YOUR FILES

This chapter covers various aspects of file management: saving and retrieving files, manipulating file lists, protecting your files from unauthorized access, using different directories, saving disk space, managing memory, and accessing the operating system from within Quattro Pro. It also covers the File Manager utility, which lets you perform disk housekeeping tasks such as copying and moving files from one directory to another, renaming or deleting files, and opening several files at once.

Using Different Directories

If you do not know how to create directories and move from one directory to another, refer to your DOS manual.

If you do not share your computer with other users and use Quattro Pro only occasionally, you will probably do fine storing all your notebooks in the Quattro Pro program directory. If you are highly organized, create dozens of notebooks a year, or share your computer with others, you will probably prefer to create additional subdirectories for your notebooks.

Loading Quattro Pro from Other Directories

When you install the program, Quattro Pro asks whether you want to include the Quattro Pro directory in your DOS search path. If you choose Yes, Quattro Pro creates or modifies a special program file, AUTOEXEC.BAT. This file is stored in the root directory of your hard disk, so the Quattro Pro program directory is included in your DOS search path every time you turn on or reboot your computer. (The DOS search path defines the set of directories in which DOS will look for any program files that it cannot find in the current directory.)

Once the Quattro Pro directory is included in your DOS search path, you can load Quattro Pro from any directory on your hard disk. You can create as many directories as you like for storing Quattro Pro notebooks and, when you are ready to work, switch to the appropriate directory and type **Q** to load the program.

If someone else installed Quattro Pro on your computer or you cannot remember whether you allowed the installation program to modify your AUTOEXEC.BAT file, type the **PATH** command at the DOS prompt. Then look for your Quattro Pro program directory—generally C:\QPRO or D:\QPRO—in the list of directories that appears. If the Quattro Pro directory is not listed in the path, refer to your DOS manual for instructions on modifying your AUTOEXEC.BAT file.

Changing the Default Directory

By default, Quattro Pro assumes that you want to store and search for notebook files in the directory from which you loaded the program (usually C:\QPRO). If you switch to the SALES directory, and then type **Q** to load Quattro Pro, your computer reads the Quattro Pro program files from the Quattro Pro directory but assumes that you want to work with notebooks in the SALES directory. Whenever you issue the / **F**ile | **R**etrieve or / **F**ile | **O**pen command or any of the save commands, Quattro Pro displays the prompt C:\SALES*.W?? followed by a list of files in that directory.

You can use the / **F**ile | **D**irectory command to designate a different default directory. This command is particularly useful when you want to work with several files that are located somewhere other than in your default data directory. For example, if your default directory is C:\QPRO, but you want to work with multiple files on a floppy disk in drive A, typing **A:** to designate the temporary directory can save you the trouble of pressing (Esc) and typing in **A:*.W*** every time you want to retrieve or save a notebook or view a list of notebook files.

To change the default directory more permanently, issue the / **O**ptions | **S**tartup | **D**irectory command. This command lets you specify a directory to use as the default directory every time you load Quattro Pro, regardless of which directory you are in when you load the program. If you later decide that you do not want a startup directory, issue the / **O**ptions | **S**tartup | **D**irectory command again, press (Esc) to erase the setting, and press (Enter). Then issue the / **O**ptions | **U**pdate command to save your change to disk.

Using Subdirectories

Whenever you issue the / **F**ile | **R**etrieve or / **F**ile | **O**pen command, Quattro Pro displays a list of files in the default directory. (These subdirectory names are always followed by a \ to distinguish them from file names.) At the bottom of this file list, it displays the names of any subdirectories of the current directory. You can display a list of all the files in one of those subdirectories by highlighting the subdirectory name and pressing (Enter).

If you tend to use files from several different directories in a single work session, you can use the following strategy to take advantage of this subdirectory listing at the bottom of file lists. First, create a data directory called QDATA for your Quattro Pro files. Do not make this a subdirectory of the Quattro Pro program directory (among other things, this can complicate upgrades); in addition, don't store any notebook files in this directory. Then make all your notebook directories into subdirectories of the QDATA directory. (You could have subdirectories such as QDATA\BUDGET, QDATA\P&L, and so forth.) Next change the QDATA directory into the default directory by using the / **O**ptions | **S**tartup | **D**irectory command (remember to use / **O**ptions | **U**pdate to make the setting permanent). Now whenever you retrieve a file or save a new one, Quattro Pro displays a file list consisting solely of the subdirectories. Select one of those subdirectories to display a list of the files in that group. Whenever you want to work with files in another subdirectory, just issue the / **F**ile | **R**etrieve command and select a different subdirectory from the list.

Manipulating File Lists

Whenever you issue a / File | Save, / File | Retrieve, or / File | Open command, or a /File | Save All command when you have unsaved notebooks open, Quattro Pro displays an alphabetical list of all the notebook files in the default data directory. There are several ways of manipulating these lists to display more detailed information, display more file names at once, and display more selective lists. You can use keyboard techniques for these tasks, or you can use the scroll bar and the six mouse buttons that appear on the right side of the file list.

Displaying More Informative File Lists

To return to the normal file list display, type − (minus) or click on the +/− mouse button again.

You can obtain more information about the files by typing + (plus) or by clicking on the +/− mouse button on the right side of the screen. Quattro Pro displays a more detailed file list, with each row containing a file name, the date and time the file was last modified, and the size of the file in bytes. If you press F3 (Choices) or click on the ↑/↓ mouse button, Quattro Pro expands the file list to show more files. If you are in a character-based display mode, the name, date, time, and size of the currently highlighted file appear just above the file list, as shown in Figure 18-1, where COLORS.WQ2 is highlighted.

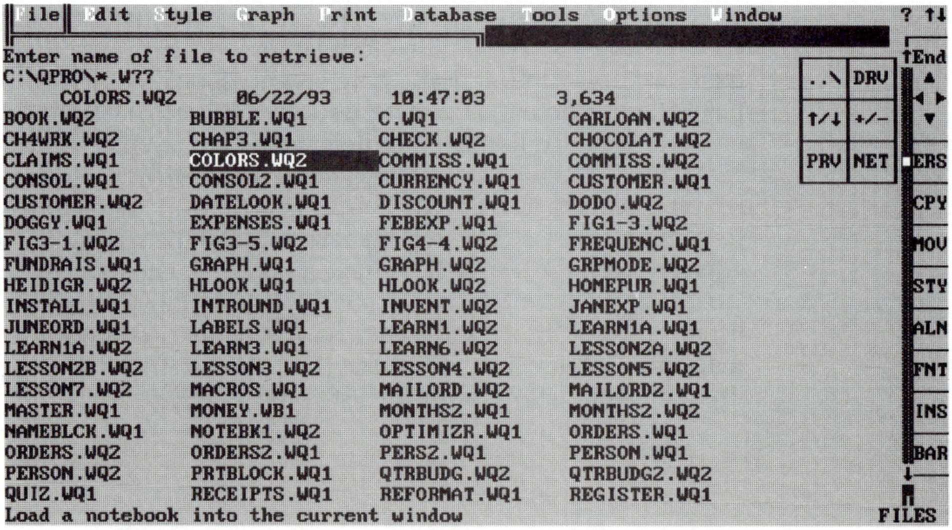

An expanded file list
Figure 18-1.

Managing Your Files

Searching Through File Lists

If you have a mouse, you can use the scroll bar at the right edge of the file list box to move through file lists. You can also search for files by letter using the [F2] (Edit) key. Whenever you press [F2] (Edit) while viewing a file list, Quattro Pro displays the prompt "Search for: *" at the bottom of the screen. As soon you type a letter, Quattro Pro highlights the first file name in the list with a name that matches the currently specified file name pattern. For example, if you type **B**, Quattro Pro highlights the first file name that starts with "B." You can type additional letters to continue honing in on the desired file name. For example, if you type **U** after typing **B**, Quattro Pro highlights the first file that begins with those two letters. You can delete a character from the sequence by pressing [Backspace].

Displaying More Specific File Lists

When you save files, the default file name pattern is *.WQ2 instead of *.W??.

By default, the file lists that appear when you use / **F**ile | **O**pen or / **F**ile | **R**etrieve include the names of all files in the default data directory that have a file name extension that begins with the letter "W." This is indicated by the file name pattern displayed immediately underneath the prompt requesting the name of the file to open or retrieve. If your default directory is the QPRO directory on drive C, the second line in the box reads C:\QPRO*.W??. The characters *.W?? indicate that the list includes files with any file name (indicated by the wild-card character *) and an extension that starts with "W" and is followed by any two other characters. This list includes regular Quattro Pro files (extension WQ1 or WQ2), Lotus 1-2-3 files (extension WK1, WK3, or WKS), and files created with Quattro 1.0, Quattro Pro's predecessor (extension WKQ).

If you press [Esc] twice by accident, you can press [Enter] to redisplay the current directory path plus the file name pattern *.W??.

As you accumulate notebooks, it can become quite tedious to hunt through a list of every notebook file in the current directory. Fortunately, you can enter a different file name pattern that specifies exactly which files you want to see. For example, if you want to see all the notebook files that begin with the letters "ABC," you can press [Esc] to erase the default file name pattern and then enter **ABC*.W??**. To see Quattro Pro notebook files that begin with the letters "BUDG," you enter **BUDG*.WQ2**. You can also use wild-cards to list files other than notebook files. For example, entering ***.DB** generates a list of all files in the default directory that have a DB extension. Quattro Pro also provides the PRV (Previous) mouse button, which displays a list of the most recently opened files.

You can also display lists of files that are stored in other directories by pressing [Esc] twice—once to erase the file name pattern and a second time to erase the directory path—and then entering the full path name of the directory followed by a file name pattern. For example, if you want to list all the notebook files in the SALES directory on drive C, you can enter either **C:\SALES*.W*** or **C:\SALES*.W??**. To list all the Quattro Pro notebook files on the root directory of the disk in drive B, you enter **B:*.WQ2**. To view the files on another drive you can also click on the DRV mouse button and select the desired drive. To display a list of notebook files in the parent directory (the directory one level above the current directory in the directory tree), you can press [Backspace] or click on the ..\ mouse button (rather than pressing [Esc] twice and entering the path and file name pattern). To display a list of notebook files in a subdirectory of the current directory, you can move to the bottom of the file list, highlight the name of the subdirectory, and press [Enter]. If you are working on network, you can click on the NET mouse button to display drive mappings (which letters are assigned to which drives).

Shortcuts for Retrieving Files

Be sure to leave a space between the Q and the name of the notebook file.

If you know which notebook you want to work with when you load Quattro Pro, you can specify the file name when you start the program. For example, if you know that you want to work with the LEARN1.WQ2 notebook, you can enter **Q LEARN1** at the DOS prompt rather than just **Q**. Once the program is loaded, Quattro Pro retrieves the file from the startup directory automatically. If you want to load a file with an extension other than WQ2, you must specify the file name extension. To load a file from a directory other than the default directory, include the path name with the file name.

If you continually work with the same notebook file or always begin your work sessions with the same notebook file, you can make it an *autoload file*—a file that is retrieved automatically every time you load Quattro Pro. The default file name for the autoload file is QUATTRO.WQ2. This means that if you ever assign the name QUATTRO to a notebook, Quattro Pro displays that notebook on screen at the beginning of every future work session. To change the name of the autoload file, issue the / **O**ptions | **S**tartup | **A**utoload File command, press [Esc] to erase the current setting, and enter the new file name. Remember to issue the / **O**ptions | **U**pdate command afterwards to make the change permanent.

Using Passwords

Occasionally you will construct notebooks containing sensitive or confidential information that you need to protect from unauthorized access. Quattro Pro allows you to assign passwords to your worksheets simply by typing a space followed by **P** after the file name when you save a file. As soon as you press [Enter], Quattro Pro prompts you for a password. The password can be up to 16 characters long and can include any characters you like.

Managing Your Files

Keep a record of your passwords; otherwise you won't be able to open the encrypted file.

As you enter the password, Quattro Pro displays square bullets on the screen in place of the characters you type, in case anyone is looking over your shoulder. If you make a mistake, use the [Backspace] key to erase characters or press [Esc] to erase the entire password and start again. Once you have entered the password, Quattro Pro asks you to verify the spelling by entering it a second time. If this second set of characters is not identical to the first set you entered, Quattro Pro displays an error message and lets you try again, starting with the entry of the file name.

Once you have assigned and verified a password, Quattro Pro encrypts the file so it cannot be retrieved or combined into another file without the password. Whenever you try to retrieve a file that has been encrypted, Quattro Pro prompts you for the password and displays square bullets as you type the password. If you enter the password incorrectly, Quattro Pro beeps and displays the error message "Invalid password." As soon as you press [Esc] or [Enter], Quattro Pro returns to Ready mode and you can try again.

If you decide that you no longer want to encrypt a file, issue the / **F**ile | **S**ave **A**s command. Quattro Pro displays [Password protected] after the file name in the dialog box. Press [Esc] or [Backspace] once to erase those characters. If you want to save the file under the same name, but without the password protection, just press [Enter]. If you want to change the file name, press [Esc] again to erase the file name and then enter or select a different name.

Managing Disk Space

As you create more and larger notebooks, you may run short of disk space. If you try to save a file that is larger than the amount of available space on your disk, Quattro Pro displays an error message. At this point, you have several choices. One option is to save the file on a different disk. If you are attempting to save the notebook onto a floppy, you can insert a new disk that has more free disk space and issue the save command again. If you are trying to save the notebook to your hard disk, you can save to a floppy disk instead. Then you can exit from Quattro Pro, delete some disk files to make more room, and copy the notebook file from the floppy disk to your hard disk.

Another option is to clear space on your disk without leaving Quattro Pro by deleting files through the File Manager or by issuing the / **F**ile | **U**tilities | **D**OS Shell command (discussed later in this chapter) and then erasing files with DOS commands. And finally, you can try compressing the file by using the SQZ! (squeeze) feature, which is explained in the next section.

As you accumulate more and more notebook files, you should perform periodic disk "housekeeping," not only to save disk space but to make it easier to find and keep track of your files. If you are using a hard disk, this

SQZ doesn't work on WQ2 files.

entails copying old notebook files to floppies and then erasing them from your hard disk. If you are using a floppy-based system, it means keeping only your current notebooks on your working data disk and periodically archiving the rest to other floppies, preferably grouping related notebooks on the same disks.

Compressing Files

Quattro Pro's SQZ! feature allows you to store files in a compressed form to save disk space. You can use this feature to squeeze a large notebook file onto a floppy disk. It can also save disk space if you frequently run out of room on your hard disk. In fact, if you do not mind the slower speed with which Quattro Pro saves and retrieves compressed files, you might want to use this option for all your files. You can direct Quattro Pro to use this compression feature simply by assigning one of the following special extensions to your file as you save it:

Use Extension	To Compress
WQ!	Quattro Pro notebook files
WKZ	Quattro 1.0 spreadsheet files
WK$	Lotus 1-2-3 WKS files
WK!	Lotus 1-2-3 WK1 and WK3 files

If you do decide to use the SQZ! feature all the time, you can assign one of these extensions as a default using the / **O**ptions | **S**tartup | **F**ile Extension command. (Remember to issue the / **O**ptions | **U**pdate command afterward.) A file saved with SQZ! occupies approximately one-third to one-half the space it would normally occupy on disk. As soon as you retrieve a file that has been compressed, Quattro Pro automatically expands it to its original form and size.

Even if you set Storage of Values to Remove, Quattro Pro recalculates formulas when you retrieve your file.

You can change the exact way in which Quattro Pro performs file compression using the / **F**ile | **U**tilities | **S**QZ! command. In the menu that appears when you issue this command, the Remove Blanks option specifies whether to store blank cells. If you change this setting from No to Yes, all numeric formatting codes in cells that are currently blank or that contain labels are deleted as the file is saved. The Storage of Values option lets you specify how formulas are saved. By default, Quattro Pro stores both formulas and their current results with a notebook. If you set Storage of Values to Remove, Quattro Pro erases the current results and saves only the formulas themselves. If you set it to Approximate, Quattro Pro saves the formula results with up to 7 digits of accuracy, rather than the usual 15 digits. If you leave the setting at Exact, Quattro Pro stores the exact formula results, with

Managing Your Files

all 15 digits of accuracy Quattro Pro uses in calculations. Lastly, the Version option specifies which version of SQZ! to use for file compression. Select SQZ! Plus for the latest and most efficient version. Use SQZ! if you want to share files with someone who is using Lotus 1-2-3 or Symphony.

If you choose an option that changes the data as the file is compressed, the resulting alteration in your data is permanent. You cannot get your formatting codes or extra eight digits of accuracy back after the fact. You are most likely to use these options when you are archiving files that you no longer intend to use or modify extensively in the future.

Managing Memory

When you work in Quattro Pro, all open notebooks must fit into the computer's memory at one time. As a result, both the size of your notebooks and the number of notebooks you can open at once are limited by the amount of memory installed in your computer. This limitation may become a concern as you enter substantial databases or build larger and more complex notebooks.

Determining How Much Memory Is Available

There are two ways to determine how much memory you have to work with at any point. The @MEMAVAIL function returns the number of bytes of "conventional" or "normal" memory (memory up to 640K) that are available. The @MEMEMSAVAIL function returns the number of bytes of expanded memory (EMS) available. You can also gauge the quantity of both types of memory at once by displaying the Options | Hardware menu, which lists the total and available amount of normal memory and EMS memory.

Running Out of Memory

If you run out of memory, Quattro Pro beeps and displays an error message. At this point, you can try any or all of the following to free up enough memory to continue your work:

- If you are using WYSIWYG, switch to a character-based display mode.
- If you have several open windows, try tiling them so that several unzoomed windows share the screen at once. If you are still short of memory, close some of the windows altogether.
- Unload any memory-resident programs that you have loaded.
- If you are using an 80x50 or 80x43 display mode, or one of the 132-column display modes, change back to 80x25.

◆ If you are trying to print in final-quality mode, try using non-Bitstream fonts. (Quattro Pro needs 125K of free memory to create Bitstream fonts.)

NOTE: Memory-resident software must be removed from RAM in reverse order to the way you loaded it. For example, if you loaded Sidekick and then Quattro Pro, you need to unload Quattro Pro and then Sidekick to reclaim memory. Do not try to unload memory-resident programs while temporarily exiting from Quattro Pro using the / **F**ile | **U**tilities | **DO**S Shell command; it almost certainly will crash the system.

Backing Up Files

All disks are fallible; if you have not already experienced a disk crash, you probably will at some point. You may also accidentally overwrite one of your files, irreversibly replacing the data previously stored under a particular file name.

By default, backup (BAK) files are stored in the same directory as your regular notebook files.

The only way to protect yourself from such mishaps is to regularly create backup copies of your data. There are several ways to do this. As you know, every time you save a file that has already been saved, Quattro Pro offers you the option of canceling the command, replacing the previous version of the file, or backing up the file. If you select the Backup option, Quattro Pro renames the older version with the BAK extension before saving the current notebook to disk with the WQ2 extension. If your WQ2 file is damaged—either due to hardware problems or user error—you can simply retrieve the BAK file with the / **F**ile | **R**etrieve command and save it with a WQ2 extension, overwriting the damaged version of the notebook.

While creating and storing a backup copy of a notebook in the same directory as the WQ2 file is useful when your notebook file is damaged, it does not protect you against damage to the disk itself. There are three strategies you can use to protect your notebook in the event of disk failure. First, you can store duplicate copies of your notebook on a different disk by issuing the / **F**ile | Save **A**s command, pressing Esc when the default directory is displayed, and entering the full path name before the file name. If you choose this method, you should save the notebook twice every time you make modifications—once on the default directory disk and the second time on a backup disk.

See your DOS manual for details on using these commands.

Alternatively, you can use the DOS COPY, XCOPY, BACKUP, or MSBACKUP (if you're using DOS 6) commands to copy some or all of your notebook files to other disks at the end of every work session. (Stick with COPY unless you are backing up a very large number of files.) If you tend to change several

Managing Your Files

notebooks in a single work session, using DOS commands with wild-card characters can save you time by allowing you to back up several files with a single command.

The third alternative for creating backup copies of your files is using Quattro Pro's File Manager utility, which is discussed in a moment.

Exiting to the Operating System

The / **F**ile | **U**tilities | **D**OS Shell command lets you either issue a single DOS command or temporarily exit to the operating system without unloading either Quattro Pro or your current notebook from memory. This enables you to execute DOS commands and then get back into Quattro Pro without reloading the program or retrieving your current file. You will find this useful, for example, when you are ready to back up your work and discover that you do not have any formatted disks. (If you have only 512K of memory or are using memory-resident programs, you may not be able to use the / **F**ile | **U**tilities | **D**OS Shell command.)

When you issue the / **F**ile | **U**tilities | **D**OS Shell command, Quattro Pro displays a dialog box with the message "Enter DOS Command, Press Enter for full DOS Shell." To issue a single DOS command, simply type the command just as you would at the DOS prompt and press [Enter]. Quattro Pro will momentarily turn control over to DOS while it executes the command and will then return you to Ready mode.

If you forget that you have only temporarily exited Quattro Pro and try to reload the program by typing Q, you'll see an error message.

If you want to issue more than one DOS command, press [Enter] as soon as Quattro Pro displays the dialog box. The notebook display will disappear and you will see the message "Type Exit to return to Quattro," followed by the operating system sign-on message and the same DOS prompt that you saw before you loaded Quattro Pro. You can then perform any DOS operation, even loading another program if it fits into system memory. When you are ready to return to Quattro Pro, you simply type **EXIT**. Your notebook immediately reappears on the screen in the same form it was in when you left it.

The File Manager Utility

Quattro Pro's File Manager utility allows you to perform disk housekeeping tasks—such as copying or moving files from one directory to another, renaming or deleting files, and opening several files at once. Using this utility, you can also display file lists by name, date, size, or extension, determine how much space a given set of files occupies, and display a graphic image of the directory structure of a disk.

To use the File Manager utility, you issue the / **F**ile | **U**tilities | **F**ile Manager command. Quattro Pro displays a File Manager window, as shown in Figure 18-2. The File Manager window initially contains two sections, or panes. Although there is no dividing line between these sections, Quattro Pro treats them as distinct areas. Only one pane is active at any time. The upper pane, known as the *control pane,* contains four prompts that let you specify a different disk drive and directory, a filter (file name pattern) that determines which files appear in the window, and the name of a file that you want to open. The *file list pane,* which appears directly below the control pane, contains a list of all the files in the specified directory that match the specified filter, followed by a list of any subdirectories of the specified directory. You can use the / **T**ree | **O**pen command to activate a third pane called the *tree pane,* which shows a graphic representation of the directory structure on the specified disk drive.

The active File Manager pane is the one that contains the highlight. This highlight appears as a small bright rectangle within the control pane, as a bar highlighting a whole row within the file list pane, or a bar highlighting a directory name within the tree pane.

You must activate a pane before you can use it. You can do this by pressing F6 (Pane) or Tab to activate the next pane in the window. You can use the ↑ and ↓ keys to move between the control pane and the file list pane. You can also activate the control pane and move the highlight directly to the File

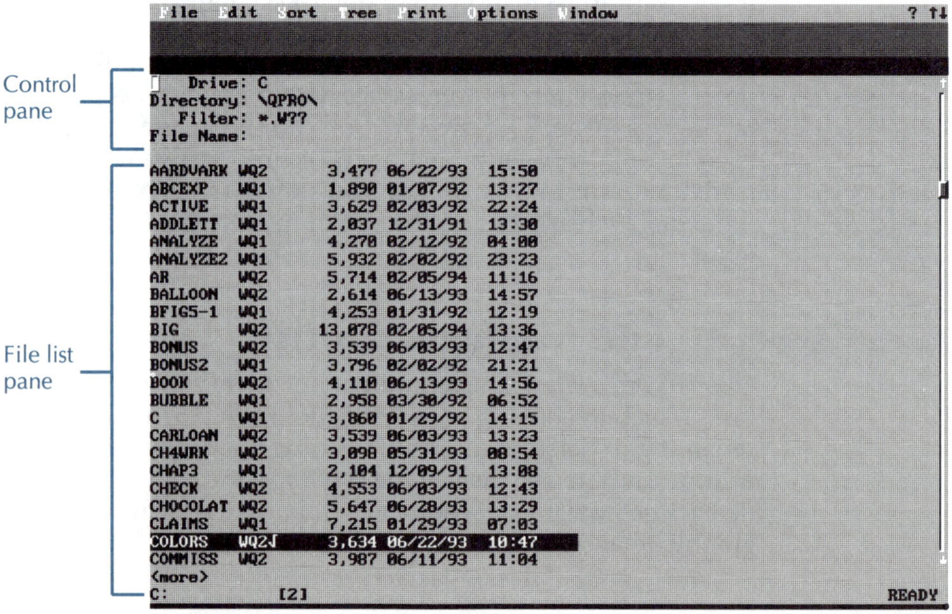

The File Manager window
Figure 18-2.

Name prompt by pressing (Shift)-(Tab). Finally, you can activate different panes by clicking with the mouse. To close an active File Manager window, issue the / **F**ile I **C**lose command.

The Control Pane

The control pane consists of four prompts: Drive, Directory, Filter, and File Name. The first three let you control which files appear in the file list. The File Name prompt allows you to retrieve a particular file.

To change any of the prompts, use the arrow keys or your mouse to move to the prompt setting, and press (Esc) to erase the whole setting or (Backspace) to erase one character at a time. You can also use any of the usual editing keys to change the entry.

Switching Drives or Directories

To display a list of files on a different disk, move the highlight to the Drive prompt and enter the desired drive letter. To display files from a different directory, press (Esc) to erase the current entry (or use the (Backspace) key to erase one character at a time) and then enter a new directory. Be sure that you include the \ (backslash) before each directory name. (Note that if you change the default directory with / **O**ptions I **S**tartup I **D**irectory, the contents of this directory will show up automatically when you get into the File Manager.)

Selecting Files to Display

The Filter prompt lets you enter a file name pattern to limit the files within the specified drive and directory that are included in the file list. By default, the file name pattern is *.W??, which displays all files in the specified directory that have an extension starting with "W." To see all the files in a directory, change the filter to *.*. You can express negative filters by enclosing a file name pattern in square brackets. A filter of [*.WQ2] displays a list of all files except those with the WQ2 extension, for example.

To create more complex filters, combine two or more file name patterns in a single filter expression. For example, the filter *.WQ2,[ABC*.WQ2] displays a list of all files with the WQ2 extension except those that start with "ABC."

The file filter remains in effect until you explicitly change it, even if you switch drives or directories. This makes it easy for you to look for the same types of files in different places. Quattro Pro also carries the file filter over from one File Manager window to the next, even if you open your next File Manager window in another work session.

Opening a File

The control pane's File Name prompt lets you select a notebook file to open. If the file you want to open has the default file extension, you do not need to type it when you enter the file name. If you enter the name of a file other than a notebook file or a database file in one of the formats that Quattro Pro knows how to read, Quattro Pro displays an error message. After you enter the file name, Quattro Pro opens a new window and retrieves the specified file.

If you specify a file that does not exist within the current directory, Quattro Pro assumes that you want to create a new file. It therefore opens a new notebook window with a blank notebook and assigns it the specified file name.

Searching for a File

For this technique to work, the Filter setting must match that of the file you're searching for.

You can also use the File Name prompt in combination with the [F5] (GoTo) key to search for a file anywhere on the specified disk drive. This technique is extremely useful when you can remember what you called the file but not where you put it. To search a drive for a file, type the name of the file at the File Name prompt and press [F5]. Quattro Pro searches through every directory on the currently specified drive. If Quattro Pro cannot find a file with the specified name, it displays an error message. Otherwise, it changes the Directory prompt to match the directory in which the file was found, adjusts the file list accordingly, and places a check mark next to the file name in the file list pane. If you want to open the file, just press [Enter]. If the current drive includes other files with the specified name, you can press [F5] again to move to the next one.

The File List Pane

The status line only appears on screen when you reach the bottom of the file list.

The file list pane contains a list of all the files that match the drive, directory, and filter specified in the control pane. At the bottom of the file list, Quattro Pro displays a status line with information about the number of files in the current list, the total number of files in the current directory, the number of bytes used, and the number of bytes still available on the specified drive. The status line in Figure 18-3 indicates that 117 files meet the filter condition *.W?? out of a total of 255 files in the \QPRO directory, that these 117 files occupy 865,533 bytes of disk space, and that there are 138,936,320 bytes still free on drive C.

As you move through the file list pane, Quattro Pro displays a check mark to the right of the file name extensions to indicate your current position within the file list. When you activate other panes by pressing [F6], the check mark

Managing Your Files

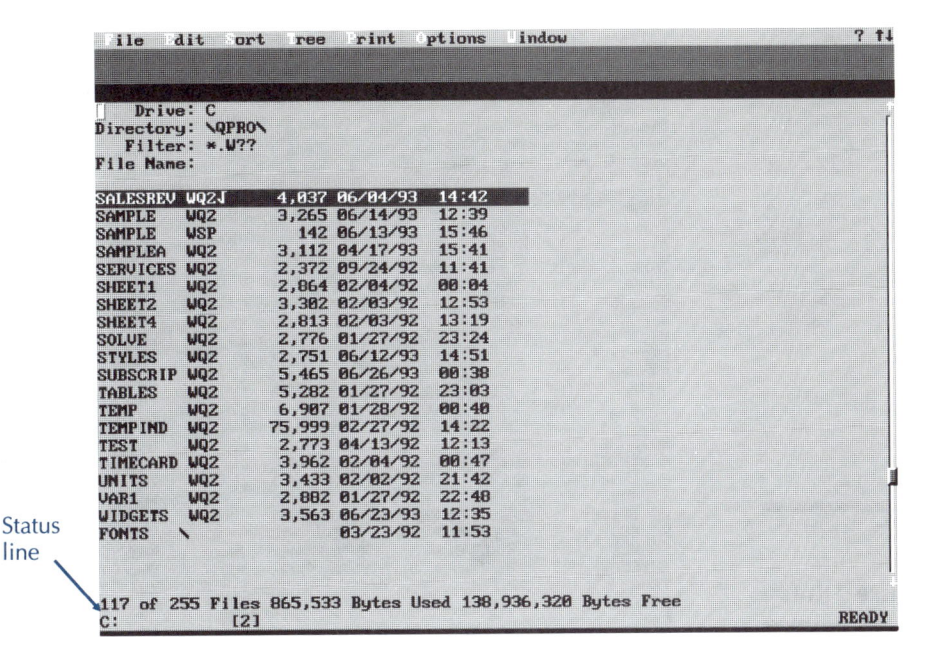

```
 ile   dit   ort   ree   rint   ptions   indow                    ? ↑↓

    Drive: C
Directory: \QPRO\
   Filter: *.W??
File Name:

SALESREV WQ2J       4,037 06/04/93  14:42
SAMPLE   WQ2        3,265 06/14/93  12:39
SAMPLE   WSP          142 06/13/93  15:46
SAMPLE   WQ2        3,112 04/17/93  15:41
SAMPLEA  WQ2        2,372 09/24/92  11:41
SERVICES WQ2        2,864 02/04/92  00:04
SHEET1   WQ2        3,302 02/03/92  12:53
SHEET2   WQ2        2,813 02/03/92  13:19
SHEET4   WQ2        2,776 01/27/92  23:24
SOLVE    WQ2        2,751 06/12/93  14:51
STYLES   WQ2        5,465 06/26/93  00:38
SUBSCRIP WQ2        5,282 01/27/92  23:03
TABLES   WQ2        6,907 01/28/92  00:40
TEMP     WQ2       75,999 02/27/92  14:22
TEMPIND  WQ2        2,773 04/13/92  12:13
TEST     WQ2        3,962 02/04/92  00:47
TIMECARD WQ2        3,433 02/02/92  21:42
UNITS    WQ2        2,882 01/27/92  22:48
VAR1     WQ2        3,563 06/23/93  12:35
WIDGETS  WQ2              03/23/92  11:53
FONTS    \

117 of 255 Files 865,533 Bytes Used 138,936,320 Bytes Free
C:        [2]                                                    READY
```

Figure 18-3.
The File Manager status line — Status line

remains in the file list pane and serves as a kind of placeholder indicating which file name will be highlighted when you reactivate that pane.

By default, the file list consists of five columns of information: the file's name, the extension, the size of the file in bytes, and the date and time the file was last altered. This type of file list display is known as the Full View. If you prefer, you can change to a Wide View which lists only the file names (including extensions), displaying as many columns of names as fit within the pane. Figure 18-4 shows a file list in Wide View. To change from one of these views to the other, issue the / **O**ptions | **F**ile List command and select either Full View or Wide View.

At the top of every file list, Quattro Pro displays two dots to represent the parent directory—the directory that is one level above the current directory in the directory structure. You can select this symbol to switch to the parent directory. For example, if the current directory is \QPRO\SALES, selecting .. changes the directory prompt to \QPRO and displays a list of all files in that directory that meet the specified filter, followed by a list of that directory's subdirectories. To switch to a subdirectory of the current directory, select one of the subdirectory names at the bottom of the file list. When you select a different directory from the file list pane, Quattro Pro automatically changes the Directory prompt in the control pane and reconstructs the file list to display all files in the new directory that meet the current filter.

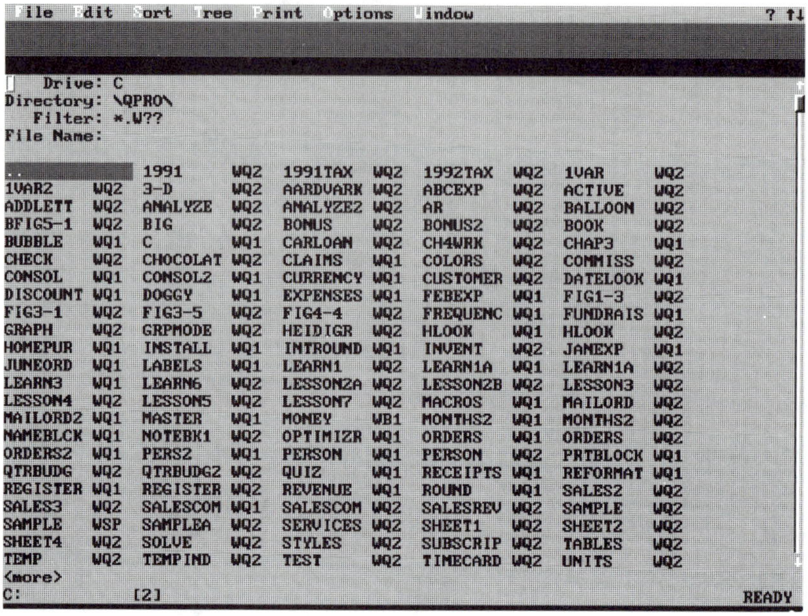

A file list in Wide View
Figure 18-4.

Several of the function keys and cursor-movement keys have special meanings within the file list pane. Table 18-1 lists all the special keys that you can use in this environment and notes which of them can be used in the control pane and tree pane as well.

Sorting File Lists

By default, Quattro Pro lists the names of files and subdirectories in alphabetical order. To change this order, issue the / **S**ort command and choose one of the following options:

- **Name**, the default setting, arranges files and subdirectories alphabetically by name.
- **Timestamp** arranges files and subdirectories according to the date and time they were last modified.
- **Extension** sorts the file list alphabetically, first by extension and then by the files' first names.
- **Size** sorts files and subdirectories by file size, from smallest to largest.
- **DOS Order** arranges files and subdirectories in the same order that the DOS command DIR would list them.

Managing Your Files

Key	Action
`F2` (Rename) *	Lets you rename the highlighted file (same as / **E**dit | **R**ename).
`Shift`-`F7` (Select) or +	Selects the highlighted file so that you can open, move, copy, or delete it. If the file is already selected, these keys unselect it.
`Alt`-`F7` (All Select)	Selects all files in the file list in preparation for moving, copying, or deleting. If any files on the list are selected, `Alt`-`F7` unselects them.
`Shift`-`F8` (Move)	Moves the selected files into the paste buffer (so that you can move them to another directory), removing them from the current file list.
`Del` *	Deletes the selected file from the disk.
`F9` (Calc) **	Reads the disk and redisplays the file list (same as / **F**ile | **R**ead Dir).
`Shift`-`F9` (Copy)	Copies the selected files into the paste buffer (so that you can paste them into another directory) while leaving them on the current list.
`Shift`-`F10` (Paste)	Inserts the file names in the paste buffer into the current file list, and moves or copies the named files into the current directory.
`Esc` **	Unselects any selected files in the file list, activates the control pane, and moves the cursor to the File Name prompt.
`Enter`	Opens the selected files. If either the .. (parent directory) item or a subdirectory name is highlighted, moves to that directory.
`Home`	Moves the highlight to the .. (parent directory) item at the top of the file list.
`End`	Moves the highlight to the end of the file list.
`Pg Up`	Moves the file list display up one screen.
`Pg Dn`	Moves the file list display down one screen.

* Works in the control pane and the file list pane
** Works in the tree pane and the file list pane

Special Keys for Use in the File List Pane
Table 18-1.

Manipulating Files

The main purpose of the File Manager is to let you move, copy, rename, and delete files on your disk without accessing DOS. If you want to manipulate a single file, you can simply highlight that file's name on the file list and then initiate the desired operation. To open, move, copy, or delete several files at once, however, you must first select all the files that you want to manipulate.

Using the File Manager can be more efficient than managing files in DOS because you can hand pick files to manipulate. In DOS, the only groups of files that you can manipulate are those that you can specify by entering a file name pattern using DOS wild-card characters. In contrast, the File Manager lets you define a filter to narrow your file list so you can hone in on the files that you want to manage. Then it lets you pick exactly those files that you want from the resulting list. Once you have selected all the files that you want to work with, you press the appropriate key or issue the appropriate command to open, move, copy, replicate, rename, or delete them as a group.

Selecting Files

You can select and unselect files with a mouse by clicking on their file names.

To select files one at a time, highlight the file name and either press [Shift]-[F7] (Select), type + (plus), or issue the / **E**dit | **S**elect File command. Quattro Pro highlights that file name and keeps it highlighted even as you move to other file names to repeat the same procedure. To unselect a file, just highlight it and again press [Shift]-[F7], type +, or issue the / **E**dit | **S**elect File command.

To select all the files in the current file list, press [Alt]-[F7] (All Select). If you can define an appropriate file name pattern—one that defines all the files that you want to manipulate—you can use the Filter prompt to display those files and then press [Alt]-[F7] to select them all at once. If you press [Alt]-[F7] when any of the files in the current list are selected, Quattro Pro unselects all the files on the list. You can also unselect all files by pressing the [Esc] key.

Opening Files

To open a single file, highlight its name on the file list and press [Enter], or double-click on the file name with the mouse. You can open several files at once—each in its own window—by selecting the files on the file list and then pressing [Enter] or double-clicking. Quattro Pro asks you to confirm that you want to open those "documents." Keep in mind that you can also open a single file by entering its name at the File Name prompt in the control panel. This technique is particularly useful if you want to open a file that is not included in the current file list.

Managing Your Files

Copying Files

There are four steps involved in copying files to a different directory:

1. Highlight the files that you want to copy.
2. Press [Shift]-[F9] (Copy) or issue the / **E**dit | **C**opy command. Quattro Pro displays the selected file names in a different color or intensity and stores those names in a section of memory known as a *paste buffer*.
3. Switch to the directory to which you want to copy the files by either choosing a subdirectory from the bottom of the file list, choosing the .. (parent directory) option at the top of the file list, activating the control pane and then entering a new directory name next to the Directory prompt, or moving to a different File Manager window.
4. Press [Shift]-[F10] (Paste) or issue the / **E**dit | **P**aste command to paste the file names from the buffer to the current directory. Quattro Pro inserts the selected file names into the current file list, positioning them according to the current sort order, and copies the files themselves into the specified directory. If the files that you copied do not match the filter in the new directory, Quattro Pro automatically changes the filter to accommodate the new files.

When you copy several files at once, Quattro Pro considers the currently highlighted file to be selected, even if you have not explicitly selected it with [Shift]-[F7], +, or / **E**dit | **S**elect File.

CAUTION: As in DOS, when you copy a file to a directory that already contains a file of that name, Quattro Pro overwrites the existing file without issuing any warnings. This is also a potential problem when you move files from one directory to another.

Copying a Group of Files to Multiple Disks

Quattro Pro includes an undocumented feature that allows you to copy or move a large group of files to two or more floppy disks with a single paste command. Start by copying or moving the files from the original directory. Then switch to the floppy disk drive and issue the / **E**dit | **P**aste command or press [Shift]-[F10]. As soon as the disk you are pasting to is full, Quattro Pro displays the name of the first file that did not fit, followed by the message "Disk full." It also presents you with three options: Stop Copying, Try again with another disk, and Ignore this file. You can then insert a new disk and choose the Try again with another disk option to copy the remaining files in the paste buffer onto a second disk.

Moving Files

The process of moving one or more files to a different directory is very similar to copying them. Once you have highlighted the files that you want to move, you press [Shift]-[F8] (Move) or issue the / Edit | Move command, copying the selected files to the paste buffer. Then you move to the directory to which you want to transfer the files by choosing .. or a subdirectory, or by moving to a different File Manager window. Finally, you press [Shift]-[F10] (Paste) or issue the / Edit | Paste command. Quattro Pro inserts the specified files in the current file list, copies them to the current directory, and then removes them from the original directory.

Deleting Files

To delete files, just highlight their names and either press [Del] or issue the / Edit | Erase command. When Quattro Pro asks if you are sure you want to "delete the marked files," type **Y** for Yes (or **N** for No if you decide you want to cancel the operation). Once you have deleted all the files in a directory, you can also delete the directory itself by highlighting its name at the bottom of the parent directory's file list and pressing [Del] or issuing the / Edit | Erase command.

Duplicating Files

If several files are selected when you issue the Duplicate command, Quattro Pro ignores all but the file marked with a check.

You can use the / Edit | Duplicate command to create a new copy of a file under a different name. This is the only way you can replicate a file within the same directory (since you cannot have two files in a directory with the same name). To duplicate a file, start by highlighting the file name on the file list. Then issue the / Edit | Duplicate command. When Quattro Pro prompts you for a file name, enter the name of the file. You must include the extension, even if you want to assign the default extension to the file. (If you omit the extension, the new file will have no extension at all.) If you want to store the duplicate in a different directory, include the directory path with the file name. If the name that you assigned to this duplicate file matches the current filter, Quattro Pro adds the file to the file list.

Renaming Files

You can change the name of the current file by issuing the / Edit | Rename command ([F2]). When Quattro Pro prompts you for a file name, enter the name of the file, including the extension. Quattro Pro removes the old name from the file list and, assuming the new name matches the current filter, displays the new one.

Managing Your Files

CAUTION: Never change the file name extension when you rename a notebook file, since the extension is what lets Quattro Pro determine how to interpret the contents of a file. If you want to change a Lotus 1-2-3 file to a Quattro Pro file, as an example, use the / File | Save As command, which directs Quattro Pro to actually translate the file contents into the format specified by the extension. Then you can use the File Manager to delete the old file from the disk.

Displaying and Using Directory Trees

A *directory tree* is a graphic representation of the entire directory structure of a disk, as shown in Figure 18-5. A directory tree pane provides two distinct advantages: It gives you a clear picture of how your disk is organized, and it makes it easy to switch back and forth among several different directories.

To display a directory tree, issue the / Tree | Open command. Quattro Pro opens a third pane, known as the tree pane, either below or to the right of the file list pane. If the File Manager window fills the entire screen, the tree pane appears to the right of the file list, as shown in Figure 18-5. Otherwise, the tree appears below the file list pane. If you have many different directories on the currently selected disk, it may take a few moments for Quattro Pro to construct the directory tree.

File Manager window with a directory tree
Figure 18-5.

The root directory is represented on the directory tree by the drive letter at the top of the tree. Below and slightly to the right of the drive letter, you can see the first level of directories. If those directories have any subdirectories, they appear below and slightly to the right of their parent directory's name.

> You can't use the scroll bar to move through the directory tree.

Use the ← and → keys to move from one level of the directory structure to another. Use the ↑ and ↓ keys to move up and down within the same directory level. (The control pane's Directory prompt can be a quicker way to move to a directory that is far from the current directory on the tree.) As you move the highlight bar through the directory tree, the Directory setting in the control pane changes to display the name of the highlighted directory, and the file list displays all files in that directory that match the current Filter setting. If your directories contain many files, your progress from one directory to another can be somewhat sluggish.

Resizing the Directory Tree

When you first display a directory tree, Quattro Pro divides the File Manager window fairly equally between the tree pane and the other two panes in the window—the control pane and file list pane. You can allocate the space differently by issuing the / **T**ree | **R**esize command and, at the Relative Tree size prompt, entering a number between 10 and 100. (The default setting is 50%.) If you change this setting to 100%, Quattro Pro devotes as much room to the tree pane as it can while still displaying the control pane and a small portion of the file list pane.

> Quattro Pro remembers changes to the size of the directory tree. The next time you open a tree pane, it is the size you last specified.

You might want to enlarge the tree pane if your directory structure contains many levels of subdirectories or if the tree is displayed below the file list pane. You might shrink the tree pane to display more file names if you are using the Wide View. To remove the tree pane from the screen, issue the / **T**ree | **C**lose command. Quattro Pro erases the directory tree and may expand the control pane and file list pane to fill its space.

Other File Manager Options

Most of the remaining options on the File Manager menus are replicates of options on the regular Quattro Pro menu tree. The few other options that are unique to the File Manager or that operate slightly differently in this context are described in the following sections.

Rereading the File List

The / **F**ile | **R**ead Dir command directs Quattro Pro to reconstruct the current file list by rereading the files on the specified drive. If you are displaying a list of files on a disk in drive A or B, you should use this command whenever

Managing Your Files

you place a new disk in that disk drive. You should also issue the / **F**ile | **R**ead Dir command when you are using a local area network and suspect that someone else may have just added files to the specified directory. The [F9] (Calc) key performs exactly the same function as the / **F**ile | **R**ead Dir command: It "recalculates" the current file list.

Making Directories

The / **F**ile | **M**ake Dir command lets you create new directories on a disk. When you issue this command, Quattro Pro prompts you for a directory name. Enter a name of up to eight characters. Quattro Pro assumes that you want the new directory to be located immediately under the currently selected directory. If you want it placed elsewhere, specify the full directory path when you enter the file name.

Printing the Contents of a File Manager Window

You can use the File Manager's Print menu to print the information in different File Manager panes. This menu is similar to the regular Print menu, except that the Block option leads to a submenu with the options Files, Tree, or Both. Files, the default option, prints the current file list, Tree prints the directory tree, and Both prints the file list followed by the directory tree.

As you work with Quattro Pro, you will create more and larger notebooks, and your ability to manage, protect, and access them will become increasingly important. In addition, as you accumulate long lists of files, it becomes more essential that you know how to perform basic disk housekeeping chores such as moving, copying, renaming, and deleting files. You can accomplish all of these tasks through Quattro Pro's File Manager utility. Learning how to manage your files is essential to working with Quattro Pro effectively.

CHAPTER

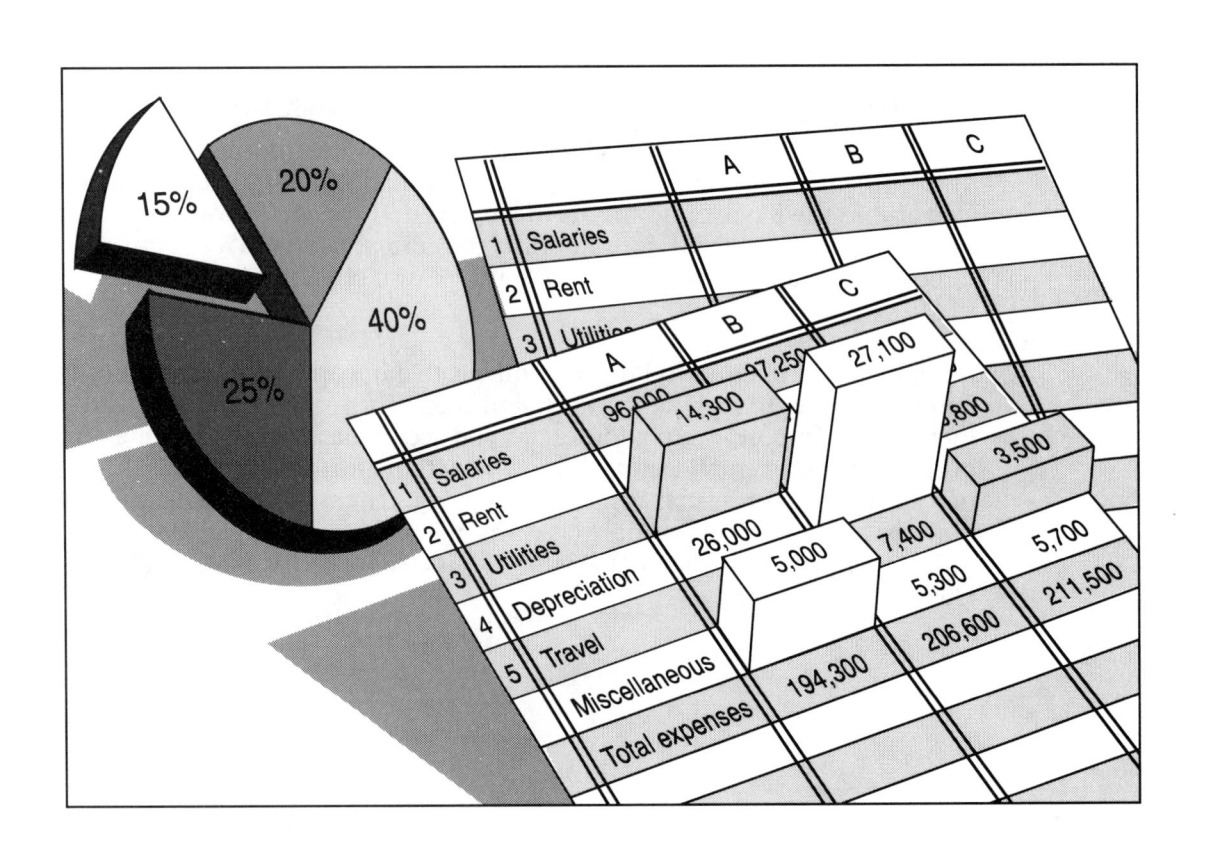

19

COMBINING, EXTRACTING, AND LINKING FILES

This chapter covers several tools for working with multiple notebook files: extracting a section of an existing notebook to create a new notebook file, combining data from two notebooks, and linking notebooks by creating formulas that refer to cells in another file.

In Chapter 12 you learned a number of techniques for working with discrete sets of data on multiple notebook pages within a single notebook. In certain cases, however, your data may be too cumbersome to be contained within a single notebook. Or, for other practical reasons—such as different people working on different aspects of a problem—you may need to work with multiple files. In these cases, you can use the techniques outlined in this chapter.

Extracting Files

The / **T**ools | **X**tract command lets you copy a block of data from your current notebook to a new file, creating a notebook that consists solely of the extracted block. When you first issue the / **T**ools | **X**tract command, Quattro Pro displays a menu containing options for Formulas and Values. If you use the Formulas option, all values contained in the extracted block are transferred "as is" to the new notebook. If you use the Values option, any formulas contained in the extracted block are converted to their end values when they are copied to the new notebook file.

TIP: You should make sure to extract all cells referenced by extracted formulas so you don't generate ERR values or unwanted adjustments in cell references.

Once you choose between the Formulas and Values options, Quattro Pro requests a name for the new notebook file and displays a list of all the notebook files currently in the default data directory. (Don't enter the name of an existing file, unless you want to overwrite that file.) When you enter a file name, Quattro Pro prompts you for a block of values to extract. As soon as you supply a block name or set of block coordinates, Quattro Pro extracts the block. All global formats, page names, and all formatting codes within the extracted block are copied from the original notebook to the new extracted file.

Copying or Moving Versus Extracting Data

When you copy as opposed to extracting data, you lose default formatting.

Copying data from one notebook window to another (as discussed in Chapter 11) and extracting data to a new file with / **T**ools | **X**tract produce similar results. Each method has its advantages. Copying data between windows allows you to see exactly what you are doing. You can use it to move data into an existing file, whereas extracting data always creates a new file. However, you can only copy data from one notebook to another if you have enough memory to load the two files at once. In addition, if you simply want to extract a section of a notebook to use later, the / **T**ools |

Combining, Extracting, and Linking Files

Xtract command is more efficient: Rather than opening a new notebook file, copying data from one file to the other, and then saving the new file, you can perform the entire operation with a single command. The / **Tools** | **Xtract** command also copies default formats as well as any formatting codes in a specific block of cells that you specify. This can save you the trouble of redefining column widths and specifying default numeric formats. In contrast, when you copy data from one notebook to another, only those formats that apply to the particular cells that you copy are transferred to the destination file. Default formats and column widths are left unchanged.

Combining Files

*You can use [Alt]-[F5] to undo / **Tools** | **Combine** commands if you act quickly.*

The / **Tools** | **Combine** commands allow you to combine data from separate notebook files. There are three options available for combining files. The Copy option copies all or part of another notebook file, as is, into the current notebook, overwriting the block of cells into which it is copied. The Add option adds the values in all or part of another notebook file to values in the current notebook. The Subtract option subtracts values in all or part of another notebook file from values in the current notebook.

Regardless of which option you choose, combining files involves the following steps:

1. Save your current notebook. The / **Tools** | **Combine** commands have a dramatic effect on the notebook and are easy to bungle.
2. Move the cell pointer to the cell you want to be the upper-left corner of the incoming block or notebook.
3. Issue the appropriate / **Tools** | **Combine** command.
4. Choose either the File or Block option from the displayed submenu. The File option allows you to combine an entire notebook file with the current notebook. The Block option allows you to combine a block of cells in another notebook with the current notebook.

It is good practice to name blocks that you want to import.

5. If you choose the Block option, specify a set of block coordinates or a block name. Because you have no way of viewing the incoming notebook or of generating a list of available block names on the second notebook, you need to know the name or coordinates of the block you want to import before issuing the / **Tools** | **Combine** command.
6. Supply the name of the file to be combined with the current notebook. If you want to use a file from another directory, press [Esc] twice, type in the name of the drive and directory, and press [Enter] to display a new file list. To designate a file, either type its name or select it from the file list.

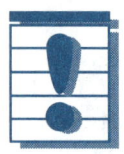

TIP: When you issue any of the / **T**ools| **C**ombine commands, Quattro Pro reads the incoming data from disk. This means that if the source notebook is open in another window, you must save any changes you have made to that file to disk before you issue the / **T**ools |**C**ombine command to ensure that Quattro Pro uses your current data.

The / Tools | Combine | Copy Command

The / **T**ools | **C**ombine | **C**opy command copies all or part of another notebook file into your current notebook. You can use this strategy for operations such as copying a lookup table or a set of column headings from another file. When you issue this command, Quattro Pro acts as if you had specified the current location of the cell pointer as the destination for a copy command. It copies the upper-left corner of the incoming data in the current cell and the rest of the data below and/or to the right of that cell. The incoming data occupies as much room as necessary, overwriting any data in its way, and assumes the column widths of the cells into which it is copied.

Quattro Pro ignores blank cells in the source file when combining files; therefore, cells on the current notebook may be overwritten with values or labels, but are never replaced with blank cells.

The / Tools | Combine | Add Command

The / **T**ools | **C**ombine | **A**dd command allows you to add values from the source notebook to values in the current notebook. Labels in the source notebook are ignored in this process; only numeric values are imported. The / **T**ools | **C**ombine | **A**dd command is extremely useful for combining figures for different corporate divisions or different financial periods to create consolidated or year-to-date financial statements.

When you add data from the source notebook, you must be particularly careful to position the cell pointer correctly before you issue the command, especially in cases where the two notebooks have different layouts. You also must be sure that the structure of the incoming block or file is identical to the section of the current notebook so like values are added to like values. If you are off by a single cell, the result can be two different line items added together incorrectly.

Values are added according to the following rules: Values in the current notebook are replaced by the sum of the original and the incoming values, except in the case of formulas; formulas in the current notebook always remain unaltered. Quattro Pro converts all incoming formulas to their results and interprets all labels as zero as it adds the values together. Any cells in the current notebook that contain labels, ERR, or NA values are not changed by the incoming data.

The / Tools | Combine | Subtract Command

The / Tools | Combine | Subtract command allows you to subtract source notebook values from current notebook values. It functions according to the same rules as / Tools | Combine | Add, except that the incoming values are subtracted from values on the current notebook rather than added to them. This command is often used to break down a notebook in which values have been previously combined with the / Tools | Combine | Add command.

Hands-On Practice

Try the various / Tools | Combine commands by creating and then merging two monthly expense statements. Start by creating an expense statement template that contains the labels and formulas used in both the two monthly notebooks and the consolidated notebook.

1. If you have anything other than a blank screen, save your work and erase the screen by issuing the / File | Erase command.
2. Change the width of column A to 17 characters.
3. Enter the following data in column A: In A1 enter **MONTHLY EXPENSE REPORT -** . In A3 enter **Meals**. In A4 enter **Entertainment**. In A5 enter **^SUBTOTAL**. In A7 enter **Hotel or Motel**. In A8 enter **Transportation**. In A9 enter **Car Rental**. In A10 enter **Car Expenses**. In A11 enter **Parking & Tolls**. In A12 enter **Miles * .22**. In A13 enter **Other**. In A14 enter **^SUBTOTAL**. In A16 enter **TOTAL**. And finally, in A18 enter **TOTAL DEDUCTIBLE**.
4. Enter the following data in column B: In B5 enter **@SUM(B3..B4)**. In B14 enter **@SUM(B7..B13)**. In B16 enter **+B5+B14**, and in B18 enter **(B5*.8)+B14**.
5. Issue the / Options | Formats | Numeric Format | Fixed command, and press [Enter] to specify two decimal places. Select Quit twice to return to Ready mode.
6. Underline the notebook title by issuing the / Style | Line Drawing command, specify a block of A1..C1, a placement of Bottom, and a line type of Single. Select Quit to return to Ready mode.
7. Create a named block for the section of the notebook that will contain the expense figures by issuing the / Edit | Names | Create command, entering the block name **EXPENSES**, and specifying coordinates of B3..B18.

8. Save this notebook skeleton under the name **EXPTEMP** (for Expense Template).

Now create a January expense report notebook.

1. Enter **JANUARY** in C1, **400** in B3, **75** in B4, **800** in B7, **300** in B8, **200** in B9, **50** in B10, **15** in B11, **45** in B12, and **30** in B13.
2. Issue the / **F**ile | Save **A**s command and assign the name **JANEXP** to the modified file. Your notebook should now look like the one shown in Figure 19-1.

Next, retrieve EXPTEMP and fill in data for February, creating a February expense sheet.

1. Issue the / **F**ile | **R**etrieve command and retrieve EXPTEMP to the screen.
2. Enter **FEBRUARY** in C1, **500** in B3, **175** in B4, **600** in B7, **400** in B8, **100** in B9, **20** in B10, **25** in B11, **145** in B12, and **60** in B13.
3. Save the file under a new name by issuing the / **F**ile | Save **A**s command and assigning the name FEBEXP. Your notebook should now look like the one shown in Figure 19-2.

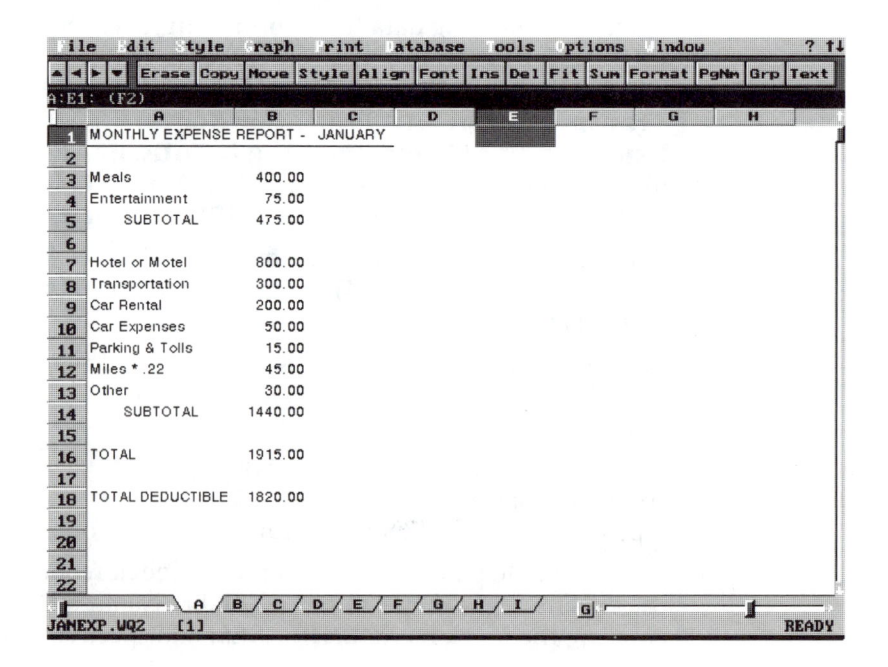

The JANEXP notebook
Figure 19-1.

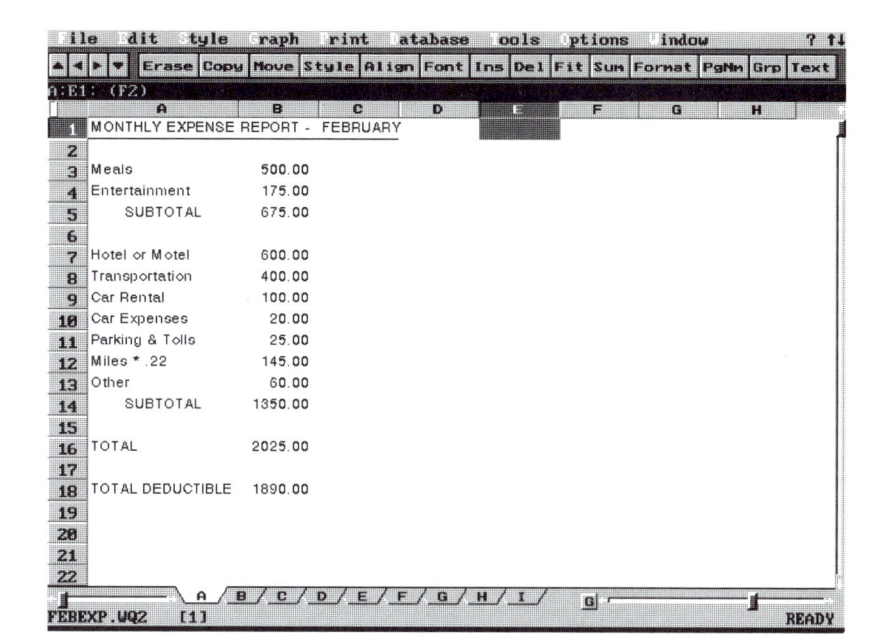

Combining, Extracting, and Linking Files

The FEBEXP notebook
Figure 19-2.

Finally, create a consolidated expense notebook.

1. Start by retrieving EXPTEMP again with the / **F**ile | **R**etrieve command and immediately save it under the name CONSOL using the / **F**ile | **S**ave **A**s command.

2. Move to A1 and enter the new notebook title **MONTHLY EXPENSE REPORT - JAN & FEB**.

3. Still in cell A1, issue the / **T**ools | **C**ombine | **A**dd | **F**ile command, and specify the file JANEXP. Because you have used / **T**ools | **C**ombine | **A**dd rather than / **T**ools | **C**ombine | **C**opy, only values are copied from one notebook to the other; the new label in cell A1 is therefore not overwritten.

4. From cell A1, issue the / **T**ools | **C**ombine | **A**dd | **F**ile command again and specify the file FEBEXP. This time Quattro Pro adds all February expenses to the January expenses, which were previously added to this notebook. Because the layouts of the notebooks are the same and you positioned the cell pointer in the identical cell (A1) before issuing the command, Quattro Pro has no trouble correctly combining the two sets of values.

5. Save the file again, replacing the previous version of CONSOL. Your notebook should now look like Figure 19-3.

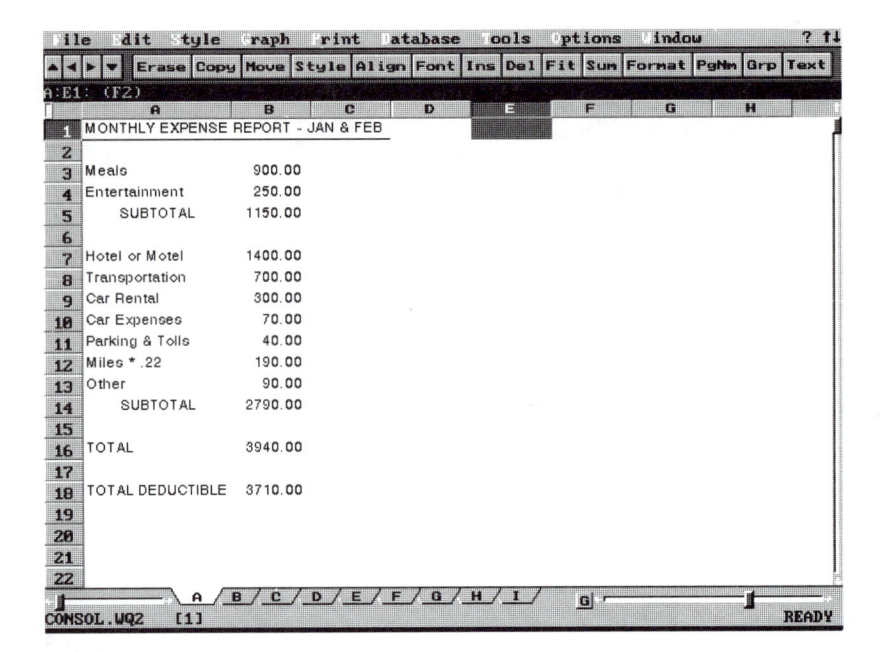

Combining JANEXP and FEBEXP values
Figure 19-3.

Linking Notebooks

Two notebooks are considered linked when a formula in one refers to a cell or cells in another. The notebook that contains the linking formula is known as the *primary notebook,* the notebook to which the formula refers is called the *supporting notebook,* and the values in the referenced cells are called *supporting values.* Once you have created a link between two notebooks, a change in the supporting values is immediately reflected in the primary notebook whenever the two notebooks are open.

There are several reasons for linking notebooks:

✦ **To break a complex model into small, specialized, easy-to-manage components** Linking lets you manage large amounts of data by linking several small notebooks rather than by creating a single huge notebook. Splitting a complicated and potentially confusing notebook into manageable sections can decrease mistakes. It also permits you to distribute work among several people, each of whom can be charged with maintaining one or more supporting notebooks. This can be a particularly effective way to organize work on a local area network.

✦ **To prevent duplication of data in several notebooks** If you need to use a particular piece of information in several different contexts, linking can save you the trouble and disk space involved in storing the same data in more than one file. By storing tax tables, price tables, and other lookup tables in notebooks of their own, you can access the data whenever you need it without copying it to multiple files.

✦ **To create models that are too large to fit in memory at one time** When you load a primary notebook, Quattro Pro lets you look up supporting values without loading the entire supporting notebook into memory. You can build models that exceed the amount of available memory in your computer by splitting an application across several files and loading only the file that you need to view or change at the moment.

✦ **To access information in an external database file** Quattro Pro lets you create links to Paradox, Reflex, and dBASE database files in order to perform database queries, generate graphs, or compile database statistics.

Creating Notebook Links

The only difference between a notebook link and a normal cell or block reference is that link references include the name of an external notebook file enclosed in square brackets. For example, [CHOCOLAT.WQ2]A100 refers to cell A100 in the CHOCOLAT notebook, and [CHOCOLAT]CALCULATIONS means the CALCULATIONS named block in the CHOCOLAT notebook.

There are four ways to create a notebook link. First, you can type the link reference while entering a formula. Second, you can point to a cell or block in another open notebook while entering a formula. Third, you can include an asterisk enclosed in square brackets in a formula. The asterisk serves as a 3-D link character (described under "Creating Links to All Open Notebooks") directing Quattro Pro to create links to the specified cell or block within all the open notebooks. If you enter the formula **@SUM([*]G10)**, for example, Quattro Pro replaces the characters [*]G10 with a list of references to cell G10 in every open notebook (except the current notebook) and displays the resulting total. Finally, you can move a referenced cell to another notebook without moving all the formulas that refer to it, or move a formula to another notebook without moving all the cells it references; doing so automatically forges a link between the two notebooks.

Typing Link References

To type a link reference, you use the form

   [*file specification*]*block*

where *file specification* is the file name, and *block* is a cell reference, block coordinates, or a block name. If the link reference is the first item in a cell, you must precede it with a plus sign to inform Quattro Pro that you are entering a value rather than a label.

The *file specification* can include from one to four parts. At minimum it must include the file's first name. If the file's extension is not the default extension (generally WQ2), you must include the extension as well. If you are referring to a file in another directory, you must specify the directory path. For example, to refer to the block F10..F15 in the CHOCOLAT.WQ2 file in a directory called \QPRO\SALES, you enter

+[\QPRO\SALES\CHOCOLAT]F10..F15

When you type a link reference, the supporting notebook need not be open, but it must exist within the specified directory (or the current directory if no directory was specified). Otherwise Quattro Pro displays the value N/A. If you later create or copy the referenced notebook, however, the link reference will be valid.

The left half of Figure 19-4 shows a notebook that contains link references to the two notebooks shown in the right half of the figure. The input line shows the formula in cell B3 of this notebook, which calculates January sales for the two divisions. Both link references refer to single cells.

Pointing to Link References

Before you can point out link references, you must open the supporting notebook in another window. Then you type an open parenthesis, a plus

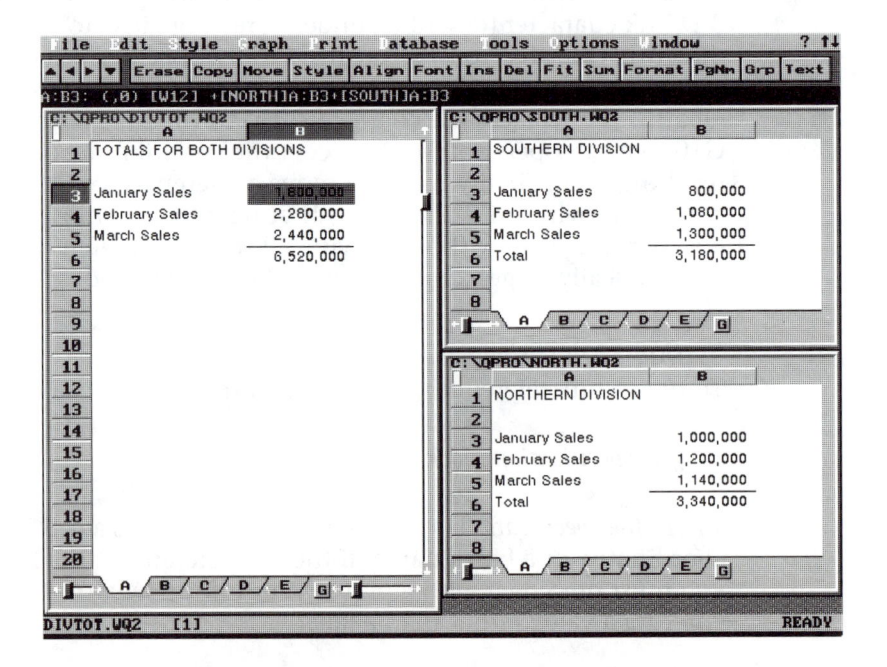

A consolidated notebook created through linking
Figure 19-4.

sign, a different arithmetic operator, or a function name followed by a parenthesis—some character or set of characters that is appropriate immediately before a cell reference. This allows you to enter Point mode. Next, either press [Shift]-[F6] (Next Window), [Alt]-[0] or [Shift]-[F5] (Pick Window), or [Alt] plus the appropriate window number to activate the supporting notebook. If you have tiled the windows so that the supporting notebooks are all visible, you can also simply activate the supporting notebook with the mouse. Move to the cell that you want to reference. If you are referencing a block, type a period to anchor the cell pointer, and move to the opposite corner of the block. Finally, press [Enter] if the link reference is the last item in your formula or type a close parenthesis or an arithmetic operator if the formula is not yet complete. Quattro Pro automatically redisplays the primary notebook.

Creating Links to All Open Notebooks

Quattro Pro makes it extremely easy to create links to an entire group of notebooks that have the same layout. You will find this feature particularly useful for consolidating a group of similar notebooks—a set of monthly income statements, for example, or departmental expense reports.

To create links to several notebooks at once, start by opening all the notebooks that you want to link. Then activate the primary notebook and enter a link reference using the form

@*function*([*]*block*)

where @*function* is a statistical function that can be applied to a block of values and *block* is a cell reference, set of block coordinates, or block name. For example, to add the values in cell B4 in all open notebooks (except the current notebook), you enter **@SUM([*]B4)**. To average the values in the same group of cells, you enter **@AVG([*]B4)**.

This type of reference is known as a *3-D link reference*. The asterisk serves as a kind of notebook wild card, signifying all the currently open notebooks. As soon as you enter a 3-D reference, Quattro Pro replaces it with a set of link references to individual notebooks. For example, if you open a set of notebooks called DEPT1.WQ2, DEPT2.WQ2, and DEPT3.WQ2, and then create a new notebook and enter the formula **@SUM([*]B4..B10)**, Quattro Pro converts the formula to

@SUM([DEPT1]A:B4..B10,[DEPT2]A:B4..B10,[DEPT3]A:B4..B10)

It is this new version of the formula (rather than the 3-D version that you entered) that is saved with the notebook. This means that if you open one or more additional notebooks the next time you open the primary notebook (opening DEPT4.WQ2 and DEPT5.WQ2 along with DEPT1.WQ2, DEPT2.WQ2, and DEPT3.WQ2, for example), Quattro Pro will not automatically extend the link to those additional files.

You can use the ? wildcard character in this context also.

You can also create links to only some of the open notebooks by including wild-card characters in the 3-D reference. For example, the 3-D reference [XY*] generates links to only those open notebooks that have names starting with "XY." The reference [X*Z] would create links to notebooks whose names start with "X" and end with "Z."

If you want to build links to several notebooks that have slightly different structures, you can still employ 3-D links by referencing named blocks. For example, to total the EXPENSES blocks in all open notebooks, you would enter **@SUM([*]EXPENSES)**.

Creating Links by Moving Cells to a Different Notebook

Copy (as opposed to move) operations do not result in linking formulas.

Whenever you move a formula from one notebook to another without moving all the cells that it references, Quattro Pro automatically creates links to the original notebook. Similarly, you can generate links by moving a cell to another notebook without moving all the formulas that reference it. You can try this yourself by moving some of the cells from the LEARN1.WQ2 notebook to a different file. Copying formulas or referenced cells from one notebook to another never generates linking formulas. Even if you copy formulas with absolute references from one notebook to another, Quattro Pro assumes that you want to refer to cells on the current notebook. The implications of moving and copying link references or cells referenced by link formulas are covered later in this chapter.

Hands-On Practice

Take a few minutes to practice linking notebooks. The following two exercises give you a chance to try two different standard linking scenarios: splitting an existing notebook into two smaller files, and creating a consolidation notebook to total values in other files.

First, try moving all the expense line items from the LEARN1 notebook to a separate notebook. (If you did not create the LEARN1 notebook, refer to Figure 19-5 and read through the following exercise.)

1. Issue the / **F**ile | **E**rase command to clear the current window in preparation for creating a new notebook.
2. Issue the / **F**ile | **O**pen command and retrieve LEARN1.WQ2 into a new window. (Do not use the / **F**ile | **R**etrieve command.) Note that at this point you have two open notebooks.

Combining, Extracting, and Linking Files

```
ABC Group Income Projection           Created:   12/25/93

                                   1993        1994
                                 Actual         Est    Variance
                                 ---------------------------------
Sales                           450,000     472,500      22,500
Cost of goods sold              193,500     203,175       9,675
Gross margin                    256,500     269,325      12,825

Salaries                         86,000      90,300       4,300
Rent                             42,000      44,100       2,100
Utilities                        15,500      16,275         775
Depreciation                     22,000      22,000           0
Miscellaneous                     8,000       8,400         400
Total operating expenses        173,500     181,075       7,575

Interest expense                 10,500      10,500           0

Profit before tax                72,500      77,750       5,250
Income tax                       29,000      31,100       2,100
Net income                       43,500      46,650       3,150
```

Figure 19-5. The LEARN1 notebook

3. Move the individual expenses for 1993 to the new notebook by issuing the / **E**dit | **M**ove command and specifying a source block of A11..B15 (Salaries through Miscellaneous). When prompted for a destination, press (Shift)-(F6) to display the new notebook, move to A3, and press (Enter). Quattro Pro redisplays LEARN1 with A11..B15 now empty.

4. Move to B16 and note the formula @SUM([NOTEBK2]B3..B7) on the input line. (The reference on your notebook may be to NOTEBK3 or NOTEBK4 if you created other notebooks earlier in this work session.)

5. Move to C16 and change the formula to (B16*1.05). This produces a slightly different result than the previous formula because it calculates the 1994 expenses by multiplying the sum of the 1993 expenses by 1.05. (The original notebook multiplied all the expense items *except* Depreciation by this growth factor.)

6. Move to row 11 and issue the / **E**dit | **D**elete | **R**ows command. Press (↓) until cells in rows 11 through 15 are highlighted, and press (Enter) to delete five blank rows (including the data still in C11..D15).

7. Issue the / **F**ile | Save **A**s command and enter **LEARN3** as the file name.

8. Press (Shift)-(F6) to display the new notebook. Widen column A to 13 characters using the / **S**tyle | **C**olumn Width command ((Ctrl)-(W) shortcut).

9. Move to A1 and enter the label **ABC Group 1993 Expenses**.
10. Issue the / **F**ile | **S**ave command (Ctrl-S shortcut) and enter a file name of **ABCEXP**.

Figure 19-6 shows the ABCEXP and LEARN3 notebooks.

In this exercise, you automatically created a link reference by moving the block of cells referenced in an @SUM formula to a different notebook. The resulting link formula referred to the block of cells containing the expense items. This is only one way of splitting LEARN1.WQ2. You might prefer to move the @SUM formula to the new notebook along with the individual expenses. Then you could reference that one cell by manually entering the link formula **+[ABCEXP]B8** in cell B11 of LEARN3 (assuming the @SUM formula is in cell B8).

Now try creating a consolidated notebook to add up the values in JANEXP.WQ2 and FEBEXP.WQ2. This is an alternative method of performing the type of consolidation that you performed using the / **T**ools | **C**ombine | **A**dd command earlier in this chapter.

1. Issue the / **F**ile | **Cl**ose All command to close all the open windows.
2. Issue the / **F**ile | **O**pen command and open JANEXP.WQ2.

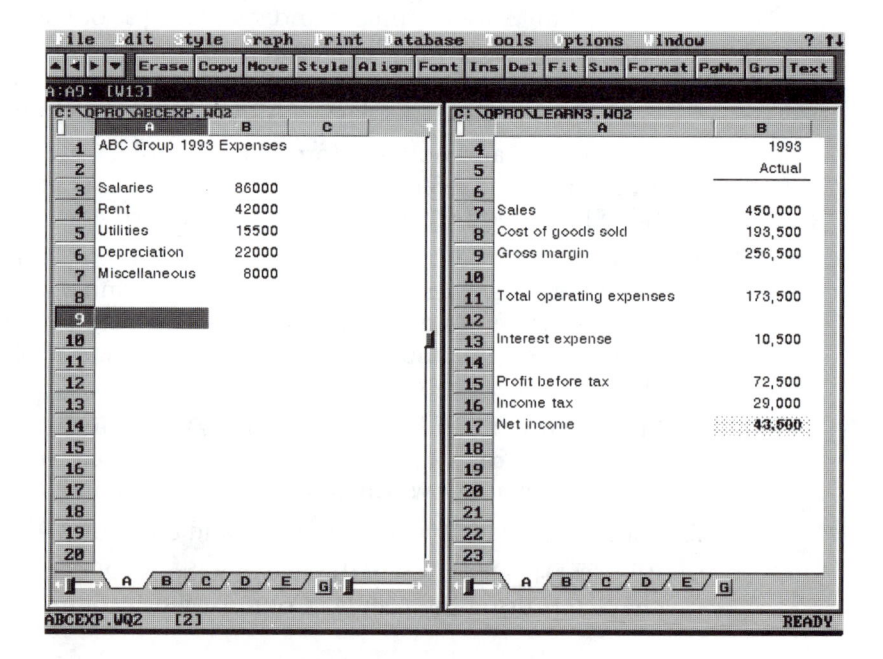

Splitting the LEARN1 notebook
Figure 19-6.

Combining, Extracting, and Linking Files

3. Open a second window using the / **F**ile l **O**pen command, and open FEBEXP.WQ2.
4. Issue the / **F**ile l **O**pen command a third time and open the file EXPTEMP.WQ2. Assign a new name to this notebook by issuing the / **F**ile l **S**ave **A**s command and entering **CONSOL2**.
5. Overwrite the label in A1, entering a notebook title of **Y-T-D EXPENSES, JANUARY & FEBRUARY.**
6. Move to B3 and enter the formula **@SUM([*]B3)**. Quattro Pro should display a result of 900.00. Note that the formula, as displayed on the input line, now reads

    @SUM([JANEXP]A:B3,[FEBEXP]A:B3)

    because Quattro Pro has replaced the 3-D link with references to each open notebook other than the current notebook.
7. Next, copy this formula to the other expense rows. Issue the / **E**dit l **C**opy command and specify a source block of B3 and a destination of B4.
8. Issue the / **E**dit l **C**opy command again, specifying a source block of B3 and a destination of B7..B13. Your notebook should now look like Figure 19-7.
9. Save the notebook and replace the previous version.

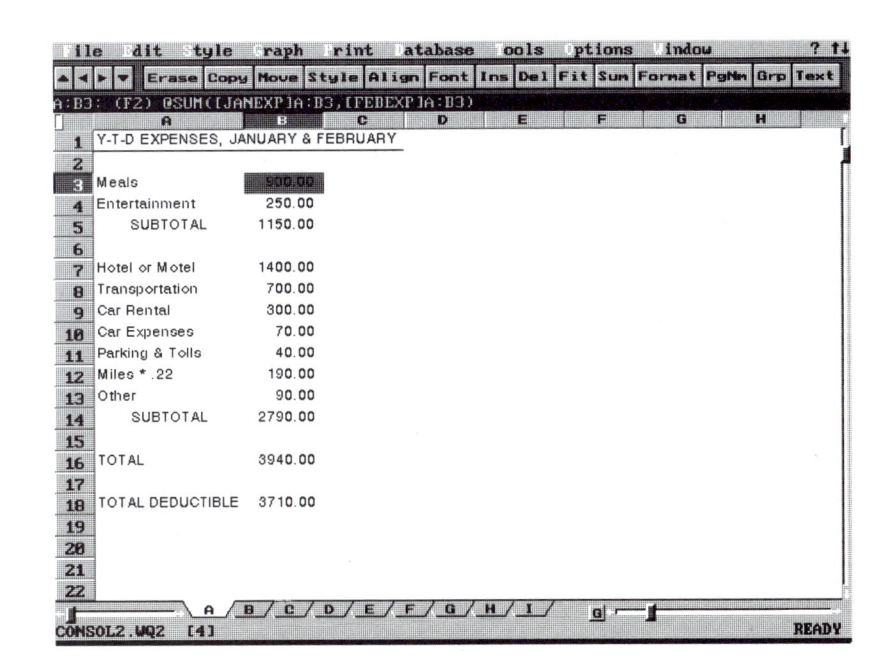

Consolidating JANEXP and FEBEXP by linking
Figure 19-7.

There is one problem with the CONSOL2 notebook at this point: It only includes links to the JANEXP and FEBEXP notebooks. As you create notebooks for future months, you will need to modify all the link references to include those new files. One way to prevent this is to create notebooks for all 12 months at the beginning of the year by saving EXPTEMP under a different name 12 times or by using the File Manager to duplicate the file. You can link CONSOL2 to all 12 notebooks using 3-D references, and then fill in the monthly notebooks as the year progresses. As a result, the figures in CONSOL2 would always refer to all the year's data, and you would not have to adjust the formulas each month to take a new notebook into account.

Opening Linked Notebooks

Whenever you load a notebook that contains linking formulas, Quattro Pro checks whether all its supporting notebooks are already open. If not, it displays a Link options menu with the choices Load Supporting, Update Refs, and None.

Workspace files were discussed in Chapter 11.

The Load Supporting option automatically loads each of the supporting notebooks into a notebook window. If any of those supporting notebooks contain links to other unloaded notebooks, Quattro Pro loads those as well, and then loads their supporting notebooks, and so on until all notebooks referenced on any of the open notebooks are loaded. This is actually one of the fastest and easiest ways to open a set of linked notebooks—you just open the primary notebook, select Load Supporting, and let Quattro Pro do the rest. Another strategy for opening a set of linked notebooks is to open them once, create a workspace file, and then open the workspace file whenever you want to work with that group of notebooks. This method of opening linked notebooks is particularly useful if you want other users, especially novice users, to work with this set of files.

When all the supporting notebooks are open, changes in the supporting values are automatically reflected in the primary notebook (unless you have changed the Recalculation mode to Manual). If you move any of the supporting values, Quattro Pro automatically adjusts the primary notebook's references. The only potential drawback to opening the supporting notebooks is that it can consume a lot of memory—possibly more memory than you have available.

The Update Refs option directs Quattro Pro to look up the current value of each of the supporting values in the supporting notebooks so that the data displayed is current. It does not, however, open these notebooks. This consumes much less memory, but it also means that you cannot view or update the supporting notebooks. If you later decide that you want to work with one of those supporting files, use the / **T**ools I **U**pdate Links I **O**pen command, described shortly.

Whenever you load a primary notebook that contains many linking formulas and select either the Load Supporting or Update Refs option, you may have to wait several seconds before the mode indicator changes to READY. Quattro Pro automatically recalculates all the link formulas on the assumption that you may have opened one or more of the supporting notebooks and changed the supporting values since the last time you saved the primary notebook.

If you select the third linking option, None, Quattro Pro does not open or read any supporting notebooks that are not already open. Instead, it temporarily replaces the links to unopened supporting notebooks with the value NA. This method of opening a primary notebook is quite fast because you do not need to wait for Quattro Pro to read the supporting notebooks into memory. You can use it to save time whenever you want to quickly scan or edit a large notebook and do not need to see the current values of the link formulas.

Linking Notebooks Hierarchically

Just as Quattro Pro allows you to enter circular formulas, even though they can create problems on your notebook, it also allows you to link notebooks in a circular fashion. This means, for example, that formulas in notebook A refer to cells in notebook B, formulas in notebook B refer to cells in notebook C, and formulas in notebook C refer back to notebook A. You should avoid this type of linking whenever possible. When you create circular links among a group of notebooks, Quattro Pro cannot properly pass updated values from one file to another unless you load all the notebooks into memory every time you make changes. If you do link notebooks in a circular fashion, be sure to open all the notebooks whenever you want fully current results.

NOTE: Unfortunately, the Update Refs option only updates references in the active notebook. For example, suppose THIRD.WQ2 refers to a cell in SECOND.WQ2 which refers to a cell in FIRST.WQ2. If you change the value in FIRST.WQ2 and then open THIRD.WQ2 and choose Update Refs, your change will not be passed along to THIRD.WQ2. Either you must choose the Load Supporting option or you must open SECOND.WQ2 and choose Update Refs before you open THIRD.WQ2.

Updating Notebook Links

The / **T**ools | **U**pdate Links command displays a menu of options specifically related to notebook linking. These options allow you to open a supporting notebook (the Open option), update data in the current notebook based on unopened supporting notebooks (the Refresh option), switch all the links to a particular supporting notebook from one notebook to another (the Change option), and remove all link references to one or more supporting notebooks (the Delete option).

Opening Supporting Notebooks Later in the Work Session

Occasionally you load a notebook without its supporting notebooks—choosing the Update Refs or None option when you retrieve the file—and then later decide that you want to work with one or more of the supporting notebooks after all. Although you can load the supporting notebooks using the / **F**ile | **O**pen or / **F**ile | **R**etrieve command, Quattro Pro also provides the / **T**ools | **U**pdate Links | **O**pen command specifically for this purpose.

If you're using a mouse, you can select notebook names just by clicking them.

When you issue the / **T**ools | **U**pdate Links | **O**pen command, Quattro Pro displays a list of the unopened supporting notebooks. To open a single notebook on the list, highlight its name and press [Enter]. To open multiple notebooks, select each notebook that you want to open by highlighting its name and pressing [Shift]-[F7] (Select), or select all the files on the list by pressing [Alt]-[F7] (All Select). Then press [Enter]. Quattro Pro opens each selected notebook in a different window.

Refreshing Linked Formula Results

Make sure the primary notebook is active when you issue this Refresh command.

The / **T**ools | **U**pdate Links | **R**efresh command directs Quattro Pro to read in linked values from one or more unopened notebooks. It has exactly the same effect as choosing the Update Refs option when you first open a primary notebook, except that you can use it whenever you like and you can specify exactly which notebooks you want to update values from.

There are three reasons to use the / **T**ools | **U**pdate Links | **R**efresh command:

- ◆ If you chose the None option when opening the primary notebook (so that NA values appear on the notebook) and then later decide that you need to use values from some or all of the supporting notebooks.

- ◆ If you only want to update values based on a few of the supporting notebooks. In this case, you would deliberately choose the None option when opening the primary notebook, and then issue the / **T**ools | **U**pdate Links | **R**efresh command and select only those supporting notebooks that contain values that you currently need.

◆ If you are working on a local area network and updated link references when you first loaded a primary notebook, but believe that someone may have changed one of the supporting notebooks since then.

When you issue the / **T**ools | **U**pdate Links | **R**efresh command, Quattro Pro displays a list of unopened supporting notebooks along with the prompt "Pick one or more spreadsheets." If you only want to update references to a single notebook, just highlight that file name and press [Enter]. Otherwise use [Shift]-[F7] (Select) or click with your mouse to select file names one at a time or [Alt]-[F7] (All Select) to select all the files in the list, and press [Enter].

If you issue the / **T**ools | **U**pdate Links | **R**efresh command when all the supporting notebooks are already opened or when there are no link formulas in the current notebook, Quattro Pro displays an error message.

Switching Links from One Notebook to Another

You can use the / **T**ools | **U**pdate Links | **C**hange command to transfer links from one notebook to another. You might use this option when you have changed the name of a supporting notebook or if you simply want to reference another supporting notebook with an identical structure. When you issue the / **T**ools | **U**pdate Links | **C**hange command, Quattro Pro displays a list of supporting notebooks for the current notebook. Highlight the one that you want to change and press [Enter]. Quattro Pro prompts you for a notebook name, displaying the selected file's name as a default. Enter the name of the new supporting notebook or press [F2] (Edit) or the [Spacebar] to enter Edit mode; then change the default name and press [Enter].

Deleting Links

The / **T**ools | **U**pdate Links | **D**elete command undoes the links between the current notebook and one or more supporting notebooks. When you issue the / **T**ools | **U**pdate Links | **D**elete command, Quattro Pro displays a list of supporting notebooks. To cancel links to a single notebook, just highlight the file name and press [Enter]. To cancel links to multiple notebooks, click with your mouse or use [Shift]-[F7] (Select) or [Alt]-[F7] (All Select) to select files, and then press [Enter]. Quattro Pro immediately displays ERR values in each cell that contains one of the canceled link references without removing the formulas themselves from the cells. Your next task is to edit or replace all those formulas with valid references.

You also can unlink notebooks by using the / **E**dit | **V**alues command to replace link formulas with their current results. This method is preferable if you no longer need the values in those cells to respond to changes in other cells. However, if you want the link formulas to remain formulas—referring to cells on the current notebook or a different supporting notebook—use the

/ **T**ools | **U**pdate Links | **D**elete command: the ERR values will help you find all the formulas that you need to change.

Copying and Moving Link Formulas

When you copy a link formula to another cell in the same notebook, Quattro Pro adjusts link references in the same way as it adjusts other cell references: Relative references are changed to fit the formula's new position and absolute references are left unchanged.

When you copy link references to a different notebook, Quattro Pro treats them in exactly the same way, adjusting the relative references and leaving the absolute references unchanged. It also leaves the reference to the primary notebook as is, even if you copy the link formula into the file that it references.

When you move a link formula from one cell to another, Quattro Pro leaves the cell references unchanged. If you happen to move the formula into the notebook that it refers to, Quattro Pro removes the file link while leaving the cell references the same. For example, if you move the formula @SUM([ABCEXP]A:B3..B7) from LEARN3 into any cell in ABCEXP, Quattro Pro changes the formula to read simply @SUM(A:B3..B7).

You must guard against one potential problem with linked references: If you move a cell (including the corner cell of a block) that is referenced by a link formula, Quattro Pro automatically adjusts the link reference *only if the primary notebook is open at the time*. It does not adjust link references in unopened notebooks, even when you open those notebooks later. The only way to correct the problem is to edit or reenter the link formulas, specifying the current addresses of the supporting values (that is, the values to which the link formulas refer). You can avoid this problem in one of two ways: You can open the primary notebook every time you modify the supporting notebook, or you can always use named blocks rather than cell addresses in link formulas. Whenever a formula contains a block name, Quattro Pro will look up the current address of that block whenever you update the notebook links or load the supporting notebooks.

For example, if you open ABCEXP without opening LEARN3, and then add an extra row in the middle of the expenses block, the link reference in LEARN3 becomes out-of-date. Even if you open both notebooks later, the formula in cell B11 of LEARN3 still refers to block B3..B7 in the ABCEXP notebook, rather than to B3..B8. To prevent this problem you must assign a name (such as 1993 EXP) to the block B3..B8 in ABCEXP.WQ2 and change the formula in cell B11 of LEARN3 to @SUM(1993EXP). Then, even if you add a row to the expenses block in ABCEXP without opening LEARN3, the link reference is adjusted properly the next time you open the LEARN3

Graphing Linked Notebooks

In Chapter 12, you learned how to graph data from multiple pages within a single notebook. In addition, you can graph data from one or more subsidiary notebooks by using link references when defining series, titles, and other graph settings. By using link references when defining graphs, you can graph data from several different notebooks without creating a consolidated notebook as an intermediate step. You will find this ability particularly useful when you want to view consolidated information only in graphic form, rather than as numbers on a notebook.

The left window in Figure 19-8 shows an inserted graph based on values drawn from the two notebooks in the right half of the figure. The Series 1 setting for the graph is [JANREV]B3..B5. The Series 2 setting is [FEBREV]B3..B5. With your workspace organized like this, you can make changes in both of the subsidiary notebooks and see them immediately reflected on the graph. You might also create a notebook with one or more graphs and even a graph slide show based on a group of subsidiary notebooks. Then, whenever you want to view the updated graphs, you can simply load the graph notebook, select Update Refs to update the graph values, and display your graphs on the full screen.

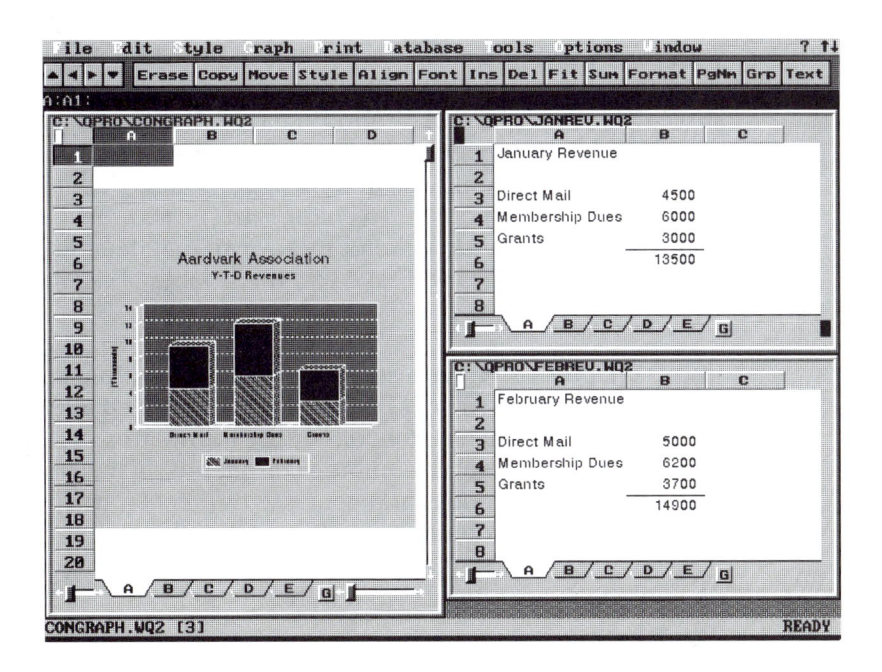

A graph based on values in other notebooks
Figure 19-8.

If you want to use link references for text, such as titles and legends, you must first enter a link reference on the current notebook. For example, if you want to use the label in cell A1 of the JANREV.WQ2 notebook as your first line title, you enter **+[JANREV]A1** in a cell of the notebook, issue the / **G**raph | **T**ext | 1st Line command, and enter a backslash followed by the address of the cell that contains the link reference. You cannot refer to another notebook directly when defining graph text. If you specify a first line title of \[JANREV]A1, for example, Quattro Pro displays \[JANREV]A1 at the top of your graph.

NOTE: Graphs that draw values from other notebooks always use the current values, even if you do not open the supporting notebooks and select the None option from the linking options menu when you open the primary notebook.

Linking Versus Combining Files

Remember, if you're working with fairly simple data, you can often use separate notebook pages instead of combining or linking.

You have now learned two different methods of consolidating data from different notebooks: the / **T**ools | **C**ombine commands and link formulas. In general, the / **T**ools | **C**ombine commands are preferable when you have no intention of changing the data that you want to consolidate. For example, if you periodically import summary data from an external database (perhaps downloading it from a mainframe computer) and simply want to combine it with earlier data, / **T**ools | **C**ombine | **A**dd can save both disk space (you end up with a single notebook filled with numeric constants rather than space-consuming formulas) and time (you issue only one command and need not wait for recalculation every time you load the notebook). On the other hand, you should use linking to consolidate data if you want your totals to remain responsive to changes in the supporting notebooks. If there is any chance that you will modify the original data, linking rather than combining notebooks will save you the trouble of reconsolidating.

In this chapter you have learned to extract, combine, and link data from different notebooks. The / **T**ools | **X**tract command allows you to extract smaller self-contained notebooks or the foundations on which to build new notebooks. The / **T**ools | **C**ombine commands enable you to combine data from multiple notebooks and generate numbers (rather than formulas) that reflect data from more than one file. Lastly, the ability to link notebooks lets you dynamically combine data from two or more files, so that changes in one notebook are reflected in another.

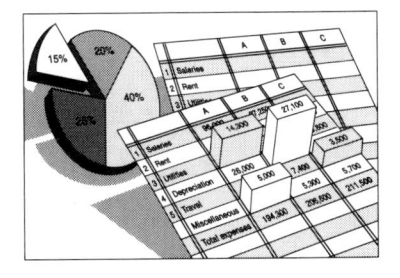

CHAPTER

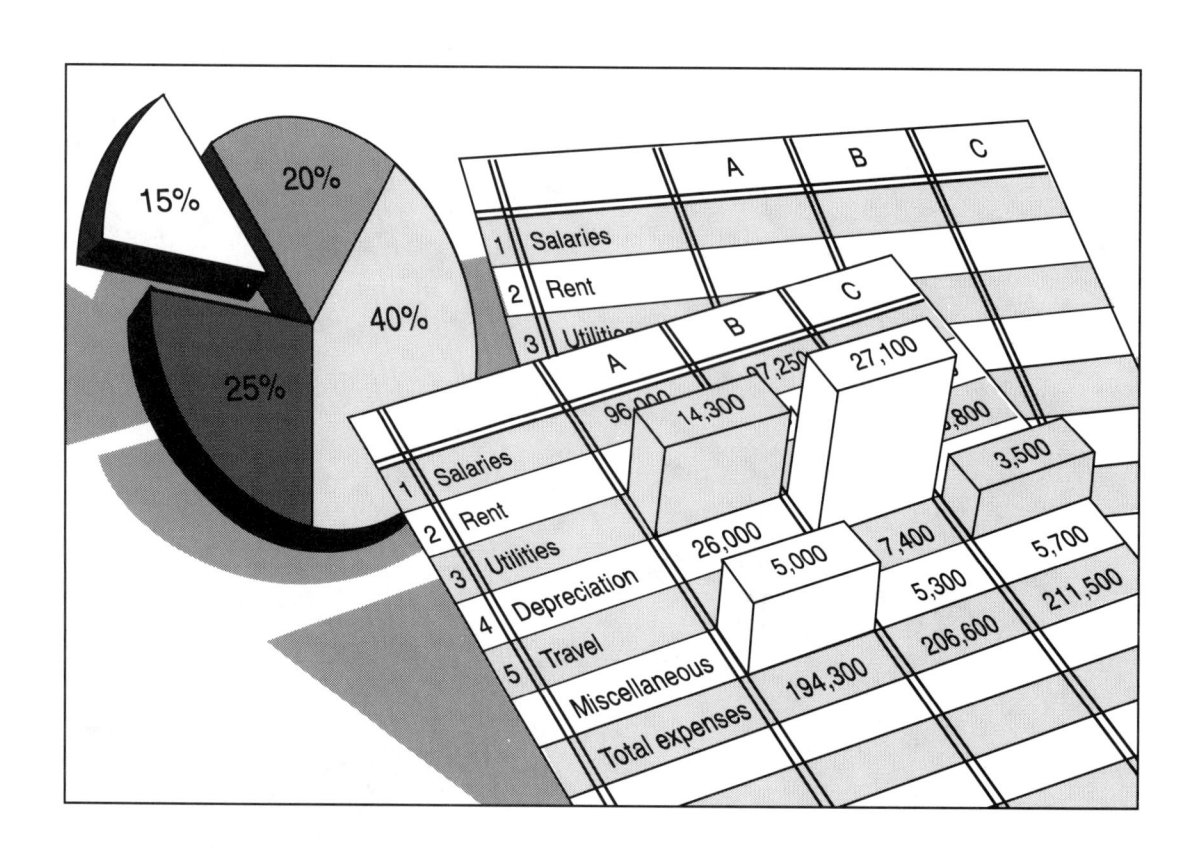

20

INTRODUCTION TO MACROS

A macro is a recording of a series of actions that can be replayed with a single command. You can use the simplest macros to automate tasks that you would normally perform by pressing keys on your keyboard or by moving and clicking the mouse. These tasks include entering and editing data, moving the cell pointer, and issuing menu commands. Using such simple macros is like speed-dialing on a telephone: You press one or two keys and the machine responds as if you had pressed a series of keys, one after another. The most elaborate macros, in contrast, carry out functions that you cannot perform by pressing keys or using the mouse—functions such as pausing to collect input from the user or making use of programming structures such as loops and subroutines. Using these special commands, expert users can develop customized applications that require little or no knowledge of Quattro Pro to use.

There are two basic reasons for creating and using macros. The first is speed. Quattro Pro can move the cell pointer and execute commands faster than the fastest typist. If you repeatedly perform the same keystrokes, macros can save time and effort, streamlining your work tremendously. The second reason is accuracy. Once your macro works properly, it will be reliable and consistent. A macro goes through the same steps every time you execute it and so is a much safer method of performing complex and delicate operations that can ruin your notebook if done incorrectly.

This chapter covers only the basic type of macros—those that can be recorded as a series of keystrokes. Even at this level macros are extremely powerful tools for automating and streamlining your work.

Creating Macros

Quattro Pro offers two ways to create macros: You can direct Quattro Pro to record a series of actions as you issue them; this is the simplest and usually the most efficient method. In addition, you can enter macros directly onto the notebook, typing in the macro commands yourself. This chapter deals almost exclusively with the process of recording macros—a perfectly adequate method for creating simple macros.

All commands related to creating and executing macros are located on the Macro menu. You can access this menu either by issuing the / **T**ools | **M**acro command or by pressing [Alt]-[F2] (Macro Menu).

Recording Macros

Before you start recording a macro, you should always do a trial run to determine exactly what you want the macro to do and which keystrokes will be required. Once you begin to record the macro, every keystroke is recorded, including all your mistakes and typos, plus the keystrokes you use to correct them. These extra actions then become part of your macro and can slow its execution considerably. It is possible to edit keystrokes out of your macro after recording, but it is a delicate operation and can usually be avoided by careful planning.

Introduction to Macros

Once you have thoroughly planned your macro, you can record it with the following steps:

1. Press Alt-F2 (Macro Menu) and type **R** to select the Record option. Quattro Pro displays REC on the status line at the bottom of the screen, indicating that your actions are now being recorded.
2. Perform all the actions that you want to record. Quattro Pro translates them into macro form and writes them in the cell or block of cells you specified. Avoid using the mouse when recording macros because Quattro Pro will not be able to record the selections that you make on various lists of choices, including lists of named blocks and files as well as some menus and submenus.
3. Press Alt-F2 (Macro Menu) again, and type either **R** to stop recording and return to Ready mode or **P** for Paste if you want to paste the macro into the notebook (as explained shortly).

You can record macros only when the Options | Recalculation | Mode setting is Background.

Quattro Pro always retains in memory the last macro that you created and lets you replay it using the Instant Replay option on the Macro menu. As soon as you record a second macro or leave Quattro Pro, however, the old macro is lost unless you already pasted it from memory to the notebook (that is, stored the macro commands in individual cells). You must paste your macro to the notebook to use it in a future work session. You also have to paste macros if you want to use more than one in the current work session. The process of pasting macros is covered shortly. You can also store macros in "macro libraries" so you can use them in more than one notebook. You'll learn how to do so under "Using Macro Libraries" later in this chapter.

As mentioned, you can replay the last macro that you recorded by selecting the Instant Replay option on the Macro menu. The steps for playing back a pasted macro depend on the type of name that you assign to the macro (as explained under "Naming Macros").

As soon as you start playing a macro, the MACRO mode indicator appears on the bottom line of the screen. If your macro is relatively long or your computer relatively slow, you can interrupt macro execution at any point by pressing Ctrl-Break.

> **TIP:** Pay careful attention to the location of your cell pointer when you run a macro. If you run a macro that inserts data in the current cell, for instance, you will overwrite any data that's already in that cell. One way to ward off this potential hazard is to include keystrokes for moving to the desired cell within the macro itself. For example, you could press Home while recording the macro to move to cell A1.

A Macro for Date-Stamping a Notebook

Remember not to use the mouse when recording macros.

The first macro that you will create records today's date in your notebook using the @TODAY function and the [F9] (Calc) key. Be sure to follow the instructions exactly. For example, do not use arrow keys to select menu options when the instructions specify typing option letters.

1. If you have anything other than a blank notebook on your screen, issue the / **F**ile | **E**rase command.

2. Issue the / **O**ptions | **R**ecalculation command, and make sure that the Mode setting on the Options | Recalculation menu is Background. Press [Esc] twice to return to Ready mode.

3. With the cell pointer in A1, press [Alt]-[F2] and type **R** to open the Macro menu and select the Record option. Note the REC indicator that appears on the status line.

4. Type **@TODAY**, press [F9] (Calc), and press [Enter] to enter the calculated value into the current cell.

5. Type **/SND4** to issue the / **S**tyle | **N**umeric Format | **D**ate command and select Date format number 4 (Long International). Press [Enter] to designate the current cell as the block to be formatted.

6. Press [Alt]-[F2] and type **R** to open the Macro menu and select Record again. The macro recording is terminated (the REC indicator disappears).

7. Move to A3, and replay your macro by pressing [Alt]-[F2] and typing **I** to open the Macro menu and select the Instant Replay option. Quattro Pro enters today's date into the current cell.

Pasting Macros into the Notebook

Remember, you have to paste your macros into the notebook if you want to use more than one macro or if you want to be able to use your macros in a future work session. Pasting macros means directing Quattro Pro to take a series of macro commands that are currently stored in memory and enter them into the notebook. Pasting a macro involves two steps: First you specify a name for the macro, and then you specify a location for the macro. Once you have supplied this information, Quattro Pro records the macro commands as a set of adjacent labels within a single column of your notebook.

You can paste a macro into your notebook as the last step in the recording process or sometime after you finish recording. To paste a macro immediately, just select the Paste option from the Macro menu (rather than the Record option) when you are done recording. To paste a macro later, select the Paste option before you either record another macro or leave Quattro Pro.

In general it is easiest and safest to paste the macro as part of the recording process. However, there are two situations in which you might hold off. First, occasionally you may want to test out a macro before committing it to the notebook. Second, you may sometimes create a macro that you intend to use for only a short time. In this case you might forego pasting altogether and just use the Instant Replay option.

Naming Macros

As mentioned, whenever you paste a macro to a notebook, you must assign it a name. This name actually becomes the block name of the first cell in which Quattro Pro stores the recorded macro commands. Later, when you execute the macro, you supply Quattro Pro with this block name. Quattro Pro then goes to the named cell and moves down that column, executing each macro command it finds. As soon as it encounters either a blank cell or a value, it stops and returns to Ready mode.

You can enter the letter for instant macro names in either upper- or lowercase.

The two types of macro names are *standard* and *instant*. The type of name that you assign determines how you replay the macro. Instant macro names consist of a \ (backslash) followed by a single letter. To execute instant macros, you simply press [Alt] and type the assigned letter. Because you can only use single letters to name instant macros, you are limited to 26 instant macros per notebook. Standard macro names, like any other block names, can contain up to 15 characters, including letters, digits, punctuation marks, and characters such as $ or %. You should avoid using mathematical operators such as +, –, *, or /. To play back a standard macro, you select the Execute option on the Macro menu and then specify the block name—either by entering the name manually or by pressing [F3] (Choices) and selecting from the list of block names. If you have assigned names to cells other than the starting cells of macros, you see those block names on the list as well.

When you name macros, try to pick names that are easy to remember and to associate with the macro's function. For example, if you create a macro to sort a database by the ACCOUNT field, you might name it ACCTSORT or SORTACCT. Even when you name instant macros, try to choose names that remind you of the macro's purpose. You might assign the name \P to a macro that prints the notebook.

You cannot assign the same name to a macro and to another block of cells on the same notebook. If you issue the / **E**dit | **N**ames | **C**reate or / **E**dit | **N**ames | **L**abels command and enter a name that was previously assigned to a macro, you will no longer be able to execute that macro.

Where to Store Your Macros

Quattro Pro allows you to execute macros that are stored either in the current notebook or in another open notebook that you have designated as a macro library. You will learn to create and use macro libraries later in this chapter. For now just be aware that macros need not be specific to one notebook. When you create macros that can be used in several different notebooks, you should store them in a macro library so that they can be executed from any other open notebook. However, when you create macros that are specific to one notebook, just use the Paste option to store them in that particular notebook file.

Whenever you store macros in a regular notebook (as opposed to a macro library), try to place them in a safe spot; it's usually a good idea to place them on a separate page set aside for macros. A macro that has been pasted to a notebook is just a contiguous block of labels and is as vulnerable to damage or deletion as any other set of data. The / **Edit** | **D**elete | **C**olumns and / **E**dit | **D**elete | **R**ows commands can be particularly dangerous to macros. / **E**dit | **I**nsert | **R**ows can also destroy macros if the inserted row falls in the middle of a macro.

If you place all your macros on a separate macros page, they'll be immune to changes that you make to other pages in the notebook. For extra safety you may want to use Quattro Pro's protection feature to protect your macros page. This strategy should prevent accidental overwriting of the macros in your notebook.

It is also good practice to place all your macros on a separate page of the notebook so you can easily find and compare them. Regardless of the location of your macros, be sure to leave adequate room underneath the starting cell. A lengthy macro can easily consume a dozen or more cells, and Quattro Pro overwrites any data in its path when pasting a macro. You should also leave at least a few empty columns to the right of the starting macro cell so you can read macro labels that are too wide to be displayed in a single cell. Also leave space in the adjacent columns for documenting your macros. (Macro documentation is discussed later in this chapter.) Finally, be sure to leave at least one blank row between the last cell of one macro and the first cell of the next.

Try pasting the macro that you just created into a separate page of the notebook.

1. Click on the page tab for page B (or press [Ctrl]-[Pg Dn]). Then click on the PgNm button on the SpeedBar (or choose / **E**dit | **P**age | **N**ame), press [Esc] to delete the default page name, type **Macros**, and press [Enter].

Introduction to Macros

2. Press [Alt]-[F2] and type **P** to open the Macro menu and select the Paste option. When Quattro Pro prompts you for the "name of macro to create/modify," enter **\D**. When prompted for a location, press [Enter] to paste the macro into cell A1 of the Macros page. Then press [Ctrl]-[S] and enter the name **SAMPMAC**. On your notebook you'll see

```
@TODAY
{CALC}~
{/Block;Format}d4~
```

These macro commands are explained in the next section.

3. Because this is an instant macro, you can replay it by moving to the desired location and pressing [Alt] plus the assigned letter. Do so now by moving to cell A5 on page A and pressing [Alt]-[D].

NOTE: If your macro contains the keystrokes /SN in place of the menu-equivalent command {/Block:Format}, the Tools | Macro | Macro Recording setting has been changed from Logical (the initial default) to Keystroke, as explained under "Changing the Macro Recording Method." Change it back to Logical for now by issuing the / **T**ools | **M**acro | **M**acro Recording | **L**ogical command. This way your macros match the figures as you perform the exercises in the remainder of this chapter.

Interpreting Macros

When Quattro Pro records a macro, it translates your keystrokes into a special form. Quattro Pro records any characters that you type—aside from those you use to issue commands—as is. In the date macro, for example, the characters @TODAY appear just as you typed them. The only difference is that Quattro Pro added an apostrophe at the beginning to designate the entry as a label. (Otherwise you would see a value in cell B:A1 rather than the characters @TODAY.) As with any other label prefix character, this apostrophe does not appear in the cell itself; it appears only on the input line when you highlight or edit the cell.

Quattro Pro represents some keys—such as the function keys, the arrow keys, [Home], and so on—using sets of characters known as *key-equivalent commands*. These sets of characters are called commands not because they are Quattro Pro commands per se, but because they are commands in the macro language. They function as commands during macro execution.

Table 20-1 is a list of all the cursor-movement, editing, and function keys and their macro representations. If you press a particular key several times, Quattro Pro uses a shorthand to record your keystrokes, using {UP 3} rather than {UP}{UP}{UP} to represent pressing ↑ three times, for example. In the \D macro, {CALC} is the key-equivalent command for the F9 (Calc) key. The ~ (tilde) character, which appears after {CALC} and again at the end of the macro, is Quattro Pro's symbol for the Enter key.

Function Keys

Command	Key
{ABS}	F4
{CALC}	F9
{CHOOSE}	Shift-F5
{COPY}	Shift-F9
{EDIT}	F2
{FUNCTIONS}	Alt-F3
{GOTO}	F5
{GRAPH}	F10
{MACROS}	Shift-F3
{MARK}	Shift-F7
{MARKALL}	Alt-F7
{MOVE}	Shift-F8
{NAME}	F3
{NEXTWIN}	Shift-F6
{PASTE}	Shift-F10
{QUERY}	F7
{TABLE}	F8
{TOGGLEGROUPMODE}	Ctrl-F5
{UNDO}	Alt-F5
{WINDOW}	F6
{ZOOM}	Alt-F6

Key-Equivalent Commands
Table 20-1.

Introduction to Macros

Cursor-Movement Keys

Command	Key
{LEFT} or {L}	←
{RIGHT} or {R}	→
{UP} or {U}	↑
{DOWN} or {D}	↓
{FIRSTPAGE}	Ctrl-Home
{LASTPAGE}	Ctrl-End
{NEXTPAGE}	Ctrl-Pg Dn
{PGDN}	Pg Dn
{PGUP}	Pg Up
{PREVPAGE}	Ctrl-Pg Up
{TAB}	Tab
{BACKTAB}	Shift-Tab
{BIGLEFT}	Ctrl-←
{BIGRIGHT}	Ctrl-→
{HOME}	Home
{END}	End
{WINDOW*n*}	Selects window *n*

Editing Keys and Other Keys

Command	Key
{BREAK}	Ctrl-Break
{BS} or {BACKSPACE}	Backspace
{CR} or ~	Enter
{DATE}	Ctrl-D
{DEL} or {DELETE}	Del
{DELETEDOWN}	Ctrl-Backspace
{DRILLDOWN}	Ctrl-Enter
{ESC} or {ESCAPE}	Esc
{INS} or {INSERT}	Ins

Key-Equivalent Commands (*continued*)
Table 20-1.

Quattro Pro also has a special way of recording menu commands in macros, using a set of codes known as *menu-equivalent commands*. Menu-equivalent commands consist of a slash followed by a space followed by two words or, more rarely, a word and a number separated by a semicolon. Like all macro commands they are always enclosed in curly braces. For example, in the \D macro Quattro Pro recorded the / **S**tyle | **N**umeric Format command as {/Block;Format}.

Rather than having separate menu-equivalent commands for each / **S**tyle | **N**umeric Format command, Quattro Pro has a menu-equivalent command for / **S**tyle | **N**umeric Format and then simply records the keystrokes used to specify different formats. In the case of the \D macro, the characters d4~ that appear after {/Block;Format} represent the keystrokes you used to specify the Date format, select Date format number 4, and accept the default block by pressing Enter.

Sometimes menu-equivalent commands contain compound words. For example, the menu-equivalent command {/PieExploded;1} represents the / **G**raph | **C**ustomize Series | **E**xplode command (with the Pie graph type selected and Slice 1 selected). Although the words used in menu-equivalent commands are rarely identical to the menu options they represent, you usually have little trouble deciphering their meaning.

Because of the way Quattro Pro records menu selections, you should generally select menu options by typing letters rather than using the arrow keys when you record macros. Otherwise, at least some of your selections will be recorded as cursor movements, which takes up more room, makes the macro harder to read, slows down macro execution, and opens up the possibility of the macro not working if you ever modify the menus. For example, in the previous macro, if you used arrow keys to select all the menu options, Quattro Pro would have recorded the application of the date format to the cell as

```
{/Block;Format}
{DOWN 7}~
{DOWN 3}~
```

meaning / **S**tyle | **N**umeric Format, press ↓ seven times and press Enter, press ↓ three times and press Enter again. As you can see, it is almost impossible to tell what this macro does without actually performing the keystrokes.

Although you can use menu command shortcuts when recording macros, avoid using shortcuts that you have created (as opposed to ones that were in effect when you installed Quattro Pro). Otherwise, your actions may be recorded as individual keystrokes rather than menu-equivalent commands, and if you change the shortcut later, your macro will no longer work.

Introduction to Macros

Now try recording a second macro so you can see how Quattro Pro records cursor movements. This macro underlines the characters in the cell above the current cell using equal signs. It uses both the @REPEAT and @LENGTH functions to display as many equal signs as there are characters in the cell above. If you are using WYSIWYG, you may want to switch to a character-based display mode since the macro's results will look better. (Due to the proportionally spaced fonts in WYSIWYG, the equal signs may occupy more space than the label you are underlining.) Before you start recording the macro, enter a label to underline.

1. Move to A:C1 and enter **This is a test**.
2. Move to C2, and press [Alt]-[F2] and type **R** to start recording the macro.
3. Type **@REPEAT("=",@LENGTH(** and press the [↑] key to move the cell pointer to C1.
4. Type **))** and press [Enter] to complete the formula and enter it into the cell.
5. Press [Alt]-[F2] and type **P** to open the Macro menu and select Paste. This terminates the recording and initiates the pasting process. When Quattro Pro prompts you for a macro name, enter **UNDERLINE**. When prompted for a block, enter **B:A5**. The Macros page of your notebook should now look like Figure 20-1. The key-equivalent command {UP} in cell A6 represents the pressing of [↑].
6. Move to A:C4 and enter **Here is a longer label**.
7. Move to C5, press [Alt]-[F2], and type **E** to execute the macro. (Since this macro has a standard name rather than an instant name, you have to issue the Execute command.) Press [F3] (Choices) and select the macro name UNDERLINE from the list of block names. Quattro Pro underlines the new label with equal signs.

By using [↑] to point to cell C1 rather than typing an explicit cell reference, you made this function generic. You can use it to underline the cell above the current cell in any spot on the notebook. In addition, because the @LENGTH function is used as an argument to the @REPEAT function, the

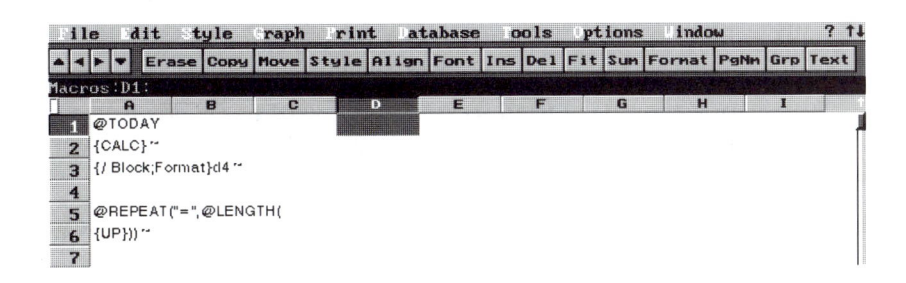

Creating the UNDERLINE macro
Figure 20-1.

number of equal signs displayed depends on the number of characters in the referenced cell.

In most cases you design your macros so you can use them in the widest possible set of circumstances. How you do this depends on the macro's function and your own work needs. For example, if you create a macro to widen a column by one character, you get a different result if, when recording the macro, you enter **10** as the width rather than changing the width to 10 by pressing the → key. In the first case, the macro always widens or narrows the column to 10, regardless of its current width. In the second case, the macro widens the column by a single character, and the resulting width depends on how wide the column was when you initiated the macro.

A similar issue arises when you refer to cells or blocks of cells in macros. Pointing to cells with arrow keys gives macros tremendous flexibility, allowing you to apply a series of actions to different cells on the notebook. In some cases, however, you want a macro to affect particular cells or blocks of cells, regardless of your current position. You can accomplish this by entering cell references or block names, rather than pointing.

In general, block names are the preferred method of referencing cells in a macro, because explicit cell references can produce problems if you later rearrange your notebook. When you use cell references in formulas, print blocks, or sort blocks, and then make changes on your notebook that affect those cell references, Quattro Pro makes all necessary adjustments on the spot. In contrast, Quattro Pro does not adjust macro cell references because macros are simply labels on your notebook; they are not dynamic formulas. If you direct Quattro Pro to move to or use a particular cell address within a macro and then subsequently rearrange the notebook, your macro will still contain the original, unadjusted cell references. You can prevent this by using block names rather than specific cell references whenever you direct Quattro Pro to go to or use a particular cell within a macro. That way, when the macro is executed, it uses the current block coordinates, which have been updated automatically as you have made changes on the notebook. Always type block names rather than using the F3 (Choices) key when recording macros so the name itself rather than a set of cursor movements is recorded. Using block names in macros also allows you to use the same (or similar) macros in different notebooks even when those notebooks are not identical in structure.

The remaining macro exercises in this chapter are more involved than the ones you have tried so far. If you want to try creating a few more simple macros first, attempt some or all of the following on your own:

- ◆ Create a macro that widens the current column by a character, as just described.

Introduction to Macros

- Create a macro that draws a double line underneath the current cell using the / **S**tyle | **L**ine Drawing command.
- Create a printing macro that executes the / **P**rint | **A**djust Printer | **A**lign command, followed by the / **P**rint | **S**preadsheet Print command, followed by the / **P**rint | **A**djust Printer | **F**orm Feed command.

Editing Macros

If you make a mistake while recording a macro, the simplest solution usually is to re-record it. Start by erasing the cells that contain the faulty macro, in case the new macro is slightly shorter than the old one. Then record the macro again. (If you haven't already pasted the macro, you can abort it just by pressing [Alt]-[F2] and then typing **R** again.)

In the case of long or complicated macros, you may want to edit the macro rather than record it again, particularly if you have made only a minor mistake. Because a macro is simply a series of labels on your notebook, you can edit it as you would any other label.

You might also edit a macro when you cannot stop recording at exactly the point you would like, because you are not in Ready mode and therefore cannot display the Macro menu. To illustrate this problem, try creating a macro to streamline the process of macro execution. This macro opens the Macro menu, selects the Execute option, and presses [F3] (Choices) to display a list of block names.

1. Move back to A:A5. Press [Alt]-[F2] and type **R** to open the Macro menu and start recording.
2. Press [Alt]-[F2] to reopen the Macro menu and type **E** for Execute.
3. When Quattro Pro prompts for a block of macros to execute, press [F3] to display a list of named blocks. This is the point at which the macro should actually stop. However, because you cannot display the Macro menu at the moment, you must continue recording until Quattro Pro is back in Ready mode.
4. Type **\D** and press [Enter] to select the \D macro from the list, and let Quattro Pro enter today's date into the current cell (overwriting the date that is already there).
5. Press [Alt]-[F2] and type **P** to stop recording and paste the macro into the notebook. When Quattro Pro prompts for a block name, enter **\M**. When prompted for a macro block, enter **B:A8**. The Macros page of your notebook should now look like Figure 20-2.

Creating a macro to execute macros
Figure 20-2.

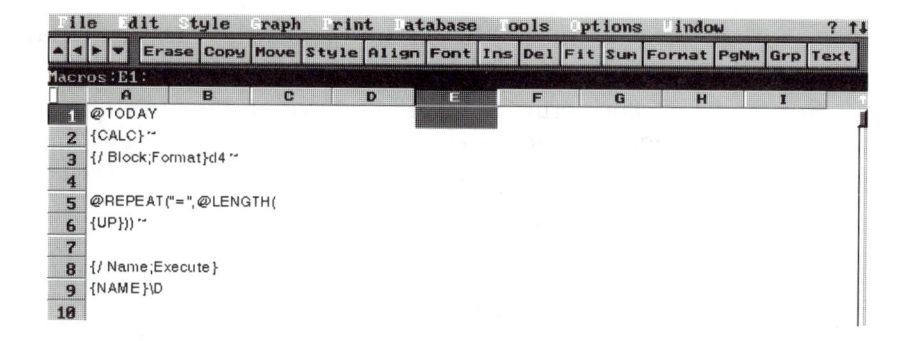

```
           A            B          C        D         E         F        G        H        I
    1  @TODAY
    2  {CALC}~
    3  {/ Block;Format}d4~
    4
    5  @REPEAT("=",@LENGTH(
    6  {UP})~
    7
    8  {/ Name;Execute}
    9  {NAME}\D
   10
```

Now you need to manually delete the extra keystrokes from the macro.

1. Move the cell pointer to the cell that contains the characters \D.
2. Press F2 (Edit) and press the Backspace key twice so that {NAME} is the last thing in the macro. Press Enter.
3. Now try playing the macro. Move to A:C6, and press Alt-M to execute the \M macro. When Quattro Pro displays a list of block names, select UNDERLINE. You should get a second underline underneath the first underline that came under the text "Here is a longer label."
4. Issue the / File | Save command and replace the previous version of the SAMPMAC.WQ2 notebook.

Sample Database Macros

You are now ready to create two more elaborate macros. Both are designed for use with the ORDERS.WQ2 database, but their functions are suitable to any database. If you did not create ORDERS.WQ2 in Chapters 16 and 17 but have another database to work with, read through the instructions first and then try adjusting the keystrokes to fit your own database's structure.

The first macro facilitates the entry of new records in your database. This macro inserts a new row within the current borders of the database and copies the last record's data into this row. It then erases all the labels and numeric constants in the last row, but leaves the formatting codes and formulas intact so that the row is perfectly prepared for a new record. Because the macro inserts the new row within the borders of the database, you do not need to adjust the block settings on the Database | Sort and Database | Query menus or the database argument in statistical functions as you add new records.

Introduction to Macros

Before you start recording this macro, you assign a block name to the column heading for the first field in the database. This named block serves as a starting point when you execute the macro, so the macro always starts from the same spot. From there the macro uses the [End]-[↓] key combination to move to the first field of what is currently the last row of the database before inserting a new row. Note that [End]-[↓] works properly only if the first field of every record is filled in, as it is in most databases and should be in this one.

If you make a serious mistake at any point, just press [Esc]. Then open the Macro menu and select Record to stop recording, and start over again.

1. Retrieve the ORDERS.WQ2 database using the / **File** | **Retrieve** command.
2. Issue the / **Edit** | **Names** | **Create** command, enter the block name **FIELD1**, and enter the address **A12**.
3. Press [Alt]-[F2] and type **R** to start recording a macro.
4. Press [F5] (GoTo) and enter the block name **FIELD1** as the cell to go to.
5. Press [End] and then [↓] to move to the first field in the last record of the database (cell A22 at this point).
6. Type **/EIR** to issue the / **Edit** | **Insert** | **Rows** command, and press [Enter] to insert a new row at row 22.
7. Type **/EC** to issue the / **Edit** | **Copy** command. When prompted for a source block, press [Esc] to unanchor the cell pointer, and then press [↓] to move the cell pointer to cell A23. Type a period to anchor the cell pointer. Then press [→] 11 times to move the cell pointer to the AMT DUE field (cell L23) and press [Enter]. When prompted for a destination, press [Enter] to accept the default of A:A22. Quattro Pro copies the data in row 23 to row 22.
8. Press the [↓] key to move to row 23. Erase all the cells in the row except those that contain formulas by typing **/EE** to issue the / **Edit** | **Erase Block** command, pressing [→] four times to extend the block to A23..E23, and pressing [Enter]. This erases the ACCOUNT, STATE, ORDER DATE, ITEM, and QUANT fields.
9. Type **/EE** to issue the / **Edit** | **Erase** command again. Press [Esc] to unanchor the cell pointer, press [→] nine times to move to column J, and type a period to anchor it again. Press [→] once to extend the block to J23..K23, and press [Enter], erasing any data in the PMT DATE and PMT AMT fields.
10. Press [Alt]-[F2] and type **P** to stop recording and paste the new macro into the notebook. When prompted for a name, enter **\A**. When prompted for a "macro block to paste," enter **B:A1**.

Pressing [→] 11 times is safer than pressing [End]-[→] twice because some fields in the record might be blank.

11. Delete row 23 by issuing the / **Edit** | **D**elete | **R**ows command and pressing [Enter]. This eliminates the extra row that you created while recording the macro.
12. Press [Home] to move to A1 so that you can prove to yourself that the macro will work from anywhere.
13. Now test the macro by holding down [Alt] and typing **A**.
14. Fill in the new record with the following data. Enter **N.L.G** in A23; enter **NY** in cell B23; enter **12/1/94** in C23; enter **32-45** in D23; and enter **3** in E23. Your notebook should now look like Figure 20-3; if not, try again from step 1.
15. Press [F5] (GoTo) and enter **\A**. Your notebook should now look similar to Figure 20-4. Don't worry about an extra keystroke or two that may have resulted from making and then correcting an error along the way, as long as the macro works.
16. Issue the / **F**ile | **S**ave command to replace the previous version of the ORDERS.WQ2 notebook.

You could have used the named block ACCOUNT (referring to the ACCOUNT field in the first record) rather than FIELD1 as the starting position for this macro. The reference to FIELD1 is safer, however, because it continues to work even if you delete the first record in the database. In

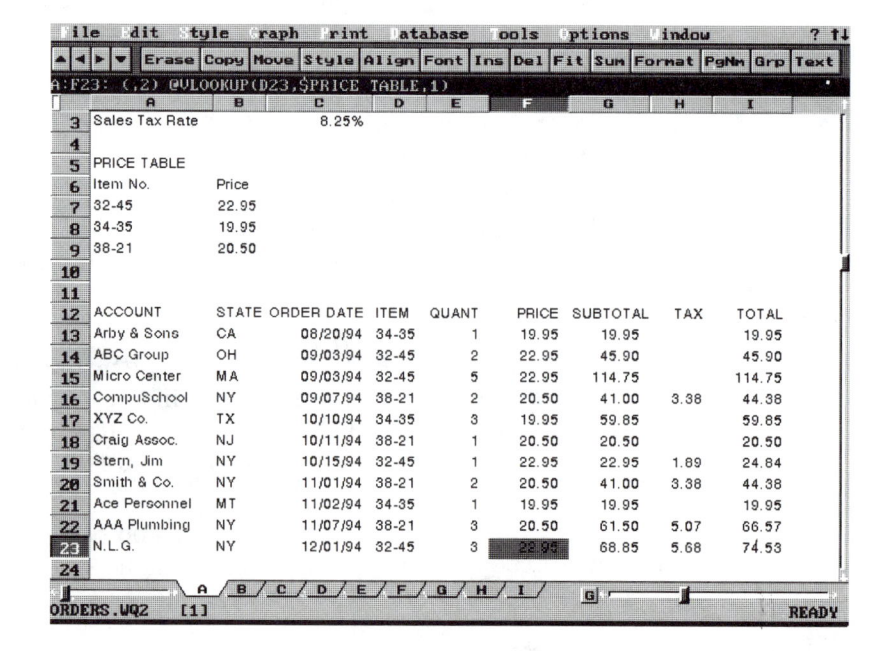

Using the \A macro to add a new record to the database
Figure 20-3.

Introduction to Macros

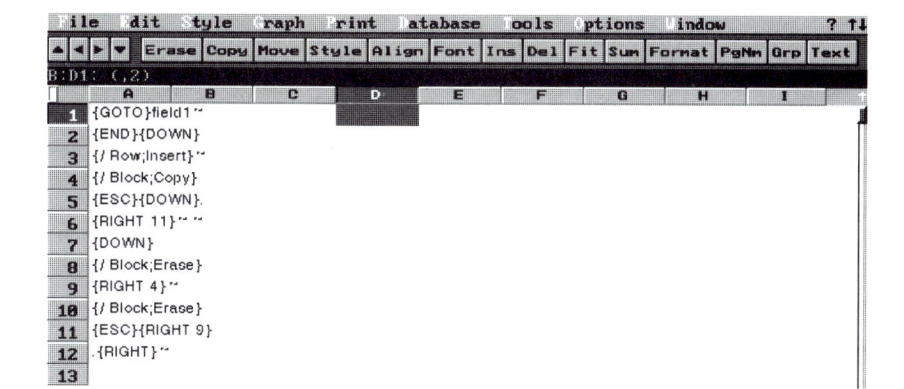

\A macro for adding new records.
Figure 20-4.

```
 1  {GOTO}field1~
 2  {END}{DOWN}
 3  {/ Row;Insert}~
 4  {/ Block;Copy}
 5  {ESC}{DOWN}.
 6  {RIGHT 11}~ ~
 7  {DOWN}
 8  {/ Block;Erase}
 9  {RIGHT 4}~
10  {/ Block;Erase}
11  {ESC}{RIGHT 9}
12  {RIGHT}~
13
```

addition, if you insert another column to the left of ACCOUNT, you only need to change the coordinates of FIELD1 rather than editing the macro to enter the new field name.

Now try creating another macro to restore the database to date order after you insert new records. Before recording this macro, you must create a new block name for the block of records to be sorted (the entire database minus the field names). Whenever you add records using the \A macro, the coordinates of the named block change to include the new data, because the \A macro inserts new rows within the block's current borders. Then, whenever you execute the sort macro, Quattro Pro looks up the current coordinates of the named block and sorts all the records currently in the database. In contrast, if you define the sort block in this macro in terms of specific cell references, those references are not updated as the database changes, and you cannot rely on the macro to sort all the records.

1. Press [F5] (GoTo) and enter **FIELD1**, moving the cell pointer to the top of the database.

2. Issue the / **E**dit | **N**ames | **C**reate command, and specify the block name SORT and the coordinates A13..L23.

3. Press [Alt]-[F2] and type **R** to start recording the macro.

4. Type **/DSB** to issue the / **D**atabase | **S**ort | **B**lock command. When prompted for a block, enter **SORT**.

You can enter any cell in column C to specify the date field.

5. Type **1** to select the 1st Key option. When you are prompted for a "Column/Row to be used as first sort key," enter **C1** to specify the date field. (It would be preferable to enter a block name, but Quattro Pro cannot accept one in this context.) When the Sort Order box is displayed, type **A** and press [Enter] to select Ascending order. (You must actually type in the "A" even though it shows up by default in this case.)

6. Type **G** to select the Go option.
7. When the sort is completed, press [Alt]-[F2] and type **P** to stop recording and paste the macro. Enter **\S** as the macro name and **B:A14** as its location.
8. To try your macro, change the ORDER DATE for Smith & Co. to 9/20/94 and then press [Alt]-[S] to re-sort the database. (If the database is not re-sorted properly, retrieve ORDERS.WQ2 from disk and start again from step 1 of this exercise.)
9. Press [F5] and enter **\S** to move the cell pointer to the new macro, which should now look like this:

```
{/Sort;Block}SORT~
{/Sort;Key1}C1~
A~{/Sort;Go}
```

10. Issue the / **F**ile | **S**ave command to replace the previous version of the notebook.

Applications for Recorded Macros

Any time you find yourself repeating the same keystrokes over and over, try automating them with a macro. And whenever you want to ensure that a particularly delicate operation is performed correctly, record it in a macro to ensure accuracy and consistency. These are just a few of the operations that you might want to automate with macros:

- Entering a set of standard column or row headings, such as the names of all 12 months or the days of the week
- Erasing data from a criteria table that you reuse frequently
- Printing a series of reports, including performing such preparatory steps as hiding or moving columns, inserting extra rows, and defining print ranges, set-up characters, and print layout
- Printing a series of graphs
- Consolidating notebooks using the / **T**ools | **C**ombine | **A**dd command

You undoubtedly will think of many more applications for macros as you continue to work with the program.

The Macro Language

You now have a good sense of what you can accomplish by recording macros. As you have seen, when you record and then paste a macro, Quattro

Introduction to Macros

Pro stores a record of your actions in the notebook using a special macro language. This language also includes several categories of commands which you cannot record, including interactive commands (which pause for user input or activate custom menus) and screen commands (which control the screen display during macro execution). If you want to use one of these commands, you must either insert it into a macro that you previously pasted to the notebook or enter the entire macro manually.

Advanced users and programmers often use the macro language to create elaborate and highly customized macros, including macros that present the user with custom menus. That level of macro usage is far beyond the scope of this book. You can also begin exploring macro commands by displaying lists of them with the [Shift]-[F3] (Macros) key or the Macro button on the Edit SpeedBar. Select a category of commands to display, and then highlight a command and press [F1] (Help) for a brief description of its use.

Maintaining and Using Macros

As you accumulate macros you must begin to think about organizing and manipulating them, performing the macro equivalent of file management. This involves documenting your macros (entering descriptions on the notebook to remind you of the macro's function), renaming them, deleting them, and copying them from one file to another.

Documenting Your Macros

If you use instant macros, create several macros on a notebook, or use a notebook infrequently, it is easy to forget what your macros do. You can eliminate the need to decipher macros later by entering brief descriptions of their functions as you create them. These descriptions need not be long or elaborate; in most cases a few words or a sentence will suffice. Figure 20-5 shows the documentation for the first macro in the ORDERS.WQ2 notebook. Note that the macro name was entered to the left of the macro and a description to its right. You can use any layout you like, as long as you include both the macro name and a description. (As described shortly, placing the macro names in a single column makes it easy to name macros after copying them to another notebook.)

Renaming and Deleting Macros

Renaming a macro is a two-step process. First you delete the old name by selecting the Name option on the Macro menu and choosing Delete. When Quattro Pro displays a list of block names, either enter a macro name or select one from the list. Quattro Pro does not ask for confirmation as it does when you delete a file; it simply deletes the macro name. The macro

Quattro Pro 5 Made Easy

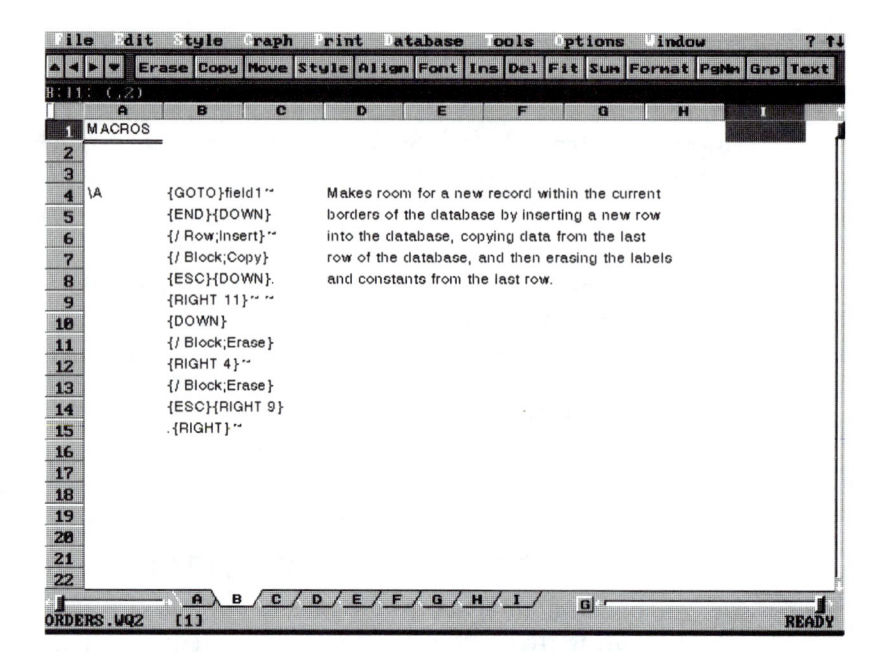

```
 File  Edit  Style  Graph  Print  Database  Tools  Options  Window      ? ↑↓
 ▲ ◄ ► ▼  Erase Copy Move Style Align Font Ins Del Fit Sum Format PgNm Grp Text
 B:11: (,2)
        A         B          C          D          E         F         G         H         I
   1  MACROS
   2
   3
   4         \A       {GOTO}field1~           Makes room for a new record within the current
   5                  {END}{DOWN}              borders of the database by inserting a new row
   6                  {/ Row;Insert}~          into the database, copying data from the last
   7                  {/ Block;Copy}           row of the database, and then erasing the labels
   8                  {ESC}{DOWN}.             and constants from the last row.
   9                  {RIGHT 11}~ ~
  10                  {DOWN}
  11                  {/ Block;Erase}
  12                  {RIGHT 4}~
  13                  {/ Block;Erase}
  14                  {ESC}{RIGHT 9}
  15                  .{RIGHT}~
  16
  17
  18
  19
  20
  21
  22
       A\B\C\D\E\F\G\H\I\        G
 ORDERS.WQ2  [1]                                                                         READY
```

A well-documented macro
Figure 20-5.

itself—the actual labels containing the representations of cursor movements, keystrokes, and commands—remains on the notebook (just as Quattro Pro leaves a block's data intact when you delete a block name). If you want to erase the labels containing the macro from the notebook, use the / **Edit** I **Erase Block** command.

You assign a new name to a macro by selecting the Name option on the Macro menu and choosing Create. When Quattro Pro displays a list of block names, enter the name that you wish to assign. (The only time you would choose an existing block name is if you want to recycle that name, removing it from one block and assigning it to another.) Then specify the coordinates of the first cell of your macro by either entering the address or pointing to the cell.

Copying Macros to Another Notebook

When you copy macros from one notebook to another, remember that the block names are not copied. You therefore need to name the macros again. If you enter the macro names in a single column to the left of the macros (see the macro name \A in column A of the notebook shown in Figure 20-5), you can name a group of macros simultaneously using the / **Edit** I **Names** I **Labels** I **Right** command. Just specify the block of cells that contains the macro names as the label block.

Using Macro Libraries

A *macro library* is a notebook that contains macros that you can execute from other open notebooks. You can designate a notebook as a macro library by choosing the Library option on the Macro menu and then changing the setting to Yes. Once you have marked a notebook as a macro library, that designation remains with the notebook permanently, unless you explicitly change it by selecting the Library option on the Macro menu and changing the setting to No.

Whenever a macro library is open, Quattro Pro allows you to execute macros from that file. When you invoke either an instant or a standard macro, Quattro Pro looks for the macro on the current notebook. If it does not find it there, it searches through every open macro library until it finds the macro and then executes it.

You should start building a macro library as soon as you start creating macros. Whenever you prepare to create a macro, consider whether the macro may have applications beyond the current notebook. Many macros, such as the date-stamping and underlining macros created near the beginning of this chapter, are completely generic (or can be made so) and can be applied to any notebook file. You should store all such macros in a macro library for the following reasons:

- You need not waste time and disk space copying macros to several different notebooks.
- You do not have to worry about damaging macros while modifying the rest of your notebook.
- You know where to look for macros when you want to use them in the future.
- You only have to edit a single notebook if you decide to change one of them.

Other macros are specific to individual notebooks but general in their basic function; they can be modified to work in other contexts but cannot be made completely context-free. The first database macro that you created falls into this category. Some of the individual keystrokes are specific to the structure of the ORDERS.WQ2 notebook, but you can use a similar macro to add records to other databases. You may also want to store this type of macro in a library to make it easy to copy into new notebooks (before modifying the macro instructions to fit the new data). This spares you the task of tracking down the macro in a notebook file.

There are a few practices that can help you use macro libraries effectively. If your macro library contains more macros than fit on a single screen, you can enter a table of contents at the top of the macro library notebook. This makes it easy to determine the names and purposes of all the macros stored in a particular library. You will find this especially helpful when you are having trouble remembering a particular macro name.

If you create dozens of macros, you may want to develop specialized macro libraries—for example, one library of editing and formatting macros and another for database macros. Although you can open more than one macro library at a time, you should do so with care. If two open libraries contain a macro with the same name, it is difficult to predict which one will execute when you invoke the macro from a third notebook. To avoid this problem either open only one library at a time or choose unique names for all your macros, regardless of where you store them.

You also encounter problems if your notebook contains a macro or any other named block with the same name as a macro in an open notebook library. Whenever you issue the / **T**ools | **M**acro | **E**xecute command or press Alt and a letter for an instant macro, Quattro Pro always looks on the current notebook for a block with the specified name. Only if it cannot find one does Quattro Pro continue its search in any open macro libraries. For example, suppose you issue the / **T**ools | **M**acros | **E**xecute command and enter **PERCENT** in an attempt to execute the PERCENT macro in an open macro library. If the current notebook contains a named block called PERCENT, Quattro Pro attempts to execute it as a macro, even if that block is simply a collection of cells that you happened to assign that name.

If you use macro libraries extensively, you may want to develop a naming scheme to help avoid such problems. For example, you could decide that the names of all macros in macro libraries will start with either a backslash (for instant macros), the letters ML (for macro library), or a special character such as an asterisk. You can then simply avoid those characters at the beginning of regular block names or macros that you create on regular (nonlibrary) notebooks.

Changing the Macro Recording Method

By default, the Macro Recording option on the Macro menu is set to Logical. This means that Quattro Pro records menu selections as macro-equivalent commands rather than as a series of keystrokes. If you change this setting to Keystroke, Quattro Pro records commands in terms of the individual keystrokes that you use to issue those commands. What follows are two versions of the same macro—a macro that assigns the Percent format with no decimals to the current cell, using the / **S**tyle | **N**umeric Format command. This macro

```
{/Block;Format}P0~~
```

Introduction to Macros

was recorded with the Logical recording method. In contrast, this macro

`/SNP0~~`

was recorded with the Keystroke recording method. You should change to the Keystroke recording method only if you must be able to import your notebook into Lotus 1-2-3.

Playing Macros Automatically

There are several ways to automate the execution of a macro, so it is replayed as soon as you load either the notebook or Quattro Pro.

Startup Macros

You can use the / **O**ptions | **S**tartup | **S**tartup Macro command to assign a particular name to a macro that you want to invoke automatically when you load a notebook. For example, if you create a notebook specifically for displaying a graphics slide show, you might create an instant macro to initiate the slide show as soon as you retrieve the file. The initial setting for the startup macro name is \0, but you can change it by entering a new name and selecting the Update option on the Options menu to save the new default. You are restricted to one startup macro per notebook.

If you no longer want a macro to be invoked automatically whenever you retrieve the notebook, you can either change its name, delete it with the / **T**ools | **M**acro | **N**ame | **D**elete command, or change the Startup Macro name. Keep in mind that changing the Startup Macro name affects every notebook that contains a startup macro, not just the current notebook. If you have created macros with the old Startup Macro name on other notebooks, they are affected as well.

Autoloading Macros

Quattro Pro offers two ways to execute a particular macro as soon as you load Quattro Pro. First, you can create a startup macro on an autoload notebook. (To do this, use the / **O**ptions | **S**tartup | **A**utoload File command in conjunction with the / **O**ptions | **S**tartup | **S**tartup Macro command.) Remember, an autoload notebook is a notebook that is loaded immediately whenever you load the Quattro Pro program. If you define a startup macro on this notebook (as described in the previous section), every time you load Quattro Pro, the autoload file is retrieved and the startup macro executed.

You can also initiate a macro from the DOS command line by typing the macro name after the Quattro Pro load command and the name of the file that contains the macro. For example, to load a macro called \A on the ORDERS notebook, you type **Q ORDERS \A**. This command loads the Quattro Pro program, retrieves the ORDERS.WQ2 notebook, and then invokes the \A macro.

As you work with any program, you inevitably find yourself repeating particular sequences of keystrokes. Macros allow you to save time and minimize mistakes by automating such keystroke sequences and letting Quattro Pro do more of your work for you. This chapter has barely scratched the surface of what you can accomplish with macros. Once you have mastered the techniques introduced here and have created new macros on your own, you may want to explore further. As a starting place, consult your Quattro Pro documentation.

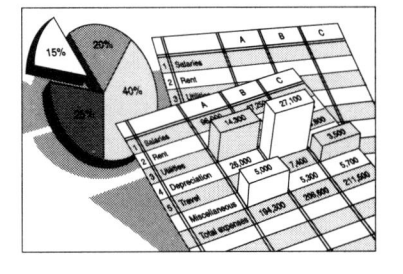

APPENDIX

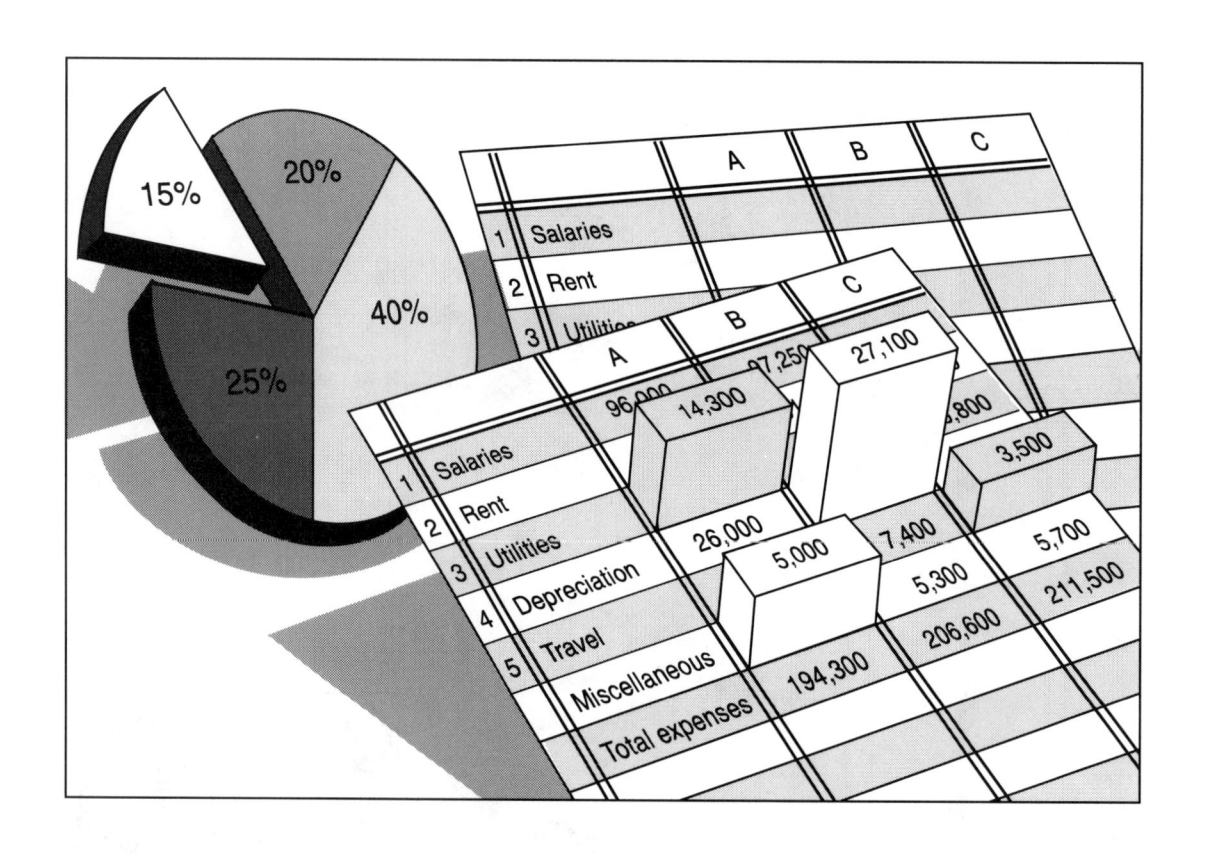

A

INSTALLING QUATTRO PRO

To install and use Quattro Pro 5, you need an IBM or IBM-compatible computer with at least 512K of Random Access Memory (RAM), DOS 2.0 or later, and at least 7 megabytes of available hard-disk space. (Once installed, Quattro Pro 5 only occupies about 4 megabytes, although it will require more as you build fonts and create notebook files.) You will get better performance with additional RAM (the more the better), particularly if you regularly work with large spreadsheets.

NOTE: If you are upgrading from a previous version of Quattro Pro, you should read the section on upgrading before you start the installation process.

Copying the Quattro Pro Disks

Before you install Quattro Pro, it's advisable to make duplicate copies of all the Quattro Pro disks. If you are using a version of DOS prior to DOS 4.0, make sure that you have blank formatted disks on hand. (DOS 4.0 and above will format unformatted disks if necessary when you issue the DISKCOPY command, so you don't need to format them first.) Place the first Quattro Pro disk in drive A. If you have two floppy-disk drives, place the first Quattro Pro disk in drive A, place the first blank disk in drive B, and enter

   DISKCOPY   A: B:

You will see a message about inserting the *source diskette* (the disk you are copying from) in drive A and the *target diskette* (the disk you are copying to) in drive B. Assuming you have already placed these disks in the appropriate drives, press [Enter] to initiate the copy process.

If you only have one disk drive of the same size as the installation disk, put the first Quattro Pro disk in either drive A or drive B, and enter

   DISKCOPY   A: A:

or

   DISKCOPY   B: B:

In a short while, your computer will prompt you to "Insert the Target diskette." Insert the first blank disk and press [Enter]. Unless you have a lot of memory installed in your computer, you may be prompted to reinsert the source diskette (the disk you are copying from) and then the target diskette.

When the copying process is complete, you will see the prompt "Copy another diskette (Y/N)?" Type **Y**. Insert the second Quattro Pro disk in drive A and, if you have a second floppy-disk drive, a second, blank floppy disk in drive B. Press [Enter] to start copying. Repeat the process again for the remaining Quattro Pro disks. Then, when asked whether you want to copy another, type **N** for No. You will be returned to the DOS prompt.

Installing Quattro Pro

Be sure to label your new set of Quattro Pro disks as Quattro Pro Disk 1, 2, and so on. Also, write the serial number on the label for Disk 1 in case you lose the original disks.

Starting the Installation

To install Quattro Pro, put the first Quattro Pro disk in drive A and enter **A:INSTALL**. The installation program will guide you through the process, asking you questions when necessary and telling you when to insert new disks. Read the screen carefully for instructions.

> **NOTE:** If you have trouble reading the installation program screens, press (Esc) to interrupt the program and then try again by entering **A:INSTALL /B**. This directs the Install program to display screens in black and white rather than in color.

In most cases, the current disk drive will be drive C. If you have a large hard disk, it may be D, E, or F.

The Install program starts by asking for the source drive (the drive that contains the Quattro Pro diskette). Then it displays the name of the directory to which the Quattro Pro program files will be copied. By default, the installation program places all the program files in a directory called QPRO on the current disk drive. To accept the default, press (Enter). If you want to place your Quattro Pro program files in a different directory, press (F2), press (Backspace) until you delete the name of the default directory, type the drive and directory and press (Enter), and then press (Enter) again to start installing.

The installation process takes longer than it would take to simply copy files from the floppy disks onto your hard disk. This is because the installation program is *unzipping* all the files—that is, converting them from a compressed format to the regular, uncompressed format they need to be in to run. As Quattro Pro is copying itself onto your hard disk, you'll see a list of which files are being installed. When all files from one disk have been copied, Quattro Pro prompts you to insert the next disk.

Once the Install program has copied and uncompressed all the files, you will also be asked to supply several pieces of information, including your name, company name, and Quattro Pro serial number. This information will be displayed on the Quattro Pro sign-on screen every time you start the program. In each case you press (F2), type the requested information, and press (Enter) twice (once to finalize the entry and a second time to move to the next item). Next, Quattro Pro asks you a series of questions about your hardware. For each question Quattro Pro supplies a default answer. You can accept this answer by pressing (Enter) or you can press (F2) for a list of other choices. If you press (Enter) accidentally, the (Esc) key will usually take you back a step. Most of the questions are self-explanatory; the few questions that may not be obvious are explained here.

- When asked whether you want to use WYSIWYG as your default display mode, you can accept Install's suggestion of Yes if you have an EGA or VGA card that supports 640x350 resolution or better. If you don't have the proper video card or if you are not sure, press [F2] and change the setting to No. (WYSIWYG display mode is a graphics-based mode that displays your spreadsheets almost exactly as they look when printed in final-quality mode.) You can always change the default display mode, as explained briefly in Chapter 1 and fully in Chapter 13.

- When Install asks whether you want to install Quattro Pro for Windows, select Yes if you plan to run Quattro Pro 5 from within the Windows program.

- When Install asks which Bitstream character set to use, accept the setting of Standard U.S. unless you need to use international or diacritical characters (such as accent marks or tildes).

When the installation process is complete, if the Install program has changed your AUTOEXEC.BAT or CONFIG.SYS file, you will be asked to reboot your computer. Press any key to return to the DOS prompt, and then hold down [Ctrl] and [Alt], and tap the [Del] key.

NOTE: Quattro Pro automatically changes your AUTOEXEC.BAT file, adding the Quattro Pro program directory to your DOS search path. If you know your way around DOS and prefer not to have this directory in your path, feel free to edit AUTOEXEC.BAT and undo this change.

Upgrading from Earlier Versions of Quattro Pro

If you are upgrading from an earlier version of Quattro Pro, you must delete that version before you install Quattro Pro 5. If you don't, Quattro Pro may behave unpredictably.

If there are any spreadsheet files, clip art data files, or custom menu tree files in your Quattro Pro directory that you want to save, start by copying them to a different directory.

1. Make a directory called QTEMP by entering **MD \QTEMP**.

Installing Quattro Pro

2. Make sure you are in the Quattro Pro directory (the DOS prompt will probably say something like C:\QPRO). Copy your spreadsheet files to QTEMP by entering **COPY *.W* \QTEMP**.
3. If you have clip art files that you want to save, enter **COPY *.CLP \QTEMP**.
4. If you have menu tree files that you want to save, enter **COPY *.MU \QTEMP**.
5. Delete the file called INSTALL.WQ2 (if there is one) from the \QTEMP directory by entering **DEL \QTEMP\INSTALL.WQ2**.

Once you have copied all of the files that you want to save, perform the following steps to erase the old version of Quattro Pro:

1. Enter **DEL *.*** to erase everything from the Quattro Pro directory. Type **Y** when asked whether you are sure.
2. Enter **DEL FONTS*.*** to erase everything from the Quattro Pro fonts directory. Type **Y** when asked whether you are sure.
3. Install Quattro Pro as previously described.

If you copied files to a directory called QTEMP, perform the following steps to copy them back to the Quattro Pro directory.

1. Enter **COPY \QTEMP*.* \QPRO** to copy the files that you previously copied to the QTEMP directory. If you know your way around DOS, you may prefer to create a separate directory for these data files, and copy them into that directory. Then, you can load Quattro Pro from this data directory as long as the Quattro Pro directory is in your DOS search path. Alternately, you can load Quattro Pro from the Quattro Pro program directory but use the / **S**tartup | **D**irectory command to define a default directory for spreadsheet files and then issue the / **O**ptions | **U**pdate command to save this setting.
2. Enter **DEL \QTEMP** and, when asked whether you're sure, enter **Y**.
3. Enter **RD \QTEMP** to erase the QTEMP directory.

Reading the README File

All last-minute modifications or additions to the Quattro Pro program are described in a file called README on the first Quattro Pro disk. You should read this file carefully before beginning your work in Quattro Pro. To display its contents, simply type **README** at the DOS prompt (you must be in the Quattro Pro program directory, usually QPRO) and press [Enter]. You can generate a printed copy of the README file by making sure that your printer is on and then entering

    COPY   README > PRN

You will need to eject the last page from the printer manually.

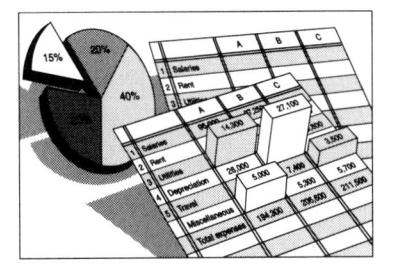

APPENDIX

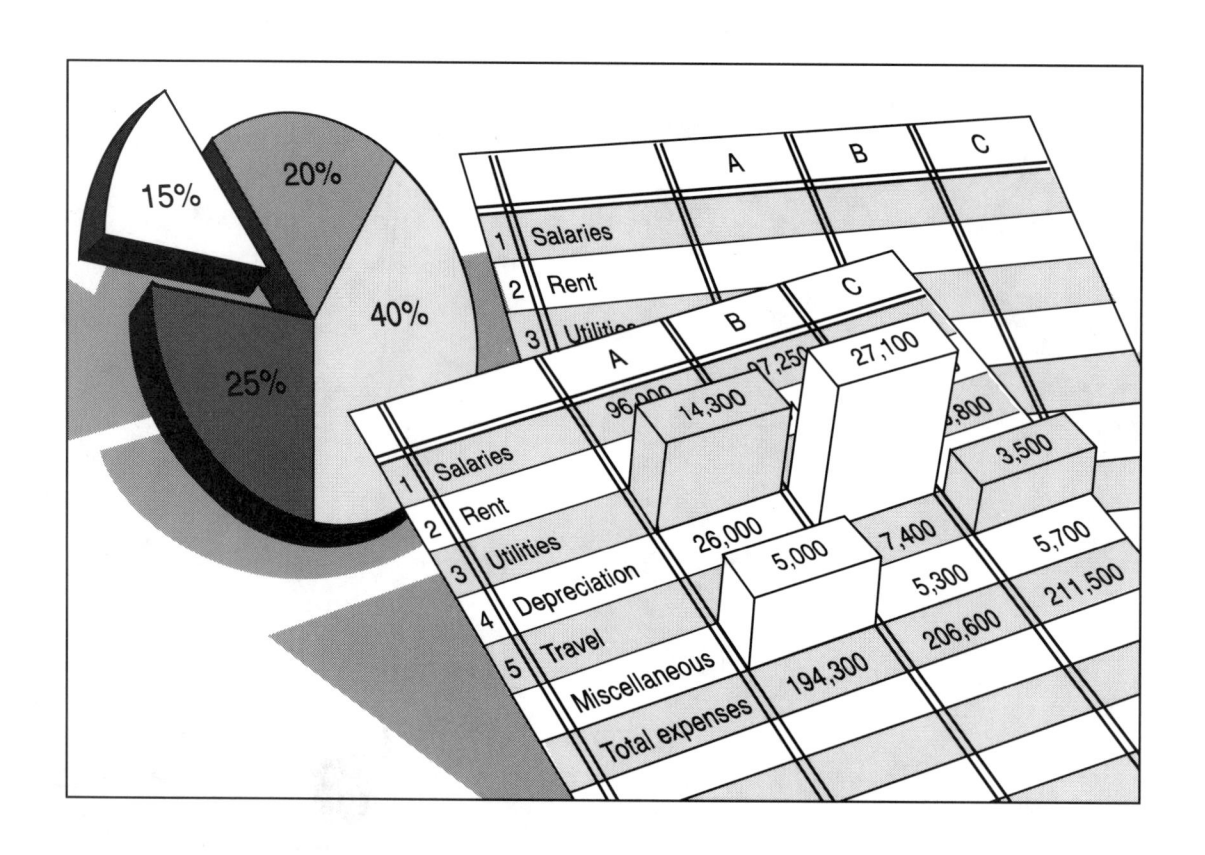

B KEYS AND SHORTCUTS

Quattro Pro offers a wide range of keyboard and mouse shortcuts to both simplify and speed up your work and suit your individual work style. In addition, there are a few dozen editing keys and function keys you should be familiar with to take maximum advantage of Quattro Pro. This appendix lists each available SpeedBar button, keyboard shortcut, editing key, and function key in Quattro Pro. You can use it to refresh your memory, or as a quick learning guide.

TIP: Remember that you can establish your own keyboard shortcuts and can also create custom SpeedBar buttons. These topics are covered in Chapter 13.

Ready Mode SpeedBar

The Ready mode SpeedBar offers a large number of buttons that you can use in place of menu options. This enables you to bypass the menu system when issuing a number of frequently used commands.

Button	Description
arrows	Have the same effect as pressing arrow keys after pressing the End key: move the cell pointer to the edge of a block of data, in the indicated direction
Erase (ERS)	Same as / **E**dit	**E**rase Block
Copy (CPY)	Same as / **E**dit	**C**opy
Move (MOV)	Same as / **E**dit	**M**ove
Style (STY)	Same as / **S**tyle	**U**se Style
Align (ALN)	Same as / **St**yle	**A**lignment
Font (FNT)	Same as / **St**yle	**F**ont
Ins (INS)	Same as / **E**dit	**I**nsert
Del (DEL)	Same as / **E**dit	**D**elete
Fit (FIT)	Same as / **S**tyle	**B**lock Size	**A**uto Width and then pressing Enter to accept one character between columns
Sum (SUM)	Creates an @SUM formula to sum values above or to the left of current cell or, if a block is preselected, creates @SUM formulas along block's bottom and right edges
Format (FMT)	Same as / **S**tyle	**N**umeric Format
PgNm (PAG)	Same as / **E**dit	**P**age	**N**ame
Grp (GRP)	Same as / **E**dit	**G**roup	**C**reate
Text	Switches to 80x25 display mode (WYSIWYG display mode only)

Keys and Shortcuts

Button	Description
WYS	Switches to WYSIWYG display mode (character-based display mode only)
BAR	Toggles between the two groups of SpeedBar buttons in character-based display mode

Edit SpeedBar

The Edit SpeedBar lets you insert arithmetic operators and toggle cell references between relative and absolute. It also lets you view lists of named blocks and macro commands.

Button	Description
arrows	In Value and Label modes, have the same effect as pressing arrow keys after pressing the End key; in Edit mode, left and right arrows move you one character at a time in the indicated direction, while up and down arrows have the usual effect
Name (NAM)	Displays a list of named blocks (similar to F3)
Abs (ABS)	Toggles cell coordinates between absolute and relative (similar to F4)
Calc (CAL)	Calculates the formula on the input line (similar to F9)
Macro (MAC)	Displays a list of menu-equivalent macro categories, each of which leads to a menu of macro commands
@	Displays a menu of functions (similar to Alt-F4)
+ - * / (.)	Same as keyboard equivalents

Editing Keys

The editing keys permit you to do everything from moving around the notebook to making alterations to existing data.

Key	Function
Esc	Discards changes and exits Edit mode
←	Moves cursor one space to the left

Key	Function
→	Moves cursor one space to the right
Backspace	Deletes character to the left of the cursor
Ctrl-Backspace	Erases entry from the input line
Ins	Toggles between Insert and Overwrite modes
Del	Deletes character above cursor
Tab or Ctrl-→	Moves cursor one screenful to the right in Ready mode and five spaces to the right in Edit mode
Shift-Tab or Ctrl-←	Moves cursor one screenful to the left in Ready mode and five spaces to the left in Edit mode
Home	Moves cursor to first character in the entry
End	Moves cursor to last character in the entry
↑	Enters data, exits Edit mode, and moves up one cell; if cursor is located after an operator, enters Point mode
↓	Enters data, exits Edit mode, and moves down one cell; if cursor is located after an operator, enters Point mode
Pg Dn	Enters data, exits Edit mode, and moves cell pointer down a screenful of lines; if cursor is located after an operator, enters Point mode
Pg Up	Enters data, exits Edit mode, and moves cell pointer up a screenful of lines; if cursor is located after an operator, enters Point mode
Ctrl-Pg Up	Moves up to previous page
Ctrl-Pg Dn	Moves down to next page
Ctrl-Home	Moves to notebook's first page
Ctrl-End	Moves to notebook's last page
End-Ctrl-Home	Moves to last cell containing data on last page containing data
Shift-Ctrl-Pg Up	Selects to same cell of previous page
Shift-Ctrl-Pg Dn	Selects to same cell of next page
Shift-Ctrl-Home	Selects to same cell of first page

Keys and Shortcuts

Key	Function
`Ctrl`-`Enter`	"Drills" an entry into all pages in the group
`Ctrl`-`Backspace`	Deletes contents from specified cell(s) in all pages in the group

Preassigned Shortcuts

Quattro Pro provides a number of preassigned keyboard shortcuts for commonly used menu commands. As with SpeedBar buttons, these shortcuts can speed up your work by allowing you to bypass the menu system.

Key Combinations	Menu Equivalents
`Ctrl`-`A`	/ **S**tyle	**A**lignment
`Ctrl`-`C`	/ **E**dit	**C**opy
`Ctrl`-`D`	Date prefix (not reassignable)
`Ctrl`-`E`	/ **E**dit	**E**rase Block
`Ctrl`-`F`	/ **S**tyle	**N**umeric Format
`Ctrl`-`G`	/ **G**raph	**F**ast Graph
`Ctrl`-`I`	/ **E**dit	**I**nsert
`Ctrl`-`M`	/ **E**dit	**M**ove
`Ctrl`-`N`	/ **E**dit	**S**earch & Replace	**N**ext
`Ctrl`-`P`	/ **E**dit	**S**earch & Replace	**P**revious
`Ctrl`-`R`	/ **W**indow	**M**ove/Size*
`Ctrl`-`S`	/ **F**ile	**S**ave
`Ctrl`-`T`	/ **W**indow	**T**ile
`Ctrl`-`W`	/ **S**tyle	**C**olumn Width
`Ctrl`-`X`	/ **F**ile	E**x**it

* Remember, this works only in character-based mode, and you can't move full-screen sized windows.

Function Keys

The function keys in Quattro Pro can be used for the following tasks.

Key	Name	Description
F1	Help	Displays information about highlighted menu option or active function
F2	Edit	Enters Edit mode; if in Edit mode, returns to Value or Label mode
Shift-F2	Debug	Enters Debug mode, so you can execute a macro one step at a time
Alt-F2	Macro Menu	Displays the Macro menu
F3	Choices	Displays a list of existing block names for the current notebook; press + to display block coordinates (if no blocks are named, F3 highlights File option on menu bar)
Shift-F3	Macros	Displays a list of macro commands
Alt-F3	Functions	Displays a list of functions; press + to see function syntax
F4	Abs	In Edit or Value mode, makes the cell address to the left of the cursor absolute
F5	GoTo	Moves the cell selector to a specified address or block name
Shift-F5	Pick Window	Displays a list of open windows
Ctrl-F5	Group	Toggles Group mode on and off
Alt-F5	Undo	If enabled, reverses last undoable action
F6	Pane	Moves the cell selector to the inactive window pane when the window is split into two panes
Shift-F6	Next Window	Displays the next open window
Alt-F6	Zoom	In character-based display modes, expands the active window so that it fills the screen; if active window is already zoomed, returns it to previous size
F7	Query	Repeats the last Query command

Keys and Shortcuts

Key	Name	Description
Shift-F7	Select	Allows you to select a block of cells in Ext mode
Alt-F7	All Select	Selects all files in the active File Manager file list
F8	Table	Repeats the last What-If command
Shift-F8	Move	Removes the files marked in the active File Manager file list and stores them in temporary memory so you can insert them somewhere else
F9	Calc	In Ready mode, calculates any formulas that have been entered or changed since you turned off automatic recalculation; in Value or Edit mode, converts the formula on the input line to its end result
Shift-F9	Copy	Copies the files marked on the active File Manager file list into temporary memory so you can insert them somewhere else
F10	Graph	Displays the current graph
Shift-F10	Paste	Inserts any files stored in temporary memory into the directory displayed in the active File Manager file list

APPENDIX

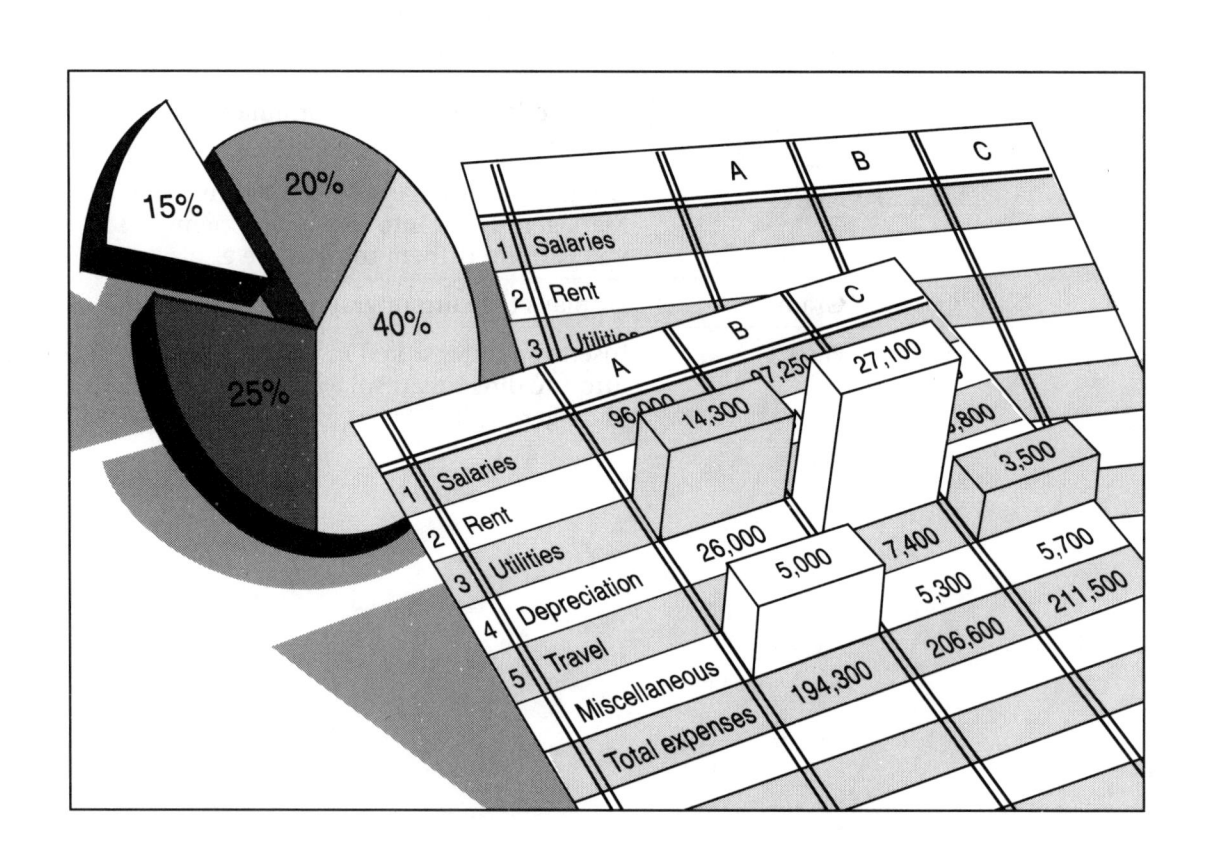

EXCHANGING DATA WITH OTHER PROGRAMS

At some point in your work with Quattro Pro, you will probably want to exchange data with another software package. You may want to export data to a word processing program so you can include a notebook in a longer report. You might wish to import stock prices that you downloaded from a bulletin board into Quattro Pro so that you can perform calculations on the data. You may want to exchange data with a mainframe, import a database initially created in another database manager, or exchange data with other spreadsheet programs. Quattro Pro offers several different methods for importing and exporting data, depending on the type of data and the type of program with which you are exchanging data. Although this chapter covers the range of possibilities, it cannot cover every program, and is designed to point out potential problems and offer general solutions rather than to provide step-by-step instructions on each situation.

Quattro Pro can interpret files in a variety of formats, allowing you to import a wide range of file types directly into Quattro Pro just by using the / File | **R**etrieve or / **F**ile | **O**pen command. In addition, you can translate Quattro Pro files into those formats just by saving them with the appropriate extension. Table C-1 lists the file types that Quattro Pro can translate, along with their file name extensions.

Exchanging Data with Lotus 1-2-3

Quattro Pro provides extensive support for the various 1-2-3 file formats, allowing you to easily exchange spreadsheets with 1-2-3 users.

Quattro Pro can read any spreadsheet created in 1-2-3 versions 1A, 2.01, 2.2, 2.3, or 3.*x*, or in 1-2-3 for Windows. Whenever you retrieve a spreadsheet file that has the extension WKS, WK1, or WK3, Quattro Pro translates the data into Quattro Pro format. This translation process is automatic; in most cases, you will not even know that it is happening.

Retrieving Version 3.0 Files

Some features in 1-2-3 version 3.*x* may present minor problems when you retrieve WK3 files into Quattro Pro.

◆ If the file contains multiple spreadsheets, Quattro Pro will ask whether you want the sheets saved as separate files. Quattro Pro can only translate a single 1-2-3 file into a maximum of 32 separate files: If your 1-2-3 file contains more than 32 sheets, you must break it up into 32-sheet files before retrieving it in Quattro Pro. When Quattro Pro divides your 1-2-3 file into separate files, each file is assigned an extension of a W followed by two characters indicating the file's spot within the original file. The last two characters of the first file's extension will be 0A, the next file gets the characters 0B, the third gets 0C, and so on up to 0Z. The 27th file's extension ends in AA, the 28th's in AB, and so on. During the conversion process, Quattro Pro converts 3-D cell references to link references wherever necessary.

You will probably need EMS to load a file that contains more than 20 sheets.

Exchanging Data with Other Programs

Table C-1. File Types That Quattro Pro Can Translate

File Name Extension	Program Name
ALL	Allways add-in
CHT	Harvard Graphics 2.x
DB	Paradox
DB2	dBASE II
DBF	dBASE III, III PLUS, IV
DIF	VisiCalc
FM3	Impress add-in (WYSIWYG)
FMT	Impress add-in
HG3	Harvard Graphics 3.x
R2D	Reflex 2
RXD	Reflex 1
SLK	Multiplan
WB1*	Quattro Pro for Windows
WK!	SQZ!, Lotus 1-2-3 2.01
WK$	SQZ!, Lotus 1-2-3 1A
WK1	Lotus 1-2-3 2.01 to 2.4
WK3*	Lotus 1-2-3 3.x
WKP	Surpass
WKQ	Quattro 1.x
WKS	Lotus 1-2-3 1A
WKZ	SQZ!, Quattro
WQ!	SQZ!, Quattro Pro
WQ1	Quattro Pro 4 and earlier
WQ2	Quattro Pro
WR!	SQZ!, Symphony 2.0
WR$	SQZ!, Symphony 1.2
WRK	Symphony 1.2
WR1	Symphony 2.0

* Can import only

✦ References to 3-D blocks are changed to complex formulas. For example, if your 1-2-3 file is named SALES and the first of its three sheets contains the formula @SUM(A:B4..C:D12), Quattro Pro will create three files called SALES0A, SALES0B, and SALES0C, and will convert the formula to

@SUM(B4..D12)+@SUM([SALES0B]B4..D12)+@SUM([SALES0C]B4..D12)

- Quattro Pro truncates any labels that are longer than 254 characters.
- Functions that are not supported in Quattro Pro (such as @SHEET) are converted to labels.
- WK3 graphing features not supported by Quattro Pro are lost.
- Formulas that are longer than 254 characters are converted to labels and followed by the comment "Formula too long." Formula annotations are ignored.
- References to external files are converted to the value of the referenced cell and followed by the comment "external reference not allowed."
- Cell references in macros are not converted.
- If your WK3 file contains multiple ranges as arguments to 1-2-3 database and statistical functions, or as print or database query ranges, Quattro Pro ignores all ranges after the first.
- Numbers larger than 10^{308} are converted to ERR and numbers smaller than 10^{-308} are converted to 0.
- Numeric formatting may change.

Retrieving Allways and Impress/WYSIWYG Files

All versions of Lotus from 2.01 on have special programs for printing (and, in some cases, displaying) spreadsheets using various desktop publishing features. Versions 2.01 and 2.2 use an add-in program called Allways. Versions 2.3 and 3.1 use a feature called WYSIWYG. Many people also use the add-in program called Impress for desktop publishing with 1-2-3 spreadsheets. When you use these special print programs, a separate supplementary disk file is created to store your formatting information. Quattro Pro 5 can read Allways, Impress, and WYSIWYG files and all the formatting information they contain except the following:

- Inserted graphs in Allways files. Inserted graphs in Impress/WYSIWYG *are* supported by Quattro Pro, unless they are based on PIC or CGM files.
- Page breaks and column page breaks.
- Label alignment with left-side spillover.
- Display (screen) colors and display zoom settings and, in Impress/WYSIWYG files, the Display options for mode, font directory, rows, and options.
- Page size, borders on the bottom, grid on printing, print settings, and frames.
- Printer type, orientation, port bin, and other print configuration settings.

Exchanging Data with Other Programs

- Formatting embedded in text, line shadows and colors defined with Format options (except for text color), and blank graphs. (All of these features are only available in Impress/WYSIWYG.)
- Some fonts. Quattro Pro can convert up to 128 different combinations of font, color, boldface, underline, italics, and font colors (in the case of Impress/WYSIWYG files). Quattro Pro converts any combinations that it does not support to Normal style.

Saving in 1-2-3 File Formats

Saving your Quattro Pro notebooks in Lotus-compatible form is simply a matter of using a 1-2-3 file name extension when you issue one of the file saving commands. To save a file for use with Lotus version 1A, use the WKS extension, for versions 2.01 and higher use the WK1 extension, and for versions 3.0 and higher use the extension WK3. If you want all your files to be Lotus-compatible, you can define one of the 1-2-3 file extensions as the default extension (in place of Quattro Pro's own WQ2 extension) with the /**O**ptions | **S**tartup | **F**ile Extension command.

Although 1-2-3 versions 2.01, 2.2, and 2.3 all use the WK1 extension, only the two later versions support linking formulas. If you save a spreadsheet that contains linking formulas and assign a WK1 extension, Quattro Pro displays the message "Formula with HotLink translated to value. Save the file?" and gives you three choices: No, Yes, and Use 2.2 Syntax. If you select No, the save operation is cancelled. If you select Yes, all linking formulas are converted to their values and the file is saved in Release 2.01 format. If you select Use 2.2 Syntax, the linking formulas are translated into 2.2/2.3 syntax whenever possible and the resulting file will not be readable in Release 2.01. There are some types of linking formulas that Quattro Pro supports but 1-2-3 versions 2.2 and 2.3 do not. If your notebook contains linking formulas that are not supported by Lotus, these formulas will automatically be converted to values, regardless of whether you choose the Use 2.2 Syntax option.

Trading Data with Other Spreadsheet Programs

Many spreadsheet programs other than Lotus 1-2-3 (including Excel) can read and write files in Lotus format. As a result, you can use the Lotus format as a middle ground between these programs and Quattro Pro. To import an Excel file into Quattro Pro, for example, use Excel to save the file in Lotus 1-2-3 format. Then include the WK1 extension when retrieving the file in Quattro Pro. If you plan to transfer the data back to Excel, use the WK1 extension whenever you save the file. Otherwise, you may want to change the extension to WQ2 so that you can make use of Quattro Pro's desktop publishing and linking features. Quattro Pro can also read and write files in

Surpass format; just include the WKP extension when saving or retrieving the file.

The "Desktop Settings Are Removed" Message

Whenever you save a Quattro Pro notebook in an external file format, Quattro Pro automatically replaces link formulas with their current results and removes all codes related to desktop publishing features that are not supported by other programs. The codes that are removed include those related to line drawing, shading, fonts, data entry restrictions (label-only or date-only designations), and alignment of numbers. Quattro Pro warns you of this removal of codes by displaying the message "Desktop settings are removed" when you issue the / **F**ile | **S**ave, / **F**ile | Save **A**s, or / **F**ile | Sa**v**e All command.

Exchanging Data with Harvard Graphics

Quattro Pro can both read and write files in the Harvard Graphics file format. Simply specify the CHT or HG3 file extension when you open, retrieve, or save the file. Because of the inherent differences between the two programs, some program-specific information may get lost in translation. In particular, when you save a Quattro Pro notebook with a CHT or HG3 extension, only the current graph is saved because Harvard Graphics does not support multiple graphs in one file. In addition, non-graph data such as notebook formatting and macros, which is not usable in Harvard Graphics, is omitted from the CHT or HG3 file. When you load a Harvard Graphics file in Quattro Pro, graphs will be converted to the closest Quattro Pro graph type and data series will be converted to values in your notebook. If Quattro Pro does not have an exact match for one of your fill patterns or graph options, it will use its closest match. Quattro Pro cannot convert multiple pie graphs, graphs that combine multiple graph types, and organization charts. In the case of multiple pie graphs, only the first pie is imported. In the other cases, you wind up with an empty file. You cannot bring CHT or HG3 files into the Annotator.

Trading Data with Paradox, dBASE, and Reflex

Quattro Pro excels at exchanging data with three major dedicated database management programs: Paradox, Reflex, and dBASE. Quattro Pro can read and write dBASE II, dBASE III, dBASE IV, and Paradox files with such ease and speed that you can use any of these programs as an adjunct or "sister program" to Quattro Pro. (Because FoxPro stores data in the dBASE III file

Exchanging Data with Other Programs

format, Quattro Pro can read and write FoxPro data as well.) Assuming your file is small enough to load into Quattro Pro, you may want to use Quattro Pro as an extension of your database program when performing extensive database management. Alternatively, if your database requires calculated fields or intensive computations, you may want to do most of your work in Quattro Pro and then switch programs to perform operations that your database management program is better equipped to handle.

Reading Paradox, Reflex, and dBASE Files

To import a Paradox, Reflex, or dBASE file into Quattro Pro, simply retrieve it using / **F**ile I **R**etrieve or / **F**ile I **O**pen. You can also use the / **T**ools I **C**ombine I **C**opy command to copy Paradox, Reflex, or dBASE data directly into an existing spreadsheet.

Quattro Pro's Paradox, Reflex, and dBASE translation skills are excellent. Whenever possible, Quattro Pro retains the data types and even the display formats used in the other program. It correctly reads date fields as dates (translating them into date serial values displayed in the Long International Date format). In the case of Paradox files, it automatically translates dollar fields into values displayed in Currency format. If you retrieve a dBASE file with a numeric field containing three decimal places, Quattro Pro displays it in Fixed format, 3 decimal places. As discussed later in the chapter, Quattro Pro can even translate dBASE memo fields into labels. In short, Quattro Pro does everything you could hope for to maintain the content and appearance of the database while translating the data to its own format. It even assigns block names to the fields in the first record, using the field names at the top of the file, just as if you had issued the / **D**atabase I **Q**uery I **A**ssign Names command. This allows you to use field names when entering logical formulas in criteria tables, without any prior preparation.

Memory Constraints

When you use a database program such as dBASE, Paradox, or Reflex, the size of your database is limited only by the amount of available disk space that you have, not by the amount of available memory. This is because these programs only read data into memory as needed, rather than reading in the whole database at once. In contrast, when you retrieve a database in Quattro Pro, the entire file must be able to fit into memory at the same time. If your computer only has 640K of installed memory, this can place severe limitations on the size of the database that you can manipulate in Quattro Pro. If you try to retrieve a database that is too large to fit in available memory, Quattro Pro displays the error message "Not enough memory for that operation" and then loads as much of the data as it can. In this case, be sure not to save the file (unless you change the file name); otherwise, the new, partially retrieved file will replace the old, complete file on disk.

A Note on Deleted Records in dBASE Files

When you delete a record in dBASE the record is not physically removed from the database file. Instead, it is simply marked for deletion at a later time. When you retrieve a dBASE file into Quattro Pro, these deletion-marked records are automatically omitted—as if you had issued a SET DELETED ON command in dBASE to screen them out. If you then modify the data in Quattro Pro and save it again, overwriting the original file, the deletion-marked records are permanently erased.

Writing Paradox, Reflex, and dBASE Files

Just as Quattro Pro translates dBASE, Paradox, and Reflex data into Quattro Pro format when you retrieve files, it can also translate that data back into the external format if you save a file with a dBASE, Paradox, or Reflex extension. The extension tells Quattro Pro to save the file using the appropriate external file format. If you intend to pass data to and from dBASE, Paradox, or Reflex regularly, you will probably want to store the data with the database extension. If you intend to do most of your future work with a particular file from within Quattro Pro, however, you can save time by storing the data with a WQ2 extension until you need to use it in your database program. This way Quattro Pro will not need to translate each time you save or retrieve the spreadsheet.

NOTE: All formulas are translated to their results when you save in dBASE, Reflex, or Paradox format. Use the WQ2 extension to save your formulas.

You can save Quattro Pro databases as Paradox, Reflex, or dBASE files using any of the save commands, or the / **T**ools | **X**tract | **V**alues command. If your notebook contains data other than the database, use / **T**ools | **X**tract. Otherwise, you will, at best, wind up with useless extra "records" containing the non-database data. At worst, the database file structure will not properly match the database. When you use the / **T**ools | **X**tract command to extract a database in an external format, be sure to select the Values option. Quattro Pro always converts formulas to values anyway when you extract a file with a dBASE, Paradox, or Reflex extension, but it will run into problems if any of the calculated fields refer to cells outside the block you are extracting—that is, outside the database. Also be sure to include the field names in your extract block.

Exchanging Data with Other Programs

To save or extract a file for use in Paradox, assign the extension DB; for use in Reflex, assign the extension RXD for version 1 or R2D for version 2. When saving or extracting a file for use in dBASE III, dBASE III PLUS, or dBASE IV, assign the extension DBF; for use in dBASE II, use the extension DB2. The DB2 extension for dBASE II files (rather than the standard DBF extension used in the program itself) is necessary to inform Quattro Pro that you will be using the earlier version of dBASE. You can then either rename the file in DOS, changing the extension to DBF, or else specify the DB2 extension whenever you open the file in dBASE II.

The process of saving data in dBASE, Paradox, or Reflex format is the same whether you entered the data in Quattro Pro or retrieved it from disk after entering it in the external database program. Each time you save a file with a Paradox, Reflex, or dBASE extension, Quattro Pro displays a File Save submenu with the choices View Structure, Write, and Quit. Choose the View Structure option to see and, if necessary, modify the names, data types, and lengths that Quattro Pro intends to assign to each field. Once you are satisfied with the file structure, press [Esc] to return to the File Save submenu and select the Write option.

When you save a file with a dBASE, Paradox, or Reflex extension, Quattro Pro automatically makes use of whatever text, number, date, and currency field types are available in the external program when designing the initial file structure. Quattro Pro does sometimes use different names for those types, however, referring to Paradox short number fields as integer fields, for example, and dBASE character fields or Paradox alphanumeric fields as text fields. Quattro Pro also allows you to change fields to still other field types. The only field types that Quattro Pro cannot write are the memo type or the formatted memo, graphic, binary, or OLE types available in Paradox for Windows. It is always a good idea to view Quattro Pro's proposed file structure before actually writing the file for the first time and before saving a file after making changes that might affect the structure.

Modifying the File Structure

To change a dBASE or Paradox file's structure before saving, select the View Structure option on the File Save submenu. Quattro Pro displays a picture of your file structure. To delete a field from the structure so it is omitted from the new file altogether, highlight the field and press [Del]. To change a field's attributes, highlight the field and press [Enter]. When Quattro Pro displays a submenu with the options Name and Type, choose the attribute that you wish to change and enter a new setting. If you select the Type option, Quattro Pro displays another submenu with the available field type options. Once you select a type, Quattro Pro prompts you for the field length, if applicable (some field types have a fixed length that cannot be changed).

This is the only way to change the length of a field; if you want to change a field's length but not its type, choose the same type, and then specify the desired field length. When you have completed your modifications, press [Esc] to return to the File Save submenu and select the Write File option to save the data using the newly modified structure.

When you alter a field type, do not expect this change to be remembered in future sessions. In most cases, when your choice of field type differs from Quattro Pro's, you must tell Quattro Pro to use this alternate field type every time you save or extract the database. You are most likely to encounter this problem when saving dBASE logical fields. Although Quattro Pro can write this field type, it never chooses it as a default; if your file contains logical fields, you must modify the file structure and adjust their field types every time you issue one of the save commands or the / **T**ools | **X**tract command.

CAUTION: If you back out of saving a dBASE, Paradox, or Reflex file by pressing [Esc] or [Ctrl]-[Break] to return to Ready mode without selecting the Write File option, Quattro Pro displays the message "Warning. File has been erased. Please try again." This means that the file has been erased from the disk, but not from memory. Unless you save the data by issuing a save command before you issue the / **F**ile | **E**rase, / **F**ile | **R**etrieve, or / **F**ile | **Ex**it command, you will not be able to retrieve it again later.

dBASE and Paradox Memo Fields

The good news about Quattro Pro's handling of dBASE memo fields is that it can translate memo field data into labels. (In contrast, Quattro Pro ignores Paradox memo fields.) This means you can actually use Quattro Pro to perform character-string manipulation on dBASE memo field data, such as searching for particular words or modifying the text with the use of string functions. For example, you can extract a list of records that have memo fields containing the name Anne Woods by entering the exact match criterion * **Anne Woods** * underneath the name of the memo field in a criteria table.

The bad news is twofold. First, because the maximum length of a label in Quattro Pro is 254 characters, any memo field data beyond this limit will be lost in the translation. Second, Quattro Pro cannot write memo fields. Therefore, you cannot create a file in Quattro Pro and then save it with memo fields. In addition, if you retrieve a file created with memo fields in dBASE, the memo field data is immediately converted into labels (and data beyond the 254th character is truncated). If you then resave the data as a DBF file, it will be saved in exactly this form. You cannot recover the truncated text or change the field type to memo. If you try to change the structure, the memo field type is not even on the list of options. This means,

Exchanging Data with Other Programs

in effect, that you cannot easily pass a dBASE file containing memo fields back and forth with Quattro Pro. You can load such a file into Quattro Pro to perform specific types of calculations if you like, but you cannot pass the results back to dBASE without losing the memo field type.

Because of the potential loss of memo field data, if you retrieve a dBASE or Paradox file that contains memo fields, Quattro Pro prevents you from overwriting the original file when you save the database. If you attempt to do so, Quattro Pro displays the error message "Cannot save without destroying family files." This message refers to the fact that memo field text is stored in a separate file, apart from the other fields in the database. When Quattro Pro says that it "cannot save without destroying family files," it means that saving the database under its original name would destroy the link between the database file and the memo file so that you could no longer access the memo field data within the external database program.

Quattro Pro will allow you to save the file in dBASE format provided you supply a different file name. If your memo field data is short and was therefore not truncated when you retrieved the file into Quattro Pro, you may want to save the file as is. Otherwise, you may prefer to remove the memo field from the file structure before saving.

NOTE: Quattro Pro 5 cannot read Paradox for Windows formatted memo fields. If your file contains such fields, Quattro Pro just ignores them.

Potential Problems in Exchanging Data with Database Programs

There are several potential problems that can occur when you retrieve external database files in Quattro Pro, modify them within Quattro Pro, and then save them again for use in the external database program. Although none of these problems are insurmountable, you need to be aware of them and take steps to ensure that your data is usable in the external program.

Most external database programs maintain index files that allow you to locate particular records quickly. If you retrieve a database into Quattro Pro, modify the data, and then save it in the external file format, you may create a discrepancy between the index file and the database file itself. To be safe, rebuild your indexes in the database program.

When you retrieve an external database file, Quattro Pro bases the width of each column on the length of the field in the external database. This means that if the field is narrow, you may not be able to read the entire field name (column heading) without widening the column. Also, if the data in a particular field is as wide as the field itself, there may be no spaces separating the data in that field from the data in the next field to the right. For these reasons, you will often alter column widths as soon as you retrieve an external database to make the data easier to read. If you save the file in this format, you will inadvertently modify the structure of your external database. To avoid this, write down the original column widths before you make your adjustments and reinstate them before you save the file.

Another potential problem relates specifically to saving and retrieving dBASE files. As mentioned, whenever you retrieve a dBASE file in Quattro Pro, Quattro Pro only retrieves records that have not been marked for deletion. If you then save the file under the same file name, the deletion-marked records will be permanently lost (as if you had performed a PACK operation in dBASE). If this is acceptable, just be sure to rebuild all your dBASE index files so that they will match the newly trimmed database. If you are not willing to part with the deletion-marked records, you can copy them to a separate file in dBASE before you retrieve the data in Quattro Pro. Then, after you save the database in Quattro Pro, you must reload dBASE and append data from that second file. Then rebuild your indexes.

There is yet another potential problem with changing and then saving Paradox files. If you change a Paradox table that has any associated indices, reports, queries, or data entry forms, Quattro Pro will not allow you to save it under the original file name. If you try, it displays the error message "Cannot save without destroying family files." If you want to save the data as a Paradox table, you must choose a new file name.

Linking to External Databases

You can query and generate database statistics on dBASE, Reflex, and Paradox database files without retrieving those files into Quattro Pro. To do this, you simply create a notebook with a criteria table containing link references to the external database.

Even though you don't need to load a dBASE, Paradox, or Reflex database into Quattro Pro to access its data, Quattro Pro acts as if you had. That is, it acts as if the database starts in cell A1, and each record occupies one row and each field one column. You therefore refer to the first field of the database as column A, the second field as column B, and so on. Quattro Pro also acts as if the first row of this database contains the field names rather than the first record. If you have a database of 100 records and 10 fields, its coordinates (as far as Quattro Pro is concerned) would therefore be A1..J101. The block A1..J1 would be considered to contain field names. The coordinates of the first record would be A2..J2.

Exchanging Data with Other Programs

When you define a database query that refers to an external database file, you do not actually need to worry about the database coordinates. You can simply enter a query block setting that uses the form

[*database file name*]A1..A2

and let Quattro Pro determine the number of fields and records (columns and rows) in the database. This block reference only works in queries, however. If you enter database statistical formulas that refer to external databases, the first argument in the function statement (the database block) must refer to all the records and fields that you want included in the calculation.

When you query an external database file, Quattro Pro also lets you refer to the fields within the first record by field name—as if you had issued the /Database | **Q**uery | **A**ssign Names command. This allows you to use field names when entering logical formulas in a criteria table.

Figure C-1 shows a notebook designed to perform a query on a dBASE database called CUSTOMER.DBF, which is stored in the DBASE directory. This figure shows the names and total orders for customers in the CUSTOMER.DBF database whose total orders are equal to or greater than $3000. This list was created by first entering the logical formula

```
+[\DBASE\CUSTOMER.DBF]TOTORDERS>=3000
```

in cell A4. Next, the block

```
[\DBASE\CUSTOMER.DBF]A1..A2
```

was specified as the Block setting on the Database | Query menu. (The block coordinates could also have been entered as A1..L500, since the database has 12 fields and 500 records.) Next, the block A3..A4 was specified as the Criteria Table, and the cells A7..B7 (the labels NAME and TOTORDERS) were designated as the Output Block. Finally, the Extract option on the Database | Query menu was selected.

Every time you open a notebook that contains link references to an external database file, Quattro Pro displays an Open Links menu with the options Load Supporting, Update Refs, or None, just as it does when you load other primary notebooks. If you choose Update Refs or Load Supporting and your database is large, it may take several minutes for Quattro Pro to recalculate the formulas. For this reason, you may want to print your notebook every time you use it. If your data has not changed, it will be far more efficient to view the printout than to load the primary notebook and wait for Quattro Pro to recalculate the link formulas.

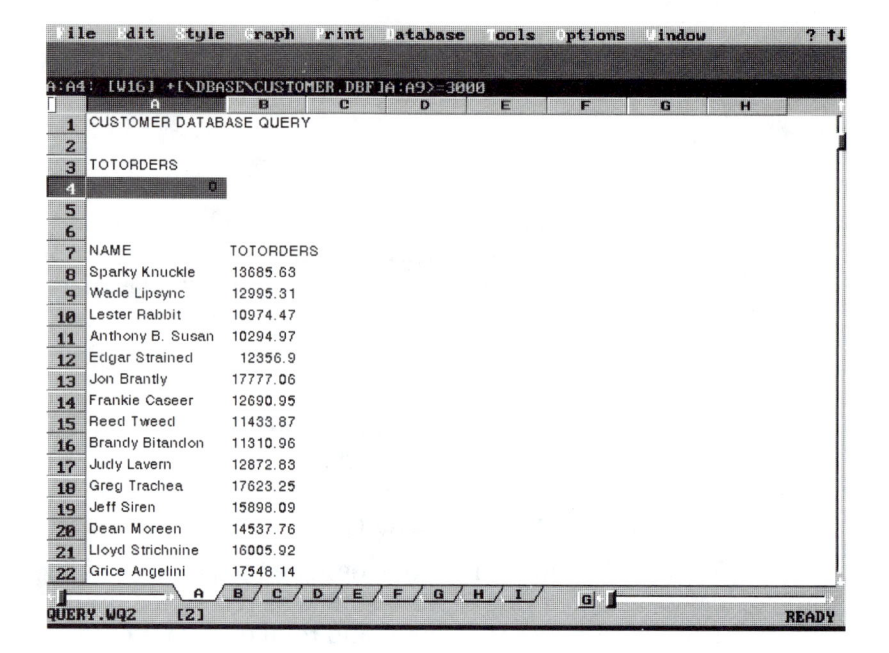

Querying an external database
Figure C-1.

> **NOTE:** When you link a notebook to an external database file, you are bound by the same memory constraints that you face when you retrieve databases: there must be room for the entire file to fit in memory at once.

Accessing Paradox

Paradox is a relational database management program distributed by Borland International, the makers of Quattro Pro. Its features include

+ A built-in report generator that lets you generate mailing labels and form letters as well as customized reports
+ Tools for facilitating data entry and for easily locating, editing, and sorting data
+ Query-by-Example, which lets you select specific records in your database more easily and quickly than you can with the / **D**atabase | **Q**uery command
+ Optional add-on called SQL Link, which allows you to access data on an SQL database server

If you have version 3.5 or higher of Paradox, you can run Quattro Pro from within Paradox, work with Paradox tables within Quattro Pro, and then

Exchanging Data with Other Programs

return to Paradox, without having to close either program. This feature, known as Paradox Access, lets you enjoy the best of two worlds—using Paradox's sophisticated database management features while exploiting Quattro Pro's graphing and desktop publishing capabilities. You can, for example, graph and create slide shows from Paradox data or use Quattro Pro's desktop publishing features (such as shading, line-drawing, and fonts) to print Paradox data. You can use Paradox's Query-by-Example feature to select data records instead of creating criteria tables, and import the resulting Paradox Answer table directly into Quattro Pro. You can also take advantage of Paradox's SQL Link feature to access SQL-hosted data residing on mainframes, minicomputers, or OS/2 servers.

In order to use Paradox Access, you must have an 80286, 80386, 80386SX, or 80486 CPU. (This means that you can't use an XT-class computer; you must have an AT-class machine or better.) In addition, you need at least 2 megabytes of installed memory, and Paradox 3.5 or later.

For more on temporary tables, see "Working with Paradox Temporary Files."

You also must take several preparatory steps before using Paradox Access. Among other things, these steps involve specifying three directories: your *working directory,* which is where Paradox will store your regular data tables; your *private directory,* which is where Paradox stores temporary tables; the directory that contains the file PARADOX.NET. If you are using a network, these three directories should already be defined in Paradox; you just need to tell Quattro Pro about some of them. If you are using a stand-alone system, you need to specify these directories in both programs.

Note: In order to use Paradox Access, you essentially fool Paradox into thinking that you are running on a network. Once you have done this, you must load a program called SHARE.EXE into memory before you load Paradox, even if you have no intention of accessing Quattro Pro. (SHARE.EXE is a DOS program that allows applications to prevent users from accessing or changing files or records that are either being used by another person on a network or that are being used by another application.) To load SHARE.EXE, you can either enter **SHARE** at the DOS prompt before you load Paradox, or you can add a line that contains the one word SHARE to your AUTOEXEC.BAT file so that SHARE.EXE is loaded every time you boot your computer. If you always load Paradox through PXACCESS (as described shortly), the PXACCESS batch file will load SHARE for you automatically.

Stand-Alone Configuration

If you are not using a network, the steps for configuring Paradox and Quattro Pro for Paradox Access are outlined here. Note that these instructions assume you are using Paradox 4.0. If you are using an earlier version, you'll need to alter the directory names accordingly.

Quattro Pro 5 Made Easy

You can also choose three existing directories for the working directory, private directory, and the PARADOX.NET directory.

1. You may want to start by creating two subdirectories underneath the directory that contains your Paradox program files: one called PDOXNET to hold the PARADOX.NET file and a second called PDOXPRIV to serve as your private directory. To create these directories, switch to your Paradox directory by typing **CD\PDOX40**. (If your Paradox directory has another name, substitute that name for PDOX40.) Type **MD NET** and press [Enter]. Then type **MD PRIV** and press [Enter]. You may also want to create a directory called DATA to serve as your working directory, just to keep your databases separate from your Paradox program files.

2. From the directory that contains your Paradox program files, initiate the NUPDATE program by entering **NUPDATE**. You will see a message about SOM files. Just press any key and then press [F2] twice to move past the next two screens. On the next screen, designate the type of network as "Other." Then enter the directory for the PARADOX.NET file. As mentioned, this directory must be different from the working directory. If you created a directory called NET in step 1, specify that directory. Remember to use the full path name, including the Paradox program directory itself. For example, if your Paradox program directory is on drive C and called PDOX40, enter **C:\PDOX40\NET**. Press [F2] to save your settings and, when asked whether to back up the serial numbers, enter **N** for No. You will be returned to the DOS prompt.

3. Enter **SHARE**. Then enter **PARADOX CUSTOM** to load Paradox and run the Custom Configuration Program script. Specify your private directory by selecting Network and entering the appropriate directory name as the Private Directory setting. (If you created a directory called PRIV in step 1, enter the full path name of that directory.) As mentioned, your private directory must be different from both your working directory and the directory that holds the PARADOX.NET file. By default, the working directory (the directory in which your Paradox databases will be stored) is the directory from which you load Paradox. Leave the other settings as is and press [Enter] to redisplay the main Custom Configuration menu. If you want to specify a permanent working directory, select Standard Settings and enter a directory name. (If you created a directory called DATA in step 1, enter the full path name for that directory.) Finally, either press [F2] or select DoIt! to save your changes. When you are asked whether to save to a HardDisk or Network, select HardDisk. Paradox 3.5 will return you to DOS. From Paradox 4.0, select Exit and then Yes.

4. Switch to the Quattro Pro directory by entering **CD\QPRO** and load Quattro Pro by entering **Q**. Issue the / **O**ptions | **O**ther | **P**aradox command and change the Directory setting on the resulting menu to

Exchanging Data with Other Programs

the directory you specified for the PARADOX.NET file. Change the Network Type setting to Other.

5. Select Quit to return to the Options menu, and then select Update from the Options menu to save all the new settings.
6. Select Quit to return to Ready mode. Then issue the / **F**ile | **E**xit command to leave Quattro Pro.

Network Configuration

If you are using a network, prepare for using Paradox Access by following these steps:

1. Issue the / **O**ptions | **O**ther | **P**aradox command and change the Directory setting to the directory that contains the PARADOX.NET file.
2. Change the Network Type setting to your type of network.
3. Select Quit to return to the Options menu and select Update to save all the new settings.
4. Select Quit and then issue the / **F**ile | **E**xit command to leave Quattro Pro.

Finishing the Configuration

The files setting determines the most disk files you can open at one time.

On both network and stand-alone systems, you should also check the files setting in your CONFIG.SYS. To do this, enter **CD** at the DOS prompt to switch to the root directory of your hard disk. (If you are on a drive other than C, switch to drive C first.) Then enter **TYPE CONFIG.SYS** to display the contents of your CONFIG.SYS file and make sure that the FILES statement sets the number of file handles to at least 40. If not, edit the file and change the statement to FILES=40.

Using Paradox Access

Now you are ready to use Paradox Access. The basic procedure is as follows:

See your DOS manual for details on the PATH command.

1. Make sure that your DOS search path includes the Paradox directory. (You can check by issuing the PATH command from DOS.) If it does not, issue a DOS PATH command or modify the PATH statement in your AUTOEXEC.BAT file and reboot.
2. Switch to the Quattro Pro directory by entering **CD\QPRO** (or the equivalent if you installed Paradox in a different directory or are using a later version of the program). Then enter **PX4ACCESS** if you are using Paradox 4.0. Enter **PXACCESS** instead, if you are using Paradox 3.5. In a moment, you will see the Paradox sign-on screen and then the Paradox main menu, as if you had loaded Paradox normally.

NOTE: If you see the message "-leaveK is no longer supported. Use SET DPMIMEMM=MAXIMEM #### command," use PX4ACCESS rather than PXACCESS to load Paradox Access.

3. Whenever you are ready to switch to Quattro Pro, press `Ctrl`-`F10`. If you have already performed at least one query, Quattro Pro will load the table ANSWER.DB by default. (ANSWER.DB is the query result table.) As explained under "Loading a File Automatically," you can choose a different file to load when you access Quattro Pro.
4. To switch back to Paradox from Quattro Pro, press `Ctrl`-`F10` (Paradox Access) or issue the / **D**atabase | **P**aradox Access command.

This hypothetical situation should illustrate the process: Suppose that you work for a health club and are using Paradox to maintain a list of club members. You want to create a pie graph illustrating what percentage each membership category represents out of the total membership. You can start by creating a query to count the number of members in each membership category in your database. You do this by loading Paradox, pressing `F10` to activate the Paradox main menu, selecting Ask, specifying the table that contains the membership data, and then filling in the query screen as shown in Figure C-2. (The query itself appears at the top of the screen; the table on which the query is based appears at the bottom.) As soon as you press `F2` (DoIt!) or press `F10` for the menu and select DoIt!, Paradox performs the

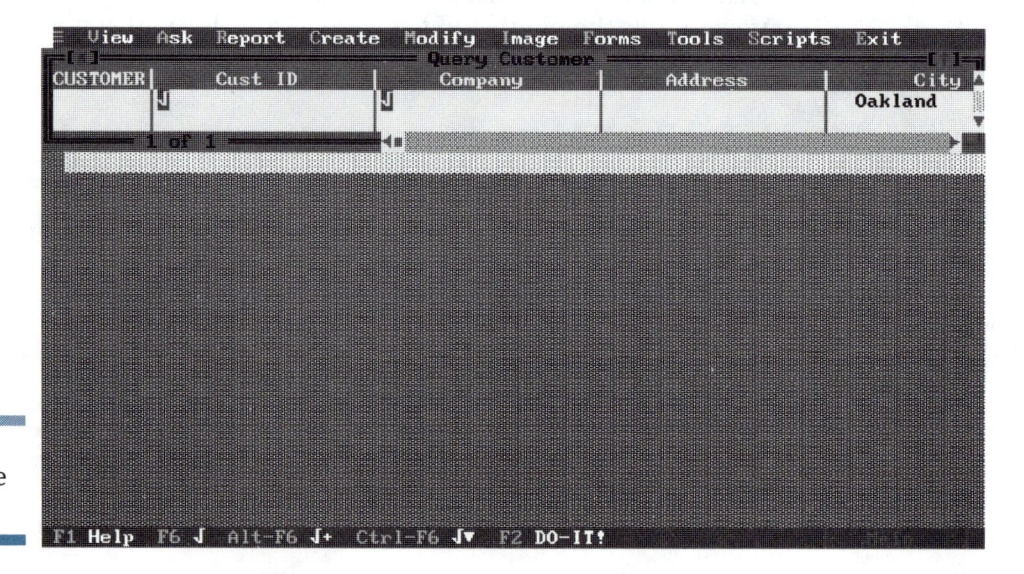

Querying a Paradox table
Figure C-2.

Exchanging Data with Other Programs

query and places the results in a temporary table called ANSWER.DB. (This entire process is analogous to creating a frequency distribution table in Quattro Pro.)

Now that you have a manageable amount of data to work with, you can press Ctrl-F10 to switch to Quattro Pro. Quattro Pro automatically loads the ANSWER.DB table into a notebook and you can create a graph based on the data. (Figure C-3 shows the ANSWER.DB table in Quattro Pro with an inserted graph. The column widths have been adjusted slightly and two rows have been inserted at the top of the notebook.) Now that the data is in Quattro Pro, you might also dress it up with fonts and line drawing, and print it in final-quality mode. Lastly, you can save your notebook by issuing the / **File** | Save **A**s command and entering any name other than ANSWER.DB. (If you attempt to save the notebook under the name ANSWER.DB, Quattro Pro displays the error message "Cannot Save or Create a Paradox Temporary table.")

Loading Paradox Tables While in Quattro Pro

To load a Paradox table while in Quattro Pro, just issue the / **File** | **R**etrieve or / **File** | **O**pen command and enter the table name (including the DB extension). If you prefer, you can select the table from a files list. Assuming you started Paradox Access from the Paradox directory, you will see a list of notebook files (if any) in that directory as soon as you issue the / **File** |

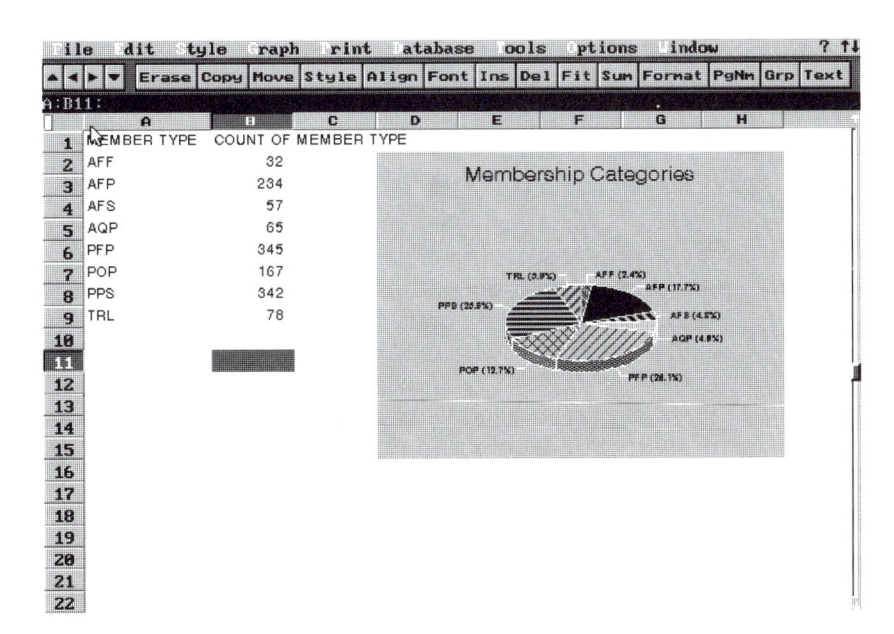

Graphing a Paradox answer table
Figure C-3.

Retrieve or / **F**ile | **O**pen command. To list the Paradox tables in that directory, enter the file specification ***.DB**. When the list of tables appears, just select the one you want. Once the file is loaded, you can perform any of the operations you would normally perform on a notebook.

If you make changes to a table in Quattro Pro and you want the changes passed back to Paradox, save your changes using one of the file save commands before you press [Ctrl]-[F10] (Paradox Access). If you modify a notebook in Quattro Pro, and then switch to Paradox and issue the Exit command, Paradox will be removed from memory and you will see the Quattro Pro screen with a message about saving your work—exactly as if you had issued the / **F**ile | **Cl**ose All command.

Remember that you cannot change temporary tables in Quattro Pro and save them under their original name. You also cannot change tables that have any associated form files—such as report files or data entry screen files. If you try, you will see the error message "Cannot save without destroying family files." In this case, you either must make the changes in Paradox or use the / **F**ile | Save **A**s command to save the file under a new name.

NOTE: If you see the error message "Unable to lock file for reading" when you attempt to retrieve a Paradox table, chances are you have one of two possible problems. Either Paradox and Quattro Pro have different ideas on where your PARADOX.NET file is stored, or Paradox is using the same directory both as your private directory and as your working directory. Refer back to the sections on configuring your system for Paradox Access to remedy these problems.

Working with Paradox Temporary Files

Paradox automatically generates various *temporary tables* (tables that are reused as necessary and erased when you leave the program) whenever you perform particular operations. For example, every time you perform a query, Paradox creates a temporary table called ANSWER.DB to hold the query results. If a table called ANSWER.DB already exists, Paradox overwrites it. Similarly, every time you delete a set of records, Paradox stores them in a temporary table called DELETED.DB, which is overwritten if you perform another set of deletions in the current work session, and is erased when you leave Paradox. Paradox creates a total of 12 temporary tables which contain everything from the last group of records that you changed (CHANGED.DB) to the results of your last crosstab operation (CROSSTAB.DB). Refer to your Paradox documentation for a full list. ANSWER.DB is the temporary table that you are most likely to work with in Quattro Pro.

Exchanging Data with Other Programs

Paradox always stores temporary tables in a directory designated as your *private directory*. (It is called private because if you are working on a network, this directory cannot be accessed by other users.) When you work with Paradox Access, this directory should always be different from your working directory (the directory where Paradox stores regular, non-temporary tables). Because Quattro Pro will look to the Paradox working directory when you issue a / **F**ile | **R**etrieve or / **F**ile | **O**pen command, the temporary files will not appear on the files list. However, you can retrieve temporary tables simply by entering the Paradox private directory when you enter the file name.

Although you can easily retrieve temporary tables in Quattro Pro, you must be careful about changing them. Paradox automatically locks all temporary tables when you access Quattro Pro, so you cannot save changes directly to those files. If you change the table in Quattro Pro and want to save your changes, issue the / **F**ile | Save **A**s command and specify a new file name.

Loading a Table or Spreadsheet Automatically

The Database | Paradox Access | Load File setting specifies which Paradox table or spreadsheet (if any) will be loaded automatically whenever you switch from Paradox to Quattro Pro. The default setting is ANSWER.DB; you can change it to the name of any spreadsheet or table that you like. If the file does not exist, Quattro Pro will simply load an empty spreadsheet. If you specify a Paradox temporary table, Quattro Pro will automatically look in your Paradox private directory. Otherwise, it will look in the working directory. If the file is stored someplace else, be sure to use the full path name when you specify the file.

The Autoload setting on the Database | Paradox Access menu determines whether Quattro Pro automatically loads the file you specified with the Load File option. The default setting is Yes. If you change it to No, Quattro Pro ignores the Load File setting and does not load any file when you switch to Quattro Pro. You must change the Autoload File setting to No if you specify no Load File. Otherwise, you will see the error message "Paradox Access Load File cannot be blank if Autoload = Yes" whenever you access Quattro Pro.

You can also automatically load a file by specifying the file name after the -qpro parameter in the PXACCESS batch file (discussed later). In this case, Quattro Pro loads this file the first time you switch to Quattro Pro and loads the Load File file every subsequent time you switch to Quattro Pro.

If you open a file other than the one specified in the Load File setting and then switch back to Paradox, the next time you return to Quattro Pro the Load File file will be selected automatically. If you close the Load File file in Quattro Pro and then return to Paradox, Quattro Pro will open the Load File file in a new window the next time you return to the program.

Both the Load File and Autoload settings on the Database | Paradox Access menu are saved automatically. You do not need to issue an update command. If you change the Database | Paradox Access | Load File setting in the middle of a Paradox Access work session, the change takes effect immediately and determines which file is loaded the next time you access Quattro Pro.

Exporting Data to Word Processing Software

Exporting Quattro Pro data to word processing software is as simple as printing a notebook. Using the same Quattro Pro print commands covered in Chapter 6, you can send any Quattro Pro report to a disk file rather than to your printer. The resulting file is a straight ASCII text file, a set of text data written in a format that can be interpreted by most standard software packages, including almost all word processing programs.

In most cases, you can obtain better results by handling all report formatting options such as margins, headers, footers, page breaks, and titles from within your word processing program rather than including them in your file when you "print" to disk. This means that you should set the left, top, and bottom margins to zero (using the / **P**rint | **L**ayout command) before "printing" to a file. You should also make sure that the right margin of the report is no wider than the page width set in your word processor. Set the Break Pages setting in the Print Layout Options dialog box to No so that the file contains one long "page" without any pages breaks, headers, footers, or headings.

When you have defined your page layout, change the Destination setting on the Print menu to Text File. When you are prompted, enter a name for the file. Unless you specify a different extension for the file, Quattro Pro automatically assigns the extension PRN. Then select Spreadsheet Print to "print" the data to a disk file. You can output different sections of the notebook to the same file by simply changing the print block and reselecting the Spreadsheet Print option.

You can also print several different notebooks to the same text file, appending new reports to the end of the existing text. Whenever you set the Print | Destination setting to Text File and specify a name that is already assigned to a disk file, Quattro Pro warns you that a file with that name already exists, just as it does when you try to save a file under an existing file name. In this case, however, Quattro Pro gives you the option of appending data to the existing file. Select the Append option to add your new report onto the old one.

Once you have printed your data to disk, you are ready to import it into your word processing program. If your word processor has an option for translating ASCII files or DOS text files, you should try using that option first. If it does not have an option for translating ASCII files, try retrieving

Exchanging Data with Other Programs

the report file as is. At worst, you are likely to find carriage returns placed a few characters to the right of where you would like them or experience minor problems with line breaks, which you can repair without much trouble. If you do experience such problems, try experimenting with different margin settings, both before creating the file in Quattro Pro and after retrieving it in your word processing program.

Exporting Data to Other Types of Software

Exporting data from Quattro Pro to other types of programs, such as database management programs other than Paradox and dBASE or mainframe computer software, is similar to the process described in the previous section. You create an ASCII text file by "printing" a report to a disk and then using your other program's facility for importing or processing an ASCII file or DOS text file.

You must observe two rules when creating the ASCII file. First, you should always include just plain data in the file, without any embellishments. This entails setting the top, left, and bottom margins to 0, changing the Break Pages setting in the Print Layout Options dialog box to No, and making sure that no headers, footers, or titles are included in your output. In exporting a database, be sure to write only your database records, not the field names, to disk. Second, you must match the structure of the file into which you will be importing data so that the other program will be able to read your file properly.

When you create an ASCII file from Quattro Pro by printing a report to disk, you create a fixed-length file, in which all blank spaces between characters are stored to disk along with the characters themselves. For example, if you have an ACCOUNT field in your database that is ten characters wide and you only fill in six characters, four blank spaces are included before the next field's data. When the data is read into another program, the only way the program "knows" when one field ends and the next begins is by counting characters: The first *x* characters are the ACCOUNT field, the next *x* characters are the STATE field, and so on. Therefore, whenever you export Quattro Pro data to a database program other than dBASE or Paradox, the order and widths of the columns (or fields) in the target database file must match those in your Quattro Pro notebook. If they do not, you can make the necessary adjustments at either end of the data transfer process: adjusting the Quattro Pro column widths to match the new database or notebook structure, or arranging your new file in exactly the same format as your Quattro Pro data.

You should also set your right margin to accommodate one entire row of data (and no more) per line because most translation programs interpret a carriage return as an end-of-record marker. For example, if you are exporting a database that is 125 characters wide (consisting of one 25-character column and ten 10-character columns), you would set the left margin to 0 and the right margin to 125.

In general, database programs for mainframe computers do not expect carriage return and line feed characters at the end of each record. You must therefore tell the program that such characters are included in the file.

Importing Data into Quattro Pro

You can import data into Quattro Pro by issuing the / **T**ools | **I**mport command. This command is similar to the / **T**ools | **C**ombine | **C**opy command in that it copies incoming data onto the current notebook, potentially overwriting data. If you do, in fact, want to add the imported data into your current notebook, just move the cell pointer to an empty section of the notebook before issuing the command. Otherwise, be sure to issue the / **F**ile | **E**rase command before importing. Quattro Pro expects you to import files that have PRN extensions, so when you issue the / **T**ools | **I**mport | **A**SCII Text File command, Quattro Pro displays a list of all PRN files in the current directory. You can retrieve files with other extensions by entering the file name including the extension.

When you issue the / **T**ools | **I**mport command, Quattro Pro displays a submenu with the options ASCII Text File, Comma & "" Delimited File, and Only Commas. Most word processing, database, and spreadsheet programs are capable of creating files in at least one of these formats. As discussed next, Quattro Pro handles ASCII text files and delimited files quite differently.

Importing Delimited Files

A Comma & "" Delimited file contains individual items of data separated by commas and character strings enclosed in quotation marks (see Figure C-4). WordStar MailMerge and some other programs use this format. When you import a delimited file, Quattro Pro places each item of data in a separate column, reading every set of characters enclosed in quotation marks as a label and every other set of characters as a value. Figure C-5 shows the same

```
C:\QPRO>type delimit.txt
"Robert Bagley","5842 Geary Blvd.","San Francisco","CA","94121",500
"Ann McAndrews","420 California Street","San Francisco","CA","94102",2200
"Elliot Dryden","25 California Street","San Francisco","CA","94111",3000
"Joseph Christian","80 Fremont Street","San Francisco","CA","94105",4500
"Anne Webster","530 California Street","San Francisco","CA","94104",2450
"Patrick Young","800 Montgomery Street","San Francisco","CA","94111",1600
"Samuel Levy","180 Bush Street","San Francisco","CA","94111",500
"Susan Walton","745 Front Street","San Francisco","CA","94111",1000
"Jeffrey Alsop","1240 Ashmont Avenue","Oakland","CA","94610",750
"Douglas O'Donnell","450 Pacific Avenue","San Francisco","CA","94133",1000

C:\QPRO>
```

A comma and quote delimited file
Figure C-4.

Exchanging Data with Other Programs

```
 File  Edit  Style  Graph  Print  Database  Tools  Options  Window        ? ↑↓
   ▲ ◀ ▼  Erase Copy Move Style Align Font Ins Del Fit Sum Format PgNm Grp Text
A:G1:
          A                B                    C           D      E       F        G
   1  Robert Bagley     5842 Geary Blvd.      San Francisco  CA  94121    500
   2  Ann McAndrews     420 California Street  San Francisco  CA  94102   2200
   3  Elliot Dryden     25 California Street   San Francisco  CA  94111   3000
   4  Joseph Christian  80 Fremont Street      San Francisco  CA  94105   4500
   5  Anne Webster      530 California Street  San Francisco  CA  94104   2540
   6  Patrick Young     800 Montgomery Street  San Francisco  CA  94111   1600
   7  Samuel Levy       180 Bush Street        San Francisco  CA  94111    500
   8  Susan Walton      745 Front Street       San Francisco  CA  94111   1000
   9  Jeffry Alsop      1240 Ashmont Avenue    Oakland        CA  94610    750
  10  Douglas O'Donnell 450 Pacific Avenue     San Francisco  CA  94133   1000
  11
  12
  ...
  22
         A / B / C / D / E / F / G / H / I /      G
DELIMIT.WQ2  [1]                                                          READY
```

Delimited file imported into Quattro Pro
Figure C-5.

data after importing with the / **T**ools | **I**mport | **C**omma & "" Delimited File command and adjusting column widths.

An Only Commas delimited file is just like the Comma & "" Delimited file, except it generally doesn't include quotation marks around character fields. Quotation marks are only used to demarcate a field that happens to contain a comma.

When you create a Comma & "" Delimited file, numeric data that includes formatting such as commas or dollar signs is usually written to the delimited file as a character string and, therefore, translated as labels when imported into Quattro Pro. When you import an Only Commas delimited file, Quattro Pro determines field types by examining the first character in that field in the first row of data. If the first character is a dollar sign, the data will be treated as a label. In both cases, the easiest solution is to eliminate these extraneous characters before exporting. Otherwise, you must use Quattro Pro string functions to delete these characters and convert the results to values.

Parsing ASCII Text Files

When you first import an ASCII text file, the data in each row consists of a single long label. Figure C-6 shows a file created with a word processing program (WordPerfect) and then exported in ASCII format. As you can see on the input line, all of the data in row 1 is stored as a single label in cell A1

Quattro Pro 5 Made Easy

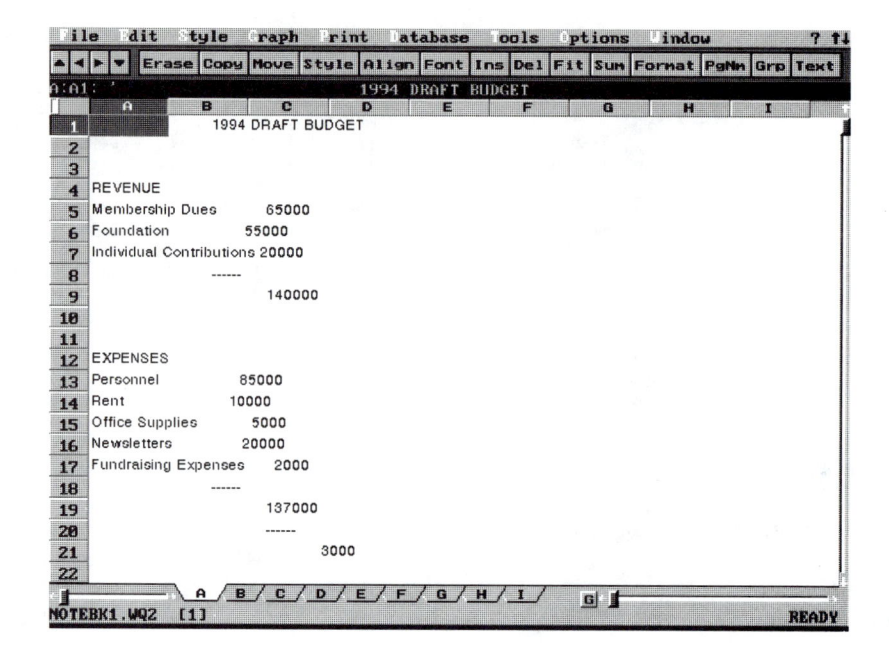

[Screenshot of Quattro Pro showing imported ASCII text file with 1994 DRAFT BUDGET data including REVENUE items (Membership Dues 65000, Foundation 55000, Individual Contributions 20000, total 140000) and EXPENSES items (Personnel 85000, Rent 10000, Office Supplies 5000, Newsletters 20000, Fundraising Expenses 2000, total 137000, net 3000).]

ASCII text file imported into Quattro Pro
Figure C-6.

even though it spills into adjacent columns on the notebook display. (The text actually looks as though it spans columns B through D.) The data in every other row in the file is stored as single labels in column A as well. Before you can effectively use this data in Quattro Pro, you need to divide these long labels by placing each item of data in a separate cell. This process is known as *parsing*, and consists of the following five steps:

1. Create format lines to guide Quattro Pro in dividing the data into columns by selecting the Create option on the Tools | Parse menu.
2. Edit the format lines as necessary.
3. Define the input block containing the labels to be parsed.
4. Define the output block where you want Quattro Pro to write the newly parsed data.
5. Select the Go option on the Tools | Parse menu to initiate the parse.

All of these steps are simple and straightforward except for the second one, editing the format lines, which can be a little tricky. If the file you are parsing is large, you should save your file with a WQ2 extension before you begin the parsing process. This way, if you need to start over because of an error in parsing, you can save time by retrieving the notebook file rather than importing again, which is a slower operation.

Exchanging Data with Other Programs

When you import an ASCII text file in WYSIWYG mode, data that originally appeared in columns may no longer line up properly, because of the proportionally spaced font. This is the case in Figure C-6. Such text will look better if you switch to either a character-based display mode or a monospaced typeface.

In most cases, it is difficult to parse data that is displayed in a proportionally spaced font because the format lines do not appear to match the corresponding data. If you are using WYSIWYG, switch to 80x25 display mode or a monospaced typeface before parsing.

Creating Format Lines

The / **T**ools | **P**arse | **C**reate command inserts a new row above the current position of the cell pointer. This row, known as a format line, contains symbols indicating how Quattro Pro intends to parse the labels below.

The following seven symbols are used in format lines:

L	Beginning of label block
V	Beginning of value block
D	Beginning of date block
T	Beginning of time block
S	Beginning of skip block
>	Additional character in block
*	Blank space between blocks

When Quattro Pro initially creates format lines it never uses the S symbol, but you can insert this symbol yourself if you want to exclude a certain section of the data from the output block. Format lines always begin with a | (vertical bar), which is the character that Quattro Pro always uses as a prefix for special codes (such as printing and page break codes).

When you issue the / **T**ools | **P**arse | **C**reate command, Quattro Pro displays a format line containing its "best guess" as to how the labels should be split. It uses the data in the row immediately below the format line (the row in which the cell pointer was located when you issued the command) to gauge the column breaks and data types to use for the entire input block. In many cases, you must generate multiple parse format lines because the layout of data is not consistent throughout the notebook. Figure C-7, for example, contains an imported database with two format lines: one in row 1, which is used as a guide to dividing the field names in row 2, and a second in row 3, which guides the division of database records into individual fields.

```
File Edit Style Graph Print Database Tools Options Window           ? ↑↓
A:A1:   :L>>>***********L>>>>>>***********L>>>***********L>>>>******L>>>*L>>*L>>>
        A           B              C              D            E              F              G         H     [End
 1      L>>>***********L>>>>>***********L>>>***********L>>>>*****L>***********U>>>>*D>>>>>>>
 2      NAME        ADDRESS        CITY           STATE        ORDER PMT DATE
 3      L>*L>>>>>>*******U>>*L>>>>***********L>>>>>>*****L>***********U>>>>*D>>>>>>>
 4      Al Simmons       262 Benita       Berkeley      CA       50.00  02/01/94
 5      Michael Smith    837 Rugby        Kensington    CA      520.00  02/03/94      ERS
 6      Alan Jones       271 Grand Ave.   Oakland       CA       90.00  02/05/94
 7      Peter Harley     241 San Pablo    Albany        CA       85.00  02/08/94      CPY
 8      Deborah Allen    421 Arch St.     Berkeley      CA       70.00  02/10/94
 9      Sonia Herrera    827 Vallejo      Emeryville    CA      320.00  02/10/94      MOV
10
11                                                                                    STY
12
13                                                                                    ALN
14
15                                                                                    FNT
16
17                                                                                    INS
18
19                                                                                    BAR
20
        ← \A/\B/\C/\D/\E/\F/\G/\H/\I/\J/\K/\L/                                        →
NOTEBK4.WQ2   [1]                                                                     READY
```

ASCII text file with unadjusted format lines
Figure C-7.

To format data correctly, you must use a different format line every time you have a long label directly underneath a format line and then shorter entries that you want to place in separate fields underneath. You also need a new format line every time the type of data changes as you move down one or more columns. In Figure C-7, for example, a new format line is required immediately above the database records because all the field names need to be entered as labels and the database records include date and numeric data. (To create additional format lines, select Quit to leave the Parse menu, move to the row where you want the new format line to appear, and then issue the / Tools | Parse | Create command again.)

As you can see, Quattro Pro does a fairly good job of "guessing" how the labels should be divided. The format line in row 1, for example, correctly breaks the first five field names into individual labels. The only adjustment that must be made is in the PMT DATE field name, which Quattro Pro proposes to split into two fields. In the second format line (row 3 in Figure C-8), both the name and the address field must be adjusted. The format line indicates a column break after the third character in the first column (the first blank space in the row below the format line) and considers the first three characters in the address field as a value field because they consist of digits in the row below. Note that Quattro Pro has correctly formatted the last field as a date field (that is, as a numeric value displayed in date format). Quattro Pro guesses that a set of characters is a date provided they are entered in any one of Quattro Pro's five date formats. It also properly recognizes times entered in any of Quattro Pro's four time formats. Although

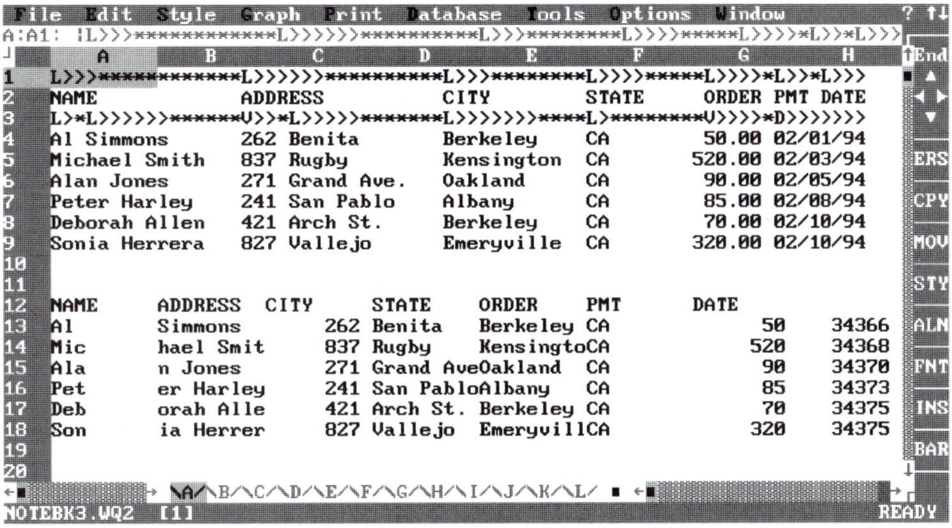

Exchanging Data with Other Programs

```
File  Edit  Style  Graph  Print  Database  Tools  Options  Window          ?  ↑↓
A:A1:  |L>>>************L>>>>>***********L>>>*********L>>>>******L>>>>*L>>*L>>>|
         A           B           C          D         E         F       G       H    End
1  L>>>***********L>>>>>***********L>>>********L>>>*****L>>>>*L>>*L>>>
2  NAME         ADDRESS     CITY       STATE     ORDER  PMT DATE                 ◄ ►
3  L>*L>>>>>*******U>>*L>>>>>********L>>>>>>****L>******U>>>>*D>>>>>>>             ▼
4  Al Simmons   262 Benita  Berkeley   CA         50.00 02/01/94
5  Michael Smith 837 Rugby  Kensington CA        520.00 02/03/94               ERS
6  Alan Jones   271 Grand Ave. Oakland CA         90.00 02/05/94
7  Peter Harley 241 San Pablo Albany   CA         85.00 02/08/94               CPY
8  Deborah Allen 421 Arch St. Berkeley CA         70.00 02/10/94
9  Sonia Herrera 827 Vallejo Emeryville CA       320.00 02/10/94               MOV
10
11                                                                             STY
12 NAME       ADDRESS   CITY     STATE     ORDER    PMT     DATE
13 Al         Simmons   262 Benita Berkeley CA              50     34366       ALN
14 Mic        hael Smit 837 Rugby KensingtoCA             520     34368
15 Ala        n Jones   271 Grand AveOakland CA            90     34370       PNT
16 Pet        er Harley 241 San PabloAlbany CA             85     34373
17 Deb        orah Alle 421 Arch St. Berkeley CA           70     34375       INS
18 Son        ia Herrer 827 Vallejo EmeryvillCA           320     34375
19                                                                             BAR
20
     ←█▌          → \A/\B/\C/\D/\E/\F/\G/\H/\I/\J/\K/\L/ ■ ←█              →
NOTEBK3.WQ2  [1]                                                          READY
```

ASCII text file after parsing
Figure C-8.

the V indicating the start of the ORDERS column is one character to the right of the first digit in the column, this will not create a problem when parsing.

Block A12..H18 of Figure C-8 shows the output produced if you simply accept the format lines created by Quattro Pro without any adjustment. (The column widths have been modified so that you can see all the data.) When you first select the Go option, Quattro Pro simply uses the column widths of the notebook. In many cases, this means that your data will appear to be truncated, and your first task should be to adjust the column widths as necessary so that you can see all the data in each column.

Editing Format Lines

To modify format lines, move the cell pointer to the row containing the format line that you wish to change and issue the / **T**ools | **P**arse | **E**dit command. You can then edit the line—deleting characters and inserting or overwriting characters using one of the seven valid format line symbols—and press [Enter] when you are done. The usual cursor-movement techniques apply: the [End] key takes you to the end of the format line, [Home] takes you to the beginning, and [Tab] moves the cursor five spaces to the right. If you press [↓], the lines of data underneath the format line move up on the screen so that you can see how data "lines up" with the format line. You can move the lines back down to their original position by pressing [↑], or they will move back automatically when you press [Enter] to finish editing.

You should watch for two potential problems when editing format lines. First, because Quattro Pro uses the row immediately under the format line as a model, each set of characters in that row that is surrounded by blank spaces is interpreted as a separate item of data. This often results in the creation of extra, unintended columns or fields, as shown in column A of the notebook in Figure C-8. You can correct the problem by extending the > symbol as far as the last character in the column that you want included in the field.

Second, watch for incorrect data types. Specifically, Quattro Pro assumes that blocks of characters consisting entirely of digits, such as ZIP codes, should be translated as values. Be sure to change the starting symbol for these blocks from V to L if you want them to be treated as labels.

Figure C-9 shows the properly edited format lines and the output produced by parsing with those adjusted lines after adjusting column widths. Note that this time Quattro Pro has properly distributed the data across the columns.

Parsing does not affect the column widths. Extending the > symbol beyond the last character of data in a column does not make the column any wider, and you will almost always need to adjust column widths either before or, more commonly, after parsing labels. The / **S**tyle | **B**lock Size | **A**uto Width command (or the Fit button on the SpeedBar) is a great tool for doing this. You will also need to use a / **S**tyle | **N**umeric Format or / **S**tyle | **U**se Style command to make any date serial numbers (such as the payment dates in the figure) look like dates.

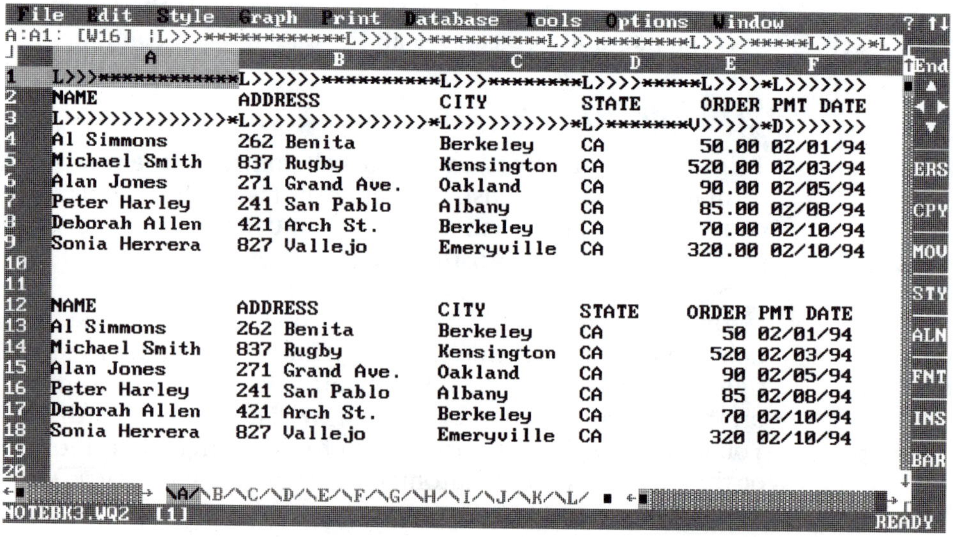

ASCII text file after adjusting format lines and parsing
Figure C-9.

Defining Input and Output Blocks

The input block for a file parse should consist of the single-column block containing the labels to be parsed and all the format lines. (Remember that the unparsed labels are displayed across several columns of the notebook, but they are actually stored within a single column.) The output block can consist of either a block of cells, or, more commonly, the cell in the upper-left corner of the area where you want Quattro Pro to place the newly parsed data. Although Quattro Pro allows you to overwrite the input block by specifying a cell at the upper-left corner of the unparsed labels, this can be dangerous. If you overwrite the unparsed labels and then discover that you have made a mistake in parsing, you can use / **E**dit | **U**ndo to undo the operation, provided that you notice the mistake right away and have previously enabled the Undo feature. Otherwise, you will need to import your ASCII text file again, or if you have already saved the data in Quattro Pro, retrieve your notebook and start over.

Initiating the Parse

Once you have created and edited your format lines and defined the input and output block for a parse, select Go on the Tools | Parse menu to initiate the parse. Quattro Pro will divide up the labels according to your specifications, delete any blank rows, and delete the format lines. In most cases, you will still need to make at least a few adjustments to the data, such as adjusting column widths and assigning numeric formats.

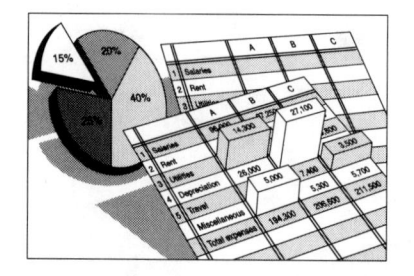

INDEX

\ character, 32
^ character, 31
#AND#, 143-144
#NOT#, 143-144
#OR#, 143-144
% scaling (in printing), 121-122
+/– format, 87
/ Database | Data Entry command, 346
/ Database | Query command, 352-353
/ Database | Sort command, 344-348
/ Edit | Copy command, 68-73
/ Edit | Copy Special command, 72-73, 100-101
/ Edit | Delete commands, 62-64
/ Edit | Delete | Pages, 238
/ Edit | Erase Block command, 74-75, 230, 231
/ Edit | Fill command, 173, 178-179, 198-199
/ Edit | Group | Create, 227, 228, 235
/ Edit | Group | Delete, 228
/ Edit | Group Mode | Disable, 228
/ Edit | Group Mode | Enable, 228, 230
/ Edit | Insert | Column Block command, 75
/ Edit | Insert commands, 61-64
/ Edit | Insert | Pages, 238
/ Edit | Insert | Row Block command, 75
/ Edit | Move command, 64, 65-66, 73
/ Edit | Names | Create command, 162
/ Edit | Names | Delete command, 164
/ Edit | Names | Labels command, 165
/ Edit | Names | Make Table command, 166
/ Edit | Page | Move, 237-238
/ Edit | Page | Name, 226
/ Edit | Search & Replace command, 174-177
/ Edit | Transpose command, 181-182
/ Edit | Undo command, 60-61
/ Edit | Values command, 167-168
/ File | Close All command, 214-215
/ File | Close command, 214
/ File | Erase command, 214
/ File | Exit command, 21-22
/ File | Open command, 213-214
/ File | Retrieve command, 39-40
/ File | Save All command, 214-215
/ File | Save As command, 37, 38
/ File | Save command, 37-38
/ File | Utilities | DOS Shell command, 376, 377
/ File | Utilities | File Manager command, 377-389
/ File | Workspace command, 219
/ Graph | Annotate command, 311-328
/ Graph | Customize Series command, 300-305
/ Graph | Insert command, 294-296
/ Graph | Name | Create command, 280-281
/ Graph | Name | Slide command, 292
/ Graph | Overall command, 309-311
/ Graph | Text command, 272-273
/ Graph | Type command, 260-269
/ Graph | X-Axis command, 307-308
/ Graph | Y-Axis command, 307-308
/ Options | Colors command, 243-245
/ Options | Display Mode command, 248
/ Options | Formats | Align Labels command, 93
/ Options | Formats | Global Width command, 82-83
/ Options | Formats | Numeric Format command, 87-88
/ Options | Hardware command, 242-243, 375
/ Options | Hardware | Printers | Background command, 130
/ Options | Hardware | Printers command, 108-109
/ Options | Other | Clock | Standard command, 15
/ Options | Other command, 252
/ Options | Other | Undo | Enable command, 60
/ Options | Protection command, 185-186
/ Options | Protection | Formulas command, 186-187
/ Options | SpeedBar command, 251-252
/ Options | Startup command, 250
/ Options | Startup | Autoload File command, 437
/ Options | Startup | Directory command, 379
/ Options | Startup | Startup Macro command, 437

489

/ Options | Startup | 3-D Syntax, 234
/ Options | Update command, 242, 250, 253-254
/ Print | Destination command, 112-113
/ Print | Format | Cells-Formulas command, 128-129
/ Print | Graph Print command, 289-292
/ Print | Heading command, 119
/ Print | Layout commands, 113-117
/ Print | Layout | Notebook Page Skip, 122
/ Print | Layout | Percent Scaling command, 122
/ Print | Print to Fit command, 121-122
/ Print | Print Manager command, 130-131
/ Style | Alignment command, 94
/ Style | Block Size | Auto Width command, 84
/ Style | Block Size | Height command, 249-250
/ Style | Block Size | Reset Width command, 83
/ Style | Block Size | Set Width command, 83
/ Style | Column Width command, 30
/ Style | Define Style | Create command, 101-102
/ Style | Font command, 123-124
/ Style | Hide Column command, 182-184
/ Style | Insert Break command, 121
/ Style | Line Drawing command, 95-99
/ Style | Numeric Format command, 87-90
/ Style | Protection command, 185-186
/ Style | Reset Width command, 83
/ Style | Shading command, 95, 99-100
/ Style | Use Style command, 102-103, 192
/ Tools | Audit command, 169-171
/ Tools | Combine command, 393-398, 412
/ Tools | Import command, 480-487
/ Tools | Macro command, 416
/ Tools | Macro | Name | Delete, 437
/ Tools | Parse command, 481-487
/ Tools | Reformat command, 179-180
/ Tools | Update Links command, 408-410
/ Tools | Xtract command, 392-393, 464, 466
/ Window | Move/Size command, 218
/ Window | Options commands, 206-213
/ Window | Options | Grid Lines command, 206
/ Window | Options | Horizontal command, 210
/ Window | Options | Locked Titles command, 206-209
/ Window | Options | Map View command, 212-213
/ Window | Options | Print Block command, 117
/ Window | Options | Row & Col Borders command, 212
/ Window | Options | Vertical command, 210
/ Window | Pick command, 215
/ Window | Stack command, 215-216
/ Window | Tile command, 215-217
/ Window | Zoom command, 217

A

Abs button, 157-158
Absolute cell references, 72, 156-160
Absolute references, 335
Accessing Paradox, 470-478.
    See also Paradox Access

Accounts receivable spreadsheet, 196
Adding data from another spreadsheet, 393-397
Adding numeric values, 44-45
Address, 7, 8
Align (ALN) button, 93
Aligning data, 92-94
Aligning labels, 31-32
Allways files, 460-461
Anchoring the cell pointer, 64-67
Annotator, 5, 311-328
    adding text and lines, 315-317, 322-324
    aligning elements, 321-322
    changing fonts, 320
    cutting and pasting, 326
    drawing curves, 317
    drawing shapes, 315-317
    gallery, 313
    linking to points on a graph, 324-325
    modifying elements, 319-322
    moving to foreground/background, 327-328
    property sheet, 313, 320-321
    resizing elements, 319
    screen, 311-315
    selecting elements, 319
    text elements, 315-317, 322-324
    toolbox, 313, 314-315
    using the alignment grid, 321-322
    using clip art, 326-327
    using the Clipboard, 326-328
Apostrophe label alignment character, 31
Area graphs, 263-264
Arithmetic, 192-193, 202
    date, 192-193
    time, 202
Arithmetic operators, 44-45
    order of calculation, 49-50
Arrow keys, 11-12
    when recording macros, 422
Art, 326-327
ASCII text files, 478-480
    importing, 480-487
Aspect ratio, 243
Asterisks, 32
Audit feature, 169-171
AUTOEXEC.BAT, 444
Autoload files, 250
Autoloading macros, 437-438
Automatic recalculation, 2-3, 47-48
Autosave edits setting, 281
Averaging values, 136, 138-139
AVG function, 136, 138-139

B

Background printing, 129-131
Backing up files, 38
Backslash, 32

Index

in graph text, 273
in macro names, 419
Backup copies of data, 376-377
BAR button, 19
Bar graphs, 261-263
Baud rate, 108
Beep, 250
Bitstream fonts, 122-123
Block names, 426
Block references in formulas, 50-52
Blocks, 160-167
   copying, 68-70
   defined, 50
   erasing, 74-75
   extracting, to new file, 392
   filling, with values, 178-179
   in macros, 426
   moving, 64, 65-67, 73-74
   moving or copying, between windows, 219-221
   naming, 162
   naming, with adjacent cells, 165-166
   pointing to, 51-52
   pointing out, in commands, 64-67, 74
   preselecting, 67
   protecting, 184-186
   selecting, with a mouse, 67
   summing, with a mouse, 52-53
   table of named, 166
   transposing, 181-182
   working with named, 160-167
   See also 3-D blocks
Boldface fonts, 124
Boolean operators, 143-144, 356-357, 360-361
Borders, 212
Boxes, 315-318
   in spreadsheets, 95
Breaking pages, 116, 117, 121
Bubble graphs, 267, 284-286
Bullets, 128-129
Buttons, 251
   mouse, 18
   switching mouse, 243

C

Calc button, 168
Calculated fields, 334-335
Calculation order, 49-50
   among complex operators, 360-361
Capitalization, 177
Caps Lock key, 9
Caret label alignment character, 31
CD (change directory) command, 5
Cell, 7
   defined, 7
   home, 8
Cell address, 7-8

Cell pointer, 7
Cell references, 45-47
   absolute versus relative, 156-160
   auditing, 169-171
   circular, 53-55
   in databases, 334-336
   linking, 398-402, 468-470
   mixed, 157, 160
   relative and absolute, 72
Cells
   copying, 68-70
   protecting, 184-186
Centering, 31, 93
CGM files, 327
Character-based display mode, 7, 9-10, 229
   SpeedBar in, 18-19
CIRC message, 54
Circular formulas, 53-55
   auditing, 170
   finding, in Map View, 213
   shown on Options | Recalculations menu, 253
Clicking with mouse, 14, 18
Clip art, 326-327
Clipboard, 326-328
Clock, 252
Close box, 20-21
Colors, 243-245
   conditional, 244
   customizing, 243-245
   on graphs, 300, 307, 311
Column, 212
Column graphs, 265-266, 283-284, 305-307
Column headings, 44
Column and row borders, 212
Column widths, 82-85
   changing, 29-30, 82-85
   defaults, 82
   resetting, 82-85
Columns, 82-85
   displaying more, 247-250
   hiding and exposing, 182-184
   inserting and deleting, 63-64
   locking, 206-209
Combining files, 393-397, 412
Comma and " " delimited files, 480-481
Comma format, 86
Comparison operators, 142
Complex operators, 143-144, 356-357, 360-361
Compressing files, 374-375
Condition, 141
Conditional colors, 244
CONFIG.SYS, 444
Consolidating spreadsheets, 224, 391-412
Constants, 48
Coordinates, cell, 7, 8
Copy (CPY) button, 68
Copying, 100-101

cells, 68-70
data, 219-221
files, 385
formulas, 70-72
link formulas, 410-411
multiple-cell blocks, 69-70
Correcting mistakes, 48-52
COUNT function, 136-137
Criteria tables, 353-361
CTERM function, 151-152
Ctrl-Break, 16
to interrupt macros, 417
to interrupt printing, 111
Currency format, 86
Currency symbols, 245-246
Current cell, 8
Cursor movement keys, 11-12
in macros, 421-423
while editing, 34-36
Custom styles. *See* Styles
Customizing the environment, 241-256
Cutting and pasting data, 59-78

D

Data, 34-36
entering, 26-28
entering in Group mode, 230-232
types of, 27-28
Data entry commands, 336
Data types, 333-334
Database management, 4
Database programs, 462-470
Database statistical functions, 134
Databases, 331-348
cell referencing in, 334-336
criteria tables, 353-361
data entry commands, 336
defined, 3-4, 331
deleting selected records, 364-365
designing, 333-336
extracting records from, 361-364
field names, 332, 334
macros for, 428-432
modifying, 341-343
querying external, 468-470
selecting records from, 351-365. *See also* Queries
sorting, 344-348
terminology, 332
Date, 246
DATE function, 197
Dates, 190-199
arithmetic with, 192-193
changing International display formats, 246-247
entering, 33-34, 190-192, 196-198
formats, 191-192
formatting with / Style I Use Style, 192

functions, 193-199
month column headings, 198-199
restricting entries to, 336
serial numbers, 190, 191
DATEVALUE function, 198
DAY function, 193, 194
Day of week, 194-195
dBASE, 462-463
exporting data to, 464-468
importing data from, 463-464
linking to dBASE files, 468-470
memo fields, 466-467
Decimal places, 85-90
functions for eliminating, 139-141
Default file extension, 250
Default font, 125
Default formats, 82, 85, 94-95
Default settings, 241-256
global, 242
notebook, 242
page, 242
saving, 253-254
Del (DEL) button, 62, 238
Deleting a cell's contents, 26-27
Delimited files, 480-481
Designing and building databases, 332-343
Diacritical characters, 247
Dialog boxes, 300
disabling, 250
Graph Overall, 309-311
Print Layout Options, 113-115
Directories, 379
creating, 389
default, 368-369
loading Quattro Pro from other, 368
startup, 250
switching, with File Manager, 379
temporary, 369
using subdirectories, 369
Directory trees, 387-388
Disk space, 373-375
Display formats, 82, 85-92, 94-95
date, 190-191
resetting, 89
table of, 86
Display mode, 7, 9-10, 247-250
switching, with SpeedBar, 10
See also Character-based display mode, WYSIWYG
Dividing numeric values, 44
Division by zero, 55
Documenting spreadsheets, 179
DOS, 377
Draft-quality printing, 111-113
Dragging with the mouse, 18
Drilling, 224, 227, 230-232
formulas, 232

Index

E

Edit key (F2), 34
Edit mode, 9
Edit SpeedBar, 19-20, 34-35, 44
    Abs button, 157-158
    table of buttons, 451
Editing data, 34-36
Editing fonts, 125
Editing keys (table), 36, 451-453
80x43 mode, 248
80x50 mode, 248
End key, 12, 74
    SpeedBar equivalents, 74
EPS file format, 292
Erase button, 230, 231
Erasing cells, 27
Erasing files, 214
ERR values, 55
    auditing, 170-171
    when copying or moving data, 73
Error messages, 53-54
Errors, 60-61
    correcting, with search/replace, 174-177
    preventing, with protection feature, 184-186
    when entering formulas, 53-55
Esc key, 15-16
Excel, 461
Exchanging data with other programs, 457-487
    dBASE, 462-478
    Excel, 461
    Lotus 1-2-3, 458-462
    mainframe computers, 479-480
    Paradox, 462-478
    Reflex, 462-478
    Symphony, 459
    word processing programs, 478-479, 480
Exiting to the operating system, 377
Exiting Quattro Pro, 21-22
Expanded memory, 252
Exponential format (scientific), 86
Exponentiation, 44
Extracting files, 392

F

Field names, 332, 334
Fields, 332
    key, 344
File extensions
    dangers of changing, 387
    W*xx*, 39
File lists, 370-372
    displaying, with File Manager, 379
    sorting, 382
    using mouse buttons with, 370-372
File Manager utility, 377-389
    control pane, 379-380
    controlling file lists, 379
    copying files, 385
    creating directories, 389
    deleting files, 386
    directory trees, 387-388
    duplicating files, 386
    file list pane, 380-383
    manipulating files, 384-387
    moving files, 386
    opening files, 384
    printing contents of, 389
    renaming files, 386-387
    searching for a file, 380
    selecting files, 384
    sorting file lists, 382
    window, 378-379
File structure, 465-466
Files, 22, 213-215, 223-224
    Allways, 460-461
    backing up, 376-377
    closing, 214-215
    combining, 393-397
    compressing, 374-375
    consolidating, 224
    copying, 385
    dBASE, 462-470
    deleting, 386
    duplicating, 386
    encrypting, 372-373
    extracting, 392
    Harvard Graphics, 462
    Impress/WYSIWYG, 460-461
    linking, 398-402
    loading automatically, 372
    Lotus 1-2-3, 458-462
    managing, 367-377
    manipulating lists of, 370-372
    moving, 386
    opening, 384
    Paradox, 462-478
    renaming, 386-387
    retrieving, 39-40
    saving, 36-39
    saving multiple, 214-215
    searching for, 371
    selecting, 384
    shortcuts for retrieving, 372
Fill patterns, 300-301, 306
Filling a block with values, 178-179
Fit button, 84
Fixed format, 86
Fonts, 113, 122-126
    applying, 123-125
    applying, to blocks, 123-124
    Bitstream versus Hershey, 122-123
    changing the default, 125

and memory, 376
printer-specific, 124
and row heights, 249-250
saving, 124-125
Footers, 114-115
Format lines, 483-486
Formatting numbers, 85-92
versus using functions, 139-141
See also Display formats
Formatting your spreadsheet, 81-105, 179-181
in Group mode, 227
Formulas, 43-57, 156-160
block references in, 50-52
cell references in, 72, 156-160, 334-336
circular, 53-55, 213, 253
common mistakes in, 53-55
converting, to values, 167-168
copying, 70-73
defined, 2, 43
ERR values in, 55
logical, 358-360
pointing when entering, 48-49
printing, 128-129
protecting, 186-187
referring to multiple pages in, 236
showing, with Text format, 87, 91-92
3-D references in, 235
types of, 43-44
Function keys, 11, 12-13, 454-455 (table)
[Alt]-[F2] (Macro Menu), 416-418
[Alt]-[F3] (Functions), 136
[Alt]-[F5] (Undo), 60
[Alt]-[F6] (Zoom), 217
[Alt]-[F7] (All Select), 384
[Ctrl]-[F5] (Group Mode), 228
[Ctrl]-[F10] (Paradox Access), 474
[F1] (Help), 16-17
[F2] (Edit), 34-35, 371
[F3] (Choices), 13, 161, 162-163, 370
[F4] (Abs), 157-158, 162
[F5] (GoTo), 12, 225
[F6] (Pane), 210, 378
[F7] (Query), 354-355
[F9] (Calc), 168, 389
[F10] (Graph), 12
[Shift]-[F3] (Macros), 252
[Shift]-[F5] (Pick Window), 215
[Shift]-[F6] (Next Window), 215
[Shift]-[F7] (Select), 67, 384, 385
[Shift]-[F9] (Copy), 385
[Shift]-[F10] (Paste), 385
Functions, 133-153
@AVG, 136, 138-139
@COUNT, 136-137
@CTERM, 151-152
@DATE, 197
@DATEVALUE, 198

@DAY, 193-194
@FVAL, 152
@HLOOKUP, 144-148, 158
@IF, 141-144, 194, 196-197
@INT, 140, 141
@LENGTH, 149
@MAX, 138
@MEMAVAIL, 375
@MEMEMSAVAIL, 375
@MIN, 138
@MOD, 194
@NOW, 200-201
@NPER, 150-151
@PMT, 149-150
@PROPER, 148
@REPEAT, 149
@ROUND, 140
@SUM, 52-53, 136-137, 139, 235
@TIME, 199
@TIMEVALUE, 201
@TODAY, 196
@UPPER, 148
@VLOOKUP, 144-148, 158, 195, 335-336, 342-343
@YEAR, 193-194
database statistical, 134
date, 134, 193-199
date and time functions, 134
defined, 50-51
financial, 134, 149-152
getting help with, 152-153
key, 136
logical, 134
lookup, 134, 144-148
mathematical, 134
miscellaneous, 135
statistical, 134, 136-139
string, 134, 148-149
syntax, 135-136
system, 134
time, 134, 199-201
types of, 134-135

G

General format, 85-87
Global column width, 82-83
Global defaults, 242
GoTo key, 12, 225
Graph Customize Series dialog box, 300
Graph Overall dialog box, 309-311
Graphics display modes. *See* WYSIWYG
Graphics printer, 108
Graphs, 4-5, 259-296
adding text to, 272-273
adding text and lines to, 315-317
area, 263-264
aspect ratio, 243

Index

bar, 261-263
bubble, 267, 284-286
changing, 280-282
changing bar widths, 301
changing colors, 300, 307, 311
changing fill patterns, 300-301, 306
changing grid lines, 310
changing lines and markers, 301
changing tick marks, 306, 308
column, 265-266, 283-284, 305-307
copying, 282
creating, 259-296
customizing, 299-311
defining a group of series, 276-279
exporting, 291-292
fast, 275-276
framing, 311-312
graphing linked spreadsheets, 411-412
high-low, 267-268
inserting, in spreadsheets, 10, 294-296
labeling points on, 301-302
legends, 272-273
line, 260
logarithmic scaling, 309
open-close, 267-268
orientation, 291
overriding graph types, 302-303
panning, 279-280
pie, 264-265, 283-284, 305-307
printing, 289-292, 296
process of creating, 269-272
resetting, 282-283, 304
resolution setting, 243
restoring, 280-282
rotated bar, 262
saving, 280-282
scaling, 307-308
second y-axis, 303-304
shortcuts for creating, 275-279
slide shows, 292-294
stacked bar, 262-263
text, 268-269, 324
three-dimensional, 269-270, 286-288
three-dimensional effect, 311-312
titles, 272
types of, 260-269
updating settings, 305
XY, 265-266, 284-286
zooming, 279-280
Grid lines, 97-99
   on graphs, 310
   display and hiding, in WYSIWYG, 206
Group button, 20-21, 228, 229, 230
Group mode, 21, 225, 228-232
   data entry in, 230-232
   deleting data in, 231
   drilling, 230-232
   formatting in, 229-230
   pointing out blocks in, 234
   saving in, 229
Groups, 227-228
   creating, 227-228
   deleting, 228, 238
   expanding, 238
   modifying, 228
   naming, 227
   removing pages from, 238
   in 3-D references, 234, 236
Grp button, 228, 229

H

Hardware, 242-243
Harvard Graphics, 459, 462
Headers, 114-115
Help icon, 20-21
Help index, 16
Help mode, 9
Help system, 16-17, 152-153
Hershey fonts, 122
Hewlett-Packard LaserJet, 123
   page length setting for, 112
Hidden format, 87
Hiding column and row borders, 212
Hiding columns, 182-184
Hiding data, 87
Hiding zeros, 91
High-low graphs, 267-268
HLOOKUP function, 144-148, 158
Home cell, 8
(Home) key, 12

I

IF function, 194, 196-197
Impress files, 460-461
Input line, 6, 8
Ins (INS) button, 61, 238
Inserting columns, 62-63
   within a block, 75
Inserting rows, 61-62
   within a block, 61-62
Installing Quattro Pro, 441-446
Instant replay of macros, 417
INT function, 140, 141
Interior labels in graphs, 301-302
International settings, 246-247
Iterations, 253

K

Key equivalent commands, 422-423
Key fields, 344

Keyboard, 10-13
Keys, 10-13
    editing, 34-36
    function, 454-455 (table)
Keywords in Help system, 16

L

Labels, 92-93
    alignment, 31-32
    changing color of, 244
    defined, 27
    on graphs, 301-302
    on pie and column graphs, 305-306
    restricting entries to, 336
    using, to name cells, 165-166
Landscape printing, 116
LaserJet. *See* Hewlett-Packard LaserJet
Leading zero, 333
Leaving Quattro Pro, 21-22
Legends, 272-273
LENGTH function, 149
LICS/LMBCS conversion, 247
Line drawing, 95-99
Line feeds, 109
Line graphs, 260
Linked spreadsheets, 3, 398-402
    auditing link references, 170-171
    creating, 399-402
    deleting links, 409-410
    graphing, 411-412
    linking external database files, 468-470
    linking versus combining files, 412
    opening, 406-407
    reasons for creating, 398-399
    switching links to another spreadsheet, 409
    updating links, 408-410
Linking, 324-325
    to external database files, 468-470
Links, 220
Loading files, 380
Loading Quattro Pro, 5
    from other directories, 368
Loading spreadsheet files, 39-40
Locked titles, 206-209
Logical formulas, 358-360
Logical operators, 143-144, 356-357, 360-361
Lookup tables, 144-148
Lotus 1-2-3, 247
    exchanging data with, 458-462
    recording macros for, 436-437
    saving graphs for, 291-292

M

Macro (MAC) button, 252

Macros, 415-438
    applications for, 432
    autoloading, 437-438
    block names in, 426
    copying, to another file, 434
    creating, 416-418
    database, 428-432
    date-stamping, 418
    defined, 3, 415
    deleting, 433-434
    documenting, 433
    editing, 427-428
    instant replay, 417
    interpreting, 421-427
    key equivalent commands, 422-423
    language, 432-433
    libraries, 435-436
    menu equivalent commands, 424
    naming, 419
    pasting, 418-419
    reasons for creating, 416
    recording, 416-417
    recording method, 436-437
    renaming, 433-434
    startup, 250
    storing, 420-421
    for underlining, 425-426
    for use in Lotus 1-2-3, 437
Mailmerge files, 480
Mainframes, 479-480
Main menu bar. *See* Menu bar
Managing files, 367-389
    with File Manager, 384-387
Map view, 212-213
Margins, 115
MAX function, 136, 138
MEMAVAIL function, 375
MEMEMSAVAIL function, 375
Memo fields, 466-467
Memory, 375-376
    freeing up, 375-376
Menu bar, 6, 13
Menu command shortcuts, 22, 453 (table)
    creating, 254-256
    in macros, 424
Menu-equivalent commands, 424
Menu mode, 9
Menu system, 13-16
MIN function, 138
Mixed cell references, 157, 160
MOD function, 194
Mode indicator, 9
    when entering data, 27
Months, 198-199
    displaying name of, 194-195
Mouse
    avoiding, in macro creation, 417

Index

buttons. *See* Mouse buttons; SpeedBar buttons; SpeedBars
   changing the palette, 251-252
   defined, 17
   editing with, 34, 35
   entering data with, 26
   other tools, 18-21
   pointer, 18
   selecting blocks with, 67
   selecting menu options with, 14
   selecting 3-D blocks with, 233-234
   selecting windows with, 215
   switching buttons on, 243
   techniques, 18
   using, in Quattro Pro, 17-21
   widening columns with, 30
   zooming windows with, 217
Mouse buttons
   file list, 370-372
   manipulating file lists with, 370-372
   See also SpeedBar buttons
Move (MOV) button, 64
Movement keys, 11-12
Moving, 64, 65-67, 73-74
   link formulas, 410-411
   notebook pages, 237-238
Moving data, 219-221
Multiplying numeric values, 44

N

Name button, 162
Named blocks, 160-167
   attaching notes to, 166-167
   creating a table of, 166
   deleting, 164-165
   in macros, 426
Narrowing columns, 82-85
Negative values, 246
Notebook area, 6, 7-8
Notebook defaults, 242
Notebook pages, 2, 3, 7-9
   absolute references, 236
   deleting, 237, 238
   inserting, 237, 238
   moving, 237-238
   naming, 223, 226
   navigating between, 225
   relative references, 236, 237
   removing from group, 238
   renaming, 226
   working with multiple, 228-232
Notebooks, 2, 223-239. *See also* Spreadsheet
   primary, 398
   supporting, 398
Notebook tabs, 9. *See also* Page tabs
Notes, 166-167
NOW function, 200-201
NPER function, 150-151
Num Lock key, 11, 12
Numbers, 94
   entering, 32-33
   filling a block with, 178-179
   formatting, 85-92

O

132-column mode, 248
Open-close graphs, 267-268
Opening files, 213-214
   with File Manager, 370, 380, 384
   linked spreadsheets, 406-407
Opening windows, 213-214
Operating system, 377
Operators, 356-357, 360-361
   arithmetic, 44-45, 49-50
   comparison, 142
   complex (logical), 143-144
Order of calculation, 49-50
   among complex operators, 360-361
Overwrite mode, 35

P

Page breaks, 116, 117, 121
Page defaults, 242
Page layout, 113-117
Page names, 224, 226
   in formulas, 226
   in Group mode, 229
   in 3-D block references, 234, 236
Page numbering, 115
Pages. *See* Notebook pages
Page tabs, 20-21, 225, 226, 229, 234, 238
   moving pages with, 237
Panes, 209-212
   synchronizing, 211-212
Panning graphs, 279-280
Paradox, 462-478. *See also* Paradox Access
   linking to Paradox files, 468-470
Paradox Access, 470-478
   loading files automatically, 477-478
   loading Paradox tables, 475-476
   network configuration, 473
Paradox temporary files, 476-477
   stand-alone configuration, 471-473
   using, 473-475
Parentheses, 50
Parsing ASCII files, 481-487
Passwords, 372-373
PATH command, 368
Payroll, 202
PCX file format, 292

Percent format, 86-87
[PgDn] key, 12
PgNm button, 225
[PgUp] key, 12
PIC file format, 292
Pie graphs, 264-265, 283-284, 305-307
    changing colors and fill patterns, 306-307
    changing label format, 305-306
    exploding, 305, 307
Plotters, 109
PMT function, 149-150
Point and shoot method of selecting options, 14
Point size, 113, 123
Pointing with the mouse, 18
Pointing method, 64-67
    in entering formulas, 48-49, 51-52
    in entering 3-D blocks, 233-234
    in macros, 421-427
    in selecting menu options, 14
PostScript files, 292
PostScript fonts, 124
Preassigned shortcuts. *See* Menu command shortcuts
Preselecting blocks of cells, 67
Print block, 117
Printers, 108
    graphics, 108
    selecting, 108-110
Printing, 107-131
    adjusting the printer, 110-112
    aligning the printer, 110-111
    in the background, 129-131
    banner, 116
    bullets, 129
    destination, 112-113, 127
    dimensions, 115, 117
    to a disk file, 478
    displaying the print block, 117
    draft quality, 111-113
    final quality, 112-113, 127-128
    fonts, 113, 122-126
    footers, 114-115
    formulas, 128-129
    graphs, 289-292
    headers, 114-115
    headings, 118-120
    inserted graphs, 296
    interrupting, 111
    landscape, 116
    large spreadsheets, 117-122
    margin and page length, 115
    multiple copies, 112
    orientation, 116
    page breaks, 116, 117, 121
    page layout, 113-116
    previewing, 127-128
    print to fit, 121-122
    print manager, 130-131
    print spooler, 129-131
    resetting print settings, 117
    saving print settings, 109-110, 116-117
    scaling, 121-122
    selecting printers, 108-110
    shading and line drawing, 113
    shrinking characters, 121-122
    sideways, 116
    on single sheets, 109
    standard reports, 110-113
    3-D blocks, 122
    wide spreadsheets, 116
PROPER function, 148
Protecting formulas, 186-187
Protecting your spreadsheet, 184-187
    with passwords, 372-373
Pull-down menu, 13
Punctuation characters, 246

Q

Quattro Pro display, 6-10
Queries, 352-353, 354-355
    complex, 356-357
    deleting selected records, 364-365
    exact match, 353-354
    extracting records with, 361-364
    locating records with, 354-355
    preparing, 352-353
    resetting, 365
    using logical formulas, 358-360
    wild cards in, 354
Querying, 468-470
Quotation mark character, 31

R

README file, 445-446
Ready mode, 9
Ready mode SpeedBar. *See* SpeedBars
Rearranging data, 59-78
Recalculation settings, 252-253
Recording macros, 416-417
Records, 340-341
    defined, 332
    selecting, 351-365
References, 71-72, 156-160, 334-336
    absolute, 72, 156-160, 335
    circular, 53-55, 213, 253
    relative, 72, 156-160, 236
Reflex, 462-466, 467-470
Reformatting text, 179-181
Relative cell references, 72, 156-160
Renaming files, 386-387
REPEAT function, 149
Repeating characters across a cell, 32

Index

Resize box, 218
Resolution setting, 243
Retrieving files, 39-40
    dBASE, Paradox, and Reflex, 463-464
    in different windows, 213-214
    with File Manager, 384
    linked spreadsheets, 406-407
    Lotus, 458-461
ROUND function, 140
Rounding errors, 140
Rounding numbers, 139-141
Row, 249-250
Rows, 61-63, 75
    deleting, 62-63
    displaying more, 247-250
    inserting, 61-62
    inserting or deleting within a block, 75

S

Saving, 214-215
Saving files, 461
    dBASE, Paradox, and Reflex, 464-465
Saving spreadsheets, 36-39
Scalable fonts, 123
Scaling (when printing), 121-122
Scaling graphs, 307-308
Scientific format, 86
Screen Previewer, 127-128
Screen types, 243
Scroll arrows, 20-21
Scroll bars, 20-21
Scroll box, 20-21
Searching for files, 380
Searching and replacing, 174-177
    in Map View, 213
Selecting blocks, 67
Sequential numbering, 178-179
Serial numbers (date), 190, 191
Shading, 95, 99-100
Shortcuts. *See* Menu command shortcuts
Shrinking spreadsheets, 212-213
Slide EPS format, 292
Slide shows, 292-294
Sorting, 247
Sorting data, 344-348
    sort order, 344-345, 347-348
    undoing a sort, 344
SpeedBar buttons, 153
    Abs, 157-158
    arithmetic operators, 44-45
    BAR, 19
    Calc (CAL), 168
    Copy (CPY), 68
    Del (DEL), 63, 238
    End key equivalents, 74
    Erase, 230, 231
    Fit, 84
    Grp, 228
    Ins (INS), 61-62, 63, 238
    Macro (MAC), 252
    Move (MOV), 66
    Name (NAM), 162
    PgNm (PAG), 225
    Sum, 52
    Text, 10
    WYS, 10
SpeedBars, 6, 18-20, 35, 44, 74
    changing buttons on, 251-252
    Edit, 19-20
    Ready mode, 19, 450-451 (table)
Splitting a window, 209-211
Spooler, 129-131
Spreadsheet, 2-3
    See also Notebooks
Spreadsheet programs, 458-462
SQZ! feature, 374-375
Starting Quattro Pro, 5
Startup macros, 250
Startup settings, 250-251
Status line, 6, 8-9
Styles, 101-104
    date, 192
    predefined, 103
    removing, 103-104
    saving and retrieving, 104
Subdirectories, 369
Subtracting data from another spreadsheet, 393, 395
Subtracting numeric values, 44
Sum button, 52
SUM function, 136-137, 139, 235
Symphony, 459
Synchronizing, 211-212

T

Tab key, 12
Tables of block names, 166
Tabs. *See* Page tabs
Tab scroller, 20-21, 225, 234
Text, 179-181
Text button, 10
Text elements in graphs, 315-317, 322-324
Text format, 87, 91-92
Text graphs, 268-269, 324
Text mode. *See* Character-based display mode
3-D blocks, 232-236
    copying, 233
    defined, 232
    erasing, 233
    methods of entering, 233-234
    moving, 237
    syntax options, 234
    using in formulas, 233

Three-dimensional effect in graphs, 311-312
Three-dimensional graphs, 269-270, 286-288
Tick marks, 308
    eliminating, in pie and column graphs, 306
Time, 199-202
    arithmetic with, 202
    changing International display formats, 246-247
    displaying, on status line, 252
TIME function, 199
TIMEVALUE function, 201
Titles, 206-209
    in graphs, 272
TODAY function, 196
Toolbox, 313, 314-315
Transposing blocks, 181-182
Typeface, 123
Typing method of selecting menu options, 14

U

Underline fonts, 124
Underline macro, 425-426
Undo feature, 60-61
    enabling and disabling, 252
Updating global defaults, 253-254
Updating spreadsheet links, 408-410
Upgrading from earlier versions of Quattro Pro, 444-445
UPPER function, 148

V

Values, 167-168
    defined, 27
    filling a block with, 178-179
VLOOKUP function, 144-148, 158, 195, 335-336, 342-343

W

Widening columns, 82-85
Windows, 205-221
    active, 215
    changing size of, 216-218
    closing, 214-215
    copying and moving data between, 219-221
    creating titles in, 206-209
    defined, 205
    File Manager, 378-379
    freezing columns and rows in, 206-209
    hiding column and row borders, 212
    map view, 212-213
    moving, 217-218
    moving among, 215
    opening, 213-214
    panes, 209-212
    rearranging, 215-218
    saving sets of, 219
    saving the spreadsheets in, 214-215
    selecting, with a mouse, 215
    splitting, 209-212
    stacking, 215-216
    synchronizing panes, 211-212
    tiling, 215-216
    zooming, 216-217
Word processing software, 478-480
    importing data from, 480-487
Word-wrapping text, 179-181
Workspaces, 219
WQ1 file extension, 39
WYS button, 10
WYSIWYG, 9-10, 248-250
    adjusting row heights, 249-250
    choosing during installation, 444
    colors, 244, 245
    displaying grid lines, 206
    fonts in, 10, 123
    group mode in, 229
    hiding grid lines in, 206
    and line drawing, 95
    Lotus files, 460-461
    multiple windows in, 215, 216
    SpeedBar in, 18-19
    zooming display, 10, 249
WYSIWYG display mode, 9-10, 248-250

X

XY graphs, 265-266, 284-286

Y

YEAR function, 193-194

Z

Zeros
    dividing by, 55
    hiding, 91
Zoom icon, 20, 217
Zooming, 249
    graphs, 279-280
    in Screen Previewer, 128
    windows, 216-217